DATE DUE

NO 30 '92	MR 13	NO 19 '04	
NO 11 93	DE 1 '99		
DE 3 '93	FE 10 00	DE 10 04	
JA 28 '94	AP 5 '00	JY 19 '07	
	JE 1 00	MY 27 08	
AP 1 '94	JY 10 00		
SE 30 '94	JY 1 '01		
JE 1 '95	OC 2 01		
SE 13 '96	NO 26 02		
OC 25 '96	NO 27 02		
NO 21 '96	DE 18 02		
MR 17 '97	NO 5 '03		
AP 17 '97	NO 24 03		
RENEW	DE 15 03		
OC 24 '97			
DE 8 97	NO 22 04		

DEMCO 38-296

GANDHI

चि० जवाहरलाल,

उपवास छोड़ो।

पश्चिमी पंजाब के स्पीकर
का तार साथ में भेज रहा
हूँ। जैसा मैंने तुमसे
कहा था वही जाहिद
हुसैन ने भी कहा।

तुम लंबी उम्र पाओ
और हिंद के नगीने
बने रहो।

बापू के आशीर्वाद

२८-१-४८

Gandhi's last letter to Jawarharlal Nehru, written in Hindi:

CHI JAWARHARLAL   18 January 1948

Give up your fast.

I am sending herewith a copy of the telegram received from the speaker of West Punjab. Zaheed Hussain had said exactly what I had told you.

May you live long and continue to be the jewel of India.

Blessings from
BAPU

GANDHI

Prisoner of Hope

Judith M. Brown

YALE UNIVERSITY PRESS · NEW HAVEN AND LONDON· 1989

Set in Linotron Bembo by Best-set Typesetter Ltd, Hong Kong, and
printed and bound in Great Britain by the Bath Press, Avon

ISBN 0-300-04595-6
Library of Congress Cataloging Number 89-51020

CONTENTS

PETER JAMES DIGGLE

dilectus fidissimusque maritus

ACKNOWLEDGEMENTS

This book is the result of two decades of a professional historian's involvement with India, during which the central theme of my original research has been the career of M.K. Gandhi. It therefore rests on so many debts of gratitude that it would be impossible for me to acknowledge all the individuals and institutions which have assisted my work. Many are recorded with thanks in the prefaces to my two earlier monographs on Gandhi. Among the bodies whose generosity has enabled my research I would mention my own universities of Cambridge and Manchester, the British Academy and the Australian National University. The notes to this study indicate the range of archival resources to which I have been given access: my main thanks go to the India Office Library in London; the Cambridge University Library; the National Archives of India, the Nehru Memorial Museum and Library, and the Gandhi Memorial Museum, all in New Delhi.

Any scholar benefits from continuous interaction wth colleagues and students, who in seminars, conferences, reviews and classes raise difficult questions, make trenchant criticisms and illuminating observations; to them all, far and near, from Manchester, Cambridge and London, to New Delhi, Canberra, Dunedin and Los Angeles, I give my thanks. Among those who at different stages have given me particularly generous encouragement and support have been Professors W.H. Morris–Jones (London), D.A. Low (Cambridge), Margaret Chatterjee (Delhi), Hew Macleod (Otago) and Barbara Ramusack (Cincinnati).

As the writing of this book coincided with a pregnancy, the birth and babyhood of our son, I owe particular thanks to a wide range of people who gave generously of their varied skills, supporting and helping me during a particularly taxing time: to the staff of St Mary's Hospital, Manchester, and Dr Madeline Osborn; to the staff of the Hallman Computer Company and the University of Manchester Regional Computer Centre, who rescued me when my word processor turned hostile;

to Mrs June Owen who read and typed part of the manuscript; to the staff of Yale University Press in London, in particular to Elaine Collins, and to Robert Baldock, my editor, who first suggested this study and saw it through to fruition with great understanding and care. Maternity and sabbatical leave would of course have been impossible without the cooperation of my immediate colleagues in the History Department of Manchester University. My family, as they have always been, have continued to be a great support. My deepest thanks go to my husband, who gallantly became both *pater familias* and resident representative of the general reading public: he read the manuscript and warded off the turgid and infelicitous. To him I dedicate this book with abiding love.

Judith M. Brown

ABBREVIATIONS

AICC	All-India Congress Committee
AISA	All-India Spinners' Association
AIVIA	All-India Village Industries Association
CP	Central Provinces
CWC	Congress Working Committee
DCC	District Congress Committee
ICS	Indian Civil Service
INC	Indian National Congress
MP	Member of Parliament (British)
NIC	Natal Indian Congress
PCC	Provincial Congress Committee
SIS	Servants of India Society
UP	United Provinces (of Agra and Oudh)

GLOSSARY

Note: foreign words are italicized in the text with the exception of those which have passed into English usage (such as raj) or those which are repeated used because they were part of Gandhi's own peculiar language (such as satyagraha).

advaita	school of Hindu philosophy which believes in the unity of all things rather than a duality, or distinction between the divine and the created.
ahimsa	non-violence (opposite of *himsa*)
ashram	religiously-orientated community, often clustered round a holy man
atman	the essence, soul of each individual
bania	person of commercial caste (*Modh Bania*: Gandhi's own sub-castle)
Bapu	affectionate name for Gandhi; 'Father'
bhakti	devotional style of Hindu spirituality
bhangi	sweeper, untouchable
brahmacharya	celibacy
Brahman	the ultimate divinity in Hindu thinking which transcends all incarnations
Brahmin	the highest Hindu caste
charkha	spinning wheel
darshan	the sight or view of a holy person, place or object, which bestows blessing on viewer; hence to take or receive, and to give *darshan*
dharma	duty; Hindi word used also for 'religion'
dhoti	loin cloth worn by men
ghee	clarified butter used in cooking and in Hindu devotional practice

gur	unrefined sugar from the sugar cane
guru	holy man, teacher
Harijans	name given by Gandhi to people formerly considered untouchable; literal meaning, 'Children of God'
hartal	strike, stoppage of work
himsa	violence (opposite of *ahimsa*, non-violence)
izaat	prestige
jalebi	Indian sweet
jati	sub-caste
karma	the ethical law of causation
khadi	hand-spun cloth
Khalifah	the Sultan of Turkey, the spiritual head of Islam
Khilafat	movement in support of Khalifah
lathi	long cane used as weapon by Indian police
lakh	100,000
Mahatma	'Great Soul'; honorific title used of Gandhi
mandir	temple
moksha	salvation, spiritual realization in Hindu thought
nabob	wealthy man; used in late eighteenth-century England to denote one who returned from India with great wealth
Parsi	Zoroastrian; members of this religious community were heavily clustered in Bombay
Patidar	name of prosperous peasant caste in Gujarat
pradakshina	Hindu form of devotion which involves walking right round a holy place or person
puja	worship
purdah	the custom of veiling women, which was found primarily among Muslims but also among some Hindu castes
raj	rule; hence 'the British raj'
Ram(a)	character in Hindu mythology seen as an incarnation of Vishnu; hence also a name of God
Ramanama	Hindu devotional practice, much favoured by Gandhi, of reciting the name of Ram
ramrajya	the rule of Ram, the rule of God
sadhana	devotional path
sadhu	Hindu wandering holy man, ascetic
sahib log	literally, the *sahib* folk, meaning the British
sanatani	orthodox Hindu
sanyassi	one who has retired from ordinary life for religious meditation

satyagraha	truth force, soul force; name give by Gandhi to non-violent resistance
satyagrahi	one who practices satyagraha
Shiva	a major Hindu god
swadeshi	literally, 'belonging to one's own country'; use of articles, particularly cloth, made in India
swaraj	self rule, Home Rule
ulema	Muslim divines, clerics (plural of *alim*)
varna	caste
varnashrama	division of society into distinct caste groups each with their own roles
varnashramadharma	word used by Gandhi to denote his ideal of a society, with groups having their own occupations but without any sense of rank
Vaishnava	Hindus giving particular veneration to Vishnu rather than Shiva
Vishnu	major Hindu god

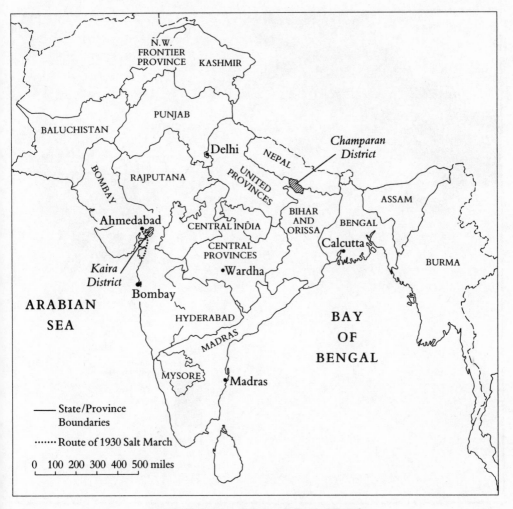

SKETCH MAP OF INDIA
*c.*1929

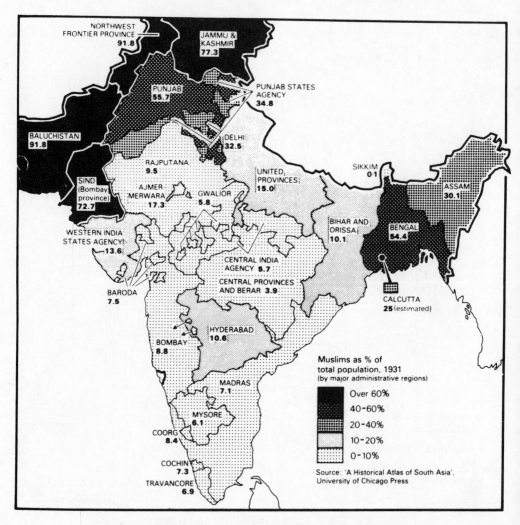

NORTHWEST
FRONTIER PROVINCE
91.8

JAMMU &
KASHMIR
77.3

BALUCHISTAN
91.8

PUNJAB
55.7

PUNJAB STATES
AGENCY
34.8

DELHI
32.5

SIND
(Bombay
province)
72.7

RAJPUTANA
9.5

UNITED
PROVINCES
15.0

SIKKIM
0·1

ASSAM
30.1

AJMER-
MERWARA
17.3

GWALIOR
5.8

BIHAR AND
ORISSA
10.1

BENGAL
54.4

WESTERN INDIA
STATES AGENCY
13.6

CENTRAL INDIA
AGENCY 5.7

BARODA
7.5

CENTRAL PROVINCES
AND BERAR 3.9

CALCUTTA
25 (estimated)

BOMBAY
8.8

HYDERABAD
10.6

MADRAS
7.1

Muslims as % of
total population, 1931
(by major administrative regions)

MYSORE
6.1

COORG
8.4

COCHIN
7.3

TRAVANCORE
6.9

Over 60%

40-60%

20-40%

10-20%

0-10%

Source: 'A Historical Atlas of South Asia',
University of Chicago Press

DENSITY OF MUSLIM POPULATION
1931

INTRODUCTION

M.K. Gandhi began his working life in India as an obscure and unsuccessful small-town lawyer, and went on to become the self-appointed champion of Indians in South Africa, turning law-breaking and gaol-going into a political strategy and religious act. On his return to India he became both a nationalist leader who attempted to refashion a whole society and polity in opposition to British imperialism, and a religious visionary widely known as *Mahatma*, 'Great Soul'. Finally, by his life and then by his death, as an assassin's victim, he became both myth and inspiration to his countrymen and to widely differing individuals and groups round the world who came to see in his beliefs and actions a remedy for hopelessness in their own situations. Understandably such a one was and is the centre of controversy, generating misunderstanding and scepticism, hostility as well as love and loyalty. Few men have elicited such vitriolic opposition or such devoted service. Churchill's ignorant jibe at Gandhi as a half-naked, seditious fakir, Muslim distrust of this Hindu holy man who purported to speak for an Indian nation, the fanatical anger of the young Hindu who killed him for 'appeasing' Muslims, were paralleled by crowds who flocked to venerate this frail, toothless man in loincloth and steel-rimmed spectacles with a commanding presence and magnetic voice, and by numerous individuals who were attracted, even enslaved, by his religious authority, his compassion and bubbling humour, even when they doubted his political wisdom or his priorities which were so alien to those of the modern world.

To present the life of such a one is exhilarating yet awesome. The primary objective is to evoke a picture of a unique individual set in a particular historical context. It is a task similar to that of the artist who with paint rather than words creates a portrait; but there is a difference, for the biographer deals with the passage of time and processes of change in the subject and his environment. Both biographer and artist, however, must assess and interpret, and their completed work, however skilled their techniques and however deep their background study, is ultimately their particular and personal response to their subject. As they enter into relationship with the one they seek to portray they also relate to those who look at or read their work, and their audience has a right to know why they chose this particular study, with what intentions, biases and credentials.

My own study of Gandhi flows from personal interest in and connection with India. I was born in India in the final years of the British raj, and my interest flowered with frequent return visits for pleasure and professional research as an academic historian, at a time when India's experience has been of absorbing fascination in many respects. India has struggled in the later twentieth century with the inheritance of an imperial structure and regime, and has firmly staked out its own political pattern, and path of social and economic modernization, ironically just as the Western world has become aware of the long-term effects of industrial civilization and disenchanted with many of them. India's venerable civilization, underpinned by the religious inheritance of its Hindu peoples, has had to adapt to the ideological and environmental changes which have resulted from intensified contact with the rest of the world.

Gandhi either played a major role in or expressed trenchant and often radical views on nearly every aspect of his country's diverse experience of change. He was a crucial figure in India's attempts to achieve political independence, and is often assumed to be the father of modern India. He made plain in word and action the priorities he expected of an independent India and its leaders. As he wrestled with the issue of non-violence in situations of conflict, and with the economic and social problems of his contemporaries, particularly the poorest and underprivileged, he questioned the assumptions of Hindu orthodoxy, Western capitalism and varieties of socialism. Although he detested the title of Mahatma and disclaimed all suggestions of sanctity, he realized he was a significant figure in determining Hindus' response to their ancient religious inheritance, and he consciously attempted to remodel it as a means for a living experience and expression of eternal truths in a changing world. The broad significance of Gandhi's life makes him therefore a fascinating and important figure for historical study. Moreover I find that Gandhi asked questions which are still uncomfortable and fundamental for people outside the Indian subcontinent. Western university students in my classes never seem to go untouched or unchallenged by him. He still inspires, aggravates and annoys. Moreover, his ideals, whether relating to politics, morals or even wholesome food and natural health care, seem to demand more serious attention, not less, as the years pass since his death.

The time consequently now seems ripe for a fresh attempt to interpret the life of Gandhi. It is not just that the dilemmas of the later twentieth century call for a re-examination of Gandhi's response to similar issues in his own context; or that historians can see more clearly his political significance in the light of the longer-term erosion of British imperial strength. A new presentation of Gandhi is actually possible now because a range of historical sources have become available for research in official and private archives, both in India and Britain. Gandhi's own *Collected Works*, ninety volumes of them, are but a part of the primary evidence now open to scrutiny. Further, the most obvious bias inherent in writing about Gandhi in the immediate aftermath of India's independence movement and its confrontations can now be left behind. Although distance in time and generation does away with the tendency towards nationalist hagiography, communal accusations or imperial justification, and though a professional historian's training guards against obvious bias, any author has to select in order to write at all. There must be choice, in the sources used and in the emphasis put on different aspects and stages of Ganhi's life. In his case the questions of selection are particularly demanding.

The sources are so extensive that the temptation is to go on delving, in acute and increasing realization of one's partial knowledge and understanding. Further, the sources can be difficult to assess and use. Many of them were generated by conflict of some kind, and their purposes have to be understood and their value as evidence judged accordingly. Some of Gandhi's religious writings are in his native Gujarati and redolent of the Hindu tradition in which he grew up, and there are subtle problems of emphasis and nuance for any who approach them from another philosophical background or read or explain them in translation. Moreover there are no papers which could be called private in the conventional sense of self-disclosure to selected confidantes, access to which enables a biographer to claim, 'Now I know the *real* Gandhi'. There are personal letters in abundance, to and from Gandhi. But his particular religious stance made him open his whole life, including his doubts and agonizings of conscience, to the public gaze. He knew that anything he wrote or said, at least in later life, was liable to become public property and indeed he welcomed such exposure. Often a personal letter was paralleled by an article in one of his journals, or he would discuss a private matter in a public speech. The sheer timescale of Gandhi's life, eight decades packed with thought and action, also poses difficulties. Not every year or phase can receive equal treatment, and the author must decide what times were the most seminal and significant, and concentrate on them to give the reader a real sense of the development of the man and his work. Without such choice of emphasis a study would become a turgid reference chronology rather than a genuine study of a human life with its varied phases of quiescence, growth and change. Finally there must be a balance between the individual and his environment, a conscious correction of the biographer's tendency to exaggerate his subject's importance, to make events revolve round him when often he may have been merely peripheral to events or moved by forces over which he had little control.

In the writing of India's history scholarly emphasis has swung firmly towards understanding the small scale political and soci. l life of local communities as the basis for comprehending change on a continental scale. Regional studies are fashionable, not biographies. This is invaluable for anyone who studies an individual: it serves as a corrective to any over-emphasis on prominent men 'making history' and demonstrates the complexity as well as the force of the circumstances in which Gandhi worked in his later years.

What is therefore offered here is a study and interpretation of a man whose life reflected many lasting human dilemmas, who attempted to resolve them in a particular historical situation, but in a way which had considerable significance in his homeland and beyond. It gives greater weight to Gandhi's Indian years because India was where his work had the deepest and longest impact, and where his ideas were fully matured and most severely tested. It sometimes breaks off from a chronological treatment to examine a particular theme or issue in the light of evidence from a considerable span of Gandhi's life, to give the reader space to consider and get the feel of the man as he would if he could engage him in conversation about his own life. This is in a sense an introduction to a person as well as an examination of the thought and work of a visionary and a politician. It is an invitation to become familiar with an enigmatic figure, both irritating and attractive; to respond to one whose life was sustained by a religious vision which created in him an abiding sense of hope and prompted him to speak and act on issues which have proved crucial to mankind in our century.

PART I

The forging of a public man

1

AN INDIAN NONENTITY

Beside the busy ring road which encircles the teeming cities of old and new Delhi in the later twentieth century there is a quiet place: *rajghat*, where a plain stone slab marks the site of Gandhi's cremation. The throbbing noises of city life, the strident voices, hooting cars and trucks, spluttering scooter-rickshaws and rumbling trains are muted here, where Indian visitors, singly or in family clusters or in parties of impressionable schoolchildren, and foreign tourists come to wonder at and pay tribute to a man who more than any other symbolized his country for a quarter of a century, both to his compatriots and to foreigners. They gaze in awe and curiosity at this symbol of a towering spirit so alien in many ways to the values of the later twentieth century, so starkly and uncompromisingly simple beside the tumultuous complexity of the India beyond the nearby road. The visitor to this national site of pilgrimage or the casual reader of accounts of India's nationalist movement might well carry away a sense of some inevitability in Gandhi's role in India's recent history. But we must cast aside such a notion if we are to begin to understand Gandhi and to appreciate his uniqueness and stature.

Mohandas Karamchand Gandhi was not born to influence, position or leadership; nor did he appear in his early life to have any wish or inner motivation to strive for power and renown. It took nearly half a century of harsh experience, of inner and exterior strugle to forge the public man known later as 'Mahatma' or Great Soul, the symbol of India, the father of a new nation. The years from his birth in 1869 to his recognition in 1919 as a force to be reckoned with in India by Indians and British rulers alike saw his development from an Indian nonentity into a mature man in public life. South Africa was the setting where a shy exile developed the incentive and skills for political and social action when confronted with the opportunity and challenge of other people's crying needs. Thus changed, he rapidly matured as a public figure in India itself on his return home early in the Great War. Underlying these outer changes a far more significant process of forging a 'public man' in a deeper sense had also occurred. The raw student of the 1880s was transformed into a visionary, passionately convinced of the primacy of truth and non-violence in all human life and relations; a searcher for truth as the ultimate meaning of life who believed that his personal life must be patent, open to public scrutiny, as he 'experimented with truth'[1] for his own and other people's spiritual realization and fulfilment.

The first part of this study of Gandhi's life concentrates on this process of forging a public man in the particular circumstance of India and South Africa at the turn of the century. Gandhi himself would have appreciated an interpretation which does not give an equal weight to every phase of his life. He saw himself as a pilgrim, and for him certain stages in his journey were more or less significant than others, as he demonstrated when he wrote his own autobiography with its highly idiosyncratic choice of events stressed or lightly touched on. The mature action and the latest illumination in the developing soul were what mattered most to him, and he scorned those who required a facile consistency over his long life as men ignorant of the deeper constraints of constant inner growth and awareness in the search for truth. The primacy given here to his Indian days is in tune with his own self-understanding, shown when he urged his contemporaries to look at what he said and did now rather than hark back to his earlier pronouncements and actions.[2]

The Indian background

Gandhi was a man whose concerns were timeless. But his career was rooted in and moulded by the context of a specific time and place. Some familiarity with India in the late nineteenth century is essential to understanding Gandhi's development, and also how extremely unlikely it was that this nonentity should have come eventually to national and international prominence.

Although a later generation that never experienced empire has glamourized India under British rule as 'the brightest jewel' in the imperial crown, to the British involved at the time when Gandhi was growing up India was the scene of hard work, a struggle against climate and frequent family separation, and often bewilderment in the face of a strange and ill-understood society and culture. Of glamour, luxury and relaxation they had precious little. Their deeply felt paternalism was often dulled by weariness, ill-health and times of disillusion.[3] Britain's commercial connections with India stretched far back into Tudor times, when intrepid merchants ventured to the Mughal court in Delhi and the East India Company was founded. But political control developed piecemeal from the late 1700s as the Mughal empire disintegrated, leaving foreigners and their trade in a context of internecine strife and uncertainty. Traders gradually turned themselves into imperialists, lured by the need to protect their financial interests from disorder and foreign competition. But often, it must be said, such sub-imperialism was greeted with reluctance on the part of the East India Company directors in Leadenhall Street and the British government in Whitehall, who alike abhorred expensive entanglements and favoured thrift and profit wherever possible. Parliament reflected this concern for sobriety and economy, well aware of the potential in British public life if nabobs, those British returned from India with vast fortunes, were to buy up 'rotten' boroughs lacking real constituencies, and turn their attentions to home politics. So parliament in its turn began increasingly to control and discipline this medley of Company servants, freebooters and other Europeans on the make, and to train them for their developing role as administrators and officials of justice. Parliament also sought to define Britain's obligations towards this expanding Asian empire. By the 1860s the East India Company had been abolished, the Indian subcontinent was under Crown government, and a regular system of imperial rule had been established. From this imperial enterprise, so little planned, various groups of Britons gained considerable benefit – from careers in the military and civilian services, from investment and trading opportunities, while Britain as a state gained a cheap barrack beyond the seas, where an army paid for out of Indian revenues stood at the ready not only to guard the pax Britannica in India but to defend imperial interests in an arc stretching from East Africa to the South China Seas. Furthermore, India's exports of raw materials to the rest of the world helped to balance Britain's trading books around the globe in a manner in which she, as a small, industrialized island, heavily dependent on imports, could never have done alone. Even India's export of desperately poor indentured labourers helped to provide vital manpower for the development of other parts of the empire, such as South Africa. Strategically and economically, therefore, India was a lynchpin not only of empire but of Britain's total position of world strength at the close of the nineteenth century.

The Indian subcontinent is the size of Europe without Russia. Only two-thirds of this vast and diverse land with its numerous peoples, languages and regions was under direct British administration. There the British constructed the tiered government of Viceroy and advisors in council, provinces with their governors and advisory bodies, and district-level administration where the District Officer bore the burden and heat of the day, and was ultimately responsible for order and good government among thousands of Indians in an area often as large as an English county. As the British parliament and electorate were notoriously bored by Indian affairs and opposed to any expense on the Indian subcontinent which fell on the British taxpayer, the Indian empire had to be self-financing. Consequently the structure of rule was as light as possible, and the British saw their role as limited to providing sound government, ready justice and protecting imperial interests. Even these limited objectives too often proved impossible, and they had no plans

for major social intervention or radical economic reform, a stance which
reflected both necessity and the *laissez-faire* understanding of a government's role widely prevalent at the time. However, at every turn they
required the help of Indians in the imperial enterprise; and the experience of differing kinds of contact and co-operation with the imperial
structure inevitably triggered changes in Indian society and in Indian
self-perception. Indian taxpayers, through the mechanisms of land
revenue, excise, customs, income tax and the like, were drawn into an
awareness of the raj and began to question its worth as its weight bore
on them more heavily. Indians were crucial in the army and the lower
ranks of civilian administration, and there was no shortage of recruits.
As the British began to develop the infrastructure of a modern state,
including the key aspects of a regular legal system and the beginnings of
English medium, Westernized education, so even more Indians were
involved in varying degrees of active collaboration with the raj, as
lawyers, teachers, doctors and students. If they belonged to the small
but rapidly expanding group of English speakers, they could begin to
co-operate with each other across the boundaries of region and
language. Their mutual awareness was sharpened by the ideological
content of their new education and aided by the metalled road, the
railway and telegraph, whose networks began to criss-cross the
subcontinent as the answer to imperial needs for military security and
swifter communications, both for the purposes of more efficient
government and the fight against famine which threatened India's
prosperity and therefore value.

In such a changing context, resources and opportunities for Indians
to become prominent in public life expanded and diversified. The
lawyer, educationalist or newspaper editor had means of wealth and
influence unknown to, though as yet not often greater than, the landed
notable of the rolling countryside or the canny family groups of traders
and bankers who accumulated considerable fortunes in the narrow,
teeming streets of India's substantial trading marts on the coasts or at
strategic river crossings. The British had always recognized from the
start of their imperial involvement in India that maintaining the raj was
as much a political enterprise as a matter of military power. Indian political weakness and intrigue had enabled them to embark on territorial
control in the eighteenth century. In the nineteenth, they refined their
political skills and acknowledged that their strength lay to a great extent
in the loyalty of notable men in the little communities of town and
countryside. To such they gave privileged access to British officialdom,
the status and powers of Justice of the Peace, and increasingly places on
the advisory councils which were meant to help Viceroy and provincial
governors to keep their ears to the ground and keep in touch, if only in
rudimentary fashion, with the sentiments of their alien subjects. By the
close of the century they had begun to recognize, unwillingly and belatedly, that men who had acquired prominence in public life through
their connection with British innovations and the British state structures

were becoming as significant foci of opinion, of loyalty or discontent as
the more traditional authority figures in Indian society. Consequently
they began to expand the advisory bodies in the capital and the provinces, though by the outbreak of the Great War these bodies were not
fully elected and had comparatively little power over the executive. Far
more significant was the conscious British expansion of Indian involvement in local government, through rural boards and municipal councils.
This was a bid to solve at least two increasingly pressing imperial
problems: to get Indians to tax themselves for local developments, and
to channel the new forms of political awareness of which they were
painfully conscious.

It would be erroneous to consider that politics in India only reflected
the emergence of men with backgrounds in English education and the
awareness and communications skills produced by their schooling and
professional expertise. Where there is power at stake there is always
politics. In India, for example, politics connected with control over
land, the sub-continent's major resource, had suffused most levels of life
in the community, right down to the level of the sturdy peasant with his
network of kin and clients, anxiously striving to expand his holding
at the expense of his neighbour or rival. The influence at stake in a
religious context bred political activity of rather different kinds as men
strove to control the resources of southern India's great Hindu temples,
or accumulated local prestige through ostentatious charity. However,
the British need for political allies, and the ideas and skills offered to
Indians through English education, the professions and the new state
structures, added a new dimension to Indian politics, a variety of new
arenas of political life. Lawyers, doctors, educationalists, administrators
and the like became increasingly aware of frustration in a political
context where the ideas found in British text books were not implemented in India. The written word might inspire with concepts of
equality, nationalism, freedom, and democracy, but the actions of the
British in India reflected little of this idealism and spoke louder of racial inequality and autocracy. Consequently there emerged the beginnings of new styles of politics geared to the issues concerning power
as wielded through the structures of the raj. Local associations
of educated Indians from the mid-nineteenth century developed to
discuss the interests of their members, such as educational provision,
the barriers to Indian entry into the prestigious Indian Civil Service,
the minimal participation of Indians in the government's councils,
or overt aspects of racial discrimination. From these self-improvement and students' societies, literary associations and overtly political
groups emerged the Indian National Congress in 1885. It was a loose association of local groups of English speakers who realized that a continental platform would enable them to speak with greater authority to
their rulers. As a body Congress was conspicuously loyal to the raj.
Although it asked for political reforms its members had no wish to
endanger or uproot the imperial structure, because it was that structure

which provided the context for their own prominence in public life. Nor was it in any real sense a popular body. Its concerns were not those of the peasant farmer or the petty urban shopkeeper. Furthermore its fears of social and religious strife made it avoid all controversies on social or religious issues. By so doing it isolated itself from what might have become a ground swell of broad support.[4] Although Congress was so limited in its base and interests, though it had no permanent organization and its finances were shaky, it nevertheless marked out a new public forum in which Indians could become influential and in which discourse was in terms of an Indian nation. It was an arena of 'high politics' where men learned to deal with each other and their rulers in the context of India as a whole, in contrast to the more local levels of politics where Indians still dealt with each other and their rulers on a more restricted scale.

The remaining third of the subcontinent continued under the control of a remnant of India's Princely families who had survived the British expansive thrust and reforming zeal of the early nineteenth century. They differed greatly in size from mighty Hyderabad in southern India to the tiny pocket-handkerchief states north of Bombay. Some of their rulers were still little more than big spenders surrounding themselves with luxury and service at the expense of their subjects. Others were earnest, foward-looking men, anxious for their people's well-being and eager to learn the practices of good modern government. Some were debauched grandees who more than held their own in the playgrounds of Europe's rich; others were deeply religious and sensitive men of affairs. Over this curious medley the British stretched a light web of control, depriving the Princes of armed force, but allowing them a great liberty within their own domains under the eye of a British Resident or Agent, whose job it was to see that the life-style and governmental practice of Princely rulers did not endanger British security. The developing politics associated with English education and the structures of the raj had no counterpart here; as society was far more deeply conservative, there were fewer educational opportunities, and the Princes, secure in British support, saw no need for political accommodation with their subjects.

Although structures of government had altered considerably in British India during the nineteenth century, generating new arenas and resources in public life, influencing and in turn influenced by the new opportunities created by a common language, English-style education and markedly improved communications, there was no fundamental change in the economic base and ordering of society. Land had for centuries been the major source of wealth and influence. Under the British it remained so, a fact reflected in their early concentration on 'settling' landed rights in return for a regular flow of revenue to government coffers, and their political realization that they must make unto themselves friends of the landholders, with their networks of connections and clients, as a guarantee of widespread acquiescence in their raj. India had no uniform pattern of landholding, and it cannot be accurately described as a feudal society in the nineteenth century. In a few areas large estates existed, but a far more prevalent pattern of land ownership was that of the prosperous peasant farmer or kin group owning some land and renting other plots in a patchwork of rights and customs. Patterns of Indian politics, particularly at village or district level, but increasingly at the level of 'high politics', reflected the concerns of such dominant rural folk, and the lines of political connection often followed those of kinship and patronage laid down in the daily routines of rural life. The local configurations of power and influence were moulded by an area's basic ecology and its patterns of landholding and usage: no individual or body aspiring to continental influence could ignore this variegated local base, but had to come to terms with it, to learn how to deal with its notables and to work within its political rules. A continental raj, an aspiring nationalist party or leader faced similar dilemmas of establishing myriads of local linkages in order to have a firm local foundation.

India's internal and external trade had been a further source of in-fluence and wealth along natural lines of communications for centur-ies. Opportunities expanded as the British presence enabled a closer integration of the Indian economy itself and with the world-wide economy through the expansion of communications. But those who took advantage of these widening opportunities were generally those whose families had generations of experience in commerce and finance. Similarly the tentative beginnings of modern industrial enterprise in late nineteenth-century India did little to disrupt existing social patterns, to place wealth into the hands of new groups of Indians or to undermine the economic foundations of society. Much of the earliest modern industry was under European control, particularly in eastern India. In the west the Indians who financed cotton mills or went into shipbuild-ing tended to be diversifying existing commercial interests and building on long-established expertise, as in the case of the Parsi community or the traditionally wealthy trading families of Ahmedabad, to the north of Bombay, who were to be so significant in Gandhi's later life.[5] The fact that existing patterns of society could accommodate and exploit these new resources, thus limiting their potential for social dislocation, was reinforced by the extremely localized nature of industrial growth, clustered within range of the port cities of Bombay, Madras and Calcutta. India remained a land of villages relatively untouched by modern economic changes until well into the twentieth century.

Given such limited economic change and the comparatively narrow range of Indians deeply affected by British culture and education, it is hardly surprising that Indian society had changed comparatively little after a century of British imperial rule. The British had never conquered India, as the Spaniards had South America, for example. The stalwart communities of village and locality remained intact and the British merely slotted into the subcontinent's politics at a comparatively high level of control where the Mughal authority had crumbled, while socially they remained aloof, recreating an English life-style insulated by a sense of community and superiority from the millions over whom they held sway. The virtual absence of white settlement by non-official British people further limited British influence in society at large. Early in the nineteenth century for a few brief years British Utilitarians, Evangelicals and free traders had dreamed of reforming Indian society, liberating its peoples from the shackles, as they saw them, of religion and tradition, and enabling the triumphant emergence of modern-minded Indians who would be indistinguishable from their rulers except by colour. Bitter experience soon showed them that Indian society was not only venerable but immensely stable, perfectly able to accommodate change in rulership, in economics and to some extent in values without falling apart. The Indian mutiny of 1857 reinforced their realization that overt social engineering was out of the question, given their limited financial resources and their radical dependence on Indian allies in the imperial enterprise.

If land is one central pillar of Indian society, religion is another. The majority of Indians were and are Hindus, though there was a very sizeable Muslim minority clustered in the north west and in Bengal. Small minorities such as Jains, Sikhs, Parsis and Christians added to the religious pluralism of Indian society. In each community religious tradition deeply affected daily life. Religion provided the boundaries of intimate social relations, particularly marriage, and laid down patterns of behaviour convering every aspect of domestic and social life, includ-ing clothing, food and family interactions. The indivisibility of the 'religious' and the 'social' in ordinary life was most marked among Hindus, where the system of hierarchical ranking of kin groups in order of ritual purity, the so-called caste system, dominated the ordering of family and community life. Western observers found this system of social stratification distasteful, having within their Christian back-ground little to enable them to understand the concepts of purity and pollution connected with certain substances and occupations. Further, they were bewildered and often frightened by the rich variety of theological and philosophical traditions and patterns of worship which made up the complexity of the Hindu inheritance. Yet to those born within this inheritance – brought up naturally to observe the strict patterns of avoidance in eating, touch and marriage between castes; told by mothers, aunts and grannies of the colourful legends of the Hindu heroes, gods and goddesses; whose childhoods were punctuated by family worship and the communal celebration of numerous religious festivals with feasting and drama – the Hindu inheritance was a vibrant one. It provided a way of life and a cognitive structure which made sense of the world, its joys as well as its perils and problems.[6]

However, those Hindus who were exposed through education and personal contact to Western and predominantly Christian values felt a tension in their lives and their understanding of what it meant to be

Hindu. Like their teachers they began to be critical of such practices as treating those at the base of the caste hierarchy as untouchable, of the way Hindu widows were cast into poverty and social degradation on the death of their husbands, and of the custom of child marriage, particularly where a child bride became the property of a far older husband, with all the attendant dangers of emotional and physical harm. New values emanating from the West challenged their values, traditions and very identity. Their response was to develop social reform associations which tried to ameliorate such practices without rejecting Hindu tradition as a whole. Simultaneously there sprang up religious reform associations which tackled the meaning of being a Hindu in a changing world. Some of those involved in this intellectual and religious turmoil were also active in new forms of political activity. But in the late nineteenth century, for most educated Hindus 'the social question' was the more pressing.[7]

The individual

Into this world of stability and encroaching change Mohandas Karamchand Gandhi was born on 2 October 1869. He was the youngest child of six, the last of three sons and three daughters born to Karamchand Gandhi who married four times, for the last time to Mohandas's mother when he was in his forties, having lost each wife in turn through death. Two scenes from the young Gandhi's childhood typify the blend of traditional forces and pressures for change even in his small world, and the tension this generated in his response to his environment. First there was his marriage, when he was barely in his teens, to the equally young Kasturbhai, daughter of one of his father's close friends in their home town of Porbandar, on India's north-west coast. It was a triple wedding, for Mohandas, an elder brother and cousin and their brides, arranged by their parents without the children's prior knowledge or consent: the first the young Gandhi knew of it was the start of the elaborate preparations which precede any Hindu wedding in order that it should be observed with due ceremony. The parents' plan was designed to fulfil the Hindu tradition of early marriage within the correct caste grouping, and also in this case to economize. Weddings were major social events at which the family's prestige was displayed, and the impact of one, let alone three in succession, was likely to impoverish any family but the wealthiest. Further, in the Gandhis' case both father and uncle were elderly and anxious to see their duty to their children well completed before their deaths. Young Mohandas enjoyed his wedding, though at the time it meant little more than feasting, processions, new clothes and a strange girl of his own age to play with. Only later was he to condemn this tradition of child marriage and the egregious display which accompanied most weddings.

But even the adolescent Gandhi was not insulated from ideas and practices which challenged Hindu tradition, though in the matter of his

marriage he may have been well content. As a schoolboy he had a friend
who told him that some of his teachers and fellow pupils were
beginning to eat meat, because they were convinced that the tradition of
vegetarianism made Hindus physically weak and had enabled the British
to rule over them. Among the schoolboys a doggerel was going the
rounds to this effect:

> Behold the mightly Englishman
> He rules the Indian small,
> Because being a meat–eater
> He is five cubits tall.

Lured by the hope of physical strength for himself and political strength
for his country, Gandhi fell for the 'reform' and for a while ate meat in
secret when his friend provided it. The first occasion was a clandestine
and unsuccessful riverside picnic when Gandhi was thoroughly sick.
Even the vomiting did not alleviate his distress as a nightmare of a live
goat bleating inside him plagued his sleeping hours.[8]

Looking back in the 1920s on his childhood, the Gandhi who by then
had become a well-known figure in Indian public life commented on
these experiences with a wry honesty. By implication the picture he
painted of those early years showed that both the circumstances of his
family and his own character as a child made it highly improbable that
he would become a continental figure of significance. The family's
material and social resources and prospects were limited. At the time of
Mohandas's birth Karamchand was living in the sleepy coastal town of
Porbandar, in one of the small Princely states of Kathiawad, in the area
which is now Gujarat State. There was no sign here of the economic,
political and educational changes that were beginning to have a significant impact on public life in British India. Even when the family
moved to nearby Rajkot when Mohandas was seven they were still
outside the mainstream of change on the subcontinent, the main
difference now being greater access to modern education for the boys
and a cosmopolitan atmosphere in which the young Gandhis met
educated men from other parts of India for the first time. In the last three
grades of high school only English was used, and Gandhi was taught by
three Parsis from one of India's most Anglicized communities, while in
Kathiawad's only college, which had been established for four years
when Gandhi enrolled there, the Principal was an Oxford graduate. The
social as much as the geographical setting of Gandhi's childhood
insulated him from much exposure to any challenge to tradition. His
family were of middle-caste ranking, *Modh Banias*, whose original
vocation was probably that of grocers, though Gandhi's father and
grandfather were both senior officials in the courts of various Kathiawad
Princes. The strength of tradition within the caste for maintaining ritual
purity was demonstrated by the fact that a powerful section of it
outcasted Gandhi when he decided to study in Britain, on the grounds
that such an enterprise would inevitably result in ritual pollution. The

youth who was outcasted had already learned as a child not to touch the sweeper who served the household, doing the polluting chores, including the removal of excrement; and as an adolescent he had seen his mortally sick father struggle out of bed to perform his natural functions lest he contravene the strict purity laws observed by the Vaishnava sect within the Hindu tradition to which he belonged. Only from a schoolboy acquaintance of whom his family profoundly disapproved did the young Gandhi learn of the reformist ideas which in other parts of India were gradually beginning to challenge conventions hallowed by time and religious tradition.

In material terms, too, there was little to precipitate Mohandas into public prominence. The family was not poor. It was well fed and housed and had its quota of servants as befitted a state official. But the father had no financial ambitions, left his widow and children little property, and money was tight after his death when his youngest son was still in his teens. It was therefore agreed by the family, as was and is so often the case in the Indian family context, that one son must receive all possible assistance so that his eventual professional standing could support the rest of his family. The choice fell on the youngest son as the most likely to prosper sufficiently to bear the family burden. Yet Gandhi's father had realized well before his death that his sons must come to terms with the new knowledge and skills opened up by Westernized education. His own formal education was slight, and conducted in Gujarati; his real resource was a wide experience of men and their affairs of state rather than book learning. But he sent his sons to benefit from the new schooling in Rajkot. Mohandas was an adequate pupil, but of no remarkable academic aptitude or interest in reading outside school hours. Moreover his schooling was badly interrupted for a year by the occasion of his marriage. Yet he managed by doggedness to progress through the high school system until in 1887 he passed the matriculation examination and moved on to a fairly local college in Bhavnagar. He had by this time a fair proficiency in English, but the experience of Bhavnagar was too much for him. Living away from home for the first time, coping with a difficult climate, and struggling both with the standard of work and of English required, he failed his first examinations and returned home to take stock.

It was perhaps the religious environment of Gandhi's childhood which was the only remarkable aspect of this otherwise unremarkable experience of growing up. Although Karamchand observed the purity rituals with such meticulous care, his was not a household marked by a rigid orthodoxy of belief and practice. Rather, it was an unusually open household in religious terms, where men of many traditions were welcomed and their insights valued as aspects of man's search for the divine. As Vaishnavas the family went to the temple of their own sect, where the worship of the incarnation Vishnu was of paramount importance. But its worship had little impact on the young Gandhi: 'I did not like its glitter and pomp. Also I heard rumours of immorality practised there, and lost all interest in it.'[9] Both parents also went with their children to temples dedicated to Shiva and Rama; monks of the Jain community were frequent visitors to the household (and even ate with the family, thus crossing traditional avoidance barriers in the sensitive area of food); while Muslim and Parsi friends were received by Karamchand with respect and interest for their beliefs. Particularly strong in surrounding Gujarat was the Jain tradition, a close sister to orthodox Hinduism, but laying greater stress on non-violence and an understanding of truth as many-sided. Only later did the Jain influence become particularly clear in Gandhi's own religious development. But its presence in his childhood was a signficant determinant of his ultimate convictions as to the nature of truth, of his personal tolerance and high estimation of all major faiths with their particular insights into the mystery of truth, and of his supreme dedication to non-violence.

Gandhi, the child, was also influenced by various devotional practices which were far more central to the Hindu tradition. His nurse tried to comfort her young charge when he was scared of ghosts and spirits with the advice to repeat the name of Ram over and over again, and this practice remained with Gandhi, the Mahatma, and became of deepening value to him. He was also impressed by hearing recitations of the story of Rama, the *Ramayana*, one of the best loved Hindu epics, at a very early age before the family moved away from Porbandar. But the greatest devotional example before him was his own mother, Putali Bhai. Her daily prayers and visits to temples, and her rigorous fasting as a religious observance, were the most lasting impression he had of her. Yet for all these influences Gandhi, on his own admission,[10] had no real and living faith in God as he was growing up. When he came across one of the key texts of the Hindu tradition, the *Laws of Manu*, among his father's books he was not impressed, and if anything moved in the direction of atheism. Ironically, in view of his later attitude and reputation, the one tradition present locally of which he was both ignorant and intolerant at this stage was Christianity. His hostility reflected the strident evangelism of missionary work in Gujarat at the time, which included street-corner denunciation of the evils of the Hindu tradition and its deities, and also the deep fear that converts had to ape European ways to the extent of eating beef, drinking alcohol and wearing European clothes.[11]

If the boy Gandhi's religious environment and his response to it gave only the feeblest hints of the religious flowering which was to occur in the adult Mahatma, the child's emotional development suggests even less the later emergence of a formidable personality, both driven by inner conflicts and drawn by an intense vision, which exerted such a compelling appeal by his mere presence. It is almost impossible from the available evidence to know whether Gandhi's childhood was a happy one. It was certainly a secure family setting, clouded by none of the insecurities of dire poverty or parental discord. Even when Gandhi's father died, the adolescent was surrounded, as is the case in the extended Hindu family, with the presence and supervisory care of other male relatives and his father's close friends, who watched over the future of the orphaned children and planned Mohandas's career. Whereas a boy brought up in the West would almost certainly find his father's death a brutal initiation into the cares and conventions of the adult male world, for the Hindu boy this was not the case. Not only did the extended family normally shield male children in such circumstances; boys would already have passed into the male world at about the age of five when their mother's early, all-embracing and providing presence was withdrawn, and they were increasingly socialized by their fathers, uncles and older brothers in their male role, including of course early marriage.[12] Mohandas was no exception. As we follow him through his autobiography we see him being inducted into the world of men, agonizing over the meaning of masculinity as he reacted to his 'reformist', meat-eating friend, and learning the role of the Hindu husband. The young Kasturbhai spent a considerable part of their early married life in her own natal home: a kindly custom which eases the young bride's transition to her new status as wife and most junior daughter-in-law in a household of strangers. In their brief periods together her young husband rapidly asserted himself, not merely as an active sexual partner, but as a reforming companion, eager to teach her to read and write, and also to subdue her self-will and to mould her into his view of the ideal Hindu submissive wife. When he tried to restrict her visits to girl friends or to the temple she understandably refused and deliberately tried to evade his wishes, with the result that 'Refusal to speak to one another thus became the order of the day with us, married children'.[13]

Although Gandhi later portrayed himself as an over-assertive and unwarrantedly suspicious young husband, a significant impression left by his autobiographical writings is of a very frightened child. He was timid and retiring among his own age group as well as among his elders at home and at school; one who did not seek out the company of his school contemporaries for companionship but went home as early as possible; the junior partner rather than leader or innovator in relationships with other boys. His childhood world was haunted by fear – of thieves, ghosts and snakes. Darkness was a well of terror for him, even in his teens, and he could not sleep without a light in the room. Even his attempts to exert his masculinity in adolescence were occasions of fear. The goat bleating inside his stomach had nightmarishly plagued him after he had eaten meat for the first time. When the same meat-eating friend took him to a brothel he became so speechless and immobile that the prostitute showered him with insults and showed him the door. The result was a severe blow to his sense of maleness and a reinforcement of his timidity both in situations and in relationships. Such episodes also served to underline another strong trait in the growing personality of the young Gandhi. He evidently had from a very early age a strong sense of morality and a tendency to self-condemnation and guilt. Two heroes of his childhood whom he encountered through books, pictures and plays, Shravana and Harischandra, were notable for their devotion to parents and truthfulness. He brooded on their stories and they became living presences in his inner childhood world. In the outer, mundane world of school he was shocked at the thought of cheating to save the teacher's face before an Inspector of Education; and he burst into tears when thought by the staff on another occasion to have been lying about an absence from class. Not surprisingly this strict moral sense conflicted profoundly with his covert attempts to experiment with Western ways, most particularly because they involved lying to his parents. He experienced this conflict as a gnawing at his heart.

Gandhi's relationship with his parents was of profound importance for his later development. But at this distance in time and across a considerable cultural gap which separates us from the late nineteenth-century inner world of the Hindu it is difficult to be precise about the nature of that parent–child relationship and the significance of particular events. Western commentators have, for example, tried to build elaborate theories about Gandhi's emotional development on the scant evidence of his relations with his father, perhaps forgetting that in the growing up processes of the Hindu boy the father's figure and role is very different from that found in twentieth-century Western and nuclear families.[14] In the context of the Hindu extended family, and Hindu patterns of child rearing, it is the mother who tends to be the more problematic parent for the maturing male child: the mother–son rather than father–son relationship is the crucial one which the growing boy must handle successfully if he is to grow to mature manhood, whereas in the West the father–son relationship, with its dark Oedipal undertones, tends to be the most difficult for the growing boy to handle. The mother in Hindu India is both the supreme giver of love, security and sustenance, yet also the embodiment of the dangerous power of womanhood which can cling to and emasculate her son. Both aspects of the mother are vividly portrayed in Hindu myths and folk tales, as well as surfacing in clinical encounters between psychiatrists and their male Hindu patients in the later twentieth century.[15] When the mother ceases the primary role in raising her son and he enters the world of the male members of the family, he sorely needs his father to help him adjust to this potentially traumatic break in his experience of security and to find a new sense of identity. Hindu fathers are culturally constrained not to show great affection for their sons until they have learned the roles of the world of masculine encounters and can be welcomed as companions and heirs. If the father is too aloof the son's development into masculinity can become fraught with difficulty.

Gandhi's autobiography makes much of his relationship with his father. The young Mohandas saw Karamchand as aloof, stern and liable to bad temper. But when he most needed him in a crisis of conscience his father proved loving and gentle. The adolescent was consumed with guilt at having stolen a golden chip out of his brother's armlet to pay off a debt for the same brother; and when he decided to tell his father the older Karamchand responded not with a beating or with recriminations but with tears. This seems to have cemented the relationship between them. However, the circumstances of Karamchand's death grievously underlined Gandhi's existing tendency towards guilt and almost certainly affected his attitudes towards sexuality later in life. Although the son was a constant nurse to his father in his last illness, at the point of his father's death the son was in bed with his wife. He wrote later,

> It was a blot I have never been able to efface or forget, and I have always thought that, although my devotion to my parents knew no bounds and I would have given up anything for it, yet it was weighed and found unpardonably wanting because my mind was at the same moment in the grip of lust.[16]

It would be wrong to see the father's death as the great trauma which affected Gandhi's later psychological development: Gandhi was not reared in the context where the son's sexuality in relation to his parents makes the father–son relationship potentially painful. But he was deeply fond of his father and vividly aware of the Hindu ideal of filial devotion, and it is probably fair to conclude that the episode coloured his attitude to sexual control later in life, though not for over a decade, and then there were other personal and cultural factors at work in his decision to become a celibate. Further, it is likely that Karamchand's death meant that his teenage son never completed his 'emotional work' in identifying with his father, and this in turn affected his response to his mother. Of Putali Bhai there is little in the autobiography except a reverent recognition of her piety. There is no hint of anxiety or ambivalence towards the mother. But from our knowledge of Hindu childhood it seems likely that the father's death made the son more vulnerable to his mother's domination, a factor which also may have influenced Gandhi's later sexual identity and interpretation of masculinity. Whatever the psychological implications of Karamchand's death, in practical terms it soon marked the beginning of a new phase in his son's life. The unremarkable youth was thrust into the bewildering and challenging world of a career in law: the one who had never travelled even as far as Bombay now set out for London.

Passage to England

The undistinguished youth whose command of English had failed him in college found himself on his father's death as the potential head of the extended Gandhi family, its guardian and major earner. Although he was not the eldest son, his family and a close family friend and advisor felt that Mohandas was the best fitted for the task and the consequent family investment needed in his future. Although medicine attracted Mohandas his father had evidently hoped he would be a lawyer, and law seemed the more certain path towards an administrative position in

the Kathiawar states, following the family tradition. With a touchingly
simple vision of the value of an English legal qualification and the
comfortable life-style back in India of barristers trained in London's Inns
of Court, the family arranged for him to study in London, much as a
century later other migrants from the subcontinent saw England as a
treasure-trove, a land of prosperity where none could fail to succeed
and in turn bring wealth and prestige to his family at home in India.

This was a dramatic cultural step not just for Gandhi but for the
whole family. None of them or their sub-caste had ventured abroad
before, and their determination was an indication of how far the
modernizing tendencies at work on the subcontinent had reached even
this remote and traditional corner of India. However, there were misgivings about the plan. Gandhi's uncle voiced the traditional wisdom,
fearing that his nephew's religion would be compromised by such a
venture, and he was critical of the overtly Westernized life-style of
Indian barristers returned from England whom he had met. 'I see no
difference between their life and that of Europeans. They know no
scruples regarding food. Cigars are never out of their mouths. They
dress as shamelessly as Englishmen. All that would not be in keeping
with our family tradition.'[17] In old age he was, as Hindu tradition
prescribed, withdrawing deeper into religious practices, and with these
as his concern he refused to give his permission for the journey. Instead he shifted the burden of decision on to Gandhi's devout mother,
and agreed to the project should she consent. Poor Putali Bhai for her
part was deeply worried by the ill-informed gossip which reached her
about the moral fate of young men who journeyed to England. In her
dilemma she turned to another old family friend, one of their own sub-
caste who had become a Jain monk. He advised that Mohandas should
vow in his presence to abstain from wine, women and meat. This done,
the mother consented. Even so, Gandhi's caste fellows disapproved,
and while he was waiting in Bombay for a passage he was summoned
before a general meeting of the *Modh Banias* and formally outcasted. To
Gandhi this was of little concern. Nor was there any sign that he
appreciated the cultural shock and hard work ahead of him. Furthermore, with little apparent concern he left behind his wife and their
first child, a son of a few months. With extreme excitement he lodged in
Bombay, booking his passage to England for September 1888, and
buying a selection of European clothes as would befit an aspiring
lawyer.

The voyage proved an ordeal. Gandhi's experiences were symbolic of
those he was to undergo in the next three years. He was still afflicted
with the crippling shyness which had marked his childhood, a sense
now compounded by his poor English. All his immediate fellow
passengers were English except for an Indian lawyer with whom he was
travelling. He found it virtually impossible to understand them or
converse with them, as he was still at the stage when he had to think out
each sentence in English in his mind before saying it. By the end of the

voyage the strangeness of it all and his homesickness overwhelmed him, and he would weep at night, remembering home and in partiuclar his mother's love. Gandhi's natural timidity and shyness, so briefly thrown off in the excitement of leaving a difficult college environment and preparing for England, were underscored by a deep social unease in the presence of English people. On the voyage this was apparent, not just in his inability to understand and be understood in English. He found the etiquette of ordinary social exchange difficult to master. He did not know how to use Western cutlery at table, and consequently ate alone in his cabin to avoid difficulty, subsisting largely on fruit and sweets he had brought with him. Even in the matter of dress he looked an absurd figure, stepping off the boat at Southampton on an autumn day, a lone figure in white flannels, so proudly acquired in Bombay! Luckily another family friend met him when he arrived in London and gave him sound advice on how to behave politely in England, and also helped him to find accommodation.

Gandhi's three years in London were a time of social, moral and intellectual ferment for him. He was confronted not only with the academic opportunities he was seeking, but with a bewildering array of intellectual, religious and cultural influences, as well as moral 'temptations' from the viewpoint of his own tradition. For him it was the first time he had had the opportunity and the necessity of taking charge of his own life, of sorting out his priorities and values. Freed from the constraining if comforting confines of his family and its cultural setting, apart from the triple vow which he rigorously observed, he had to work out who and what he was and wanted to become, what it meant to be an Indian adrift in the cultural and economic capital of the empire whose influences had only just reached the home he had left.

Gandhi's life-style underwent remarkable changes in London. After the first shock of the voyage and landing in England he threw himself into an overt strategy of Westernization, attempting to learn all the skills and graces he thought befitted an English gentleman. He started out on lessons in French, dancing, violin and elocution. He rapidly saw that the 'European' clothes he had bought in Bombay looked out of place in England, and went to the solidly respectable Army and Navy Stores for new ones. He even had an evening suit made in Bond Street. Mirrors had been unheard of luxuries at home except for the family barber's visit, but now he struggled for ten minutes each day in front of one to master the art of tying a tie, and to tame his unruly hair. A contemporary meeting him in Piccadilly Circus was left in no doubt about the impression the young man was now seeking to create. He was dressed in the morning clothes of an English gentleman, from his high silk hat down to his spats and patent leather boots, even carrying a silver-mounted stick. He seemed 'a student more interested in fashion and frivolities than in his studies.'[18]

This proved a passing phase. Gandhi soon gave up the unequal struggle with music and dancing, abandoned elocution, and began to think seriously about legal study. He continued, however, to wear European clothes and, on his own admission, to be punctilious about dress for years. A major factor in this change was the need for economy, reinforcing a sense that he was endangering his cultural identity and primary goal by such frivolous experimentation. The moral seriousness of the child resurfaced in the London student and set him on the path of increasing frugality and simplification of life-style. The expense of living in London horrified him and he moved rapidly out of a hotel into a landlady's house. Then for greater economy he moved into rooms on his own, and eventually into one room where he had a stove on which he cooked breakfast of oatmeal porridge and cocoa, prepared an evening meal of bread and cocoa, and only had his lunch out. He lived on 1s 3d a day – a grand economy on the £3 hotel bill for his initial weekend in London. At the same time he learned to walk everywhere within London wherever possible. This habit saved him money on fares and also toughened his physique so that decades later he could still walk younger men off their feet. This capacity marked him out on his return to India, where conventionally the influential and well-to-do walk as little as possible, in sharp contrast to the daily physical toil of the working man and woman. Walking like ordinary people, touring the land in face-to-face contact, was to become part of Gandhi's peculiar style of popular leadership. Another habit which he acquired in London and which later stood him in good stead as a public man handling considerable public funds was that of keeping regular accounts. He kept a daily tally of every farthing spent in London, including postage or a daily paper, a meticulousness which stayed with him all his life.

Gandhi's vow to his mother was also a dominant element in his changing life-style. Because he could not eat meat and found it difficult to distinguish the ingredients in English cooking, and was often too shy to ask for something different, he found that his early months in London were marked by extreme hunger and disgust at the blandness of such vegetarian food as he was offered by his landlady. He dared not ask for more food and even the extra slice or two of bread the daughters of the house offered him could not satisfy his gnawing hunger: 'little did they know that nothing less than a loaf would have filled me.'[19] Eventually he found a vegetarian restaurant in the city, and ate his first good meal since his arrival in England. In the same restaurant he saw and bought Salt's *Plea for Vegetarianism*. He read it voraciously and claimed that from that day he became a vegetarian by choice. The book opened to him a whole new world of thought, linking diet with morality, religion and science. He began to ponder on the relations between men and animals, on the role of food as strictly a means of life rather than an enjoyable experience. With all the moral seriousness of his younger days he began to experiment with different diets, abandoned the sweets and spices sent from home and earnestly set his mind to live on the bland food he had found so insipid on his arrival. Thus began a concern for an

interlocking approach to diet, health and religion which lasted a lifetime. Such concerns were far removed from those of most Indian
politicians with whom he was to deal; but they were integral to the
vision Gandhi was to evolve of a new India founded on healthy,
self-supporting village communities. Gandhi also mixed with vegetarians through the Vegetarian Society. He found himself on its executive committee and so began his first experience of voluntary, organized activity, and included not only the conventions of committee
work but also writing for the society's journal. But even their sympathetic company made it no easier for him to speak either in committee
or in bigger public gatherings. Even at a farewell dinner among vegetarian friends he proved incapable of more than one sentence of thanks.

Gandhi's association with like-minded English folk is a reminder that
there was in late nineteenth-century England little of the racial prejudice
and tension which faced later Indian visitors to England. When Gandhi
journeyed west his Indian fellow travellers were either students or
highly Westernized Indians, and there was little occasion for cultural
clashes between them and their host society, and no economic tension of
the kind generated when immigrants and poorer sections of the indigenous population are in competition. Consquently Gandhi was to find
racial arrogance and discrimination particularly galling when he encountered it on his return to India and then more acutely in South Africa.
Despite the comparative ease with which Gandhi was received in
England, he felt real tension between the standards of English society
and his Indian perceptions of proper behaviour. There were the obvious
temptations which low life in any city offered the young and lonely
male visitor. These Gandhi avoided, thanks to his shyness and his vow
to his mother. He also felt reluctant to admit that at that young age he
was already a husband and a father, lest Westerners should misunder-
stand and think ill of Hindu culture. It was particularly problematic
because there were opportunities for friendship with young women
whose openness and freedom in a totally respectable manner were far
removed from the conduct expected of their counterparts in India.
Eventually when he thought that a kindly English woman had eyes on
him as a match for one of her younger friends, he admitted his real
family status – with no ill effect on the friendship. But the young Indian
had little experience of English families and their domestic habits, so
aloof did he keep himself, and so debilitating was the shyness which
overcame him if there were more than a few people in the room.

One striking change the English experience worked in the young man
was a widening of his religious horizons and sympathy. Ironically it was
through two Theosophists, bachelor brothers, whom he met after
nearly two years in England, that he encountered with real interest and
responded to some of the roots of his own religious heritage. They
introduced him to Sir Edwin Arnold's translation of the *Bhagavad Gita
The Song Celestial*, and also to Arnold's *The Light of Asia*, which Gandhi
read with even more interest than the *Gita*, so appealing to him was its

account of the Buddha's teachings, many of which echoed his Jain inheritance and his own movement through vegetarianism towards non-violence and compassion for all life. The *Gita* seemed to him even at that early age to be 'of priceless worth', but it was only some years later that it became part of his daily reading.[20] The same brothers were his introduction to Theosophy. Although he declined to join the Theosopical Society, it was Madame Blavatsky's *Key to Theosophy* which helped him shed the uneasy suspicion, fed by missionary preaching in Rajkot, that Hinduism was rife with superstition. Of profound significance also was Gandhi's contact in England with kindly and tolerant Christians, so different from the strident street-preachers he had encountered at home. The genuine piety of such friends, and the welcome news that Christianity did not inevitably mean joining the ranks of meat-eaters and alcohol-drinkers, impressed him. But even more so did the Christian scriptures. He plodded through the Old Testament, invariably falling asleep under the influence of the earlier books. But the New Testament, and particularly the Sermon on the Mount, spoke directly and powerfully to him. There seemed in the Sermon much in common with the *Gita*. The themes of compassion, non-violence and self-renunciation from various religious sources began to combine in his estimation as the highest manifestations of religion. His experiences and reading in England turned him even more resolutely against atheism than before; but though he returned home with a deeper sensitivity to a wide range of religious teaching and experience, as yet he himself had no real religious commitment, no vision to inspire his adult life.

The primary objective of Gandhi's visit to England was legal study and qualification. In this he showed himself remarkably conscientious, taking the Bar Examinations with utmost seriousness. He bought and read all the prescribed text books, many of them weighty tomes, even studying Roman Law in Latin, whereas many of his contemporaries muddled through the comparatively easy examinations on the basis of last minute study of students' notes. He was called to the Bar in 1891. In preparation for this he had also in his early months in London striven to improve his English and his general educational qualifications. He studied for the London Matriculation and passed, at the second attempt, after failing initially in Latin. It says much for the young man's natural ability as well as his tenacity and courage that after an unremarkable educational record at home he was prepared to tackle this hurdle, including two foreign languages, French and Latin, and all of this in a language of which his initial command was worryingly weak.

The Gandhi who set sail for home in mid-1891 had made immense strides in self-knowledge and growth in personal identity since his naïvely eager departure from Bombay, ignorant of the turmoil in store for him. He had a new fluency in English, a professional qualification, and was far more cosmopolitan than the youth in white flannels who had stepped ashore in Southampton. In his three years in England he had met a wide social range of people, learned the ways of Western social life, had expanded his intellectual and political horizons not just through books but also the newspapers, which he had never read at home, and had even visited Paris for the Great Exhibition. However, on his departure from England he still had few of the resources needed to make good in India, and his family had had totally unrealistic hopes about what an English legal qualification alone could give their brightest son. He was still shy. He was poor and lacked the wealthy or influential contacts essential for a career in law. Even his study of law did not equip him to practise in India. He knew little of Indian law, and even less of the ways of the Indian courts or of the lives of his potential clients.

Homecoming was not the joyous or triumphant experience for which he might have hoped. He was already anxious about his ability to practise law, uneasy about his caste's likely attitude to him, and concerned about the life-style he should adopt as one who considered himself a 'reformer'. But the bitter blow which awaited him was the news of his mother's death, which the family had kept from him while he was abroad. He had been longing to see her, and his grief, though publicly restrained, was far deeper than that felt at his father's death. Quite what the psychological impact of this bereavement was is impossible to determine at this distance in time and culture. But it would not be surprising if the mother whose piety had restricted his actions in England now after her death exercised a continuing and powerful influence over him. The natural distancing from her which would have taken place as the son established himself as an adult family head was now cut short: emotional work was ended abruptly before its completion just as it had been in his father's case. The young man's later development of his self-image as a caring public servant, his identification with women and willing performance of female roles such as nursing and tending children, as well as his withdrawal from male sexual activity, may well reflect in part the still powerful mother figure in his life, rendered the more potent by her death.

However, Gandhi's immediate concerns were to take up the threads of social life and to embark on his new profession. To please his brother he underwent a ritual purification in order to placate a section of the *Modh Banias* in view of his ritual pollution by foreign travel, and the family gave a caste dinner back in Rajkot to the same end. Gandhi disliked having to do this and never thereafter tried to placate the diehards in the community who refused to forgive his disobedience in going abroad. Gandhi's 'reformism' found further outlet in his family life. His brother had thought he should welcome him into a more English atmosphere at home, and crockery among other domestic items was already provided for daily use, whereas it had been reserved for special occasions before. The reforming home-comer added his customary oatmeal porridge to the changes, and cocoa became an item in the housekeeping! He also continued to wear European dress. However, in his relations with his wife the old patterns re-emerged. He was still jealous, suspicious and domineering, both physically and mentally. For a while he even sent her home to her father's house, thoroughly distressing her. In fact they spent very litle time together in the months after his return as he set up an establishment alone in Bombay for professional reasons. But their relationship became less stormy and more one of partnership as they shared in household reforms and in the care of their son and now a second child. When Gandhi left India again in 1893 for a year's contract in South Africa he felt a wrench on parting from Kasturbhai, an emotion never mentioned in his account of his earlier departure for England.

In his professional life, however, he experienced nothing but setbacks. His growing household expenses to support his modified lifestyle urgently demanded that he should earn good fees. But his inexperience made this impossible in Rajkot where his pretensions would have caused ridicule. So he left alone for Bombay, to gain experience of the courts, study Indian law, and if possible begin to build up a practice. Expenses of another household further burdened him; ignorance and shyness debilitated him professonally. His first case was an utter fiasco because he did not have the courage to get up and cross-examine. In despair he tried for a teaching job on the strength of his London Matriculation and his command of English. Even this door was slammed in his face, because the high school concerned was looking for a graduate, and he had no degree. So after six months he returned, a failure, to Rajkot. Here he was at last able to make ends meet, with the humble legal work of drafting applications and memorials – so far removed from the career his family had envisaged for their returning London barrister. But even in Rajkot his low status dogged him. His brother had asked him to intercede with the Political Agent for the Kathiawar states on his behalf, on the strength of having met him in England. But when he made the approach to the British official he was curtly told that his brother was an intriguer who should put his case through the proper channels, and he was forcibly shown the door. His English experience had not prepared him for this sort of arrogance, and his initial reaction was to proceed legally against the official for insult and assault. He was only dissuaded by one of Bombay's most distinguished lawyers who was visiting Rajkot and told him roundly to pocket the insult and learn the ways of life in India lest he ruin himself. Learn he did, and fast, as he worked in Rajkot. The petty politics of the small states, the constant intrigues of their officials, sickened him. Both he and his brother began to look for a way out of this atmosphere, so alien to the idealistic but briefless barrister. The opportunity came when a Porbandar trading-firm wrote to Gandhi's brother offering Mohandas a year's contract if he would go to South Africa, where they had business and were involved in a big court case, in order to advise their local lawyers; his English would also be a significant help to them. He was offered a first class fare, all expenses paid, and a fee of £105, all of which he realized he could contribute to the household expenses he and his brother shared. When the terms had been clarified he agreed without haggling. In April 1893 he set sail once more from Bombay, an Indian nonentity, his once high hopes dashed on the rocks of reality, now bound for a routine legal job which seemed like an escape from failure rather than a challenging opportunity. But Gandhi's South African experience led to the radical remaking of the man, and the fashioning of one of the twentieth century's most remarkable spiritual and political figures.

SOUTH AFRICAN EXPERIENCE I

The self-taught political apprentice

The context

Gandhi's name is identified with India's achievement of independence
and his non-violent resistance to the British raj, but he spent a significant
part of his adult working life in Africa. From 1893 to 1914 his home and
work were in South Africa, a land where he had no intention of settling
permanently. These African years were crucial in forging Gandhi into a
public man, inwardly and outwardly. In his self-understanding, too,
Africa was a seminal experience; but it was only the spiritual and
political prelude to his life's work, which he was always convinced
could only be in India. Looking back he wrote of finding his true self
and realizing his vocation in this unexpected place.[1] It was here he had
his first real experience of public work, and, overcoming his shyness,
developed an undreamed-of capacity for political and social action, and a
measure of self-confidence in his own abilities in public life.[2] It was in
Africa, too, that Gandhi's spiritual and moral questioning bore fruit in a
singular philosophy of life and an overwhelming vision of man as a
spiritual being created to find fulfilment in a lifelong pursuit of truth.
Coeval with this religious transformation was a fundamental optimism
about people and their relationships as individuals and groups which
remained a hallmark of his subsequent thinking. Africa, a land of exile,
provided the context for the development of a man of action, of vision
and of hope.

Most obvious were the outer manifestations of this change in Gandhi:
the transformation of the timid, failed barrister into a skilled lawyer,
political spokesman and organizer, equipped to play a public role in
India. His accumulated reputation and experience were to compensate
for the conspicuous lack of resources which had so far marked his life,
despite the ambitions and endeavours of his family. The origin of these
changes was his response to the conditions experienced by Indians in

South Africa and their challenge to his own values and expectations. The young barrister anticipated a due respect for his legal training, his Anglicized appearance and general bearing as a prosperous, English-educated Indian. His rebuffs in India had not dulled his sense of total equality with white subjects of the British empire, born largely of his experiences in London in training for the Bar and mixing easily in English society. But his expectations were rudely shattered a week after he reached South Africa as he travelled from Durban to Pretoria. Despite his appearance and his first class ticket, a white passenger objected to sharing a compartment with him, and because he refused to move out he was physically ejected by a police constable into the freezing night at Maritzburg station. Similar racial insults were launched at him as he continued his uncomfortable journey. This was a personally traumatic experience of colour prejudice, and was but the start of Gandhi's rapid awakening to the insulting and degrading conditions in which his compatriots were forced to live, and to their quiescence in the face of injustice and prejudice.[3]

Indians had first come to South Africa, and primarily to Natal, in the second half of the nineteenth century as indentured labourers to work on sugar and coffee plantations. As such their presence was welcomed by their white employers, though the treatment of this cheap labour-force caused considerable concern to the Indian government. Those who stayed on after their indentures had expired tended to become servants, unskilled labourers or market gardeners, and were not perceived as an economic threat to the white community or to 'white civilization'. But by the last two decades of the century white perceptions had begun to change. Indian traders known as 'Arabs', who were mostly Gujarati Muslims, arrived in considerable numbers and began to compete with white merchants, and the overall Indian population began to outstrip the European community as a result of immigration and a high birth rate.[4] By 1894 there were 43,000 Indians in Natal compared with 40,000 whites. In Transvaal, too, the influx of 'Arab' traders caused growing concern, though the total number of Indians there was smaller than in Natal: in 1899 there were 17,000 Indians of whom about 5,500 were merchants or hawkers. By contrast, in the Cape and the Orange Free State there were far fewer Indians.

Only the Indian merchants were likely to complain about the attitudes of the Europeans, which were manifested not only in humiliating, discriminatory social conventions such as Gandhi had experienced on that first journey, but also in legislation and municipal ordinances restricting Indian civil rights, franchise and freedom to enter, live and trade at will. Even they, Gandhi quickly discovered, often preferred to pocket insults in the interests of making money. By contrast the immigrant labourers were predominantly low caste or untouchable, totally uneducated, inarticulate and defenceless. For them conditions in South Africa might be bad, but they were worse in their homeland, from which they had been driven by poverty.

South Africa's Indians were in theory citizens equal to those of European descent within the British empire. However, the famous 1858 Proclamation which promised Queen Victoria's Indian subjects freedom from discrimination on grounds of religion, race or colour seemed of little consequence when confronted with the increasingly strident and locally present determination of white settlers to maintain white superiority in matters social, economic and political. Before the close of the century Natal legislators made it plain in their restrictions on trading licences that their objective was to get rid of the Asian trader, having already disenfranchised the majority of Indians in effect, if not in overtly racial terms. Even the labourers, known as 'coolies', elicited white hostility though once they had been considered an economic asset. The *Natal Mercury* in 1895 spoke of 'evils attendant upon the immigration of coolies, their low standard of living and morals, the introduction by them of disease and the ever-threatening outbreak of epidemics'.[5] Similar attitudes were being voiced in the Transvaal:

> Apart from the question of his loathesome habits, the coolie is not an immigrant to be encouraged. He lowers the standards of comfort and closes the avenues to prosperity to the European trader. Economically he is of no advantage to the country he visits – for, be it remembered that he does not settle. He accumulates money by virtue of the wretchedness in which he lives – a wretchedness constituting a terrible danger to the rest of the community – and he takes 80 per cent of that money back again to Asia. In Natal we actually have the spectacle of European trade being gradually destroyed by the impossible competition of the coolie. The Asiatic is thus a menace to the European's life, an obstacle to his commerical progress.[6]

There, too, restrictions were being placed on Indian residence and trade; Indians had no vote and were required to register in order to remain in the colony. Like the African population, they were not allowed to be out of doors after 9.00 p.m. and could not walk on public footpaths, though 'Arabs' were exempted as a favour. Gandhi had galling experiences of these regulations. He eventually acquired a permanent exemption which he had to carry in case he was stopped by the police. As he commented,

> I thus made an intimate study of the hard condition of the Indian settlers, not only by reading and hearing about it, but by personal experience. I saw that South Africa was no country for a self-respecting Indian, and my mind became more and more occupied with the question as to how this state of thing[s] might be improved.[7]

Gandhi was not alone in his convictions. In 1912 the then Viceroy of India, Lord Hardinge, voiced the unease increasingly felt by India's imperial rulers that the empire presented an ambivalent face to its Indian subjects. He told the Governor of Bengal that he had 'no sympathy with the bare-faced manner' in which Indians were treated in South Africa.[8]

However, the political and constitutional position of the South African white colonists was so complex that in practice the imperial government in London had little leverage which it could use on behalf of its Indian subjects. Cape Colony and Natal, the two most British parts of South Africa, had both received responsible government within the empire by the time Gandhi arrived, and anti-Indian feeling was gaining strength. Although the London government could theoretically disallow acts passed by self-governing colonies, in practice it was extremely reluctant to do so except on some major imperial issue; Although the treatment of Indians in white South Africa challenged the imperial ideal of equality, London preferred not to jeopardize the loyalty of white settlers by direct confrontation with them on this issue, it contented itself with the face-saving formula of insisting where possible that restrictive laws should not be based on overtly racial grounds. By contrast, in the Boer-dominated areas the British imperial government had even less influence. It had no legal basis for intervention on behalf of Indians in the Orange Free State. Transvaal from 1881 had self-government subject to the 'suzerainty' of Her Majesty's Government; but London and the Transvaal disputed the meaning and range of this supposed over-arching control.

It might have been thought that the Boer War of 1899–1902 would have clarified the position and enabled London to act more decisively on behalf of its Indian subjects. Certainly this was what Gandhi and the Indian community hoped. But the contrary was the case. When imperial issues were at stake, the contentment of white South Africans, Boer and British, so crucial in maintaining the security of the Cape route east to the rest of the empire, was more important than the position of a small minority of immigrants who posed little threat to imperial stability or communications. When the Union of South Africa came into being in 1910 this became even clearer: London's restraining influence was now largely gone, the Sovereign only having power to disallow a law within a year of its being granted assent by the Governor-General.

Gandhi – the public man

Political and constitutional realities worked against the Indian community in the long term. But in the short term the divisions of authority and the various governmental and public audiences concerned in the Indian case gave Gandhi and his colleagues an immense range of options as they resorted to political pressure. Not only were there the local governments and London to be approached. Pressure could be put on white settlers in South Africa and appeals made to liberal opinion in England and educated opinion in India. Furthermore, the Indian government was keenly interested in the problem, largely because of the effect that discrimination against South African Indians had on its own educated Indian public, and consequently on its own standing. Hardinge as Viceroy made the point bluntly to his Secretary of State, Lord Crewe, in

mid-1913: in view of educated Indian feeling it was 'very important
that the Government of India should be able to show that' it was doing
its 'utmost to protect Indians in the Colonies.'[9] Gandhi's many-angled
campaign to suit this particular situation consequently became self-
education in handling the complexities of government and political
decision-making within situations of divided authority, which was to be
an asset when he returned to India with its own particular setting of
authority shared between London, Delhi and the provinces. The plight
of the Indian immigrants as an issue, which attracted the attention of
Delhi and educated India, gave Gandhi a high political profile in India
where he had previously been unknown, without involving him in any
anti-British sentiments or action. For what was he but a champion of the
empire's highest ideals, however embarrassing that might prove to that
empire's rulers?

Gandhi did not accept the role of a public man with any eagerness.
Rather, it was thrust on him by the growing urgency of the Indians'
situation and the incapacity of any other Indian to champion the
community. He even pleaded with a venerable Indian politician, then an
MP at Westminster, to guide him, so profoundly did he feel his own
inadequacy.[10] His initial agreement to stay in South Afrcia after completion of his original court case was only for a short period, to help the
Natal Indians with the threat to their franchise which was being proposed in the Natal Legislative Assembly. What was intended as a farewell
party for him, given by grateful 'Arab' traders, turned into a planning
session for a political campaign. Gandhi's intentions of staying on for a
month were confounded by events, and it was not for three years that he
was able to return to India. By then he had realized that his African work
was likely to be prolonged, and he wanted both to fetch his family and
to publicize the cause at home. Even that brief visit to India in 1896 was
cut short by a cable from Durban urging him to hurry back. Eventually
in 1901, towards the end of the Boer War, Gandhi thought he could go
home for good. He felt his real work was in India, and feared that his
success as a lawyer in South Africa might corrupt him into concentration
on money-making. His associates in South Africa reluctantly agreed,
but extracted from him a promise that he would return if needed within
the year. On his return to India Gandhi travelled, making political
contacts and attending the annual Congress session, and he paid a
prolonged visit to one of the most significant Indian politicians of
the day, G.K. Gokhale, who was greatly respected by his compatriots and the British alike. Gokhale was anxious that his protégé
should settle in Bombay, practise at the bar, and become involved in
Congress politics. But Gandhi was wary after his earlier professional
failure in Bombay and decided to work first in provincial Rajkot where
he had contacts and repute. With the encouragement of Rajkot friends
who promised to supply him with work in Bombay, he eventually
plucked up courage to move with his family to that mighty
cosmopolitan centre. He began to make professional headway, and

maintained a considerable life-style in a large bungalow in the suburb of Santa Cruz, travelling daily first class into the city to work. But yet again a cable from South Africa drew him back there late in 1902 to help the Indian community prepare to meet the Secretary of State for the Colonies. Still he did not contemplate a more permanent life away from Indian and left his wife and children behind.

As Gandhi became inextricably entangled in the struggle of the Indian community he set his face against the idea of developing a political career in the accepted sense. If he was to be a public man, then his role would be one of service rather than self-aggrandizement. He refused to accept any fees for public work, preferring to support himself by his legal practice; and when he was showered with parting gifts on his vain attempts to return home to India he refused to accept them and they were converted into a trust to be used for the community as needed. Here were visible some of the first signs of Gandhi's deep trans- formation into one concerned not with self and an immediate circle of family and friends, but committed to service of an ever-widening circle of people who became as important to him as his own kin, because they were human and in need. Whatever the possibly harmful effects of this expanding love on his physical family, those who naturally expected his primary concern, it became a central pillar of his self-understanding as a public figure, and an ideal he tried to inculcate into those who associated with him in his political and social work throughout his life. Most observers would call this self-denial. Gandhi saw it rather as the pathway to true self-realization; for only by service of humankind could one draw close to truth, to ultimate reality, and thus to one's own deepest self.[11]

When challenged about his aims in South Africa, Gandhi insisted that he was not ambitious for himself, and that he did not seek political power for the Indian community. Rather, their goal was an end to discrimination and degradation, and conformity by local governments to the spirit of the British constitution and the 1858 Proclamation.[12] His own role in this he envisaged as that of interpreter between different racial groups, as one whose task was to achieve conciliation. When confronted with extreme white hostility, culminating in violence to him personally on his return from India in 1897, he demonstrated this in word and action. He refused to launch a prosecution against those of the white mob who had attacked him after his ship had docked, and insisted to the press that he came back not to make money or to fulfil his own political ambition, noting that he received no money for his public work and had not even tried to be enfranchised.

If the European Colonists can believe me, I beg to assure them that I am here, not to sow dissensions between the two communities, but to endeavour to bring about an honourable reconciliation between them. In my humble opinion, much of the ill-feeling that exists between the two communities is due to misunderstanding of each other's feelings and actions. My office, therefore, is that of an humble interpreter between them.[13]

Gandhi the householder

As Gandhi reluctantly accepted the role and status of a public figure his personal life also became increasingly public. This process was not complete until he was firmly established with his extended family and close followers in an Indian style of community living in 1916 in Gujarat.[14] While in Africa Gandhi still had some 'private life'; and he was essentially still a Hindu householder, working out the role considered appropriate in his religious inheritance after the student years for mature adulthood – as husband, parent and provider[15] – although his perception of his duties in this stage of life changed markedly. A glimpse into the private life of the Gandhi family complements an understanding of his expanding public role. It is vividly illustrated by a succession of photographs through his African years in which the gawky student, ill at ease in European clothes, became a comfortable, prosperous lawyer and family man, and then embarked for India so assured of his adult identity that he wore Indian dress with ease and price.

The economic base of Gandhi's personal and public life was his legal practice. In terms of his profession the first year in South Africa was a turning-point, just as it was in his experience of racial discrimination. Working on the details of the business case on which he had originally been employed he learned the nuts and bolts of legal practice, and, significantly, gained a confidence in his own professional abilities. In this particular instance he realized that however strong his client's case in fact, the processes of litigation might well ruin both parties, not only in financial but in personal terms, as they were related and lived near each other. Consequently he arranged a compromise by which both parties saved considerable expense and also rose in public repute. From this beginning Gandhi made a cornerstone of his practice constant attempts to bring about private compromises between contestants, commenting later, 'I lost nothing thereby – not even money, certainly not my soul.'[16] Gandhi's legal work also embodied his rigid adherence to high standards of probity: he refused to take on doubtful cases or to coach witnesses as to what they should say, with the result that some potential clients stayed away from him. Despite these self-imposed standards – and Gandhi argued it was because of them – his practice flourished, so that he was not only able to support his wife and family, which had now increased to four children, but also to bear a large part of the cost of a newspaper he founded and largely edited from 1904, *Indian Opinion*. By the end of his time in Africa he was pouring all his savings into it, remitting as much as £75 a month.

Meanwhile Gandhi had to make a home for himself and his family, at a time when his ideas about an appropriate life-style, marital relations, education and health were all undergoing radical transformation. The external manifestations of his heart-searchings on these matters fill out the picture of the political apprentice, showing how Gandhi's personal and public life developed in conjunction, the personal being simplified and freed from the desires and primary obligations normally associated with family life, as his concern for public service expanded.

When Gandhi was joined by his wife, children and the son of his widowed sister in 1896, he had to decide what dress and kind of life they should adopt abroad. He chose for his wife the Parsi style of sari and for the boys Parsi coats and trousers, because the Parsis were 'regarded as the most civilised people amongst Indians'.[17] As yet he did not feel he could let them appear for what they really were – banias from 'backwoods' Kathiawad. Poor Kasturbhai and her brood submitted to his authority though they found getting used to wearing shoes and stockings a sore trial, for their feet became painful and their stockings stank from perspiration, so strange was the constriction to them. Although dress may seem a small issue it is immensely symbolic of the way people perceive themselves and of the image of themselves they wish to project. For people caught in cultural conflicts, as were Gandhi and his generation of Indians, dress indicated as much as words their ambivalences and compromises. When Gandhi first adopted Indian dress late in his South African campaign it was a gesture of solidarity; and then as permanent garb in India it was a sign that he had come through the turmoil which had begun in childhood under the influence of his meat-eating friend, and had 'come home' to a new sense of ease and security in his understanding of Indianness.

Even though Gandhi dragooned the children into uncomfortable clothes for the sake of a 'civilized' appearance, he was by the 1890s sufficiently critical of the European schools available in Africa to decide to educate his children at home. At such mission-founded schools they would have been oddities, the only Indians allowed in as a favour; and they would have been educated in English with little chance of learning Indian vernaculars. So he engaged an English governess, and supplemented her efforts with his own, speaking to them only in Gujarati. As he later admitted, their education was consequently lacking in many of the areas then considered essential to a liberal education, but he felt he had given them more experience and a far less artificial life-style than would have been the case if they had attended Westernized schools in Africa or India. In his own family circle Gandhi was clearly already developing the passionate concern for the proper education of young people for a new India which was to come to fruition in the 1930s. He also began experiments with health with those nearest to him; these too were manifested in India as concern for a whole nation's health, as well as that of his closest associates. In preparation for the birth of the two sons born in South Africa he read up on the subjects of birth and child care. He actually delivered the last child as the doctor and midwife could not be fetched in time, and himself took on much of the daily care of the babies for several months. In his insistence on parental care for the

Facing page: (top left) Gandhi age 7; (top right) age 17; (below) outside his Johannesburg law office with his staff – to his left is Henry Polak and to his right Sonja Schlesin.

Gandhi and Kasturbhai in South Africa, 1914, having adopted Indian dress during the campaign on behalf of indentured labourers.

In 1915, after their return to India from South Africa.

child and the vital significance of a child's earliest years and even its
pre-birth experiences, he sounds remarkably modern. However his
growing alienation from modern medicine and increasing reliance on
natural methods of healing caused him considerable heart-searching
when the health of his family was at risk, and required considerable
courage from all of them. Gandhi's second son, Manilal, had severe
typhoid and pneumonia during their time in Bombay, but Gandhi as a
strict vegetarian would not allow the doctor's recommendation of
chicken and eggs for nourishment, ministering to him personally with
hip baths, wet sheets and a restricted diet of orange juice. In Durban
Kasturbhai was severely weakened by haemorrhages and minor surgery
to prevent these, and in Gandhi's absence was given beef tea by the
doctor. Gandhi removed her at once from the doctor's care, though this
involved a journey by rail, rickshaw and hammock, and nursed her
himself with hydropathic remedies, and later with a diet free of salt and
pulses.

Gandhi's wife and children acquiesced in his medical experiments; but
though Kasturbhai permitted what might have threatened her own life,
her relations with her husband were not unmarked by turmoil as he
launched out on a spiritual journey which had a profound impact on the
life of his whole family, touching areas hallowed by religion and social
convention. When he insisted, for example, on returning the parting
gifts, including ornaments which were given when they tried to leave
Africa, Kasturbhai let loose a torrent of arguments, saying that he might
not need these things, but what might befall the family in the future and
might not her daughters-in-law eventually need them? She complained
that she had slaved for Gandhi and accepted his wishes; he had deprived
her of her own ornaments and was now trying to make ascetics of her
sons. Eventually and despite the arguments and tears she acquiesced,
though Gandhi admitted that he had 'extorted a consent from her.'[18] An
even fiercer altercation occurred when Gandhi demanded that
Kasturbhai clean the chamber pot of a Christian clerk who came to their
Durban home, and was in her eyes untouchable. Such work was
anyway deeply offensive to one of her caste standing. He insisted that
she do it, and with a good grace; for a moment they stood at the
entrance to their home, locked in public conflict, as he threatened to
push her out. In shame they desisted, and peace was restored as it always
was after their 'numerous bickerings'.[19]

Kasturbhai's greatest acquiescence in the wishes of her husband must
however have been in a far more private matter, though little is known
of her feelings and wishes concerning it. Gandhi had wrestled with
conflicting ideas about contraception as early as his days associating with
vegetarians in London, and felt increasingly that self-control should
replace artificial means. He was also becoming deeply concerned with
the nature of the sexual bond between husband and wife, and the
destructive effect of lust on this and wider relationships. Eventually he
became convinced that public service and the normal obligations of

family life were inconsistent. These thoughts began to take shape around 1900 but it was only in 1906 that Gandhi decided to take the full step of a vow of celibacy or *brahmacharya*, though husband and wife had already been sleeping apart for some time. *Brahmacharya* is normally associated in Hindu thought with the final stage of earthly life when the householder withdraws from worldly cares to devote himself to religion. In Gandhi's case he was convinced that a vocation to wider public service demanded that he should relinquish the desire for children and wealth, and should become open to the needs of a far wider circle around him. Of Kasturbhai he noted that 'she was never the temptress', and that the fight to control passion was only on his side.[20] Looking back on the strains in their marriage, their intellectual and educational disparity, and the demands for change he made on her as his vision of right and duty broadened, Gandhi could nevertheless speak of their contentment and happiness.[21]

Such was not the case with his eldest son, Harilal, who broke away from his father and his changing values while the family were in Africa. He insisted in 1911 on going to a high school in Ahmedabad rather than acquiescing in his father's homespun educational experiments, and felt that the earliest days of his father's professional success were the best, compared with the growing austerities and unconventional practices of the later years which he called delusion. He resented the fact that he and his three brothers had come last in their father's priorities rather than first, as he would have expected. Gandhi agreed to support him in India, but the break hurt him, as did his absent son's long silences. He blamed himself for the breakdown of this relationship, not for the same reasons as Harilal, but because he felt that his own earliest and undisciplined years as a teenage father were being echoed in all his son's undesirable traits.[22]

The Gandhis' family life was marked in South Africa by growing simplicity, and a gradual merging of Gandhi's 'home' and 'public' domain. Their first home in Durban was initially a place of considerable ease and comfort, befitting a prospering barrister and Indian who wished to proclaim the equality of Indians and whites within the empire. Rapidly Gandhi began to pare down his initial expenses, as he had done in London. For example, he realized that the washerman's bill was heavy and that he had to have a far larger number of shirts and collars than was necessary to see him through should the laundry be returned late. So he bought a book on washing. He and Kasturbhai learned a skill which in India was the preserve of a far lower caste group. His early attempts at starching collars won the ridicule and amazement of his fellow barristers. So did his first efforts at cutting his own hair, when they asked if rats had been at it. In this his self-help was prompted not so much by economy as by the experience of discrimination, when an English barber in Pretoria refused to cut his hair for fear of losing white custom. But again he was taking on tasks which in India were reserved for people of low caste. A further rejection of material standards

currently accepted as natural was Gandhi's decision to abandon an
insurance policy which would have provided protection for his wife and
children. This caused a temporary rift with his brother, who considered
that Gandhi was neglecting his family. Gandhi's growing religious
convictions and his attempts to extricate himself from entanglement
with possessions encouraged him to rely far more on a good providence
than on secular prudence, and distanced him from the Indian insistence
on the primary obligations owed to the joint family. Although his
brother could expect nothing from him in the future, this action fell into
its right perspective, he insisted, if only his brother could expand his
understanding of 'family'.[23]

In 1905 the Gandhis set up a new home in Johannesburg as political
work drew Gandhi increasingly into the Transvaal. There they lived in a
large villa in a pleasant surburban neighbourhood, their immediate
family expanded by two European associates of Gandhi and their wives.
Everyone, regardless of age or sex, began to contribute physical labour
to the running of the household as its style became more simple and
self-reliant. They began to bake their own bread, hand-grinding their
own flour. The children helped with the grinding, as they did with the
general cleaning work, including that of the lavatories, thereby receiving practical education totally at variance with that of the average Indian
bania child who would have learned that manual labour was degrading
and that the sweeper's job was polluting.

Gandhi's simplification of his family's style of living was further
expanded in two experiments in communal living which were to be the
precursors of his Indian communities at Sabarmati in 1916 and in central
India from the 1930s. The first of these, the Phoenix Settlement, was
started in 1904 to house the press for Indian Opinion and help finance the
paper. It consisted of 100 acres near Durban, on which were fruit trees
and little else. The first building to go up, financed by the generosity of
a Parsi, Rustomji, was the printing shed. Gradually the band of settlers,
which included Gandhi's close European friend, Albert West, and his
cousin, Chhaganlal Gandhi, built simple wood and corrugated-iron
houses to replace the tents in which they had first camped. The aim was
a self-supporting community which kept itself by its own manual
labour and also financed and ran Indian Opinion far more cheaply than if
it had been a commercial enterprise. Although this experiment reflected
financial and political necessity it also demonstrated the deep effect the
work of Ruskin was having on Gandhi. He hoped after reading Unto
This Last to retire from practice and live a life of manual labour at
Phoenix and put his new-found truths into practice in this simple place.
But politics called him away to the Transvaal. Even there he maintained
a close interest in Phoenix and wrote admonitions to the inmates on
such apparently mundane matters as cooking and the right sort of
packed lunches to take if they had to eat in the nearby city. For him such
concerns were as significant for the right development and living of the
whole person as were the great public concerns which occupied him

more obviously. He felt passionately that Phoenix was a 'nursery' for producing a new kind of human and a new kind of Indian, and that experiments could be made there without any of the restraints inevitable in India. Such was the case of the women of Phoenix who were able to take on new roles in freedom compared with their home environments.[24]

The ideal of a communal and simple style of life remained and deepened in Gandhi when he was in Johannesburg, and in 1910 he launched another experiment, this time named Tolstoy Farm after the great Russian whose ideals confirmed those which were already maturing in Gandhi's own mind. Tolstoy Farm was both a gesture of idealism and a response to political necessity, as by this time the families of those who had followed Gandhi into passive resistance and jail needed homes and maintenance. Another European associate bought a farm of over 1,000 acres near Johannesburg and allowed Gandhi and his motley group of dependents and followers the use of it without charge. They included Indians from many regions of the subcontinent, Hindus, Muslims, Parsis and Christians. About 40 were young men, 20 to 30 children, and there was a handful of old men and women. They built their own houses, and lived on as simple a diet as possible, grinding their own flour, making their own bread, butter and marmalade, and growing their own oranges. Generally they walked into Johannesburg rather than travel even third class on the train, though the round trip was 21 miles – Gandhi's London habits stood him and his flock in good stead! He also paid detailed attention to sanitation, as was to become habitual with him, insisting that for public health and comfort all excrement should be collected and buried in a deep pit, where eventually it would become valuable manure. All food and vegetable refuse was similarly turned into manure, and other rubbish was buried in special trenches. The community began to make its own sandals and to teach its own children, and Gandhi supervised the health of the members according to his faith in natural medicine. Not once did they have to call in a doctor or use drugs.[25] Politically this experiment was vital in sustaining the later stages of Gandhi's political campaign. For him personally it was deeply significant as an enactment of ideals he was forging in the first decade of the century whereby his 'private' and 'public' life became one, and he became the idealist and spiritual leader who returned to India to continue his peculiar style of political work infused with practical morality and down-to-earth religion.

Gandhi the political apprentice: practice and ideas

Gandhi, the Hindu householder who was reinterpreting his religious duty in this stage of his life, was also the self-taught political apprentice. The details of Gandhi's political campaigns, the causes he espoused and their tortuous progress within the complexity of South Africa's constitutional position in the empire, belong properly to a history of the Indian community in South Africa. But their broad outline is important here as we examine Gandhi's political apprenticeship, for several reasons. His political techniques were not the result of preconceived patterns of politics or of training at the hands of an experienced political patron or within an established political party: they were his pragmatic response to the particular circumstances of South African Indians, coloured by his legal training and his sketchy knowledge of Indian political behaviour at home. Those same circumstances dictated the kind of people with whom he was to work politically, both as associates and clients, and as opponents. The nature of Indian grievances also had a profound effect on his attitude to India itself and her relationship with Britain.

The main causes Gandhi espoused in South Africa related to Indians' experiences in Natal and the Transvaal. He was not uninterested in developments in the Cape and the Orange Free State, but as Indians were most heavily clustered in the first two areas it was there that they bore the burnt of white settlers' sharpening fear and hostility. As he made clear from the outset, his main concern through all the particular problems that arose was the status of Indians as equal citizens of the empire, and their protection against discrimination on overt racial grounds. In his eyes the whole meaning of the British empire was on trial in South Africa; and against white prejudice and political power he held out the banner of the 1858 Proclamation as the source of Indians' equality as imperial subjects, calling it their Magna Carta.[26]

In Natal the main problems Indians faced and on which Gandhi campaigned were connected with the franchise, immigration, licences to trade, and a tax on indentured labourers who wished to remain when their indentures expired. These were the occasion of Gandhi's plunge into politics, and his involvement in the Transvaal only came in the first decade of the new century. The threat to Indians' voting rights had kept Gandhi in Natal in the first place, but despite his vigorous campaigning, in 1896 Natal effectively disenfranchised Indians who did not already have the vote, on the grounds that they were of non-European origin and came from countries which had not hitherto possessed elective institutions. As long as Indians were not mentioned by name, London was content to withhold its potentially restraining hand. Simultaneously burdens had been imposed on ex-indentured labourers who would not return to India; and from 1895 they had to pay an annual tax of £3 which, though lighter than the £25 originally proposed, was crippling for a large family on a labourer's small wage. But it was the 'Arabs', free Indian traders, who were the most grievous threat in white perceptions; they were the target for an act of 1897 restricting immigration to propertied persons with knowledge of a European language. It, too, passed through London's supervisory net because it was not overtly anti-Indian, though in practice its administration meant that very few Indians were permitted to enter Natal. 'Arabs' were further hounded by a licensing act of 1897 which exposed Indian traders to the mercies of municipal licensing officers who had to check that books were kept in

English and that premises were in a satisfactory and sanitary condition. Furthermore, appeal against a refusal of a licence was to the municipal boards rather than the courts, boards which were the bastions of those who wished to end Indian competition. Despite Gandhi's vigorous fight in the press, in the courts and through petitions, the substance of discrimination remained, and the Indian position actually deteriorated in the next decade. In 1902 the £3 tax was extended to children of indentured labourers brought to Natal after 1895, when they reached the age of 13 for girls and 16 for boys: their alternatives were to go to India or to become indentured in Natal. A year later the 1897 immigration law was further tightened – by the way it was adminstered rather than by specific racial discrimination against Indians written into any statute – and in 1908 the position of Indian traders was further eroded.

Although Gandhi continued to be concerned over Natal Indians at this later stage, the main thrust of his campaigning after the Boer War was in the Transvaal. There the change in the constitutional position did not help Indians as they had envisaged, and an acknowledgement of Indian equality seemed even further removed despite the defeat of the Boers. The first blow was the virtual re-enactment of a law dating from 1885/6 by which Indians were confined to separate locations for trade and residence, an exception being made for any highly educated Indian who conformed to a European life-style. But the issue on which relations between Indians and white settlers came to breaking-point, and on which passive resistance was first launched, was the control of Indian immigration and settlement. In 1906 the Transvaal legislature passed the infamous 'Black Act' by which all Indians wishing to reside legally in the colony had to register: without a valid registration document no Asian could reside or trade, and in Indian eyes this amounted to a draconian pass system, applied to people who were meant to be free citizens within the empire. At the end of that year the colony received responsible government and was thus able to overcome the political stumbling-block of the London government which had disallowed the 1906 law. It re-enacted without hindrance the 'Black Act', which was supplemented by a futher law restricting immigration by those unfamiliar with a European language. Following the Indian campaign not to register, a compromise was reached between Gandhi and J.C. Smuts, then the minister responsible for Asian questions: Indians would register voluntarily but not under compulsion, for this was degrading to their status. This of course did nothing about the new immigration law or the numerous restrictions on Indian freedom to move and trade at will. Even that compromise was short-lived. Gandhi understood that the 'Black Act' would be repealed once the voluntary registration was complete; Smuts maintained he had never made such a promise. In 1908 an act was passed legalizing this voluntary registration and making further provision for Asian registration, and the hated original act was not repealed.

Indian resistance continued, souring Indian relations with the new

Union Government which came into being in 1910. This state of virtual war was ended only in 1911 when Smuts, now Minister of the Interior in the Union government, and Gandhi came to a provisional agreement which included the repeal of the 'Black Act' and the legal equality of Indians under any new immigration law. But as with their earlier compromise, in this case, too, peace was short-lived. Three major problems continued to concern Gandhi and his compatriots, and were exacerbated by a visit to the colony by the Indian politician, Gokhale, as Indians were assured by him, following discussions with the government, that very specific improvements would be made in their position. Their main grievances, which eventually led to renewed passive resistance, were proposals for a new immigration law which culminated in 1913, conceding little, the unsolved problem of Natal's £3 tax, and in 1913 the bombshell of a judgement in the Cape division of the supreme court declaring only marriages performed by Christian rites and recorded by a registrar as legal. This made all Hindu, Muslim and Parsi wives nothing but mistresses and rendered their children illegitimate. Gandhi's political campaign spanning two decades had now escalated from polite representations to conscientious law-breaking and gaol-going on a large scale. It involved the governments in Britain, South Africa and India, and the varied sections of public opinion in each country which could influence political decisions. It only ended when the Pretoria government, hard pressed at home by passive resistance and an Indian miners' strike, and publicly berated in India by Hardinge, the Viceroy, agreed to appoint a commission of enquiry into Indian grievances. Despite Gandhi's suspicions of its impartiality and his refusal to co-operate in its hearings, its recommendations, enacted in 1914, settled some of the most outstanding problems, including that of the status of Indian women and the repeal of the 1895 Natal Act which had imposed the £3 tax.

When Gandhi left for India in the same year, 1914, feeling that his work was done, it was certainly true that the Indian community's response to white-settler hostility had provided the environment in which a political apprentice had matured into a skilled and publicly respected leader and campaigner. But longer term the campaigns and supposed settlements proved to have done little to secure Gandhi's goal of giving Indians actual equality of status as imperial citizens in South Africa. The franchise, licenses and locations all remained unsolved problems; and Indians were to find, as did the black community, that white South African governments, backed by their voters, were determined to maintain white supremacy in the face of any imperial ideal of equality.

Gandhi learned the skills and methods of political action and leadership in a hard school, without benefit of any of the personal or organizational help which would have been available to his contemporaries in India or England. But they proved an immense resource on his return to India. His first lesson in South Africa was that anyone who claims to represent a particular group and wishes his words to carry weight must in effect create his own constituency. As he worked among South Africa's Indians he found that this involved the founding of organizations, attempts to unify the community, and a programme of what later political and social activists would have called conscious-ness-raising. These three patterns, observable in his African work, re-emerged repeatedly in India as he attempted to create his constituency, first among smaller groups whose interests he championed, and then eventually throughout a whole nation which he sought to make anew and for which he strove to speak with authority to its imperial rulers.

To found and organize political associations was an immense step for one who only a few years earlier had been unable to make even an after-dinner speech of thanks to vegetarian friends on his departure from England. But in 1894 he was instrumental in founding the Natal Indian Congress, the first in a long line of associations for political and social ends which were to bear his stamp and feel his rigorous guidance. He knew virtually nothing about the Indian National Congress at this time, but decided to use the name because the INC had such prestige among Indians at home.

Gandhi and his 'Arab' associates learned through this initiative the disciplines of providing regular subscriptions to finance their work, and of the more Western style of regular meetings with minutes and rules of procedure. Not only Gandhi, but also his colleagues who had shown only a limited ability to organize themselves or to articulate their grievances before his arrival, became accustomed to speaking in public, and to working amongst the Indian community, recruiting support. Although it came into being as an instrument in the fight to save a remnant of the Indian franchise, the stated aims of the NIC were far wider: to promote goodwill among the European and Indian com-munities in South Africa, to inform Indians at home about their com-patriots' predicament in Africa, and to educate African Indians about their homeland, to examine and promote the conditions of all kinds of Indians in Africa, and to improve their moral, social, economic and political situation. Its records show that it spread its net far wider than strictly political work, though its major preoccupations were necessarily organizing petitions and generating propaganda for the Indian cause, and also helping to finance Indian court cases under the various discriminatory laws in operation. It also attempted to politicize those Indians born in the colony who did not have even the minimal impetus and skills for public activity of the 'Arab' traders among whom Gandhi initially worked. It provided funds for charitable work, such as an Indian hospital and a girls' school for daughters of Indian railway employees, and gave emergency accommodation in its own permanent buildings to Indian refugees from the Transvaal during the Boer War. But even at this early stage in his career, and on this small scale, Gandhi found that political enthusiasm and participation were ephemeral. He noted with regret that when he was back in India in 1902 the Congress work declined.[27] When he transferred his work to the Transvaal, as the crisis in Indian conditions developed there, he became the guiding force behind two more political organizations, the Transvaal British Indian Association, whose range of concerns was much the same as the Natal Indian Congress, and later the 'Satyagraha Association', created specifically for that aspect of the Indian campaign which culminated in law-breaking.

However, in establishing a coherent Indian constituency, Gandhi found that mere organization was insufficient. In South Africa Indians were divided by religion, regional origin and the gulf separating those born there, mostly of indentured labourer parents, and those who came as migrant traders. Gandhi realized early on the necessity of welding these groups into one if the case he was making out for Indians was to have any public credibility. Under his aegis the Natal Congress extended its political and charitable work to the indentured labourers and their families, and it also founded and funded a Natal Indian Educational Association for young Indians born in Natal who spoke English, to give them a place to meet and air their views, to learn about India, and to realize their unity with the 'Arabs' who were more politically active. As Gandhi noted this unifying process was intended to be two-way: 'It was also intended to impress upon them that free Indians considered them as their own kith and kin, and to create respect for the latter in the minds of the former.'[28] Gandhi's deep personal commitment to the indentured Indians and compassion for their plight, and in turn their growing response to him as their particular champion, was a further aspect of his unifying work. It stemmed from the very early experience he had as a lawyer of a few months' practice, when a Tamil indentured labourer, bleeding and with broken teeth after an assault by his employer, came to seek his help.

The division between Muslims and Hindus, which to some extent reinforced the economic and social divide between colonial and Indian-born Indians, also deeply concerned Gandhi, and he fought in word and action any tendency for this religious difference to inhibit the growth of truly Indian feeling. In 1906 when he master-minded a deputation to England, he insisted that a Muslim should go with him to make the deptuation properly representative. Even earlier in his paper, *Indian Opinion*, he had appealed for Indian unity, in the context of a wider article on religious toleration:

> India, with its ancient religions, has much to give, and the bond of unity between us can best be fostered by a whole-hearted sympathy and appreciation of each other's form of religion.... Is it not a fact that between Mahomedan and Hindu there is a great need for this toleration? Sometimes one is inclined to think it is even greater than between East and West. Let not strife and tumult destroy the harmony between Indians themselves. A house divided against itself must fall, so let us urge the necessity for perfect unity and brotherliness between all sections of the Indian community.[29]

By 1909 he had concluded that cementing Hindu–Muslim unity was a massive task, and that someone would probably have to die in the cause: he would, he said, count himself fortunate if he were to be this one – a prophetic statement in the light of his death four decades later. Even at this stage he could write that he felt there could be no Hindu–Muslim divide in the campaign for South African Indians, and that his own life was devoted to that unity in an even wider cause, namely 'to demonstrating that co-operation between the two is an indispensable condition of the salvation of India.'[30] While on deputation in London in 1909 he put this principle into practice by drawing the attention of the Secretary of State for India to the Transvaal government's refusal to give Muslim prisoners facilities to observe the Ramzan fast obligatory on them. He also urged his associate, Henry Polak, who was touring India while he was in London, to make contact with leaders of the Muslim League, to seek the help of Muslim organizations and to stress how significant Muslim interests were in South Africa.[31] As he travelled back to South Africa later that year he wrote his extended meditation on the meaning of Indian home rule, *Hind Swaraj*, and the urgent need for unity among Indians of all religions was one of its great themes: 'In no part of the world are one nationality and one religion synonymous terms; nor has it ever been so in India.'[32]

In training a new generation of Indians on Tolstoy Farm Gandhi laid great stress on courteous toleration and understanding for each other's religious beliefs and practices, even to the extent of non-Muslims keeping the Ramzan fast with the Muslims, by all eating one meal a day only in the evening. However, his attempts at unifying the Indian community were not entirely successful even in the limited context of South Africa. Throughout his African years there were signs that some Indians thought he was too aligned with Muslim associates and their particular interests. When Gokhale's visit was being planned communalism reared its head, as a Hindu group attached to a temple in Durban planned a specifically Hindu address to the great Indian visitor rather than co-operate in one from the whole Indian community. Some Muslims, on the other hand, were so dissatisfied with the 1914 settlement of the status of Indian marriages that they even denied that Gandhi had any right to represent Muslims and their interests. In 1908 Gandhi had already encountered similar hostility when he was beaten unconscious by a small group of Muslims, angry at his settlement with Smuts. But he refused to take legal action against them, hoping that his suffering would help the cause of communal unity. Then, as later in India, Gandhi found that the protagonist of communal unity was a difficult if not perilous role.

Preaching unity was of course one of Gandhi's ways of creating an Indian consciousness. Much of his work was of a far more practical and mundane nature in the same cause. His large legal practice helped to sustain Indians' awareness of their restricted position and the possibility of fighting through the courts to challenge discrimination in practice. He also involved himself in attempts to raise the standard of living

among Indians, to protect them against accusations that Indian areas
were filthy and insanitary, and a menace to decent living standards and
white civilization. *Indian Opinion* was a major vehicle for his educational
campaign among Indians, and its inaugural edition specifically noted
that one of its functions would be pointing out Indian faults and
suggestion their remedy.[33] This schoolmasterly role was one Gandhi
and his paper constantly performed, commenting on a wide range of
social issues, instructing Indians in international examples of service and
patriotism, as well as imforming them of their political and legal
position and the progress of the campaign on their behalf and how best
they could participate in it.

Once the Indian community was in process of creation as a self-
conscious and visible entity, Gandhi set about giving it the voice it had
so far lacked. His fluency in English and his ability to construct sustained arguments were virtually his only qualifications for this task at
the outset, apart from his burning personal commitment to their cause.
But he rapidly taught himself and his associates the political skills of
petitioning authority. Given the constraints on the Indian position in
Africa this was one of the only avenues of political action open to them.
It reflected Gandhi's staunch belief in the rule of law and the significance
of the 1858 Proclamation in imperial ideology, and was sensible tactically,
given the divided constitutional authority in the South African colonies
and the various power-centres which could influence the outcome of
any situation in which Indians were involved. By engaging in a political
style that was peaceful, constitutional and acceptable in Western politics,
Indians would also reinforce their claim to be the civilized, rational
equals of white citizens of the empire. A record of the petitions Gandhi
organized in his two decades in Africa would fill volumes: the two
months of June–July 1894 alone indicate the range and volume of
Gandhi's formal appeals in connection with the Indian franchise.
Petitions in writing or through deputations were sent to the Natal
Assembly (28 June), to the Premier of Natal (29 June), to the Governor
of Natal (3 and 10 July), to the Natal Council (4 and 6 July), and to Lord
Ripon, the Secretary of State for the Colonies (mid-July). This last
petition to London was no mean feat of organization when communications were poor and Indian literacy low; 10,000 signatures were collected in two weeks, and Gandhi's main helpers were Muslim traders
who used their own transport without payment. One opened his house
to Gandhi and other volunteers, giving them office space and meals.
One thousand copies of the petition were printed and circulated to the
press, and distributed among Indians to inform them of their position.[34]

Gandhi also went twice in person to London to plead the Indian case,
first in 1906 and then again in 1909. In 1906 Gandhi and a Muslim
colleague met not only Lord Elgin, Secretary of State for the Colonies,
but Lord Morley, the Secretary of State for India. They co-operated
closely with a number of MPs and public men sympathetic to their
cause, including Lord Stanley of Alderley, Sir Lepel Griffin, Sir George

Birdwood, Sir Henry Cotton, and the two most politically significant Indians in London at the time, Sir Mancherjee Bhownagree and Dadabhai Naoroji. Gandhi's letters also show that he was busy canvassing the support of a range of influential individuals by writing and seeking interviews with them: they included Winston Churchill, Lord Milner, A.J. Balfour, and Alfred Lyttleton.

A more permanent result of the England visit than the strong impression made on Elgin was the establishment of a South African British Indian Committee on 15 December 1906, presided over by Lord Ampthill, a former Presidency Governor in India and acting Viceroy. Gandhi had been considering such a development for a while as he could see that with constitutional changes coming in South Africa there would doubtless be further anti-Indian legislation, and he felt, rightly, that a permanent committee to act as watchdog and to express Indian views at the seat of the imperial government would be more effective and economical than a transitory deputation. Ampthill's importance was clear in 1909 on the occasion of Gandhi's visit to London. He worked extremely hard on the Indians' behalf, advising on the best tactics, in the knowledge that Gandhi and his compatriots probably overemphasized the influence of the committee and its support in England, and were dangerously enthusiastic about a large campaign in England when a quieter approach would be more politic.[35] Gandhi's petitions even reached India's Viceroys, indirectly, or directly as in a telegram from Gandhi to the Viceroy in 1896.[36]

Gandhi's work in London showed that he recognized that the support of public opinion was as vital to his political campaigns as the inherent strength of coherent and moral argument based on facts. The lawyer needed the skills of the publicist, and his South African experiences taught him to perfect techniques of appealing to as wide a public as possible, if necessary across several continents. This aspect of his political style was to become even more significant in India when the use of non-violent resistance to injustices, and ultimately to the raj itself, relied for its effectiveness in large measure on the sense of moral concern even amounting to outrage which it could arouse, and the pressure this in turn could put on the authorities being resisted. At this early stage in his career Gandhi saw the importance of appealing to public opinion in England, South Africa and India itself, and bent his energies to the task, even though at the outset he was a lone voice and a political nonentity.

In England Gandhi extended his appeals to public opinion beyond the range of the influential men he personally contacted on his two visits. He maintained a list of friendly newspapers and individuals, and probably utilized these contacts for the distribution of open letters on Indian problems, as in September 1897 and in April 1901.[37] He was also in touch with the London-based British Committee of the Indian National Congress using its wider channels for publicity, including its journal, *India*. In South Africa Gandhi constantly appealed to white-settler opinion, as befitted his self-perception as an interpreter between the European and Indian communities. His main tactics were those of the open letter and letters to the white press. His first open letter – to members of the Natal Legislatures – was probably written early in December 1894 on the whole problem of Indians in Natal, pleading for an end to ignorance in South Africa about India and her peoples. This was followed by another open letter more widely distributed among Europeans in the colony. One of his more substantial pieces of publicity aimed at the white community was a pamphlet on the Indian franchise, written a year later, subtitled, 'An Appeal To Every Briton In South Africa'.[38] He also attempted to bridge the gulf between the races by articles and letters in his own *Indian Opinion* and in the white press.

Even more copious were Gandhi's attempts in person and through the pen to tell Indians in India what was happening in South Africa and to elicit their support. His first and most substantial piece of writing for Indians at home was the 'Green Pamphlet', describing the Indian condition in South Africa, written while he was visiting India in 1896, and so called because its cover was green.[39] From then onwards open letters to public men in India followed, though Gandhi had doubts about their efficacy as in India there was no equivalent of the British permanent committee to watch over Indian interests and co-ordinate publicity and protest. Soon, as Gandhi became known as a legitimate and knowledgeable spokesman for South African Indians, his letters and articles were hospitably received in India's English language press, both Indian and British owned. Among the welcoming papers were *The Times of India, The Hindu, The Statesman,* and *The Englishman.* In 1899/1900 *The Times of India*'s weekly edition published a series of articles by Gandhi from Durban on a whole range of Indian problems in the South African colonies. G.A. Natesan, a well-known Indian liberal politician, journalist and businessman who edited the *Indian Review*, was a significant contact who did considerable practical work for Gandhi's cause, sending substantial donations from himself and others and helping Indians deported from the Transvaal. By the end of his time in Africa Gandhi's main ally and adviser in India was G.K. Gokhale, the Bombay politician who moved so freely in government as well as Indian circles, and had actually seen Indian conditions in Africa with his own eyes.

When Gandhi was in India to lobby in person he threw himself into public meetings and contacts with important politicians and political organizations in the interests of his compatriots in Africa, casting off the inhibitions which had crippled him as an aspiring lawyer, and for the sake of the cause ignoring the fact that he was young, inexperienced and virtually unknown in his own country. His personal campaign culminated in December 1901 in a speech to Congress itself.[40] After outlining Indian problems he pleaded with the delegates not for mere 'lip sympathy' or donations. What was needed, in his view, was a publicity effort by those who edited papers and journals, and actual settlement in South Africa by professional men, for they could help to create a rounded Indian community of settlement like those produced by European emigration from a wide social span, and could then educate and minister to their compatriots, teaching them their rights, while simultaneously breaking down the ignorance and suspicions which marred relations between Indians and whites. When Gandhi was busy in England in 1909 his close colleague, Henry Polak, toured India for him, addressing public meetings and visiting influential individuals. But lest the South African Indian cause be tainted by any suspicion of contact with Indian politicians the raj might consider 'extremist', Gandhi gave him strict instructions to follow the advice of Gokhale, the editor of *The Times of India*, and the Aga Khan.[41]

As Gandhi contrived ways of appealing to public opinion in three continents he rapidly learned the power of the well-directed and well-informed pen, and the stumbling student of Rajkot days trained himself to become a competent publicist and journalist in a language not his own. His first two pamphlets, aimed at the white community in South Africa, were written in his first brief stay in Natal; but his first major essay in journalism was the 'Green Pamphlet' written while he was at home in Rajkot in 1896, which ran to 10,000 copies. This was journalism on a shoe-string, and Gandhi later recalled how in order to get the pamphlet ready for the post he gathered together local children from near his home and they did the wrapping for the reward of used postage stamps which Gandhi had collected. By 1904 he had realized that occasional writings and the hospitality of newpapers were inadequate to the broad and urgent campaign on which he had embarked, and in that year he launched *Indian Opinion*, a weekly in English and Gujarati sections. Its stated aims were broad and conciliatory: to voice the feelings of the Indian community, to remove the misunderstandings which had bred the prejudice of white settlers against Indians, to point out to Indians their faults and give them practical and moral guidance and a knowledge of their motherland, and to promote harmony in the empire.[42] Gandhi lavished on this paper his time, skill and savings, the last being necessary because it was not a commercial venture and except at the very beginning the paper accepted no advertisements to buoy up its finances, and its press took on no outside work. Its continuation was secured by the move to Phoenix which enabled economy and the support of the labour of a committed community. Gandhi hoped it would thus be free of outside pressures and so enabled to concentrate on service to the wider community, which he perceived as the fundamental duty of the press. To Gandhi, editing *Indian Opinion* was an immense education – in the discipline of regular and restrained writing, in the power and potential perils of the press, and in understanding his compatriots as they inundated him with letters, friendly, critical and bitter. It became a means for expressing his personal views on a wide range of social, political and religious topics, as well as a co-ordinating organ for the political campaign. It was thus a direct precursor of the two weeklies Gandhi was to found and control in India.

Gandhi rated his training in journalism very high among the lessons he learned in South Africa. But as significant in his estimation was the experience he received in handling money for the first time, some of which were deposits from clients who had no other place of safety, while other amounts were those collected for general political work and for the satyagraha (civil resistance) campaigns. In the first year of its life, for example, the Natal Indian Congress's income was about £500; by mid-1896 its expenses were treble that amount, and it had acquired a permanent property for over £1,000. When satyagraha was under way lavish donations came from India, including £400 from G.A. Natesan, and two gifts each of 25,000 rupees from Ratan Tata of the big Parsi industrialist family. Three Indian Princes, Bikaner, Mysore and Hyderabad, also gave rupee donations running into four figures, at the instigation of Natesan.[43] Although these were great benefactions Gandhi had learned about the difficulties of extracting regular subscriptions the hard way in the early years of the NIC when members promised funds readily enough but were dilatory about handing over the money. As a result he decided never to carry on public work on borrowed money, but only with cash in hand. He also began to distrust the use of interest from invested capital for public work, preferring the immediacy of funds donated by people enthused with a cause who would demand that their gifts were rightly spent. As he commented wryly some years later,

> An institution run with the interest of accumulated capital ceases to be amenable to public opinion and becomes autocratic and self-righteous. This is not the place to dwell upon the corruption of many a social and religious institution managed with permanent funds. The phenomenon is so common that he who runs may read it.[44]

He remained a stickler for keeping accounts as he had been in London. But now this was the more vital because he was dealing with money entrusted to him rather than his own. In 1896 he kept a daily record of out-of-pocket expenses for the NIC to account for expenditure of £75 it had given to him for its work in India during his brief visit. He included not only hotel bills, transport and porters, but tips, expenditure on soap, drinking water, fruit and individual meals. He did the same during his deputation in England in 1906, later insisting that it was incumbent on voluntary workers to be scrupulous in the matter of accounts.[45] His skill as a fund-raiser and repute as an honest trustee of public funds were resources which were of considerable importance when he eventually returned to India and far greater sums were at stake. Without his financial acumen, acquired by trial and error in Africa, the political campaign against the raj, and the numerous linked campaigns for handspinning and weaving, and for social uplift, would have been significantly poorer and weaker.

However, it was the tactic of satyagraha, non-violent resistance to injustice and wrong, which became the hallmark of Gandhi's mature political style. This above all marked him out from other Indian politicans, and it originated in his response to the experience of South Africa. For him satyagraha was of much wider significance than a mere technique to be deployed in political conflict, and its inner meaning for him in the context of his total spiritual reorientation will be examined closely in the next chapter. Here our concern is with the birth and manifestations of a strategy which revolutionized the course of the Indian struggle in South Africa.

Varieties of non-violent resistance had occurred long before Gandhi's South African experiments, and he almost certainly knew of many of them. He used the British suffragette movement, for instance, several times in *Indian Opinion*, and even went back to figures in European history such as Tyler, Hampden, Bunyan and Socrates, as men who had obeyed their consciences rather than bow to the dictates of the ruling authority. Deep within his own Gujarati culture there was also a stress on the positive power of suffering and, surviving into the nineteenth century, a tradition of public action whereby an aggrieved party would publicly call to attention his grievance, shaming the offender, by fasting outside him home. Gandhi became aware of Tolstoy's writings and how they were in sympathy with his own developing ideals very early in his South African stay. But he did not read Thoreau's work on civil disobedience until he was in gaol for that offence. When Gandhi and the Indian community reached the point of open-eyed and morally committed law-breaking it was not so much the result of ideology but of sheer necessity in their eyes. In 1906 the 'Black Act' seemed a humiliation to Indians' honour and a threat to their whole existence in South Africa. Recalling the meeting held in September 1906 in a Jewish theatre hired in Johannesburg so that as many Indians as possible could gather to decide on a course of action, Gandhi admitted that this first satyagraha was pragmatic. 'But I must confess that even I myself had not then understood all the implications of the resolution I had helped to frame; nor had I gauged all the possible conclusions to which they might lead.'[46] When one of the most venerable members of the Indian community suggested that they should pass, in the name of God, the proposed resolution not to obey the new ordinance, Gandhi soon began to see the moral seriousness of the proposed action and the great hardships it might involve. He pronounced himself willing to endure whatever came, even if he was the only one to do so. Not only the meeting's president joined him in a sacred oath: so did the whole gathering.

However, Gandhi was soon pushed to define what the Indian strategy was, as Europeans immediately equated it with what they knew as passive resistance, and called it a weapon of the weak who had no other recourse left to them. Gandhi argued that the Indians were using what he called 'soul force' rather than passive resistance: it was the power of the courageous, loving spirit, pitted against wrong. In it there was no place for hatred or the idea of violence; there was no idea of harrassing or injuring the opponent. Nor was it a weapon taken up by the weak as a last resort, but an attitude and practice which flowed from inner strength. It was based on a belief in 'the conquest of the adversary by suffering in one's own person'; or, as he put it in a letter to the *Rand Daily Mail*, 'not resistance but a policy of communal suffering'.[47] In order to avoid confusion he organized a competition through *Indian Opinion* to find a name for what the Indian community was doing. The outcome was the name, satyagraha, from the words for truth and firmness, which he used thereafter, sometimes in English using alternatively 'truth force' or 'soul force'.

The manifestations of satyagraha in South Africa were varied, even at that early stage giving an indication of its potential flexibility and its 'feel', at least when Gandhi controlled it. Breaking a law deemed to be immoral or profoundly unjust was its main thrust, as in the case of Indian refusal to register under the 'Black Act' and deliberate entry into the Transvaal without permits. In these cases gaol was the penalty; and Gandhi argued that imprisonment in such circumstances was a glorious outcome rather than an ignominy. Right at the start of satyagraha against the 'Black Act' he wrote, 'We believe that, if the Indians in the Transvaal firmly stick to this resolution, they will at once be free of their shackles. The gaol will then be like a palace to them. Instead of being a disgrace, going to gaol will enhance their prestige.'[48] This attitude was visible again in India as satyagraha against the raj gathered strength: Gandhi's exposition of satyagraha invited Indians to believe in themselves and in their inner strength in a new way – in complete contrast to the Indian self-image as cowering before the mighty meat-eating Englishman in the schoolboy doggerel he had known so well. Gaol in the national cause became the badge of this new confidence, and a valued qualification for office when Congress came to power in India.

However, satyagraha in Gandhi's hands was not just a matter of courageously breaking the law at issue: it was also an occasion for a range of symbolic acts which would enhance the community's self-awareness, increase its internal cohesion, and shame the opponent. Here in South Africa he demonstrated his great skill in the use of symbol, which was to become more highly developed in India. A great bonfire of registration certificates in August 1908, when the government had in Indians' eyes gone back on its acceptance of their voluntary registration in the Transvaal, was one of the most striking examples. A huge iron cauldron was set up on a platform in the grounds of a mosque in Johannesburg, and several thousand certificates were soused in paraffin and burned in it as a prelude to the renewal of the struggle. Again in 1913 Gandhi contrived the symbolic 'invasion' of the Transvaal by a select group from Phoenix without permits, deliberately courting arrest. They were followed by a group of women who were also gaoled – a fate deliberately chosen to arouse the moral sense of Indians in Africa and India, accustomed to the seclusion of women and their high valuation as symbols of purity and family life. Later the same year

Gandhi led a long march of over 2,000 men, women and children across the Transvaal border; all were deported to Natal, prosecuted and jailed. There seems to have been little elaborate organization behind satyagraha as it developed in complexity of action and the numbers involved. Gandhi had created a separate satyagraha organization but he seems to have been the planning and driving force behind all the action, both in person and through the columns of *Indian Opinion*. Through satyagraha he learned to manage large numbers of activists and to handle considerable sums of money donated to the cause. But if his close associate, patron and admirer, Parsi Rustomji, is to be believed, he had not yet learned the art of delegation. He attempted to do far too much himself, and the organization of satyagraha became muddled.[49]

Within satyagraha Gandhi envisaged a crucial place for personal discussion and compromise between antagonists, even at the height of a struggle. These were aspects of Gandhi's style which became prominent in India, as well as an indication of the spiritual conviction behind satyagraha. In 1908 and 1911 Gandhi met Smuts face to face, and worked out the basis for a settlement of outstanding problems. For a satyagrahi (an exponent of satyagraha) there was no shame or sign of weakness in achieving a compromise provided fundamental principles were preserved. The actions of a satyagrahi were founded in an implicit trust in human nature, in the conviction that truth would always triumph, and concessions from both parties except on central principles could bring peace, thus compromise marked no defeat for either but the far greater and more desirable triumph of truth and the strength of the human spirit.

Gandhi's practical apprenticeship in the craft of politics was obviously important for his future in India. But in the light of the Indian political context and his later career it is evident that in other, less obvious ways the South African experience was a rich and formative one, moulding him into a very special kind of public figure, far greater in range and experience than most politicans of his day. His contemporaries who were active in India's political life tended to work in the sophisticated arena of the Indian National Congress, with its high proportion of lawyers and professional men, using English as their all-India language, while simultaneously working from a local power base often circumscribed by caste and language; or they were active predominantly in the restricted public world of province and district, concentrating their efforts on more local problems, having few if any contacts on a national scale. Gandhi's South African work, by contrast, enabled him eventually to become both an all-India figure and one closely concerned with the affairs of a great variety of men and women in their local situations. In South Africa he encountered in microcosm many of the Indian subcontinent's diversities and the divisions among Indians, originating in region and mother tongue, religious community and caste, which in the African situation almost crystallized into a class ordering among Indian migrants. Because of the pattern of Indian migration these distinctions tended to reinforce each other. As Gandhi became aware of these divisions, he committed himself to their abolition, or their sublimation in a common Indian identity reflecting a national community whose varied components treated each other with mutual respect. In so doing he worked with a range of Indians far wider than he would have done had he received his political apprenticeship in India.

Although a Gujarati Hindu, he found his earliest associates among the Indian Muslims of South Africa, and initially campaigned on issues most closely touching them. Here was no leader who confined his interests to those of his own religious community, and the shared background and the Gujarati language helped him to overcome the religious barrier. As he stayed on in South Africa he learned more of the rough conditions in which indentured Indians lived and worked; and his compassion increased for the low caste, poor labourers, many of whom came from South India and spoke Tamil. His active work among them increased markedly. In his autobiography he told the pathetic story of the Tamil labourer, Balasundaram, beaten by his master, for whom he contrived to gain a new employer, as the incident which marked the start of his work among his most degraded and helpless compatriots. Indentured labourers began to pour into his lawyer's office, seeking help, once Balasundaram's case became known among them, and Gandhi commented, 'I hailed this connection with delight.'[50] Public work among men of lower and even untouchable caste from a region far removed from his own by geography, customs and language would never have been a natural social and political pattern for Gandhi in India. Furthermore, his growing identification with the poor, and determination to better their position, was an attitude of mind and style of behaviour at variance with Hindu perceptions both of a stratified society based on religious merit, and of charity and patronage rather than personal involvement in reform and service as the role befitting the higher caste or more economically privileged.

Early signs of Gandhi's rebellion against Hindu social assumptions are visible from this time, though they probably reflected his deepening religious vision more than his work amongst the indentured labourers. Gandhi claimed as early as 1905 that in his eyes there was no distinction between Brahmins and untouchables.[51] In his own family circle he insisted that no one should consdier work normally done by a sweeper as polluting. This had become a source of contention with Kasturbhai in their first Durban home, and a decade later in 1907 he was advising his cousin, Chhaganlal, at Phoenix to see to the cleanliness of his baby son's bedding and clothes himself and not to 'allow the useless and wicked superstitions about untouchability to come in your way.'[52] Soon he was publicly decrying the notion that there were 'high' and 'low' castes, though he did not as yet feel that the caste system as a whole was wrong or useless. He berated as cowardly satyagrahi prisoners who would not eat food touched by untouchables or sleep near them in gaol for fear of tyrannical caste reaction at home; and he told a Tamil meeting that they would have come to South Africa in vain if they brought with them the caste divisions which were so strong in their native Madras.[53] Gandhi thus became practised in dealing with a very wide religious, economic and social spectrum of his compatriots, an experience and commitment which marked him out from other politicians on his return to India.

South Africa's unique circumstances also gave him the opportunity to work with Indian women in a way which would have been socially unacceptable as well as politically unnecessary at home. In Phoenix and Tolstoy Farm he had encouraged women settlers to participate in new life-styles where they were not only treated as equals with the male members of the communities, but educated in far more open social relations between people of different communities and castes than would have been possible in India, where women were early in life socialized within the family environment to conform to and perpetuate conservative social and religious conventions of seclusion and avoidance. But it was not until the very end of his South African campaign that he involved women in active political campaigning even to the extent of breaking the law and courting imprisonment, following the court judgement jeopardizing the status of Indian marriages. With some hesitation he explained to the women of Tolstoy Farm and Phoenix the ordeal and dangers of appearing in court and going to gaol, not wanting them to break down at critical moments and thus damage the whole satyagraha movement. But their eagerness and fortitude proved remarkable. One was pregnant and several had babies in arms, but they responded enthusiastically to Gandhi's call. One almost died in gaol because of the poor food, and another died within days of release after contracting a fatal fever in prison.[54] Gandhi's work with Indian women in South Africa provided the foundation for his involvement of women in politics in India, so convinced had he become of their potential strength of character and will, as well as the publicity value of their sufferings in a satyagraha campaign.

In South Africa Gandhi formed close living and working relationships with sympathetic Europeans. This was most unusual for an Indian, whether at home or in Africa: in India religious and social conventions inhibited close association between races, while in Africa white prejudice reinforced the prohibitions of caste and custom. Gandhi recognized that these close relationships were unconventional and disturbing to his Indian friends, and particularly to his immediate family. But he later insisted that it was right to welcome such contacts as part of an expanding circle of identification and service. 'I hold that believers who have to see the same God in others that they see in themselves must be able to live amongst all with ... detachment.'[55] He had two female European stenographers who worked for him in succession and were trusted with accounts and the handling of money, and became far more to Gandhi than mere typists, both in their responsibility and in their personal relationships with him. The second, a Miss Sonja Schlesin, virtually ran the publicity and business side of satyagraha when the main leaders were in gaol, working on a far lower salary than she could have commanded, because she sympathized with Gandhi's ideals.

Gandhi's closest male colleague was a journalist, Henry Polak, whom he met casually in a vegetarian restaurant in Johannesburg. Polak joined the staff of *Indian Opinion*, went both to India and England as Gandhi's spokesman in the cause of satyagraha, and eventually became a lawyer in partnership with Gandhi. The two men held similar views of fundamentals from the start, and it was Polak who lent Gandhi Ruskin's *Unto This Last* which had such a profound influence on his way of life. He joined Gandhi in the Phoenix community and then, with his wife, lived virtually as a joint family with the Gandhis in Johannesburg; neither of the Polaks feared the manual labour and simplicity involved as Gandhi experimented with an increasingly spartan life style.

Albert West was another European Gandhi met in the same Johannesburg vegetarian restaurant. At the time he was in a printing partnership with another European, but he agreed to look after *Indian Opinion* for Gandhi, even though the remuneration was small. At once he realized that it was a loss-making concern as it stood, and agreed to live at Phoenix when it was moved there to put it on a more secure foundation; and he accepted a monthly allowance under a third less than Gandhi had originally given him. He in turn brought a wife, mother and sister-in-law to join the community. Like Miss Schlesin they became crucial for the back-up of satyagraha as Indians were gaoled, maintaining Phoenix, the press and paper. Another European colleague, Mr Ritch, eventually left for London to become a barrister and was important in the activities of the South African British Indian Committee.

A German architect, Herman Kallenbach, gave Gandhi free house-room when he closed his own Joahnnesburg home, and lent Gandhi without rent the site of Tolstoy Farm. He, too, came to share Gandhi's ideals of simple living, and lived on Tolstoy Farm as simply as any of the Indian settlers, giving up the comparative luxury he had been able to afford, though some Europeans thought he was a fool. He engaged with Gandhi on many religious topics, and was eventually converted to the ideal of non-violence. So far did he carry this that he actually experimented with taming and befriending snakes, though Gandhi gently chided him for this.

Gandhi's experience of living and working closely with Europeans who sympathized with his ideals and were prepared to adapt to a modified Indian way of living was replicated in India, where numerous foreigners joined his ashram communities for short or long periods; he also welcomed close European colleagues in his political and social work, such as C.F. Andrews, whom he first met in South Africa.[56] His freedom from racial prejudice and ability to form relations of trust across chasms of colour, creed and race, contributed to his remarkable ability to mix with representatives of the raj, and reinforced his constantly stated belief that although he had come to abhor the institution and ways of the British raj in India, he did not hate the British themselves. The response of men like Polak, West and Kallenbach to him suggests something of the immense charm and appeal Gandhi was beginning to exert. When the mature Gandhi's relationships with Europeans are compared with those of the diffident student in London with his hosts and hostesses it is clear what a watershed South Africa was in his personal development.

The circumstances of Indians in that alien land also helped to mould Gandhi's range of public work and his expectations of the role of a public figure, and they were far removed from the vision of an English-returned lawyer commanding a high salary and public deference which had fired his family's decision to send him to London. Increasingly he became involved in humanitarian work as he identified with the poor and ill-treated, and interpreted his role as one of service rather than the pursuit and use of power. In the first decade of the new century, even when his legal career was at its busiest and most lucrative, he was unsatisfied, and hankered not only for a simpler life but for the opportunity to do some specific caring work. He found this in a small charitable hospital financed by the generosity of Parsi Rumstomji and directed by a European mission doctor. He took an hour or more each day from his office work to help in the hospital, taking case notes and dispensing what was prescribed by the doctor. Thus he attained some solid medical knowledge as well as tending patients who were mostly indentured Indians from areas other than his native Gujarat. He used his medical skills more publicly on two occasions when he organized an Indian Ambulance Corps in South Africa, once in the Boer War and again in the Zulu Rebellion of 1906. The latter brought home to him particulary vividly the horrors of war, as he nursed Zulus whom no white men were willing to tend. Such war work demanded courage and physical strength as well as humanitarian dedication. In the Boer War the ambulance corps was at one point asked to serve within the firing line, and in both outbreaks they had to march up to 40 miles a day.

Gandhi also attended in person to distasteful jobs in the service of the Indian community which he discussed forthrightly in *Indian Opinion*. Decent sanitation was then and later one of his major concerns, and in Durban he took part in regular inspections of hygiene in Indian homes though he found his compatriots were often insulting or politely uncooperative in response to his efforts. In Johannesburg he master-minded a temporary hospital in a storage shed lent by the Municipality for Indian victims of an outbreak of plague. He and his fellow volunteers cleaned it up and nursed the patients at considerable personal risk, large numbers of them died, as did the nurse loaned by the authorities. Gandhi's willing acceptance that such humanitarian activities were a part of his work as a public figure distinguished him from most of those who were active in Indian politics when he returned home. Far from receding in importance, such actions enlarged as a proportion of his concerns and actions on his return, as he confronted for the first time the subcontinent's vast economic and social problems as well as its political dilemmas.

Gandhi's experience of gaol in Africa was also of profound importance for the development of his inner resources as well as for his political

style. He was imprisoned in 1908, 1909 and 1913 as the penalty for
satyagraha. For an Indian of respectable caste and good standing, exposure to the routines of gaol, to prisoners who were there for crime rather
than conscience, to the erratic behaviour of warders, as well as the sheer
fact of being gaoled, were deeply shocking. But Gandhi wrote about
them with detachment as he tried to educate his compatriots through
Indian Opinion about what to expect if they joined the satyagraha
struggle. He detailed the day's routine, the accommodation, the diet and
the work demanded, sparing his readers nothing of the strangeness and
possible sense of humiliation. Food was one of the worst problems for
Indian prisoners. The mealie porridge and bean diet served to non-white
prisoners wreaked havoc with the Indian digestive system, causing
either constipation or diarrhoea. In 1908 Gandhi managed to get this
regime somewhat modified. The same problem occurred in Gandhi's
second imprisonment, later in 1908. On this occasion Indian nutritional
needs and religious feelings were heeded after Gandhi and 36 others had
sent a petition to the local magistrate, and Indians were permitted *ghee*
and vegetables in place of the other prisoners' meat allowance. In 1909
after a longer tussle over food Gandhi again managed to ameliorate the
diet of all Indian prisoners, but in the process he lived for six weeks on a
single meal of beans only at midday.

Lack of privacy for bathing and in the latrines was another source of
shame for Indians exposed to prison life, but Gandhi argued that they
should take this equably and feel no sense of shame since prisons could
not provide privacy. He himself had some unpleasant experiences in this
matter, being physically ejected from a lavatory by a strong and heavy
African prisoner, though eventually the Indian prisoners were given
separate facilities. On other occasions he was harrassed by warders
weary of having to stand guard while he took a long time to move his
bowels. Gandhi also found that he and his compatriots were expected to
do physically tiring work, though few of them were used to it. They
had to dig, to garden, to clean out cells and privies, to polish floors and
doors. Lighter work like sewing blankets came Gandhi's way when the
authorities realized that his health was suffering. But he never complained about the terms of his sentences and urged Indians to consider it
their duty as satyagrahis to do whatever was imposed even if it was
apparently 'polluting' or degrading.[57]

South Africa taught Gandhi to face gaol for the sake of conscience
with pride and resilience. It was one of the main lessons he proceeded to
pass on to his fellow Indians then and back in India. He wrote of his gaol
experience in *Indian Opinion* in such detail because he felt this would
increasingly be part of the struggle and it was necessary for Indians to
welcome it as an honour despite the apparent degradation involved.
'Those who have gone to gaol have been the gainers. Those who have
not gone to gaol have been the losers. Those who have sacrificed their
wealth for the sake of their motherland have in reality earned it.'[58] He
was profoundly concerned that prisoners should realize that the impact

of prison on them reflected their attitude to it: it could be a hell or a paradise, could improve and instruct a man or degrade him, depending on his state of mind and ability to take advantage of the opportunities for experience and growth it offered. For himself he found that accepting physical suffering willingly increased his peace of mind and his inner strength.[59] He also eagerly made use of the time and opportunity available for reading. In 1908–9, for example, he read not only the Bible, the Koran in English and the *Gita* with a commentary by a Gujarati Sanskrit scholar and other Hindu devotional and scriptural writings, but also works by Bacon, Carlyle, Emerson, Huxley, Tolstoy, Ruskin and Plato. Books, he claimed, saved him from boredom and a sense of isolation from his friends, and fed his inner intellectual and spiritual life. He recommended to all Indians the habit of reading good books if they wished to be happy in gaol.[60] Such an experience of inner growth and strengthening encouraged Gandhi to see gaol for the sake of conscience and experienced in the right spirit as not only a necessary element in satyagraha in certain political situations but a moral good which could refine the satyagrahi's spirit and make him or her a worthier exponent of a political style which presupposed a whole way of life and thought.

Gandhi's wide reading as well as his actual experience of living and campaigning within a part of the British empire sharpened and modified his thinking on political issues, particularly the nature of government and the character and worth of the British empire to Indians both at home in India and abroad. He never became an academic political theorist, but his circumstances in South Africa made him forge his own distinctive political attitudes which marked out the mature man who left Africa from the gauche lawyer who had arrived there twenty years earlier.

One of the most striking aspects of Gandhi's thinking on political relations between Indians and the British throughout the turmoil of his South African years was his loyalty to the British empire. It is a strange contrast: the heroic rebel of the 1930s and 1940s who ultimately challenged the British to quit India, and the devoted imperialist of the turn of the century who sang the National Anthem with gusto, planted a tree to celebrate Queen Victoria's Dimanod Jubilee and helped to circulate to Indian children in South Africa in 1901 a memorial souvenir of the late Queen which would not have been of place in any patriotic schoolroom in Britain. He was at this stage convinced that the British imperial connection with India was providential: the work of God which would ultimately be for India's good. It had occurred because the British exhibited strength of character in so many of her people which in his view Indians did not; and he reckoned that under British rule India enjoyed considerable protection.[61] The hinge of this loyalty to the empire was a deep-rooted belief that its fundamental values were those of the British constituion, and he was not swayed from this by local practice in parts of the empire or temporary aberrations which seemed at variance with these basic values. Looking back from the 1920s he thought he had probably not known anyone who cherished such loyalty to the British constitution as he did then; and in his 1895 pamphlet on the Indian franchise he maintained that Indians 'are proud to be under the British Crown, because they think that England will prove India's deliverer.'[62] Those basic values of the constitution included love of justice, fair dealing, equality and liberty; and he spoke and wrote of them continuously in connection with the empire, despite evidence to the contrary in South Africa. Against the apparent odds he continued to hope that the empire would live up to its ideals. As he wrote in 1906, about a case where an Indian was cleared after two Europeans had attempted to blackmail him,

> we have no hesitation in saying that one of the greatest secrets of the success of the Empire is its ability to deal out even-handed justice. A case such as the one we have referred to makes up for many a defect in the legal administration in the various British possessions. It serves as a beacon-light to tell Indians ... that they need not be without hope, so long as the fierce sun of pure justice beats on the chill surface of broken promises.[63]

Gandhi insisted that there could only be a true imperial community and sentiment if one standard was observed throughout the empire; and it was for this reason that he encouraged Indians to cling to the promises of the 1858 Proclamation and used it continuously in his exchanges with the authorities while he worked in South Africa. But he reminded his compatriots that justice would only come if they continued their demands: 'Even a mother, says an Indian proverb, does not serve without being asked – much less does a British Government.'[64]

Gandhi's loyalty to the empire was most vividly displayed during local South African crises when Indians might well have attempted to exploit the situation to better their own position. Gandhi was adamant that this should not be so, despite Indian voices to the contrary. Instead, during the Boer War and Zulu Rebellion he volunteered his services as a non-combatant. Although his personal sympathies lay with the Boers and the Zulus in each case he felt that if he demanded rights as a citizen of the empire so it was his duty to participate in its defence. Offering his own and other Indians' services to the Colonial Secretary in 1899, Gandhi wrote that they would consider it a privilege to do whatever the government required, freely and without pay: it was an earnest of Indian loyalty. Reflecting on this after a decade's work in India and a significant shift in his attitude to the British empire, he had no regrets, and he wrote in his detailed account of satyagraha in South Africa that he would do the same again if he still had the faith he had then in the empire, and the hope that Indians would achieve liberty within it.[65]

Despite his words and active service in support of the empire, there were growing signs of disquiet in Gandhi's mind as he thought about the Indians' actual position in South Africa. As early as 1903 in connection with difficulties Indian trustees were experiencing in acquiring legal rights to the Pretoria mosque, even after British administrators had replaced the Boer regime, Gandhi wrote ominously,

> It is a pretty outlook for people living under the British flag, which takes under its protecting fold all the religions. We may, therefore, well ask, what are the Indians coming to in the Transvaal? Is the British Constitution going to be revised at Pretoria? Or will justice ultimately triumph?[66]

He wrote in 1904 of the exclusive attitude of the colonies making a deep impression in India, and making the task of ruling India itself more difficult as it became clear that for Indians British citizenship was of little value in the other parts of the empire. And in 1907 he told the High Commissioner in Johannesburg that he was recommending to Indians that they should resist the 'Black Act' precisely because as 'a lover of the Empire' he saw in it the seeds of danger to the empire. In 1910 he was associated with what he himself called a momentous step – namely, Indian avoidance of any identification with a public welcome for the visiting Duke of Connaught, as a sign of grief at continuing Indian disabilities in the Transvaal and the uncertain outlook under the new Union of South Africa.[67]

However, much more significant than any local South African crises in forging Gandhi's attitude to India, Britain and the empire was a far deeper disillusion growing in him with Western civilization itself. Discussion of this belongs properly in the next chapter, but understanding the general trend of his wider thinking is necessary here as the background to his major work on Indo–British relations and Indian home rule, *Hind Swaraj*, written in 1909, which was the nearest he came to producing a sustained work of political theory. The Anglophile student of the late-Victorian era had gradually divested himself of the trappings of a successful lawyer, had simplified his life and home and abandoned the outward manifestations of Westernization with which he had been so concerned when he set up his first family homes in India and Africa. By October 1909, writing from London, he was expounding a total disillusion with the values of Western civilization. He felt it inadvisable for any Indian to visit or live in England, which he saw as in the grip of a 'crazy civilization' where material values reigned supreme and people were losing their inner peace. In a personal letter to Polak written the same month, he was beginning to expand this into a complete reappraisal of India's relations with Britain, which he worked out in full on board ship returning home to South Africa at the end of the year.[68]

Hind Swaraj ('Indian Home Rule') was published in *Indian Opinion* late in 1909, and then issued as a booklet in 1910. Within months it was proscribed in India, and Gandhi hurried on with an English translation and a preface in which he refuted the idea that it contained any approval of violent hostility to the British, and argued that he was still loyal in his own particular way to the empire, despite his condemnation of the methods of the British raj. For him the crucial question was an even deeper one than political loyalty, namely that of the clash of modern civilization with what he understood to be India's ancient civilization:

> My notion of loyalty does not involve acceptance of current rule or government, irrespective of its righteousness or otherwise. Such notion is based upon the belief – not in its present justice or morality but – in a future acceptance by Government of that standard of morality in practice which it at present vaguely and hypocritically believes in, in theory. But I must frankly confess that I am not so much concerned about the stability of the Empire as I am about that of the ancient civilization of India which, in my opinion, represents the best the world has ever seen. The British Government in India constitutes a struggle between the Modern Civilization, which is the Kingdom of Satan, and the Ancient Civilization, which is the Kingdom of God. The one is the God of War, the other is the God of Love. My countrymen impute the evils of modern civilization to the English people and, therefore, believe that the English people are bad, and not the civilization they represent. My countrymen, therefore, believe that they should adopt modern civilization and modern methods of violence to drive out the English. *Hind Swaraj* has been written in order to show that they are following a suicidal policy, and that, if they would but revert to their own glorious civilization, either the English would adopt the latter and become Indianized or find their occupation in India gone.[69]

Hind Swaraj is in the form of a dialogue between an editor and a reader, Gandhi speaking through the mouth of the editor. Briefly summarized, his attitude differed from those in India who wanted to remove the British, whether by violent means or not. As he said in the English preface, his concern was with India's far deeper predicament, namely the stranglehold of modern civilization with its purely materialistic values on India under the aegis of the British raj. Consequently, ousting the British and gaining what most people considered to be 'home rule' or 'freedom' was a delusion. They would not have achieved true freedom, but merely the same type of government run by a different set of men. The editor rounded on his reader.

> [You] want English rule without the Englishman. You want the tiger's nature, not the tiger; that is to say, you would make India English. And when it becomes English, it will be called not Hindustan but *Englistan*. This is not the Swaraj I want.[70]

The British were in the same parlous state as Westernized Indians, gripped by a value system and life-style which denied their fundamental spiritual identity and stifled it with erroneous values of wealth and gain. True swaraj consisted in returning to India's traditional values, as he perceived them. So swaraj could not be given to India by any political act: every Indian would have to experience those values for himself, would have to learn to rule himself, and only on such a foundation of transformed individuals could true swaraj be built. Even the British could be accepted within this swaraj if they followed the same path and abandoned their materialistic values and habits. Not only could swaraj not be 'given' to Indians, but rather it had to be created by them. It could not be achieved by violent methods, as these would destory the end in view. Means and end were, according to Gandhi, indistinguishable, as intimately connected as the seed and the eventual tree. Thus the only sure road to swaraj was satyagraha, the force of love or of the soul. Only Indians trained in this way of self-suffering would be able to stand up to their present rulers and by quiet and probably painful persistence begin to achieve a reformation of India's polity and society by refusing to be party to any action which was at variance with India's own values.

Although *Hind Swaraj* was a condemnation of, rather than an incitement to, violent rebellion, and though the author pitied rather than hated the British, there were evident here seeds of radical rebellion against the raj, potential for a movement against the whole machinery and values of existing government in India far greater than that perceived by existing Indian politicians. Not only did Gandhi envisage a total reversal of all the patterns of Westernization the British presence had set in motion in India, including education, medical practice and industrial development, as well as the practice of government. He had also realized that the raj depended on Indian co-operation; and if that could be knocked from under the raj by a reorientation of Indian values, particularly those of Westernized Indians, then the seemingly mighty edifice would crumble. However, the Gandhi of 1909 was still groping towards these ideals. He had no idea of translating them into a wide political movement, and as yet attempted to work them out only in a personal life-style for himself and in his communities of sympathizers. In the world of practical politics he still maintained an uneasy loyalty to the empire in the hope that it might live up to its professed ideals, as he showed in his advice to Indians to tender loyalty to their new king in 1911 on the occasion of George V's coronation.[71]

Gandhi wrote *Hind Swaraj* as an essay in the proper sense of the word, as a trial discussion of his hopes for India. But what were his links with the real India of the early twentieth century? He had left home, unknown in public life, unconnected politically, a failure in his profession, and socially rejected by a section of his caste. Did South Africa enable the maturing public figure to make new connections on the subcontinent; and did the South African experience influence his own expectations of a personal role in Indian life?

Ties with India

As Gandhi embarked on political work in South Africa, he soon saw the need to appeal to public opinion in India on behalf of the exiled

Indian community. He made this appeal on a consciously broad and
non-party basis through his own visits to India and that of Polak in
1909, when they addressed public meetings in many parts of the country
and made contact with press men and individuals influential in public
life, and through Gandhi's constant communication with Indian newspapers from South Africa. In this way he met within a few years of
starting his African campaign some of the most venerable and significant of the Congress leaders who had been among its founding fathers
in the 1880s and were still central to its discussions. They included Mr
Justice Ranade, Mr Justice Badruddin Tyabji, and Sir Pherozeshah
Mehta, giants in Bombay public life as well as in the all-India Congress;
D.E. Wacha, Chimanlal Setalvad, the fiery Tilak and his more moderate
opponent, Gokhale, and the great Bengali, Surendranath Bannerjea.
Mehta, though nicknamed the 'Uncrowned King' of the Bombay
Presidency, condescended to help the young Gandhi, and in 1896 gave
him invaluable advice on how to handle public meetings and publicity
for his speeches. But it was to Gokhale that Gandhi felt immediately and
most powerfully drawn:

> He gave me an affectionate welcome, and his manner immediately
> won my heart. With him too this was my first meeting, and yet it
> seemed as though we were renewing an old friendship. Sir Pher-
> ozeshah had seemed to me like the Himalaya, the Lokamanaya [Tilak]
> like the ocean. But Gokhale was as the Ganges. One could have a
> refreshing bath in the holy river ... the Ganges invited one to its
> bosom.... He ... assured me that he was always at my disposal ...
> and sent me away exultantly happy. In the sphere of politics the place
> that Gokhale occupied in my heart during his lifetime and occupies
> even now was and is absolutely unique.[72]

The grievances of South African Indians were the basis for the
connections Gandhi was able to forge in Indian public life on a national
scale, such as he would never have achieved had he been a small-town
Gujarati lawyer. But though he was willing to pay his respects to these
great figures and to receive their advice, he remained very much his own
man, and was soon making a definite and personal response to the
institutions and people prominent in India's public life. For example,
although he attended the annual session of Congress in 1901 and was
anxious to publicize his cause through it, he had considerable doubts
about its ethos and methods. He noticed the lack of training among the
volunteers whose duty was to look after the domestic arrangements of
the great gathering, noted with disgust that the Tamil delegates
observed caste separation so rigidly that they insisted on a special
kitchen, screened for privacy, and was shocked at the lack of sanitation
and the dirty habits of some of the delegates, and the refusal of
volunteers to do the cleaning they considered untouchables' work. He
thought that the political discussions of Congress were badly organized,

and much time was wasted; and it saddened him how important English seemed to be for communication among Congressmen.[73]

By 1909, as his own convictions and political skills matured, he became more exasperated with Congressmen's seemingly petty concerns and lack of vision. Discussing the absence of hope and conviction in Indian political circles about ameliorating the Indian position in South Africa, he urged Polak to try to make the Indian leaders see that the struggle was of profound significance for India's own future, was adding to India's mature national identity, and was training an army of men who would in future be able to serve India's own cause, in the face of violence if need be. By contrast, to him the demands made by Congress were limited, and tainted by attention to immediate problems rather than fired with a true vision of a renewed India. In a message for Congress some days later he explained what he considered to be the political and moral significance of the African struggle – a struggle for India's honour that was pure in its methods as well as its goal – and he contrasted this with the Congress programme which was all ideas and talk and no action, certainly none of the disciplined work of self-suffering present in South Africa. He pleaded that Congress should therefore give its exclusive attention to the exiled community's campaign, suggesting that they might then also discover that satyagraha might be the solution to many of India's problems. Echoing *Hind Swaraj* he claimed,

> . . . it is the only weapon that is suited to the genius of our people and our land, which is the nursery of the most ancient religions and has very little to learn from modern civilization – a civilization based on violence of the blackest type, largely a negation of the Divine in man, and which is rushing headlong to its own ruin.[74]

Two years later there was a tentative enquiry as to whether Gandhi would be prepared to serve as Congress president. He responded very hesitantly, knowing that his views might sound peculiar and contrary to those of many Congressmen.[75] When it became clear that it was not a firm invitation he was profoundly relieved, as he would have felt unable to conceal his strongly held views on so many questions Congress debated annually and they might well have embarrassed the Congress leaders; but his current state of mind was so passionately earnest, as he admitted, that he could not have held his peace, and would have been made useless by any curb on his expression.[76]

Similarly Gandhi did not hesitate to point out, even publicly, where he differed from individual political figures with whom he would have to deal on his return to India. Gandhi corresponded with and met Tilak, for example, as early as 1896, and realized his political significance both in his own western India and in all-India politics. But when in 1908 Tilak was deported after being found guilty of sedition in two press articles in which he had supported violent political methods, Gandhi did not hesitate to distance himself from this attitude, and urged South

African Indians to do likewise, rather than blithely following the policies of those regarded as great. They should venerate him for his scholarship and patriotism, but should reject his views. 'India's welfare does not consist in merely uprooting British rule. It will be harmful, even useless, to use force or violence for uprooting that rule. Freedom gained through violence would not endure.' By comparison their satyagraha would have an incomparably better outcome.[77] Gandhi was also reserved in his attitude to Annie Besant, the maverick Theosophist leader, who was briefly influential in Indian politics at the time of Gandhi's return to India and had a considerable following based on the Theosophical Society's members. He had been impressed by her when he was a student in London, took care to pay his respects to her in 1902, and in 1905 initiated a reprint of her translation of the *Gita*. By 1911 he had, however, concluded that she was credulous though not a hypocrite, and he disapproved of the Theosophists' search for occult powers, and felt that there was much fraud at their headquarters in Adyar, near Madras.[78]

Gokhale was the one Indian leader with whom Gandhi formed an enduring political and personal tie. His empathy with Gokhale sprang from their first meeting in 1896 and his prolonged stay with Gokhale in 1901–2, when his host treated him with the ease of a relative and enabled him to meet a range of interesting people. The young man found this visit a great education, and was deeply impressed by Gokhale's dedication to the public good. Looking back in 1921 he remembered,

> He seemed to me all I wanted as a political worker – pure as crystal, gentle as a lamb, brave as a lion and chivalrous to a fault. . . . He was and remains for me the most perfect man in the political field. Not, therefore, that we had no differences. We differed even in 1901 in our views on social customs, e.g., widow remarriage. We discovered differences in our estimate of Western civilization. He frankly differed from me in my extreme views on non-violence. But these differences mattered neither to him nor to me. Nothing could put us asunder.[79]

Thereafter the two men kept in constant touch on South African matters. Gandhi informed Gokhale of the problems faced by Indians and the progress of their campaign, and commended Polak to him when his friend visited India in 1909. In 1912 Gokhale came to South Africa in person, and Gandhi devoted himself to the honoured guest, acting as his personal assistant, interpreter and companion. He even took him to Tolstoy Farm without thinking that the walk from the station and the Spartan accommodation would be a trial to his mentor, who bore the experience serenely despite catching a chill and insisting on sleeping on the floor in order to share the life of the inhabitants. Local officials viewed this close relationship with unease. The Secretary of State for India told the Viceroy of a letter received in the Colonial Office from the Governor-General's private secetary. It stated,

... that Gandhi, the Indian leader there (who is considered a straight and rather high-charactered person, but an undoubted fanatic), has got complete hold of Gokhale and never lets him see any visitor alone.[80]

Official misgivings were not unfounded, since it was the aftermath of Gokhale's visit and Gandhi's allegations of government breach of pledges given to Gokhale on Indian grievances which precipitated the final satyagraha.

Even with Gokhale Gandhi had his differences, as he admitted in his 1921 reminiscences on their relationship. He was saddened by the Servants of India Society, founded by Gokhale in 1905, feeling that it was far too Westernized, that its members did not live simply enough, and that it was a 'superstition' that only a graduate could belong. To him Phoenix surpassed the Society both in its aims and its way of life; and indeed he felt that the political and educational work of the Society did not forward swaraj as he envisaged it but 'is likely to add to our slavery.'[81] The greatest strain in their relationship came in 1913–14 when Gokhale strongly disapproved of Gandhi's decision to lead the Indian community into satyagraha and then in a boycott of the inquiry into Indian grievances set up by the South African government. As one long-used to treading the corridors of power in Whitehall, Calcutta and Delhi he recognized the danger Gandhi ran of jeopardizing the discreet but strong support the Indian government was giving the Indian community in their campaign. However, their relationship survived the tension and culminated in South Africa in Gandhi's stated wish to return to India and work under Gokhale's direction. He had mentioned the possibility in 1911, but early in 1914 he was definitely envisaging a rapid return to India and work under Gokhale's guidance. He recognized his own inexperience on the subcontinent and wanted to remedy it under Gokhale's tuition, agreeing to keep silent on all matters except South Africa for a year after his return. His ambition, he told his friend and political tutor, was 'to be by your side as your nurse and attendant. I want to have the real discipline of obeying someone whom I love and look up to.'[82] For his part Gokhale had for years hoped that Gandhi would come home and work in the SIS, as he thought, according to Polak, that Gandhi was the greatest of the younger men coming into Indian public life. But as they worked increasingly closely he became well aware that their views differed and might prevent Gandhi from joining the SIS, particularly Gandhi's attitude to swaraj. His suggestion that Gandhi should remain silent for his first year back in India was a measure of his hesitation about how his protégé would fit into the Indian public context and his wish to prevent him making early blunders out of ignorance and enthusiasm which would lessen his potential for public work. He was also, on Gandhi's own admission, aware of the younger man's forceful personality and the tendency of people round him to give in to his views rather than argue against his high moral tone and almost fanatical convictions.[83]

An important facet of Gandhi's links with his homeland was what in the language of later twentieth-century political life would be called his public image. This was a time and place far removed from the professional moulding and manipulation of the image of public figures in the mass media. Nevertheless, a politican's standing and repute was a critical element in Indian public life, not least because the British, conscious of their ultimate dependence on Indian loyalty or acquiescence in their rule, were anxious to involve prominent men in their complex network of allies, and reluctant to alienate those who could arouse public sympathy in India and even abroad. Gandhi's name became known in India as far from his native Gujarat as south India, and there largely because of his work among Tamil indentured labourers. Polak in 1909 reported, probably with some exaggeration and reflecting the sympathetic circles in which he was moving on his Indian tour, that Gandhi was 'regarded as one of India's greatest men today'; and in 1910 when G. A. Natesan spoke in Congress, calling Gandhi an indomitable, brave and saintly man and a true patriot, his words were greeted with cheers.[84] It was significant that in the following year there was a faint possibility that Gandhi might be asked to become Congress president. But this reputation was only among those active in all-India politics and was primarily based on his South African work. It was no guarantee of support in Indian public life on issues nearer home, where connections and patronage were still of crucial significance in determining attitudes and alignments.

Among officials of the raj there was an extreme wariness in response to this unusual political figure. *Hind Swaraj* had been proscribed soon after its publication; yet the government felt constrained to assist him and the exiled Indian community in their campaign against white-settler discrimination. Hardinge, as Viceroy attempting to help the community, and his emissary, Sir Benjamin Robertson, found Gandhi extremely hard to handle in 1913–14, not least because they considered that he combined unpredictability with an excess of conscience. The Secretary of State for India, unaware of the repercussions of what he was suggesting, wrote to the exasperated Hardinge in 1914,

> The best possible outcome will be if Gandhi will return to his native land. He is a quite astonishingly hopeless and impracticable person for any kind of deal, but with a sort of ardent, though restrained, honesty which becomes the most pig-headed obstinacy at the critical moment.[85]

As yet British officialdom did not see Gandhi as a serious threat to imperial stability, or a potentially powerful public figure in his homeland. He was thought of more as a crank; possibly as a saintly figure in his own way, but devilishly difficult to deal with in the realms of practical politics; yet one who must be humoured and used as far as possible, because he represented concern on an imperial issue which could disrupt significant sections of Indian public opinion.

Gandhi's own expectations of his role in India were markedly different from those of the government. For him his real life's work lay at
home rather than in South Africa, whatever the repute he had built up
there and the significance of the cause he had championed. In 1911 he
was trying to run down his African commitments, and wrote of all his
work being but a preparation for work in India. He hoped to become a
public servant in this new sphere, under Gokhale, and envisaged that it
would be geographically restricted to his native Gujarat, and probably
only to Kathiawad.[86] The following year Gokhale urged him to come
home within twelve months and began to prepare him for his return by
describing to him in detail all the leading Indian politicans, in the course
of long talks on board ship as Gandhi sailed with him as far as Zanzibar
on his departure after his visit to South Africa. The political crisis
following Gokhale's visit prevented Gandhi's rapid return to India, but
in 1913, as the crisis deepened, Gandhi's thoughts were turning to India,
not so much with a view to a career or a particular type of public service,
but as a spiritual necessity for himself. Increasingly he was saddened by
his own spiritual state, feeling that the pressures of work in South Africa
were exacerbating his faults and undermining his spiritual peace. India
he saw as the land of duty where he could find release from the shackles
of earthly life, and could build the courage to live the life of a true
satyagrahi.[87] It is therefore to Gandhi, the inner man, that we must now
turn our attention, to see how in South Africa he had changed from one
who had welcomed that land as a release from professional failure and
moral ambiguity into a spiritual seeker who yearned for India as a
personal spiritual need.

3

SOUTH AFRICAN EXPERIENCE II
'The satyagrahi'

'The saint has left our shores', wrote the harrassed J.C. Smuts in mid-1914; 'I sincerely hope for ever.'[1] We now investigate the making of the 'saint', and see how the very ordinary Indian lawyer who had arrived in South Africa two decades earlier, moved by necessity and convention and lacking any real religious conviction, became a deeply religious man, a visionary whose insights drove him to action and public involvement; one who, if not a saint as Smuts half-mocked, was of growing spiritual stature, nurtured by a mighty hope in and for mankind. The transformation of Gandhi's inner world was worked out at its fullest and clearest in his practice of satyagraha and his self-moulding into a satyagrahi.

To trace a spiritual pilgrimage is a task fraught with difficulties, because of the complexities of the inner world where conscious belief, unconscious forces, new external influences and inherited traditions all blend. Gandhi's own attempt in his *Autobiography* is erratic and often confusing if the reader is seeking some clear chronological development or reasoned analysis. In Gandhi's case the difficulties are compounded by the fact that there is no 'conversion experience' as a landmark, as is so often the case in a Christian context. Although there were in his South African years certain times and experiences crucial in his inner development – his first year of religious ferment, reading a seminal book, the vow of celibacy, the writing of *Hind Swaraj* – his experience was more a process of deepening enlightenment and discovery, influenced by a multiplicity of sources which reinforced each other. By 1914 some called him a political leader, some a saint or Mahatma, for he had become so much more than the conventional politician or religious teacher. He saw himself as a seeker after truth; and it was for his 'experiments with truth', his inner turmoil and its results that he would have wished to be remembered, rather than his political achievement. To him the latter were ephemeral: the spiritual quest was of eternal and universal significance.

Whereas the boy and youth in India and England had merely been exposed to a range of religious influences, now in South Africa the adult Gandhi experienced a time of *conscious* religious searching and experiment. By contrast with his earlier interest in religion he now, during his first year in Pretoria, experienced real religious conviction. 'Here it was that the religious spirit within me became a living force', he recalled. 'I had gone to South Africa for travel, for finding an escape from Kathiawad intrigues and for gaining my own livelihood. But . . . I found myself in search of God and striving for self-realization.'[2]

There was no single reason for or experience behind this change. Certainly that physically and emotionally bitter experience of being ejected from a train on his first journey in Africa challenged his previous experience and values. But his religious turmoil and quest stemmed also from the wide range of contacts he made in Africa among deeply religious people of various persuasions, whose convictions and way of life as well as preaching forced him to re-evaluate their traditions and in the process to study more deeply the Hindu tradition to which he belonged.

In South Africa he made friends and colleagues of many Christians, mostly evangelicals. Their sincerity was patent, as was their anxiety for Gandhi's salvation, though this was expressed in a more courteous and loving fashion than the strident evangelism of the missionaries of Gandhi's boyhood. They invited him into their homes, to their prayer meetings and conventions. But though he valued their honesty, though he venerated Jesus and was powerfully moved by parts of the Bible, he could not accept their insistence that salvation could only come through Jesus. To him it seemed impossible that there should be only one son of God: all men were such and could become God-like, he felt. Further, the Cross of Jesus was a great example of sacrifice, but not an instrument of universal redemption; and Christian lives did not bear witness to any greater reformation than that visible in the lives of men of other faiths. The difficulties Gandhi found in the theology of his Christian friends reflected the inclusive, eclectic nature of the Hindu tradition with its diverse strands and many paths to salvation, its multitudinous manifestations of the divine in human and natural form, and its understanding of *moksha*, salvation, in the sense of liberation from a series of lives and their *karma*, rather than as liberation from sin and its consequences into a new relationship with the divine.

Gandhi's new Muslim associates urged him to study Islam, and we know that he bought and read a translation of the Koran and acquired other books on Islam at that time. The attraction of aspects of Muslim devotion for Gandhi was clear in an article he wrote in *Indian Opinion* in 1907 on a thirteenth-century Persian Sufi poet. He quoted the poet at some length:

'I saw the Cross and also Christians, but I did not find God on the Cross. I went to find Him in the temple, but in vain. I saw Him neither in Herat nor in Kandahar. He could be found neither on the hill nor in the cave. At last, I looked into my heart and found Him there, only there and nowhere else.'[3]

Whereas Muslims and Christians commended their creeds to Gandhi, some Theosophist friends a little later tried to extract help from Gandhi, believing that he was conversant with the Hindu tradition and could enlighten them on such beliefs as rebirth. Despite his limited knowledge of the great Hindu texts and his virtual ignorance of Sanskrit, Gandhi agreed to read some of the sources with them; and for this purpose delved even deeper into the *Gita* and began to learn it by heart as he brushed his teeth for fifteen minutes every morning, staring at *Gita* verses pinned on the wall. Gandhi summed up the 'mental churning' produced by his exposure to other traditions and his search for truth amidst them:

> ... if I could not accept Christianity either as a perfect, or the greatest, religion, neither was I then convinced of Hinduism being such. Hindu defects were pressingly visible to me. If untouchability could be a part of Hinduism, it could but be a rotten part or an excrescence. I could not understand the *raison d'être* of a multitude of sects and castes. What was the meaning of saying that the Vedas were the inspired Word of God? If they were inspired, why not also the Bible and the Koran?[4]

In this inner turmoil Gandhi returned to his roots, and wrote a series of letters to people in India asking for help. Chief among them was a young Jain jeweller, poet and deeply religious man, Rajchandra Rav-jibhai Mehta, whom he had first met in 1891. Referring to him as Raychandbhai, he recalled the immensely spiritual impression he had made on him at this first meeting, though at the time, as he admitted, he was full of his own achievements, so recently home from England, and not interested in serious religious discussion. But when religious turmoil surged over him he turned naturally back to Raychandbhai as his 'refuge'.[5] Raychandbhai dealt patiently and at length with a range of questions Gandhi launched at him in 1894. They covered a wide spectrum of issues, from the nature of the soul and of God, the meaning of salvation, rebirth, the nature of the Hindu scriptures and major Hindu deities, to Christian belief, the Bible and Jesus; and they clearly reflected the questions with which Gandhi was wrestling as a result of his new religious contacts.[6] His mentor also suggested a number of Hindu books his young questioner should read. As a result Gandhi gained peace of mind and was reassured that all he needed could be found within his own Hindu tradition.[7] Looking back he felt that three contemporaries had influenced him most powerfully: Raychandbhai, Tolstoy and Ruskin – but he gave the pre-eminence to Raychandbhai. From him he gained not only answers to specific questions but the example of a life grounded on a passion to see God face to face. The jeweller–businessman combined a busy involvement in daily affairs with this religious quest, and exhibited the supreme virtue of non-attachment, the precondition for the soul if it is, in Hindu thought, to achieve *moksha*, salvation or freedom from enslavement to the transitory and illusory. It was a pattern of life which Gandhi was to strive to perfect until his death, and one which was infinitely more demanding than the way of total renunciation of worldly cares and commitments. A passionate but detached involvement with humanity involved compromise, misunderstandings and constant self-questioning.

In Raychandbhai he also saw a man who strove ceaselessly for self-knowledge, for illumination from within as to his own duty or *dharma* in human life, rather than accepting *dharma* as that prescribed by a particular creed or dogma. Consequently he was open to the truth available in all religions, and passed on to Gandhi a strong sense that all faiths were both perfect and imperfect, all contained aspects of truth but did not encompass truth, and that the soul which truly seeks salvation can do so within its own tradition. This tolerance reflected the Jain doctrine of the 'many-sidedness' of truth which was a powerful element in Gandhi's emerging religious vision. Finally, the aspirant saw in his friend and advisor a man committed to non-violence, also central to the Jain tradition, but a non-violence far broader than saving aged cattle, for example, which so often went by the name of non-violence in India, for it extended to the whole of humanity. As Gandhi's life unfolded and his vision of truth matured, the extent of the influence of this jeweller–poet on him and the similarity of much of their thinking became even clearer.

If one person directed Gandhi firmly back within his own religious tradition, one book did likewise. That was the *Gita*, a spiritually luminous poem within the epic *Mahabharata*, of profound significance in the developing understanding of the nature of the divine and of man within Hindu tradition. In it the divine graciously manifests as person to the warrior hero before a great battle, and they discuss deep issues of morality and human behaviour. Many of the other Hindu books Gandhi read at this early stage deepened his knowledge of Hinduism and his valuation of it; but the *Gita* became the supreme authority in his daily life. He was inspired by its teaching on non-possession and equability (so close to the detachment which shone from Raychandbhai), and he wrestled with the meaning of these qualities in his own particular context.

> How to cultivate and preserve that equability was the question. How was one to treat alike insulting, insolent and corrupt officials, co-workers of yesterday raising meaningless opposition, and men who had always been good to one? How was one to divest oneself of all possessions? Was not the body itself possession enough? Were not wife and children possessions? Was I to destroy all the cupboards of books I had? Was I to give up all I had and follow Him?[8]

Although Africa encouraged Gandhi to seek spiritual nourishment in his

Indian spiritual roots and enabled him to call himself a Hindu with
increasing conviction, at this stage he had not had to come to terms with
the actual practice of Hinduism in India, except peripherally in the
matter of caste and untouchability. It was not until his return to India
forced him to do so, and his leadership of an ashram and his growing
correspondence imposed on him duties of religious guidance, that his
relationship to the Hindu tradition evolved into its mature form.

The studies Gandhi undertook as a result of contact with his new
Christian friends led him in directions they had not contemplated,
particularly when he encountered Tolstoy's *The Kingdom of God is
Within You*. He noted that it 'overwhelmed' him and made on him a
lasting impression.[9] In it Tolstoy condemned the modern state as
unnecessary and aggressive, and counselled abstention from participation in its activities. By contrast the true Kingdom was to be found
deep in the hearts of individuals transformed by truth and love.
Gandhi's youthful scepticism and residual belief in violence were dealt a
mortal blow: from the moment of reading the book in that first year in
South Africa he gained an enduring faith in the efficacy of non-violence.
Later reading of other works by Tolstoy confirmed this, and Gandhi
began to perceive new dimensions and possibilities of 'universal love'.
He expounded Tolstoy's teaching of returning good for evil to Indian
readers in Africa in 1909: to follow this precept constituted 'real courage
and humanity'. In his estimation Tolstoy more than anyone else, either
in India or the West, understood the real nature of non-violence.[10]
Summing up Tolstoy's beliefs for his Indian audience he noted his
insistence on returning good for evil, and on refraining from fighting or
wielding political power; man's primary duty is to his Creator, and
therefore he should always concentrate on his duties rather than on his
rights. Man is not set in the world to accumulate wealth, and his natural
and proper occupation is agriculture, whereas industrial cities only
enable the few to wallow in wealth by exploiting the poverty of the
many.[11] Tolstoy had taken on from another Russian writer, T.F.
Bondareff, the idea of 'bread labour': that every one should do some
daily manual labour before he had a right to eat. This also appealed
profoundly to Gandhi, echoing themes of sacrifice he found in the *Gita*;
he later expanded the theme of sacrifice to mean any work done in the
service of others.[12]

Right at the end of Tolstoy's life he and Gandhi exchanged letters,
after Gandhi had first written to him from London in October 1909,
telling him of the South African Indian struggle, of his own firm belief
in satyagraha when confronted with evil, and of the impression Tolstoy's writings had made on him. He also asked for and was gladly
given permission to publish a letter Tolstoy had written to an Indian
editor which had not been published because the editor disagreed with
its views. Expressing thoughts similar to those Gandhi was to expound
in *Hind Swaraj* (written very soon after Gandhi had first come across this
letter) Tolstoy urged Indians not to attempt to eject the British by force,

but to use the weapon of non-participation in the state; for they could only be slaves if they accepted that status and willingly co-operated in the system of enslavement. Gandhi sent Tolstoy a copy of *Hind Swaraj* in April 1910, and Tolstoy replied that he thought Gandhi's theme of passive resistance was 'a question of the greatest importance not only for India but for the whole [of] humanity.' As his own strength failed and he felt that death was imminent he experienced an impulse to share with others beliefs which were to him supremely important, and he wrote later in 1910 a powerful and moving letter to Gandhi about 'the discipline of love'; and he urged Gandhi on in his work in the Transvaal because he felt it was of fundamental significance in showing how Christian civilization had left the ideal of its founder and become blind to the fact that violence in any form is incompatible with love.[13]

Aspects of Tolstoy's writings echoed many of the themes Gandhi was hearing from the mind of Raychandbhai, particularly the ideal of non-violence, the sense of God in the depths of the soul, and insistence on life as duty. Similarly, and equally fortuitously, another book which was to be seminal in Gandhi's life came into his hands a decade later and reinforced and expanded the ideas on society and the economy which Tolstoy had awoken in the young searcher. His friend, Polak, lent him a copy of Ruskin's *Unto This Last*, and he read it voraciously through the whole of the twenty-four hour journey from Johannesburg to Durban, scorning sleep, so much did it grip him. He recorded that he had 'discovered some of my deepest convictions reflected in this great book of Ruskin, and that is why it so captured me and made me transform my life.' As he understood the book, Ruskin was arguing that the individual's good lies in the good of all, that all work is of equal value, and that the supremely desirable life is one of labour, whether as a farmer or a craftsman.[14] The practical result of Gandhi's sleepless night's reading was Phoenix, his first experimental community founded on the simplicity of life, equality, and labour of its members. In 1908 Gandhi produced a Gujarati version of the work, exhorting his Indian readers at its conclusion to remember that swaraj for India must not be an imitation of the industrial West, but a state where the economy was founded on morality rather than on conventionally accepted economic principles, as a result of which the rich amass wealth and the poor become even more impoverished, and none is happier as a result.[15] The extent of Ruskin's influence on Gandhi was clear throughout his life, as he began to expound his economic ideals when faced with the reality of India. They were to differ not just from those currently accepted in India and the West on the desirability of economic growth based on industrial production, and on the operation of market forces; they differed profoundly, too, from traditional Indian assumptions about a radical inequality between occupations, displayed in the caste ordering of society and the horror of the higher castes at the thought of manual labour, and contemporary Indian display of wealth for the honour of family and community on such occasions as weddings.

Such were the key influences on the young Gandhi as he searched for a deeper truth by which to conduct his life than any of the creeds curently available. Some people have wondered, and even did so in his life-time, whether Thoreau, too, had influenced his ideal of satyagraha. Although Gandhi was profoundly impressed by Thoreau's essay on civil disobedience he did not read it until the Indian struggle had developed from petitioning into satyagraha and he was himself gaoled for that offence. In his mind its origins lay in the Hindu tradition of non-violence, *ahimsa*, as mediated by Raychandbhai and his own childhood, and in Tolstoy's writings on the power of love translated into practical action.

Gandhi never ceased his spiritual quest, even when he was an acknowledged spiritual leader in India, answering numerous questions on spiritual matters and honoured with the title of 'Great Soul', Mahatma. He saw himself as always waiting for inner guidance, to which he tried to open himself by prayer, a disciplined life, and increasing detachment not only from possessions but also from excessive care about the results of his earthly actions. He claimed to be perpetually experimenting with satyagraha, examining the possibilities of 'truth force' as new situations arose. He was, right to the end, supremely a pilgrim spirit.[16] He wrote no coherent religious treatise or *apologia*, insisted that he propounded no new religious system, and that there was no such thing as 'Gandhism', though people came to use the word in India. The nearest he came to extended theological discourse was a series of talks on the *Gita* originally prepared for the members of his ashram at Sabarmati in 1926.[17] So understanding of his beliefs must be gleaned from his *Autobiography*, and his numerous letters, articles and speeches, most of which were responses to particular problems and situations. Or as Gandhi himself put it, his life itself was his message.[18] However, the main themes of Gandhi's religious beliefs were visible by about 1906; he had emerged from a decade of reading, encounter and soul-searching still a Hindu, nourished by his tradition's scriptures and many of its central tenets, yet powerfully aware of and moved by the scriptures of the world's other great religions, particularly Christianity and Islam. He had become a man of vision and of hope, whose life was increasingly marked by self-discipline in pursuit of that vision, and inner calm reflecting that hope.

Gandhi's religious vision was both profoundly God-centred and man-orientated. It stemmed from an unshakeable sense of a divine power ordering, sustaining and suffusing the created order. Yet it emphasized man's response to this central reality: each man and woman must recognize the divine, work hard to co-operate with it, and ruthlessly shed all encumbrances on the individual spiritual journey towards the divine which was the only true human goal. The sceptical student had matured into a man of faith and hope: faith in the existence and beneficence of a divine providence, and hope that all people were ultimately capable of spiritual and moral perfection, however long the process of reformation, however hard the struggle. This hope sus-

tained, one might even say imprisoned, him even when events demonstrated the ignorance of those with whom he tried to share his vision,
their lethargy in matters he felt to be of crucial importance, and their
violence towards each other, whether displayed in family squabbles, in
discord within his ashrams, in national and world-wide economic
disparities or in communal killing. He spoke of God in many names,
slipping easily from Ram to Allah, to 'God' in English, and increasingly
and simply to 'Truth'. He used the stories of Hindu mythology as he
spoke on religious matters, but he showed little of the veneration of
particular Hindu deities common among Hindus who expressed their
beliefs in temple-going or in cults of devotion to specific gods. He
engaged in none of these popular practices and was closer to the more
austere, philosophical Hindu perception of *Brahman*, the fundamental
divinity sustaining and pervading all things, and the *atman* or soul which
is a spark, as it were, of *Brahman* in each person. When the *atman* is
turned and freed to realize its essential self, that self-realization is truly
moksha, or salvation, liberation to perceive reality, to embrace the vision
of God and be embraced by it, and it is signified by freedom from the
cycle of births and deaths piled up by the law of *karma*, according to
which men must work out the results of their past deeds.[19] He felt that
work towards this self-realization should be started as early as possible
in life, and directed the education of the children on Tolstoy Farm to this
end, despite the commonly held assumption among Hindus that this
development was proper only in the final stage of human life, that of
renunciation.[20]

Although the Hindu tradition remained Gandhi's spiritual home he
maintained from this early stage in his life that true religion was beyond
all 'religions'. For him each separate religious tradition had valid insights
into the nature of truth and devotional practices which aided the vision
of truth, but no one of them perceived truth in its totality. Truth, like a
diamond, has many facets (or as the Jains put it, is 'many-sided') and
men can only glimpse some of them. Consequently adherents of particular religions must treat those of other traditions with tolerance and
charity, recognizing that they, too, have glimpsed something of the
totality; but each believer should stay within his own tradition to
pursue his own pilgrimage, rather than change allegiances in the belief
that one rather than another religion offers the only path to salvation.
He wrote of this toleration as early as 1905, and in *Hind Swaraj*,
commenting on Hindu–Muslim strife he asked, 'Is the God of the
Mahomedan different from the God of the Hindu? Religions are different roads converging to the same point. What does it matter that we
take different roads so long as we reach the same goal?'[21] In such an
eclectic and tolerant way he resolved for himself the crisis posed by
his Christian friends' insistence on their faith as the one true road to
salvation; and he interpreted salvation in a way fundamentally different
from their understanding of it as a free gift of redemption from sin
bestowed by divine generosity through the Cross of Christ. In Tolstoy

Farm he tried to put into practice his ideal, seeing that the children of different religions learned about their own inheritance, yet also respected the practices of other faiths and helped other children of these faiths to observe them. When asked in 1913 whether he thought the world would ever have one religion, he replied that he did not think so, nor did he deem it necessary.[22]

Gandhi used the usual Hindi word, *dharma*, duty, for religion. It meant the fundamental ordering of society and the individual, which both in turn had to uphold; and by extention in the plural, *dharmas*, indicated the duty of each person within his caste, if society was to remain an integrated and stable whole. For Gandhi, however, *dharma* was not a matter of caste occupation decided by birth, but an individual calling to pursue truth. It was all-encompassing, not a religious compartment of life, and it had practical implications for every aspect of life, from religious devotions to personal health and public sanitation. True religion, *dharma* closely followed, was morality in action, as well as faith and devotion. A glimpse of what he perceived as the content of *dharma* is possible from a speech he gave in 1905:

> The way . . . is to do pure and good deeds; to have compassion for all living things, and to live in truth. Even after reaching this stage, one does not attain liberation, for one has to enjoy embodied existence as a consequence of one's good deeds as well. One has, therefore, to go a step further. We will, however, have to continue to act, only we should not cherish any attachment to our actions. Action should be undertaken for its own sake, without an eye on the fruit. In short, everything should be dedicated to God.[23]

Yet Gandhi recognized that man's knowledge of *dharma* could never be final. True religion was not a matter of rules and regulations, but a journey though the realities and vagaries of life, in the midst of which *dharma* must be sought and worked out. The only true guide on this journey was the inner voice of truth, to which each must train himself to listen. Gandhi's personal awareness of an inner voice, a sense of guidance, was one of the outstanding characteristics of his spiritual life. As the years passed he spoke of it more often and more freely, and it had major implications for his public activities, causing some consternation among his contemporaries who wondered where this unpredictable inner authority would drive him next. He dated his awareness of it for the first time to about 1906, when he also started praying regularly. But he said it was no dramatic new experience or conversion, and that he felt his spiritual life had developed as unselfconsciously as one's growing hair.[24]

From this central core of belief there flowed in Gandhi's understanding a number of necessary attitudes or stances for the genuinely religious man, the follower after truth. In the first place, the truth-seeker had a constant need and duty to work for 'self-purification' in order to release his own capacity to perceive truth. It meant a discipline of casting away inessentials and care for them, freeing oneself from self-concern and from debilitating passions, such as lust, envy and anger, and also from worry and concern over the results of one's actions. Increasingly he tried to live according to such discipline, for example by his experiments with fasting and restricted, even bizarre, diets. Undertaken at first for health reasons, his experiments with living on fruit and giving up milk and cereals became from the middle of that first decade of the new century an adjunct to his wider concern for sexual self-restraint. His dietary peculiarities remained a controversial and much publicized aspect of his life from now onwards, and earned him considerable criticism and misunderstanding. But to him it was not faddishness but an essential element in his *dharma*, his need to strip himself of all that hindered a single-hearted quest for truth. If love of food, as much as lust after a person or consuming concern over the results of particular actions, threatened his search for truth, then it must be rooted out in the process of self-purification.

Such a concentration on ridding the self of impurity might have become an introverted spiritual athleticism, feeding the ego rather than weakening it. Indeed the Jain insistence on self-purification, which must have influenced Gandhi, came close to intense spiritual individualism. But for Gandhi the discipline was never for the sake of the individual's spiritual state alone or perhaps even primarily: it was self-purification for true vision, but also for the sake of service. This insistence on a life of service as the practical working out of the search for truth was firmly established in Gandhi after his first decade in South Africa. He was never at rest in the purely contemplative tradition, but believed passionately that as sparks of truth, of ultimate reality, lay in each person, so the truth-seeker must find truth, must find his God, in encounter with and compassion for his fellow men. He wrote in 1910 of *moksha* being obtainable only through service,[25] and work for the poorest and sick, both within the Indian community and outside it, increasingly became a feature of his life. One of his fullest expositions of this theme dated from much later, but the commitment to a life of compassionate caring was present by the early years of the century. In 1936 he explained to a Polish visitor why he was immersed in work for India's villagers.

> I am here to serve no one else but myself, to find my own self-realization through the service of these village folk. Man's ultimate aim is the realization of God, and all his activities, social, political, religious, have to be guided by the ultimate aim of the vision of God. The immediate service of all human beings becomes a necessary part of the endeavour simply because the only way to find God is to see Him in His creation and be one with it. This can only be done by service of all. . . . If I could persuade myself that I should find Him in a Himalayan cave, I would proceed there immediately. But I know that I cannot find Him apart from humanity.[26]

Yet his knowledge of humankind made him see the pitfalls in 'service' if it was carried out for the sake of public acclaim rather than from conviction, and with wry realism he criticized the killjoys who helped people with long faces and grudging spirits. Such joyless service helped no one, neither giver nor receiver, though he believed that joyful service outweighed all other pleasures and possessions.[27]

The third hallmark of the truly religious man in Gandhi's eyes was non-violence, that quality of spirit and of living he had met when he turned to Raychandbhai, to the Christ of the Gospels, or to His radical follower, Tolstoy. Now *ahimsa* and 'universal love' fell into place in Gandhi's vision of truth. It alone could safeguard truth in all situations, particularly those of conflict; it alone could preserve the integrity of every individual involved because it would not force those against whom it was used to abandon their understanding of truth, while they who used non-violent means would be strengthened and purified by their use. He wrote in *Hind Swaraj* that non-violence as displayed in satyagraha 'blesses him who uses it and against whom it is used.'[28] Sooner or later all those who are fired by conviction encounter the problem of ends and means. Are all means legitimate and helpful if the end is of overwhelming importance? For Gandhi the answer was 'no': the wrong means distort and corrupt the end. As the 'Editor' in *Hind Swaraj* he chided his 'Reader'.

> Your belief that there is no connection between the means and the end is a great mistake. Through that mistake even men who have been considered religious have committed grievous crimes. Your reasoning is the same as saying that we can get a rose through planting a noxious weed. If I want to cross the ocean, I can do so only by means of a vessel; if I were to use a cart for that purpose, both the cart and I would soon find the bottom.... The means may be likened to a seed, the end to a tree; and there is just the same inviolable connection between the means and the end as there is between the seed and the tree.[29]

Believing this, he held passionately to non-violence as the one means universally valid and applicable because it could never distort the end. It was in a real sense the goal itself, the end sought for in action: it was truth acting through the courageous man who was prepared to follow it to his own cost. Concluding his account of the South African struggle he underlined the point: 'Satyagraha is a priceless and matchless weapon, and those who wield it are strangers to disappointment or defeat.'[30]

However, as he had insisted to Indians in South Africa and those who used the English phrase 'passive resistance', thinking non-violence was a weapon of the weak, Gandhi maintained that it required in its exponents lengthy and hard discipline. It demanded not only faith and hope, but courage, physical endurance and abandonment of care for all those worldly possessions and attachments which men value. 'Those alone can follow the path of passive resistance who are free from fear, whether as to their possessions, false honour, their relatives, the government, bodily injuries or death.'[31] He was also keenly aware that however dedicated to *ahimsa* the truth-seeker might be, however disciplined, life inevitably involved for everyone a degree of violence. Eating, drinking, just moving about, all meant some destruction of life. But Gandhi did not become weighed down by this ambiguity or take refuge in the extreme measures of some Jains who wore masks to prevent themselves ingesting tiny insects with their breath. More robustly and realistically he argued that followers of the way of non-violence must live normally, aware of the inevitability of a degree of violence in their actions, but safeguarded if the spring of those actions was compassion.[32]

Gandhi's understanding of the qualities essential in the pursuit of truth were summed up in his own life in the decision to become a celibate, to take the vow of *brahmacharya* or chastity. He did so in 1906, although for some years he and Kasturbhai had slept apart, and his time and energy had been increasingly deflected from normal family life and consumed by his public work. Looking back, he felt it was Raychandbhai's discussions on true service which first set his thoughts working in this diection, while on a more mundane level he had come to feel that he had no wish for more children and that restraint was the proper method of birth-control. But by the early 1900s *brahmacharya* had taken its place in his understanding of the truly religious life and he felt it had a crucial role in the pursuit of truth. He interpreted it to mean more than sexual restraint. It was control of the senses in thought, word and deed, though aspects of it, such as fasting, were also a buttress to sexual abstinence. On his own admission he found the physical side of the vow difficult to observe; but mastery of thought was even harder, and he wrestled with it to the end of his days. Yet he was convinced that this was the broad high road to the self-purification so vital for the truth-seeker. Without it life was 'insipid and animal-like', whereas man's true nature could be liberated and revealed only if it was observed.[33] Furthermore, the man who sought truth in his fellow men through a life of service would be inhibited by the concerns and obligations of fatherhood and family life. It was the Zulu Rebellion which showed him this dramatically in his own life, as he left his family for the hard conditions of a medical assistant, and his meditations on this event ultimately precipitated the actual vow in 1906. Without the vow family obligations would come first, and he would be unable to embark on the life of widening service he saw opening up before him; but aided by this vow he felt his care for his family would be consistent with service of the community.[34]

Finally, *brahmacharya* had essential links with man's capacity for non-violence, demanding as it did such a degree of inner and outward strength. As satyagraha developed in South Africa he came to argue this increasingly strongly, asserting its essential role in satyagraha in *Hind Swaraj*.

Chastity is one of the greatest disciplines without which the mind cannot attain requisite firmness. A man who is unchaste loses stamina, becomes emasculated and cowardly. He whose mind is given over to animal passions is not capable of any great effort.[35]

Three years later in one of a series of articles on health he noted the place he attributed to celibacy in good health. He likened it to the proverbial philosopher's stone, because its jealous care markedly increased the physical, mental and moral strength of those who observed it.[36]

Because Gandhi's attitude to sex is so at variance with contemporary understanding of the essential and creative role of sexuality in human growth and life, this aspect of his religious development has generated much theorizing and speculation, and not a little criticism for its apparent harshness. For he argued that *brahmacharya* was not just for a few specially chosen souls, but for all truth-seekers. Even within marriage there should be abstinence from physical relations except on the few occasions when a couple specifically wanted a child.[37] Many have speculated whether the circumstances of his father's death when Gandhi was in bed with his young wife crippled his process of maturing in this area of his life, and culminated in this spectacular renunciation of masculinity as normally understood, because he found it too painful a psychological burden to bear. It would also be possible to argue that his mother's profound influence on him and his inability to distance himself naturally from her because of her unexpected death made him accept it by renouncing his maleness and devoting his energies to caring roles most often associated with the female. It is also true that each individual carries within him or her self aspects of femininity and masculinity which can become creative without there being anything abnormal in personality development.

Ultimately we cannot know what inner forces and ambiguities made celibacy so significant, indeed necessary, for this man in the prime of his life. Undoubtedly he was a personality subject to extreme inner stress, a theme which recurs throughout his life. He wrestled with guilt, anger, depression and lust. But to attribute his vow of celibacy to the inner needs of a haunted soul is to do less than justice to his vision of man's ulitmate destiny, and also to forget the strong resonances it had with central aspects of the Hindu understanding of man. Strength and virility are major concerns of Hindu mythology and literature as well as of contemporary Indian life, for religious and social reasons. Conservation of semen has long been thought to conserve a man's vital strength; and this interlocks with the ambiguous view of woman as creator and sustainer, but also temptress and, by extension, the destroyer of man's power and identity. This theme of conserving strength by sexual abstinence is clearly present in Gandhi's article on *brahmacharya* in the series on health in 1913. He must therefore be understood as a man of his time and culture, even though psychology can now suggest other elements in his development of which he was unaware.

Gandhi insisted that religion could never be boxed up in a separate compartment of life: true religion would always be the mainspring of a person's attitudes and actions, and in consequence would overflow into the whole of life. In his own case once the core of his religious vision had taken shape it began to affect his attitude to the right way of living. Once his central vision is clear to the outside observer his changing attitude to civilization falls into its rightful place. *Hind Swaraj* was not quirky romanticism but a reflection of his inner transformation. He expounded his new understanding of civilization fully during and after his visit to London in 1909, when the renewed experience of the pace and quality of Western life reinforced his growing inner doubts.

> Looking at this land, I at any rate have grown disillusioned with Western civilization. The people whom you meet on the way seem half-crazy. They spend their days in luxury or in making a bare living and retire at night thoroughly exhausted. In this state of affairs, I cannot understand when they can devote themselves to prayers.[38]

But far earlier than this visit he had been wrestling with the problem of what constituted civilization, and the nature and value of the Western way of life, as his own values changed, and his vision of God and the true destiny of man began to take its distinctive shape. In 1894 he wrote in *The Natal Mercury* about books which might help readers who found that materialism did not satisfy their soul and were hankering after something other than 'the dazzling and bright surface of modern civilization' with its luxuries and feverish activity; he offered to talk quietly with anyone who was concerned with such matters. He returned to the same theme a few weeks later in another paper, noting 'the utter inadequacy of materialism', which was alleged to have produced a great civilization but had in fact generated terrible weapons of destruction, anarchism, strife between capital and labour, and cruelty to animals in the name of science.[39] In 1903 an accident in the Paris Metro prompted him to warn Indian readers of 'the tinsel splendour of modern civilization'; that it could offer no real certainties, while 'that alone is worth having or worth cultivating which would enable us to realise our Maker and to feel that . . . on earth we are merely sojourners.'[40] By 1908, as he concluded his summary of Ruskin's *Unto This Last*, he warned that Western civilization, built on the accumulation of wealth, had brought in its train violence, and in under a century had reduced Western people to 'a state of cultural anarchy'.[41]

His growing criticisms culminated in a total attack on Western civilization in 1909, first in a letter[42] to Polak from London, and then at length in *Hind Swaraj* as he sailed from England to South Afrcia. Now he had abandoned any notion that there was a distinctive Western or European civilization; rather there was 'modern civilization' and it was purely material, based on industrial production in factories and the rise of large cities, and its standards were determined by the accumulation of wealth. He believed that such a civilization threatened man's true nature and goal, by inculcating false wants generated by the capacity for excessive consumption; and futhermore, through the unequal distribution of wealth and the factory system of production, inevitably led to competition and violence between man and his fellows. It was truly the reign of the devil and unrighteousness, as opposed to the reign of truth and morality: it had the West in its grip and through Western influence threatened to strangle the life out of India. Among its manifestations which attracted his particular condemnation were, not surprisingly, factories and modern machinery, as well as rapid means of transport, which all fed the desire for material goods and pleasure. But the modern medical profession, too, stood for Gandhi as a symbol of a way of life which had forgotten morality. In his eyes doctors merely patched up the patient's body which had become diseased through wrongdoing and intemperate living, and so encouraged him to repeat his vices. Hospitals were 'institutions for propagating sin'.[43] When pressed by the 'Reader' in *Hind Swaraj* as to the nature of true civilization, he defined it as 'that mode of conduct which points out to man the path of duty. Performance of duty and observance of morality are convertible terms. To observe morality is to attain mastery over our mind and our passions.'[44] Whereas modern 'civilization', so-called, bade man forget the path of duty and indulge his passions, he looked back in India's history to what he perceived as true civilization in action – when men had limited their needs and these were fulfilled by man's own labour rather than machinery which only produced beyond essential needs and so generated greed and immorality; where life was simpler and slower, and people had time to be true to their essential nature as they lived in villages, uncorrupted by town life which encouraged thieves, prostitutes and all kinds of vice and provided the environment where the rich could exploit the poor. Whether such a civilization had ever existed in India is highly debatable historically, as is Gandhi's contention that villages encouraged equality and peaceful neighbourliness. But the point is that Gandhi believed passionately in what he perceived as the Indian way of life before the spread of Western influence, and built much of his social and political programme upon that belief.

What then were men and women of vision to do to extricate themselves and their fellows from the life-threatening coils of material civilization? To his friend, Polak, he explained that as a satyagrahi, one who believed in truth force, the right path was to enunciate the truth and follow it as far as poossible. There was no point in waiting for the majority to see the need for change. If he was right, then others would eventually follow, drawn by the power of truth. But, as in the matter of non-violence, he was realistic about the compromises and ambiguities this would involve for the satyagrahi. Every time he used a train, for example, he would realize that he was violating his sense of what was most deeply right, but this would have to be endured. 'The theory is there: our practice will have to approach it as much as possible. Living in the midst of the rush, we may not be able to shake ourselves free from all taint.'[45] Gandhi therefore turned his thinking and his life to the immediate tasks a satyagrahi could undertake in his attempt to live according to the standards of true civilization, to the key areas of concern if he was to awaken Indians to their plight. Three of these – the simple life, education and health – marked Gandhi out for the rest of his life and became increasingly important to him after his return to India and his encouter with its realities. These were concerns not generally within the compass of the political activists with whom Gandhi was to mix. But he insisted that they, even more than the structure and personnel of government, were crucial to true swaraj, and that they were proper ingredients of political discourse and action. For him life could not be compartmentalized into 'political', 'social' and 'religious'; if his vision of truth dictated that these were essential areas for change, then he must pursue such changes or risk his own integrity.

Gandhi's early experiments in divesting his life of the trappings of Westernization and drastically simplifying it have been sketched in already as the personal background to his emergence as a public figure. At that stage they owed as much to economy as to idealism. Then his liberating experience of reading Ruskin, reinforcing Tolstoy's rendering of the idea of 'bread labour', helped to crystallize his ideas and led eventually to the start of the Phoenix community, which was the working out of Gandhi's views on the simple life, as later was Tolstoy Farm. These were attempts to build communities removed as far as possible from the standards of materialistic civilization and its modes of production. Their hallmarks were the 'self-abnegation and abstemiousness' which Gandhi felt would be the only possible pattern for Indians if they wished to solve the dilemmas of their motherland, increasingly entangled in the clutches of modern civilization, and to deal with the problems of British rule.[46] When in 1914 he heard rumours of plots against his life in Johannesburg he wrote to Chhaganlal Gandhi, explaining how he wished his extended family to order their lives after his death. Their's should be a life of genuine service to the community (unlike the paid political work of so many of their older relatives which he now denigrated as the pursuit of selfish interest). To this end, they should live in the manner of the Phoenix settlement, as farmers or craftsmen, subsisting on a limited vegetarian diet. There should be none of the usual family commotion about arranging marriages and providing dowries, and the widows in their charge should be provided with the means for a simple living. It was a life-style based frankly and consciously on poverty, which he felt was 'the only sound basis', though he realized that to others it might sound harsh. Yet it was the only way he knew to be true to what he saw as man's ultimate goal. 'The secret of life seems to consist in so living in the world as it is without being attached to it, that *moksha* might become easy of attainment to us and to others.'[47]

An integral part of Gandhi's thinking on simplicity of living was the idea of swadeshi, literally meaning 'belonging to one's own country'. It was a politico – economic strategy which had been employed against the British in India while Gandhi was in South Africa. But to him it had a far deeper and wider meaning than the mere boycott of British goods in an attempt to erode the financial aspects of British interest in India. For Gandhi it was inextricably tied to the values of simplicity and self-reliance, of limiting one's wants, and of the worth of manual labour. Writing early in 1909 he encouraged South African Indians to see its significance. 'Swadeshi carries a great and profound meaning. It does not mean merely the use of what is produced in one's own country ... there is another meaning implicit in it which is far greater and much more important. Swadeshi means reliance on our own strength.[48] Once he had returned to India the symbol of the spinning-wheel became the hallmark of Gandhi's swadeshi teaching and activity. In South Africa he had not yet worked out the implications – one might even say the 'theology', so significant would it eventually be for him – of hand-spinning. But the ideas which were later to come to fruition were partially visible in Hind Swaraj. There he expounded the need to end the use of imported goods, whether cloth, matches, pins or glassware. What they could not make they could do without, as their ancestors had done. He hoped that mill owners would contract their business and encourage the ancient craft of hand-weaving, and he recommended that English-educated Indians such as lawyers and doctors should abandon their professions and take up hand-weaving, and encourage both it and the wearing of hand-made goods.[49]

Given Gandhi's changing values and his vision of what constituted a truly civilized and free India, it was not surprising that he developed firm views on education, as education not only moulds the new genera-tion but reflects a society's fundamental assumptions about itself and the individuals which compose it. Watching Gandhi in South Africa, we see him moving away from his earliest acceptance of the contemporary wisdom that Western-style education was appropriate for Indians and was the high road to success, influence and prosperity for the individual who received it and his relatives. He, together with his family and countless other Indians for decades, had believed in the desirability of the educational system as first envisaged in the early nineteenth century when the East India Company began to set aside an annual sum of money for education, which under Macaulay's eloquent guidance was invested in English language education for the few, who would receive a liberal higher English education much on the lines of their British contemporaries, and become like their rulers in manners and values. While in South Africa Gandhi still encouraged Indians who had the means to embark on this style of education, as he himself had done. In 1898 he drafted a congratulatory address to the first Indian who had appeared successfully for the local civil service examination, and in passing praised his father for financing both his education and that of an older brother who was studying medicine in Glasgow. As late as 1908 he congratulated another young Indian and his family for their enterprise in sending the youth for further education in England, and argued that an English education, including study of English and the sciences, was essential in the contemporary world. Without it they would be crippled and backward.[50] However, the first hints at his disquiet over the effects of such education were clear in the unorthodox way in which he educated his own children, eschewing the regular school system, whether in South Africa or India, with its literary tradition, and speaking to them as much as possible in their mother tongue, Gujarati. At Phoenix he began experimenting with alternative styles of teaching and learning, and in 1909 was prepared to accept a few pupils from outside the immediate circle of settlers.[51] They were to be boarded with Phoenix families and would share their simple life-style. The school's main object would be to strengthen the pupil's characters and there would be considerable emphasis on religious instruction, each child being taught his own tradition. Vernacular languages would be used, as well as English, and subjects would include arithmetic, history, geography, botany, zoology and the history of India. Almost simultaneously he castigated young Indians who used bad and broken English among themselves, and urged that though Indians needed good knowledge of English as the language of government and international communications, they should cherish their vernaculars, enrich them and speak them among themselves. This, too, was part of swadeshi, and a way in which they could make themselves true Indians.[52]

By late 1909 Gandhi's rebellion against his own original views, against English education as available in India, and against Indians' striving after it, was complete. Speaking of the importance of India's vernaculars, he exhorted Indians to spend more time on them instead of wasting it on English, and so increase their self-respect. 'India's uplift is ... bound up with this. I had been under the sway of Macaulay's ideas on Indian education. Others, too, are. I have now been disillusioned. I wish that others should be.'[53] In *Hind Swaraj* he devoted a whole chapter to education, arguing that the English system of education had enslaved India and enabled English-speaking Indians to exploit the common people. English might still have a limited place in India, but it could only be useful once Indians had begun the real process of education, which was learning how to control the senses, and acquiring an ethical basis to life. Character-building, not the acquisition of a foreign lanuage or irrelevant knowledge, was the need for India's millions. Although he did not expound in detail a proposed alternative scheme, he made it plain that Indian vernaculars would have in it a high priority, as would religious education.[54] In Tolstoy Farm he had the chance to make practical experiments with a new style of education. There the traditional pedagogical approach was abandoned and Gandhi, as the chief teacher, aided by other adult members of the community, tried to live more as a father to the pupils, teaching by example and shared experience. The primary aim of the education given was character-building, as at Phoenix. In practice this included physical labour on the farm and some craftwork, such as shoe-making and carpentry. What literary instruction there was was given in the vernaculars, though English was also taught, and all the children learnt elementary history, geography and arithmetic. Apparently they had few textbooks, and Gandhi believed from his own childhood experience that the teacher himself was the pupil's best textbook. Finally there was 'spiritual teaching', which again depended largely on the example of the teacher, though Gandhi also used hymns and books, and tried to impart to each child a knowledge of the scriptures of his or her own faith.[55] So far these were only experiments, required because the children on Tolstoy Farm needed education. Ganhi's scheme to replace existing Indian education only matured later as he wrestled with the problem of a genuinely national education for all Indians, coming to fruition near the end of his life in his plan for Basic Education. But the principles were already taking shape, as he discarded Macaulay's ideals and emphasized character-training rather than accumulation of knowledge, vernaculars as opposed to English, and learning through practical skills rather than book-bound study.

Health, like education, concerned Gandhi profoundly, though it was scarcely considered by most contemporary activists in Indian politics. For him it was of such importance because it was an aspect of man's relationship with his Creator. Good health spoke of being in tune with mankind's basic law of life, and attention to healthy habits in public denoted care for one's neighbour and the community. So health matters were as spiritual as prayer and religious devotions. They were a constant element in Gandhi's experiments and writing, almost from the start of his working life, though they became more urgent for him when in later life he attempted to tackle the problems of Indian villages, among which was chronic sickness for which neither traditional nor modern medicine seemed to be providing remedies, let alone preventing from the outset. Gandhi's earliest experiments in healthcare, as in education, had been within his immediate family circle, when he tried 'natural' remedies such as water and changed diet for his wife and sons, often deliberately contravening the advice of Western-trained doctors. Typical of him in so many ways was a letter written to Chhaganlal Gandhi in Phoenix. Sandwiched in the middle of a discussion relating to *Indian Opinion*, he chided his relative for suffering from boils. 'This is inexcusable. There must be some irregularity about the diet.' The cure suggested was simpler food, and Gandhi urged him to follow his own example if he had to eat away from home, and have a simple packed lunch taken to work in the city consisting of 'Kuhne bread, nut butter and jam'.[56] By late 1909 Gandhi made his own attitude to modern medicine abundantly clear in *Hind Swaraj*. It was irreligious because it involved vivisection in its researches; and he claimed that many medicines contained 'animal fat or spiritous liquors' taboo to Hindus and Muslims. But at an even deeper level it invited men to ignore religion, to violate the true laws of their being, because it offered to patch and mend bodies diseased by wrong living. Rather than serving mankind, doctors were positively injurious to their fellow men, taking up the profession for the sake of honour and high fees. He recommended that doctors should leave their profession and take to the handloom, realizing that it was better for patients to be ill or die rather than benefit from the results of vivisection or drugs which he considered useless in relation to the real cause of their diseases. Rather than mending bodies, doctors should make their priority mending souls.[57]

Gandhi's alternative to modern medicine was given free play on Tolstoy Farm, where he was not only schoolmaster but physician. Firstly he ensured that all dirt and waste was buried, so there was no smell and no flies, and the end product could be used for manure. Commenting on Indian habits when he described the farm's communal hygiene, he echoed the distaste he felt when he first attended the Indian National Congress:

> A small spade is the means of salvation from a great nuisance. Leaving nightsoil, cleaning the nose or spitting on the road is a sin against God as well as humanity, and betrays a sad want of consideration for others. The man who does not cover his waste deserves a heavy penalty even if he lives in a forest.[58]

Looking back he felt he had been somewhat naive at Tolstoy Farm in his faith that a simple life prevented disease and that when illness occurred it could be cured by natural remedies. But at the time it worked. 'I held that all kinds of diseases could be cured by earth and water treatment, fasting or changes in diet. There was not a single case of illness on the Farm, in which we used drugs or called in a doctor.'[59]

In 1913 Gandhi shared his ideas about the care of health in a series of articles in *Indian Opinion*.[60] These are a fascinating mixture of sound common sense on such matters as the need for fresh air, clean water, restrained eating and adequate exercise, and treatment for a range of diseases and physical discomforts with hot and cold water, steam and earth, and changed diet which sounds bizarre from the standpoint of modern medicine. He totally abhorred vaccination against smallpox, and suggested that for a patient suffering from it the best cure was wet sheet packs, mud packs, and a diet of rice, lemons and light fresh fruit. For the expectant mother he particularly recommended wheat, bananas and olive oil: she should reject all spices and resolutely resist any odd pregnancy cravings for weird foods. Gandhi argued that humans were designed to be vegetarian, and extolled a purely fruit diet, and warned against tea, coffee, cocoa, spices and even milk. Yet even in the middle of these perhaps idiosyncratic recommendations there were elements which sound very modern, such as his denunciation of shop-bought white bread in favour of home-made wholemeal bread from home-ground flour, and his insistence that purges did more harm than good for the constipated, for instead they should be eating such fruit as figs, plums, raisins, grapes and oranges. His advice covered celibacy as

necessary for good health and strength, what clothes to wear, and the
bad effects of ornaments so cherished by Indian women, which only
collected dirt in the ears and nose. Underlying all this was his
conviction that ill-health occurred when man so used his body that he
was out of tune with his essential nature, when in fact he disobeyed
the laws of God. Furthermore, he had a duty to care for his health, not
so much for his own comfort, but because it is the 'place where one may
meet and recognize God. It is called the House of the Lord.'[61] This
theological conclusion to a down-to-earth, not to say earthy, series of
articles, showed plainly why Gandhi was so concerned with health care.
It was an integral part of his search for the deepest truth within man, and
his religious vision drew him on to see the importance of areas of life
which religious and political leaders equally would have avoided as
outside their proper concern. For Gandhi religion was life; he had to be
concerned with the whole of it, whether this meant digging pits for
night-soil, applying mud packs, teaching children, fighting a law case or
going to gaol. This was true religion as much as prayer or reading the
Gita.

During his South African years Gandhi's inner life was transformed,
as was his outwardly visible life, in his mode of living and in his career.
But it was the inner changes which were the most significant because
they undergirded the outer ones, and remained with Gandhi when he
returned to India, where the very different circumstances elicited yet
further changes of work to be consistent with the inner vision by which
he was now consumed. He had become a public man in the obvious
sense. But in a deeper way, too, his life was now lived on a public stage,
because as a truth-seeker, a satyagrahi, he felt he could not conceal his
inward journey with its struggles of conscience, its triumphs and
failures. Whether it was his vow of celibacy and his difficulties observing it, or his experiments with different diets, or his changing attitude to
modern civilization and its effects of India, he felt bound to share them
with close associates like Polak and Kallenbach, relatives such as Chhaganlal, and his readers in *Indian Opinion* and ultimately in his *Autobiography*. Such openness would help to spread his convictions, but would
also be a check on his 'experiments with truth' and help him to search
for truth with clearer eyes and a keener conscience. A satyagrahi should
have nothing to hide, and nothing to fear from such scrutiny. When
Gandhi returned to India in 1915 he offered his homeland the ideals and
insights of a changed man. But as Gokhale envisaged when he recommended to him a year of silence, most of those who engaged in modern
styles of politics in India, and were concerned with the Congress and the
hope of home rule, would have felt more at home with the values of the
young Gandhi of the 1890s than with the ideals of the angular visionary
who wrote *Hind Swaraj*, the 'saint' whom Smuts was relieved to see
departing for his motherland.

4

INDIA AND THE RETURNING EXILE

Gandhi's return to India early in 1915 was a turning-point in his own life, and in restrospect momentous for his homeland. But at the time the public implications of his home-coming were not obvious and his welcome was low-key and domestic, confined largely to his family and those small groups in Bombay and Gujarat who had followed his work abroad with interest. South Africa had forged Gandhi, the man, the satyagrahi and the public figure. Now when the garlands of welcome had faded and the speeches in recognition of his African work had died away, he had to face the reality of middle age, a time in life which demands of every individual a reassessment of capacities and priorities, a coming to terms with oneself and one's surroundings, and he had to do this in a new and little known environment. Although he had come home in many senses, there could be no rest, for he had to rediscover himself in this new setting and work out afresh the implications of his vision of man and of truth. He was deeply moved at the thought of returning to India, writing late in 1914 from London of his longing to be there, in contrast to the 'artificial' and 'materialistic and immoral' environment of the West which seemed to be atrophying his spirit.[1] As he voyaged home he wondered what the future held in store, seeming content to receive what providence offered rather than making any elaborate plans for a public career.

> I have been so often prevented from reaching India that it seems hardly real that I am sitting in a ship bound for India. And having reached [India] what shall I do with myself? However, 'Lead Kindly Light, amid the encircling gloom, lead Thou me on.'[2]

Soon he was writing with relief of the 'holy atmosphere' of India.[3]

Having left behind the roles he had performed for twenty years – of family man, lawyer, public notable – he envisaged for himself a more obscure life, tackling at their roots in a local setting the problems of man and society as he saw them: he did not see any prospect of launching a satyagraha for at least five years. He deliberately dressed in simple Gujarati clothes, spurning the outward trappings of the wealthy, the Westernized and the publicly successful. But if Gandhi had harboured any notions of easily finding a place in Indian public life he was sharply reminded of his own limited physicial capacity, the differences between so many of his attitudes and those of his compatriots, and the difficulties he would face in making himself understood at any deep level. Experiences in England, where he briefly halted en route for India, and then before he even attempted to make a settled Indian life for himself, symbolized the gulf between him and his countrymen as much as between him and British officialdom.

Gandhi reached England in August 1914, clearly a sick man. After the prolonged strain of his satyagrahas and his periods in goal, he had subjected himself to lengthy fasting in response to incidents in the Phoenix community, which he saw as moral lapses, and for which as the community's leader he felt he must do penance in order to purify the atmosphere. In London he suffered from pleurisy and piles, and needed considerable bed rest and medical treatment. It was typical of him that he tried to remedy his condition largely by attention to diet – living on a variety of cereals, fruit and vegetables, and even experimenting with raw food. Although he was weak and frail, and in considerable pain, he refused to take milk, despite the doctors' insistence and the pleadings of his mentor, Gokhale. For him, abstaining from milk and meat were religious issues, far greater than the prospect of his own death, and he found an ally in Dr Allison, renowned for his vegetarianism and for his brown bread.[4] Gandhi's battles on issues of food with his friends and the space he devoted to the incident in his autobiography show his personal priorities at a time when most other men would have been preoccupied with the outbreak of war and its possible repercussions on relations between India and Britain.

Gandhi did not ignore the war, but again his response was highly personal, the result of prolonged agonizings of conscience. He was the leading spirit in the formation in the autumn of 1914 of a Field Ambulance Training Corps, largely for Indians in London, to enable them to serve the empire in its crisis, and particularly their own compatriots who were fighting in considerable numbers in Europe.[5] Not surprisingly some Indians felt such co-operation was ill-judged and that they should be taking advantage of their rulers' need to press for political concessions. Gandhi did not then consider the imperial relationship to be totally enslaving or intolerable and hoped that co-operation would enhance Indians' status in British eyes. Even his close friend, Polak, and other intimate Indian colleagues in South Africa, could not understand how he could be a party to the war, given his dedication to non-violence. But Gandhi reasoned that *ahimsa* was rarely an easily discernible path, given men's inevitable involvement with violence by the sheer process of living. He was even more implicated in violence while in London because he was protected there by British arms. As he was unable to escape this situation he felt the best, though not the perfect, course for a devotee of *ahimsa* was to serve with a much courage and compassion as possible.[6]

Once decided on this action, he found that the Commanding Officer officially allocated to the Ambulance Corps a retired member of the Indian Medical Service, was intent on a more than formal exercise of his command, and refused to deal with and through Gandhi as unofficial leader and representative of the Corps. Here Gandhi was claiming the representative capacity he had claimed and often *de facto* enjoyed in South Africa and which he was to seek in India; and here he encountered the rigid perceptions of rank and role which he was to find so prevalent among officials of the British raj. A compromise was patched up by the India Office, made easier by the fact that Gandhi was bed-ridden just when the Corps was needed to nurse a large contingent of wounded Indian soldiers who were arriving in England. But both parties to the controversy had had a taste of Gandhi's will-power, even stubbornness, in the face of what he perceived as insensitive and domineering officialdom.

The different facets of Gandhi's short London stay were not the only signs of his potential isolation in India and the likely breakdown of understanding and sympathy between him, his countrymen and their rulers. On his return to India early in 1915 he accepted the shrewd advice of Gokhale not to speak on public matters for a year and to travel widely to familiarize himself with his homeland and its problems. His journeys took him to many places in the Bombay Presidency, to Bengal, Burma, the United Provinces, Delhi, Madras and so back to Bombay and his native Gujarat. He insisted on travelling third class by train, and was appalled by the curt way the poor were treated by railway officials, but was equally disgusted by the rude and dirty habits of the passengers themselves which made travelling conditions well-nigh intolerable for him and his wife. The dirt, the numbers, and the lack of facilities made third-class carriages little better than cattle trucks. Such was Kasturbhai's distress that he allowed her to use the bathing facilities in a second-class waiting-room when a member of Gokhale's Servants of India Society recognized them on a station and offered his help.

During his travels Gandhi spent some time at Shantiniketan, 'the abode of peace', an experimental educational community led by the Bengali poet, Rabindranath Tagore, which had offered hospitality to the party from Phoenix which Maganlal Gandhi had brought directly from South Africa while Gandhi journied via England. There they had striven to replicate Phoenix, its disciplines and simplicity, in their own special quarters. But when Gandhi came in person, changes began. He urged the students and teachers of Shantiniketan to learn self-help, to cook for themselves and thus do physical work probably for the first time. They began to cut vegetables and clean grain, and to cleanse the kitchen areas in line with Gandhi's standards of hygiene. (He noted, 'It was a delight to me to see them working spade in hand.'[7]) The experiment was short-lived. But it demonstrated that wherever Gandhi went, even where he was most welcome and at home, his critical eye was on people's habits and relationships, and he could not rest content without attempting reform according to his own ideals.

Later in the year he went to Hardwar, the holy city on the banks of the river Ganges, on the occasion of a great celebration held every twelve years which attracted thousands of pilgrims. Here the Phoenix party found themselves digging and tending the latrines. Gandhi himself wandered the streets when not receiving visitors and recoiled at the cruelty to animals, the credulity, hypocrisy and dirt which passed for religious experience. He saw 'more of the pilgrims' absent-mindedness, hypocrisy and slovenliness, than of their piety. The swarm of *sadhus*, who had descended there, seemed to have been born to enjoy the good things of life.'[8] In reaction he pledged himself to even greater simplicity and self-discipline, curtailing his eating to five items in a day and total abstinence after dark. The whole train of his thought, as a satyagrahi, was that even one truth-seeker by self-sacrifice could begin to cleanse the surrounding atmosphere and start the processes of personal and social renewal. It was a response to life which imposed immense strains on the individual, whether himself or those who strove to follow him, and it was at odds with the wider political and social strategies of many of the educated Indians with whom he was to deal.

The Servants of India Society, founded by Gokhale, was the only organization Gandhi contemplated joining at this early stage, and his experiences in relation to it demonstrated as starkly as had Hardwar how out of sympathy he was with so many aspects of the Indian environment. Even in South Africa he had been dubious about the SIS for its 'Westernization'. His relations with it reached a crisis when Gokhale died in February 1915. This deprived Gandhi not only of a deep friend but of his surest guide in Indian public life. His reaction was to attempt to join the SIS out of deference to Gokhale's memory and spirit. Lat in the month there was a crucial meeting in Poona between Gandhi and members who had gathered to mourn Gokhale; they made it plain that they disapproved of his 'anarchical' views, both political and social. Some felt they were poles apart from him in vital matters and his presence would imperil the Society. Gandhi, according to one senior member, V.S.S. Sastri, 'sat like a man rebuked.'[9] A final decision about his membership was postponed as Gandhi went off on his travels. But by the end of the year he was sure enough of himself to stand alone, and he preferred to work happily and informally with the Society's members when opportunity offered rather than press on with a request for formal membership. His sensitivity in not forcing the issue was a profound relief to Sastri.

The returned exile had an ambiguous public image among his countrymen. Those who had heard of his work considered him a remarkable patriot. But the Western-educated had many hesitations about his ideals and his life-style. Sastri, who was nearer to him in sympathy than many, wrote privately in amazement of his 'queer food' – fruit, nuts, no salt, no animal products, as little cooking as possible.[10] A prominent Bombay journalist took him to task privately for his wholesale condemnation of Western civilization, though he agreed that there were features of that civilization which merited criticism. 'Your career and character is such a vast public asset that one feels that it is a pity it should be rendered less useful than it might and should be ... by this prejudice, as I must hold it to be, against modernity as such.'[11] Other public figures and journalists did not hesitate to make similar criticisms of Gandhi in public, and were evidently perturbed that he might embark on a programme of passive resistance. However, he was already gaining the repute of being a deeply religious man, and was increasingly referred to as Mahatma; wherever he went people came to him for *darshan*, that 'sight' or 'seeing' of a holy place, object or person which in Hindu spirituality bestows blessing on the onlooker by its presence. Gandhi noted this rather wryly as he described his visit to Hardwar, where the *darshan*-seekers would not even allow him privacy to bathe or eat. British officials were also somewhat mystified at this eccentric and enigmatic figure. He was given the official honour of a Kaiser-i-Hind Gold Medal in 1915, and both the Governor of Bombay and the Viceroy took steps to meet him informally when he returned to India. But the official image of him as a well-meaning, idealistic subject of the empire, whose allegiance was worth retaining, began to tarnish as he became more vocal and active in public life. Although at first his movements were not shadowed, by February 1916 the publication of one of his speeches was banned in the UP and plans were made for his surveillance, though the Lientenant-Governor regretted this necessity as he gathered that 'Mr Gandhi ... is a man of personal probity and high ideals.'[12]

His first and to him most significant work was the establishment of an ashram community, reminiscent of Phoenix and Tolstoy Farm, where those 'high ideals' could be enacted, demonstrated to his countrymen and placed at the service of the nation. Looking back after two years he called his ashram 'the finest thing in the world'; 'a humble attempt to place at the disposal of the nation a home where men and women may have scope for free and unfettered development of character, in keeping with the national genius'.[13] It was also a practical necessity, as the group of twenty or more relatives, pupils and colleagues from Phoenix needed a permanent Indian home. Gokhale had liked the idea of an ashram and promised to finance it, but on his death Gandhi had to look for a place where there would be local support, material as well as moral. Gujarat was the general area he had in mind from the start; by the end of March 1915 he had decided on Ahmedabad, the region's cultural and economic capital, indeed sometimes called the 'Manchester of India' for its modern textile industry. Maganlal Gandhi had been there to sound out the

prospects of some of the major mill owners providing funds, and their
attitude to Gandhi's views on caste and the importance of reviving
cottage rather than factory industry, and Gandhi felt reasonably assured
of financial support for at least a year from some of them, while they got
to know him better. He was also persuaded by the fact that he could
work in his mother tongue rather than in English – with all the cultural
and political significance that held for him. He also hoped Ahmedabad
would be a good base for the revival of hand-spinning since it had once
been a centre for hand-loom weaving.[14] From its small beginnings in a
hired bungalow in May 1915 the ashram developed into an organized
community on the banks of the river Sabarmati on the city's outskirts,
with its own acres for agriculture, and starkly simple living quarters. It
was called the Satyagraha Ashram as Gandhi wanted it to be a sermon in
action, to teach India about the ends and means he had come to value
supremely in South Africa.

The ashram's constitution was worked out during 1915:[15] the life-
style envisaged and the vows to be taken by the permanent members
bore all the hallmarks of *Hind Swaraj* and were in effect the enactment of
that vision on a personal and small-scale community basis. Although its
heart lay in a religious vision and it stood in the Hindu tradition of a
community of devotees, the emphasis was far more on the committed
ideals of a community of permanent members than on the authority of
any one *guru*, and its scope was far more broadly social than that of a
more traditional ashram. The primary vows of truth and non-violence
were to be buttressed by vows of celibacy (even for married couples)
and self-denial over food – in keeping with Gandhi's personal experience
of the manner of life which fortified the truth-seeker in his pilgrimage
and his commitment to non-violence. A total commitment to simplicity
and sufficiency as opposed to unnecessary consumption was enshrined
in vows of 'non-stealing' and 'non-possession'. Further, members
promised not to observe untouchability, pronouncing their belief,
though there were Hindus, that the practice was 'a blot on the Hindu
religion'. No caste *dharma* was observed in the ashram, as members
were *sanyassis*, those who had renounced the world; but, significantly,
caste as social discipline (as opposed to untouchability) was not
condemned.[16] A spartan life-style was laid down, and the daily time
table from 4.00 am to 10.00 pm presupposed morning and evening
prayers and considerable stretches of time for manual labour, specifically work on the land and hand-weaving, as well as the routine domestic
work of cooking, cleaning and drawing water. Communication would
be in the mother tongue. Outlines of an educational programme were
sketched for those who came as 'students', whether they were adoles-
cents, adults, or children with their parents. So Gandhi tried to work
out in the Indian context the issues at stake for India which he had
outlined in South Africa: truth, non-violence, moral economics, true
education and an equitable social order.

However, even the limited challenge to the social order offered by the ashram, the abandonment of untouchability, caused such a crisis that the community nearly disintegrated.[17] In September 1915 Gandhi accepted into the ashram an untouchable couple and their toddler. There was talk of social boycott by the residents of the city, and abuse by the man who controlled their water supply. Outside funds dried up. Potentially even more destructive was the upheaval within the ashram. Various members threatened to leave or actually left. The rebels included those dearest to Gandhi, Kasturbhai and Maganlal. Gandhi was prepared to face even this because it would be a demonstration both of satyagraha and his commitment to the untouchables, both of which were integral to swaraj. Eventually Kasturbhai endured alongside her husband, though Gandhi remarked in November that she was still smouldering inside, though she was outwardly calmer. But Maganlal left temporarily. When the District Magistrate visited the ashram in October he found it in a rather sorry state, its numbers much reduced by the storm of protest. It consisted of Gandhi and his relatives and virtually no local recruits, though there were still curious visitors who came to see both it and the notable eccentric at its head. There had been a real danger that the group would have to take refuge in the untouchables' quarter of the city and live there by their own manual labour. They were saved from this by a generous donation in cash of 13,000 rupees from an 'anonymous' local businessman who had never even visited the ashram and insisted in handing over the money swiftly from his car without entering. He was in fact Ambalal Sarabhai, a young mill owner in his twenties whose own life had been built on social rebellion as he had married out of caste. He was deeply attracted by Gandhi and his reforming zeal, though not to the ashram life itself; and this gift marked the beginning of a long and close, if ambiguous, relationship between the industrialist and the saint of the spinning-wheel, the wealthy urban prince and the man who chose a poor and rural way of life. Ambalal's generosity was in a long religious tradition of charity still practised by the wealthy of Ahmedabad and other towns, though his support developed into a wider political calculation as Gandhi became prominent in public life.

Criticisms other than those on the caste issue were also levelled at the ashram. It was thought to be too severe, too monkish, too backward-looking. But despite such doubts among observers it recovered from the crisis of 1915 and grew in size and public repute. It was never the home base Gandhi had originally intended: as he became increasingly involved in all-India public life he was often away and had to leave the daily management to the trusty Maganlal. Nor was it a perfect community. It had its share of petty squabbles, of moral dilemmas, and even its thefts; but Gandhi was to make a virtue of these, for in handling them he publicly demonstrated his striving for a swaraj society on a small scale. The ashram was his powerhouse for the next decade, as he hammered out his ideals in practice, and drew on its members to be his front-line helpers in his public campaigns.

Since Gandhi's concerns were with sanitation in pilgrim sites, spinning-wheels and the acceptance of two untouchables and their baby
girl as symbols of the ills of India, it was little wonder that he was
considered strange by the majority of those who were active in Indian
political life. They were all overtly or by implication concerned with
India's cultural and spiritual identity in a time of change, and most were
willing to accept and welcomed a degree of Western influence in their
lives and value systems. Further, at this juncture in time, most of them
were deeply concerned with the impact on India of world war, and the
opportunities it might provide for India's political advancement. While
Gandhi founded his ashram, what was at stake for them was the survival
of the empire and India's role in it. Ironically it was the war, which
Gandhi so lamented and had refused in London to 'exploit', that
produced the circumstances which in turn enabled his emergence as a
prominent Indian public figure.

Although the main theatres of war were thousands of miles from
India, the subcontinent provided a major contribution to the British war
effort – British officers and men who would otherwise have served in a
civilian or military capacity in India, Indian soldiers, animals, raw
materials and money through taxation and war loans. But this effort
in the imperial cause badly stretched the framework and resources of
the raj, and highly placed officials noted this with considerable
apprehension. Apart from the much depleted military pressence on the
subcontinent, they saw three main areas of danger.[18] Prices were rising
inexorably, and the effects on ordinary people were compounded by
shortages of basic necessities of life, such as kerosene. This was the type
of situation when widespread hardship could, and did, create sporadic
disorder, and theatened to undermine the acquiescence of the population. More particularly the war strained the loyalty of many of India's
Muslims, as their Khalifah (the spiritual head of the world-wild Islamic
community), the Sultan of Turkey, was opposed to the British and their
allies. Further, the empire's peril was a gift to those involved in modern
styles of politics and concerned about India's status within the empire.
With the evidence of Indian troops fighting alongside British soldiers in
France, and the ideological ammunition of the assertions by British
spokesmen and their allies that this was a war to defend small nations
and to asserrt the sanctity of treaties, Indian politicians naturally claimed
that the British should rethink their position in India in the light of such
statements and proclaim their intentions for this brightest jewel in the
imperial crown. What deeply worried British administrators in India
was the possibility that unmeetable demands might come not just from
a small vocal wing of politicians, but would represent the attitude of
those they called the 'Moderates' inside and outside Congress, on whom
they had come increasingly to rely for political support. In the four
decades since the foundation of Congress, the raj had come to realize the
significance of its members and its fluctuating penumbra of supporters.
They represented a major and increasingly vocal element in public life

whose perceptions were vital for the legitimacy of the raj. Their co-operation was also highly desirable, not only in the modern professions, but in the legal and administrative structures of empire, and the political institutions – from urban and rural boards up to the provincial and all-India consultative councils – through which the British haltingly tried to keep in touch with Indian public opinion and elicit Indian collaboration in the daily running of the empire. The steel frame of the raj might still be the Civil Service, backed by the army, but imperial control was increasingly a matter of political awareness and acumen in a world where educational and economic change were shifting the balances of power and opinion in Indian society and public life.

What ultimately convinced the British that they must take into account this wartime shift in Indian political thinking was evidence of the spread and invigoration of Indian political organization, and signs of a new unity among Indian politicians behind a claim that Britain should announce self-government within the empire at an early date as the objective of her imperial rule in India. Two political leaders, Tilak in Bombay and Annie Besant in Madras, started in 1915–16 two Home Rule Leagues to publicize the call for home rule and to sway opinion in Congress in support of this claim. Their publicity methods were far more populist than those used previously by the scrupulously loyal and socially conservative Congress, and they attracted a wider range of people than had previously been concerned with all-India political demands. These two also engineered a new unity in Congress behind the home rule demand. Their strategy was enabled partly by the death in 1915 of two of the giants of the early Congress, Gokhale and the Sir Pherozeshah Mehta who had so overawed the young Gandhi. They had held a stalwart loyal line within Congress for a whole decade to the discomfort of those who would have liked Congress to have taken a more radical and aggressive stance towards the British.

Even more dramatic than Congress's internal display of unity in 1916 was the Lucknow Pact in the same year, reached by Congress and the Muslim League, which supported the Congress demand and proposed a joint scheme of constitutional reform. Few Muslims had joined the early Congress: their reluctance reflected apprehensions as a religious minority, and the fact that so few Muslims had the educational and professional standing to enable them to participate in modern politics, a deprivation stemming from the social and geographical background of India's Muslims rather than any specifically religious inhibitions. Many educated Muslims had preferred to rely on the assurances of the British that in any political reform they would by given special protection and a recognized separate identity, as in the 1909 reforms, when they had been granted separate electorates in the expanded consultative councils. The Muslim League, founded in 1906 in part to press for this special treatment, now gained Congress's agreement that Muslims should have special electorates and reserved seats in the provincial and all-India councils in return for the League's support as Congress put political pressure on the raj. Although this was a significant and disquieting development to British eyes, sensitive as they were to Muslim feeling about the war, it was only a bargain amongst a small group of politicians, and not a sign of any large-scale political co-operation between Hindus and Muslims. Just as Congress was still limited by region, education and caste in its support among Hindus, so the League had no solid claims to represent all India's Muslims and had a membership of under 1,000, most of whom were educated men from northern India.

None the less, at the highest levels of the British raj, in Delhi and in London, it was now decided that in order to stabilize moderate Indian political opinion, a significant wartime gesture should be made. The result was a declaration in 1917 by E.S. Montagu as Secretary of State for India, that the goal of British policy was 'increasing association of Indians in every branch of the administration, and the gradual development of self-governing institutions, with a view to the progressive realization of responsible government in India as an integral part of the British Empire.' Even though it was a compromise wording, and envisaged no radical reform or relaxation of British control of the timing or nature of political change, it was a turning-point in imperial policy. In the cold weather of 1917–18 Montagu visited India and in company with the Viceroy, Lord Chelmsford, toured the country, listening to individuals and groups who wished to make their views known. The result was their joint report on possible post-war reforms, which laid down the outlines of what became the Government of India Act of 1919, popularly known as the Montagu–Chelmsford Reforms. Under their provision the councils in Delhi and the provincial capitals became more like real legislatures, with enlarged memberships free from an official majority. The franchise was reformed, and in general linked to tax liability, with the result that about one in ten of the male population gained the vote. Separate communal electorates were given to Muslims and other religious minorities, and they were linked to reserved seats in the legislature on lines similar to those suggested in the Lucknow Pact. Certain key topics like foreign affairs, currency and criminal law remained firmly the preserve of the Delhi government. But other topics were delegated to the provinces. Of these provincial topics, some were reserved to the control of the governor and his executive council, while others were transferred to Indian ministers responsible to the legislature and through it to the electorate. So the British, pushed into political concessions by the war, greatly extended the significance for many Indians of the legislatures as arenas of politics, and expanded the range of political discourse. By reforming the franchise they also modified the avenues for political influence and success, and altered the terms of political leadership. Although their aim was to stabilize their raj and attract the working collaboration of a range of the Western-educated and moderately well-to-do, they opened the way for more popular styles of politics and a broader spectrum of political activities.

First public steps

Not surprisingly when Gandhi emerged in 1916 from his year of silence on public matters, most prominent politicians were caught up in this process of working out the role of India in the empire after the war. Gandhi's concerns and activities were far more diverse and often seemed to have little direct connection with either the war or the prospect of political reform. He seems to have had no particular political ambition, no plans for a public career. Rather, he tried to 'experiment with truth' in whatever area of his life seemed necessary, whether in the ashram or in the more public realm. 'I have taken up things as they have come to me and always in trembling and fear.' To the outsider this might have seemed like pragmatism: to him it was following the guidance of a good providence.[19]

Some of the causes Gandhi espoused when he began to speak in public were a natural development from his African work, or were ideals which he had begun to value and work out in South Africa but which now demanded development and clarification in the light of actual Indian conditions. His handling of them contributed to his standing as a high-minded patriot with a distinctive, indeed idiosyncratic, public stance. The system of indentured labour and the plight of the poorest Indians caught up in it had concerned Gandhi for twenty years. It had also perturbed the Government of India, which in March 1916 had announced that the system would be ended in due course. But as the months dragged by and thousands of Indians abroad remained shackled by their indentures, a public campaign began in India, involving among others Gandhi's friends, Henry Polak and C.F. Andrews, and Gandhi himself. Gandhi moved a resolution on the subject in Congress in December 1916; in the new year he obtained an interview with the Viceroy, who proved sympathetic but gave no definite promises as to timing. Thereafter Gandhi began an all-India tour to press for the end of the system by 31 May, starting on home territory in Ahmedabad and Bombay, where he used friends and the Imperial Citizenship Association, which had welcomed and encouraged him while he was based in South Africa. In September the campaign achieved its goal when the Viceroy announced that the indenture system would soon be ended. Gandhi's role as champion of the indentured was significant, perhaps less for his contribution to the ending of the system than for the all-India platform it gave him in his homeland and the connections it forged for him in Indian public life.[20]

For Gandhi indentured labour was not a stick with which to beat the government: it was a moral issue, involving 'moral degradation'.[21] Similarly, for him the cause of swadeshi, on which he also campaigned publicly in these early years in India, was a moral question. His concern for it likewise originated in Africa, and much of what he now said was foreshadowed in *Hind Swaraj*. Significantly, and despite the hopes of Gokhale, the actual experience of India did not cure Gandhi of the ideals for India he had expressed in 1909: when the pamphlet was republished in 1919 he adhered to his views in it as strongly as ever.[22] In its widest sense swadeshi for him meant 'that spirit in us which restricts us to the use and service of our immediate surroundings to the exclusion of the more remote.' It was the humble way of love, of serving in the immediate context in which one found oneself; it excluded ideological or material aggrandizement or violence, and it included matters of religion, politics and economics.[23] However, it was this last and more narrowly economic aspect on which Gandhi spoke most widely and which became inextricably linked with his name at home in India and abroad. The use of locally-made articles was one of the principles of ashram life because members, as truth-seekers, could not be assured of the morality in the manufacture of articles from abroad. But for India as a whole Gandhi preached the necessity of a moral economics. Acknowledging with humour his alleged crankiness and ignorance of economics, he argued passionately that material 'progress' as commonly understood was in fact the enemy of real, moral advancement. Indians should fight the disease of materialism by holding fast to their ancient civilization and cherishing a simple live-style where the principles of sufficiency and compassion would overcome the evils of grievious poverty, over-consumption and economic violence.[24]

An aspect of the revitalization of Indian civilization and identity which Gandhi stressed as particularly important was education: for to him, as he had expounded in *Hind Swaraj* the present system of education in India perpetuated immoral ideas, bred generations of Indians eager to collaborate in an imperial regime which was importing an evil civilization and threatened to create a widening gulf between the so-called 'educated' and the masses. His concern focused on the actual content of the educational syllabus and the language in which students were taught: he argued trenchantly for the use of vernaculars as opposed to English, and the abandonment of the current over-literary and foreign syllabus in favour of study soundly based on spiritual values in the context of practical labour. By early January 1917 he was so involved in this problem that he wrote of his whole time being taken up with 'preparing a big educational scheme'.[25] The plan was for a genuinely national school in Gujarat, a measure of Indian self-help, on the assumption that relying on attempts to persuade the government to change the current system would mean enormous delay in any reform. The plan incorporated all the educational principles which Gandhi was trying to spread in his speeches, and was similar to the schemes laid down for education in Phoenix and Tolstoy Farm. It came to fruition on a small scale in the ashram at Ahmedabad by the middle of the year. Gandhi set immense store by it as an experiment which might become a pattern for other voluntary institutions and eventually prove to government the need for and right way to achieve reform of the current system. His criticism of contemporary education in his appeal for the ashram was robust, comprehensive and

typical of the many public pronouncements he was making on education.

> The system of education at present in vogue is wholly unsuited to
> India's needs, is a bad copy of the Western model and it has by reason
> of the medium of instruction being a foreign language sapped the
> energy of the youths who have passed through our schools and
> colleges and has produced an army of clerks and office-seekers. It has
> dried up all originality, impoverished the vernaculars and has dep-
> rived the masses of the benefit of higher knowledge which would
> otherwise have percolated to them through the intercourse of the
> educated classes with them. The system has resulted in creating a gulf
> between educated India and the masses. It has stimulated the brain but
> starved the spirit for want of a religious basis for education and
> emaciated the body for want of training in handicrafts. It has crimi-
> nally neglected the greatest need of India in that there is no agricultu-
> ral training worth the name.... The experiment now being carried
> on at the Ashram seeks to avoid all the defects above noted.[26]

Many decades later, when the more disruptive and uncomfortable
aspects of Gandhi's vision of India have been ironed out of the myth
surrounding him, it is difficult to appreciate quite how radical and
abrasive Gandhi would have sounded to educated Indians as he castigated their educational training and their values and told them they were
traitors to their motherland by being willing 'victims' of the current
system. His increasing emphasis on the divisiveness of contemporary
Indian education showed his growing identification with the poor in his
homeland rather than with the educated with whom he would naturally
have fitted by virtue of his own education and professional training. His
concern for what education was doing to India and Indians also led him
into deeper consideration of the problem of finding a genuinely national
language rather than English, with all its drawbacks of social exclusiveness and association with the political and cultural rejection of the
nation's own rich heritage. As early as December 1916 he presided at a
conference on this issue; in October 1917 he was president of a Gujarat
educational conference at which he dealt with the question of a national
language as well as wider educational issues. His preference was for
Hindi as spoken by north Indians, Muslim and Hindu, which could be
written in either Devanagri or Persian scripts.[27] This was to be a significant aspect of his work for a new national identity and true swaraj until
the end of his life.

The returned exile was not merely a somewhat quirky public speaker,
expanding on themes he had first tried out in Africa and daring to
challenge the values prevailing among many of those who were active in
Indian public life. Very rapidly his concern for truth drew him into
situations which were totally new to him, in an Indian setting which
was still largely unfamiliar. He came to the point of trying out satyagraha

much earlier than he had anticipated, as a result of three issues in Gujarat and one in Bihar on the opposite side of the subcontinent. It is tempting with any great figure, and particularly in a biographical study, to assume that the individual was always the initiator of action and the major influence in any set of circumstances. Yet it is misleading to see Gandhi in these early days in India as the prime mover in the causes with which he became involved, as one who deliberately sought out wrongs on which to campaign, or as a man who was purposefully building a public career. He was at this stage very much at the mercy of local groups or individuals who invited him to participate in their problems because of his reputation and his distinctive political style which offered modes of action which might be effective where the techniques of the established politicians were of little avail. How far he understood these situations into which he was drawn or how fundamentally he was able to take control of them or alter them is very questionable.

The first issue on which Gandhi began to contemplate an Indian satyagraha, now little known or considered in accounts of his life, shows very clearly how he was still only a small part of a long-standing local situation. Gujarat was a honeycomb of native states and English-administered territory, and controlling the customs on the borders of British India was problematic since the Kathiawad princely states occupied the coastline. The particular problem of an inland customs control at Viramgam railway station had perturbed the Government of India for some time, was a topic of local complaint in the press, and was a real source of aggravation to railway travellers, not only because of the inconvenience but because of the manner in which officials dealt with them. Gandhi, as a Kathiawadi, travelled widely in the area after his return, and was rapidly recruited by local people into their protest campaign about the customs barrier; he began to work publicly against the barrier when his year of silence ended. He spoke at various public meetings and began to raise in private and public the question of satyagraha as a method of protest. He took the case in person to the Governor of Bombay and the Viceroy, and in November 1917 the matter was resolved by government's removal of the customs control. Although this was a small, local issue, even trivial by comparison with the great issues at stake for India's future as a result of the war, and a situation in which Gandhi's role was limited, it was significant because it was the occasion for his first public discussion of non-violent, direct action as appropriate in the Indian context. He was forthright and blunt about his reasoning, telling the secretary to the Governor of Bombay,

It is my duty to place before the people all the legitimate remedies for grievances. A nation that wants to come into its own ought to know all the ways and means to freedom. Usually they include violence as the last remedy. *Satyagraha*, on the other hand, is an absolutely non-violent weapon. I regard it as my duty to explain its practice and its limitations. I have no doubt that the British Government is a powerful Government, but I have no doubt also that *Satyagraha* is a sovereign remedy.[28]

The occasion to try out this 'sovereign remedy' was close at hand. While Gandhi was still working on the Viramgam customs issue he was also drawn into another local problem, this time not on familiar territory but in Champaran district of Bihar, on the opposite side of the subcontinent. Here he was an outsider, ignorant of the people and their particular problems; he could not even speak the local vernacular or understand with ease the local variant of Hindi. He reluctantly became involved in the district's affairs by the insistence of a prosperous agriculuralist, Rajkumar Shukla, who contacted him at the 1916 Congress gathering and pursued him on his travels thereafter until in April 1917 Gandhi agreed to visit Champaran. Shukla had tried to persuade other prominent public figures to take up the cause of the Champaran peasantry, but had succeeded in obtaining no practical aid or personal commitment – only a general Congress resolution. Only Gandhi, the outsider both to Bihar and to the politics of Congress, the maverick in public life, would give his time and attention, and ultimately his peculiar expertise. He found a situation which he considered might be worse than that of indentured labour in Fiji and Natal – a wrong indeed – and it became the issue for his first satyagraha in India, involving only himself in opposition to a local magistrate's order to leave the district. Yet at the outset he was not a particularly welcome figure in Indian eyes and his reception at the small town of Bankipur on the way to Champaran was almost as chill as his first experience of a railway journey in South Africa, though in this instance the barrier was caste not race. Shukla dumped him in a strange house where the servants were suspicious of the stranger, and refused to share food or a bathroom with him. He treated the whole incident philosophically but wondered it he would ever reach the place where his help was allegedly needed.[29]

Champaran was a deeply rural district in north Bihar, little touched by the economic, social or political developments which were influencing urban life. But, unlike many areas of the Indian countryside, it was characterized by the presence of large estates and was dominated by landlords, rather than peasant proprietors. Most of the large landlords had let their land to temporary tenure-holders, a substantial number of whom were European planters, and they in turn either cultivated the land directly or let it to peasant tenants. Not that all these peasant tenants were abjectly poor, ignorant and downtrodden, as Gandhi tended to depict them. Many, like Shukla himself, were of high caste and combined cultivation, money-lending and the management of lands other than those they actually rented. The hardships of Champaran's peasants were exacerbated by wartime conditions. Scarcity of rolling-stock hit this isolated area hard, for prices of basic necessities imported by rail rose, while the foodstuffs normally shifted by rail out of the district could not be moved and their price fell, to the discomfort of all involved in commercial agriculture. But the district's basic problems were far more deep-seated and had for several decades generated discontent, erupting on occasion into public violence. The planting community was rooted in the industry of indigo production, and planters leased lands to the peasantry on the condition that they would grow indigo on certain parts of the land. This indirect cultivation of indigo enabled the planters to dominate the area and their tenants' lives, often by very dubious means. By the beginning of this century indigo was ceasing to be a paying proposition, as German-manufactured synthetic indigo began to undercut the natural dye on world markets. The planters proceeded to pass their losses on to their tenants, by commuting indigo-growing agreements into money payments either in the form of a lump sum or of enhanced rents. The result of these long-standing and more immediate social and economic conditions was a 'planter raj' causing considerable discontent and perturbing even government officials.

Gandhi came to Champaran intending to stay a few days; but he was so appalled that his involvement in person or through a small band of helpers lasted for a year. He saw his role as one of public service, of attempting to bring peace to the rural community, but with honour. However, the Divisional Commissioner and the District Magistrate thought otherwise: fearing that Gandhi's objective was agitation and that his presence would further disturb the public peace, they ordered him to leave the district. This he refused to do and explained in the District Magistrate's court why he had come to Champaran and why he felt he could not leave as ordered. His disobedience and willing acceptance of the penalty were not, he claimed, a sign of disrespect to the lawful authority but obedience to the higher law of conscience. The Magistrate, confronted with such an unexpected event and such an unpredictable person, postponed judgement while he conferred with his superiors. The Bihar government was doubtful that the order had been legal in the first place, as Gandhi had showed no signs of disturbing the peace; moreover, it was determined that Gandhi should have no opportunity to play the martyr role as he was known to have done in South Africa. A sharp rebuke reached the district officials, and they were instructed to allow Gandhi to investigate, providing he was warned not to stir up trouble.

So Gandhi began work, investigating the condition of the peasant tenants, taking down statements from them, and also contacting members of the planting community. He was assisted in this by a group of small-town lawyers and businessmen, and a small number of articulate peasant tenants (often admittedly with personal grievances against the planters as well as a broader concern for conditions in the district) who were his links with the countryside and interpreted the peasants' statements for him. This travelling caravan of investigators penetrated deep into the countryside where Western-educated politicians had never been. Gandhi spoke not of political demands for home rule nor for reformed legislatures and voting rights, but of the troubles which the rural folk poured out to him – how they were forced to grow indigo on their best lands, of the weight of the money payments in place of the indigo obligation, how the planters' servants bullied them, and how the planters enforced illegal demands on them.

Gandhi generated an amazing atmosphere wherever he went. A young English ICS man commented that Gandhi seemed to the peasants 'their liberator, and they credit him with extraordinary powers. He moves about in the villages, asking them to lay their grievances before him, and he is daily transfiguring the imaginations of masses of ignorant men with visions of an early millenium.'[30] Gandhi soon became convinced that the courts, the current land-settlement operations and private agreements with the planters would not bring a lasting end to the cluster of problems: the government would have to act firmly to end abuses and also appoint a commission of inquiry. Eventually in June such an inquiry was set up and Gandhi was given a seat on it, although official records show that it was the Government of India which pushed an extremely reluctant provincial government into this course of action rather than risk a public outcry on a matter where there were obviously very real problems which needed investigation and rectification. The Committee's findings confirmed many of Gandhi's suspicions, and the Bihar legislature passed an act incorporating its recommendations, including the abolition of the system under which tenants cultivated indigo, and reduction of rents which had been raised in lieu of indigo cultivation. Other aspects of high-handed planter pressure on peasants were dealt with by executive orders. However, this did not produce the peace with honour Gandhi had hoped to achieve in Champaran. Relations between planters and peasants continued to be strained, with both groups virtually fighting a guerilla war against each other; the planters remained convinced that they had been sacrificed by the government to appease Gandhi and a pack of political agitators.

Gandhi's experience of Champaran showed him that satyagraha was indeed a remedy he could use in India, even if it was restricted to himself. It also brought him into direct contact with the realities of Indian rural life in a new way. The urban, Western-educated English-speaker now saw in all their starkness, villagers' problems of disease, poverty, ignorance and the unequal division of power. He became deeply convinced that India's rural problems needed long-term solutions and were of the utmost significance for the country's future. Only knowledge, not just in the sense of schooling, but about health, cleanliness and the individual's worth, could eradicate the fear and deprivation of India's poor and provide a firm foundation for true swaraj. He told his companions that their work in Champaran was real work for home rule when they were perplexed, even frustrated, at his insistence that they must keep that work politically neutral rather than aligning it with the agitation which bore the name of home rule. His attempted solution to Champaran's deepest problems was a number of village primary schools, whose teachers would not just make the children their concern, but would involve themselves in attempts to clean up the villages and provide rudimentary medical care. Women were particularly recruited into the work to reach village women. Kasturbhai was summoned to assist her husband, as was their youngest son, Devadas. Most of the volunteers came from outside Bihar, and a sizeable contingent came from the ashram. To Gandhi's sadness the rural work was short-lived because no one in Bihar was willing to continue it.

If the realization of a desperate need for village work and the sight of its collapse were major lessons Gandhi learned from Champaran, others began to recognize that there was a new and important public figure in their midst, and this was as crucial for Gandhi's future as was his own reaction to the experience. The widespread response to Gandhi, which remained throughout his life, was apparent there almost for the first time. At the grass roots of Indian society ordinary people, ignorant by the standards of the Western-educated, flocked to see him, to receive his *darshan*, though this wonder and adulation did not make them malleable political material in his hands, and often went with a distaste for the type of disciplined self-reform he advocated. Some Champaran villagers bluntly told him how they disliked the untouchables' work he was prescribing as the cure for public insanitation. Gandhi also became more widely known throughout India among those who read newspapers or attended public meetings as a result of reports of his work in Bihar. Reactions to him among the educated varied. Some, like the young Jawaharlal Nehru were excited and enthusiastic. Others were perturbed at the possible repercussions of disobedience to the law, or were mystified at this deliberately simple life-style. The government, too, realized that it could not ignore Gandhi. Local officials had been seriously embarrassed by his presence and were anxious that his 'philanthropy' was taking him into the company of politically motivated urban lawyers who were manipulating him, or that he was a budding anti-European demagogue. Further from the actual pressures of coping with Gandhi, his entourage and the admiring crowds, the government in Delhi was disposed to see Gandhi as a high-minded social worker, and to wish to avoid any confrontation with him, particularly in wartime when it needed maximum public acceptance and could ill afford gratuitous squandering of its legitimacy by unnecessary conflict.

In retrospect Gandhi's first major encounter with India's real social and economic problems and with the raj, as opposed to the scene sketched in *Hind Swaraj*, illuminates many facets of his subsequent career. The effectiveness of his personal satyagraha depended primarily on the fact that he had engaged with one tier of officialdom while higher tiers, for reasons of their own connected with provincial or continental politics, wished to see him placated and were in a position to countermand the actions of their subordinates. If in future circumstances there was no such leverage satyagraha could exert by its influence on higher authority, its effectiveness might be very limited. But even at this early stage official concern at Gandhi's impact on public opinion indicated that satyagraha was an encounter at the level of legitimacy – an aspect of imperial rule which was highly significant and was to become even more so as political awareness developed on the subcontinent and as Gandhi began to campaign on wider issues.

Gandhi's style of work in Champaran also bore many of the hall-marks of his later campaigns. Here in action was his eagerness to talk with the opponent at the outset, whether government or planter, and to arrange a compromise if possible rather than reach the point of con-frontation, the duty of the satyagrahi as he perceived the role. Here also was the willingness to compromise on non-essentials to achieve a settlement. (Some of Gandhi's associates felt he should have pressed for a full reduction of rents enhanced in lieu of indigo production instead of the limited reduction he had negotiated with the planters.) Here was a meticulous concern for the collection of properly documented evidence, more akin to the lawyer's brief than the politician's rhetoric. In poor Bihar, where he was at the outset a total stranger, he showed that financial flair for attracting donations which meant that his campaigns were rarely ill-funded. He also showed his awareness of the importance of the media, and in this case he deliberately discouraged wide press coverage of his work, to enable him to pursue it in his own style, unaffected by the political turmoil of the war years. Moreover, he chose to work with a trusted group of local men who would be his links with the local situation and his agents in his absence – a strategy of connection via devolved responsibility which contrasted with his greater personal control in South Africa. This reliance on a local group was essential, given the size of India and his personal limitations of time, energy, language and knowledge. In turn it also provided a training-ground for a significant number of young men who rose to prominence in provin-cial and all-India politics through working with Gandhi initially on prosaic, local concerns. Rajendra Prasad, a local lawyer who helped him in Champaran, became a prominent 'Gandhian' Congressman, provin-cial leader and eventually President of independent India. Champaran was, before Gandhi appeared, an area with its own problems and its own politics, particularly in the form of power conflicts between the European planters and their tenants. Some of the latter, like Rajkumar Shukla, tried to make connections with a wider political world in order to pursue their goals. But Champaran, indeed Bihar as a whole, was generally considered backward and uninvolved in terms of the politics of the Western-educated and of Congress. Gandhi's work in Bihar and the development of the province as a base of support for him suggests the potential of such areas in continental politics if a leadership could make connections between the two, and if the issues important to Bihar could be ventilated and pursued in a continental pattern of politics.

It was Gujarat, Gandhi's home region, which became his firmest base in public life, as he emerged first as a local and then as a continental figure of influence. Like Bihar, Gujarat had produced none of the early pioneers of new Westernized styles of politics whose work had culmin-

ated in the founding of the Indian National Congress. But as the
northern part of the Bombay Presidency, within an easy train journey
from the great port-metropolis of Bombay itself, Gujarat had for some
decades been exposed to the influences of the new education, the
expanding cash economy, and ultimately of new political ideas and
organizations. When Gandhi began to be active in Gujarat on his return
from South Africa he entered a public arena where there was considerable new political activity and awareness. Recognizably nationalist
sentiment had reached not only Gujarat's main city, Ahmedabad, but
her small market towns and some of her substantial villages. In this
process the new Home Rule League, founded by Annie Besant, was a
significant mechanism, with its meetings and volunteers, intent on
spreading awareness of the potential for political change during the war.
Gandhi's reputation for his work in Champaran made him admired and
much sought-after by political activists, even those who had at first
wondered and even mocked at his anti-Western attitudes and simple
style of life. Increasingly he became locally known as he spoke at public
meetings on a range of all-India and local issues, and he gained his first
institutional political footing in 1917 as elected President of the Gujarat
Sabha and invited President of a Gujarat Political Conference. Both
these positions he welcomed, not so much for their possible implications for a political career for himself, but for the way he was able to use
them to bridge the gap between India's ordinary people and her Western-educated. He insisted, for example, that the Political Conference
should conduct its proceedings in Gujarati. Of his work through the
Gujarat Sabha to organize a huge public petition in support of the
Congress–League scheme of constitutional reform he wrote, 'For me
the value of it lies in the education that the masses will receive and the
opportunity that the educated men and women will have of coming in
close touch with the people.'[31] His main opportunities to be this new
sort of political educator and public bridge-builder, and also to experiment with his satyagraha technique on a far broader scale, came when
two issues peculiar to areas of Gujarat were brought to his notice, one in
Kaira district, and one in Ahmedabad itself.

Kaira district and its farming community were very different form
Champaran.[32] It was a fertile and well-irrigated area which has prospered on the growth of cash crops and the remittances of its sons who
had travelled to East Africa to trade. Its most favoured central tract was
famous for its agriculture, its trees and its well-built villages behind high
hedges. The farming families who shared in this prosperity were known
as *Patidars*. They were a tough, enterprising and well-organized caste
who prided themselves on their skill, thrift and independence. Over
several generations they had developed into substantial yeomen farmers,
controlling between them much of the region's land. They despised and
were often in conflict with the lower caste labourers who worked for
them. As for the government, most of them had little knowledge of or
contact with British officialdom, which was remote and awe-inspiring.

They dealt when they had to with the Indian police or with the local Indian revenue official who worked beneath the District Officer, but preferred to have as little as possible to do with either and to regulate their own affairs as a community. They had a political tradition in which as a community they supported each other in land revenue payments; and as part of their dominant position the richer would refuse payment if they felt the demand was exorbitant and threatened to weaken village solidarity and harmony. As a last resort they could move away to new lands, but this option really no longer existed by the twentieth century because of pressure on land, except in the form of temporary flight to the princely states whose borders ran close to their fields. For them the revenue demand was part of a well-understood moral order in which both official and farmer had a proper role: if government overstepped its role then protest was a moral as well as an economic act. The British, by contrast, saw any such refusal as a political action because it was a threat to a crucial element in the raj's financial stability, and spoke of peasant stubbornness and recalcitrance. Gandhi became involved in such a conflict early in 1918 when rising prices, a poor season and outbreaks of plague and cholera prompted Kaira's *Patidars* to protest at the level of land revenue demand. As in Champaran it was a local problem in which he became involved at the request of local people because of his repute, which he then appropriated with considerable significance both for the public life of the area and for himself.

Before Gandhi's personal involvement in the Kaira land revenue controversy the *Patidars'* discontent had been orchestrated by two local, educated men with considerable political experience who linked the embryonic agitation with the newly active local Home Rule League, contacted the two Bombay lawyers who represented Kaira on the Bombay Legislative Council, talked to the district's Collector, and eventually put the problem to Gandhi as President of the Gujarat Sabha. Little practical was done, however, apart from exchanges between the government and the Sabha until Gandhi returned from Bihar. At once he mentioned publicly the possibility of satyagraha, and embarked on a pattern of work similar to that he had followed in Champaran, contact-ing officials (in this case from the local revenue officers up to Lord Willingdon himself, the Presidency's Governor), requesting an official inquiry into the problem, and making local investigations himself with the help of local, educated men, most of whom were prominent in the Gujarat Sabha. When the government refused both an enquiry and any postponement of revenue collection Gandhi pursued his satyagraha proposal, though several prominent local politicians, including Home Rulers, were nervous at the long-term implications of deliberate law-breaking. In late March the Sabha agreed that resistance was the only course left; Gandhi launched the campaign of refusal to pay revenue with a vow to be taken by the wealthier farmers that they would withhold payment, even if it meant confiscation of their land, and would only stop their satyagraha if the government would postpone

Gandhi in 1918

revenue collection from the poorer villagers. Gandhian satyagraha was thus in the deep-rooted tradition of a moral order in which the *Patidars* supported each other and the more powerful dealt with the outside world in order to maintain the stability of the whole community. It lasted until June 1918 when local officials agreed that in view of the government's need for tranquility and support during the war no pressure would be put on those who were really too poor to pay. Here was no success for satyagraha, no real yielding by government because the different levels of the administration stood firmly together, recognizing that any major concessions would undermine their whole land revenue system. What little leeway there was in official attitudes certainly stemmed from all-India priority, just as in Champaran there had been a much more dramatic intervention by the higher reaches of government. But Gandhi was right in reflecting sadly that satyagraha had achieved little directly for its participants.

The details of the Kaira satyagraha and the controversies about the precise level of the crops and the proper revenue demand really belong to an account of the rural life of Gujarat. Yet the campaign is important in an understanding of Gandhi's development as a public figure. His own account of it indicates that although he considered the farmers' complaint fully justified and consequently that this was a public wrong which could be rectified by the use of truth-force, he was far more concerned with the potential of the struggle as an educative mechanism, not only in the use of non–violence, but in a wider political sense. He claimed that it raised the whole issue of government by consent.[33] If people would recognize that governments could only rule with the co-operation of their subjects and that they need not tolerate insults, threats and stonewalling, then true swaraj would be on its way. Furthermore, such political awareness must not and need not be the preserve of the educated: India's peasantry must be taught their power as citizens in contexts which had practical meaning in their daily lives. Although Gandhi was not a committed Home Ruler, nor a recognized politician, this campaign was a sign that political issues were central to his vision of a new India and that he would be prepared to deploy his satyagraha technique in situations where it would have considerable political repercussions.

In Champaran Gandhi had deliberately insulated his work from the politics of the press and political organizations. In Kaira he used political means and connections, showing the skill he had developed as a publicist in South Africa. Not only did he deploy the mechanisms of the petition, the mass meeting, speeches and the press, he was also happy to use donations from outside the area, for example from Bombay businessmen, many of whom were Gujaratis with known sympathies for the Home Rule movement, and to work with and through overtly political bodies such as the Home Rule League and the Gujarat Sabha. He made it plain that he was primarily courting public opinion rather than funds, for he realized that in a political battle with the raj the issue of legitimacy was paramount. Without standing and acceptance, without *izzat*, that quality of prestige which the British so prized, the raj would crumble from within. But the core of his work was among the Kaira farmers themselves, teaching them their potential strength, and stiffening their courage with his presence and the power of a holy vow which had such profound resonances within the Hindu tradition. By contrast with later local satyagrahas in Gujarat the campaign was patchily organized and often Gandhi's presence was badly needed to sustain local determination and morale, and he went wherever he could in person. He also showed his political acumen in recognizing the power of the symbolic act. As an object lesson in and a symbol of courage he advised one of the early leaders of the agitation to remove a standing crop of onions which had been officially designated in lieu of a revenue payment. The onion 'thief' and his helpers were then escorted to prison by a procession of admirers. As in South Africa and later in India, Gandhi made goal-going the hallmark of integrity and national commitment, rather than an experience of degradation and public shame. Social pressure was also put on those who broke the vow not to pay the revenue and those who worked for government in collecting revenue. At the peak of the campaign probably between 2,000 and 3,000 actually signed the pledge of resistance.

In terms of Gandhi's public standing and influence the Kaira satyagraha was significant for more than just the opportunity it gave him to demonstrate in India skills and patterns of work he had refined in South Africa. It offered the chance to forge long-term link with groups of people in Gujarat which were to remain a source of strength through his Indian career. The *Patidar* community, though by no means converts to his deeper ideals, saw in him a man whose strategies worked in their traditional framework of reference; who linked their political behaviour to a wider vision of politics; and whose sense of Indian nationalism was expressed in terms they could understand and see, as in the instance of the onion thief. Gandhi also gathered round him, as he had in Bihar, a group of local professional men who acted as his links with the country-side when he could not be present in person, who became his trusted colleagues in a broader political scene. Among them was the local lawyer and civic politician, Vallabhbhai Patel, himself a *Patidar*, who became one of his stalwarts in the all-India Congress as well as the man he trusted most closely to organize political work in Gujarat. The Kaira campaign also boosted Gandhi's India-wide public image, and particularly his prestige in the Bombay Presidency among those who read the papers in which satyagraha was reported. But among them there was often concern at the implications of passive resistance, despite their respect for this political saint who had appeared in their midst. In Government circles Gandhi was now increasingly suspect. Bombay's Governor even went so far as to describe him as 'honest, but a Bolshevik & for that reason very dangerous.'[34] Lord Willingdon's assessment was somewhat ironic as just three years earlier Gandhi's name had gone forward with Lady Willingdon's for a Kaiser-i-Hind gold medal as honour for public service.

The Kaira satyagraha consolidated Gandhi's standing in Gujarat, despite its limited practical success. Here the government stood firm because it recognized that any major concession would undermine its land revenue system and open the way to constant questioning up and down the land of this most crucial financial buttress of the raj. So the Kaira episode showed, at least in retrospect, how satyagraha was effective only when the opponent was vulnerable in some respect, and the more so if the issue was one on which there was a widespread moral concensus that something was amiss. In Gandhi's second Gujarat satyagraha in 1918 the opponent was a group of Ahmedabad mill-owners; their vulnerability lay in Gandhi's local prestige and the close personal ties he had with some of their families.

Ahmedabad was Gandhi's chosen home on his return to India, the place where he felt he could best work with people of his own back-ground and language, who were likely to be sympathetic to his ideals and his vision of a new India. Yet in some ways it represented the antithesis of Gandhi's values and plans. The second-largest city in the Bombay Presidency, it was aptly called 'the Manchester of India': its long-established urban traditions and its prosperous trading communities were now working in the development of a large textile industry, whose mills, substantial profits and unequal division of wealth and power were evidence of the characteristics of an industrial society which Gandhi had condemned in *Hind Swaraj*. Wartime opportunities had greatly expanded the millowner's profits, and in order to attract mill-hands they were prepared to pay high wages and to top them up with a special 'plague bonus' in 1917 when outbreaks of plague threatened to drive workers back to their villages in order to escape infection. This bonus could amount to nearly three-quarters of a worker's normal pay. However, this equilibrium between the interests of owners and work-ers, betwen high profits and high wages, was broken early in 1918. The crisis in industrial relations was the result of the war. At this juncture Gujarat, like the rest of India, was taking the full brunt of wartime inflation; but the owners found themselves short of coal to power their mills because of the shortage of rolling-stock to bring their fuel from central India, and they decided to withdraw the plague bonus, knowing that temporary disruptions in their labour supply as a result would be no real economic deprivation for them. Gandhi became involved in the controversy over mill wages because various interested parties appealed to him to intervene in a situation of potential conflict. The millworkers were disorganized and leaderless, but those who spoke to Gandhi on their behalf were a secretary of the Gujarat Sabha, and Anasuya Sarabhai, sister of the millowner Ambalal Sarabhai, who had saved Gandhi's ashram from financial disaster after Gandhi had taken in an untouchable family. Anasuya was a voluntary philanthropist and social worker who worked with the millhands and also became interested in Gandhi's work in Kaira. Ambalal also saw Gandhi when they were both in Bombay at the beginning of February, and warned him of the possible repercussions of a strike on the city they both valued so highly, and asked him to intervene. When Gandhi reached Ahmedabad within a few days the British Collector also asked him to use his good offices to avert the impending conflict, as he understood that the owners were amenable to Gandhi's advice. So Gandhi became implicated in a fraught and potentially violent industrial situation, not of his own choosing. Champaran had brought him up against the realities of rural India: Ahmedabad's mills taught him something of industrial India. The record of his work suggests that the returned exile was still feeling his way and in this industrial setting was often out of his depth. Yet he felt he must respond to the pressures on him to become involved because the conflict raised issues central to his hopes and fears for India in the twentieth century. If the owners succeeded in withdrawing the bonus without raising their standard wages, it would be a sign that even in India, the land he saw as retaining something of true civilization as he had portrayed it in *Hind Swaraj*, money rather than morality held sway. It would be a triumph for 'the arrogance of money' over compassion and fraternity, and would have serious consequences for the whole of Indian society.[35]

Gandhi's involvement in the mill dispute spanned February and March of 1918. His failure to persuade Sarabhai to pay his weavers increased wages brought him to Ahmedabad in person to investigate the economics of the textile industry and the plight of the workers. He appealed to the millhands to seek a solution which would not lead to bitterness between them and their employers, and recommended arbitration if no solution could be reached by an appeal to the owners. The Collector of Ahmedabad agreed to chair a board of arbitration, when the owners somewhat reluctantly agreed to this strategy, having realized that there was no one else with whom they could expect to deal as a representative of their workforce unless they dealt with Gandhi. However, Gandhi could not control the millhands, and when sporadic strikes broke out, despite his careful and peaceful strategy, the owners withdrew from arbitration and a powerful group of them forged a common front and locked out the weavers in late February. This lock-out lasted until mid-March when they offered to take back the weavers who were prepared to accept a small increase in wages. Gandhi meanwhile had begun to organize the weavers, with daily mass meetings and leaflets through which he explained the nature of the struggle, and exhorted them to remain peaceful and disciplined. The mainstay of the campaign was a pledge not to return to work until an adequate increase was granted. Daily the pledge was repeated at the evening meeting, and processions through the city carried banners exhorting workers to keep the pledge. When the owners offered terms lower than those stipulated in the pledge, the workers' refusal to work became a genuine strike.

However, Gandhi could not control all the weavers, despite the moral aura generated around him and the campaign with a sacred pledge as its focus. Attendance at his meetings began to drop, some began to drift back to work, and some muttered that Gandhi was doing all right because he was a friend of the owners, enjoying their hospitality and the convenience of their cars, while they, the strikers, bore all the hardship. Probably as a result of these grumblings and to stiffen the resolve of the strikers, Gandhi decided to fast until their demands were met. Inevitably some people interpreted this as moral blackmail against his millowner friends; the police dismissed it as a theatrical gesture when he knew a settlement would have to come soon. He himself professed to be profoundly peaceful and full of joy at his steps: he told those who attended an ashram prayer meeting that this was his way of demonstrating the sacred nature of a vow and the religious implications of satyagraha, of relying on the ultimate triumph of truth. 'That a pledge once taken, at my instance, should be so lightly broken and that faith in God should decline means certain annihilation of dharma.'[36] He realized that his fast might well put pressure on the owners and would have wished that any concessions they made flowed from justice rather than charity towards him. Agitated consideration for him was, despite his protestations, forthcoming: within days the owners agreed to negotiate. A compromise was reached which saved face for both parties, and an arbiter, a local academic, was accepted. He eventually awarded the increase the workers had been claiming, though by then most of the mills were paying that amount or more. Although the context was so different from Gandhi's two rural satyagrahas, his Ahmedabad campaign demonstrated not only the viability of satyagraha in a further type of conflict but also many of the characteristics of his campaigns which were to recur wherever he had some real control – the search for a peaceful solution at the outset, the sacred pledge as the heart of the struggle, strict discipline and self-improvement among the participants, careful publicity and the generation of an ambience of moral authority and pressure, and finally a compromise solution to save the face and honour of all concerned. These were the hallmarks of satyagraha as he saw them, the procedures worthy of the true satyagrahi.

This comparatively brief incident helped in the long-term to establish Gandhi in the public life of urban Gujarat, to ensure that he could always turn for support to his home city, among both the labour force and the owners. The latter became some of his most generous financial backers, partly for reasons of personal and regional affinity, but partly also because they saw in his relations with their workers and his attitude to industrial relations the promise of harmony and productivity rather than destructive or even revolutionary conflict. The 1918 wage dispute made Gandhi face the reality of industrial relations in India; this was an urgent contemporary issue, whatever his fundamental hostility to the industrial mode of production. He based his vision of harmonious industrial relations on his existing belief that all wealth over and above one's basic needs was a trust, and that grabbing at or exploiting it at the expense of others amounted to theft. He lamented in one of the leaflets produced during the strike that 'pure justice ... inspired by fellow-feeling and compassion', the ancient, Eastern way of justice as he perceived it, was now being obliterated by Western conventions governing relations between employers and employed: everybody appeared to be looking to their own interests rather than acting from a sense of mutual obligation. On their part owners should treat their employees generously, as he urged Ambalal Sarabhai.

> Why should not the mill-owners feel happy paying a little more to the workers? There is only one royal road to remove their discontent: entering their lives and binding them with the silken thread of love. This is not beyond India. Ultimately, the right use of money is to spend it for the country; if you spend money for the country, it is bound to yield fruit.[37]

In saying this Gandhi was also in the long Hindu tradition that the privileged had a religious duty to extend charity. He was quite consciously trying to modernize what he felt to be traditional religious values and attitudes and adapt them to industrial relationships. In working out this modernization he argued that good industrial relations depended not only on employers regarding their workers' interests; the latter also had a duty to consider their employers' position, and in any dispute to act peaceably, with discipline, trying the way of negotiation and arbitration before resorting to anything like a strike. In the economic turmoil following the war he encouraged the establishment of trade unions, and in Ahmedabad a Textile Labour Association, to act on these principles for the protection of their members. He was adamant that unions were protective rather than coercive, and should foster unity between employers and employed; he claimed that he never had been nor would be party to any move to coerce the Ahmedabad owners or harm their interests.[38]

Some argued that his fast in 1918 was a coercive act. Gandhi was clearly worried at its possibly excessive influence on his owner friends, but he realized that for the satyagrahi there were rarely clear-cut moral issues, and that the truth-seeker must weigh the greater good and the lesser evil in any particular situation. In this instance the most significant consideration was to underline the value of a religious vow even if this risked an element of coercion. He had now come to the point when he felt that fasting, a traditional, religious method of self-purification and appeal, well known in the family context and not least in his own childhood, could properly be used in the public sphere; though until this time he himself had fasted only in private situations, such as his own family-like communities. Fasts on public issues became a permanent part of his public style and he refined the concept and laid down strict conditions for their use as he gained more experience; one can speak of him in subsequent years as working out both a theology and a practice of fasting. It became such an important element in his thinking and action that in 1925 he wrote that fasts were 'a part of my being. I can as well do without my eyes, for instance, as I can without fasts. What the eyes are for the outer world, fasts are for the inner.'[39]

Wider political involvement

Such an attitude marked Gandhi out from his contemporaries in Indian politics. Whereas they spoke of constitutional schemes for independence to take advantage of Britain's wartime vulnerability, he spoke of creating a new society from the roots upwards, and not only spoke but acted with whatever material came to hand – in the ashram, among farmers, and with factory hands. The terms for growing indigo, land revenue assessment, or the wages of one small group of factory workers were as significant to him as imperial policy and Congress schemes; indeed, even more so, because the solution of such problems was evidence that Indians were making anew their nation, and not relying on concessions from their rulers which would only amount to a spurious home rule, not real swaraj. Yet he was convinced that a truly religious man could not avoid politics as commonly understood. The traditional role of the religious recluse was not for him, despite his advancing years and loosening family ties: middle age called him not to withdrawal from ordinary life but to a deeper and wider public involvement if he was to be true to his religious vision, and to seek God in his creation and identify himself with even the meanest and lowliest in that creation.

> ... a man who aspires after that cannot afford to keep out of any field of life. That is why my devotion to Truth has drawn me into the field of politics; and I can say without the slightest hesitation, and yet in all humility, that those who say that religion has nothing to do with politics do not know what religion means.[40]

Gandhi's local satyagraha campaigns were the basis for such a wider involvement in politics, because of the personal connections he formed through them, the support he generated among local groups, and his growing public repute. They also increased his self-confidence for wider work in India, and particularly for satyagraha in an Indian context earlier than he had anticipated. Yet he seems still to have been feeling his way, using haphazardly the causes and people who offered themselves rather than planning a coherent strategy for himself or for swaraj. He thought back to his African experiences for guidance and longed for the sort of support and companionship he had enjoyed there.[41]

Ironically, as the crowds began to flock to see a Mahatma, as the politicans began to take note of his attitude and to court his alliance, Gandhi was profoundly aware of his loneliness and isolation in the midst of extreme business. Most particularly in the world of all-India political issues and people he felt an outsider. From the time when he wrote *Hind Swaraj* it had been evident that his vision of a free India was peculiarly his own, originating in his deepening convictions about the nature of a truly moral social, economic and political order. He refused to condone the peripheral, minority element of violence in Indian nationalist political thinking and practice, visible in response to the partition of Bengal in 1905, and in the sporadic and localized terrorist movments which attracted small groups of young men generally of high caste, and embarrassed the core nationalist leadership of Congress. Yet he also condemned as too Westernized those who were cast in the mould of liberal, constitutional nationalists; though ironically his own understanding of India's national identity owed a profound debt to his contact with Western political thought and example, and he accepted the geographical boundaries of an Indian nation as demarcated by the extent of the British raj, though for him the essence of Indian nationhood lay in the genius of Indian civilization as he perceived it. Now in public at political meetings and in private dealings with political figures he asserted that he belonged to no party and supported no particular programme wholeheartedly. He told leaders of both the more moderate and more extreme wings of Congress that he held strong and probably peculiar views which distinguished him from them all.[42] When the Secretary of State for India met him on his Indian tour in November 1917 he called him a social reformer. 'He dresses like a coolie, forswears all personal advancement, lives practically on the air, and is a pure visionary.'[43] But Montagu underestimated Gandhi's political commit-

ment and potential. His very presence at such an interview was a sign
that he saw the significance of all-India politics as a means of swaraj.

However, Gandhi was only willing to venture into that political
arena, to take a stand on continental issues, and become involved with
or against prominent individuals and organizations, on very restricted
occasions: only when he saw obvious moral issues at stake or the
opportunity for forwarding his vision of swaraj. For example, in 1917
when he was approached by a group of Bombay men on the issue of
Annie Besant's internment as a prominent Home Ruler, he toyed with
the idea of some form of passive resistance by concerned individuals in
her support. Gandhi did not like this maverick foreigner with her
suspect pseudo-religion of Theosophy and her wartime politics of
aggressive publicity and pressure on a beleaguered raj; but he felt that
the government had blundered in interning her and risked provoking
violence in support of her. However, political opinion was deeply
divided on the wisdom of passive resitance when it was discussed in
connection with her, and the issue was dropped by Gandhi and the
concerned groups of politicians when the government released her as a
device for achieving a peaceful and co-operative public mood for the
Secretary of State's visit.

Far more urgent and committed was Gandhi's public stand for the
Muslim brothers, Shaukat and Mahomed Ali, who were interned for
their Pan-Islamic and pro-Turkish sympathies and journalism soon after
the war began. This was for Gandhi not just an affront to a sincere
religious belief, and therefore a public wrong which needed righting; it
was also an opportunity to forge in India the sort of Hindu–Muslim
co-operation he had valued so highly in South Africa. He thought that
communal harmony was essential for the creation of true swaraj, and
also the measure of the strength of *ahimsa* which he believed would
receive its severest trial in the matter of relations between the two
communities. Quite bluntly he told the Alis that he was interested in
their plight because of its crucial role in his own wider vision and
experiments: 'my interest in your release is quite selfish. We have a
common goal and I want to utilize your services to the uttermost, in
order to reach that goal. In the proper solution of the Mahomedan
question lies the realization of Swarajya.'[44] Gandhi's campaign in public
speeches and personal approaches to the Government of India in 1918
was of little avail. He was not allowed even to visit them. After an
inquiry into their case had been undertaken, the government still refused
to release them, on broad political grounds, despite its own inquiry's
recommendations. The Alis' case was the first all-India issue on which
Gandhi showed his political skills and his potential as an all-India
political protagonist. Equally significantly it showed the high value he
placed on having the alliance of Muslim public figures as part of his
work for swaraj. The Alis were actually in no sense representative of
India's diverse Muslim population, as they belonged to the radical
educated group who were anxious to align their demands and activities

with Congress, and were essentially UP politicians. But Gandhi fastened on to their cause, hoping that they would enable him to continue in India the role he had achieved in Africa, of a Hindu who spanned narrow religious allegiances and worked to weld together a nation in search of swaraj. His wisdom in his choice of Muslim allies at this stage is debatable, given the Alis' foreign loyalities and their proclivites towards violence in tone and action; but Gandhi's move demonstrated the real concerns which moulded the pattern of his relations with the Indian Muslims until his death.

To most Indian politicians the fate of two strident Muslim journalists was far less pressing than the prospect of significant political reform during the war. Gandhi's understanding of swaraj was idiosyncratic, and he differed from other politicains also on the question of appropriate methods of politics.[45] Yet he was willing to participate in his own way in the campaign for home rule as popularly understood because of the opportunities it provided to break down barriers between educated Indians and their compatriots; hence his part in generating a monster petition from Gujarat in support of the Congress–League scheme of constitutional reform. He publicly supported the scheme though he admitted that he had little interest in it and did not share the premises on which it was based. He did not accept 'the Western model' of swaraj on which the Home Rule campaign was founded, and argued that swaraj could not be clamoured for as a concession from the British, but had to be earned and achieved, by hard work on such issues as domestic and communal unity and civic government, including public cleanliness. These were the appropriate fields in which Indians must learn to manage their own affairs.[46] Not surprisingly this approach embarrassed the politicians and pressmen who hoped to make capital out of Gandhi's support for the Congress–League claim. When the Viceroy and Secretary of State put forward their reform package in 1918 Gandhi was broadly sympathetic. But he refused to align himself on the issue with either of the main groups in Congress, as he disagreed with their views and ultimately would have been prepared to go to the length of passive resistance to wreck the scheme if his objections to it had not been met. He was profoundly sure of his own rightness but was not prepared to fight for his position in Congress. "I must therefore bide my time patiently and plough my own solitary furrow.'[47]

Gandhi's real concern, which distinguished him most radically from his contemporaries, was his belief that Indians should support the war effort to the extent of fighting for the empire, just when the politicians were out to exoploit the war and just when he was becoming known as an apostle of non-violence. On the issue of recruiting he stood alone, misunderstood and opposed: by becoming the raj's 'recruiting sergeant' he alienated his potential political allies, bewildered his friends and jeopardized his local power bases. But he felt it was the greatest problem he had faced in his life: his struggle with it devoured both his interior and physical energy. He made his priority plain in private letters and in public, not least by attending two War Conferences in Delhi and Bombay organized by the central and provincial governments to rally and publicize support for the war. In the behind-scenes committee work of the Delhi conference he opposed those who demanded responsible government as the *quid pro quo* of mobilizing Indian manpower and resources, while in the conference proper he supported recruitment with a single Hindi sentence. Although he offered his services to the Viceroy he was not prepared to fight in person. He made plain his own deep reservations about government action and policy on numerous issues but he was not going to bargain on these and take advantage of the government's embarrassment.

Instead, he plunged into a personal recruiting campaign in Bihar and Gujarat, in the belief that *this*, rather than political bargaining and appeal, would achieve swaraj. Almost incredibly he told someone who had known him for years, 'You must be watching my work of recruitment. Of all my activities, I regard this as the most difficult and the most important. If I succeed in it, genuine swaraj is assured.'[48] To fight for the allies was to fight for their own cause of swaraj; and in his view the gateway to India's freedom was on French soil. He reasoned (as he had done in London in 1914) that Indians must help in the war if they wished to enjoy the benefits of the state in which they lived. Further, this was a war being fought for freedom and demanded participation by those who wanted freedom for their own country. But perhaps even more importantly, Indians could never hope to be equal to the British unless they learned to defend themselves; courage and self-help were essential qualities for a nation which hoped to enjoy true swaraj, and the war gave Indians a chance to develop and display such qualities. For a committed follower of non-violence a recruiting campaign seemed as contrary as it did for a committed nationalist.

On this deepest moral issue of violence, quite apart from the immediate issue for Indians in 1918, Gandhi seems to have moved decisively in his understanding as a result of his Indian experiences. Privately he admitted that he was now convinced that such were the moral dilemmas of human existence that violence could on occasion be part of *ahimsa*, indeed its training-ground. Real *ahimsa* was the quality of people who were courageous and strong enough to be violent: only those who could use *ahimsa* could genuinely renounce it. He explained to a close disciple from the West that he was going through new experiences and struggling with himself and with words to understand and explain his conclusions in this matter. 'I am praying for light and guidance and am now acting with the greatest deliberation.'[49] His experiences in Champaran and Kaira had made him realize the Indians' satyagraha was, as yet, a weapon of the weak. Only he himself and some of his closest colleagues genuinely practised it from a position of courage and fearlessness. Now the opportunity had come to teach his countrymen how to cultivate courage and even the ability to fight, in the long-term cause of teaching them true *ahimsa*.[50] If Gandhi was struggling with a new understanding of the implications of non-violence forced on him by his experiences of using satyagraha in India, those around him were nonplussed or bluntly hostile to its practical application in his recruiting drive. In the localities where he had generated enthusiasm and awe a few months earlier he was now met with refusals and isolation. In Kaira, for example, of the few hundred recruits only about one hundred were local men, and they were not *Patidars*. Few would help him in the campaign, or even lend carts free of charge to the campaigners; Gandhi and his colleagues often had to tour on foot, covering as much as twenty miles a day.

Gandhi's struggle with his conscience, with those near to him, and those who had flocked to him, combined with physical exhaustion to precipitate a radical collapse in his health from the second half of 1918, virtually removing him from public life. In mid-August as he travelled Gujarat in search of recruits he contracted dysentery and aggravated it by eating some food Kasturbhai had prepared in celebration of a religious festival. His condition deteriorated rapidly and Ambalal Sarabhai and his wife came to Nadiad, where Gandhi had become ill, and removed him to their comfortable Ahmedabad home to be nursed. But he insisted eventually on going home to his ashram. It was the severest illness he had had in his life: he wrote of being in unbearable pain which brought him almost to screaming point, and at least once he thought he was going to die. Once the acute phase of the attack was over the main problem was his extreme weakness. In late-September he could just walk on the verandah, and in early-November was still virtually bedridden. Even by February when he insisted on public work again he was still weak and his health was erratic. By then he had also undergone surgery for piles. The main obstacle to his recovery was his refusal to eat a normal, mixed and sustaining diet. His doctors, friends and the faithful Kasturbhai despaired of his 'crankisms' as he called them.[51] His wife's dumb misery (cow-like as he described it) put considerable pressure on him, as did friends' concern and his natural will to live. Early in his illness he had asked about substitutes for cow's milk which he would not drink because he had vowed not to in South Africa. Eventually he agreed to drink goat's milk to build up his strength. Although he did not thus break the letter of his vow and was at pains to justify himself at the time, he later came to feel that he had broken it in spirit.[52] This time of enforced rest not only made Gandhi brood deeply on the nature of truth and truth force; he also experienced during it the outpouring of concern from friends, and thus, as he put it, the love of God to man. In response he felt he was called the more to serve humanity, and pondered long on how to purify his life for this role of service.

All-India satyagraha

By February 1919 Gandhi felt that an issue of such proportions was at stake in public life that, despite his continuing weakness he must resume a public role, even from his sick-bed, if he wanted to be at ease with his conscience. The occasion was the government's decision to arm itself in peacetime with powers to deal with terrorism through the so-called Rowlatt bills, popularly named after the chairman of the committee which had reported in 1918 on 'revolutionary conspiracies in India' and advised the adoption of strong powers to deal with them.[53] Gandhi was greatly agitated by them and as early as 9 February envisaged that he might now 'have to fight the greatest battle of my life.'[54] His subsequent all-India satyagraha of protest was the final phase in the forging of a man ready to play a public role in India's national affairs, a process of forging which had begun in South Africa and culminated in the gradually expanding work of the returned exile during the First World War. The Rowlatt satyagraha, as it has become known, crystallized Gandhi's inner determination to begin a new phase in his life. Henceforth he was prepared and even eager to carry his deep private convictions to the public test and to challenge both the government and the country's leading politicians. Through this experience he also began to refine and refashion satyagraha into a continental movement on a broad political issue, rather than a sharply focused mode of opposition to a specific wrong, using well-tried elements as well as new ones such as the *hartal*, or temporary stoppage of work. He also began to test out an India-wide network of publicity and support, and generated an even broader and more definite public image.

The immediate issue facing Gandhi early in 1919 was the Government of India's determination to have adequate powers to deal with terrorism when the Defence of India Act lapsed after the war. The powers sought in the Rowlatt bills were not excessive when judged by the measures deemed necessary even by democratic governments to combat terrorist violence in the later twentieth century. They included special trials without juries and powers to restrict and imprison suspects. The liberal Secretary of State was profoundly uneasy, finding much in the proposals 'most repugnant'; but Delhi pressed on hurriedly, pushing the main measure through the Viceroy's Legislative Council, despite the votes of all the Indian members and widespread political hostility to the measures manifested outside that decorous arena of debate. The powers were ultimately hedged with safeguards. They did not of course apply to ordinary citizens and political activity but only in cases of anarchical and revolutionary movements, and were only for three years. A further measure which would permanently have altered the criminal law was dropped. A public furore continued, despite these concessions. Those active in politics saw it as proof that despite the projected reforms the imperial government was concerned to retain, if only in reserve, its capacity to use the iron fist in defence of imperial rule; and it seemed to make a mockery of any politics of co-operation within the legislatures if government could override political opinion in this manner. In the end the act turned out to have been more trouble than it was worth to the government, for the powers were never used.[55] Gandhi responded to the news of the bills and the government's use of its official majority to achieve their passage through the legislature with unwonted anger and forthrightness. His criticism challenged the government in that crucial and sensitive area of *izzat*, prestige, and legitimacy, where it was particularly vulnerable. In his eyes this was hypocrisy and immoral repression.

> To me, the Bills are the aggravated symptoms of the deep-seated disease. They are a striking demonstration of the determination of the Civil Service to retain its grip of our necks. There is not the slightest desire to give up an iota of its unlimited powers and if the Civil Service is to retain its iron rule over us and if the British commerce is to enjoy its present unholy and privileged position, I feel that the Reforms will not be worth having. I consider the Bills to be an open challenge to us. If we succumb we are done for.... If the Bills were but a stray example of lapse of righteousness and justice, I should not mind them but when they are clearly an evidence of a determined policy of repression, civil disobedience seems to be a duty imposed on every lover of personal and public liberty.... For myself if the Bills were to be proceeded with, I feel I can no longer render peaceful obedience to the laws of a power that is capable of such a piece of devilish legislation ... and I would not hesitate to invite those who think with me to join me in the struggle.[56]

To the uneasy Secretary of State he privately argued that government insistence 'in the teeth of universal opposition is an affront to the nation. Its repeal is necessary to appease national honour.'[57] Gandhi's response to the Rowlatt bills also dealt with the tactical problem of Indian helplessness in the face of the government's insistence. This had shown up the ultimate impotence of the politics of petitioning as practised by Congress and the Westernized politicians for decades; yet it also invited the opposite and potentially destructive political reaction, namely violence. He offered non-violent civil disobedience as a viable alternative and asked some of the most traditionally moderate political leaders to co-operate with him for this reason. 'I think the growing generation will not be satisfied with petitions, etc. We must give them something effective. Satyagraha is the only way, it seems to me, to stop terrorism. From this point of view, I am justified in seeking your help.'[58]

From late February Gandhi was active in orchestrating protest on the issue and channelling it into satyagraha.[59] To his ashram came a perplexed group of Bombay and Ahmedabad Home Rulers, looking for guidance on a national and political issue from the ailing man whose local campaigns they had assisted or followed with sympathy. From that meeting emerged a new organization, the Satyagraha Sabha, and a pledge to resist the Rowlatt legislation. Gandhi took ultimate responsibility for this outcome, and the pledge as a mode of action as well as its wording bore all the marks of his guiding hand.

Being conscientiously of the opinion that the Bills ... are unjust, subversive of the principle of liberty and justice, and destructive of the elementary rights of individuals on which the safety of the community as a whole and the State itself is based, we solemnly affirm that, in the event of these Bills becoming law and until they are withdrawn, we shall refuse civilly to obey these laws and such other laws as a Committee to be hereafter appointed may think fit and we further affirm that in this struggle we will faithfully follow truth and refrain from violence to life, person or property.[60]

Gandhi told the Viceroy of this by telegram, saying that unless the government reconsidered its stand he would feel bound to publish the pledge and recruit more signatories. He used the same arguments as he had before – the legislation was symptomatic of a basically wrong official attitude and augured ill for the reforms – adding the affirmation he had made in Kaira, that all governments ultimately owe their power to the will of the people. Having at last taken a public stand on the issue he felt at peace with himself, and prepared for a struggle which he saw as a step towards swaraj.[61] There followed a phase of intensive publicity as Gandhi made known his views and suggestion, in person, through the press, the Satyagraha Sabha and his adherents from the Home Rule Leagues. In the Bombay Presidency at least the campaign centred on the pledge was carried to district towns and villages, to industrial workers and to Bombay's commercial communities. Gandhi seems to have intended Bombay city and Gujarat to be the heart of the movement rather than trying to organize from the grass roots a continental campaign, because there in his home region he and his most trusted colleagues like Vallabhbhai Patel knew the area and people and could control the campaign. Whatever his intention, that area was the most warm in its response: by mid-March between 600 and 800 had signed the pledge in the Prsidency. Elsewhere support was patchy, and the politically active and aware showed in their meetings and newspapers considerable hesitation at his proposal; some publicly denounced it, including a group of senior politicians in the Imperial Legislative Council, and others felt for less high-minded and more personal reasons that he was a Gujarati upstart, intent on rocking the political boat, and threatening to undermine the followings of existing leaders.

Satyagraha in opposition to powers designed to control terrorists was difficult to contrive for high-principled protesters committed to non-violence, a difficulty some of Gandhi's friends as well as critics pointed out. He wracked his brains to find a solution to the problem experiencing sleepless nights as he agonized. Inspiration came at last in the early hours of one morning – the *hartal*, a traditional expression of mourning by stopping work, to be pressed into political service and observed for a day with prayer and fasting as a prelude to this holy fight. The day was fixed, at very short notice, for 6 April. Despite the small numbers of converts to his cause, Gandhi went on his way, cool, unruffled and single-minded, insisting that the press and his supporters should adopt a high moral tone and refrain from bitterness and abuse.[62] Amazingly, the call for *hartal* received some support throughout India, particularly in towns and cities, though not working and attending meetings was the common form rather than prayer and fasting. In Bombay, for example, four fifths of shops shut, and the police admitted that it was a strategic success for Gandhi. In UP, Punjab and Bihar *hartal* was very evident in large towns though confined to them. But in Madras, CP and Bengal response was less widespread. However, the number of committed satyagrahis who actually signed the pledge as opposed to shutting businesses or attending meetings was very small – somewhere around one and a half thousand in Bombay Presidency by the day of the *hartal*, but far fewer in the rest of the sub-continent taken together. Some more permanent protest had to be achieved, however, and, as Gandhi had told the Viceroy, a committee (headed by him) decided on laws other than the offending Rowlatt act as the targets for civil disobedience. The choice fell on prohibited literature because this was possible for individuals, was unlikely to lead to violence and indeed would be educative as the literature selected included *Hind Swaraj* and an unregistered (and therefore illegal) news sheet, *Satyagrahi*, which Gandhi began on 7 April.

The records of these uprecedented days of widescale public participation in novel styles of politics show, however, that where Gandhi's call to satyagraha was supported it owed its strength not to any true mass support for his ideals but to the momentum of local politics in each particular area, often reflecting genuine dislocation of public and individual life by wartime pressures; and to the availability of political leaders who saw some reason to publicize his views – reasons which might include genuine commitment, but might also lie deep in pre-existing political loyalties and circumstances. Gandhi's valiant attempts at publicity and at control through his own presence, through the press, the Satyagraha Sabha and his Home Rule League supporters were patchily organized. Most obviously this was evident when Delhi observed *hartal* a week early. It also proved easier to arouse feeling by an emotive call and strategy for a particular day than to generate longer-lasting and disciplined action; and further, it was all too possible for the campaign to slip entirely out of control of recognized local political leadership and to degenerate into violence, as in Delhi and Lahore, and even in Gandhi's own Gujarat.[63]

Violence ultimately destroyed the Rowlatt satyagraha. The government treated Gandhi with as light a hand as possible and in the hope of avoiding trouble kept him within the Bombay Presidency. But taking him off a train heading north and returning him to Bombay was widely publicized as an 'arrest'; rumours spread and precipitated violence in several Gujarati towns, including Ahmedabad, and with even more disastrous political consequences in Amritsar in the Punjab, where Gandhi's plight coincided with the arrest of two local politicians. In the

ensuing mob violence there four Europeans were killed, the civil
authorities lost control of the city and during the subsequent state of
martial law troops fired on a civilian and unarmed crowd in the
Jallianwalla Bagh, a walled-in space from which there was no easy
escape, killing nearly 400 and inflicting numerous other casualties.
Gandhi was devastated by the violence. Of Ahmedabad he wrote to the
Viceroy's Private Secretary:

> ... in the place I have made my abode I find utter lawlessness
> bordering almost on Bolshevism. Englishmen and women have
> found it necessary to leave their bungalows and to confine themselves
> to a few well-guarded houses. It is a matter of the deepest humilita-
> tion and regret for me. I see that I overcalculated the measure of
> permeation of satyagraha amongst the people. I underrated the power
> of hatred and ill will. My faith in satyagraha remains undiminished,
> but I am only a poor creature just as liable to err as any other. I am
> correcting the error. I have somewhat retraced my steps for the time
> being.... My satyagraha ... will, at the present moment, be
> directed against my own countrymen.[64]

Gone were the heady days of the previous week when Gandhi had
marvelled at the Bombay crowds who bathed in the sea and then
processed to a meeting on the *hartal* day, and when he had with his
friends and volunteers sold prohibited literature and been showered
with rupee notes by people insisting on paying more than the asking
price. Now he tried in person to soothe the crowds in Ahmedabad and
Bombay, urging them to realize that swaraj would never be achieved
through violence, and himself underwent a three-day fast of personal
penitence. Just as in the face-to-face situation of the ashram he had
imposed suffering on himself as a result of wrong-doing among the
members, now in the context of the nation he fasted because of the
actions of those who purported to follow him, thereby in a new way
personalizing and moralizing politics, as well as using a well-known
theme within Hindu tradition. On 18 April he advised the end of civil
disobedience, though the preaching of satyagraha in the sense of truth
and non-violence was to continue. He admitted that he had made the
mistake of a 'himalayan miscalculation' in inviting people to disobey the
law before they knew how to obey the law freely and intelligently out of
a sense of duty. In private, however, he argued that the roots of violence
lay not in satyagraha or any spirit of disobedience it was alleged to have
engendered, but in public distrust of the forthcoming reforms, resentment at the Rowlatt bills and Muslim fears of allied intentions towards
Turkey. It was these deep and widespread causes of violence which
satyagraha had proved unable to restrain, and he argued that there could
be no peace in India until something was done about these issues. The
government should in fact regard satyagraha as an ally![65]
 Satyagraha in its attenuated form was still formally operative until
June when Gandhi began to consider the renewal of civil disobedience.

Despite the searing experience of the April violence he still believed passionately in his method. 'A movement like satyagraha, designed as it is to work a moral revolution in society so far as the method of attaining reforms are concerned, cannot be stopped for the vague fear of unscrupulous or ignorant persons misusing it.'[66] He envisaged it being restricted to people and places carefully chosen by himself precisely to avoid such 'misuse'. He planned to be the first satyagrahi himself and laid down detailed instructions for controlled, individual satayagraha to follow if he were arrested, after a period of peace and propaganda. In the end the Delhi and Bombay governments came to a compromise with him because they were convinced he really wanted an opportunity to end the movement. For his part he argued publicly that though the Rowlatt legislation remained, there were signs of government's willingness to listen to public opinion on this and other key issues and that he, as a satyagrahi, had a duty not to embarrass the government. Almost certainly further elements in his thinking, beside his perception of the satyagrahi's proper role, were the signs that a wide range of public figures were deeply worried by satyagraha and its destructive potential; even in Bombay and Gujarat, the heartland of his support, public apathy had replaced enthusiasm, and some of his closest supporters on whom he relied were wavering. Satyagraha was in effect disintegrating, and Gandhi's gesture at least saved some moral prestige for the method and for himself.

Although the Rowlatt satyagraha did not succeed in gaining the repeal of the Rowlatt act and precipitated violence rather than preparing the way for swaraj as Gandhi had hoped, its somewhat inglorious end masks the immense significance it had in Gandhi's own life. From now on he was an all-India public figure, both in his own estimation and in the eyes of those around him, in government circles and among the politically aware and active. For himself, he still believed that his calling was essentially religious, but that in following it he could no longer keep out of politics on a wide scale. He wrote in mid-1919,

> My bent is not political but religious and I take part in politics because I feel that there is no department of life which can be divorced from religion and because politics touch the vital being of India almost at every point. It is therefore absolutely necessary that the political relation between Englishmen and ourselves should be put on a sound basis. I am endeavouring to the best of my ability to assist in the process.[67]

In his political activity Gandhi was now prepared to challenge the established politicians, even in their own citadel of Congress, whereas in 1918 he had refused to take a stand against them. In the Congress meeting of December 1919 he urged members to respond to the Royal Proclamation which accompanied the reforms as the earnest of a new era of co-operation and to implement the reforms despite their inadequacy. He announced that if they declined to do so he would challenge their

position in a country-wide campaign, saying that they had failed their
cultural tradition and the duty that culture demanded of them if they did
not respond to the hand which had been offered. In retrospect he
thought that this session marked his real entry into Congress politics.
But despite this new all-India role, he felt isolated and lonely by
comparison with his work in South Africa; he admitted that even his
closest colleagues did not give him the sense of fellowship and security
he had enjoyed there.[68] The ebbing of support for satyagraha increased
his loneliness. Yet even those who opposed Gandhi's novel stance and
technique were forced to acknowledge that he was now a political
power to be reckoned with. One venerable Bombay political veteran
wrote of Gandhi working grave mischief and possibly provoking
incipient rebellion, and even the sympathetic Srinivasa Sastri who led
the SIS on Gokhale's death feared Gandhi would injure their country,
even if unwittingly.[69]

The government, too, recognized that it had on its hands a man who
held his beliefs with embarrassingly fanatical intensity, whose public
repute and influence might well be of use to them, but whose activities
it would henceforth have to watch and control in as wary and delicate a manner as possible. The exasperated Viceroy commented to the
Secretary of State,

> Dear me, what a d ... d nuisance these saintly fanatics are! Gandhi is
> incapable of hurting a fly and is as honest as the day, but he enters
> quite lightheartedly on a course of action which is the negation of all
> government and may lead to much hardship to people who are
> ignorant and easily led astray.[70]

Above all the Government of India was determined to avoid making a
martyr of Gandhi by interning him. Rather than make him a focus for
discontent they hoped to enlist him on the side of law and order, though
they were prepared to deal with him firmly and were convinced they
were on good ground in so doing. The Viceroy's private secretary
engaged with Gandhi in a series of personal letters which were friendly
and even bantering in tone when Gandhi himself asked that they should
keep in close touch, as he had done in South Africa with Smuts' private
secretary. Maffey now exhorted Gandhi to see that his personality and
repute gave him a huge responsibility to act circumspectly and for the
public peace. In one letter at the time of Gandhi's penitential fast he even
warned him against fasting too much because the government needed
his influence working at full horsepower, having acknowledged earlier
in the letter Gandhi's 'almost incredible work in calming excited
feelings'.[71]

Latterly officials were well pleased that Gandhi did seem to be acting
as a soothing influence. Their main problem was his extreme unpredictability – highly unsettling to the orderly official mind which liked
to predict and plan. The Governor of Bombay was astounded when

Gandhi actually asked him in the early days of May 1919 to sign a pledge to wear swadeshi clothes! Later he wrote of Gandhi that 'the proper place for a saint is heaven, not the Bombay Presidency and he is paradoxically trying to make it into a hell.'[72] As the government came to its strategic compromise to enable Gandhi to stop the campaign entirely it admitted that it really did not know what his plans were.[73] Ironically and in a way which was to be repeated in subsequent decades, by treating Gandhi as a special case rather than as a run-of-the-mill agitator, by using his influence and co-operating in the style of highly personalized political contacts which he had fashioned in South Africa and wished to repeat in India, the government boosted Gandhi's all-India role and standing. His easy access to and informal relations with government officials increased his own confidence in his ability to perform a national role, and was also an element in his expanding political influence and repute in the estimation of his compatriots.

Yet Gandhi was still weakly founded as an all-India campaigner, compared to his strength as a magnetic personality and wielder of emotive public symbols. The course of the Rowlatt satyagraha and its ultimate disintegration showed that his new style of political action, if it was to become a mass rather than individual mode, depended on the co-operation of local leaderships and on the nature of provincial or even more local circumstances which prompted people to participate in it. So far Gandhi did not have the support of disciplined local leaders who could do his work for him: he realized belatedly that the only method of real control was drastically to circumscribe the numbers of participants and to direct them himself. He did not have the organization to lead and control a sustained campaign even in the Bombay Presidency, let alone throughout the subcontinent. It was not until he entered Congress politics on a permanent basis, in some measure captured it and began to refashion it into a properly structured organization for disciplined action, that he began to make good this lack.

However, in 1919 he took a great step towards becoming a national communicator and educator through the press. In South Africa he had learned how important the press could be in politics, for good and ill. He had taught himself there to use the written word and he continued to do so in India, for example using leaflets in organizing and explaining the Ahmedabad and Rowlatt satyagrahas. Now he acquired in May 1919 editorial control of two weeklies, *Young India* and *Navajivan*, run by sympathetic Bombay men who had co-operated with him in his local campaigns in Gujarat. These paper in English and Gujarati were to become the heirs of *Indian Opinion*, published from Ahmedabad. They were intended by him to educate the public in satyagraha, and in order to preserve their independence from commercial considerations and pressures Gandhi refused to let them take advertisements, just as he had when he began to operate *Indian Opinion*. Besides giving him a permanent public platform, continual 'media exposure' as later experts in the moulding of public personalities would call it, these outlets gave Gandhi personal contentment; for, whether or not a satyagraha campaign was in operation, he could publicly pursue his quest for truth and spread his ideals.

Thus was Gandhi forged into a public man, ready and equipped to become a national leader with a new message and a new style. The South African exile had found his feet in Indian public life, but his stance was still idiosyncratic and even ambivalent, for neither politicians nor officials knew what to make of him or could predict his attitudes and activities. Almost certainly Gandhi could not either. How his specifically Indian identity and career would develop, how the Mahatma would relate to the Indian nation, was still an open question.

PART II

Indian identity: Mahatma and nation, 1920–34

5

NON-CO-OPERATION

The road to swaraj?

In 1931 Winston Churchill proclaimed that he found it nauseating and humiliating that Gandhi, a 'seditious fakir', should hold talks with the Viceroy of India. Despite his angry misunderstanding of Gandhi and of the realities of the Indian situation, Churchill highlighted with characteristic vividness the measure of the change in that situation, and Gandhi's position within it. In little more than ten years the man who was profoundly shocked by his own ignorance of his homeland and the violence his attempted satyagraha had triggered in 1919 was able to speak for Congress to the sovereign's representative during a hiatus in a powerful national movement of non-co-operation against the raj. In the decade and a half following the Rowlatt satyagraha Gandhi found his Indian identity and forged his Indian public role, and the personal resolution of issues left open in late 1919 was inextricably linked with the problem of India's own identity. As an individual taking up a permanent public and political role Gandhi had to come to terms with the realities of Indian society and politics. He did so in the context of slackening British control and the devolution of power to Indian 'representatives' in the provinces under the 1919 reforms, which forced Indians increasingly to consider their public, common identity. Were they a nation or a conglomerate of peoples, communities and interests jostling against each other for power? On their answer would depend the relationship they would seek with their rulers. Gandhi was fervently committed to the belief that India was one nation, and to the task of building what he saw as true swaraj, a new society and polity, where imperialism had no place. In his work towards this goal the identity of the Mahatma and an Indian nation were interwoven.

Although Gandhi had used satyagraha briefly in India against certain aspects of the British raj, such as its land revenue structure, it was not until 1920 that he attempted to launch non-co-operation against it as a total system. In March 1922 he stood trial for inciting disaffection towards the legally established government in India, technically on the evidence of articles in *Young India*, but in effect for leading a movement of non-co-operation from late 1920 to 1922. He pleaded guilty, calling himself 'an uncompromising disaffectionist and non-co-operator' in contrast to his former stance as a 'staunch loyalist'.[1] He pointed to 1920 as the critical time in this change, when British handling of the fate of the Muslims' Khalifah after the war and of those responsible for the Jallianwalla Bagh shooting convinced him that he must totally oppose the raj. It would be too simple to accept this statement at its face value, to contrast a loyal and disloyal Gandhi before and after 1920: his 'loyalty' in 1919, indeed from 1909, was of a very guarded and conditional quality, depending on a hope for the future rather than the present practice of the raj. However, in 1919 he had still retained that hope, and had urged Congressmen to co-operate with the British in the constitutional reforms. But during 1920 he became severely critical of the raj and almost devoid of any hope that a connection between India and Britain would allow Indian equality and growth to full nationhood. In July 1920 he wrote publicly of his disaffection; within weeks was speaking of the raj as satanic, and saying that it was his moral duty to work for the end of British rule unless it was radically transformed.[2] Yet, even then, he still hoped that such a transformation might occur and that an equal India and Britain could retain a special bond.[3]

Of the two reasons Gandhi gave for his changed attitude to the British raj in 1920, the most wide-ranging in its implications was the status of the Sultan of Turkey, the Muslim's Khalifah, after the war, and the frustration by the British and their allies of the claims made by the Khilafat movement in India, with which Gandhi became increasingly involved from 1919. At first sight it seems strange that a Hindu Mahatma and self-professed nationalist should keep company with ulema and fierce believers in a pan-Islamic community. But his stance was essentially a natural progression from the status he had prized in South Africa as spokesman for Muslim grievances, and from his championship of the Ali brothers during the war, in an attempt to achieve a similar position in India. The claim of the Khilafat movement was that the Sultan of Turkey, despite defeat, should retain sufficient temporal power to defend the faith, should remain guardian of Islam's major holy places, and that the geographical centre of Islam should remain under Muslim control. Indian Muslims in the movement claimed that these were issues of faith, and that they were entitled to protection of their faith under the 1858 Royal Proclamation (which Gandhi had himself invoked in South Africa in defence of Indian equality). If their faith was endangered, their loyalty to the crown would be endangered. They also claimed that several statements by Western leaders, including President Wilson's famous Fourteen Points, were 'pledges' that the Khalifah's status would be protected. The Viceroy was apprehensive about Muslim sentiment, as he and his predecessor had been throughout the war, but the terms of the eventual treaty of Sèvres lay with London and its allies, and there the protests of Indian Muslims had no effect.

It was in fact a minority of Indian Muslims who sympathized with the cause of Pan-Islam or were greatly perturbed at the Sultan's plight after the war, and therefore it was a minority with whom Gandhi chose to make common cause. But he spoke grandiloquently as if all the subcontinent's Muslims were united behind the Khilafat movement and its claims. It seems that in its early stages the movement attracted only some younger, educated Muslims from north India and a group of prosperous Bombay Muslim merchants who were prepared to finance it provided it did not degenerate into violence. The evidence of a 'Khilafat day' in October 1919, when Gandhi urged Muslims and Hindus to observe *hartal* on the lines he had recommended in protest against the Rowlatt legislation, suggests very patchy support from Muslims, and that even in Muslim majority areas such as Bengal and the Punjab, few were interested. However, at the end of December 1919 a range of those interned as a wartime security measure were released, including the Ali brothers, and they joined forces with the more extreme exponents of the Khilafat cause. Control of the movement slipped out of the hands of the more cautious and judicious Bombay men, passing to the fiery sparks from northern India and their supporters among Islam's religious leaders who controlled what was said in local mosques and could reach the poor, ignorant and illiterate. As a result the movement deepened and widened, particularly among the large and predominantly undeucated Muslim populations of Bengal and Sind, and in UP among younger educated men, disgruntled at the political conservatism of the older Muslim politicians, and among small landowners and urban artisans, already disturbed by Pan-Islamic propaganda and wartime economic hardship. In Sind, for example, at a Khilafat conference in February 1920, the largest day's attendance was 15,000; local Muslim clerics were the main speakers, and thousands of rupees were collected for the cause.[4]

Gandhi's involvement with the Khilafat movement laid him open to considerable Hindu misunderstanding and criticism. But he countered this with the assertion that he felt morally bound to campaign on the issue as one of right and wrong, just as he had in Champaran and Kaira and against the Rowlatt legislation. He believed this was a religious issue for Muslims, as well as a case of broken official pledges to which he could not be party by inaction. But it was not just to satisfy his conscience as one who claimed to serve the public that Gandhi sought out such unlikely colleagues. He also hoped to be able to use the Khilafat movement to mould public life according to his own standards and to forward causes he had consistently made his own as central to the creation of swaraj. He proclaimed this intention openly in *Young India* in May 1920.[5]

I hope by my 'alliance' with the Mahomedans to achieve a threshold end – to obtain justice in the face of odds with the method of

Satyagrah[a] and to show its efficacy over all other methods, to secure Mahomedan friendship for the Hindus and thereby internal peace also, and last but not least to transform ill-will into affection for the British and their constitution which in spite of its imperfections has weathered many a storm.

Privately he had just written to the trusted Maganlal Gandhi about how important he felt the movement to be for creating communal unity and displaying the nature and potential power of non-violence; he confided that he believed that if he did not pursue this work he would be disregarding his real *dharma* or duty, and would risk jeopardizing everything he hoped to achieve, and his own *moksha* or salvation. So significant was the Khilafat work to him that it became part of his subconscious life, and he admitted to dreaming about it.[6]

Campaigning for the Khilafat cause did not just bring Gandhi peace of mind in following his particular sense of vocation. It also profoundly influenced his role and standing in Indian politics. Personally it brought him to the point of advocating non-co-operation with the British in a broad spectrum of activities which were crucial to the functioning of the raj, and it gave him a receptive audience, unlike the stony gound he had encountered when he mooted satyagraha on the issue of the Rowlatt legislation. Late in November 1919 at an all-India conference held in Delhi on the Khilafat question Gandhi first used the expression 'non-co-operation', though he had not worked out its implications then. By early March 1920 he was advocating withdrawal of services by those who held honorary and paid positions with the raj as a last resort; and in mid-March he became the principal member of a committee to discuss details, which suggested several stages of non-co-operation, starting with relinquishment of titles and honours, then resignation by legislative council members, and culminating in refusal to pay taxes. Late in June he also began to advocate refusal to participate in the forthcoming elections under the 1919 reforms, as a further element in non-co-operation.

The Khilafat movement also brought Gandhi to a new position of leadership and leverage in Indian politics. Increasingly Muslim politicians looked to him for ideas and sections of the Muslim population saw him as their spokesman. But as the movement gained in popularity and its tone became more strident Gandhi was hard pressed to control the violence inherent in it. Initially as the ally of the Bombay leadership he had not found this a problem, but when the leadership swung into the hands of the more extreme early in 1920 he felt constrained to think out a more radical plan of campaign to contain them, and insisted in lengthy meetings with Muslim religious leaders that non-violence was absolute precondition of any assistance he might give them. However much they disagreed at heart with such a total ban on violence, the Khilafat leadership needed Gandhi, not just for his creativity in forging new styles of political opposition to the raj, but because of his growing popular repute, and also – most crucially – because he seemed to be able to secure sizeable support for their cause among Hindu politicians, who would otherwise have had little truck with such a specifically Muslim and international issue. Without Hindu support non-co-operation would merely weaken the public position of Indian Muslims, leaving offices open for Hindus to step into and replace them. At least some Hindu politicians also saw a need for Gandhi, as the means to a broader cross-communal alliance in order to put more pressure on the British, and as a guarantee against the eruption of violence as Muslim disquiet became more widespread and populist. The new standing Gandhi had acquired as a linchpin between Hindu and Muslim politicians, as well as the deep reservations about him in both groups, was clear in June 1920 when there was an important gathering of Khilafat and Congress leaders at Allahabad. Many Muslims were riled by Gandhi's apparently dictatorial behaviour, although they supported his idea of non-co-operation; and some of the Hindus were deeply worried about his new strength through his Muslim alliance, yet saw the perils of opposing him, given his increasing all-India influence. This influence was in contrast to the débâcle of the attempted Rowlatt satyagraha. Then Gandhi had lacked any network of supporters who could put his plans into action across the subcontinent. Now through the Khilafat committees which spanned India there was something more like a genuine continental framwork of organization which he could use to implement non-co-operation.

A Muslim cause alone, however, could never have given Gandhi the position of dominance he achieved in Indian politics by the end of that year. A broader issue, on which Hindus were particularly sensitive, became central to his public work and added greatly to his continental standing. This was the issue of military violence in the Punjab in response to public violence during the Rowlatt satyagraha, hurtfully sharpened for Indians by the official report into events in the Punjab, and by public reaction in Britain. E.S. Montagu, a liberal Secretary of State, had always disliked the stern paternalism for which the Punjab government had been famous for decades; when he realized that allegations of brutality during martial law were being made he instituted an official enquiry by a committee headed by a former Solicitor-General for Scotland, Lord Hunter. Indians immediately criticized its composition and status, Congress's own committee of inquiry refused to co-operate with it, and its report, published in May 1920 was condemned as a racially insulting cover-up. In retrospect what is perhaps more surprising than the Indian response was the degree of condemnation the Hunter report contained of General Dyer's implementation of martial law, including the Jallianwalla Bagh firing, and the Government of India's even severer criticism of Dyer. His career in the Indian army was forcibly finished; but Indian opinion, already sore, was even more offended by the support given to Dyer in Britain among politicians and the public. At issue was not just the truth about events in the Punjab, but in Indian minds the likely sincerity of the raj in granting political reform if its officials were capable of treating Indians as anything but equal, and if some of the British electorate and members of Parliament were overtly racialist.[7]

The timing of the outburst of Indian political feeling on the questions generated by events in the Punjab played fortuitously into Gandhi's hands, coinciding with the deepening of Muslim agitation on the Khilafat issue. It gave him the cause which boosted his standing among Hindu politicians who were now even more doubtful of the value of the 1919 reforms. But Gandhi had been involved in the Punjab affair for months as a member of the Congress's own committee of enquiry. Furthermore he had become the most influential member of that committee, partly because some of its members were busy with their professional affairs, and partly because its amateurishness seems to have so affronted his sense of the necessary accuracy and rectitude in the conduct of public affairs that he assumed control of the final stages of compiling its report. Motilal Nehru, senior UP Congressman and eminent lawyer, was another of the committee members, and he acknowledged Gandhi's centrality in this Congress enterprise when he wrote that an All-India Congress Committee (AICC) meeting to discuss the committee's findings held without Gandhi, who was ill, would be like playing *Hamlet* without the Prince himself.[8] Not ony did the Punjab issue give Gandhi his first important organizational and leadership role within the Congress, it was through this work that he came to know personally and to be accepted and valued by a range of prominent Congressmen such as Motilal Nehru and the Bengali, C.R. Das, who formed the core leadership of Congress between its annual seesions. Gandhi's experience and his reaction to the Hunter report had a profound effect, also, on his own view of the raj and commitment to non-co-operation as an immediate necessity. In June 1920 he condemned the official report and the government response to it as pages of 'thinly disguised official whitewash' and called on the nation to rise against 'an intolerable wrong' – not by armed rising, but by non-co-operation: '... if we are worthy to call ourselves a nation, we must refuse to uphold the Government by withdrawing co-operation from it.'[9]

By mid-1920 Gandhi's involvement with the issues of the Khilafat and the Punjab had markedly changed his position in Indian politics, both in outward terms of people's relationships with him, and inwardly as his self-perception altered. To any observant onlooker it was clear that in contrast to 1919 Gandhi now had a position of very considerable political prominence and influence, in and outside Congress, having attracted by his actions in the intervening months a range of allies and followers far broader than most existing Congress politicians. Established Congress leaders began to feel distinctly threatened by this development, and even the British were forced to recognize that they were being confronted by a new political force – moreover a very subtle one which it would be impossible to stifle with the blunt instrument of prosecution and internment. Gandhi had seen the fundamental vulnerability of the raj: its dependence on a broad range of Indian co-operation. However, advocacy of non-violent withdrawal of that co-operation was not seditious in strict legal terms, at least in the early stages of the non-co-operation plan; and even if he could have been successfully prosecuted, the government had no wish to alienate public opinion by appearing to hound a holy man.

Some months later the new Viceroy, Lord Reading, an eminent lawyer and experienced man of affairs, met Gandhi; his reaction demonstrated official recognition that the raj was no longer dealing with a backwoods lawyer who had a reputation for social work, but a fanatical idealist who was an unknown and potentially explosive force.[10]

> There is nothing striking about his appearance. He came to visit me in a white *dhoti* and cap, woven on a spinning-wheel, with bare feet and legs, and my first impression on seeing him ushered into my room was that there was nothing to arrest attention in his appearance, and that I should have passed him by in the street without a second look at him. When he talks the impression is different. He is direct and expresses himself well in excellent English with a fine appreciation of the value of the words he uses. There is no hesitation about him and there is a ring of sincerity in all that he utters, save when discussing some political questions. His religious views are, I believe, genuinely held and he is convinced to a point almost bordering on fanaticism that non-violence and love will give India its independence and enable it to withstand the British Government. His religious and moral views are admirable and indeed are on a remarkably high attitude [sic], but I must confess that I find it difficult to understand his practice of them in politics.

Gandhi's own perception of his proper role in Indian public life had also changed significantly in the early months of 1920. Now he was prepared for political work, as ordinarily understood, as a permanent concern and occupation. This was symbolized by his agreeing to take on the presidency of the Home Rule League which Annie Besant had founded. It seems that Motilal Nehru, so recently impressed by this newcomer to Congress politics, was behind the invitation to Gandhi to break out of the careful isolation from political institutions which he had preserved since his return to India. In mid-March Gandhi agonized with friends over the wisdom and propriety of accepting the honour, given his pronounced views on a wide range of public issues, particularly the need to introduce high standards of honesty into politics, to accept swadeshi as an immediate goal, Hindustani as a national language, an early redistribution of the boundaries of India's provinces on linguistic lines, and the necessity of Hindu – Muslim unity, currently via work for the Khilafat cause.[11] Late in April he agreed to accept the presidency, and published an open letter to all the League's members saying that this was a momentous decision for him, but he believed he could use the League to forward the causes with which he had identified, and which he felt would lead to self-government far more quickly that constitutional reform – he admitted the latter was of secondary importance to him. He listed the same issues he had discussed with friends, and promised to plunge the League into work on these lines, though he said it would not become a party organization or an instrument of civil disobedience.[12] However in October at a League meeting – just over 60 out of 6,000 members attended – some of the members were so disquieted at the idea that Gandhi might take the League into outright and unconstitutional opposition to the raj that they resigned, as the League's constitution was altered and its name was changed to the Swarajya Sabha. Significantly, among those who resigned was M.A. Jinnah, later leader of the Muslim League and architect of the separate state of Pakistan.[13]

A further aspect of Gandhi's plunge into the established institutions of politics was his new role in Congress. Not only was he central to the preparation of the Congress report on the Punjab, he was also asked to be a trustee of a fund for a Jallianwalla Bagh memorial – a recognition of his fundraising skills, develped in South Africa. Even more significantly, he was entrusted with the job of drafting a new Congress constitution, to make Congress more streamlined in discussion, more representative in character and equipped with officials who could maintain a year-round momentum of decisions and actions. Gandhi seems to have been the main architect of this new constitution, as other major leaders were too busy to do this laborious and time-consuming work. He noted succinctly, 'With the assumption of this responsibility I may be said to have made my real entrance into the Congress politics.'[14]

Gandhi was realistic about his new political position, having made a conscious decision to abandon his former isolation. But he still saw his political role as an aspect of his total vision of the proper goal of man and of the Indian nation in particular: as a religious vocation rather than a self-motivated urge for power in public life. He disclaimed 'sainthood' but agreed that he saw his vocation, even to political work, as essentially a religious one.[15]

> ... the politician in me has never dominated a single decision of mine, and if I seem to take part in politics, it is only because politics encircle us today like the coil of a snake from which one cannot get out, no matter how much one tries. I wish therefore to wrestle with the snake.... Quite selfishly, as I wish to live in peace in the midst of a bellowing storm howling round me, I have been experimenting with myself and my friends by introducing religion into politics. Let me explain what I mean by religion. It is not the Hindu religion, which I certainly prize above all other religions, but the religion which transcends Hinduism, which changes one's very nature, which

binds one indissolubly to the truth within and which ever purifies. It
is the permanent element in human nature which counts no cost too
great in order to find full expression and which leaves the soul utterly
restless until it has found itself, known its Maker and appreciated the
true correspondence between the Maker and itself.

Because in Gandhi's vision there was no distinction between ends and
means he was able to pursue his understanding of religion through
politics with ease of conscience. Satyagraha in its multiplicity of forms,
including non-co-operation, was truth-seeking in action – one might
say, was religion in action: its very activity would achieve the end
sought, in this case the transformation of individual and public life in
India according to the dictates of truth. In the specific context of India
under British rule it was also a novel mode of direct but non-violent
political action which offered an alternative to existing Western-style
politics which had come to appear increasingly stagnant and powerless
against British determination to control the nature and pace of reform.
Gandhi did not mince words when describing most of the contemporary practitioners of politics in the provinces, quite apart for the current
impotence of their methods. He told one lawyer,[16]

The lawyers today lead public opinion and conduct all political
activity. This they do during the few leisure hours they get for their
tennis and billiards. I do not expect that by dividing their leisure hours
between billiards and politics lawyers will bring us substantially near
Swaraj. I want at least the public workers to be whole timers and
when that happy day comes, I promise a different outlook before the
country.

Non-co-operation was also Gandhi's answer to those who argued that
only violence would move the raj. The need to offer a credible form of
political action to the coming generation was close to the forefront of
Gandhi's mind, as it had been in 1919, when he argued to those who
were timid at the prospect of satyagraha that nothing less would prevent
the spread of terrorism.[17]

Having consciously adopted the role of leader of a new form of
politics Gandhi had to expound what he envisaged as its culmination –
what was to replace the raj which he castigated as devilish. To a
somewhat incredulous political audience he offered swaraj in one year.
At a special Congress session in September 1920 he claimed that they
could achieve swaraj by late 1921 if they carried out his scheme of
non-co-operation. Laughter erupted at the very idea; but he reiterated
his belief in *Young India*. He looked to a state in which Indians could
manage their own affairs, could settle their own disputes, educate their
children, feed and clothe themselves, and keep peace between their
different communities without reference to or help from the British.
Non-co-operation properly enacted would demonstrate this capacity.[18]

All this means discipline, self-denial, self-sacrifice, organizing ability, confidence and courage. If we show this in one year among the classes that today count, and make public opinion, we certainly gain swaraj within one year. If I am told that even we who lead have not the qualities in us, there certainly will never be swaraj for India, but then we shall have no right to blame the English for what they are doing. Our salvation and its time are solely dependent upon us.

But in practical political terms at this juncture swaraj meant to Gandhi not what he had envisaged in *Hind Swaraj*. He felt that India was not ready for this, and though he worked for it in his personal life, his public, corporate activity was aimed at securing parliamentary swaraj according to the wishes of the Indian people. This would imply control over the army, the economy and taxation. As for himself, when such swaraj came he hoped to have a very long and much needed holiday![19] Such vagueness about the precise nature of swaraj was in fact part of the strength and inclusiveness of Gandhi's appeal. Young and old, rich and poor, could and did put their own interpretation on it; and no one needed to feel apprehensive about his future position. Motilal Nehru's son, the young Jawaharlal, then emerging into active politics for the first time, remembered the exhilaration he had experienced under the influence of Gandhi's appeal, but later noted, too, that Gandhi had discouraged clearer, more precise interpretations of swaraj, which might have engendered divisions and fear.[20]

In late 1920 Gandhian politics became praticable politics on an all-India scale for the first time. On 1 August Gandhi returned his own Kaiser-i-Hind, Zulu War and Boer War medals to the Viceroy as a symbol of his estrangement from the government and his belief that because political methods so far tried in India could not move such a regime he felt it encumbent upon himself to launch non-co-operation. In forging ahead with the movement rather than waiting for Congress's deliberations, Gandhi was trying to pressure Congress into accepting the new style of political agitation. He claimed that this was one of the rare moments in life when conscience (the 'still small voice' as he frequently called it) demanded an individual stand. In this instance he was so sure of himself that he did not wish to invite Congress discussion as a way of cultivating public opinion, but aimed to 'act and demonstrate its efficacy so as to command acceptance by the nation.'[21] In the September speical session held in Calcutta and in the normal December session convened that year in Nagpur, Congress agreed to most of Gandhi's strategy; to his own surprise and that of many contemporaries, he had for the time being 'captured' Congress.

Gandhi captures Congress

Yet meticulously piecing together the jigsaw of historical evidence about the way Gandhi became poised to launch a new political and the reaction of Congressmen to him in the Calcutta and Nagpur sessions does not alone bring to life either the dynamism of this small, superficially unremarkable individual, or the passionate reactions of people to him, of support, criticism, incomprehension and fear. The reality and impact of Gandhi, the living and changing personality, is hard to sense and depict, depite his outpourings in speeches and the press of his beliefs and struggles of conscience, and in part because of them, for so often they read as the required formulae of a satyagrahi searching his soul in public, rather than as the private agonizings of a real individual. Furthermore, many of the surviving records of reaction to him which provide our historical evidence tend to set him up either as a cardboard figure of piety or as a wilful and wiley destroyer, for dubious 'religious' reasons, of so much in public life that was cherished by Indian and British political practitioners alike.

To Western readers Jawaharlal Nehru's early reactions to Gandhi are possibly the best lens through which to perceive the man behind the image of a Mahatma. The two men could not have been a greater contrast. The young Nehru, immaculately turned out, carrying effortlessly the privilege of his Brahmin ancestry and the polish of his Harrow and Cambridge education, faced a middle-aged man who admitted his *bania* background with jokes about his ability to bargain and do business, and deliberately rejected his own Western training and rejoiced in his chosen peasant style of life and dress. Jawaharlal, the apple of his father's eye, who was swathed in a family's doting care, faced a celibate who had abandoned the warmth and support of normal family life. One went home to a palatial house in Allahabad, where money was no problem and discreet luxury was the norm; the other disciplined himself to the simplicities of an ashram, the plainest food and few possessions, apart from scant clothing, spectacles and a typewriter. The son of one of India's most eminent lawyers, whose life was moulded by work within the public institutions of the raj, encountered this self-confessed rebel whose vision of *Hind Swaraj* was the antithesis of the Nehrus' way of life. Jawaharlal indeed admitted how difficult Gandhi was to understand, how his language was almost incomprehensible to modern Indians, and how he and his contemporaries discussed Gandhi's quirkiness and, half-laughing, said that his fads should not be encouraged once swaraj was achieved.[22]

Yet Nehru was powerfully attracted by the personality of the older man. Gandhi was not a genial, sociable man in Western terms; there is little of the type of evidence there would be in the case of a Western politician, of the private man displayed in the intimacies of social gatherings, a few close friendships and ordinary family life. His life was organized according to a strict, puritanical regime: meals were a time for careful regard for health and self-discipline rather than for pleasure and sociability, he allowed himself little relaxation and had no time at all for hobbies. Yet we know from the observations and experiences of contemporaries that he was capable of warmth and tenderness in relationships, and showed concern for the most private details of his

Gandhi with baby, 1931

colleagues' emotional and physical lives. The man who had nursed his
own son and wife in South Africa increasingly became dietician and
physician to many Indian public men; the celibate who mourned his
early treatment of his own wife involved himself in marital counselling
when his friends were in need. His habitual sternness would relax as he
watched children play, particularly his granddaughter, Manu. It is
indicative of Gandhi, the man, that to many his pet name was 'Bapu', or
Father, and he acquired a paternal status in their families. He gave
people from varieties of Indian and European backgrounds a singular

sense of their importance and potential. He grieved for the death of friends and family, and at times he longed for the ease of companionship he had found among friends in South Africa. Beside the fanatical idealist who could be harsh and dictatorial in pursuit of what he considered right, there was also a man with a considerable sense of humour, who was often exasperated by the pomposity of many in public life, and the self-abasement and adulation of himself which so often characterized those who clustered around him.

In Gandhi Nehru found personal warmth and concern of a degree he had only encountered within his own family. As a Westernized Indian he also received from Gandhi the ability to return to his Indian roots, to take pride in his Indianness, and to relate to his poorer compatriots in ways that would have been unthinkable to his patrician father, Motilal. As Gandhi's colleague, Jawaharlal became as familiar with the farmers in the fields as the lawyers in their courts and clubs; he came to see the raj's gaols as houses of honour rather than places for the punishment of criminals which men of good standing should shun. He also experienced in 1920–1 a great sense of intoxication at being a crusader involved in a political campaign of high morality with a glorious goal in view, a campaign which actually seemed to be changing India and draining away the moral and political authority of the British.

This complex, often enigmatic yet compelling personality offered not only himself to India's politicians in 1920. He suggested as a practical alternative to existing political modes, a technique which could cut at the roots of the raj, by withdrawing from co-operation with it all those whose services, taxes and tacit support were of far greater importance than the British force of arms the raj could muster. But further, non-co-operation practised with the total non-violence he suggested also threatened the *moral* credibility of the imperial regime within India, in Britain and in the eyes of a wider international audience. Martyrdom and repression are the stuff of which nations are made, and the British realized, often with acute frustration, that they could not adopt Dyer-like tactics against a Mahatma and a non-violent movement if they wished to retain the support of what they called 'moderate' Indian opinion, not actively aligned with Congress, and of sections of their own electorate and of their allies in the Western world. It was little wonder that some Indian politicians, particularly younger men who had fewer vested interests in older styles of politics, threw in their lot with Gandhi at this stage and became his permanent colleagues and supporters for the rest of their lives. Jawaharlal Nehru was the best known. Others who rose to the highest eminence in political life before and after 1947 were two comparatively backwoods lawyers who had encountered Gandhi during his local campaigns in 1917–18, Rajendra Prasad from Bihar and Vallabhbhai Patel from Gujarat. They became respectively President and Deputy Prime Minister of India. Others with no wish for prominence or aptitude for great achievement also changed their lives in association with the Mahatma, becoming true 'Gandhians' in belief and life-style, either as individuals in their own towns and villages, or in his ashram communities at Sabarmati or later in Sevagram. Such people had little influence or role in India's main political organizations, but they provided front-line exponents of satyagraha who could be trusted to preserve non-violence.

Gandhi's emergence as a continental political leader who could sway Congress policy was not, however, a simple matter of great numbers being converted to his beliefs and style of action. Those who were truly convinced by his teachings were few in number both in 1920 and throughout his Indian career, and the decisions of Congress in 1920 to give his methods a trial were neither a foregone conclusion nor a permanent swing away from the politics of collaboration with the raj. Political leadership, in whatever context of time and palace, is a complex phenomenon. It is essentially a relationship between the leader and those who actively follow him or acquiesce in his role, because in a certain situation he has particular resources that he can deploy to achieve the ends his adherents seek. These resources can be authority of birth or of office, access to wealth or honour, or perhaps skills vital in a specific situation, such as the ability to make a broad public appeal, to raise funds, to achieve maximum publicity, to mediate between conflicting groups, or to create a viable political strategy. In Gandhi's case this was particularly true, as he lacked initially any inherent political authority by virtue of birth or subsequent grooming by an established politician. Yet he offered his compatriots such different things as a new way of relating to their rulers and to other Indians, new opportunities for public careers, as well as (for a few) a convincing ideal and ideology. One of the clearest examples of calculated 'following' of Gandhi at this early stage was the leadership of the Khilafat movement in general, and the Ali brothers in particular. The Alis aligned themselves with him for the political benefits he could deliver to them personally and to the Khilafat movement, but only for a limited time, so long as the alliance seemed beneficial, and never as total converts to non-violence. Political leadership is always to an extent dependent on the running calculations of existing and potential followers, and is a phenomenon which, like all relationships, changes, can flourish and expand, or shrivel and decay. To penetrate more deeply into the realities of 1920 we must look at the different calculations people made in response to Gandhi's personality and plan in that particular context of Congress decision-making. Evidence from that time shows the conditions and institutions within which Gandhi had to work, and the raw material out of which he had to fashion swaraj, and the conditional quality of his leadership. Pressures, constrictions and limitations on Gandhi, even when his leadership seemed triumphantly secure, were always a reality of his Indian career. To recognize them is to acknowledge the stature of the man far more realistically than portraying him as a cardboard cut-out, a figure without humanity, whose relations with those around him were unchanged or simple.

The fact that Gandhi launched the non-co-operation movement in the press and through the Khilafat committee network before Congress met obviously put pressure on political leaders to support it to some extent if they did not wish to appear timid in the national cause. Although there was no dramatic reaction to his call on 1 August there was a degree of response in the shape of meetings and *hartals* in most provinces, most significantly in Sind, Gujarat and Punjab, areas which had never before been prominent in Congress politics. By coincidence Gandhi was appealing to new areas and levels of political support just when some of the politicians in the Presidencies, where Western-style politics had been longest established, were in disarray because of the death of their old leadership. Pherozeshah Mehta and Gokhale, who had both helped to set Gandhi on his way politically in western India and in Congress, had both died in 1915; Annie Besant was a spent force by 1920; and on the very day Gandhi launched non-co-operation the old tiger from western India, B.G. Tilak, died. The result was that virtually no one could stand out as a continental figure against Gandhi and rally those who were sceptical of non-co-operation or opposed it outright. In each locality and province Congressmen manoeuvered for position before Congress met, and often a provincial Congress's decision about non-co-operation depended on local issues and the state of local factions. Gandhi's politics became a pawn in local power struggles and where the long established Provincial Congress Committees (PCCs) did accept the strategy, as in Bengal, Bombay or UP, it was often because a faction strong enough to sway the vote feared worse results for themselves if they opposed Gandhi rather than appearing to support him or hedging their bets with a fine choice of words. The Madras PCC had to meet three times before it could make a decision, and then its views were deliberately unclear because it approved of non-co-operation yet opposed Gandhi's programme.[23] It is significant that Gandhi received particularly strong support from Congressmen in Gujarat and Bihar, where his local satyagrahas had generated enthusiasm for him and his tactics. In fact some Congress veterans like the Bengali Surendranath Banerjea decided not to attend Congress at all, so convinced were they that Gandhi's new supporters would sweep the field.

Yet Calcutta was the cradle of Western-style politics, and Gandhi himself was fearful lest the old leaders and their vested interests would effectively block any new departures at the Special Congress in September. Some of them did attempt to form the nucleus of an opposition and joined forces as they converged on Calcutta by train. But in any Congress the crucial arena was the Subjects Committee which met before the open session, hammered out resolutions to be placed before the full session, and in so doing virtually swung the whole Congress. In Calcutta Gandhi's supporters won seats in every provincial bloc on the committee, specifically fighting on the issue of non-co-operation. One Bengali paper commented that no one stood a chance in the election unless they declared for non-co-operation. The committee quickly disposed of the other resolutions for Congress, and then for two days engaged on the issue of non-co-operation, Gandhi's plan being set against a modified plan proposed by the Bengali, B.C. Pal, which would have temporarily shelved the controversial parts of Gandhi's proposal. The discussions were not only prolonged but also acrimonious: at one point Shaukat Ali had to be physically restrained from attacking M.A. Jinnah! Gandhi was determined not to agree to a compromise, possibly sensing how much support he had among the delegates. Eventually his proposal was carried in committee by the slender majority of twelve, 144 voting for it and 132 against. In the open Congress it soon became clear that opinion was flowing in his favour. Annie Besant was howled down when she attempted to speak; and when it came to the choice between Gandhi's plan and Pal's amendment (which he had lost in committee) Gandhi's plan was accepted by a majority of about 1,000, though, significantly, about half the registered delegates did not vote.

Gandhi's success, unexpected as the delegates assembled, but increasingly likely as the days passed in Calcutta, depended partly on the strength he had in the Subjects Committee, and on the fact that from it emerged only two suggested plans of non-co-operation: outright opponents had no means of registering their opposition, which probably accounted for the mass of abstentions in open Congress. But he had a substantial bloc of support in the open Congress and this was essential for his triumph. Some people muttered of 'packing' the session, but even some of his opponents discounted the accusation. It is impossible to analyse the composition of his supporters, but a considerable number appear to have been Calcutta-based businessmen, particularly those of the Marwari community, who rather like the Jews in Europe had fanned out across northern India from their original home in the west of the subcontinent, carrying in their close-knit kinship networks strong religious traditions that echoed Gandhi's own background. Another solid bloc of support for Gandhi seems to have been Muslims anxious to secure Congress support for the Khilafat movement. A 'Khilafat Special' had brought over 200 delegates, mostly Muslims, from predominantly Hindu Madras, and nearly half the Madras members of the Subjects Committee were Muslims; 43 of the 217 Bombay delegates who voted for Gandhi were Muslims simultaneously attending a Khilafat conference; and western Indian opponents of Gandhi complained bitterly of his playing 'the Muslim hand' and flooding Congress with Khilafat activists. As striking as the new Muslim influence in Congress behind Gandhi was the support he attracted from regions which had previously had little influence on Congress decisions, particularly UP, the Punjab, Bihar and the Gujarat area of the Bombay Presidency. All these were areas where he had worked as a local leader, or where he had championed a cause particularly significant locally, such as the Punjab question, and the Khilafat cause which appealed to UP Muslims. The new politics were attracting new supporters, and this was to influence established Congress groups powerfully in the ensuing months of discussions and decisions about non-co-operation. Gandhi had broken down the walls of their comparatively cosy politics and they had to consider how best to safeguard their positions in the changing situation. One Gujarati politician, for example, appealed to Sir P. Thakurdas, a substantial Bombay businessman of moderate political stance, to speak out to a wide audience to stop Gandhi undercutting existing politicians by his mass appeal.[24] He was only one of countless others anxiously reassessing their standing after the Calcutta Congress.

Deep reservations about non-co-operation and considerable remaining hostility to it and its author were evident after Calcutta. Even the AICC, which as a smaller body had to issue detailed instructions for the campaign, contained opponents and doubters, and it watered down Gandhi's plan in order to protect some of the interests of India's educated, specifically the legal profession and their precious Western education, by suggesting that boycott of courts and schools should be gradual. The main elements of the plan suggested for immediate adoption were boycott of the forthcoming elections to the reformed legislative councils, boycott of foreign goods, and surrender of titles and honorary offices. Outside official Congress bodies many politicians still complained in private and public that non-co-operation threatened their whole political style and its achievements, and that it was likely to precipitate social chaos and violence. Among the critics were two long-standing and trusted friends whose attitude must particularly have hurt Gandhi, Srinivasa Sastri and Henry Polak. One old warrior wrote in a private letter that he and Pherozeshah Mehta had always been dubious of Gandhi's

> ... sagacity and political circumspection. The man is so full of overweening conceit and personal ambition and the vast unthinking multitudes, let alone the so called 'leaders' of the hour, and the lip 'patriots', seem to be quite mad & willing ... in following like a flock of sheep, this unsafe shepherd who is bringing the country on the very brink of chaos & anarchy ... [time] will be the avenger of the wrongs this madman is now inflicting on the poor country in his mad and arrogant career.[25]

Yet most political activists hesitated to oppose Congress's official programme, and moved tentatively in support of it. Taking India as a whole, however, very few lawyers gave up their practices, few people resigned from posts or handed back their titles, and boycott of schools and colleges was an isolated phenomenon. But this masks the fact that in some areas there was real and deep public enthusiasm for the idea of the movement – in Gandhi's own Gujarat, and in Punjab, for example. The November elections give an opportunity for a clearer indication of the strength of non-co-operation, though as these were the first to be held under the new and wider franchise there is no valid comparison. The elections were duly held: for all but 6 out of 637 seats there were candidates, but few of them were Congressmen. The polls varied dramatically, from a high turn-out in Madras (over 50% in some districts) – where there was that rarity, an effective local party opposed to Congress, which made the most of its opportunity – to a low 8% in Bombay among city Hindus and 4.4% among city Muslims, and 8.5% among Hindu and Muslim urban voters in Punjab. In every province the preaching and organization of non-co-operation had some effect, and the raj's strategy of conciliating the political nation with the 1919 reforms was seriously weakened.

It had been painful for Congressmen to abandon the new legislative councils, though for some at least it made some political sense, because they feared that they would be fettered in council by a plethora of men from speical seats, such as those reserved for the landed. But they could comfort themselves with the knowledge that this was a temporary self-denial: elections would come round again when the worth of a seat was clearer. But the other facets of non-co-operation, particularly relating to their professions and their children's future, and their own Westernized life-styles enabled by the import of a range of foreign goods (particularly clothing materials) threatened to be more permanently damaging; and it was with this knowledge in mind that they came to Nagpur in central India for the regular Congress session at Christmas time. A group of them led by the Bengali, C.R. Das, floated an alternative plan to local men before the delegates began to arrive: they hoped to avoid any dramatic and immediate boycott of schools and courts, yet, realizing the new significance of a far broader range of those who were now politically aware, including those who had recently been enfranchised, they suggested a more streamlined organization for Congress to represent more people and to turn Congress into an efficient, active body.

Fourteen and a half thousand delegates converged on Nagpur – the largest number ever to attend Congress to date. Some opponents of non-co-operation stayed away; others left when they sensed how opinion was moving. But most activists with strong views took care to be there and to bring with them a contingent of supporters. The Bengal Khilafat Committe, for example, sanctioned 6,000 rupees for a special Congress train and nearly twice that for their expenses in Nagpur. C.R. Das was thought to have paid 36,000 rupees out of his own pocket to bring 250 delegates from Bengal and Assam. Gandhi himself toured the area round Nagpur in early December and elicited a wave of support. The ever-sober Times of India noted, 'it is said that he has succeeded beyond even his own expectations in converting the Central Provinces to not merely the principle and policy of non-co-operation, but into aggressive "whole-hoggers".'[26] Gandhi's proven following in western India combined with this new support was crucial, for virtually 80% of the delegates came from those areas. Observers realized that this was a Congress of a totally different order from its past history of decorous, educated discussion. No longer did the Western-educated predominate in numbers, and this had wide consequences for the future of effective political leadership. A senior government official noted the dawn of a new era of political leadership and participation.[27]

> As regards the class of persons attending, whilst many of the prominent politicians were present, the Bengal contingent included hundreds of ex-detenus and the intelligentsia, which dominated earlier Congresses, seems to have been swamped in a mass of semi-educated persons swept up from all parts of India. At the same time it would be wrong to overlook the fact which this Congress clearly brings out, namely, that the extremists have at their disposal many thousands of men who are available for propaganda amongst the masses of the most unscrupulous, reckless, and dangerous character.

As at Calcutta, so in Nagpur the composition of the Subjects Committee was vital to Gandhi's eventual strength in the open session. In the voting for every provincial bloc of the committee's members Gandhi's supporters made a clean sweep or gained a large majority, except in the case of Bengal. (Two attempts to elect the Bengali bloc failed because of differences of opinion which ended in a free fight.) Three main topics were at issue in the session – the Congress creed, the plan of the forthcoming campaign, and the new constitution on which Gandhi had been working all year. The Subjects Committee first tackled the Congress creed. The Ali brothers wanted Congress to change its professed objective to independence, while at the opposite end of the political spectrum there were still those who felt it politic to aim for a continuing connection with Britain. It was Gandhi who provided a compromise formula, that Congress's goal should be swaraj for India, but by legitimate and peaceful means. When this came before the open session most of the opposition had melted away; two of Gandhi's opponents even supported the proposal publicly, and it had an easy passage when the delegates cast their votes.

Non-co-operation also provoked hours of debate in the Subjects Committee. But out of committee came what was called the Das–Gandhi pact. C.R. Das, the wealthy Bengali lawyer and local Congress leader, who had tried before the session to co-ordinate opposition to withdrawal from courts and schools, actually moved the resolution confirming the one passed at the Calcutta Congress. It was seconded by a strange combination of known supporters of Gandhi, Khilafat leaders, and various Hindu politicians who with Das had been publicly opposed to Gandhi's plan. It was obvious that a compromise had been reached, and the question of whether those parts of non-co-operation which threatened the Western-educated and professional groups should be immediate or gradual was carefully fudged by a new choice of words. In the face of this powerful combination most of the few remaining opponents of non-co-operation sat silent, mourning the almost unanimous acceptance of it by the Congress delegates.

At the very end of the session Congress approved its new constitution which Gandhi had in effect drafted. Almost without controversy a decision was thereby made which was arguably far more important in the long term for India's political development than the decisions which had provoked such dissension in the previous days. Under this new dispensation Congress prepared to cut its links with its moderate London committee, and henceforth to rely on its strength in India alone, as a more streamlined, representative and popular political body. In future it would have a permanent executive in a Working Committee of 15; this was to be the year-round brain and power-house of Congress politics, chosen by the AICC. (The President and his allies, or those who controlled the President, were influential in the choice: and so the selection of President rather than the Congress venue was to become increasingly important.) The AICC was relegated to a lesser position under the Working Committee. Congress was divided into areas which coincided with India's natural linguistic boundaries rather than with the borders of existing administrative provinces; the number of delegates to each session was fixed in proportion to the population of each area (so preventing local swamping or 'packing'); and Congress organization was to extend down to the district level. So a shambling debating society, which could easily by swayed by canny manoeuvres, was turned into a potentially formidable national organization and fighting force.

The changes reflected all Gandhi's criticisms of current political practice, and his belief that only Indians could win swaraj for themselves. But the remaking of Congress suited many of the established politicians who had made their way under the old dispensation. C.R. Das had made the point when he paid his pre-Congress visit to Nagpur to tout for support. 1920 had shown them all that elitist styles of politics were at an end: the extended franchise was one reason, so was the achievement of the Khilafat leaders and Gandhi in reaching new and broader groups in society with an overt political appeal and recruiting them into the effective political nation. He who aspired to political leadership in the future would have to engage with the new voters and those who for the first time now saw the value of new styles of political action: either he would have to become a popular leader in his own right or construct around himself networks of allies who could reach deep into the urban sprawl or the far-flung villages of the subcontinent.

As Congress deliberated at Nagpur, *The Bombay Chronicle* reported, 'There is no manner of doubt about it that this is a Gandhi Congress.'[28] In retrospect the Chief Commissioner of the Central Provinces in whose territory these dramatic events had occurred made the same point in a letter to his chief, the Viceroy.[29]

The outstanding feature of the Congress has been the personal domination of Gandhi over all political leaders and followers alike. He has carried through the policy that he had decided for this Congress without any material modification. All opposition to his views has been overcome without difficulty, owing to his strong hold over the bulk of the delegates and visitors, with whom his word is law.

Gandhi's success at Nagpur did not mark a wholesale conversion to his ideals among the political leadership of India. Their decision was the product of complex calculations about their present and future political positions in a changing political environment. Gandhi had drawn on support both at Calcutta and Nagpur from areas, religious and social groups who had previously been of little significance in Congress. The advent of politically conscious and radical Muslims, of men from Bihar, Gujarat and CP, who had barely been on the periphery of Congress, of men whose background was rural and whose education was limited to the vernacular, changed the whole political scene. Leaders who had succeeded when politics was a matter of organizing little cliques, and occasionally drumming up wider support for a Congress session, who had controlled the local Congress from a lawyer's office, realized that they might have to change their style and that they must respond to the pressure of this new political force in their midst, Gandhi, the man whom many of them had dismissed as a crank and a do-gooder. Their decisions were often complicated by their divisions among themselves, particularly in the areas where their style of politics had been long established. Nowhere could they unite and confront Gandhi with a consolidated opposition. In each area the most radical dared not take cover with their old moderate opponents for fear of losing their local position of being in the vanguard of politics; yet they feared Gandhi might undercut them locally or defeat them in an all-India arena by virtue of his wider appeal. Therefore they chose to make alliance with the force which threatened them. C.R. Das came to his pact with Gandhi almost certainly to re-establish his reputation in Bengal, particularly among the younger generation of political activists. Those who had swung to Gandhi earlier on the matter of the creed were acting in a similarly self-defensive manner. A crisis had occurred in their cosy political world, and many of them turned it into an opportunity for rehabilitating themselves locally as more populist political leaders and acquiring for themselves all-India renown by their association with the Mahatma. Their decision was one of political expediency; it was also temporary. Their continuing attitude to Gandhi would depend on what his leadership and style of politics could do for them as individuals and for the national movement.

Satyagraha in action

So dawned 1921 for Gandhi and for Congress: to observers it seemed that a new leadership would remake the party and give it new life and style; for Gandhi it was the year in which he hoped to see swaraj. However, Gandhi found the ensuing fourteen months a time not only of great hope, but also of great grief, as it ended with murderous bouts of violence in Bombay and UP. The year which was meant to see the

advent of a new, moral politics ended with his abandonment of its
ultimate manifestation, civil disobedience, in the wake of strife and
violence which equalled the debacle of 1919. The year was one of
frenetic activity for this middle-aged saint-politician: and it concluded
with enforced rest and seclusion for him in gaol.

Although non-co-operation proved not to be the road to swaraj
Gandhi had envisaged, it was during this campaign that his public
repute was consolidated throughout India and he evolved the pattern of
life and work which was to become the foundation of his Indian
identity. We know in some detail the punishing routine he set himself
from odd comments in his correspondence, the despair of close
colleagues, and the record of some who acted as his secretaries and bore
the brunt of his astounding output. Despite his apparent physical frailty
he was capable of extraordinarily hard work, as a young student helper
during non-co-operation discovered. He marvelled at the way the
Mahatma quietly got on with correspondence and journalism, and
preparing speeches, despite streams of visitors, and milling crowds
wherever he travelled.

> So many people would be constantly crowding round him that if
> perchance he could snatch a few moments of spare time, he would
> spend them wholly on his work of reading and writing. One was
> simply amazed to find how in the midst of all this confusion he could
> keep his head cool and get through the scheduled course of his work.
> Under such circumstance, ordinary people would go mad. . . . Once
> or twice, I had even seen him cooling his forehead and head with ice.
> And yet everyday [sic], whether in his room or in the train, he would
> go on calmly and patiently writing articles for the Navajivan and
> Young India, while all round him people were making [a] noise and the
> crowds were howling outside. Such complete mastery over the mind
> seemed to me unique.[30]

Gandhi's work was extremely varied and demanding. A day would
always include receiving and writing letters, both to the well-known
and important and to the unknown who appealed to him for advice and
help; preparing press articles, particularly for the two journals which
became his mouthpiece to India; often attending and speaking at several
public meetings, particularly if he was away from home; and during this
campaign which demanded his closest attention, constant informal and
formal meetings with political leaders. No detail was too small for his
personal concern. As his colleagues prepared for the 1921 session of
Congress at Ahmedabad, he thought and wrote not only of the great
issues of policy to be considered, but of the most basic housekeeping
details for the great gathering – arrangements for bathing, siting and
cleanliness of lavatories, provision of drinking water, and kitchens for
people with different dietary habits. In the same way his letters ranged
from matters of state to the details of his correspondents' health. His

serious application to work, his gravity of face, was sometimes pierced with flashes of impish humour. He had been aggravated, for example, by the waste of paper when he had been in the habit of tearing up telegrams which flooded into his hands daily during non-co-operation. Gleefully he discovered he could turn them into envelopes, and derived singular pleasure from this ingenious economy![31]

To keep up such pressure of work he went to bed early and rose well before dawn. Often he started his correspondence between 3.30 am and 5.00 am, particularly if he had been brooding on a problem and illumination had come in the night. Besiders his work and simple meals (which took considerable preparation by those around him to conform to his standards of purity and simplicity), his days included a regular walk, which he often used to befriend a particular visitor, regular prayer, and spinning. As he had brooded in 1921 on the meaning of swaraj, using things made in one's own country, swadeshi, had gained in important for him, and within it the role of hand-spinning as an answer to many of the country's economic ills and as a symbol of each individual's dedication to the renewal of Indians' personal and corporate life. From late October 1921 he made it a solemn rule to spin for half an hour a day.[32] About the same time he also changed his mode of dress to demonstrate his concern for swadeshi and his identification with the poor of India. Clothes had always been highly symbolic for him: and now again his exterior garb was to reflect his inner conviction as he took to the swadeshi loin cloth and a shawl in cold weather, abandoning the more adequate Indian-style clothing he had worn since his return from Africa. Gandhi's routine also included a weekly day of silence to order his cluttered mind and renew his vision, as well as to complete outstanding work; from November 1921 this, too, became a regular habit backed by a vow. When he heard of the communal violence which had broken out in Bombay, not only did he fast immediately as a personal reparation to the injured, but proposed henceforth until swaraj came to fast weekly on Mondays, which was also to be his day of silence.[33]

During 1921 Gandhi was constantly travelling the length and breadth of India to publicize his programme. Unlike any politician before him he spent himself in travel, which he referred to as a pilgrimage or *pradakshina*, a Hindu form of devotion which entails walking around a holy place or person.[34] Not for him the comforts of air travel, jeeps, air-conditioning and other amenities which ease the way of a later generation of Indian politicians. Ill-sprung trucks and lorries, bullock carts, third-class railway carriages and his own two feet were his means of transport in the Indian heat and dust. It was no wonder that by the end of the year he looked worn and thin. This was to be the pattern of his public work in India – constantly available, working himself to the bone, and often saved from ultimate collapse by gaol or a bout of ill health which enforced rest on him. The social worker of Gujarat, the *guru* in his ashram, gave way to the peripatetic publicist and preacher, campaigning for truth and the national cause in his own idiosyncratic way.

Non-co-operation set the mould for Gandhi's life and work in India and clarified his own Indian identity. But as a campaign to bring the raj to a grinding halt by withdrawal of Indian co-operation it did not succeed. British administration carried on in its usual cumbersome fashion, the work of the legislatures continued and taxes were collected. (Ironically, the one area of financial embarrassment to the raj resulted from an aspect of the campaign which Gandhi and Congress had not planned – a temperance movement which hit excise revenue! Several provinces were badly hit and in late February 1922 the Governor of Madras admitted that his government's financial position was 'really desperate' largely as a result.[35]) The courts, too, continued to function, packed with lawyers and their clients. Yet something new had happened, of a different order a from anything which had previously occurred in Indian politics. Here was a widespread political agitation of striking power and novelty, directed in the name of an Indian nation against the very structures and supports of British dominion; at its helm was a master of political symbolism who had stirred the popular imagination. This was obvious to any contemporary who read the vernacular or English newspapers, or had contacts with India's towns and cities, as many of the movement's manifestations were highly visible and widely reported. Thousands, for example, attended public meetings whereas a decade earlier a turn-out of several hundred would have been significant. People of many different backgrounds took part in the wide range of activities suggested by the politicians, for non-co-operation did not require education and professional skills as qualifications for participation. Men and women, old and young, townsman and rustic could choose the action appropriate to them, from attending a meeting to closing a shop, staying away from classes, or persuading local shopkeepers to stop selling foreign cloth and liquor. The handspun cloth which Gandhi hailed as the symbol of a swaraj society became the virtual uniform of Congressmen who in an earlier generation had prided themselves on their semi-Western sartorial elegance. 'Gandhi caps' became the hallmark of the radical and patriotic. Gandhi himself presided over a great ceremonial bonfire where foreign finery was consigned to the flames – the ties and shirts reminiscent of the registration documents he had burned in a huge cauldron in South Africa as symbols of slavery. Even such notable and law-abiding Indians as Motilal Nehru now went to gaol as an honour, though before 1921 they would have considered it a shameful disgrace.

The details of non-co-operation properly belong to accounts of Indian politics;[36] but its essential features illuminate Gandhi's real position in public life and his state of mind during these tumultuous months. It was the first all-India agitational campaign which the central Congress organization attempted to lead and control. Previous 'popular' agitations had tended to be localized, run by local Congressmen, often in ways embarrassing to Congress as an all-India body with continental priorities of unity and moderation. Now through the new and vigorous Working Committee non-co-operation was developed from the centre in clear stages, starting with an emphasis on fund-raising and recruiting members for Congress, a somewhat guarded boycott of schools and courts, and the acquisition of spinning-wheels; progressing in mid-summer to the boycott of foreign cloth and the manufacture of *khadi*; and finally in late 1921 encouraging government employees to with-draw from service and permitting each area to undertake civil dis-obedience, including non-payment of taxes, if very strict conditions of preparation had been fulfilled, such as adoption of swadeshi and belief in non-violence and communal unity by those involved.

In the preparation of a plan of campaign Gandhi's role was central and his position extremely strong. He did not hesitate to use his influence. Late in July, for example, he steered Congress towards concentrating on the boycott of foreign cloth, a position mid-way between those who favoured all-out civil disobedience and those who hankered after work in the new legislatures. Reporting on this AICC meeting to the Secretary of State, the Viceroy commented, 'Gandhi's personal in-fluence was the outstanding feature, and when there was any danger he adopted the attitude that he would retire from the movement and this brought about the result he desired.'[37] Gandhi's personal dominance was equally apparent in the December session of Congress at Ah-medabad, as he again fought off attempts to change Congress policy; and most obviously when Congress gave hm 'dictatorial' powers over the movement.[38] And it was Gandhi who effectively called off civil disobedience in February 1922.

Perhaps the most significant thing about the novel movement Gandhi master-minded was not that it failed to achieve swaraj but that it had such a wide and deep effect in public life. No part of India was untouched by it, and virtually every aspect of the campaign elic-ited some public response. Few title-holders or government servants actually resigned. But several hundred lawyers gave up practice, though for many this proved a temporary holiday. Various unofficial 'courts' sprang up to deal with cases withdrawn from the government courts, notorious for their expense and delays; but just as quickly these substitutes collapsed, often because they dispensed strange justice and had only violence and social boycott to back their decisions. Attendance at schools and colleges did drop, but often this was a temporary demonstration for a few weeks, or if longer-term reflected difficult post-war economic circumstances for parents rather than political will. Economic difficulty was the main official explanation for the very marked drop in imports of foreign cloth in 1921–2. But the impact of the swadeshi aspect of non-co-operation was significant, as it was also in boosting the imports of yarn most suitable for hand-spinning. Under pressure from the politicians and local groups of pickets, some cloth merchants turned themselves temporarily into swadeshi–dealers, and many cashed in on the new fashion for *khadi* to publicize their businesses. Temperance movements, which originated as aspects of social reform, also gained the blessing of Gandhi and Congress, and several provincial govenments became anxious that the social motivation had combined with the political to reduce their excise revenue.

It is impossible to estimate the numbers of people involved in the non–co–operation movement over all. But patchy evidence suggests that the numbers of activists, quite apart from silent sympathizers, ran into thousands in each province. Groups of Volunteers, encouraged by Congress in late 1921, often attracted several thousand per province: in January 1922 the Congress in UP reckoned it had about 80,000. Many aspects of the campaign were not of course illegal: no one could be prosecuted for wearing *khadi* or drinking tea rather than toddy! So figures for convictions are barely the tip of the iceberg. But in 1921 to mid-1922 four areas each produced well over 1,000 convictions arising out of the movement. As significant as the actual numbers involved in non–co–operation was the fact that many of its sympathizers and activists were not the educated men who had made up the effective political nation in earlier years and had run the all-India and provincial Congress organizations. Country folk as well as townsmen, shop-keepers and substantial farmers, labourers in tea-gardens as well as lawyers, teachers and students heard and responded to Gandhi's call for a new sort of political campaign.

The 'popularity' of non–co–operation raises real problems for the historian, just as it did for Gandhi himself. On close inspection wher-ever the movement became genuinely popular, attracting a large-scale response, it seems that a local issue of significance to ordinary people was finding on outlet through the all-India campaign. Some of these issues were of long standing; others stemmed from the effects of a post-war economic depression in India and the resulting strains and dislocations in many relationships. Gandhi's name was often misused and his teaching misunderstood; and the appeal of the campaign was primarily its local relevance rather than its national meaning as proc-laimed by Gandhi and the central Congress bodies. As the national movement became entangled with local-level politics, local activists and protagonists used and manipulated the all-India campaign and certainly generated local support for it but at times also threatened to wreck it. In jungly Assam, for example, non–co–operation became the instrument of migrant workers in the tea-gardens who left their work and made for home in protest at their wages as the tea industry suffered in the post-war depression. In UP various local peasant movements which existed before Gandhi mooted non–co–operation in Congress found a new name, although the grievances that powered them had nothing to do with swaraj as Gandhi or Congressmen envisaged it. Here burning the hillside forests was more a protest against forestry regulations; the peasant movement in the plains was directed against landlords who were trying to make ends meet by squeezing their tenantry. Far away to the south on the Malabar coast there was a history of tension and bloody strife between Muslim cultivators and their Hindu landlords, and this erupted again in 1921. Khilafat campaign propaganda was probably the spark, but the power behind the violence of the 'Moplah Rebellion', which left some areas totally outside government control for several weeks, was long-standing local economic and communal tension. In the Madras Presidency there seem to have been four separate local campaigns, ranging from urban protest to opposition to forest regulations, which fed into the all-India movement and temporarily gave it local popularity and strength.[39]

What was happening throughout India was a new type of interaction between all-India and local politics, as a result of Gandhi's novel political style, but also because of the pressure by government and the economic effects of war and its aftermath on Indian society. Congressmen who thought and worked at least partly in national terms were indeed welcoming the interest and support of men whose sights were far more local; but the latter in turn had begun to see that a national dimension to their local activities might be beneficial, endowing them with greater political significance and strength. Yet this interaction between local and national politics, between different levels of political awareness and expertise, was fraught with difficulty for any all-India leadership – as Gandhi was ruefully to discover. He might be highly skilled in making connections in people's minds and actions between swaraj and their local experiences; but campaigns which had locally a momentum of their own proved embarrassingly divisive in Indian society and often hard to control. A national leadership might, as in 1921, cobble together a range of local agitations under the nationalist, anti-British banner of non-co-operation, but non-co-operation was consequently always in danger of falling apart, either wrecked by internecine strife, or drained of strength as local interest died away.

As Gandhi lived through 1921 he became more aware of the differences between central and local political priorities and the resulting tension within what was ostensibly 'his movement', sadly recognizing that it had a life of his own which he could not direct or control in the way and to the degree he would have wished. For example, he blessed the various temperance movements which developed once they had taken off locally, seeing that they could be used in the cause of swaraj. Other local developments were less tractable. He was deeply worried by what was happening in Assam in his name, and he tried to curb the simmering violence of the anti-landlord movement in UP.[40] It was the incipient violence in the campaign as it became localized and conformed less and less to his central blueprint which distressed and threatened him most. Finally, as the campaign moved on to the brink of civil disobedience in the form of non-payment of taxes in selected areas, it was violence which made Gandhi first postpone civil disobedience and then abandon it altogether.

In November 1921 the Prince of Wales arrived in Bombay at the start of a royal progress through India; the local Congress, in line with central Congress strategy, staged a *hartal* and a public meeting of protest which Gandhi himself addressed. But at least some of the people who listened to his impassioned speech on the need for non-violence and communal harmony were within hours responsible for violent rioting, which left injured and dead among the city's Europeans, Anglo-Indians and Parsis, victims of a lethal Hindu – Muslim alliance. Gandhi was horrified by the news, and toured the city, witnessing the destruction and attempting to bring peace. He was sickened by the admiring crowds who hailed him but had shattered his hopes, and proclaimed that there was no chance now of mass civil disobedience, given the evidence of the public mentality in Bombay.

> I have personally come deliberately to the conclusion that mass civil disobedience cannot be started for the present. I confess my inability to conduct a campaign of civil disobedience to a successful issue unless a completely non-violent spirit is generated among the people. I am sorry for the conclusion. It is a humiliating confession of my incapacity, but I know that I shall appear more pleasing to my Maker by being what I am instead of appearing to be what I am not. If I can have nothing to do with the organized violence of the Government, I can have less to do with the unorganized violence of the people. I would prefer to be crushed between the two.[41]

For two days he agonized over what to do: the 'swaraj' he had seen in Bombay 'has stunk in my nostrils', he admitted.[42] Eventually he decided to fast to make amends to the victims of violence, and advised the city's Hindus and Muslims to stay at home, repent and befriend the injured minority communities. Hardly surprisingly, local Congressmen rushed to retrieve the situation, leaders of all communities appealed for peace and reassured Gandhi of their commitment to non-violence. After three days he publicly broke the fast in a meal of fruit with representatives of each community and leading politicians, including the Congress Working Committee. But he was realistic enough to know that assurances of good will would need to be backed by solid work in implementation. 'Though a born optimist, I am not in the habit of building castles in the air.' During the fast he had experienced great inner peace, as he followed the voice of his conscience, heard after lengthy prayer and meditation in the early hours; but now he plunged back into the 'stormy ocean' of everyday politics.[43]

Stormy ocean it proved to be. He had to fight hard at Congress in Ahmedabad six weeks later against both those who wanted compromise with government and those among his supporters, particularly Muslims, who hoped for a more aggressive stance. He and the Congress Working Committee moved once more towards civil disobedience in February 1922, almost certainly with reluctance, but knowing that once they had ruled out the option of negotiation with government which a group of moderate politicians had hoped to arrange they could not continually postpone the ultimate form of non-co-operation and still retain the momentum of the movement. Then a massacre of twenty-two policemen occurred in Chauri Chaura in UP of such sickening savagery, that Gandhi decided to abandon civil disobedience whatever the results for the movement. A burnt-out police station and the charred corpses of the victims was the evidence which finally convinced him that 'the foetid smell of violence' was in the air. He admitted that he had pushed ahead despite other evidence that violence was rife, though with considerable misgivings; now he knew he must stop if non-co-operation was not to be permanently polluted with violence. By this time the young Nehru was in prison, and he and his associates were deeply agitated by Gandhi's reaction and apparent withdrawal from the crusade for swaraj. But the Mahatma reassured him by post that 'The cause will prosper by this retreat. The movement had unconsciously drifted from the right path. We have come back to our moorings, and we can again go straight ahead.'[44] Although he had realized that a mass campaign must be allowed to have a natural momentum, he had become increasingly aware in the days before the Chauri Chaura slaughter of the lack of real preparation for civil disobedience as he had advised it, even in the Gujarati district of Bardoli where civil disobedience was first envisaged. Relief probably blended with sorrow and desperation as he made the fateful decision. Satyagraha must be preserved in its purity as the road to swaraj. Congress had given him full powers over the movement at Ahmedabad; but the Working Committee and the AICC met soon afterwards and confirmed his decision, though there were some who, like the imprisoned Jawaharlal, felt that the time had come for all-out confrontation with government.[45] Following the withdrawal of the planned experiment of civil disobedience in Bardoli, and the prosecution of Gandhi himself within weeks, non-co-operation began to falter, and soon ceased to bother the government or to be a viable political strategy for those political leaders who remained at liberty.

The fate of the non-co-operation strategy and its varied manifestations, from 'Gandhi caps' and temperance to arson and murder, reveals much about the nature of Gandhi's leadership in practice after his dramatic claims to leadership in the Congress sessions of 1920. It was evident that his public reputation had spread throughout the subcontinent, and had developed in an extraordinary way, when compared with his mainly local standing in Gujarat on his return from South Africa, just six years previously. Now he found his repute as a Mahatma both embarrassing and uncomfortable. He wrote in *Navajivan* in August 1921 that in his recent travels in Bihar even in small towns thousands of people had crowded noisily round him, trying to touch his feet in the traditional Hindu greeting of reverence, and wanting his *darshan* (the sight of a holy object or person): 'they do not give me a moment's respite. I get no peace anywhere, by day or night. As for going out for a walk, it is out of the question.'[46] Others bore surprised testimony to the Gandhi phenomenon. An intelligence report in March 1921 noted the unprecedented quality of his appeal in a small UP town when it was announced that Gandhi had been invited to visit.[47]

> But the fact of his being invited was taken to mean that he was coming and it was a sight to see Hindu and Moslem villagers coming from long distances – on foot, with their bedding on their heads and shoulders, on bullock carts, on horse back, as if a great pilgrimage was going on, and the estimate was that nearly a lakh of persons had come and gone back disdappointed. It was simply touching to see how eagerly they inquired if there was any hope of his coming. Never before has any political leader, or perhaps even a religious leader, in his own lifetime stirred the masses to their very depths throughout the country and received the homage of so many people.... His influence is certainly phenomenal and quite unprecedented.

The Indian who wrote that account might possibly have been indulging in a measure of over-dramatic statement; but the sceptical Governor of Madras, who lost no love on Gandhi, was equally forced to recognize that they were now dealing with a new political phenomenon.[48]

> Gandhi is here with the whole of his gang. It is amazing what an influence this man is getting. One of my ADCs came from Calcutta with them in the train and was tremendously impressed with the huge crowds at every station, their orderliness, and absolute devotion to their leader.... *Now* I admit the position is becoming one of extraordinary difficulty. There is no doubt that Gandhi has got a tremendous hold on the public imagination ...

Part of Gandhi's public image was that of a Hindu holy man, and in places this almost shaded into veneration of him as semi-divine. There were reports of regular Gandhi *puja*, the worship offered to images of Hindu deities, of prayers to him for the birth of sons, of stories spreading about miracles he had performed and the evils which befell people who did not believe in him, of people flocking for his *darshan*, and women putting their babies in his lap and on his feet.[49] It is no wonder, given such evidence, and later idealization of Gandhi's memory after his death, that much has been made of his 'charismatic' leadership. Charisma he certainly had – that quality of personality which, independent of birth of office, attracts and compels the onlooker. But charismatic appeal was not the foundation for a stable and disciplined political following, as Gandhi found to his cost in 1921. Those who venerated him could easily turn to violence and arson. Yet this public aura of sanctity and popular devotion was a potent political resource: his compatriots and British administrators alike had to reckon with it in their political calculations of viable policies and alliances. To oppose or suppress the Mahatma was now a risky business. One senior moderate politician and lawyer, who kept close links with Congress though he was at this point the Law Member of the Viceroy's Council, meditated late in 1921 on Gandhi's place in public life, and he hinted at the complexity of Gandhi's position and the different public responses to him.[50]

> During the last twelve months or so, his influence has extended over a much larger area than perhaps we can realize. The masses may not understand exactly the full significance of his propaganda or the meaning of the Swaraj, but he has eminently been successful in exploiting their discontent, which may be attributable to half a dozen causes, and enlisting their active sympathy and support on his side. He is not a mere politican in the eyes of the masses. He has all the sanctity of a holy man attached to him, and therein lies, to my mind, the secret of his hold and also the danger of it. To the Muhammadans he has made himself invaluable, for the simple reason that but for his personality and influence they would not have been able to command the active support and sympathy of the Hindus in their agitation on behalf of Turkey. Probably, the landed classes are the only classes about whom it may be said that they are not affected by his doctrines for obvious reasons. It is intolerable to them that there should be any disturbance of vested interests which his propaganda undoubtedly entails. As against them, however we should set off the monied classes in Bombay, and to a certain extent the Marwari community in Calcutta. With the labouring classes he and his party unquestionably wield a most powerful influence which cannot be ignored. Even those who differ from him among the Moderate party, respect him for his personal character.

Although a charismatic appeal could temporarily mobilize large crowds and could make opponents wary of voicing their opinions and fears, the real foundations for continental leadership for any individual had to be a complex network of lesser leaders who, through personal commitment to him or by virtue of his position in an organized political party, could galvanize their own locality or particular group of followers or clients on his behalf. In 1920–22 Gandhi had a really strong personal political base only in Gujarat and possibly Bombay city. The Congress 'party' was not yet sufficiently strong and organized to yield him disciplined followers at the grass roots just because the central Congress had decided to follow him in 1920. As the intricacies of Congress decision-making had shown in late 1920, his acceptance as an all-India leader was the result of three distinct groups moving to support him – new areas and people finding a voice in Congress for the first time, Muslims concerned with the Khilafat issue, and established politicians making a calculated move to back him at least temporarily. In 1921–22 these three bases for continental leadership began to crumble beneath him; the ambiguities and weaknesses of his public position became increasingly clear, just at the time when his reputatioin as a charismatic figure was growing.[51]

The support of areas and groups of people who had previously had little connection with Congress or seen the relevance of its style of

politics proved in 1921 to be a two-edged weapon. The drive of their
local political interests and styles might temporarily give strength to a
continental campaign; but equally as local politics fed the national
movement local divisions and feuds began to weaken that movement,
and in places people began to feel that other political styles were
more productive than non-co-operation. In the Madras Presidency, to
take one small example, as time passed temperance societies began to
court official financial support; and many one-time 'agitators' and 'non-
co-operators' preferred the substantial benefits which accrued from
co-operation with the raj through the system of elected municipal
government or the new legislature.

More dramatically, the Muslim support which had weighed so heavily in Gandhi's favour at Calcutta and Nagpur became an embarrassment
and threat to the Mahatma. The main issue at stake between the Khilafat
leaders and Gandhi was that of violence. For the former non-violence
was an expedient, not a holy obligation, and they made no bones about
this difference. In May 1921 Gandhi was involved in delicate negotiations with the Viceroy over the Ali brothers' penchant for violence, and
he saved them from immediate prosecution by extracting from them an
assurance that they would remain non-violent while they were associated with non-co-operation. But he could not restrain them for long,
and within months they were gaoled after proclaming that it was now
wrong for Muslims to serve in the army. As the year wore on the
Khilafat leaders still at large chafed at Gandhi's restraint: he had to fight
them at the Ahmedabad session of Congress and to restrain them at
subsequent Khilafat meetings right up until the day before he was
himself arrested. His Muslim following and the communal alliance
which rested on it were frail indeed as a basis for leadership by the time
he was removed from effective politics by the British.

Finally it became clear that many of the established provincial politicians who had accepted Gandhi's leadership, often reluctantly and after
considerable opposition and bargaining, were continuing their running
calculations of political expediency through 1921, and during the year
concluded that other political strategies than those Gandhi offered
would be more productive. The former followers of Tilak in western
India had by late 1921 concluded that non-co-operation as guided by
Gandhi was ineffective; privately and publicly they suggested that he
should either go the whole way to civil disobedience and confrontation
with government, or retire and allow them to use the legislatures to
confront the government. In Bengal the most striking example of a
one-time ally rethinking his strategy was C.R. Das. A reluctant colleague in 1920, making his pact with Gandhi with an eye to his local
power base, by November 1921 he had decided that Gandhi's tactics
had proved to yield little in the way of political dividends. Like the
ex-Tilakites he scorned Gandhi's deeper hopes for social and political
transformation as symbolized by the spinning-wheel, and when Gandhi
drew back from civil disobedience after the Bombay violence he argued

for a more aggressive strategy. The final straw for him was when, at the close of 1921, and now in gaol, he heard that the government was willing to consider a political conference, to conciliate moderate opinion worried by official force against non-co-operation and to prevent further violence during the Prince of Wales' visit. Das urged Gandhi to seize this offer and so regain the political initiative; he was horrified when Gandhi imposed conditions unacceptable to the government, including the release of all those imprisoned in connection with non-co-operation. (Gandhi was no stranger to the delicate process of concluding a satyagraha campaign by negotiation: indeed he said the satyagrahi must always be prepared to compromise on inessentials. But he had to ensure in advance that enough would come out of any conference or meeting with the authorities to satisfy his followers and display some success for satyagraha. Conditions for negotiation which he imposed now and later in his career seem always to have been with this in mind.) Das, however, decided that the Mahatma was no longer a strong leader and productive ally and began to consider afresh the tactic of entering the legislative councils. Gandhi's suspension of civil disobedience only confirmed Das in his new attitude and resolve.

So by early 1922 Gandhi was a 'leader' of a campaign which had not succeeded on the lines of his central plan for disciplined and sacrificial behaviour worthy of swaraj, and was disintegrating in violence; many of his 'followers' were slipping out of his control; and many of his allies were convinced that his tactics which had looked so novel and attractive in 1920 now constrained and weakened them and prevented their adoption of more profitable political strategies.

The course of non-co-operation also showed that quite apart from those who reacted to Gandhi out of political expediency there were many in public life who for varied reasons were deeply disquieted by his innovations in politics and his insistence that personal and social transformation alone would bring swaraj. They were the so-called 'Moderates', mostly well established men in public and professional life, who feared Gandhi's radicalism and populist politics, though they were apprehensive of opposing him outright because of his personal probity and public repute. These were the men whose sympathy government feared to lose as official policy towards exponents of non-co-operation became tougher in late 1921 and many prominent politicians like the Nehrus and Das found themselves in gaol; it was to soothe their apprehensions that the Viceroy was prepared to consider a conciliatory conference.[52] When that enterprise collapsed many of them continued to attempt – fruitlessly as it turned out – to achieve a more conciliatory atmosphere through an informal conference convened by the prominent UP politician, Pandit Madan Mohan Malaviya, who had had the courage to express his opposition to non-co-operation as Congress adopted it at Nagpur, though most others who felt the same way had remained silent.[53] The leading Moderates who now supported Malaviya included Jinnah, who had abandoned the Home Rule League when

Gandhi became its president and began to mould it in his own fashion in 1920 and had spoken against non-co-operation at Calcutta; the Bombay men, P. Thakurdas and M.R. Jayakar, Ambalal Sarabhai, the Ahmedabad millowner who had befriended Gandhi as he started his ashram there, and the southern Indian journalist, K. Natarajan. It was his paper, the *Indian Social Reformer*, which plainly stated Moderate apprehensions.[54]

> On principle . . . we cannot and do not rule out civil disobedience as inadmissable in any circumstance whatever. But, as we have repeatedly declared, and as Mahatma Gandhi himself will not deny, civil disobedience on any appreciable scale in the present political conditions of India, spells ruinous civil war the result of which is incalculable. A large section of Indians, and that by no means the least intelligent or patriotic, while keenly feeling the grievances of the country and strongly holding that the Government policy is utterly unjustifiable, is at the same time seriously apprehensive of the consequences of civil disobedience which, it believes, is a remedy worse that the disease it is intended to cure. Mahatma Gandhi will be making a serious mistake if he thinks that he need pay no heed to these men so long as he has got a large following among the masses.

Natarajan feared not only the possible repercussions of civil disobedience, but also what he saw as the negative side of Gandhis's vision – its rejection of so much that was modern and Western. He was not alone in this: the most eloquent critic of Gandhi in the name of a cosmopolitan civilization and liberty of thought was none other than the poet, Tagore, who had given Gandhi and his flock a temporary refuge when they returned from South Africa.

At the other end of the religious and cultural spectrum, many orthodox Hindus were alienated by Gandhi's activities and pronouncements, particularly his rejection of untouchability. They relished the prospect of swaraj as the Mahatma painted it as little as the Moderates did. Even in his own Gujarat, higher-caste ladies who attended his gatherings were reported to have taken purificatory baths on their return home lest they be polluted by the lower caste people with whom Gandhi freely associated.[55]

In the turmoil of non-co-operation it was not only Indians who had to respond to Gandhi and weigh the challenge he presented both to their politics and many of their deepest assumptions. The government, too, had to consider how to handle the new phenomenon of a charismatic politician with a motley following and an even wider and more varied range of sympathizers. Although there were many influential people in government, both in London and the provincial capitals, who favoured a tough line with Gandhi, the Delhi government, in particular the Home Department, pursued a calculated, delicate and risky policy of not making a martyr of Gandhi by refusing to arrest him until it was absolutely essential; not least because a harsh policy of repression would undermine the new reforms and alienate the Moderates who were anxious and sceptical as Gandhi preached non-co-operation. But by March 1922 the Delhi government calculated that it was appropriate to arrest and prosecute Gandhi. Moderate opinion had been conciliated by government tactics and was now genuinely perturbed at the prospect of violence; Congress had not abandoned non-co-operation even if mass civil disobedience was no longer in prospect; and Delhi, having committed itself in early February to arresting Gandhi when civil disobedience was imminent, was merely awaiting the best time to rouse the least agitation in response, knowing well the pressure in the Cabinet in London and among its own senior officials for the ultimate blow at Gandhi and his movement.[56] The policy was vindicated when on 10 March the Mahatma was politely arrested in the Sabarmati ashram and no disturbance occurred in protest.

Gandhi himself had been expecting this for days and had made preparations for the running of the ashram and his journals. He went quietly and graciously to the nearby Sabarmati gaol and thence to his trial a week later before the Ahmedabad district judge. Not only did he plead guilty to inciting disaffection towards the government, he also made a long statement expounding his changed attitude towards the British connection. In conclusion he invited the judge to impose on him the severest penalty available for that offence; or, if like Gandhi he thought British rule was evil, to resign his post. The ICS man who had the uncomfortable position of sitting in judgement sentenced Gandhi to six years imprisonment, but he made it plain that he saw Gandhi as a man of high ideals and noble life and regretted that such a one should have made it impossible for the government to leave him at liberty. After such courtesies between judge and prisoner, Gandhi, frail but serene, was removed to gaol in Yeravda, near Bombay. It might have seemed that this was the end of Gandhi's bid for leadership in Indian politics. But in a very real sense government action only consolidated his public position and repute. Gaol saved Gandhi from dealing with recalcitrant and uncontrollable followers and increasingly critical allies, and from facing the reality of his disintegrating political position. Furthermore his Indian identity was now confirmed by the government, for it had accepted him as the main leader of the national movement by being prepared to parley with him, and by treating him differently from other major politicians in the timing of his arrest. Now his repute as a patriot was assured as the doors of Yeravda closed behind him.

In the course of non-co-operation Gandhi had to a significant degree forged a truly Indian identity: by 1922 he had assumed the appearance and life-style which were to be his until his death, had launched his politics on the national stage, and had begun to come to grips with the realities of Indian life. As he went contentedly behind bars he also left behind real changes in politics and in the Indian sense of nationhood. Congress was now in a geographical sense, and increasingly in a social

sense, a nationwide political organization, indeed the only organization
with any realistic claim to be the mouthpiece of a nation. It now
couched its claims overtly in the name of a broadly-based Indian
nationalism; and few radical politicians relished the prospect of working
outside it, however dubious they were of the tactics and ideology of its
current leadership. Not only did work in its name carry the cachet of
nationalism, but also held out the prospect of consolidating a broad
following, for if its new constitution could be properly implemented
it had the potential to became a truly popular political party. In 1921–2
Congress did indeed seem to be changing markedly, though in retrospect these changes were only temporary, and Gandhi and his allies had
to attempt to re-establish the Congress organization on a regular and
popular basis in the last years of the decade and into the 1930s. But for
the moment membership increased, though there are no accurate statistics for this phenomenon. Funds available to Congress were swollen by
the Tilak Swaraj Fund, which had attracted ten million rupees between
April and June 1921. This enabled Congress to fund a far broader range
of activities, including the promotion of *khadi*, and to pay at least some
full-time workers. About two million rupees were also raised for a
separate Khilafat fund. Gandhi's success as a fund-raiser was again
well-proven, providing another reason for many aspiring politicians to
prefer alignment with him. The Congress organization, which should
under its new constitution have spread down to village level, was more
a blueprint still than an actuality. But despite its patchy implementation,
the number of district committees increased and the organization spanned nearly the whole of that part of India which was under direct British
rule; in 1921–22 there were 213 District Congress Committees compared
with the 220 districts of British administration. However, where details
of Congress work below the provincial level are available it is clear that
despite the boom year of 1921 for local membership and activity,
Congress in the districts could not permanently sustain or finance
itself.[57]

The months of non-co-operation had also seen changes in the depth
of political awareness and participation in an overtly nationalist movement. Gandhi's preaching, the highly flexible and adaptable style of his
campaign plan, as well as Congress attempts to broaden its clientele and
organization had made new connections between the politics of nationalism at continental level and the no less political but localized
concerns of men in villages and small towns. Some at least of the latter
were also beginning to realize that as their local isolation was broken
down by the structures and policies of the raj and the pressures of a
wider economy they, too, needed a broader framework for their political reactions: Congress and non-co-operation were conveniently to hand.
It seemed briefly as if local awareness and activities would become the
building blocks from which a popular nationalist movement might be
formed. But the connections made during non-co-operation turned out
to be tenuous and ambiguous. Many of the newly recruited Congress

sympathizers and non-co-operators of 1921 reverted to their former concerns and styles during 1922, while even before the collapse of the national campaign after Gandhi called off civil disobedience it had become clear that local political drive carried with it the threat of divisions between Indians on lines of geography, caste community and faction, as much as it also held out the hope of a popular political nationalism. India was not yet a nation in actuality, but in the process of self-definition and self-creation. Nowhere was this clearer than in the matter of communal relations. Gandhi had deliberately attached himself to the Khilafat movement and used his unique position between that movement and Congress to create an alliance for the purposes of non-co-operation in the short term, and in the longer term a swaraj society which would include Hindus and Muslims and other minorities as equals. But the campaign deepened Indian awareness of community, and the Muslim violence on the Malabar coast and the incipient violence of the extremer Khilafat leaders generated fear and resentment in other communities, while some Muslims were offended at the high profile of an overtly Hindu religious leader in the movement.

Non-co-operation had proved not to be the road to swaraj which Gandhi had planned with such optimism in 1920, either in relation to the British or in terms of Indian creation of a new national polity through social and economic reform and the generation of fraternity among the country's different religious groups. Yet the Mahatma was an optimist, still fired by a zeal for true swaraj and a trust in the potential for change in the human heart and mind. For him prison marked not failure but the next stage on his pilgrimage of hope.

6

FRUITS OF REFLECTION; ROOTS OF IDENTITY

The historian's besetting danger is hindsight. In examining Gandhi's life it is tempting to describe his Indian years in terms of the peaks and troughs of his political influence as discerned from a later perspective[1]: a natural enough temptation as so often he is seen primarily in the context of political changes and the emergence of nationalism. This tendency to treat his life as if it were just a political career is reinforced by the nature of the records: he generated much more historical evidence in times of great political activity, and particularly during satyagraha campaigns. Meditations in the ashram, spiritual growth in gaol or on a sick-bed leave fewer records than political controversies. Yet it is wrong to dismiss these times of apparent political withdrawal as phases of weakness or inaction, as the British tended to do. Lord Birkenhead, Secretary of State for India, commented with grim satisfaction in 1925, 'Poor Gandhi has indeed perished! as pathetic a figure with his spinning wheel as the last minstrel with his harp, and not able to secure so charming an audience.'[2] Even the more sensitive Viceroy, Lord Irwin, wrote of Gandhi as a political force which had suffered a great decline, and as 'rather remote, and moving in a rarefied atmosphere divorced from the practical facts of the situation', interested in social matters rather than politics.[3]

However, in the broader terms of the development of Gandhi's personal identity and his vision of a free India's true identity, these quieter years when he was not leading civil disobedience were arguably more seminal and productive. From his imprisonment in 1922–4 until 1928 he was certainly not pre-eminent in Congress politics; gaol, ill-health, the year of 1926 deliberately spent in the Sabarmati ashram, and a studied distance from politics as commonly understood, removed him from the position he had briefly held in 1920–2. But these were years of intense reflection. He went back to his own personal roots. He recounted and commented on his own life as he wrote both *Satyagraha*

In South Africa and *An Autobiography*. He meditated, too, on the religious resources which nourished and sustained him, the results being apparent in his speeches, writings and his ashram talks on the *Bhagavad Gita*. It is surely right to interpret this introspection as, at least in part, a mid-life reassessment of his priorities and capabilities, so often forced on the middle-aged by some particular event or crisis which marks unmistakably the passing years. For Gandhi this crisis of imprisonment, ill-health and the erosion of his political leadership was an opportunity not just to return to the roots of his identity, to renew his vision and his hope, both for himself and his country. He reflected, too, on the identity of the Indian nation. Around him before he was gaoled and more particularly after his release he witnessed the disintegration of fraternity, a decline in selfless public work, and disregard by the majority of public men for his style of moral politics. Swaraj had not been attained within the year; and he recognized that the bulk of non-co-operators had used his plans as a political expedient without sharing his commitment to non-violence.[4] He saw on his release from Yeravda the political factions and parties that were fighting each other in the wake of non-co-operation, and the tragic signs of increasing communal hostility and violence. In response to this evidence he plunged himself into a range of work to plant and nurture what he saw as the real roots of a swaraj society and polity. The British might think he was a spent force, divorced from practicalities: he maintained that he was engaging with the real problems of Indian society and working for the reform of that society in a truly radical way – from the roots upwards.

This chapter therefore largely steps aside from chronology and examines Gandhi's main concerns in the middle 1920s. He appears as a tireless spirit, wrestling with problems of ultimate reality, and, in-extricably linked with these, the problems of his and India's present, contingent and contradictory realities. Like many great visionaries he combined the contemplative calling with a capacity and need to be involved in active, even frenetically active, work. In this he bears a resemblance, for example, to a Teresa of Avila or a John of the Cross in the Christian tradition. But – like others of vision and action – exaltation and certainty had a reverse side: the experience of despair and phases of dark depression, and a tendency to extreme physical and emotional exhaustion. Gandhi, the man and the wrestling visionary, is more accessible in these phases of conscious withdrawal from active politics and redirection of energy into the work of radical social and political reconstruction, though for him this and active political leadership were equally aspects of one work, one *dharma*, one hopeful pursuit of a vision of truth.

Gandhi's work of reflection began in gaol, from March 1922 until January 1924 when he underwent an emergency operation for ap-pendicitis and was thereafter released unconditionally.[5] In Yeravda he gained a much-needed rest, and at one point acknowledged with a huge laugh to a visitor that gaol was as good as a nursing-home! Right from

Addressing a conference in Bangalore after a period of illness, 1927.

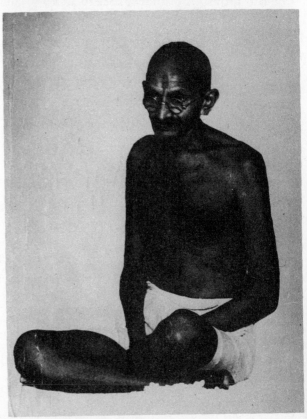

Gandhi during a fast.

the start in the Sabarmati gaol, before his sentence had been passed, he claimed to be enjoying himself and to be completely at peace; and once established in Yeravda he was happy with his isolation and silence, for it reflected his natural tendencies and allowed him time to study.[6] He had a clean and airy cell, ample bedding, was allowed to sleep outside, and had a reasonable amount of open space in which to exercise.

He soon settled into a routine not dissimilar to that followed in the ashram. He rose at 4.00 a.m. to pray, using hymns and prayers that would have been used in the ashram. He worked during the daylight hours, from 6.30 a.m. to 7.00 p.m., as no artificial light was allowed, and went to bed at 8.00 p.m. after reciting the usual ashram evening prayer. Six of his working hours were given over to reading, and four to spinning and carding.[7] Compared to his experiences of gaol in South Africa, in Yeravda his creature comforts were well catered for. He was allowed a private and daily bath; sanitation was also excellent, he commented approvingly. He had adequate food, nearly his usual diet, and was allowed extra fruit, for example, sent by friends. In general he kept in good health apart from the occasional stomach disorder and his eventual appendicitis. His weight, however, remained low, around seven stone, and it was not surprising that after his operation he needed several months of convalescence.

However, there was a range of matters relating to visitors, letters, reading material and the welfare and conditions of other prisoners, which concerned him and on which he clashed, courteously, with the gaol authorities. His status in official eyes was so special that he even received a visit from the Governor of Bombay in August 1923. He was content with the medical care he received when he became ill, and both thanked the surgeon and took care that his contentment should be publicly known. He later wrote at length of his gaol experiences, adding how he felt Indian gaols should be reformed. He was convinced and wished to convince his colleagues that imprisonment, with all its curtailment of liberty and its possible pains and humiliations, should be seen as work in the cause of truth if properly approached.[8]

I wish I could convince the workers that imprisonment of a comrade does not mean so much loss of work for a common cause. If we believe, as we have so often proclaimed we do, that uprovoked suffering is the surest way of remedying a wrong in regard to which the suffering is gone through, surely it follows as a matter of course that imprisonment of a comrade is no loss. Silent suffering undergone with dignity and humility speaks with an unrivalled eloquence. It is solid work because there is no ostentation about it. It is always true because there is no danger of miscalculation.

Apart from the rest gaol afforded, its most important gift to Gandhi was time to read. He read well over 100 books and the range of his reading was as remarkable as the quantity. He used the gaol library and those books and periodicals permitted by the authorities when

they were sent to him.[9] He read history, biography and fiction, and
much on the great religious traditions, including Hinduism, Islam,
Zoroastrianism, Sikhism, Buddhism and Christianity. Among the most
valuable works to him were the sources of Hindu tradition, many of
which he was able to plunge into properly for the first time: he revelled
in the *Mahabharata*, the *Upanishads*, the *Ramayana*, and the *Bhagavata*.
Indeed he hoped to come out of gaol a Sanskrit scholar as well as one
competent in Urdu and Tamil, but release cut short his studies.
Although he did not emerge from Yeravda the scholar he would have
wished, his two years apart from ordinary life and the country's politics
were a time of reflection, renewal of vision and a deepening and
broadening of his spiritual awareness. They enabled him to study
religions other than his own and to ponder on their meaning and power.
He read about the lives of the Prophet Mohamed and his followers as
well as studying the Koran, and in consequence felt far closer to the
Muslim mind. However, he interpreted the Prophet as a man who tried
to walk in the fear of God, whose simplicity, self-effacement and trust in
God was the power behind early Islam, not the sword. This reading
of Muslim origins, so at variance with that of many Muslims, enabled
him to cling to the hope of communal unity in India and to
dismiss contemporary Muslim intolerance and methods of proselytization as 'un-Muslim'. Books sent by Christian friends did not
alter his attitude to Christianity. He could not accept that Jesus was in a
unique sense the son of God, but he deeply revered Jesus, the man, his
ethical teaching and his sacrificial death. He was appreciative of his
Christian friends' concern for him while he was in gaol, but to them and
to Muslims he clarified his religious position on his release.[10]

> I regard both the religions as equally true with my own. But my own
> gives me full satisfaction. It contains all that I need for my growth. It
> teaches me to pray not that others may believe as I believe but that
> they may grow to their full height in their own religion. My constant
> prayer therefore is for a Christian or a Mussalman to be a better
> Christian and a better Mahomedan. I am convinced, I know, that God
> will ask, asks us now, not what we label ourselves but what we are,
> i.e., what we do.

Gaol gave Gandhi time also to think about the sources of Hindu
tradition, and his conclusions were to be crucial as he proceeded along
the path of social and religious reform, claiming that he was not thereby
irreligious but working for the purification and growth of that tradition.
Writing on his release of the enormous task of reading the *Mahabharata*'s
6,000 pages in full for the first time, he described how his initial
prejudices against it had vanished and how he now saw it as an
inexhaustible mine of spiritual finds. But to him it was 'hopeless' as
history: it should be understood as an allegorical treatment of eternal
truths, of the eternal battle between good and evil. It had also, he
thought, suffered accretions over time so that it was now difficult to

know how much was original.[11] The *Ramayana* of the poet, Tulsidas, also gave him deep consolation. He had in youth and manhood abandoned the devotional practice of reciting the name of God, Rama; but now this came back to him as he read Tulsidas, and the recitation of the Name calmed him when he was lonely and helped him to experience the divine, and to feel that his life and work for India were not in his hands alone.[12]

Perhaps even more significant for the imprisoned Gandhi than his overtly religious reading or devotion was the practice of spinning. For years he had regarded swadeshi as spiritually as well as economically important, and found in it a way of identification with and service of the poor, and through them of encountering the divine. Yeravda deepened this sense, and the wheel gained an immense practical and symbolic significance which was to be apparent on his release. He wrote to a Muslim colleague early in his sentence:[13]

> This spinning is growing on me. I seem daily to be coming nearer to the poorest of the poor and to that extent to God. I regard the four hours [of spinning] to be the most profitable part of the day. The fruit of my labour is visible before me. Not an impure thought enters my mind during the four hours. The mind wanders whilst I read the *Gita*, the Koran, the *Ramayana*. But the mind is fixed whilst I am turning the wheel . . .

He alluded to this growing conviction again when in January 1925 he summed up what he saw as the divine purpose in his Yeravda experience and early release: 'the purpose is that I should . . . put before you the fruit of profound meditation in prison, namely, the key to swaraj lies in fulfilling three conditions alone – in the spinning-wheel, Hindu–Muslim unity and in the removal of untouchability.'[14]

Once released from gaol Gandhi had to rediscover in practice his identity and role in public life. The immediate issue to be resolved was his political role and his relationships with the politicians who had been his allies in Congress and the Khilafat movement, and the question of the viability of non-co-operation, which was still nominally Congress policy. However, once civil disobedience had been abandoned in 1922 the non-co-operation campaign had rapidly disintegrated, as the links between an all-India movement and local politics had snapped. Moreover the value of using official political institutions, from the municipality up to the all-India legislature, had become increasingly apparent and attractive, and a body of 'pro-changers' had challenged Congress policy, and now, led by Motilal Nehru and C.R. Das, had formed swaraj parties which worked in the legislatures, hoping to wreck them in order to prove the hollowness of the 1919 reforms. Ultimately even the Swarajists, as they were called, could not agree among themselves, and split up often on local lines, as they calculated whether to obstruct or co-operate with the work of government.[15] In such confusion the function of an all-India leader of a continental agitation, such as Gandhi had once exercised, was redundant.

Gandhi went to the seaside near Bombay to convalesce, and it was not until late May that he returned to the ashram. Even then he found it impossible to tolerate noise, make speeches or attend meetings. To conserve his energy and concentrate on writing he observed Mondays and Wednesdays as silence days, but found that all his energy was taken up with correspondence and editing *Young India* and *Navajivan*, which he had resumed in early April. He maintained that he had no new message or programme, and that his faith in the programme he had preached before he was removed from public life was 'just as bright as ever, if not brighter.'[16] He still opposed work in the legislatures, but tactfully refrained from talking about the work of the pro-changers until he had had time to talk with them.

In late March Motilal and other prominent supporters of council entry had visited him and attempted to persuade him that a new policy was essential. However, he remained unconvinced, and in the ensuing weeks began to formulate a declaration of his considered opinion, in co-operation with Nehru and Das. In the mean time he was conspicuously tolerant in public, observing that there was room for many different honest opinions and no one had the monopoly of truth.[17] Eventually he released a statement of his views at the end of May: it was plain that he was still unconvinced. For him non-co-operation was inconsistent with council entry; but though he maintained a full faith in the constructive programme laid down in 1920–1 he refused to obstruct the work of the pro-changers.[18] Later he made it clear that he felt council work had nothing to do with the real problems of ordinary people, nor could it involve them in a national movement; furthermore, it only generated divisions in Congress as people scrambled for power. But he was determined as far as he could to strengthen Congress, and above all to avoid any acrimonious split in its ranks; it was with this in mind that he approached a crucial AICC meeting in Ahmedabad in June.

Gandhi resolved to test opinion in Congress and to see how far its core members shared his belief in the old programme, particularly the use of *khadi* and the practice of spinning, his insistence on non-violence, and to gauge how far they were prepared to submit to all-India discipline. (Among the resolutions he proposed was one enjoining daily spinning on all Congress office-bearers!) Quite consciously he was laying down the terms for his renewed leadership of Congress. If Congress did not agree with him he would not complain or feel bitter, but would cheerfully remain outside it and work independently in the way he thought best.[19] It might have looked as if he was aggravating division, but his aim was to clear the air. The show-down was dramatic. At one point Das and Nehru walked out with over 50 supporters in protest at Gandhi's resolution on spinning. In the end a compromise was reached on spinning, and the resolutions were passed. However, the one relating to non-violence received a narrow majority of under 10, and this nearly broke Gandhi's heart. He wept publicly and described

himself as 'defeated and humbled'.[20] He really wanted to retire from
Congress and to concentrate on Hindu–Muslim unity, *khadi*, and the
abolition of untouchability; but ultimately he yielded to the pro-
changers who feared his loss to Congress and he agreed to work on his
own programme and travel the country to see the situation for himself.

Gandhi's position in the ensuing months was perplexing as he struggled to end the wrangling in Congress, to find a way in which the
pro-changers and no-changers could follow their different policies to
complement each other, and to extricate himself from Congress without
a great uproar. He urged those who agreed with him not to obstruct
those who wished to use the councils, but to let them control the
Congress organization. He realized he was alienating a wide range of
people, cherished friends included, and confessed to Jawaharlal Nehru
that it was a 'wretched situation', but he knew he would stop being
useful if he was not true to himself: 'but I do not despair. My faith is in
God. I know only the moment's duty. It is given to me to know no
more. Why then should I worry?'[21] He had already begun to brood
on the idea of 'surrendering', as he called it, to the men of Motilal's
persuasion, and demarcating zones of work between the disputing
groups who were locked in 'domestic wrangling' which sickened him.
He was determined not to divide Congress because he felt it was the
most national and representative of all India's organization; he even
began to regret having forced a vote at the June meeting.[22] It was
government which precipitated his final decision. Its resort to a firmer
policy in Bengal brought Gandhi in November into agreement with the
Swarajists, and into a wider attempt to forge a joint front between
Congress and the Moderates through an All-Parties Conference. What
was proposed to heal the wounds Congressmen were inflicting on each
other was an agreement to end non-co-operation (except for refusal to
wear foreign cloth), and to allow the swaraj parties to do work in the
councils as an integral part of Congress. As President of the December
session of Congress, held at Belgaum, Gandhi helped to secure the
ratification of this agreement, and further, selected in co-operation with
Das and Nehru a Working Committee dominated by pro-changers. He
determined to do and say nothing of a 'party' nature in the forthcoming
year.[23]

Gandhi had not abandoned his own faith in non-co-operation: as part
of satyagraha it was integral to his personal search for truth, though he
recongnized that India was not yet ready for it. He admitted to being
disheartened by this recognition and the necessity of abandoning the
1920 boycott programme, but he increasingly felt that quiet, solid work
at the roots of society for *khadi*, communal unity and an end to
untouchability was the surest way to a new order, and to generating
strength from within for a new Indian polity. As this consumed his
attention he became less and less interested in politics: he claimed
(somewhat ingenuously) that he had no aptitude for politics or faith in
that aspect of Congress work, and that it was ably conducted by the

Swarajists. His role should be the attempt to generate a new economy and a new society based on fraternity and a recognition of common nationality which transcended caste and community.[24] Time in gaol and the evidence before his eyes after his release had evidently helped him to understand the enormity of the work for swaraj in his terms, and forced him to reconsider the most appropriate strategy for the country and his right place within it. His place as a sympathizer aloof from Congress, but willing to give it what he could while he concentrated on what he could do best and valued most, was further crystallized in late 1925 when, after the death of Das, he offered Motilal the suggestion that the Swarajists should henceforth carry on Congress's political work and use all its organization to that end, whereas under their agreement in 1924 the Congress organization was to have worked solely on the constructive programme. In September an AICC meeting discussed and ratified this idea. Now the former position was precisely reversed. Congress was in effect a political body rather than the constructive body Gandhi had envisaged on his release, and the pro-changers had all its organization and funds to use, while Gandhi concentrated on the constructive work through a new body, the All-India Spinners' Association (AISA) which would be an independent though integral part of Congress.[25]

Although Gandhi had by late 1925 resolved the complex and distressing problem of his role in relation to Congress and his one-time adherents in non-co-operation by carving out a separate sphere of work in the AISA, he remained closely connected with the Congress leadership, even in 1926 which he spent in the ashram. He was often consulted in Congress affairs, and attended its annual sessions. In April 1926, for example, he attempted to act as peacemaker among the Swarajists who could not agree on their strategy in the councils. But he saw his relationship with Congress as similar to that in 1915–18, when he had only spoken on subjects he had made particularly his own. In 1927 Motilal drew him into discussions about the next Congress President, and Gandhi threw his weight behind M. A. Ansari in order to promote communal unity and 'prove' that Congress was not a Hindu body. But the anxious Motilal was deeply concerned at the Mahatma's evidently failing health in early 1927, and reported to his son that Gandhi was half-famished, seriously ill and virtually killing himself in his work to publicize the spinning-wheel.[26]

Despite his studied distance from the main political stream of Congress work there was an issue on which Gandhi took up the cudgels – that of independence from Britain. As his plans for swaraj in a year had failed, an important part of his rediscovery of a personal identity was his attitude to the still-continuing raj which he had called satanic and hoped to undermine. His understanding of true swaraj did not change, but its political *form* was something on which he was conciliatory. Immediately after his release he spoke of political self-rule as a state of partnership with Britain similar to that enjoyed by the white dominions, and some weeks later he reiterated that he would welcome this type of home rule even though it was not the swaraj that could be generated by Indian efforts alone.[27] As President of the Belgaum Congress of 1924 he repeated that it would be possible to have swaraj *and* a British connection;[28] and as the demand for total political independence began to grow among a section of Congressmen, Gandhi warned them to be careful of playing with words and to be realistic in their aims. When a resolution was passed at the 1927 Congress demanding independence, Gandhi was angry and scathing. For him it was divisive and unrealistic and would only exhibit Congress's weakness: 'we have almost sunk to the level of the schoolboys' debating society.'[29] Yet he was second to none in his detestation of the current system of rule, and still maintained that it was the duty of any nationalist to promote disaffection.[30] In retrospect Gandhi's distancing of himself from the rough and tumble of politics stood him in good stead: as an outsider, devoting himself to the cause of swaraj along his own lines of work, he retained an image of probity and commitment to the national cause, unsullied by the strife of factionalism which characterized much political activity in the later 1920s. Motilal Nehru was deeply distressed by the lack of dedication to the national cause he saw around him. Gandhi saw the same deterioration in public life, but drew a more hopeful conclusion: 'I regard all this rising of the poison as a necessary process in national up-building.'[31]

Gandhi had been right in assuming on his release that many of the problems he faced were infinitely more complex than they had been when he had felt constrained to call off civil disobedience, in particular that of relations between India's diverse religious communities.[32] Taxing and distressing the readjustment of his relations with Congressmen might have been; but his identity in relation to India's Muslims became to him a far more grievous, even agonizing, problem. As he emerged from Yeravda he saw that the alliance he had constructed between Hindus and Muslims had collapsed. Tension in this alliance had always been near the surface, but when an aggressive strategy was abandoned in 1922 the Khilafat leaders lost the reason for their temporary adherence to non-violence, Congress and the Mahatma. Soon the whole issue of the Khilafat was taken out of their hands by the rise of Mustafa Kamal and Turkish nationalism: in 1924 the Caliphate was abolished. In the 1920s the main thrust of Indian Muslim politics was the choice of strategies to buttress their local and all-India positions, as the British seemed increasingly likely to devolve more power to elected Indians, particularly in provincial legislatures and governments. The signs of this new priority in Muslim politics were the separate meetings of League and Congress in 1924 for the first time since 1918, the collapse in Muslim attendance at Congress from the spectacular high of 1920, and the discussions among Muslims in different provinces on their best strategies, according to whether or not they were in a local majority. Punjabi and Bengali Muslims, safe with provincial majorities, had profited from the 1919 reforms and looked to a future where provincial

autonomy and the maintenance of communal electorates would safeguard their influence; leaders of provincial Muslim minorities, however,
toyed with the idea of offering to abandon communal electorates and
instead seeking their security in an Indian federation in which there
would be more Muslim provinces than there were in British India at that
time. Amid such discussions Muslim became divided from Muslim, and
Muslim from Hindu. Congress could not claim to speak for India's
Muslims; but nor could the Muslim League, which itself split.

Even more disastrous than political bickering and rivalry for office for
one such as Gandhi, who had laboured for communal fraternity and
co-operation, was the evidence of deteriorating communal relations at
local level. Serious communal riots became increasingly commonplace,
and there were ugly signs of extreme religious intolerance and revivalism in both Muslim and Hindu strategies for achieving conversions and
the reintegration of those who had fallen from faith. Historians have
wrestled with the evidence of sharpening hostility between the two
communities and the emergence of overt 'communalism' in Indian
public life, and have concluded that it was a complex phenomenon
with no single cause; though in the past many tried to interpret these
developments as the result of devious British schemes to divide in order
to rule, or of inevitable divisions between two nations, one Muslim and
one Hindu. In an environment where resources and access to them
were changing, relations between communities were often disturbed,
and the British tendency to see Indian groups in terms of community encouraged aspirant politicians to couch their appeals in terms of
community to gain the rulers' notice as well as supporters. Yet when the
issues at stake are examined closely they often seem to have been not
inherently 'communal', but long-standing economic problems, for
example, which acquired a communal label. Once religion was thus let
loose in politics it became uncontrollable and self-perpetuating: fear and
violence bred fear and violence, and prominent all-India politicians
could not contain it. In this cumulative process the passions and dis-
appointments roused during non-co-operation were probably of minor
significance, though some heaped blame on Gandhi's head.

Soon after his release Gandhi showed how perturbed he was: he called
Hindu–Muslim unity 'the greatest question before the country', and
admitted he had been thinking about it, night and day, since he regained
his liberty.[33] Such unity he believed to be vital, not just for religious
reasons of tolerance among truth-seekers: it was essential to prevent any
opportunity for the British to play off one group against the other and
so hinder swaraj. He was not convinced that British policy was the sole
cause of communal tension, but he saw how it could play into their
hands.[34] But as in the reorientation of his role among Congressmen, so
in relation to Indian Muslims, he remained reticent after his release until
he had had time for discussions with such prominent figures as Motilal
Nehru and Pandit Malaviya, both Hindus, and the Muslims, Mahomed
Ali, Dr M.A. Ansari and Hakim Ajmal Khan. Late in May, soon after

he had formulated his attitude to the pro-changers in Congress, he dealt at great length in *Young India* with the whole range of matters at issue between Hindus and Muslims, and strenuously denied that his alignment with the Khilafat movement had helped to strain communal relations or rouse the Muslim masses in a new religious awakening which was then vented on the Hindus. He suggested arbitration rather than fighting as the remedy where Hindus and Muslims were opposed, and asked Hindus as the majority to bow to Muslim wishes in political matters; he called for mutual tolerance and trust, but recognized that the dominant prevailing attitudes were passion and prejudice.[35] As the weeks passed he admitted that he felt a solution was becoming more difficult and he was convinced – prophetically – that some leaders would have to sacrifice their lives in the cause. His own position he felt to be 'most pitiable' because so many people were looking to him for guidance in 'this sea of darkness, doubt and despair'. Just at this point he was also deeply distressed by the wrangling in Congress over its proper strategy and role, and his desire to solve the communal problem was an element in his decision to allow Motilal and his party to follow their bent and thus resolve at least that problem which was consuming his time and perhaps more important, his limited physical and emotional energy.[36]

Communal disunity erupted dramatically in early September 1924 in Kohat on the North-West Frontier. Over 150 people were killed or injured, considerable damage was done, and the whole Hindu population fled in terror. This was for Gandhi the final straw. Discussions with leaders, reasoned articles and pleas for tolerance were dead-ends. He felt he must do something, and after days of emotional and spiritual anguish, prayer and soul-searching, in the hours before dawn he received the answer to his searching in a sudden illumination: he must fast for three weeks from 18 September, living on water alone. It was a personal penance, but also a prayer to the heads of all communities 'to meet and end this quarrel which is a disgrace to religion and to humanity. It seems as if God has been dethroned. Let us reinstate Him in our hearts.'[37] As he wrote to his old friend from South African days, C.F. Andrews, 'dearest Charlie':[38]

> Don't you fret over my decision. It has been taken after deep prayer and clearest possible indication. This fast of 21 days is the least I can do. Oh the agony of it all! Every day has been a day of torture. But I shall soon be at peace. I was longing to see my duty clearly. The light has come like a flash. Can a man do more than give his life?

Even some of his closest colleagues were perplexed by this, and in the early days of the fast – which took place under Mahomed Ali's roof as a symbol of unity – he tried to get them to understand his heart while he still had the strength. He blamed himself for the violence around him, believing that if he had been perfectly non-violent this would not have happened; and he said that right from the outset of non-co-operation he

had believed that he might have to pay willingly with his life if the
weapon he offered to his country was abused. He claimed that there
were examples of such penance in Hindu tradition and in Islam, and that
it was the Prophet himself whose example had taught him that fasting
depends on faith in God and opens the way to divine revelation. He was
convinced that the soul's strength grew in proportion to the degree to
which a man disciplined the flesh; after this he would be all the stronger
in his work for communal unity.[39]

The fast may have been primarily a matter between Gandhi and his
Maker, as he prayed helplessly out of his anguish, 'Rock of Ages cleft
for me, Let me hide myself in Thee.' But it was also an appeal, and it
had an immediate effect. Motilal Nehru organized a Unity Conference
in Delhi on 26 September; to it came about three hundred religious
luminaries, including the head of the Anglican Church in India, Bishop
Foss Wescott, Shaukat Ali and H.A. Khan speaking for Muslims, and
the prominent Hindus, Swami Shraddhanand and Pandit Malaviya.
Gandhi sent a message asking for real unity rather than a patched-up
peace in deference to his fast. In the resolution the conference ultimately
passed (which was largely drafted by Gandhi) it deplored communal
dissension, gave its opinion on various flash-points between Hindus and
Muslims such as music before mosques and cow-killing, and suggested
a board of arbitration to decide all disputes between Hindus and
Muslims. The conference also pleaded with Gandhi to break his fast and
give it the benefit of his co-operation. He refused, on the grounds that it
was an unbreakable vow, an expression of faith, and a matter between
himself and God. But he assured Motilal that he had no intention of
dying: this fast was to enable him better to serve the country and if he
reached the point of death he would certainly eat rather than die.[40] He
ended the fast on the due day with his particular talent for theatre and
symbolism. The well-wishers had gathered in a highly emotional
atmosphere, in the dark before the dawn, to pray. All morning crowds
of people flocked for his *darshan* or stayed to watch the climax, and
Gandhi insisted that even the servants should be allowed to attend,
making a point of giving special thanks to the sweeper. When all were
gathered round his bed a Muslim declaimed the opening of the Koran, a
Christian said the devotional hymn, 'When I survey the wondrous
cross', and finally his young follower, Vinobha Bhave, recited from the
Upanishads and another Hindu sang a Vaishnava hymn. Gandhi was so
weak his words to his Muslim friends were barely audible; the ceremony ended with him drinking a glass of orange juice. However it took
him several months to recover from the fast and to recoup the health
which even before this deprivation had been frail, for in the turmoil of
1924 he had lost weight and found it hard to eat because of the pressure
of work.

Great as the emotional impact of the fast was, in practical terms it
solved nothing; nor did the method of the conference have an enduring
influence on communal relations. Increasingly Gandhi became aware of

his changed position: by the end of the year he acknowledged that he could no longer claim with any truth that he was a spokesman for India's Muslims.[41] This was proven to him in 1925 when he and Shaukat Ali could not agree on the causes of the Kohat riot, and when he roused Muslim hostility by criticizing the stoning of two Muslim 'apostates', arguing that even if this punishment was permitted in the Koran, it should be subject to the scrutiny of reason and justice. Just as he refused a literal, fundamentalist interpretation of Hindu scriptures, so he treated the Koran.[42] In early March he acknowledged publicly that despite all his efforts he could put forward no workable solution to the communal problem; he proposed to keep aloof from it and wait on divine guidance. Vividly he used the simile of a tangled spindle:

> Indifferent spinners amongst you know how sometimes when you are unwinding your yarn from the spindle it becomes ... a tangle. You know the more you try to undo the tangle the more knotty it becomes, and a wise spinner leaves his tangle aside for the moment when he has lost his temper and approaches it after he has cooled down. So it is with the Hindu–Muslim question. It has become a hopeless tangle at the present moment. I thought I was an expert in solving that tangle as I think I am also an expert in spinning. But for the time being I have put away in my cupboard this Hindu–Muslim tangle. This does not mean that I have despaired of a solution. My mind will eternally work at it till I find out a solution. But I must confess to you today that I cannot present a workable solution that you will accept.[43]

So by 1925 Gandhi had resolved the issue of his relations with the politicians who had once been his allies, and had recognized that his priorities were shared by few in public life. As his public image and role changed he had also to come to a satisfactory self-perception and to return to the roots of his personal identity in order to live at peace with himself, his ideals and his limitations. It would have been fatally easy to succumb to despair in 1924–5 or to compromise on ideals in order to retain his public role. But Gandhi was a man of integrity who could not live at peace if he was being false to himself. He also proved to be extremely resilient. The source of this resilience was his continued self-perception as a seeker after truth. The fundamental purpose of his life was to see God face to face, for 'God I *know* is Truth'.[44] Despite his increasing years and the Hindu understanding that later middle age is a time for preparing to withdraw from worldly affairs, he maintained that the search for truth did not necessitate retirement; he was a householder, not a cave-dweller who had withdrawn to contemplate or a Hindu *sanyassi* who had abandoned ordinary life for a peripatetic search for holiness.[45] He believed passionately – and in stark contrast to those wandering holy men whose sanctity he often dismissed as a sham – that the search for God, for true salvation, the finding and realization of oneself within that ultimate Truth, could only be through service of his fellow men, more particularly the poorest of them.

> I count no sacrifice too great for the sake of seeing God face to face. The whole of my activity, whether it may be called social, political, humanitarian or ethical, is directed to that end. And as I know that God is found more often in the lowliest of His creatures than in the high and mighty, I am struggling to reach the status of these. I cannot do so without their service. Hence my passion for the service of the suppressed classes. And as I cannot render this service without entering politices, I find myself in them.

He wrote that in the year of his release from Yeravda, but as the turbulent months passed he became even more closely identified with the poor in his own mind: 'I see in the fellowship with them the God I adore. I derive from that fellowship all my consolation, all my hope and all the sustaining power I possess.'[46] The idea of trying to separate out politics from the rest of his life was as incredible as the idea of trying to serve India and her poor without political involvement, and his definition of politics was idiosyncratic in its inclusiveness.[47] Because he felt that politics was an integral part of his vocation he could not give up that side of his life when circumstances seemed against him and he was opposed or misunderstood, though he maintained that he would have chosen – if the choice had been there – to devote his time and creativity to the ashram community.[48]

Given that politics was essential to his personal religious quest, Gandhi was quite clear about his political priorities. He was not out for a political career in the ordinary sense, and therefore temporary withdrawal from a leadership position or an institution such as Congress could be as clear and valid a political action and part of his essential work as leadership of a nationwide movement. Indeed in 1926 when he was by choice spending the year in the ashram, he wrote, 'The condition of the country certainly makes me unhappy, but sometimes even silence is a form of action. I am sure that my silence is.'[49] A silent witness to true goals would be more effective than active involvement at the price of his own integrity, as he had told the Swarajists when they wanted the cachet of his alliance. His basic goal in public life remained the one he had envisaged in 1909. He explained to the wife of his British surgeon in 1924:

> My own motive is to put forth all my energy in an attempt to save Indian, that is, ancient culture, from impending destruction by modern, that is, Western culture being imposed upon India. The essence of ancient culture is based upon the practice of the utmost non-violence. Its motto is the good of all including every living thing, whereas Western culture is frankly based upon violence.

He certainly called himself a nationalist, but insisted that this involved a desire for the well-being of all nations, not India's exclusively to the disadvantage of others. His basic message was for the whole world, but had first to be preached and proven in India: he resisted attempts in the mid-1920s to lure him on foreign tours, to Europe or the USA, attempts which became more common as he became internationally known and began to attract a range of foreign admirers and devotees.[50]

In the very particular circumstances of Indian politics after his release, and given the rejection by most Indian politicians of his satyagraha programme, Gandhi felt he had two main tasks. The broader one was to generate power within the Indian nation so that Indians would no longer have to bow to their rulers' wishes. He was humiliated and saddened by their manifest weakness and division as a nation once they had re-nounced his 'moral politics' and the steely resolve and inner strength he had thought it would bring. Now he would work for those qualities in different and radical ways, nurturing the very roots of national identity.[51] His other and more specific task was, as the originator of and expert in civil disobedience in the Indian context, to remain its guardian; just as in 1922 he had told the young Nehru that he must abandon it to preserve it in its full purity and strength for the future. His faith in the 1920 strategy was firm, and if he could have carried his Congress colleagues in the 1920s he would still have wished to maintain that course. Now, even in his year in the ashram, he brooded on the future of his ultimate weapon. How could it become a mass weapon until they could control the masses? Each time he had had to call it off the reason was Congressmen's involvement in violence. But now he maintained, 'I should not hesitate to go forward even if there were a thousand eruptions in the country if I was sure that they had nothing to do with the political upheaval and that Congressmen had no hand in them directly or indirectly.'[52] Such a development in his thinking as he meditated on past disasters makes it quite clear why now and in the coming years he laid such stress on Congress organization and disci-pline, as well as strategies such as the khadi movement which extended a truly national mass organization. He alone was the true 'keeper of the lighthouse called satyagraha in the otherwise chartless sea of Indian politics', though he saw his creed as being on trial, such was his contemporaries' contempt for it.[53]

Gandhi realized that as he felt his way in the changed political circumstances of the 1920s and carved out his identity and role he was often accused of being shifting and changeable. He responded that this apparent changeability was in reality the hallmark of one who sought truth. His deepest beliefs remained, as unchanging as a rock; it was their manifestation and implementation which had to change as the world changed about him, and to him this was a sign of growth. Indeed it was one of his basic convictions that mankind was not spiritually static, but could make inner progress, could experience moral growth, just as it could make physical discoveries and inventions.[54] It was the duty of the spiritually tuned – and he clearly counted himself among them – to spread an atmosphere of morality around their own particular sphere of work, even if society at large seemed like an unthinking flock of sheep. However bad the times, the moral individual life could have profound implications, for he believed that the moral triumph or moral fall of each individual affected all.[55]

Such thinking was the cognitive context of many of the decisions which perplexed observers and still make him a figure much misunderstood. The 1924 fast was a case in point. He was well aware that public regard for him as a man of moral stature was still very high, and that the title, Mahatma, was frequently used of him; but he loathed the undisciplined and often mindless adoration he was forced to witness. His repute as a Mahatma he said was worthless because it was the result of his external political actions.

> What is of abiding worth is my insistence on truth, non-violence and *brahmacharya* which is the real part of me. That permanent part of me however small, is not to be despised. It is my all. I prize even the failures and disillusionments which are but steps towards success.[56]

His struggles as an individual were significant precisely because he did not claim to be spiritually 'special': 'I have often said that I do not claim to be an extraordinary man unless one who is mad after the search for truth be called extraordinary ... I have disclaimed the title of a saint for I am fully conscious of my limitations and imperfections.'[57] He was consequently willing to share, even publicize, his own weaknesses and struggles, whether they were to do with prayer, maintaining chastity or controlling anger. The significance of his life, he felt, was not that he was special: he was a piece of ordinary humanity and therefore showed what was spiritually possible for all.[58] Although he believed in the Hindu tradition of a guru or spiritual master for each individual, he had never found a guru for himself, much less was he one himself.[59]

At heart in all his endeavours, whether they were apparently political, social or spiritual, Gandhi was a man of deep, unquenchable hope. He called himself time and again an 'irrepressible optimist'. His optimism was grounded in his belief in God and dependence on him. In the press of events after his release, at the time of his fast for communal unity, as he disentangled himself from the dilemma posed by the Swarajists in 1925 he spoke of depending on God for guidance, in whose hands he believed was the future for India and for humankind. A man with faith in God could never lose hope, because he believed in the ultimate triumph of truth.[60] Were it not for his faith he would have gone out of his mind, he said repeatedly – when he faced the public world on his release in 1924, when he heard of natural disasters, or in a speech to missionaries in some of the most difficult weeks of 1925: 'if I did not feel the presence of God within me, I see so much misery and disappointment every day that I would be a raving maniac and my destination would be the [river] Hooghli.'[61] After taking a brief respite from public activity in Vinobha Bhave's Wardha ashram in late 1925, he spoke of his enjoyment and relaxation, and the world of turmoil to

which he had to return, for this was just days before the annual
Congress session. But turmoil did not dismay him: 'we should get our
peace not from the external environment, but from within us, and so I
do not worry.'[62] There are signs that he was progressively internalizing
his own search for peace and for meaning, drawing on his deepest inner
resources, rather than depending on the ebb and flow of external events
or outward stimulation. He spoke of his growing need for silence each
day, and also as many as two silent days per week. He admitted that art
played no part in his own spiritual journey: enough for him the beauties
of nature, particularly the night sky, on which he must have constantly
gazed, as he liked to sleep in the open, and he often sensed his deepest
convictions in the dark hours before dawn when the world's silence was
at its most profound. Even reading was becoming less important to
him, compared to his eager search for spiritual enlightenment through
books in his earlier years, right until his Yeravda gaol sentence. Now his
desire was to think, pray and then act on the light God illuminated
within him: the experience of others offered him little help.[63]

So Gandhi in later middle age turned inwards to renew his sense of
meaning and his vision of truth, and to receive guidance, as he came to
terms with the external changes in his public position. Yet his deepest
convictions and his peace of mind were hard won. The reality of
Gandhi, the man, was one of changing moods and of struggle with
himself, often bitter and exhausting, particularly when he was faced by
error or defection among those closest to him. He admitted that at times
he sank into deep gloom, almost despair, and spoke of his inner
struggles without shame, as in the days before the prolonged fast in
1924, or in early 1927 when he thought he might not live more than a
year, and saw little for his future. 'I have nothing new to say or give. I
may collect more, give a little more guidance and patch here and there.
But really the clock has struck for me.'[64]

This particular admission came at the point when he suffered a serious
collapse in his health, and it is essential to realize that the context of
Gandhi's self-assessment in these years was nearly always one of massive pressure of work on an extremely frail body. Little is made of this in
most interpretations of his life, but except when gaol, illness or impending collapse enforced rest on him, he lived at a furious pace, driving
himself to the bone, exhausting his colleagues and dismaying those who
saw his value for India or simply loved him. Soon after his re-emergence
into public life in 1924 he was trying to control the number of his
visitors and correspondents, pleading with people to read his two
journals if they wished to know his mind, and protecting himself by
taking extra times of silence. When he began touring for the propaga-
tion of khadi in 1925 and then again in 1927, the burden of work and the
strain of travel and public speeches was even greater. He was constantly
on the verge of exhaustion, and his frail physique was frequently
wracked by bouts of fever, and he continually experimented with his
diet, often with dire consequences. Only gradually did he begin to come

to terms with his physical limitations. Late in 1925 he agreed after consultations with colleagues and his doctor, M.A. Ansari, to spend a year at Sabarmati, partly to tend the ashram and consolidate his infant foundation, the AISA, but also to take as much rest as possible.[65] But even during that year he regained strength very slowly, and his weight was only just over seven stone, though he took care of himself, had time for regular meals and exercise. But he could not resist dietetic experiments and in mid-year attempted to live on fruit alone.

After the year's sabbatical, he *professed* to be working in a limited field only, and to be observing his own limitations, yet he was determined to do what he did do well, and with utmost concentration, and again he rapidly brought his body to the edge of a very serious collapse. In the middle of a tour late in March 1927, after four months of travelling, speaking, cajoling and persuading, he had to stop, his blood pressure having shot to dangerous heights because of over-work and nervous exhaustion. It was not until early July that he was able to speak in public again, and not until September than he began to travel. Though he wished to convalesce in Sabarmati, his doctors insisted on a cooler climate, and he went first to the Nandi hills in Mysore, and then to temperate Bangalore. His wife and youngest son, Devadas, came to be with him, and an army, as he described it, of devoted volunteers and co-workers who nursed him through and assisted with the limited work he still insisted on doing. His doctors kept a close watch on his blood pressure and his diet, controlling his attempts even then to experiment with different combinations of his already very limited diet, as he still insisted on living on five items of food a day. Lying in bed and coping with unanswered letters, he wrote to his old friend, H. Kallenbach, and told him of the sudden collapse, and his sense that it was his own fault for trusting in his own judgement and overworking, rather than relying totally on God. His chief problem as he convalesced was not so much the enforced discipline of rest, but the unceasing work of his mind, his constant thinking about communal relations and the poverty of the masses in particular.[66] Despite his good intentions to reform his mode of work, when he began touring again late in 1927 and into 1928 his blood pressure was a persistent danger signal that he was pushing himself beyond the limit.

The origins of this need to drive himself are a matter of conjecture. Some would argue that he worked out his childhood tensions and guilts through self-punishing service of his fellows; others that his identification with and service of the poor, taking a female, caring role rather than an aggressively masculine role of dominance, stemmed from his inner conflicts over sexual identity, originating in his own early marriage and his father's death. Less often mentioned by those who try on slender evidence to probe the recesses of the Mahatma's psyche is the strong possibility that his troughs of depression and his ceaseless activity were the repercussions of unacceptable and inexpressible anger – at his own physique and personality, at the stubbornness and cruelties of his compatriots, at the untrustworthiness of his closest – turned inwards and redirected into channels which served the country but also undermined his own stability and strength. The evidence of his health certainly suggests that here indeed was a personality in travail, who despite what he *said* about finding peace through trust in a benevolent God, despite the consolations of conscious religion, was at the deepest levels of his being still wrestling with profound conflict.

The way Gandhi spoke of trusting in God could equally have been the idiom of a Christian, Muslim or Jew. (Indeed he was accused of being a secret Christian.) As he drew on his deepest resources in the 1920s and discovered afresh his unique identity he had to clarify his relationship with formal religion, particularly his own Hindu tradition. His voracious reading in gaol had taken him back to his religious roots as well as broadening his religious sympathies. Once out of Yeravda his role as ashram leader demanded of him advice and teaching; his public image as a Mahatma laid him open to persistent religious questions; and in his work to rid Indian society of customs which stemmed from Hindu tradition he had to make plain his attitude to that tradition. However, he retained even more strongly his belief, stated publicly, that true religion was beyond all distinct religious traditions: it was that inner core of a man which tries to find and express itself, and sees its identity with God.[67] He did not think there was any need for one religion, gathering together the best insights of all traditions:[68] rather, he urged people to stay within their own traditions and to be religious in the most profound sense of that word *within* those formalised religions.

> ... all religions are more or less God-given and ... therefore one must work out one's own salvation in the religion of one's own forefathers; for, a seeker after Truth finds out that all religions melt and become one in God who is one and the same for all His creatures.[69]

For him the hallmarks of true religion, wherever found, were service and devotion: he robustly insisted that true spirituality, in contrast to outer piety, always resulted in practical work.[70] Given his wide tolerance of the varied religions found in India and his sense that they were sufficient for each individual's particular pilgrimage towards truth, it was hardly surprising that he opposed attempts to convert people from one religion to another. His criticism of proselytization, particularly if it included force or material inducement, was aimed at all; not only Christian missionaries, for example, but those Hindus who practised *shuddhi*, a purification and reintegration movement, which had a role in the escalation of communal hostility, as did a Muslim equivalent.[71] Gandhi's treasuring of all religious traditions included the sense that all of them were able to change, to deepen and to grow: only God was changeless, not the partial human formulations of the vision of God and its practical repercussions.

When challenged on his own position Gandhi denied that *he* was working to create a new religion. He proudly proclaimed himself to be a Hindu. Born a Hindu, he found in the tradition of his fathers all the resources he needed for religious vision and growth; for him it had the particular merit that it was tolerant and able to accept new insights from other sources. Indeed, his study of the scriptures of other traditions had deepened and broadened his own understanding and experience of being a Hindu.[72] He defined being a Hindu as one who believes in God, immortality and transmigration of the soul, *karma* and *moksha*, who tries to practise truth and non–violence (including protection of the cow) and acts according to *varnashrama*, the division of society into distinct groups with their own roles. He realized of course that other Hindus disagreed with him over what being a Hindu meant, and some of his bitterest clashes with the orthodox were over the issue of untouchability as an essential part of Hinduism or a terrible excrescence.[73] Gandhi never hesitated to condemn aspects of Hindu tradition: 'today it has become moribund, inactive, irresponsive to growth', he wrote in 1924. But he insisted that it had never been unchanging, and was still capable of growth and renewal.[74] He defined his position still further by saying that he was a *sanatani*, or orthodox Hindu, though he knew many of the orthodox vigorously refuted this. But he based his claim on the asser-tion that he tried to live out the oldest ideals in the tradition and believed in its scriptures.[75] He stood in the *advaita* tradition which asserted the unity of all things, rather than a duality of the divine and the created order.

> I believe in *advaita*, I believe in the essential unity of man and for that matter of all that lives. Therefore I believe that if one man gains spiritually, the whole world gains with him and, if one man falls, the whole world falls to that extent.[75]

This was no mere matter of theology to him, but a living principle on which he based his whole work. It undergirded his belief in satyagraha's efficacy, even if practised by a lone individual; it was the reason why he valued his own 'experiments with truth' as universally significant, and why his lapses and weaknesses caused him such profound pain. Although a Hindu he acknowledged his deep debt to Jain teaching, and in particular to the way it made explicit the insight that truth can be seen from many aspects; for it was this which helped to strengthen his own tolerance.[77]

Gandhi's public position meant that he had to grapple with far more precise religious queries than his own position as a Hindu. To a greater extent than ever before in his life, he was inundated with queries about the practicalities of religious observance. One major problem with which he constantly engaged was the worth and authority of the Hindu scriptures. He had struggled with the question in Yeravda, and after his release it was clear that his position was both radical and modern. Although he valued the great corpus of writings, he rejected any fundamentalist interpretation of them. The magnificent stories should not be taken as literal history, but as allegorical writings, depicting fundamental truths. It should be recognized that all literature, including scripture, is the product of human minds and hands, and therefore the divine truths are filtered through the lens of a particular historical time, and may have to reviewed and understood afresh at a later date. Consequently all the practical prescriptions of tradition must, without exception, be judged in the light of reason and contemporary understanding of true morality and compassion; customs and ideas which failed this test should be rejected even if there was apparent scriptural authority for them, and this of course included untouchability.[78] For himself the *Bhagavad Gita* remained the most treasured scripture, from which he derived increasing consolation and guidance, and in his year of rest in the ashram he gave a series of discourses on it.[79] But even to this text he consciously gave his own interpretation, finding in it many of the beliefs he held most firmly, and using it as a vehicle for the process of growth he wished to see in the Hindu tradition.

The multiplicity of Hindu modes of worship and devotion also drew Gandhi's attention. Its great temples, so full of riches, so venerated, yet so often places from which untouchables were excluded and extravagance and vice abounded in the name of religion, drew Gandhi's severe criticism. He felt they had been forsaken by God, and He would only return to them when Hindus accepted untouchables as their fellow equals and allowed them into the temples; many temples he dubbed as no better than brothels.[80] But what of the gods and goddesses of the Hindu pantheon whose images were central to much popular Hindu worship in the temple and the home? He clearly did not believe in these deities in any literal way, but rather as man's attempts to depict the passions and powers at work in the world. He replied to a teacher anxious about telling the scriptural stories to children:

> I do not believe that gods ... reside in the sky and that they are separate individuals, or ... are separate entities. But I certainly believe that gods and goddesses represent the various powers. Their descriptions are sheer poetry. There is a place for poetry in religion. The Hindu religion has lent to everything that we believe in a scriptural form. In a way, all those who believe that God has innumerable powers may be said to believe in gods and goddesses. Just as God has innumerable powers, He has innumerable forms also. One should worship Him by the name and in the form one likes. I do not think there is anything wrong in that. Whenever and wherever necessary, the symbols and metaphors may be explained and their inner meaning made clear to the children.[81]

He grieved when communal violence took the form of Muslims desecrating Hindu temples and their images, and felt that veneration of these images had its proper place in religious devotion, provided that the 'idols' were used as an aid to contemplation and worship rather than being worshipped themselves as physical objects. Far more idolatrous in his view were those who blindly worshipped a holy book rather than using it with reason, or fanatically refused to see that people outside their own tradition had genuine faith and modes of worship. 'This form of idolatry is more deadly for being more fine and evasive than the tangible and gross form of worship that identifies the Deity with a little bit of stone or a golden image.'[82] In forms of worship and religious observance the touchstone was the human heart and understanding rather than the outward action. But though he could see the potential for good in popular worship of images, he felt that Hindus in the twentieth century were cluttered with a multiplicy of ceremonies which meant nothing, and he consciously encouraged people to pursue this sort of reform. 'There can be no doubt that it is necessary for this generation to strike out an original path by giving a new form and even meaning to many old ceremonies.'[83] In the ashram he set an example: there, ceremony was minimal, worship was spartan in its setting, and marriages were so simple that they were more like the taking of monastic vows, instead of the lengthy and elaborate display of most Hindu weddings. When questioned on prayer he declined to give elaborate instructions. For him the core of prayer was the heart's yearning to merge with its maker: without such a movement of the heart prayer was parrot-like repetition; with it any form of prayer the individual chose was valid. To learn this, so to tune one's heart, could only be done through service of the poor and suffering. 'God comes unsought, comes because He must, and dwells in the heart of one who serves others.' Gandhi did advocate regular, daily prayer, and said he could go without food but not without prayer, as it was a daily purification of the heart, just as the daily bath cleansed the body.[84] In his personal devotions the prayers and hymns of many traditions had a valued place, but now the recitation of the name of God, the practice of *Ramanama*, grew on him after his rediscovery of it in Yeravda, and he recommended it to those who sought peace and comfort, particularly those 'whose faith is not damped [*sic*] by over-much learning'! In the hour of real danger or temptation learning was useless; faith alone could save, and here was the place for a humble calling on the name of God.[85]

Gandhi might decry learning as an aid to genuine devotion, but within the Hindu tradition some of the greatest minds had wrestled with the philosophical problem of the nature of God, and it was inevitable that he would be faced with it, particularly as he spoke so naturally, though certainly not casually, of a close, almost intimate, experience of the Divine. He certainly believed in a 'Supreme Unseen Force': a God who is unfathomable, everywhere, all-seeing, yet allows Himself to be worshipped under many forms and by many names, who comes deep in the heart of men. He is pure being and yet is personal to those who need a personal deity. But ultimately after all attempts to define, visualize and understand Him He transcends speech and reason. To Gandhi only the ignorant disputed the existence of God; reason could never reach Him, only faith.[86] Yet his belief in God as utter goodness raised the perennial question of evil in the world. Rather than become involved in tortuous argument Gandhi rested on an acceptance of ambiguities and unresolved questions; enough for men to know that evil existed and should be avoided.[87] In a real sense he felt that these philosophical questions were an irrelevance and a diversion from the practical matters of ordinary living for which he and others had sufficient guidance: 'we should ... cure ourselves of the disease of asking abstract questions', and attend to immediate duties in a spirit of devotion.[88] The more Gandhi pondered on the nature of God and tried to conform his life to the guidance of God, the more he was forced to deal with the innumerable questions people raised with him as a reputed holy man, so his understanding became more simple and more profound. By the close of these years of reflection he come to the point when he could write that the guiding principles of his life were truth and love.

> If God who is indefinable can be at all defined, then I should say that God is TRUTH. It is impossible to reach HIM, that is TRUTH, except through LOVE. LOVE can only be expressed fully when man reduces himself to a cipher. This process of reduction to cipher is the highest effort man or woman is capable of making. It is the only effort worth making, and it is possible only through ever-increasing self-restraint.[89]

The Sabarmati ashram was home for Gandhi, and it was here that he tried to create an environment infused with his religious vision where people could grow into servants of God and thus into servants of India. He had poured his heart and soul into it, and he called it his best and only creation, despite its failures and problems.[90] Yet he was so seldom there, except in 1926, and in his absence it was run by a council of members, and its dominant spirit was Maganlal Gandhi, the grandson of Gandhi's uncle who had followed him home from South Africa. Even in that year of residence Gandhi was desparately busy, not only with running the ashram, but his vast correspondence, his writing for *Navajivan* and *Young India*, and his serialized autobiography, his discourses on the *Gita*, and his work to establish the AISA on top of daily prayer and spinning and receiving the many guests and visitors who pressed on the ashram while he was there in person. By the late 1920s it was not the small family group who just managed to survive its foundation: it was well over 200 strong, including 133 men, 66 women and 78 children. It was more like a little village with its own farming, dairying and tannery. Furthermore, it was sound financially, living on considerable charitable donations. (Its annual upkeep cost at least 18,000 rupees in 1925, and by 1928 its monthly expenditure was 3,000 rupees; by 1925 over 200,000 rupees had been given for land and buildings and by 1928 it had 132 acres and buildings worth over 300,000 rupees.[91])

Although its basic aim had not changed, in the 1920s the emphasis of the community's life turned firmly towards manual labour – cultivation, spinning, carding and weaving, dairying and tanning, as well as the

domestic labour needed to keep the communal life going. Gandhi's
strong streak of anti-intellectualism, which surfaced in his discussion of
religious problems, was clear at Sabarmati as early as 1924 when he
wrote, 'I am convinced that we have had an overdose of philosophical
and politcial studies. The faculty of working with our hands and feet is
all but atrophied. An attempt is being made at the Ashram to revive the
taste for hand labour.'[92] The daily schedule began with congregational
prayer from 4.15 to 4.45 a.m. and the day closed with prayer again from
7.00 to 7.30 p.m. The hours between were taken up with manual
labour, and two times for cooking and eating. The food was simple and
vegetarian. However, Gandhi found the running of the ashram immensely taxing; he claimed that it took more thought than a satyagraha
campaign, and he believed that even being Viceroy would stretch his
spiritual resources less![93] His burden in running the ashram when he was
so often far away and could only deal with problems by letter was
increased by the death of Maganlal in 1928, for he had been the one
whom Gandhi had trusted implicitly, not only on practical matters, but
to uphold the values the ashram enshrined. Gandhi never hesitated to
admit that the ashram's problems were many, and that it was not yet the
sort of place he longed to create. Despite the emphasis on simplicity and
non-possession, Gandhi realised that the ashram maintained a considerable standard of living compared with the really poor; even in 1927 he
was having to exhort the women not to hanker after jewellery and fine
clothes. Laxity over spinning and prayer, particularly in his absence,
grieved him sorely, and the problem of giving the daily prayer meetings
life and depth continued to disturb him throughout this period. But he
persisted in the practice in the hope that the genuine devotion of a very
few would ultimately infuse the rest. Other problems, endemic in any
such group, continued to plague him, in person or when he was far
away on tour. There were constant squabblings and personality clashes,
particularly among the women, disagreements when they attempted to
have a single kitchen for the whole ashram, and sexual experiments and
relationships which defied the principles of purity and chastity. It was
one of these fairly minor incidents among the boys in the ashram school
which in 1925 made Gandhi fast for a week. He told the readers of *Young
India* that experience had taught him that punishing children did not
purify but only hardened them; therefore out of love *he* was doing the
penance. 'If I am to identify myself with the grief of the least in India . . .
let me identify myself with the sins of the little ones under my care.' He
warned his readers that almost certainly this was not the last fast he
would undertake; fasts were like eyes to him, though they enabled him
to see the inner rather than the outer world, and he would abandon them
as willingly as he would his eyes.[94] Something of the moral compulsion
in a small community of these self-inflicted penances can be sensed if one
visualizes the frail man propped on a pillow, still determined to do his
daily spinning, or carried to the daily prayer meetings on his bed. His
weight had never risen over 8 stone since his release from Yeravda, and
now he lost 9 lbs in a week. But he rapidly regained this with a careful

return to 'normal' food, through two weeks of goat's milk and fruit juice, and was soon walking and sleeping normally. (It was on the occasion of this fast that he publicized the careful way in which these fasts were conducted, with regular drinks of water mixed with salt and soda, a daily enema and a sponge bath.[95])

The ashram community constituted Gandhi's family, and the rare glimpses we can still get of his relationships with his blood kin suggest that though he cared about them deeply in an idiosyncratic way, they bore a great burden because of their kinship with a Mahatma and his expectations of them. Kasturbhai kept doggedly to her place in the ashram, despite Gandhi's frequent absences. On some occasions she helped in his work outside Sabarmati, as, for example, in his campaign in 1927 to dissuade women from wearing heavy ornaments – work of which she specifically approved. But in 1928 changes in the ashram (which was the only married home she had) weighed her down mentally and physically, and she seemed so listless and uninterested in her surroundings that Gandhi attempted, unsuccessfully, to perusade her to take a break in the cooler climate of the Himalayan foothills.

Of their sons the eldest, Harilal, was the most resentful of his father's life-style and values. Although he remained tenuously in touch with his father he was totally outside his control, and his business escapades, for example, proved profoundly embarrassing when the public expected a Mahatma's son to be a model of rectitude. Manilal Gandhi, the second son, still in South Africa, distressed his father in early 1926 when he fell in love with a Muslim girl, and Gandhi argued that such a match was contrary to *dharma*. He warned his son of his mother's predictable and inconsolable bitterness at the prospect – indeed he did not even dare to put the idea to her! But then he used the public argument. 'Your marriage will have a powerful impact on the Hindu–Muslim question. Intercommunal marriages are no solutioin to this problem. You cannot forget nor will society forget that you are my son.'[96] The next year he was busy, like any ordinary Hindu father, arranging his son's marriage to a suitable Hindu girl. Such was his timetable that he had to plan to journey part of the way from Bombay to the wedding with Manilal in order to have any time at all to talk with him before the ceremony. It was a profoundly novel wedding: Gandhi enjoined total simplicity and an atmosphere of devotion and discipline. No presents were accepted, and it cost virtually nothing. When Ramdas, his third son, was married at the ashram in January 1928 the ceremony was also marked by a total lack of ostentation. Yet observers at this event saw that he was moved almost to tears as he spoke of Ramdas and his last born, Devadas, who were the sons closest to him. His human warmth, so seldom publicly displayed to his kin, prompted a compassionate letter to Manilal and his new wife, now back in South Africa, when he heard news of his daughter-in-law's miscarriage: he not only suggested treatment but urged them not to keep back such news from him because they feared his views on celibacy even within marriage.[97]

Even dearer to him than his sons was Maganlal. In controlled lan-

guage in *Young India*, he said his death hurt him even more that it hurt
the weeping widow, and but for his faith in God, he would be
distraught at the loss of one so close for 24 years, and so trusted that he
had been Gandhi's hands, feet and eyes. To Jawaharlal Nehru he did not
soften his words about this 'calamity'. 'It is well-nigh unbearable.
However I am putting on a brave front.'[98]

Meditating on the death of Maganlal in *Young India*, Gandhi had said
that Maganlal's life had shown how service of India and self-realization,
the true and deep knowledge of God, were synonymous. In the breadth
of practical work in the ashram Gandhi displayed his conviction that
the individual and society are interwoven: here was no private piety,
no spiritual individualism. The men and women who truly lived the
ashram life, like Maganlal, found their deepest selves and learned to
serve India simultaneously. So, too, was it in Gandhi's own life. He had
returned in the 1920s to his deepest roots as an individual in order to
become a better nationalist. Serving his nation meant working at the
very roots of its corporate life. Once he had withdrawn from active
Congress politics by the close of 1925 his public role was radical labour
for swaraj: to generate power within society, particularly by overcoming its deepest fissures, and to work for a moral and harmonious social
order. As he reflected on the roots of his own identity, so he wrestled
with the problem of the roots of a new Indian identity.

Harmony, tolerance and interdependence of equal but different
groups were in Gandhi's eyes the hallmarks of a society capable of
swaraj, and to him India's greatest flaw and tragedy was communal
conflict. Although he thought about it constantly and spoke of it often,
he was convinced from 1925 that he had no practical plan to suggest for
closing the widening chasm between Hindus and Muslims. He told
readers of *Young India* in August 1925, 'I have ceased to regard myself as
an expert or an authority on the Hindu–Muslim qustion', and when
people asked him to intervene or arbitrate in communal disputes he
refused.[99] He wrote privately to a businessman friend and supporter that
anything he might say would 'just be a cry in the wilderness'; he
repeatedly said that the most productive work he could do to promote
unity was to watch and pray and to wait on divine guidance. But when
that guidance came he would have no hesitation in emerging into public
work again for the cause.[100] When he heard from his Muslim doctor,
M.A. Ansari, that people were saying he had lost faith and interest in
communal unity he immediately denied this in *Young India*. His passion
and hope for that unity remained, but neither Hindus nor Muslims
seemed to share it, so his methods had to change. Meetings and
resolutions had once seemed hopeful, but now in an atmosphere of
'distrust, fear and hopelessness' he relied on prayer and individual acts of
friendship.[101]

Much of his amazing energy was at this time poured into the cause of
khadi, the spinning and wearing of truly swadeshi clothes, whose
symbol was the *charkha* or hand spinning wheel. He had consciously

narrowed down his earlier and broader call for swadeshi to this one issue. The wheel became so much a national symbol by the time of independence that its novelty as a symbol and cause can easily be forgotten. Indeed to the British and to many educated Indian politicians it was at least initially a cause for derision as well incomprehension. As Gandhi threw himself into promotiong the wheel and *khadi* after his release from Yeravda he had constantly to expound what it meant to him and why he saw it as central to radical labour for swaraj. It was of course an aspect of his rejection of the economics of Western civiliza-tion, but its benefits in Gandhi's eyes were far more specific in the work for swaraj. *Khadi* to him was the means by which Indians would be able to learn the essentials of widespread organization and mass discipline. (Indeed he would have done the same for the art of cooking if it had needed revival and demanded the same capacity for organization.[102]) Plying the wheel regularly and wearing *khadi* would also break down the barriers of caste, community and educational level. If Indians could learn these lessons and put them into practice then they would actually demonstrate their capacity for true swaraj – a capacity which in his eyes seemed singularly lacking after decades of nationalist politics. Further, organization, discipline and unity were prerequisites for the proper setting for civil disobedience.[103] More obviously, *khadi* would alleviate unemployment, prevent idleness (which he abhorred as the root of evil and the reason for poverty), and bring real help to the very poor, while simultaneously undermining one powerful element of the imperial interest in India, namely the profits of the cotton exporters.[104] The products of the wheel, being Indian rather than foreign, should have a particular beauty in the eyes of anyone who loved the Indian nation.[105] Gandhi's concern for the right means in the furtherance of any cause also drew him strongly to *khadi*, for in this work he saw no possibility of abuse, while the other means that had been tried seemed to have brought to the surface of Indian society 'the ugliest of our passions' – anger, mistrust, division and strife.[106] These were the themes he hammered home as he toured the country, preaching the gospel of *khadi* he had made peculiarly his own, as he wrote about it in his two weeklies, as he tried unsuccessfully to impose a 'spinning franchise' within the Congress organization, and as he himself spun daily, whether in the ashram, in a train or on a sick-bed.

It was to promote *khadi* and the revival of the *charkha*, a forgotten art among most Indians, that Gandhi worked for his own national spinning organization which would have none of the drawbacks he had seen in Congress politics since his release from Yeravda, and would allow him to escape from the impossible position in which he found himself in relation to the Swarajists in Congress. Such a foundation was being publicly discussed by him and among Congressmen in July 1925.[107] He had drafted a constitution for an All-India Spinners' Association by late September and the AISA came into being then as a result of an AICC resolution at its Patna meeting. So the Swarajists had control of Con-

gress, while Gandhi had his own area of work where his values and his
terms were unquestioned. As President he unashamedly called it 'a one
man's show'.[108] Its thrust was to be economic reform, as an expert
organization for the development of hand-spinning and *khadi*; and
Gandhi insisted that by its very constitution it was precluded from
participation in politics, just as its separate identity would shield it from
the ups and downs of Congress politics.[109] But inevitably the existence
of such a body and Gandhi's predominance within it had a significant
impact on Gandhi's standing, giving him access to funds, a platform and
an independent all-India base. He stayed at Sabarmati in 1926 partly to
establish the association on a firm foundation, but in 1927, when his
health became so precarious, it was evident that he could not continue
to bear so large a burden in relation to it. In May of that year the AISA
council appointed an officiating Chairman, though Gandhi remained
President and the final authority on controversial matters. But the daily
administration of the association was now in the hands of the new
Chairman, Jamnalal Bajaj, a cotton-merchant, banker and Congressman
from the Central Provinces (a prime cotton-growing region), and the
Secretary, the Gujarati politician, Shankarlal Banker, both of whom
were twenty years younger that Gandhi. The organizational burden of
the association must have been considerable, and at times intensely
frustrating. Apart from collecting funds for *khadi* work, it collected yarn
supposed to be spun by its members as a condition of membership, it
employed spinners and weavers, helped to distribute *khadi* and ran *khadi*
stores. Perhaps not surprisingly much of the fund-raising depended on
Gandhi's personal efforts and connections. When he retired to the
ashram in 1926 and gave up touring, the AISA's finances came 'to a
standstill', in his words, and he gratefully accepted a loan from his
Marwari businessman friend, G.D. Birla. By contrast, the following
year his tour of south India and Ceylon brought in very substantial
donations.[110] By the end of its first year the AISA had distributed over
nine lakhs of rupees to 110 carders, 42,959 spinners and 3,407 weavers,
in 150 production centres. The numbers involved grew in the following
year, but organizational inefficiency made it impossible to obtain fully
accurate figures. The association's annual report calculated that there
were now over 83,000 spinners, that it was organizing weaving in
nearly two and a half thousand villages, compared with one and half
thousand in the first year. Despite this expansion it was only a drop in
the ocean of rural India. Gandhi also bewailed the fact that members
were not sending in their voluntary donations of yarn – for this to his
mind suggested that they lacked the sense of discipline and duty to
progress towards swaraj. 'Public work has not yet risen from the status
of a pastime or patronage to that of a primary duty. And yet for one
who desires a healthy social and public life, public service is as much a
duty as is service done to oneself or to one's family.'[111]

Khadi was Gandhi's main work for economic reform in India, unlike
those few in public life who as a result of contact with Western political

theory believed that economic change was the key to all the necessary changes in India. Gandhi was far more concerned with changing people's hearts and attitudes than with attempting to reform the economic order: for him people rather than systems were the core of historical change. Of course he was also a realist about what he could actually attempt, given his age and limited strength, and he preferred to concentrate on what he felt he could do and not dissipate his energy on problems that could only be effectively tackled after independence. Yet he did comment briefly on his hopes for India's economic order.

Compared with Indian socialists like Jawaharlal Nehru he was far from radical: he wanted no forcible dispossession of the wealthy, whether they were landholders or factory owners, and he abhorred the vision of some inevitable class struggle and the organization of labour to that end. The key notion behind his economic theory (inasmuch as he had one) was trusteeship: those with wealth must consider themselves its trustees and use it for the good of all. The right relationship between capital and labour was co-operation, not conflict. Reflecting on the work done in Ahmedabad among mill-workers, under his guidance though not directly by him, he stressed its emphasis on educating labour and uniting the local work force. He saw this not as anti-capitalist or as in any direct sense political; and he rejected utterly the idea that he was exploiting labour for a political end. Given the disorganization of labour in other regions and its manipulation by unscrupulous and often communally-minded leaders, he shunned the idea of an all-India union. He believed it was he who was truly radical, by attempting to work on the hearts of owners and workers, and to generate internal self-consciousness and strength among the workers, rather than imposing on them some spurious political programme.[112]

Gandhi's understanding of economic relations was shot through with emphases originating in Hindu tradition, such as the duty of the wealthy to extend charity, the vision of a harmonious society where different groups with their own functions were interdependent. But in the 1920s he was forced to confront very precisely some of the aspects of India's social order which were rooted in Hindu tradition: for he believed that radical labour for swaraj meant attending to society's most basic attitudes and relationships. Swaraj in his eyes was impossible if the social order was corrupt.[113]

His primary social concern at this time was the problem of untouchability, the rejection of a whole group of the poorest and most menial in society as a result of Hindu ideas of hierarchy, and purity and pollution. Now, as he travelled widely, he saw in harsh practice the power of this social division, and the poverty and degradation it caused, though he had rejected the whole idea far earlier and inveighed and worked against it even in South Africa. Once home in India, having tested the temper of public opinion, he was aware of the strength of Hindu orthodoxy and he took care not to equate his campaign against untouchability with the question of caste as a whole, for fear of holding back the work on what he saw as the most vital and urgent reform. Rather, he argued, his was a campaign to purify and strengthen caste by abolishing this pernicious custom.[114] For Gandhi untouchability was primarily a religious problem.[115] He believed that there was no warrant for it in scripture: it was a late and evil accretion which actually harmed and threatened the Hindu tradition he so treasured, and its observance was positively sinful. If it continued he feared that Hinduism would not survive. However, he was also clear that its observance impeded India's journey to swaraj at an obvious level, for such a profound fissure in Hindu society might well generate violent rebellion among untouchables against the higher castes,[116] and would give leverage to any imperial authority wishing to maintain Indian divisions in order to rule.

Personal example was one of Gandhi's strategies to end untouchability. He mixed freely with them, as everybody knew; he ate with them, and the untouchable whose admission to the ashram had jeopardized its early existence ate as an equal with the other ashram members. But Gandhi did not expect everyone to go this far. For most caste Hindus the obligation was to treat the untouchables as a caste *within* Hindu society, affording them citizens' right. They should be allowed to use wells, roads and public transport, attend schools and enter temples, though conventions prohibiting marriage or meals with them would remain, as they did between members of 'clean' castes. Gandhi's main method of attack was his battery of public pronouncements, in speeches and the press. Most of his exhortations were addressed to caste Hindus. Theirs was the penance; theirs was the primary obligation to change their attitudes and practices. To untouchables he preached a different gospel of purification – to change the habits that distinguished them from and horrified many caste Hindus, such as eating meat or drinking alchohol, and to attend to their personal cleanliness and stop observing distinctions of untouchability even among themselves. However Gandhi did not feel it necessary to attack the tasks that made the untouchables so degraded and filthy. To him latrine cleaning, for example, done well and consciously as service, was a godly work. It was not surprising that as his campaign gathered strength some untouchables began to complain that Gandhi was no better than an orthodox Hindu, and that his calls for changed attitudes did not tackle the basic economic and occupational aspects of untouchability which would continue to shackle them, whatever changes of heart occurred among caste Hindus. The issue of temple entry was a particularly symbolic one: if untouchables were admitted to Hindu temples it would be a very significant sign of changing values. But on this, too, Gandhi was wary. He totally supported a satyagraha campaign in the Princely state of Travancore in 1924 to allow untouchables to use the roads around the temples. But he opposed any forcible entry into temples by untouchables, and in 1926 was maintaining that the time had not yet come for satyagraha on this issue.[117] But while he was convalescing in Bangalore in 1927 he floated the idea of a new all-India association to work with a definite constructive programme for the uplift of untouchables, and discussed it with a prominent orthodox Hindu politician. Experience of the depths of the problem, and realization of the need to involve the known exponents of orthodoxy in plans to make untouchables acceptable to caste Hindus seem by this time to have convinced him of the need for some new departure. Later that year he had come to the point where he was planning to leave aside his *khadi* work and devote his attention to the solution of the untouchability problem.[118]

As the enormity of untouchability as actually practised in India dawned on Gandhi in the 1920s he began to confront the far broader but related question of caste itself. Soon after his return from Africa he had written with guarded approval of caste as a social system inculcating discipline, and said he was opposed to movements for its destruction, though he recognised it had its evils.[119] Now he began to distinguish between the many castes and sub-castes (known as *jatis*) actually found in India, clinging to severe forms of separation and breeding an intense feeling of social superiority and inferiority, and an ideal he called *varnashramadharma*. This owed much to ancient scriptural accounts of caste as a four-fold division of society in which each of the four castes or *varnas* had a peculiar function for the good of the whole, be it fighting and ruling, trading or exercising priestly functions, or performing essential labouring tasks. Gandhi visualized a harmonious social order of four castes or *varnas* into which men were born, but which were not inferior or superior to each other. He was beginning to describe this ideal in late 1924, and to assert it more forcefully in 1925. Early in 1926 he answered a question in his attitude to caste categorically:

> I do not believe in caste as it is at present constituted, but I do believe in the four fundamental divisions regulated according to the four principal occupations. The existing innumerable divisions with the attendant artificial restrictions and elaborate ceremonial are harmful to the growth of a religious spirit, as also to the social well-being of the Hindus and therefore also their neighbours.[120]

But it was in 1927 that he began to assert bluntly that his ideal had nothing to do with caste as currently found in India: the latter was a monstrous parody and distortion of *varna* as properly understood.[121]

Gandhi realized that in practical terms a frontal attack on caste as a total social structure was impossible. His specific suggestions for immediate reform were restricted to a limited range of practices. He decried the practice of giving lavish caste feasts at weddings and funerals as intolerably wasteful: money would be better spent on education and social welfare for the benefit of the caste and, through it, of the whole society.[122] On prevailing restrictions in marriages between people of different castes he was critical where the restriction of choice merely confirmed the division of society into a plethora of sub-castes; he believed in four castes only and therefore at this stage supported marriage within broad caste groups, just as he felt that marriage should be confined to people of the same faith.[123] On the question of eating with people of other castes Gandhi was frankly undecided at this point.[124] His whole approach was to put an ultimate vision of a purified fourfold caste order before Hindus, but in practice not to force the pace and stir up bitter feeling on issues which were minor compared with the great iniquity of untouchability. He always advocated civility and consideration for others in matters of social reform, hoped that caste leaders themselves would take the lead in reform, and countenanced an individual's stand in defiance of his caste only if the practice in question was positively immoral. In his handling of the problems of untouchability and more widely of caste as a social system, Gandhi's relationship with Hindu tradition was as clear as in his overtly theological pronouncements. He was deeply commited to that tradition, but undoubtedly saw himself as a reformer of it. He preached and acted in the name of a *purified* tradition, using its sources selectively, judging accepted scriptural authority by the standards of reason and morality. His aim was not just to renovate tradition, but to enable it to grow and evolve, using the power and authority of its own resources.

The other great social issue with which Gandhi felt bound to grapple in his grass-roots work for swaraj was the place and treatment of women in Indian society. Here he faced a complex problem, where tradition was reinforced by economic constraints on women. Whatever the high value placed on womanhood in Hindu scripture, and the possible equality of women and men at the earliest stages of Hindu civilization, in practice by the late nineteenth and early twentieth centuries Hindu women were treated as adjuncts of the males in a family, and primarily as bearers and rearers of children. A woman's spiritual identity was achieved through marriage and motherhood, and widows were not permitted to remarry. Further, the control of women through arranged marriages was a powerful buttress of the caste system. Women were so poorly educated that they had little chance of individual development or achievement and were often seen as an economic burden on their families, except in their capacity for domestic and agricultural labour. In poor rural households they were often staggeringly overworked in the house and the fields, over and above their frequent pregnancies; while in rich households they all too easily became idle gossips and display stands for lavish jewellery which reflected the family's status. A host of interrelated social problems therefore faced the would-be reformer: most families' initial preference for baby boys rather than girls, knowing the eventual financial burden of a marriage and dowry; arranged marriages between child brides and much older men to conform to caste restrictions on choice; the plight of child widows unable to remarry; the harsh conditions often suffered by older widows; and women's general seclusion and lack of participation in public life, to name only the most pressing.

It is impossible at this distance in time and from a different cultural environment to understand fully Gandhi's personal and undoubtedly complex attitude towards women. He must have been deeply influenced at a conscious and subconscious level by the ambiguities in Hindu perceptions of womanhood: the sense of woman as temptress and a source of mysterious power, as well as the vision of the self-sacrificing wife and mother. He had his own memories of a strongly religious and iron-willed mother, and the incomplete nature of his relationship with her because she died before he could approach and relate to her as a well-established professional and family man. His relations with women were also deeply affected by his vow of celibacy and his belief that sexual activity was degrading and weakening. His publicly proclaimed celibacy and struggles to maintain an absolute standard of *brahmacharya*, or restraint upon the physical senses, gave him an unprecedented freedom to work with women. Many who flocked to his women's meetings or lived in the ashram evidently found him compelling. There was no doubt that unlike most Hindu men, and certainly unlike most public figures, he had a sense of empathy with women: he saw himself as 'mothering' many of his colleagues and dependents, and tried to equate himself with women in order to serve them.[125] He acknowledged that they had received rough treatment in the past at the hands of men, and argued strongly that if women's role was to change, if they were to be treated as equal human beings, the attitude of men as well as women's self-perceptions would have to change, and there must be no double standards of morality expected of the two sexes. When he arranged the marriage of his son, Manilal, he appealed to him to uphold his father's ideals. 'You know my attitude towards women. Men have not been treating them well. I have proposed this alliance assuming you to be capable of coming up to my ideals.' Manilal should treat his wife with compassion, not as a slave, should care for her as he would himself, and never force his sexual attentions upon her.[126] Gandhi's concern for women stemmed not just from the combinations of experiences and influences within his own psyche, he sensed that they were formative influences in the lives of their children, and that in their attitudes lay part of the secret of achieving changes of heart which he saw as necessary for true swaraj. (Indian social reformers had long known that women within the home were often the main protagonists and buttresses of tradition.) Whatever the tortuous workings of the Mahatma's psyche, his belief in sexual restraint which finds so little sympathy in the modern world, and however complex the sublimated urges which found an outlet in Gandhi's maternal instincts and self-imposed caring roles, it must never be forgotten that in him the women of India found a very considerable champion.

However, his female ideal was not the 'modern woman', liberated from traditional social, economic and physical restraints by birth control, the right to divorce and a new economic independence. He would have seen no moral good in claims by later twentieth-century feminists for 'freedom' to rule their own lives and to compete with men. Indeed he stated specifically that there was much in tradition which should be retained and cherished: 'we should not give up the ideal of woman's duty while espousing the cause of her rights.'[127] The symbol of his ideal woman was drawn from Hindu epic tradition – Sita, the wife of King Rama, who cruelly rejected by him, nonetheless maintained a brave constancy and purity, courageously bearing her ordeal until they were reunited. So within the symbolism of tradition Gandhi preached female virtues of bravery and independence, and a capacity to bear suffering; the model he offered to Indian woman was the virtuous and faithful wife.

As in the matter of caste, he consciously and selectively used elements of tradition to enable a new response to a changing situation. He was convinced that Indian women must draw on the deep resources available within themselves as women and within their religious inheritance to participate in public life, and in particular to play the vital role he saw for them in the struggle for swaraj. Unless they did so, and unless society tackled the evils in contemporary treatment of women, he argued that there could be no real swaraj.[128] When the question of the priority of political or social reform was raised he refused to distinguish between them or place one before the other: social, economic and political reform must proceed simultaneously. 'The sooner it is recognized that many of our social evils impede our march towards swaraj, the greater will be our progress towards our cherished goal. To postpone social reform till after the attainment of swaraj is not to know the meaning of swaraj.'[129] All through the 1920s he hammered home that *purdah*, enforced seclusion of women, practised among some Hindu castes as well as Muslims, was inhumane, immoral, and deprived the emerging nation of the work for swaraj which its women could perform. Indian women must become conscious of their potential, must exercise their right and duty to serve outside as well as inside the home, and must participate on equal terms with men in the work for swaraj.[130] He realized that this changing role would need readjustments by men unused to working with women, and by women who would have to learn how to work in formal organizations and not bring to that work bitchiness, suspicion and intrignes; indeed he noted wryly that even Indian men found selfless and open-handed organization of public work difficult.

It was not just that the seclusion of women in the private domain prevented half of India from working for swaraj. Gandhi believed profoundly that there were certain particularly female qualities and capacities which were much needed in the radical labour for a new society and polity. He often spoke of women as having a special capacity for self-sacrifice, learned early in the cause of the family, which must now be put to the use of the emerging nation.[131] It was little wonder that the apostle of satyagraha, of self-imposed suffering in the cause of truth, should see women as his natural allies. Moreover he felt women were so socially situated that they were particularly fitted to work at the three central elements of his national programme: reviving the art of spinning and making honourable the wearing of *khadi*, treating untouchables as

fellow humans, and extending hands of simple friendship across communal boundaries, where men's work in public meetings and speeches
had failed. Increasingly in the 1920s Gandhi became aware of his need
for more women workers, and it was partly because of this that he cared
so deeply about the attitudes of women in the ashram, and exposed
them to the new experiences of equality with men, communal living
and fraternity across traditional social boundaries.

As Gandhi toured India, often speaking at women's meetings and
encouraging women to break out of some traditional social moulds and
follow him into public work, he became more deeply aware of the
attitudes and suffocating practices which restricted women and reduced
their esteem in their own eyes as well as those of men. Inevitably too his
public position meant that he was asked very specific questions about
the treatment of women. He was not slow in response, and as on the
question of untouchability he argued that there was no religious warrant
for many of the practices he condemned, and that their abolition would
purify and strengthen Hindu society. Of course he was not alone in
arguing for change: there was a tradition of social reformers and their
organizations stretching well back into the nineteenth century. But
Gandhi argued so strongly in the context of Indian and Hindu values
that he could never be accused of 'Westernizing' or undermining traditional values with foreign influences; and he placed social reform square-
ly in the centre of the work to achieve swaraj, whereas earlier social
reform movements had been kept apart from the political work for fear
of alienating the orthodox.

Among the specific issues affecting women which concerned him was
the basic preference of most families for sons. He condemend this
outright as sinful superstition, and also the mercifully rare but not
unknown practice of quietly killing off baby girls. Realizing that part of
the sense of burden which accompanied the brith of a girl stemmed from
the inevitable expenses of a wedding and dowry, he condemned these,
too. Ostentation, commercialism and bargaining should have no place
in arranging a sacramental union which was to be a lifelong and holy
bond. The weddings celebrated at the ashram were examples of de-
corum and solemnity without traditional displays and transactions. The
plight of child brides and child widows disturbed him particularly, and
some of his fiercest criticisms were reserved for 'ill-matched unions'
between young girls and much older men. He argued that no girl should
be married until several years after puberty: child marriage was nothing
but rape and undermined both morality and the physique of the nation.
Further, if young girls of 15 or under became widows they should be
remarried by their fathers' arrangement, for no child could be expected
to understand what holy widowhood could mean for an older woman.

The sanctity of widowhood must be felt by the widow, [and] cannot
be imposed upon her. Divorce and other irregularities going on in the
West have surely nothing to do with the very simple question of

doing elementary justice to the thousands of our own sisters. Hinduism is in grave danger of being undermined by our own fanaticism
and the habit of defending every practice of Hinduism no matter how
repugnant it may be to the moral sense of the world.[132]

Gandhi's desire to purify Hindu tradition meant that in some respects he
was 'traditional' as well as being a reformer. For example, he saw
nothing wrong in arranged marriages, but did insist that the girl should
have the final decision over her parents' choice for her. Although he
condemned *enforced* widowhood (of older women as well as of young
girls) he cherished the Hindu *ideal* of widowhood for older women if
they freely chose it. A widow's life marked by self-control, sacrifice and
service was an ornament and benefit to religion and society. He argued
that women should be educated so that they not only became better
wives but could support themselves as widows and undertake such
useful work as nursing or teaching uneducated village women. (He was
well aware that some widows tended to become idle or travel on
'supposed pilgrimage'!)[133]

Gandhi's sharp eye for the realities of Indian society and his sympathy
for women drew him into discussion not only of major social assumptions and practices, but also of the most mundane of female experiences.
He advised on the traditional custom of social avoidance of women
during menstruation which arose from Hindu belief that menstrual
blood was polluting; he felt that this custom was neither necessary nor
obilgatory, and that all that was necessary was that women should avoid
hard physical work or sexual intercourse. But he suggested that women
such as his European disciple, Mirabehn, should tread delicately in this
matter, and have a regard for the feelings of Hindus around her. Gandhi
also challenged the custom of wearing heavy or lavish jewellery. In
Bihar in 1925 he was horrified by the heavy bangles and nose rings he
saw and decided to make public his criticism of a custom which he had
for some time deprecated; it was not only uncomfortable but liable to
lead to dirt and disease.

> I had never seen so much ornamentation anywhere else. Heavier
> articles I have seen, as for instance the unbearable heavy ankle-hoops –
> I cannot call them rings – of Kathiawar ladies, but never so much
> body space covered over with so many bangles and what-nots.

Economy and health should be sufficient argument against 'these articles
of personal furniture.'[134] Later he protested that it was barbarous to
pierce a girl's ears or nose, and warned one close woman associate that
the craze for jewellery was only a cover for sensual desire. He appealed
to women to give him their ornaments, so that a symbol of female
subservience to custom could be put to the work for swaraj.

In one of his articles on virtuous widowhood Gandhi wrote, 'It is
good to swim in the waters of tradition, but to sink in them is
suicide.'[135] This perfectly described his own position: working in the
ambience of tradition, accepting its buoyancy and capacity for move-

ment, using it to make progress, yet being its master rather than its
victim. However, his selective use of tradition to promote limited
reform has laid him open to considerable criticism. In retrospect and by
later standards his critique of women's treatment and roles did not
extend to some of the fundamentals of women's position in society; nor
did participation in his work for swaraj radically affect women's roles
and expectations. Struggle for women's rights, personal, social and
economic, still has to continue late in the twentieth century. Yet his
achievement was to invite and enable women to perform certain public
roles, even if these were restricted, and to make discussion of women's
position a legitimate and essential part of the movement for freedom.

During the mid–1920s Gandhi's range of concerns was very broad. He
had been forced by external circumstances to ponder in depth on his
own identity, and on the identity of an emergent India capable of
swaraj. He visualized a total renewal of society from its roots upwards,
so that it would grow into a true nation, characterized by harmony and
sympathy instead of strife and suspicion, in which castes, communities
and both sexes would be equal, complementary and interdependent.
Experience of politics had convinced him even more deeply that such a
radical work could only be done by people trained to disciplined and
selfless living; he believed that his recipe for individual life, for social and
political change, which culminated in satyagraha, was a message of
eternal value which must not be sullied by the use of wrong means.
Apparent withdrawal from politics had been essential to preserve his
integrity of vision and action, but he was willing to resume a political
role in the work for swaraj provided it was on his own terms. In
mid–May he made this abundantly plain in a private letter.[136]

> I am keeping fairly fit. I am biding my time and you will find me
> leading the country in the field of politics when the country is ready. I
> have no false modesty about me. I am undoubtedly a politician in my
> own way, and I have a scheme for the country's freedom. But my
> time is not yet and may never come to me in this life. If it does not, I
> shall not shed a single tear. We are all in the hands of God. I therefore
> await His guidance.

7

CIVIL DISOBEDIENCE

The quest for legitimacy and unity, 1928 – 1934.

Gandhi's return to active politics was not inevitable. He was doubtful early in 1928 if his health would ever again 'stand the awful strain of public speaking and public demonstrations'; and towards the close of the year he maintained, as he had done since 1924, that he could only exert a leadership role on his own terms – if his priorities were accepted. 'I shall only lead India when the nation comes to me to be led, when there is a national call.' He added that he must feel certain of his hold over the masses, and their ability to follow him in non-violence.[1] Before Gandhi could contemplate such a reassertion of leadership two developments were necessary. Within himself he would have to be convinced that people would heed his priorities and that he would not be enmeshed in the sort of strife which so distressed him and weakened the possibility of any strong common action in 1924–5. External circumstances would also have to change so that people actually called him into action because they needed him and his skills.

Gandhi's career once again raises the whole question of the nature of political leadership, particularly in an all-India context. Was the all-India, national leader one whose ideals and practical skills at least temporarily served the needs of the majority of his politically active compatriots, enabling productive relationships among themselves, with less educated Indians, and with their rulers? Gandhi's role as an all-India leader was particularly complex because it occurred at the intersection of so many political relationships: between British and Indian in the imperial enterprise, between Indians of different regions, communities, castes and generations in the enterprise of building a nation. In Indian political life one of the critical and often fraught relationships was between the regions of the subcontinent, with their own histories, languages and social structures, and any actual or potential all-India organization, be it the raj itself, or more particularly in Gandhi's experience, the would-be national Congress. Further, he was active for such a long time in Indian public life in a period when the political system itself was actually changing. Indian politics were never static between 1915 and 1948: the passing years changed the people involved as generations came and went, the issues altered, and the very structures of political life were in the process of reform and transformation as India moved in stages of liberalization from being an autocratically ruled part of a British empire to becoming an independent state. Could Gandhi in the next decades be an effective and credible leader, or was his assertion of authority in 1920–2 a 'one-off', a unique position enabled by the upheavals caused by the First World War? Some detail of the complicated political changes occurring in 1928–34 is inevitable, lest analysis of Gandhi's role becomes simplistic, ignoring the ambiguities of his position and the constraints upon him. Readers with a particular interest in the environment in which Gandhi worked will be pointed to specialist studies.[2]

Late 1928 to 1934 forms a unity in Gandhi's life because during these years he saw himself and was accepted by others, both British and Indian, as Congress's major leader and spokesman – whether he was actively organizing a resumption of civil disobedience, was attending a Round Table Conference in London, or was in gaol, for even in gaol he was active and dominant in political decisions compared to his seclusion from public life in Yeravda in 1922–4. These were years when Indian politics were dominated by civil disobedience, either active or imminent. The new campaign lasted from 1930 to 1934 with an intermission for most of 1931 when Congress negotiated with the raj and eventually sent Gandhi to the constitutional conference in London. But civil disobedience was not a simple matter of a conflict between imperialism and nationalism, though it has often been portrayed in this way, by those wishing to build up a new nation's self-conscious identity and history, or Western devotees of the Mahatma anxious to display a conflict between 'might' and 'right'. Civil disobedience in the 1930s was not essentially an attempt to dislodge the British. It was far more Congress's quest for legitimacy as mouthpiece and representative of a unified Indian nation, designed to prove and establish Congress in a unique role in relation both to Indians and to the British, so that its spokesmen were formidably positioned and armed to *negotiate* India's future with the British. Civil disobedience was also a test of the raj's legitimacy, as the rulers planned a package of constitutional reform in British India and a federal union with Princely India to create a new polity where Indian political aspirations and activities would be channelled into governing India without undermining ultimate imperial supremacy. The British, like Gandhi in his idiosyncratic way, were seeking to build a new order in India; they knew they needed Indian collaboration if the exercise was to be successful and long-lasting, and for this reason they were particularly sensitive to the mood of different sections of public opinion on the subcontinent as they responded to civil disobedience and balanced control and suppression at times with a willingness to negotiate with Gandhi and Congress. In their handling of civil disobedience both the Gandhi-led Congress and the British were consciously playing for the hearts and minds of the Indian people.

Gandhi's 'return' to politics

Gandhi's initial rise to power in politics had been occasioned and enabled by a particular set of circumstances created by the repercussions of the First World War on the sub-continent. His re-emergence as a dominant figure in all-India Congress politics late in 1928 occurred in the context of the ebbing legitimacy of the reformed political structures the raj had created in 1919 as an attempt to buttress British dominion with Indian co-operation. The reformed constitution had actually functioned during the 1920s, despite initial non-co-operation by Congress and the subsequent desire of the Swarajists to wreck the legislatures by their actions within them. In only two provinces did a breakdown in the political structures occur. Increasingly constructive legislation was passed and Indian politicians began to work with British administrators and to exercise real influence over government. (It was no conincidence that the British offered special terms of early retirement to ICS men who felt unable to serve India in the new political environment where they would be expected to behave as colleagues of Indians rather than paternalist administrators, though comparatively few took up the offer.)

One of the most striking developments in political life as a result of the reforms was the way the province, so often to become a state within independent India's federal union, became increasingly the most significant arena for most politically conscious and active Indians. Much of the drive of local politics was channelled into the provincial structures of power and into the struggles to control them. As the province became the natural context of much political action so was reinforced each province's unique historical experience and identity. In the future any all-India political party or leader would be constrained by these deepening and consolidated provincial identities, and would have to come to terms with leading provincial politicians whether to form a national entity such as a party or even a state on a viable base, or to construct a viable continental strategy or policy which could evoke popular support. However, there were real strains in the working of the 1919 reforms. There was as yet no organized party system such as sustains the parliamentary system of government in Britain at any level of Indian politics; consequently Indian ministers rarely had reliable support in the legislatures and tended both to rely on the government's nominees in the legislatures and to support the government. Provincial governors still retained considerable powers, including authority to certify legislation Indian legislators would not pass. And real financial stringency meant that there was a limited and actually decreasing amount of money to spend on the aspects of provincial government such as education which had been transferred to Indian control. Quite apart from the beginnings of a demand among some, mostly younger, politicians for total independence, which had evoked Gandhi's scorn in late 1927, there was unease about the working of the reforms and clear recognition among rulers and ruled that they could not last long as an acceptable framework for stable government.

The 1919 reforms had built into them a review after a decade, but a Conservative government in London, fearful lest a government further to the left should be in power by then, appointed the Statutory Commission of enquiry into the working of the reforms late in 1927. Headed by Sir John Simon, it was an all-white committee of British parliamentarians, who were to report to the British parliament for *its* decision on India's future; it seemed a blatant negation of imperial promises of increasing Indian participation in the government of their own country. The only role accorded to Indians was to give evidence to the peripatetic commissioners. A wide cross-section of Indians active in politics, including many Congressmen, preferred to boycott the Commission, and wherever Simon and his colleagues travelled they were greeted by hostile crowds exhorting them to go home.[3] Gandhi told Motilal Nehru that he thought the Simon Commission was an 'organized insult to a whole people', and he confided to his old friend, C.F. Andrews, that he distrusted Simon and saw 'no truthfulness about anything emanating from the Commission' (perhaps the most severe condemnation he as a self-perceived truth-seeker could have made).[4] He took no interest in the Commission's work; neither it nor other attempts to formulate a new constitution for India interested him much, as he admitted to the British editor of the Calcutta paper, *The Statesman*, who tried to involve him in some broadly-based constitutional discussions in mid-1928. 'I confess ... that neither the Statutory Commission nor constitution-making interests me much. I am concentrating my attention upon the means of attainment of swaraj'[5] Although he felt the boycott of the Commission and the huge demonstrations against it were good and useful in their way, he lamented that they had no reality behind them, no solid work for swaraj, and he could not envisage himself leading such an insubstantial gesture.[6] He would indeed have been prepared to welcome Simon at the Sabarmati ashram had Simon sought him out, but he had no intention himself of seeking an interview since he felt he could in no way help Simon in his work.[7]

The other aspect of political life which drew Gandhi back into active politics was that same one which had made him strike out on his own path to swaraj – disunity among Indians. Although the raj and its structures were beginning to lose their legitimacy in the eyes of many Indians, there was no alternative focus of loyalty or plan for the country's furture. Congress in the 1920s was opposed by an increasing number of politically-minded Muslims, by a range of experienced Liberal–Moderate politicians who felt its policies of opposition to the raj were too radical and destructive, and by a loose coalition of orthodox Hindus who feared its sensitivity to Muslim feeling. It was itself riven by internal feuds, conflicting provincial priorities and increasingly a gap in sympathy and aim between the established leaders and the growing generation, symbolized by the different stances of Motilal Nehru and his son, for example within one family. However, in response to the Simon Commission, Motilal and his legal colleague and friend, the Moderate ex-Congressman and former Law Member of the Government of India, T.B. Sapru, organized an All Parties Conference to try to achieve a widely acceptable alternative constitutional plan. Its fruit, known as the Nehru Report, appeared in August 1928.

This report envisaged India's future as a federation of British and Princely India within the British empire, but having the same status as the white dominions. It did not suggest the road marked out by the 1919 reforms, of devolving more power to the provinces. Residual power would remain firmly with a central government responsible to the electorate. Such a central government would inevitably be dominated by Hindus because of the logistics of numbers and the presence of Princely India in the new state. However, Muslims were guaranteed religious freedom and offered new Muslim majority provinces such as Sind and the North-West Frontier, they were to have reserved seats in the central legislature and the legislatures of those provinces where they would be a minority, but they would lose their separate electorates, written into British reforms in 1909 and 1919. The Nehru Report was a major achievement both in vision and in constitutional drafting, reflecting the legal eminence and wide political experience of Nehru and Sapru. It was also a real attempt to deal with the communal problem and reassure Muslims of a valued and secure position within a new united nation state.[8] However, it rapidly became the target for a broad range or opposition – from Muslims, from orthodox Hindus and from Congressmen themselves, particularly the pro-independence group which included younger radicals like Jawaharlal Nehru and the Bengali Subhas Chandra Bose, and older men who opposed Motilal on less ideological grounds.[9]

Gandhi, with his professed lack of interest in constitutional schemes, whether emanating from British or Indian pens, took no part in the All Parties Conference and its work, though he was always present behind the scenes and was kept informed of developments by the two Nehrus. In fact it was he who saved the conference's work from collapse at one point by suggesting the formation of a small committee to draft the constitution.[10] He lamented such disunity to Motilal, comparing the Conference and its work with that of the Simon Commission. 'We are engaged in an unequal duel; on the one hand are clever whole-timers acting with one mind and with the greatest deliberation; on the other we are part-timers having many irons in the fire and having as many minds as our numbers.'[11] Gandhi gave public support to the Nehru Report, urging that it would be anti-national to resist it to the point of creating disunity; he argued that what was now essential was 'a little forbearance, a little mutual respect, a little mutual trust, a little give and take and much confidence not in our little selves but in the great nation of which each one of us is but a humble member.'[12] However, he was convinced that unless Indians had some sanction with which to back the report, they would still be in the position of beggars, and the only means he could see of generating such internal strength was the boycott of foreign cloth.[13] Despite Gandhi's misgivings, of which Motilal was well aware, Motilal pleaded with him to come to the annual Congress session in Calcutta when the Nehru Report would be a major issue. He could envisage the conflicts that might emerge, for as the weeks passed the opposition to the report even among Congressmen was becoming alarmingly apparent. Gandhi agreed to go to Calcutta at Christmas, not least because he had urged poor Motilal to accept the Congress Presidency in the belief that he was a senior figure who might be able to unify the warring groups behind his report. The stage was thus set for the 'national call' without which Gandhi had asserted he would not return to an overtly political role.

Gandhi's own priorities for work were national unity and the development of national strength. To this end he had laboured since his release from Yeravda. To this end he had stood aside from Congress politics. But now in 1928 his own inner perceptions of what he could do began to change, and prepared the way for his reassertion of political leadership. Probably the greatest single cause of this inner change was a local satyagraha in the Bardoli district of Gujarat, which suggested to him that in contrast to his shattered hopes of 1922 civil disobedience might now be properly used by Indians *en masse* as the sanction behind their demands.

The Bardoli satyagraha lasted from February to August 1928.[14] During it the district displayed the qualities of courage, cohesion, and strong direct action which Gandhi simultaneously perceived as so singularly absent in the politicians' reaction to the Simon Commission and their attempts to achieve an alternative plan for India's future. Its objective was to obtain a government inquiry into the level of land revenue demand, which had recently been raised by 20 percent. (Land revenue work was a major part of British administration; its proceeds were vital to government solvency. But it was an area in which the raj was particularly vulnerable; revenue asssessments depended on painstaking field-work to gauge changing productivity and annual crop yields, and this work had little scientific basis and depended on the efficiency and judgement of fairly low-level officials, many of whom were Indian. Refusal to pay land revenue threatened to undermine not just government finances but also the raj's crucial alliance with substantial yeomen farmers and to destroy government's prestige, its zealously-guarded *izzat*, unless compromise could be quickly achieved.)

Bardoli would have been one of the districts to start civil disobedience in the form of non-payment of taxes in 1922 had not Gandhi called off the movement. It was a prosperous area, dominated by a wealthy land-owing peasantry, the *Patidar* community, whose caste fellows had found in Gandhi their champion during the Kaira satyagraha of 1918. Not only was the community knit by bonds of caste and kinship, it also had a range of caste welfare organizations which in the 1920s had been put to political and social use, as they took up Gandhian constructive politics, spreading the art of spinning and doing constructive village work not just for themselves but among poorer labourers in the district whose position in relation to the *Patidars* was often little better than that of serfs. When the richer *Patidars* decided to resist the revenue enhancement it was this organizational structure and the district's at least temporary social cohesion across caste barriers which the local Congress leader, Vallabhbhai Patel, was able to use. There was solid refusal to pay revenue, government officials were boycotted, and so were the abortive auctions of lands confiscated in lieu of revenue. Eventually a settlement was reached and an inquiry was set up.

Bardoli, like Champaran in 1917, showed how powerful satyagraha could be if it was conducted on a small and tightly disciplined scale, on a restricted issue, where the opponent was already vulnerable. In the case of the Bombay government in 1928, it had already recognized the inexperienced work at the base of the settlement operation and had reduced the originally proposed enhancement. The Governor was also worried that he would face boycott by Hindu Bombay and Gujarati members of his legislative council and possibly the resignation of his Hindu Ministers on the issue, just at the point when he hoped the legislature would agree to a committee to co-operate with the Simon Commission; and further, a new Governor was about to arrive and a long-running battle with a major group of agriculturalists would not be a propitious start to his term of office. Bombay was also subjected to pressure to reach a settlement by the Government of India, which felt it had mismanaged the whole business and was playing for far higher all-India stakes of Indian collaboration in constitutional reform.

Vallabhbhai Patel was the acknowledged practical leader of the satyagraha, and Gandhi made this plain himself, though he acknowledged that Bardoli was also in a real sense 'his' campaign, though physical frailty restricted what he could actually do.

Let it be known ... that I have associated myself with the Bardoli Satyagraha from its very beginning. Its leader is Shri Vallabhbhai and he can take me to Bardoli whenever he needs me. Not that he needs my advice; but, while taking any important decisions, he consults me. He does all the work whether small or big on his own responsibility. I do not go to attend the meetings, etc., but this is an understanding reached between him and me before the struggle began. My health does not permit me to carry on all kinds of activities ... I have full sympathy with all the steps undertaken in the struggle ... neither he nor I have seen any need for me to go to Bardoli or take any active

part so long as he is there. Where complete mutual trust exists, there
is no room for outward show or politeness.[15]

The evidence suggests that Gandhi and Vallabhbhai were in constant
touch and that Gandhi actually drafted some of the key letters in
negotiation with the government. He also conferred with Gujarati
businessmen and legislators and sent some of his most trusted ashram
associates to help in Bardoli. But his main role was to use the columns of
his two journals to publicize and interpret the significance of the
campaign, and to encourage and instruct the satyagrahis.

Gandhi's press articles make it clear just why he felt the Bardoli
satyagraha was so important – for him personally and for the nation as a
whole. Although it was a local satyagraha on a local issue it was a step
towards swaraj. 'Whatever awakens people to a sense of their wrongs
and whatever gives them strength for disciplined and peaceful resistance
and habituates them for [sic] corporate suffering brings us nearer
swaraj.'[16] It was an opportunity for communal unity, and for work for
the welfare of all sections of society; he urged the satyagrahis to go on
working after their settlement with the authorities in the same spirit
of fraternity and to attend to social reform and uplift of the less
privileged.[17] But – and particularly significant in the case of a raj that
relied on collaboration and acquiescence – Bardoli had also shown people
that they were in fact far stronger than they thought, that they could
oppose government and undermine it if they rid themselves of the fear
of punishment. 'It is indeed true,' he reminded his readers, 'that man
forges his own fetters and he himself can break them.'[18] For himself and
his personal future, the lesson of Bardoli was no longer to be haunted by
the blood and flames of Chauri Chaura. The Bardoli satyagrahis had
shown to him and to India at large that mass non-violence was possible,
even if most people adopted it from expedience rather than moral conviction. As he told the sympathetic Charlie Andrews, then in London,
'Bardoli victory was indeed a victory for Truth and Non-violence. It has almost restored the shattered faith in non-violence on the
political field.'[19] Historians may now see just why satyagraha 'worked'
in this particular set of circumstances in the Bombay Presidency in 1928.
What mattered then was how it appeared to Gandhi. For him here was
indeed the true sanction to back the demands the politicians were
formulating, the type of public work in which he was the expert, whose
expertise had at last been vindicated in a well-publicized campaign.

If Bardoli convinced Gandhi both of the strength and practical
viability of non-violence and of his power over a mass movement, his
other inner need before he could resume a politically dominant role was,
as he had said, the sense of a national call for his services. This came to
him at the 1928 Christmas meeting of Congress in Calcutta, to which
Motilal had virtually dragged him. He came to the exhausting series of
private meetings, Subjects Committee meetings and plenary sessions,
knowing full well the disunity within and outside Congress, and sensing

that now non-violence was on trial as the true style of the national movement. Clashes between police and demonstrators against the Simon Commission made the viability of national satyagraha immensely urgent in Gandhi's mind, particularly after the death of a senior Punjabi Congressman, Lala Lajpat Rai, following a police beating, and an aggressive police clearance of demonstrators in Lucknow, where Jawaharlal Nehru fell foul of police *lathi* blows. He exhorted demonstrators against Simon to remain peaceful but wrote and spoke of the imminence of a 'final struggle':

> That day is fast coming, faster than most of us imagine. So far as I can see, sacrifice of precious lives will have to be made before we come to our own, whether in a struggle wholly non-violent or predominantly violent. I am hoping and praying that non-violence will be maintained even up to the last . . .[20]

At Calcutta it immediately became clear that Gandhi's services as a peacemaker and as the expert in satyagraha were desparately needed. At the Subjects Committee on 26 December he urged acceptance of the Nehru Report with the sanction behind it that if the British did not accept it by the end of 1930 Congress would revive non-violent non-co-operation and would advise people not to pay taxes or render any aid to the government. There was, face-savingly, no abandonment of the previous year's decision that independence was the goal of Congress. But even this did not prove acceptable to the 'independence faction', including Bose and the younger Nehru, who wanted to give the British no time to agree to the lesser goal of Dominion Status. Intensive negotiations to achieve a compromise followed over two days which greatly taxed Gandhi's conciliatory powers. The result was a further resolution moved by Gandhi in Committee in place of his previous one: this set the end of 1929 as the deadline before the Congress took to non-co-operation. Gandhi made no secret of the fact that he himself preferred his earlier suggestion but was prepared to adjust his position for the sake of unity within their ranks just as those who had been out for an immediate independence campaign were willing to modify their stand behind the new resolution. This conciliatory role was his 'sacred duty' to India. Not only was Gandhi prepared to meet the more fiery souls half-way; to mend the widening rent in the Congress he tried to convince them that there was no fundamental difference between Dominion Status and independence as their goal and urged them not to stir up strife over a non-issue; words were misleading and what they all wanted was a political status in which India could devleop its full potential. Again, as in 1920, he promised that if Congressmen really followed his programme they could achieve swaraj within the year. Gandhi's resolution was passed in the Subjects Committee by 118 votes to 45, and then in open Congress with deafening shouts of support for the Mahatma. But even in the open session Bose tried to carry on the battle with Gandhi and overturn the compromise to which he had agreed, and to insist on independence as Congress's immediate goal; the younger Nehru, his loyalties cruelly torn between the younger and older men, between idealism and realism, supportd Bose, though he had kept away from the Subjects Committee when the compromise resolution was discussed.

Massive demonstrations of affection and support when the open Congress passed Gandhi's compromise resolution, or the uproarious greeting given to him when he arrived at the plenary session were doubtless gratifying, but Gandhi now had no illusions about his compatriots and the worth of their public effusions. He had stated in the Subjects Committee that having performed his sacred duty of conciliation at Calcutta he would retire to Sabarmati – unless Congressmen were prepared to work on his 'terms'. Bose felt this take-it-or-leave-it stance was blackmail; but Gandhi was so convinced of his own ideals that he could perceive of leadership in no other way. His terms were made plain in the resolutions buttressing the central one on the Nehru Report and the sanction of non-co-operation. Congress would have to revive its nationwide organization and insist on strict discipline within it. Congress should also in 1929 throw itself into a thoroughgoing programme of social reform and integration, including *khadi*, boycott of foreign cloth, temperance, removal of untouchability and encouragement of women in new social and public roles. Bardoli should be the pattern for rectification of any specific grievances. These terms were also accepted by the full Congress. Whether they would be implemented remained to be seen.[21]

So came Gandhi's 'national call'. When relations between Indians and the raj and between Indians themselves were in a state of flux, partly as a result of pending constitutional reforms, Congressmen had called on him to effect a face-saving compromise which would at least temporarily unite them across chasms of ideal, faction and generation and enable them both to deal with the government and to play for popular support. He had not expected to be called upon to take such a crucial and central role preventing the disintegration of Congress's unity, as he admitted privately and publicly. To Motilal he wrote several days later,[22]

No apology whatsoever is necessary for taking me to Calcutta. Of course I had never expected to have to take such an active part in the deliberations as circumstances forced me to take. But it was as well. I was quite happy over it and it gave me an insight into the present working of the Congress organisation which I certainly did not possess. And after all we have to battle both within and without.

To Gandhi the 'battle without', against the raj, depended on the 'battle within'. Unless Congress could radically reconstruct itself into a popular organization, engaging with issues that really mattered to ordinary people, making them see that swaraj meant for them a new quality of life, and unless it had a working organization spreading wide and deep through India, it could not be the instrument of independence, whatever the brave claims of those who shouted for complete independence from the British. His aim as he returned to political leadership was still fundamentally to create swaraj from the roots upwards; but more nearly in time, and more possible politically, he hoped to put Congress in the position whereby its delegates could go to London and negotiate with the British Parliament as true and legitimate national delegates, as genuinely contracting parties rather than as beggars awaiting constitutional handouts as the Simon Commission procedures envisaged.[23] Yet Calcutta was keenly fought. Gandhi had emerged dominant; but the forces he had only just controlled would inevitably constrain his future choices, and if he was to reconsolidate a true position of leadership he would have not only to achieve as a base for action the newly revived Congress organization he envisaged; he would also have to go on proving to his compatriots as the political circumstances changed that his presence and programme continued to enable productive political relationships among themselves and with the raj.

Prelude to civil disobedience

With hindsight 1929 could be called a prelude to civil disobedience. But in Gandhi's mind there was no certainty that a confrontation with the government would occur, and he manifestly did not wish for such a conflict. He exhorted people not to break the law while boycotting foreign cloth, and said that although he was 'mad' and 'hungry' for freedom, he would strain every nerve to avoid civil disobedience and to settle with the government without conflict. His expectation was that they could rapidly gain Dominion Status; and with this he would be content. 'If it means a partnership at will on a basis of equality with full freedom for either party to secede whenever it should wish I for one should be content with it.'[24] Among Congressmen there were many who shared Gandhi's hopes of a peaceful accommodation with the government and were anxious that Congress should be able to present its case in some forum in London; their views were made known to the Viceroy, partly through the good offices of the Liberal–Moderates such as T.B. Sapru who were so near to them in hope but would never become non-co-operators.[25] Hardly surprisingly, Gandhi had no clear plans for civil disobedience, if it proved necessary, and when the year offered at Calcutta to the British to review policy was nearly through, he was clear in his own mind that his compatriots were willing to talk, to make grand speeches and demonstrations, but they had shown little of the solid groundwork necessary for satyagraha.

It is a gross misrepresentation of the true situation to say that the masses are impatient to be led to civil disobedience, but that I am hanging back. I know well enough how to lead to civil disobedience a people who are prepared to embark upon it on my terms. I see no such sign on the horizon.[26]

Gandhi's main work rather than planning a new civil disobedience campaign was to achieve Indian unity and strength, focusing on Congress; to weld a viable and cohesive nation behind Congress's claim for India and to undermine the psychological foundations of the raj. He had said when reflecting on the Bardoli satyagraha that Indians made their own chains. In *Young India* he now reiterated that British rule over so many million Indians was not the result of force, but of Indian acquiescence: if Indians could only believe in themselves, the raj's days would be numbered.[27] Much of his energy went into the campaign for *khadi* and the boycott of foreign cloth, the best way he knew of inculcating discipline in a common cause under Congress direction. In January he prepared a detailed scheme to this end, under which the AISA would co-operate to maintain *khadi* standards, but the brunt of the campaign would be borne by the local Congress committees and a new central Congress Foreign Cloth Boycott Committee. Work would include burning foreign cloth, picketing foreign cloth shops, preaching *khadi* and boycott, and organizing distribution of *khadi*.[28] This scheme was accepted by the Congress Working Committee (CWC) in February and Gandhi was appointed Chairman of the new committee; but the routine work during 1929 was done by a Congressman from Sind, J. Daulatram, working out of Bombay. His labour proved slow and unrewarding, not least because so many local Congress committees failed to co-operate with him.

Gandhi's main contribution to the campaign was his series of personal tours to publicize *khadi*. He worked as hard as ever, covering vast distances, penetrating deep into India's remote villages; to enable him to do this without repeating his 1927 collapse he demanded strict discipline and attention to detail from local hosts and organizers. He refused to let his Western devotee, Mirabehn, accompany him on his south Indian tour in May because of the pace he set, the increasing heat, and the lack of food she might find reasonable.

> This does not mean that I am myself put to any inconvenience. So many look after me and, what is more, I insist on my requirements being met. I have to if I am to finish the tour without collapsing. You need not therefore feel the slightest anxiey about me. I am in first-class health. But I am a big enough morsel for the people.[29]

Among his demands were no noise, no processions, not too many engagements in a day, not more than six hours work daily, and the simplest food. He would tour as many villages as possible between about 6.00 and 9.00 in the morning, when the day was at its coolest, and then again between 5.00 and 8.00 as the evening sun set. Over and above that he needed as much as six hours for his correspondence and journalism. He came to know rural India in a way unique among India's public men: he was seen and heard by vast crowds of quite ordinary people as he travelled by train, car and on foot. He exhorted local Congressmen wherever he went on the need for organization, discipline and the proper handling of funds; demanded statements on local *khadi* work and the state of Congress finances, and maps to show the scale of Congress activity; and he collected thousands of rupees in cash and jewellery for the *khadi* cause. It was little wonder that his popularity grew among people who would once have been outside the range of political appeals. Yet he found popular outpourings distressing and actually destructive of his precious time and energy. As he was about to start on a tour of UP he pleaded.

> I have a horror of touching-the-feet devotion. It is wholly unneces-sary as a mark of affection, it may easily be degrading. It inter-feres with free and easy movement, and I have been hurt by the nails of the devotees cutting into the flesh. The performance has often taken more than fifteen minutes to pass through a crowd to a platform only a few yards from the farthest end.[30]

To escape some of the worst excesses (and to save the expense and possible danger of a special platform) he took to speaking from the back of a car parked in the centre of the meeting.

Gandhi had realized from the outset that the success of the *khadi* and boycott programme would depend on a thorough overhaul of the Congress organization at local level, and a vigorous recruitment drive. He spelt this out in his original scheme, just as he had made Congress self-reform a precondition of his return to political work. Whenever he heard of irregularities in Congress's organization and Congressmen's behaviour he castigated them, and urged Jawaharlal as Congress General Secretary to make the reorganization of Congress committees his first priority – without a streamlined and efficient Congress any future call for civil disobedience would be totally ineffective.[31] His worst suspicions were justified, as the young Nehru began to investigate. Congress finances were in disarray: large debts were owed to the AICC by individual Congressmen and by whole provinces (139,003 rupees from the Bengal PCC alone), and both the AICC and many PCCs had relied on the generous support of Bombay and its politically committed businessmen. Further, in early 1929 seven PCCs had failed to pay their required contributions to central funds, while those which had contributed were egregiously stingy. UP, for example, sent 300 rupees and Maharashtra a paltry 50 rupees. This financial chaos was symptomatic of the chaos and lethargy into which the Congress organization had sunk in the 1920s, after the heady days of non-co-operation and the paper plans for a truly national organization in breadth and depth accepted in 1920.

Only eight PCCs were actually functioning as proper offices, and even in their areas organization at district level was often non-existent. In Punjab, for example, only ten out of thirty districts had District Congress Committees (DCCs). Even in politically experienced UP, the home of the Nehrus, Congress was in a parlous state, as the provincial Congress Secretary reported to Jawaharlal in May 1929.

During the last few years the Congress organization in our province, as perhaps, in other provinces also, had become dormant. Soon after the upheaval caused by the Non-co-operation movement had subsided, propaganda and work in the villages was more or less given up; and as the natural result of this the Congress machinery could not function at all effectively. Work came to be totally confined to the headquarters of districts and larger cities. Once in a while when the elections of the PCC or for the official Councils approached, interested persons enrolled some members and set up some sort of Congress committees. During the past year or two in many districts even this was not done: in more than half of the districts, the district committees, [sic] have either disappeared or have existed only nominally on paper. Even the provincial office suffered from the prevailing reaction and remained only in name.[32]

Where there was no PCC, conditions were naturally even worse. It was little wonder that at the AICC, which received these gloomy reports in May, Gandhi called for a thorough reorganization of Congress from PCC to village level and for recruitment of members in proportion to the population on pain of disaffiliation. An intense recruiting drive followed this meeting, and by late 1929 there were probably about 500,000 properly enrolled Congress members. But the statistics were unreliable and indicated little about the support Congress could really muster or the discipline to which these 'members' would submit.

Even within the far smaller circle of active Congressmen there were acute differences, and Gandhi spent some of his time trying to effect compromises and accommodate differences. Work in the legislatures, for example, was an issue on which deep rifts opened up in Congress on provincial lines. The Viceroy, Lord Irwin, had extended the life of the legislatures pending Simon's report, and when the CWC called on all Congress legislators to abstain from attendance and devote their time to building true national strength through Congress work in the country, there were howls of protest from those who saw the power available in the assemblies and often had legislation on the stocks which was important for their constituents – and therefore for their future support. Gandhi had predictably supported the idea of withdrawal to concentrate on productive national work; but when the AICC became deadlocked on the question it was he who in July produced an acceptable compromise – that the issue should be held over until the forthcoming Congress. His aim was to maintain what fragile unity Congress possessed.[33] A similar concern for unity lay behind his refusal to preside at the critical 1929 session, and his pressure on Jawaharlal to take up the position. Although a majority of provinces wanted Gandhi to preside he refused, thereby precipitating an AICC meeting on the issue. Publicly he argued that so few Congressmen really accepted his priorities that as President he would be a liability and a source of contention. Privately he told Jawaharlal that he felt few people would really follow his lead and that their calls for his presidency were essentially exploitation of him. He had thrown his full weight behind a reluctant Jawaharlal, arguing that young men must be given a role, hoping that this would mellow and train him, and also that it would heal the rifts of generation and ideology which had opened so wide at Congress in December 1928.[34] Predictably the AICC elected Gandhi's protégé.

Gandhi's conciliatory skills were stretched by disunity within Congress. It was therefore not surprising that there was very little he could do about the strong Muslim opposition which had built up against the Nehru Report. This focused on a new grouping, the All Parties Muslim Conference, which opposed the report, sought to unify the different Muslim political groups in existence, and urged Muslims not to attend Congress. Even Gandhi's two meetings in February and August with the former Congressman, M.A. Jinnah, who had so feared Gandhi's politics in 1920 and now began to sense that the Nehru Report was a critical divide between the two communities, yielded no tangible results. As Gandhi sensed his powerlessness to sway Muslim opinion, and even his unpopularity among some Muslims, he began to rely more heavily on those few from the community who adhered to Congress, and became known as Nationalist Muslims, men like his doctor colleague, M.A. Ansari. To them he now looked to give credence to Congress and himself as they claimed to represent the Indian nation; consequently they became a significant factor in any decision he might make about future strategies.

While Gandhi was concerned with matters of high politics in 1929 and with a campaign for nationwide organization and discipline, he still concerned himself with much more ordinary, small-scale problems, particularly the activities and weakness of those whose lives he most closely controlled. It had often perplexed and perturbed his sympathizers that at moments of high political significance he would attend to apparent trivia. In 1928 he wrote to a Western Quaker, whom he was to know better in the future, on just this issue.

> You seem to think lightly of my having invited suggestions with reference to sanitary matters. In my own humble opinion we needlessly divide life into watertight compartments, religious and other. Whereas if a man has true religion in him, it must show itself in the smallest detail of life. To me sanitation in a community such as ours is based upon common spiritual effort. The slightest irregularity in sanitary, social and political life is a sign of spiritual poverty.... Anyway, the Ashram life is based upon this conception of [the] fundamental unity of life.[35]

In 1929 he returned to his long-running battle against public filth, public defecation and the total absence in India of a clean and ecologically productive system of sanitation, with articles entitled *A National Defect* and *Does a Village mean a Dunghill?*[36] But as he had explained to his Quaker friend, his life and work were all of a piece. Now he reiterated this to a black South African. If Indians or any people were to effect public reform, they must also attend to people's private lives.

> Unfortunately a belief has today sprung up that one's private character has nothing to do with one's public activity. This superstition must go. Our public workers must set about the task of reforming society by reforming themselves first. This spiritual weapon of self-purification, intangible as it seems, is the most potent means for revolutionizing one's environment and for loosening external shackles.[37]

In accordance with this prescription Gandhi continued in 1929 to concern himself with the tensions and defects still present in the life of the Sabarmati ashram, and urged Chhaganlal Joshi, who now directed the community, to keep in constant touch with him, however trivial the problems might seem. His concern for Sabarmati ranged from advice to Joshi on how to cure cracks in the soles of his feet, to tension among the women about whether they should have separate rooms, and to far more damaging events such as the discovery that one of his own cousins, whom he had brought up like a son, had been thieving petty cash, that a widow living in the ashram had been seduced by another of its members, and that even the long-suffering and devoted Kasturbhai had kept money given to her for her personal use, despite the ashram rule to the contrary. Some of these problems he discussed publicly in the press, following the principle of the indivisibility of public and private life. He did not wish to suggest that he was more virtuous than those who had failed in the ashram; rather, their failure reflected and originated in his own imperfections. Despite this, he still felt that the ashram was his most significant and best creation.[38] It assumed even more importance in his mind after he had refused to be Congress President, as he told Chhaganlal Joshi in October:

> And if my responsibility has increased, that of the inmates of the Ashram also increases. If the country is able to do nothing and if I see the fitness of the Ashram inmates, something can certainly be done through them ... This, of course, does not mean that I have now a plan of action. That will come when God inspires it.[39]

Even more amazing to many onlookers, and in contrast to the preoccupations of most political leaders, in the middle of this crucial year Gandhi made the dietary experiment of living on raw food! He ate such things as sprouting wheat, ground nut paste, spinach, raisins, lemons, honey and coconut milk, and a number of brave souls in the ashram joined him in the attempt. Eventually he had to abandon the project because of its effects on his health: at one stage he had been very weak and his blood pressure dropped, and eventually he suffered from dysentery or colitis. He aroused much interest by this experiment, and he wrote about it at length in his journals. To him it was not just a private fad: it had implications for health, for non-violence, for the

life-style of women in particular, so often chained to the kitchen by the
need of their families to have cooked food. It would make the life of
busy public workers much simpler as they travelled in areas with
different food habits. It was also part of his continuing search for the
food which aided the observance of celibacy, and he hoped to revert to
the experiment when he was stronger. He pleaded with one of his most
important supporters and financiers not to be anxious about the experiment but to understand his need to do it. 'Such experiments are an
integral part of of my life; they are essential for my mental peace and
self-realization.'[40] Gandhi's mind and emotions were, however, often in
turmoil in 1929; so often he felt overwhelmed with anger, particularly
with those he thought were his closest and most trustworthy.[41] The
strain of re-immersion in politics and the burden of resoponsibility he
felt as a result was very real.

Like Gandhi the government was preparing its men for the renewal of
confrontation, but hoping that such a conflict might not occur. Irwin
well realized that, as in 1920, there must be a balance between the ability
to control Congress and its activities, and the need to attract as many
politically active Indians as possible into the impending processes of
reform. So he had his eye on the reactions not only of Congressmen but
the Moderates who sympathized deeply with their Congress friends and
would be swayed by govenment action towards them. His government
accordingly prepared instructions to provincial governments on how to
deal firmly with a potentially grave situation;[42] but he also cast about
for a conciliatory gesture by which to integrate Congressmen into
constitutional discussions. As early as January 1929 he stated his belief to
the Secretary of State 'that in nearly all quarters except the most extreme
there would be very genuine relief if some face-saving device which
afforded an excuse for the introduction of saner counsels could be
found.'[43]

In July he returned to England for mid-term leave and found in the
new Labour government welcome support for the conciliatory device
he now had in mind after watching the development of Indian political
attitudes and consulting with some of his senior colleagues. What he
proposed was a British declaration that their goal for India was Dominion Status, and that to facilitate discussion there should be a broadly
based conference in London of representatives of government, British
and Princely India. This idea was lucky to survive the cross-currents of British party politics, Liberal and Conservative hostility, and
the opposition of eminent jurists with Indian experience, including
Birkenhead and Reading, respectively former Secretary of State and
Viceroy.[44] But after his return to India Irwin and his governors paved
the way by interviews and correspondence with prominent Indian
politicians, and on 31 October the famous declaration was made, that
Dominion Status was the natural outcome of the declaration made by
Montagu in 1917, and the subsequent reform policy, and that there
would be a Round Table Conference to discuss reform which would

include representatives of British and Princely India. Despite official assertions that this was no new policy, but a plain statement of what was implicit in the 1917 statement and the Viceroy's own instructions on his appointment, what made it significant now was that it occurred after Balfour had defined dominionhood in 1926 as a status of complete autonomy in internal and external affairs: India was on the path to a status of independence within the Empire–Commonwealth which only white domininions had so far enjoyed.

The development of government's two-pronged policy of conciliation and control shows how the Delhi government and Gandhi were in analagous positions in 1929. Both were playing for legitimacy and support. Both had to evolve policies which would unify and sustain their supporters and followers, and also have a wide appeal that would convert Indian and international opinion in their favour. Both realized that if confrontation did occur between Congress and the raj it must be so handled, even staged, to retain the highest moral ground. Gandhi had often underlined the psychological aspect of the struggle from his point of view. The ethos of collaboration and acquiescence must be broken. The government, too, realized that its legitimacy was at stake – as the acting Home Member of the Delhi government made plain when he noted in May 1930, 'I confess I have been getting the impression during the last week or two from various parts of India that ... Government may not be retaining that essential moral superiority, which is perhaps the most important factor in this struggle.'[45]

Gandhi's response to the Irwin Declaration between November 1929 and his initiation of civil disobedience in the spring of 1930 demonstrated clearly the many consideration which pressed on him, and the almost unbearable constrainsts which resulted from the nature of his following, and the divisions among those he wished to retain as allies within or connected with Congress. The first stage in deciding the response Congress would make to Irwin's gesture occurred in November–December. It involved the CWC and a group of prominent Moderates such as Sapru, and culminated in an iterview between Irwin and Gandhi, Motilal Nehru and Sapru among others.[46] In these weeks of intricate discussions and negotiations Gandhi was the key figure and recognized as such by all those involved. It was to him that government and Moderates looked to swing the decision. They thought initially that he would advise a generous support of co-operation. Indeed co-operation had many advantages: it would avoid a costly and painful conflict for which Congress was ill-prepared; it would satisfy many of the more moderate Congressmen including the Nationalist Muslims, would please the men outside Congress of Sapru's persuasion and strengthen Congress's hand in relation to the British by binding them closer to Congress. It might also bring Congressmen to an important position and role at a negotiating table, and India to a definite constitutional advance. However, co-operation with government would alienate Jawaharlal and the younger men whom he represented

both in Congress and in the country at large; and if it split apart the
Congress on lines so dangerously apparent in December 1928 it would
wreck Congress's negotiating strength and claim to legitimacy as a
national mouthpiece. It was also not at all clear that Congress had a
strong enough national base to negotiate successfully in London if
confronted with representatives of other political groups and communities. Gandhi therefore had to find a course which would unify Congress
and assure Congressmen of a secure and powerful role if they went to
London.

Initially after an informal meeting on 1/2 Novemeber, Gandhi, the
two Nehrus, Sapru and a range of others signed a document presaging
co-operation; but they made the provisos that the planned Round Table
Conference should actually frame a Dominion Status constitution
(rather than discussing *when* Dominion Status should be achieved), that
Congress should be the main representative of Indian political opinion at
the conference, and that in the meantime government should adopt a
more conciliatory policy and grant an amnesty to political prisoners. To
gain Jawharlal's signature even to this document Gandhi had had to
exert considerable pressure. But Jawaharlal and Bose resigned from the
CWC almost immediately and Jawaharlal also resigned as General
Secretary of the AICC. Gandhi's strategy for unity seemed to be
disintegrating, and his public pronouncements became tougher towards
the government. A further CWC meeting in mid-Novemeber confirmed the Delhi statement, but only as a holding operation until the
meeting of the full Congress in Christmas week.

Moderates began to fear – and rightly – that Gandhi was less able and
inclined to control the young Nehru and that their attempts to achieve a
co-operative Congress response might be in grave danger. Word
reached Irwin in early December from a young American who had just
spent three days in Sabarmati that Gandhi was quiet but determined,
and not looking for a compromise. The points made in the original
response to government were his last word, and if they were not
satisfied by 31 December he would advocate complete independence as
the Congress goal and would be ready to start civil disobedience. He
also seemed concerned that the Labour government would not prove a
united and powerful enough ally to get a satisfactory solution through
Parliament.[47] Certainly hostility in Parliament to the Irwin Declaration,
reported in India, had made many in India reassess its worth. Evidence
was building to convince Gandhi that co-operation with government
was not the most productive course, despite its initial attractions; by the
time of the meeting between Viceroy and leaders in late December there
was no real hope of a compromise, not least because Irwin could not
satisfy them on the points they had raised, particularly whether any
conference would be bound beforehand to frame a Dominion Status
constitution. The meeting was inconclusive but Gandhi's position was
clear. Co-operation would wreck Congress unity and would only land
Congress representatives in London, with their hands weakened by

Congress splits and the communal divisions in the country, with the backing of a weak British government. The alternative – confrontation through a carefully staged satyagraha – seemed far more likely to unite Congress and eventually position its representatives as strong negotiators and legitimate national spokesmen in London. And of course in Gandhi's eyes satyagraha was the most potent force he could use to purify public life and neutralize violence: it could work for swaraj from the roots upwards in the way negotiations and conferences could never do. As Srinivasa Sastri remarked, 'I thought he was genuinely struggling on our side. Now, however, a doubt has begun to cross my mind. Is he not after all thirsting for a great opportunity for his mighty weapon?'[48]

From the comparative quiet and privacy of face-to-face negotiations with people he knew well, Gandhi turned to the annual Congress session at Lahore for the crucial discussions on what Congress would do now that 1929 was virtually over and the British had responded to the 1928 ultimatum with the Irwin Declaration and its doubtful implications. Gandhi's skills of conciliation and strategy-making were tested in the forum of the Subjects Committee and then in open Congress.[49] In the former the continuing moderation of many established and seasoned Congressmen was apparent. Men as different as the Muslim, Ansari, and the orthodox Hindu, N.C. Kelkar, argued against a destructive confrontation and for use of the resources and potential in constitutional collaboration. In open Congress, however, the turbulence of many of the younger men was plain. Gandhi again found himself in a central position in the attempt to achieve some agreed policy. On his own admission he 'had to conceive and frame practically every resolution',[50] and onlookers acknowledged that he dominated the session. He pushed through the hesitant Subjects Committee the main resolution endorsing the CWC's action on the original Delhi statement of early November, but now rejecting the government's offered conference, and declaring Congress's goal to be complete independence, envisaging an immediate boycott of the legislatures and civil disobedience at the AICC's discretion. However he did not have it all his own way in committee: he had to abandon suggestions to streamline Congress further and tactics he would have supported such as boycott of schools and courts, and non-co-operation in organs of municipal government, realizing that these went against the interests of many Congressmen. He clearly became very annoyed with the obstructive attitude of the Subjects Committee as it rejected carefully worded proposals. In open Congress many of his moderate opponents returned to the attack, while some of the radicals argued for an even more offensive campaign than the one he was suggesting. Eventually the main resolution was passed almost unanimously with shouts of triumph for Gandhi; but the very narrow majority for the resolution deploring a recent bomb attack on the Viceroy's train showed how near to supporting violence were many in Congress as well as outside it. Gandhi's victory was sealed with the election of a CWC of his choice, from which opponents such as Bose were deliberately excluded.

Many Congressmen however adhered to the Mahatma with heavy hearts, not because they agreed with him, but because of the degree of unity his suggestions attracted, and because without him no mass campaign would be possible. A senior Punjab police officer reported in detail on the multifarious forces pulling Congress apart and noted that it was Gandhi, the *bania*, the dealer in bargains, not Gandhi, the idealist, who carried the day.[51] As Gandhi entered on 1930, apparently the main Congress leader, expected to lead a mass civil disobedience movement, he realized that many of his 'followers' were so as a matter of expediency rather than conviction, that their priorities meant that any campaign he planned would have to be carefully contrived to retain their co-operation, and that the Congress organization was still unwieldy and feeble as a fighting machine. Indeed he seemed to be leading an ill-assorted rabble rather than disciplined troops. Furthermore, they did not represent the whole nation; Muslim and Sikh opposition to Congress was clear, though he had hoped that now the Nehru Report was a non-issue some new communal co-operation would be possible.

Civil disobedience

In the early weeks of 1930 the burden of decision-making and planning lay heavily on Gandhi's shoulders. Although the AICC nominally had to decide on the nature and timing of any civil disobedience, this effectively meant Gandhi would make the key decisions, as he told readers of *Young India*. But he could not see his way forward:

> I must confess that I do not see the atmosphere for it today. I want to discover a formula whereby sufficient provision can be made for avoiding suspension by reason of Chauri Chaura. A time must come when there may be a fight to the finish with one's back to the wall. With the present temper of many Congressmen, with our internal dissensions, with the communal tension, it is difficult to discover an effective and innocent formula. It may be impossible to offer civil disobedience at this stage in the name of the Congress, and it may be necessary to offer individual civil disobedience without the Congress *imprimatur* and apart from it. But just now everything is in the embryonic state.[52]

Few of those who had supported his resolution at Lahore had clear ideas about what civil disobedience was expected to achieve. A few like Motilal Nehru thought that their aim was the collapse of the administration; most accepted it as a dramatic anti-government protest which they could tailor locally and individually to their needs without risk of any great sacrifice. (Gandhi's concession over the boycott of schools, courts and municipal government made this clear, as did the number of Congressmen who did not resign from the legislatures after

Lahore, or did so reluctantly.) Gandhi, however, was sure of his goal for civil disobedience. It was to generate among Indians the strength and unity essential for swaraj in the long run, and which in the short term would legitimize Congressmen as national spokesmen in constitutional discussions. Therefore the ground and strategy of any campaign must be carefully chosen to influence not only Indians in their relations with each other, but also the British raj, and wider international opinion. As Gandhi retired to Sabarmati to brood on strategy he had to consider such disparate groups as the outright opponents of Congress and civil disobedience, particularly the minority communities; the Moderates on the fringes of Congress; the Nationalist Muslims within Congress who feared civil disobedience might precipitate communal violence and wreck any prospects of future unity; Congress's business financiers; and British administrators who would be embarrassed by non-violence but greatly strengthened in moral authority in India and abroad if the campaign precipitated such violence as had occurred in 1921–2. Running in his mind were his previous experiences of satyagraha, particularly in South Africa and in Bardoli; he realized that he must contrive some new form of satyagraha rather than embark on a repetition of non-co-operation. He told Jawaharlal in mid-January,

> Even since we have separated at Lahore, I have been evolving schemes of civil disobedience. I have not seen my way clear as yet. But I have come so far that in the present state of the Congress no civil disobedience can be or should be offered in its name & that it should be offered by me alone or jointly with a few companions even as I did in South Africa ...[53]

In early February he still had no definite plan though he felt morally bound to launch non-violent action to counteract what he saw as the double violence increasing both in government and among the people.[54] Srinivasa Sastri had been near the truth when he sensed in December that Gandhi was anxious to use his ultimate and most moral weapon.

As befitted a satyagrahi Gandhi's first public move towards confrontation was to offer a way to peace to the opponent. He was also setting the stage for conflict as he wished it. This took the form of 'eleven points', eleven vital needs, which if the British could satisfy would mean that there need be no civil disobedience and Congress would gladly co-operate in a conference. Here was no discussion of ultimate goals or preconditions for negotiation, but a statement of mundane requirements; they included total prohibition, reduction of the rupee–sterling ratio, reduction of land revenue, abolition of the salt tax, reduction of military expenditure, reduction of the salaries of high officials, a protective tariff on foreign cloth, abolition of the CID and discharge of all political prisoners.[55] To many, including his closest friends such as the two Nehrus, this seemed irrelevant and fantastic, and smacked of surrender. To Gandhi it was an attempt to fill out the practical meaning of independence to make it relevant to as many people as possible, from political activists to businessmen to small peasants, and to soothe minority fears of the nature of the independence sought by the Congress. It was also a last attempt to achieve a compromise with the British.

In mid-February the CWC met in close and very private confabulation at the Sabarmati ashram. From this meeting came a resolution endorsing Gandhi's proposal that only those who believed in non-violence as an article of faith rather than a matter of expediency should start and control civil disobedience: otherwise the nature and timing of the campaign was to be left to Gandhi. So was the dilemma of possible violence resolved. Gandhi would use only those he could trust to maintain *ahimsa*, and if violence erupted among others then he would not be directly responsible. Finally the issue of confrontation was chosen – salt. This might now seem an amazing ground for conflict between an imperial regime and a party which claimed it spoke for a nation; a bewildering irrelevancy from one who had been discussing the possibility of a solemn Round Table Conference in London. But it was Gandhi's ingenious resolution of many of the problems of staging a non-violent confrontation with the government on high moral ground. It did not touch Indian vested interests (which inhibited so many possible strategies), nor was salt revenue vital to government, so harsh reprisals were unlikely. It was a highly emotive issue – a tax by an alien regime on a basic necessity of life, on which there was a long tradition of Indian political opposition to the raj. Further, as an issue touching all people it might become common ground on which Hindus and Muslims could unite, and which ordinary Indians would appreciate. Even Motilal, who had been so scathing of Gandhi's 'eleven points' saw the ingenuity of this, not least as a means of attempting to achieve communal unity.

Early in March Gandhi courteously informed Irwin that he proposed to start civil disobedience on the salt tax issue on 11 March,[56] though even then the plan for civil disobedience was vague. On 5 March he announced at the ashram prayer-meeting that he and a column of satyagrahis would march from the ashram, carrying copies of the *Gita*; their destination would be the coast where they could easily break the law by making salt. Using the tactic of the march by resisters which he had deployed in South Africa, he now proposed to stage a live drama, to educate his compatriots and enact with disciplined ashram colleagues the confrontation between the empire and a nation wishing to handle its own resources and control its own destiny. So he removed independence from the forum of political discussion and definition where it had only created disunity within and outside Congress; he used men he could trust in place of the ramshackle Congress organization he had failed to perfect and discipline in 1929.

Gandhi's 240-mile march from Ahmedabad south to the Bombay coastline at Dandi took nearly a month. In many ways it was one of the peaks in his career as an apostle of non-violence and as leader of a national movement. For nearly four weeks he kept the eyes of all those in India interested in politics on himself and his band of disciplined followers, as he preached non-violence and the meaning of swaraj, and ultimately courted arrest by making salt on the sea-shore. The movement was totally under his control, and as he advanced deliberately towards confrontation with the government on the issue he had chosen he had the government paralysed as it waited for the best time to arrest him and speculated on the plans of this enigmatic saint–politician. Looking back several years after Gandhi's death Jawaharlal felt that it was this episode which best recalled the nature and impact of this man whose presence had enlightened and given significance to the lives of so many.

> Many pictures rise in my mind of this man, whose eyes were often full of laughter and yet were pools of infinite sadness. But the picture that is dominant and most significant is as I saw him marching, staff in hand, to Dandi ... in 1930. Here was the pilgrim on his quest of Truth, quiet, peaceful, determined and fearless, who would continue that quest and pilgrimage regardless of consequences.[57]

Gandhi walked with about eighty male companions, chosen from the ashram and people he could trust to represent most regions of India, Muslims, Christians, untouchables as well as Hindus, and a wide generation span. They travelled in the early morning and cool of the evening, stopping in two villages to stay for the day and for the night. Gandhi announced that they would sleep in the open, and all he required was a clean, sheltered place to sleep, a clean washing-place and the simplest possible food; he saw this as a sacred pilgrimage in which discipline and purity were essential. Indeed, a religious aura surrounded the whole enterprise. He and his followers kept quoting the Gospels, presumably drawing comparisons between Gandhi and Christ deliberately setting his face towards Jerusalem and confrontation with the authorities; the sale of Bibles among Ahmedabad Hindus shot up. The government noted that Gandhi's position in the public mind was completely different from that of any ordinary political leader.[58]

Gandhi consciously used the march to educate the villagers in places where he stopped, the crowds of thousands who gathered to hear him in the larger towns *en route*, and those untold numbers who followed the reports of the march in the press. He asked not for money, as he had in his *khadi* tours, but for the changed attitudes which would enable true swaraj; and he filled out the meaning of swaraj and expounded the duty of disobedience to a corrupt state. For him this was evidently a crisis in his life, a unique and profoundly significant opportunity. The self-confidence he had lost during the weeks of political wrangling had now returned: '... the voice within is clear. I must put forth all my effort or retire altogether and for all time from public life. I feel that now is the time or it will be never.'[59] His companions did feel the strain of the march, some complained of the harsh conditions, and some fell sick; but the Mahatma continued, in the Viceroy's words, 'regrettably hale and hearty. I suppose if you have no vices, such as drink or anything else of that kind, there is no particular reason why you should crack up.'[60] It was a physical achievement for an ageing man whose health had collapsed in 1927 and whose blood pressure was erratic and often too high: his calm stamina and strength probably reflected his interior peace as he staged this most Gandhian of demonstrations, confident that the hour had come for the vindication of his own life and vision, and of satyagraha as a practical moral alternative to currently accepted modes of politics.

The march generated great India-wide publicity and drew large numbers to meetings. As Gandhi travelled through southern Gujarat where he and Vallabhbhai Patel had over a decade and more attracted the dominant agricultural community and organized them for sat-yagraha and constructive village work, he appealed to village officials to resign from their posts which buttressed the imperial regime. Resig-nations began to occur in large numbers, under pressure of publicity and social boycott, and the Viceroy reported to London how grave the situation was as Gandhi challenged the legitimacy of govern-ment. In Gujarat 'the personal influence of Gandhi threatens to create a position of real embarrassment to the administration ... in some areas he has already achieved a considerable measure of success in under-mining the authority of Government.' As the government of Bom-bay saw it, the real problem was that more and more people who used to be judged sane and reasonable were joining Gandhi, 'not because they expect any definite results from anti-salt laws campaign but because belief that British connection is morally indefensible and economically intolerable is gaining stength among educated Hindus, Gujaratis mostly but others also.'[61]

The Delhi government knew it would eventually have to act against Gandhi in order to shore up its authority and strengthen its servants and adherents; but it wanted to choose a time when this would generate the least possible disturbance, and avoid as far as possible endowing Gandhi with a martyr's halo or giving him the chance to go on hunger-strike in gaol. Irwin confided to the Secretary of State in mid-March that most of his thoughts were concentrated on the best method of tackling the Gandhi phenomenon; in early April he admitted that they would be 'clumsy-footed' if they thought the law could successfully treat Gandhi 'as it treats any other mundane and immoral law-breaker.'[62] Eventually Gandhi was arrested, not when he picked up the symbolic lump of mud and salt at Dandi, nor as his followers proceeded to break the law by boiling sea water in pots and pans, but a month later when government was under extreme pressure from various quarters, and from circumstances unconnected with Gandhi, to exert its authority. The ordinary penal law was left unused and he was interned on the night of 4/5 May under a Regulation of 1827 which did away with the need for a trial or a fixed sentence. Once again he was taken to Yeravda, and the

Civil disobedience: Gandhi and followers breaking the Salt Laws, 6 April 1930.

senior police officer who received him commented that he was fit and smiling, and looked years younger than when he saw him last in 1922: clearly the open-air life of the previous weeks had suited him. He left the new prisoner as he was about to have a bath, clutching a cake of Sunlight soap![63]

So ended Gandhi's personal involvement in civil disobedience. But the weeks from the Lahore Congress to his arrival at Dandi had shown how this man whom contemporaries had considered a spent political force in the mid-1920s was now central to Indian politics, and had a public reputation unique in range and quality. Indians looked to him for guidance for mundane political reasons as well as reverence for a reputed Mahatma. The government had feared his return to such a position and had striven not to reinforce his position with martyrdom. But now it was forced to concede that he was a special case, and, moreover, one whose reaction was vital as they played for legitimacy for the raj and its plans. As such his value to this colleagues and followers increased, even though he was behind bars. Not only had he enabled new relations among Indians in politics by his conciliatory presence and ingenious policies; he was also a key figure in the leverage they could exert on the raj and in any future negotiations with the raj.

Chronologically an account of Gandhi's life should now turn to his experiences in gaol for virtually a year. But his work in gaol in part reflected what was going on outside Yeravda, particularly the course of civil disobedience and the government's alternative offer of a political future in the Round Table Conference. Only the briefest sketch of civil disobedience between the salt march and the 'truce' between Gandhi and Irwin in early March 1931 is relevant here as a background to Gandhi's activities and standing, though in itself it is a subject of great fascination and complexity.[64] Like non-co-operation, civil disobedience in 1930 coincided with a severe economic crisis, which increased the varied discontents and fears which fed into the continental political campaign. Now it was not inflation but the world-wide depression and a catastrophic fall in prices which dislocated social and economic relations on a broad scale – from importers whose stocks piled up for lack of purchasers, to tenants whose crops fetched too little to enable them to pay their rents, to landlords and cultivating owners who were hard pressed to pay their land revenue. The government, too, with falling revenues, had to cut back staff and reduce salaries just when it badly needed maximum loyalty and all available manpower (not least in the police and prison services) to cope with the challenge of civil disobedience.

The movement was conceived as a far looser campaign than non-co-operation, and from the start the CWC recognized that provinces would have virtual autonomy over their own styles of and issues for civil disobedience compared with the all-India strategy and control unsuccessfully attempted in 1921–2. Although it laid down strategies and broad issues for confrontation, such as the salt monopoly, foreign cloth boycott and the Ordinances the government adopted to control civil disobedience, the CWC's communications with the provinces were more suggestions than directives. Given the nature of Congress, still a loose coalition of local groups rather than the tightly organized national party Gandhi and Jawaharlal had striven to create, and its financial instability, lack of central control was not surprising. What was surprising was that the Congress organization actually worked to a considerable extent throughout India, and that in certain areas such as Gujarat and Bombay city it had a very extensive organization, which spread instructions and news, and controlled and financed campaigns. Government action also hampered any central direction of the campaign, as it took special powers under Ordinances rather than the ordinary law to remove the leadership, cripple the organization and stifle the publicity necessary for a centrally directed movement.

The first major aspects of civil disobedience were attacks on the government's salt monopoly and the boycott of foreign cloth. The salt satyagraha affected virtually every province, though obviously in some areas for geographical reasons there was little opportunity for this except token gestures. Bombay Presidency bore the brunt of the salt campaign. There, one main manifestation was illicit salt-making by satyagrahis who boiled sea water but were surrounded by rings of Congress volunteers who linked arms, thereby making it virtually impossible for the police to stop the exercise without using force – thus creating precisely the moral outrage towards government which Congress intended. Even more dramatic were non-violent raids on government salt works, again designed to force the government into violent retaliation, which was then publicized in lurid detail. In all, the salt phase of civil disobedience scarcely harmed the government's salt monopoly or revenues; but it did generate an atmosphere of contempt for government and a moral enthusiasm for breaking laws seen as oppressive, even to the point of suffering severe personal injury from police retaliation.

In contrast the boycott of foreign cloth became a very forceful India-wide campaign, organized by Congress volunteers who perfected methods of social pressure on vendors and buyers alike, sealed foreign cloth stocks, inspected them periodically and physically obstructed attempts by merchants to move them. Many of India's major centres of the foreign cloth trade such as Amritsar, Delhi and Bombay, came to a virtual halt for much of 1930, and imports dropped dramatically. In part this fall was due to the wider economic situation of falling prices and declining Indian purchasing power, and many merchants were disposed to co-operate with the boycott at least temporarily because trade was so difficult anyway.

Beyond these two common strategies civil disobedience varied in style and intensity from region to region, and even from district to district and village to village, according to who controlled local politics and the extent to which local needs and drives meshed with the all-India campaign. Bombay Presidency was much the hardest hit, the two main storm centres being Gujarat and Bombay city. In Gujarat Gandhi and Patel were assured of a local following among many of the *Patidars*, and the civil disobedience organization rested on the Congress ashrams which had been built up in the region in the 1920s and often dominated the villages both physically and psychologically. There civil disobedience took the form of social boycott of government servants, leading to resignations, and refusal to pay land revenue. Because Princely territory interwove with British territory in this part of the Bombay Presidency many defaulters chose to migrate and take refuge with relatives across the borders, leaving whole villages desolate. For months the British administration virtually collapsed in parts of Gujarat, and even the elected local government bodies co-operated in the campaign. In Bombay city, too, the raj was totally undermined and Congress could run the city when it chose, with its bodies of volunteers and its support among white collar workers and businessmen, many of whom were Gujaratis and also suffering badly from the depression. The Government of India's Home Member had no doubts about the strength of Congress after he had visited the city in June.

The Congress House openly directs the movement of revolt against Government, Gandhi caps fill the streets, volunteers in uniform are posted for picketing with the same regularity and orderliness as police constables. One sees an occasional body of earnest young men in *khaddar* marching along. It is not surprising that all this intense feeling with its open and apparently successful defiance of Government has produced a profound impression on Bombay as a whole. . . . [particularly] the series of processions that have been organized by the Congress. The numbers, the discipline, the organization and the brushing aside of the ordinary functions of police control of traffic have combined to produce a vivid impression of the power and the success of the Congress movement.[65]

The only other places where government disarray compared with Bombay were some rural parts of Bengal and Peshawar on the Frontier, both for distinct local reasons.

All provinces had a share in the movement, however, and most provincial governments came under pressure at one time or another. The movement's appearance varied, chameleon-like, according to the pre-existing nature of local politics, from Andhra farmers in the south already protesting against enhancement of their land revenue obligation, to the men of Central Provinces who burnt trees and cut grass in defiance of forestry regulations, to Biharis who broke liquor laws with a glad heart! By the second half of the year, however, the Congress was unable to launch new offensives and government felt more secure. By early 1931 civil disobedience was hardly a problem.

In retrospect this first wave of civil disobedience seriously challenged British rule on a continental scale and in a way quite unlike non-co-operation, particularly in those areas where normal government almost collapsed for a time. Further it was a mass movement in quite a new way, in the numbers, areas and types of people involved. No part of India escaped, and though only about 60,000 were gaoled in the course of the movement this represented only a fraction of the numbers who had heard of the campaign, made local donations to it, avoided buying foreign cloth, or became involved to the extent of attending meetings. From the government's point of view it was disquieting that in certain areas it had become a deeply rooted rural movement rather than an urban phenomenon, as had been the case with previous 'extremist' movements. Further, a significant number of women, of good family and considerable education, were participating in the movement, proving adept at the picketing and pressure necessary to achieve a boycott of foreign cloth, and helping to run the Congress organization when their menfolk were gaoled, and even going to gaol themselves. Young people, too, were prominent in the movement, and even children of school age became involved. Gandhian tactics had to some extent succeeded in his intention of integrating the generations within Congress. But they failed conspicuously to achieve what he had so hoped – common action by Hindus and Muslims in the national cause. In contrast to non-co-operation Muslim participation was paltry, except on the Frontier, where Gandhi's gospel of non-violence received an unexpected following. In Muslim majority areas such as Bengal and Punjab civil disobedience was much weakened by Muslim abstention and in all only just over 1,000 Muslims were in gaol in mid-November, out of a total of 29,000 prisoners. But civil disobedience showed that Congress had to a very significant extent achieved a mass audience of sympathizers. The Moderate, Sapru, told the Viceroy of this in plain language:

I have been compelled by personal experience to revise some of my opinions. The Congress has undoubtedly acquired a great hold on popular imaginations. On roadside stations where until a few months ago I could hardly have suspected that people had any politics, I have seen with my own eyes demonstrations and heard with my own ears the usual Congress slogans. The popular feeling is one of intense excitement. It is fed from day to day by continuous and persistent propaganda on the part of the Congressmen – by lectures delivered by their volunteers in running trains and similar other activities. Very few people understand what they say or what they do, but there is no doubt whatever in my mind that there is the most intense distrust of the Government and its professions. Indeed I have little doubt in my mind that racial feeling has been fanned to a very dangerous extent.... It seems to me that the Congress is really fighting for its own supremacy in the country.[66]

Among educated Indians who did understand what Congress was about there was a similar and growing sense of distrust. As the authority of the government began to ebb in the public mind and as the repute of Congress as the nation's vanguard grew, so those articulate politicians who wished to see a successful outcome to the constitutional plans for a new era of collaboration between the raj and political India, and whose support was so vital to government, were increasingly embarrassed and pushed unwillingly towards opposition to the government. Such was the backdrop to Gandhi's imprisonment and to the government's assessment of his role and strength as a political leader, and of his 'value' to the British as a potential negotiator of peace and a vital element in their broad plan of building a new political order in India based on a wider and deeper span of political collaboration. It was also the broad context in which Gandhi and his colleagues had to decide on the worth of peace compared with the benefits to Congress of continued confrontation with the government.

Gandhi in gaol

Meanwhile Gandhi was having a welcome rest in Yeravda gaol (or as he preferred to call it on his letters, Yeravda *mandir*, or temple). He relaxed happily into his new mode of life, and seized the opportunity to make up for lost sleep and days of fatigue. Although it was the hot weather, the Poona climate was reasonably temperate, and the nights were cool, which Gandhi savoured as he slept out in the open.[67] He was offered comparatively luxurious extra facilities by the government, but he pleaded that his life-style should be as simple as possible. 'It is an obsession . . . with me that we are all living at the expense of the toiling semi-starved millions', he told the Bombay Inspector-General of Prisons, and he sent word to Anasuya Sarabhai in Ahmedabad that she should send no money to Poona to pay for extra comforts, as she had apparently done during his previous sentence there. Even when he was sent luxury fruit such as mangoes by well-wishers he gave them to the prison staff, disdaining them when such a 'conflagration' was going on outside.[68] It grieved him that the diet he found necessary for health was comparatively expensive: it consisted of fruit, bicarbonate of soda, curds and milk, and the goat which provided the last item was actually milked in his presence. Later he also ate vegetables, nuts and bread, though he maintained the discipline of only five items of food in a day. He had been given the same 'suite' of two roomy cells, with wide front and back verandas and a small garden plot in front, which he had occupied in 1922. He was allowed all the exercise he wanted and had ample space for it, and his bathroom facilities were scrupulously clean. A gaol steward did any shopping he needed, and six fellow convicts were detailed to perform duties for hm, from the Indian who milked the goat to the two Europeans who each day carried his bed outside and back again. After several weeks he received a companion prisoner, Professor D. Kalelkar, a valued colleague and principal of a Gandhian educational institution in Ahmedabad, whose son had been on the salt march. When Kalelkar was released, a young man from the ashram, Pyarelal, who later became his secretary, joined him instead.

Gandhi's day lasted from 4.00 a.m. to 9.00 p.m., and he also slept for about an hour and a half during the day. Two hours were taken up with his ablutions, three hours with preparing and eating food, and an hour and a half with exercise. He spent six hours on various aspects of spinning and carding, and two hours reading or meeting gaol authorities. An hour was spent in prayer. He was allowed to receive and send a generous number of letters and kept up a voluminous correspondence. He had any books and papers he wanted, and these included his own two journals, *The Times of India*, *The Bombay Chronicle*, *The Modern Review*, and the *Indian Social Reformer*. However, reading was far less important to him than in his previous sojourn in Yeravda, and he never read until he had completed his daily spinning, which he saw almost as a religious rite. He began to sew as part of this craft-work, and at one stage made gaol caps. He also began to study Marathi and to learn the *Gita* by heart, even using leisure in the lavatory for this godly purpose, though he cheerfully recognized that some tender souls might be shocked by this. His robust spirituality reasoned that as God was present everywhere his work could be done everywhere.[69]

Much of his correspondence was with members of the ashram, and it covered a wide range of religious, dietetic and practical problems. He sent to Sabarmati a series of discourses on the ashram vows, to be read out at the ashram prayer time, and between May and December he also translated into English a large number of devotional songs which he used in the ashram prayers for his English devotee, Mirabehn. He had decided not to mention political subjects at all in his correspondence, and had told Kalelkar that he felt totally unable to guide the political struggle because of his seclusion.[70] He kept in sound health in gaol, despite the occasional stomach upset, and his weight remained around seven and a half stone, with little variation, except when he voluntarily fasted to reorder his temperamental digestive system. The gaol superintendant noted wearily to the Bombay government which showed anxiety about Gandhi's meagre diet, that there was really no need to worry. 'I do not think that anybody could influence Mr Gandhi in his diet, he sticks to his own opinions, and does not listen to the advice of others.'[71] Half-way through the sentence the Bombay politician, M.R. Jayakar, who saw him in the course of abortive negotiations for a settlement with the government, noted that he had never seen Gandhi in such good health; Gandhi admitted when he was released in the following January that he felt he was leaving peace and quiet and exchanging it for turmoil.[72]

Indeed his only major sources of disquiet in gaol were the terms for receiving visitors and whether he could see other civil disobedience prisoners in Yeravda as he had gathered from the press that some were being ill-treated. He came to an agreement with the authorities on the latter issue, but over visitors there was deadlock. Gandhi insisted that permission granted to see relations should include those he considered *as* relatives, and submitted a list of over 150 names, many of them ashram people, and children, none of whom was a recognized politician. When this was refused Gandhi decided to see no one, arguing that for years he had obliterated from his mind the idea that kinship was a special tie.

Consequently the only intrusion on Gandhi's tranquillity came at the behest of the government. From the start of the new campaign Gandhi had the prospect of negotiation with the government near the surface of his mind.[73] As a realist he knew the confrontation would have to end in compromise; as an idealist the doctrine of satyagraha taught him that compromise on inessentials was the best end to a movement of civil resistance. But it was only as the conflict deepened and the authorities became aware of the impact of the campaign on the public, on their structures of control, and on the men in public life whose support was crucial to them that they began to consider seriously the prospect of talks with Gandhi – and it was to Gandhi they looked, calculating that his opinion was critical in determining the way Congress moved.[74] Not that the government was prepared to negotiate directly with him: at most it would give an indication through mediators of what it would do if civil disobedience were to be called off.

A group of Bombay politicians and businessmen had already begun to discuss how to capitalise on Gandhi's known willingness to talk to the government; M.R. Jayakar and Sapru shouldered the responsibility and approached the Viceroy, who with the backing of his Council agreed that these two eminent Moderates should visit Motilal Nehru and Gandhi in their respective prisons to see if they could secure an end to civil disobedience if they were convinced that the British really intended an agreed solution of the constitutional problem. So, late in July they intruded on Gandhi's peace and quiet, buttressing their own arguments for peace and their interpretation of the government's position with the news that a number of his Congress colleagues, including the Nationalist Muslim, Ansari, and Bombay commercial opinion had swung in favour of peace, so destructive was the campaign. It seemed at first that Gandhi was willing to co-operate, but he insisted that he could only act in conjunction with the Nehrus, and that Jawaharlal's must be the final voice. Jayakar and Sapru then shuttled north to see the Nehrus and received a tough reception. But the two mediators carried on their efforts, and the government gave permission for the father and son to visit Gandhi in Yeravda and whisked them to Bombay in a special train. (It was an amazing demonstration of the nature of the raj that it was prepared to co-operate with its own prisoners in this way for the sake of political co-operation from their self-confessed opponents as well as the range of men of moderate opinion represented by the painstaking mediators. As is so often and rightly pointed out, Gandhi's role and achievements would have been very different had he confronted a different type of imperialism.) Conversations between Gandhi, the Nehrus, the mediators and one or two other Congressmen lasted through 13–15 August, and during them the belligerents were firmly told now Bombay businessmen were pressing for a settlement, so grave now was the city's economic position. But the upshot was an even stiffer Congress response to the government and a statement of essential conditions to be met before the CWC would halt civil disobedience. Not surprisingly Irwin could do little with such a response; and at the end of August, when the Nehrus heard in person from the mediators of the official reply, they, too, felt there was no basis for further discussion, though they wanted Gandhi to have the final say. Having travelled yet again to Poona in early September, Sapru and Jayakar found a Gandhi whose attitude was much tougher than when they had first broached the subject to him over a month previously, and on 5 September they told Irwin by telegram that negotiations had broken down.

Gandhi's centrality to this whole abortive manoeuvre was clear. It was to him that the government, the mediators, Bombay businessmen and his own Congress colleagues turned for a lead. But he felt he could only maintain his position if he kept Jawaharlal with him, and he preferred to be swayed by Jawaharlal's continuing belligerence and the evidence of the campaign's strong momentum by mid-year than to listen to the mediators and those who craved peace. It would take more than the evidence then to hand to persuade him that conflict was not still the best preparation for eventual discussions, the surest way of strengthening the position of Congressmen as national representatives. It is indicative of the man, however, that this heavy responsibility took its physical toll: by late August he had lost noticeable weight, which the official medical report attributed in part to the worry of the negotiations.

Eventually the government broke the deadlock in this war of attrition with Congress. In mid-1930 Irwin had played for Congress co-operation in the forthcoming London conference. This took place in the closing weeks of the year without a Congress presence, but 58 politicians of varying hues and different communities joined 16 Princely representatives and a group representing the British political parties to discuss India's future. It proved a breakthrough, and took the prospect for India far beyond the limited reforms envisaged in the Simon Report, which had been published in mid-1930 but now sank into oblivion as a working proposition. Indian members of the conference proposed a future federation between British and Princely India, and the British government now felt able to envisage a central government for the whole country responsible to the electorate because it was assured of the presence in that government of a conservative Princely bloc. So were Conservative and Liberal fears assuaged, and Dominion Status became a practical possibility.[75] Now Irwin had to play for far higher stakes than he had six months previously, a chance he thought unlikely to recur in years. After consultation with London, he and his Council agreed to release the members of the CWC unconditionally, hoping that Congress would now decide on co-operation in formulating the new plans, and that the returning delegates from London would add their voices to those within Congress that were arguing for the end of conflict. So Gandhi left Yeravda on 26 January 1931, reinvigorated for active political life, though he professed to have an open mind about the future rather than a plan or policy already mapped out.[76]

Gandhi the peacemaker

He needed all the strength he had recovered in gaol, for he was at once exposed to the full impact of conflicting views and evidence about civil disobedience and the worth of the current British offer. As in late 1929 he had the unenviable task of trying to achieve a united Congress response to government. But now, compared with that episode and with the abortive peace discussions in mid-1930, the evidence seemed to weigh heavily for peace as the best strategy whereby Congress could retain its unity and reach a profitable deal with the government in the name of the nation. It was not only many Congressmen, including Ansari representing Congress Muslims, who were anxious for peace: the rank and file who had given the campaign such momentum and strength were tired and demoralized. Business opinion was even more strongly voiced in favour of a settlement, and was reinforced by the arguments of the men who were just returning from London, enthusiastic for what was now within their grasp. Yet Gandhi also knew

that Jawaharlal was still uncompromising, and that the trusty
Vallabhbhai was deeply worried lest any settlement should sacrifice his
Gujarati peasant proprietors who had lost their land by refusing to pay
their land revenue. They, after all, were the archetypal peasant supporters whom Gandhi had hoped to mobilize *en masse* as committed
nationalists; if he abandoned them now in any settlement his
programme would have less popular credence in the future. In the
middle of this confusion Motilal Nehru died. (He had already been very
ill during the prison meetings a few months before.) His son was now
more open to Gandhi's paternal influence in a time of personal distress,
and his absence from the political scene threw an even greater burden of
responsibility for a decision on the Mahatma.

Gandhi was by his own admission bereft of the guidance of the 'inner
voice', and he wrote a very personal letter to Irwin, asking for an
interview as a way forward and before the CWC made any decision. 'I
would like to meet not so much the Viceroy of India as the man in
you,'[77] he wrote – undoubtedly recalling the way his good personal
relationship with Smuts in South Africa had enabled the resolution of
apparently intractable conflict. Irwin at once agreed, not standing on
ceremony, and approaching the meeting with a similar hope of a
personal rapport. As he explained to the Secretary of State, he gathered

> ... that it is really going to be a question of personal appeal and
> conviction, rather than of any argument. The cards I fancy are
> sympathy; understanding of his hopes, suspicions and disappoint-
> ments; some play on what everybody says is a characteristic, namely,
> vanity of power and personality; but above all, striving to convey to
> him, through what one says, a real echo of the sincerity that pervaded
> your doings in London. You may trust me to do my best, and one
> can't do more. Sastri, whom I saw yesterday, summed it up by
> saying: 'He is like a woman; you have got to win him; therefore
> before you see him, perform all your ablutions, say all your prayers
> and put on your deepest spiritual robes'! ... I think I understand
> enough of his character to realize that nothing is impossible if one can
> only manage to touch the right note.[78]

So Gandhi's work as a leader was expanded to include the role of sole
mediator and negotiator between Congress and Government. He gained
a unique position of political leverage because Congressmen, Liberals
and the British all needed some means of achieving an accommodation
with each other. His work in the next few weeks probably represented
the highest point of his political career, when his actions were highly
significant for the future of Congress and therefore of India, when
Indian politicians and officials alike waited to see what he could achieve.
It was a role which he was particularly fitted to play, by inclination and
experience. His repute was as an immensely popular and revered figure,
standing apart from the infighting of so much Congress politics, and
bridging the gulfs of ideology within it and between it and men like

Sapru and Sastri, by his love of India and his talent for friendship and personal warmth. But it was critical that his counter-player in this drama of peacemaking was Irwin, the sensitive patrician and devout Anglican who had a deep sympathy for Indian political aspirations and recognized the power of the religious vision in Gandhi's life and character. Conversations with later Viceroys, the stolid Linlithgow or the gruff and shy soldier, Wavell, would have yielded very different results.

The talks took place in Delhi, and Gandhi stayed at M.A. Ansari's home on the borders of the old and new cities, with the CWC in attendance, and constant visits from Sapru, Jayakar and Srinivasa Sastri, who kept in touch with the Congressmen and Secretariat officials, smoothing out difficulties and misunderstandings. Gandhi and Irwin were in remarkably similar positions. Both had constantly to refer back to their advisors and colleagues, and Gandhi would even wake the members of the CWC in the night to discuss matters; both had to bear in mind the repercussions of their decisions on those who had borne the brunt of the conflict at the grassroots, be they landless *Patidars* or village officers who had resigned their posts, or beleaguered police and ICS men. They met first during 17–19 February, duly prepared by the Moderate mediators to perceive each other as spiritually sensitive men rather than implacable political opponents. Sastri reported to his brother on the first day, 'This afternoon 'the two uncrucified Christs' meet. Sapru, Jayakar and I have prepared each for the other! ... If they hit it off, then serious negotiations will begin.'[79]

The atmosphere and content of these preliminary talks convinced Viceroy and Mahatma that they could profitably continue working together, and on 27 February they met again for the start of the really tough phase of their talks. The broad constitutional question proved to be the least of their problems: future constitutional discussions would be about the implementation of the scheme mooted in London, of which the fundamentals were a federation of British and Princely India, responsible government, and certain necessary safeguards for matters like British control of defence, the position of minorities and India's financial credit. The real problems were immediate and practical ones, particularly picketing in the cause of a boycott of foreign cloth, an inquiry into police behaviour during civil disobedience, the government's salt monopoly and the question of lands forfeited during civil disobedience. These nearly became an insurmountable barrier to a settlement. But on 5 March they were able to publish the terms of a settlement which became known as the Gandhi–Irwin Pact, which government and the CWC were willing to accept. Congress agreed to stop civil disobedience, and government would withdraw the special powers it had taken to deal with civil disobedience and its punitive police; it would release all civil disobedience prisoners, and would restore forfeited lands which had not yet been sold and treat liberally village officers who applied for their old posts, provided these had not been filled. But there was to be no inquiry into police conduct. Only peaceful picketing could continue; and government would not modify the salt laws although it agreed that people in salt-producing areas could make or collect it for home consumption. As a result, Congress would participate in discussions on the constitutional scheme now on the table.

Both Mahatma and Viceroy recognized with great warmth that it was the other's sincerity and directness that had enabled this positive outcome to their talks. Yet they both had exhibited political skill and realism as they battled to safeguard the interests of their respective 'troops', and eventually reached a formula which neither could claim as outright victory, but both could argue to be respectable and productive for the future. Together they consoled each other that they must have done a good job, as both were being criticized for having 'sold' their countries, the Mahatma by the tearful bitterness of Jawaharlal, the Viceroy by the parliamentary tirades of Winston Churchill. When questioned whether he had achieved anything more than he was offered in late 1929 or in gaol, and whether he had backtracked on Congress's demand for independence, Gandhi replied that now they *knew* Britain had accepted the claim for responsible government, and, moreover, having shown their strength in civil disobedience, they were going to London not as beggars but as true negotiators from a position of strength. He urged Congressmen to implement their side of the settlement and further increase the prestige of Congress. The goal of independence stood: it did not necessarily exclude a link with Britain, and anyway Congress could raise this at the forthcoming conference, as Gandhi had confirmed with Irwin at the outset of their discussions.[80]

Congress met in the last week of March to consider the settlement.[81] Its venue was Karachi, which made access easy for Gandhi's many Bombay supporters. Bombay funds from businessmen anxious for peace helped to bring candidates favourable to Gandhi to Karachi, thereby consolidating his position; he was further strengthened by the CWC's rapid election of Vallabhbhai as president, cutting short the usual pre-session manoeuverings and lengthy discussions about possible candidates. Opposition to Gandhi was none the less evident. Young men with black flags paraded on the station shouting abuse, and tried to break into Gandhi's quarters in the Congress camp. But among the Congress delegates there was no such hostility; even those potential leaders who opposed the pact, such as Jawaharlal and Bose, saw that leading an anti-Gandhi revolt would only weaken them all and strengthen the government's hands. The pact was a *fait accompli* and there was no strong opponent of it who could act as focus for those who were uneasy about it, particularly now that Motilal was dead. As one of them had put it during Gandhi's talks with Irwin, 'Howsover great an individual, this sort of autocracy in a matter of such supreme importance is undemocratic & undesirable; everyone feels it but is afraid to speak.'[82]

Jawaharlal in fact agreed to Gandhi's astute request that he should move the resolution ratifying the settlement, and it was carried by a large majority. Although Gandhi had not deferred to Jawaharlal in the weeks since his release in the way he had done in late 1929 and in gaol, he did now encourage the young idealist to think deeply about the future. He had lavished attention and affection on him, particularly during their early morning walks in Delhi while Gandhi was working with Irwin, and Jawaharlal was grieving both for his father and the civil disobedience struggle. As a result they drafted a resolution on fundamental rights which was also passed at Karachi, committing Congress to a future in which Indians enjoyed rights of association, speech and conscience, and an independent government would work for an egalitarian society. Here, Gandhi's ideals, preached so often in the past decade and particularly spelt out in his famous and much misunderstood 'eleven points' the previous year, dovetailed with the younger man's more doctrinaire socialism and helped to convince him that together rather than apart they could best work for a new India, despite the retreat from active confrontation with government.

The Karachi Congress was a signal triumph for Gandhi, as onlookers admitted. Outside the circle of decision-makers crowds gathered everywhere he went to revere him as a Mahatma and as a political hero. In the public eye and among the politically active this was possibly the pinnacle of his prestige, as even Bose reluctantly admitted. The strain of public exposure and the hard political work to ensure the ratification of the pact exhausted Gandhi. 'Karachi washed me out completely', he confided to C.F. Andrews; and even by the end of April he was still having to have two or three daytime naps to overcome his fatigue.[83] Despite the political success and public acclaim at Karachi, Gandhi's political leadership was not firmly founded on a bloc of supporters, as, for example, Vallabhbhai's was in Gujarat. This was the difference between a regional and an all-India leader. Gandhi, as the latter, could only lead when his skills and repute were needed, when people adhered to him and even used him, because of what he could do for them – be they Congressmen at Karachi, *Patidars* resisting land revenue, Bombay businessmen anxious for peaceful trade, or government dignatories playing for the high stakes of Britain's future relations with India. In early 1931 he had been pivotal in a wide range of interlocking political relationships. In consequence not only had his own role become crucial in Indian politics, he had brought Congress to the doors of a conference room, recognized by Indians and government alike as a powerful political voice, though not as the sole voice of the nation.

Within days of the Karachi Congress the new CWC (chosen in effect by Gandhi, Jawaharlal and Vallabhbhai) had decided that Gandhi alone should represent Congress at the second Round Table Conference in London. Contemporaries speculated at the reasoning behind this decision, but it seems most likely that Gandhi and his close colleagues calculated that the austere and manifestly Indian Mahatma would create a bigger impact in England than a delegation which might not speak with one voice and would certainly not give such dramatic visual credence as would Gandhi alone to Congress's claim to represent India's poor.[84] Even while accepting this role Gandhi was arguing that the real work for swaraj was to be done in disciplined constructive work at home rather than in constitutional discussions in London, and throughout the middle months of 1931 it was evident that while he wanted to go to London, he wished to ensure that his position when he arrived was as strong as possible. In particular, he felt it would only be productive to go if Congress were first proven to be the legitimate voice of the Indian nation, not if he found himself speaking for a Congress which seemed to be only one party among many.

In retrospect it would have been better for Gandhi's public repute and possibly for his freedom to manoeuvre in London if he could have gone to London in the spring of 1931. But the conference was scheduled for the autumn. In the intervening months his position proved to be exceedingly uncomfortable; the man who gained such repute for his pact with Irwin was increasingly distrusted and misunderstood by government, Muslims, non-Congress Hindus and even his own Congress colleagues as he seemed to hesitate, to change positions, and to bargain with government about the terms on which he *would* go to London.[85] He still appeared the most outstanding and influential man, in Congress and in Indian politics: he was destined to represent Congress in London, and in the meantime he was the key leader in ensuring that Congress maintained its side of the March settlement and was the pivotal figure in relations between Congress and government when the terms of the settlement needed clarification or when either side felt that the other was not keeping it. He travelled endlessly, visiting areas where the settlement seemed fragile, and much of his time and energy was spent in interviews and correspondence with officials, from local ICS men to Governors, key Secretariat officers and the new Viceroy himself, Lord Willingdon. Perhaps even more than in February–March his all-India role was enabled by the need of so many different people for his good offices. Government needed him as a control over local Congress leaders who chafed at the settlement as it applied to their locality and were hard pressed to discipline their local followers. Non-Congress Hindus continued to work through him for a Congress presence in London, lest their constitutional hand should be weakened in relation to government and the minorities. Congressmen themselves needed him as a means of gaining access to and pressurizing various levels of government. Yet the months while he worked to uphold the settlement and prepare for London showed the constraints on his leadership, the very restricted parameters of his leadership function and capacity. His position was also highly vulnerable since he as an individual responded to such diverse needs: if those who looked to him for leadership found he could not 'deliver the goods' they wished they might abandon him and look elsewhere.

Gandhi's main task in mid-1931 was to ensure that Congressmen throughout India kept the terms of the settlement. This was essential because if Congress could not enact what it had promised then its claim to speak for Indians was a hollow nonsense. It would also alienate public opinion in Britain, and Gandhi, like all Indian politicians then and in earlier years, knew how important this was if Parliament was to enact reforms. Moreover, Congress's organization and finances had not recovered from the earlier confrontation with government, and Gandhi also knew that if a further conflict developed government would have no hesitation in hitting Congress fast and hard. From mid-April the Delhi government had been preparing a new and comprehensive Emergency Powers Ordinance for this purpose. The policy shift coincided with the arrival of a new Viceroy, Lord Willingdon, an experienced Indian administrator who had been Governor of Bombay from 1913 to 1918 and was therefore predisposed to sympathized with the problems of local governments such as Bombay in times of acute administrative strain; he was a man of less sensitive and flexible political style than Irwin and tended to see Gandhi as an astute and wily politician rather than as a man of vision and high integrity. But the policy now in reserve against a renewed onslaught by Congress originated in a deeper logic than a change of Viceroy. The Government of India would only work the settlement, with all its tensions and ambiguities, if it knew it would never again have to subject the men in its services and their local allies to pressures like those they had endured in 1930, when civil disobedience was at its peak.

Gandhi found that being the national guardian of a settlement was far harder than being one of its architects. Whereas Jawaharlal and Vallabhbhai had been only warning voices in February-March, now they both spoke for regions where the all-India terms of the settlement appeared to be very hard in its operation on local people. In Gujarat the main problems were the continuing non-payment of revenue, and the question of whether lands and posts should be returned to those who had lost them during the conflict. In UP there was real economic distress because of the slump in agricultural prices which precipitated non-payment of rents. Gandhi did what he could to smooth over these local problems, but he could not personally control what went on in the fields of UP or even Gujarat; his colleagues, Jawaharlal and Vallabhbhai, were themselves ambivalent, realizing that an all-India settlement might have long-term value, yet being reluctant to abandon those to whom they had appealed and might again need to rally in any future confrontation with the government. Allied to Gandhi's activities as guardian and guarantor of the settlement on the Congress side was his wish and need (if he were to be strong in London) to build on the foundations of the pact with Irwin and confirm in the eyes of Indians, officials and the wider world that Congress was in effect the sole representative of the Indian people. He continuously forwarded this claim in words and his own actions as mediator – for example, in dealings with the

Commissioner in charge of Gujarat in April, in his June request for a permanent Board of Arbitration to decide on matters of the settlement disputed between government and Congress, or in his later modified suggestion of an independent tribunal. The government refused to budge on this issue: it could not concede that Congress was its equal as a *contracting* party or that Congress alone could speak for Indians, though its willingness to use Gandhi came perilously near to this. Eventually, as a result of three days of discussion between Gandhi and Willingdon in Simla, the government conceded an inquiry on one issue as a means of getting Gandhi to London, in what became known as the 'second settlement'.

Finally, as part of the broad strategy of working to go to London as the representative of a truly national party, Gandhi attempted to reach an agreement with a significant bloc of Muslim spokesmen in the All India Muslim Conference, and he maintained that he could not go to London without a communal agreement – a stance which was in line with his arguments from the time of the Irwin Declaration of 1929. Personally he would have liked to concede all the Muslim demands, but his hands were tied by the views of Congress's own small group of Muslim supporters; in the end his attempts to achieve a new unity collapsed on the question of separate electorates. The CWC decided in June that Gandhi should go to London even if there was no communal agreement, provided other circumstances were favourable, and to this Gandhi reluctantly agreed. Now he could not claim to represent all Indians he would have preferred that Congress abandon conferences and concentrate on consolidating its mass base and on doing constructive work for what he saw as real swaraj.

Gandhi in England

So, after months of hard labour and in an atmosphere of growing scepticism about his political acumen and value as a leader, Gandhi sailed for London in August, though he had not completed the tasks before him in the previous months of precarious peace. His role as mediator between so many different groups, as an all-India strategist who tried to assuage local aspirations and fears, had brought him almost to the point of political stalemate at home, in contrast to the hopes generated by his pact with Irwin. Neither the conference nor renewed conflict seemed profitable alternatives. But to London he went, perhaps hoping that in a different setting, away from immediate pressures, he would be able to use his manifold political skills to better advantage. Even Willingdon reluctantly conceded to the Secretary of State that Gandhi would probably be constructive and helpful in the conference context.[86]

You will find him I think amenable and anxious to help, with a real desire to work out a satisfactory constitution. I do not think you will find him in any way a violent extremist, or that he will be likely to

Gandhi age 62 (1931).

walk out in order to create a demonstration. I must confess to a sense
of extreme relief at having got rid of the little man for a few short
months, for while we are the best of friends he certainly is the most
difficult man to pin down in the matter of negotiations. He may be a
saint, he may be a holy man; he is I believe quite sincere in his
principles; but of this I am perfectly certain, that he is one of the most
astute politically-minded and bargaining little gentlemen I even came
across. Still, I feel that in his new surroundings . . . he will be a help
and not a hindrance.

Gandhi was accompanied to England by a considerable entourage,
including his son, Devadas, two secretaries, Mahadev Desai and the
young Pyarelal who had been with him in gaol; his English devotee,
Mirabehn; his businessman friend and financier, G.D. Birla; and the
orthodox Hindu, Pandit Malaviya, who brought gallons of ritually pure
milk with him because he was forbidden to have a cow on board. Even
without livestock they were a curious band and attracted considerable
attention, not least from the children on board, with whom Gandhi had
a special empathy. He insisted, naturally, on travelling second class; he
slept on deck, ate his usual meagre diet, mainly dried fruits and goat's
milk, wore his customary scanty clothes, and kept up his habitual round
of prayer, spinning and correspondence. (There could hardly have been
a starker contrast with his first passage to England as a shy, unknown
student bent on becoming an English gentleman and lawyer: one

suspects that this occurred to him, too.) Mahadev Desai wrote a series of personal letters to Jawaharlal, giving an intimate and delightful insight into their enterprise. During the voyage the faithful secretary reassured Jawaharlal how deeply Gandhi cared for him, particularly since his father's death. He commented of their journey, when so many passengers were laid low by rough weather, 'There have been no 'talks' of a political character for the simple reason none but Bapu is in a condition to carry on a talk. Bapu is thoroughly enjoying himself – if I may use the word 'enjoy' about anything that he does.'[87] Gandhi badly needed the modicum of relaxation he allowed himself after his hard labours in the middle of the Indian hot weather, for once in England he was swamped with visitors, journalists and broadcasters, and became an object of very considerable curiosity. Unlike some of his compatriots at the conference he spurned luxurious living arrangements and chose to stay at Kingsley Hall, a settlement in Bow, though he worked from an office in Knightsbridge. The enormous welcome he received, particularly from the people of the East End, touched him profoundly; he was also agreeably surprised by the warmth of the officials and politicians he met, including the Secretary of State for India, Sir Samuel Hoare, and the previous Viceroy, Lord Reading (who must have been eating his words in the 1920s about Gandhi being like the last minstrel with his harp!). Soon Gandhi's appointment book was filled for weeks in advance, with individual encounters, public gatherings and of course the work of the conference, primarily the meetings of the Minorities and Federal Structure Committees of which he became a member.

Despite Willingdon's sanguine farewell to Gandhi, the Mahatma from the outset expected little to come of the conference. During the voyage he had said he expected nothing from it, but that being an optimist he hoped that something would turn up to make it a success from the Indian national point of view. The alternative was a renewed confrontation with government.[88] Fundamentally he had no belief that true swaraj could be achieved through the exercise of political power; more immediately he was deeply dispirited by the communal deadlock. If he was to exercise a leadership role in London he had in the context of detailed constitutional discussion and in the informal contacts between delegates outside the conference room to offer them something they needed, or threaten them with something they would prefer to avoid. However, his hands were tied, both by the Congress position and by his perception of Congress and therefore of himself as Congress's representative. The Congress mandate to him consisted of the relevant resolution passed at the Karachi session and a gloss on it made by the CWC in early September and sent to Gandhi by Vallabhbhai and Jawaharlal. It demanded that India's relationship with Britain should be more than Dominion Status (including the right to sever the connection), and should also mean control of defence and finance. It stipulated that in any future federation with Princely India representatives of the latter should be elected to the central legislature. (Congress's fear was that it might be swamped by conservative nominees of the Princes.) It also stood by the Congress formula to solve the communal problem, which the CWC had worked out in early July, giving minorities reserved seats, accepting the formation of more Muslim provinces, but not conceding separate electorates.[89]

Gandhi's room to negotiate was further curtailed by his blunt assertions in public and private that Congress (and therefore he) represented all Indians, including Muslims, and that the other Indians present were not true representatives but only government nominees. This was deeply offensive to the members of minority communities at the conference, and the Muslims particularly opposed his attempt to get Ansari to London to 'prove' Congress's representative character. Simultaneously he alienated and frightened almost all the Hindus present by his assertions that Hindus should give Muslims 'a blank cheque'.

Gandhi's impotence to achieve any progress on the communal problem was painfully clear when despite a week of intensive, informal discussions by the minorities, which he chaired, there was complete deadlock. Eventually the minorities reached an agreement which included separate electorates, for untouchables as well as such obvious minorities as Muslims and Anglo-Indians, and they requested the Prime Minister to make a 'communal' award of seats on this basis. Gandhi opposed this bitterly, for it undercut Congress's claims and weakened what he perceived as the nation in its struggle against the bureaucracy. He was particularly vehement about the work of the spokesman for untouchables, Dr B.R. Ambedkar, himself an untouchable, as a party to this minorities' pact. He claimed it was he, Gandhi, who really represented the untouchables: if they were given separate status by the constitution, he who had fought against their separation from caste Hindus and their degradation would resist the proposal with his life.[90] Despite his emotional appeal and unpremeditated pledge to wager his life on the issue it was clear that he could not lead the minorities to a solution because of his prepared position: there was nothing he could offer them, and they realized that they could exert more strength if they acted together in relation to the raj.

In the Federal Structure Committee Gandhi was equally hamstrung by the Congress claim. Doggedly he went on, attending the seemingly interminable and tedious meetings; on virtually every issue he found himself a dissenting voice. The Secretary of State concluded, after hearing Gandhi in the meetings and in many private talks with him,

... that we cannot possibly make an agreement with him. He cannot accept anything like our terms and we cannot possibly accept his. Unless, therefore, something very unexpected turns up, I am afraid we must accept the fact that he will not agree to our conditions and that the most that we can hope for is that we will send him back personally friendly to us and other people, even though he may be politically opposed to us.[91]

Gandhi representing the Indian National Congress at the Second Indian Round Table Conference, London, September 1931.

By early November the conference was grinding unproductively into the ground, largely because of the communal impasse; but also because many of the Princes were becoming less interested in co-operating in a federal scheme, which they had seen as a defence of their power against the potential threat of a united British India, now that such a unity lay in pieces before them. Even the last-minute private discussions of a two-phased advance to central responsibility via provincial responsibility in which Gandhi became involved, to the serious disquiet of the other Hindu delegates, came to nothing. At the close of the conference he pleaded with government to accept the Congress as representative of the Indian nation and to trust it. He said he had come looking for compromise and partnership with Britain. Now he felt he was at a crucial parting of the ways – though he would still work for peace, not confrontation. But as he looked ahead his real hopes focused on satyagraha, that self-strengthening and moral enterprise which could in his view achieve what the words and bargains of a conference could not. He told journalists early in December:[92]

I am no more pessimistic that when I left India. I never believed that we would get anything more that what our own internal strength entitled. The Round Table Conference negotiations have been a method of finding out the measure of our strength compared with those with whom power resides. We have evidently failed. The

Congress, therefore, must refill the battery so that it will be powerful enough to do its work.

Gandhi's performance at the conference was harshly criticized by many Indian participants and commentators. His style was certainly not suited to intricate negotiations even though he was a lawyer: but more significantly, he was bound by his vision of Congress and the Congress mandate, which meant he had no true negotiating position, no leeway for give and take which could have convinced either Indians or the British that he was a profitable ally or leader. In fact his own fears about going to London in a weak position were more than fulfilled. However, he had another task in England: to publicize the Congress claim and to make himself well known in England; for it was the British electorate which ultimately would sway British policy towards India. He therefore seized every opportunity to mould British public opinion, eagerly expanding his views to the press and arranging meetings with individuals and groups, and in this he was assisted by a group of English friends, including C.F. Andrews. Although he was often tired, depressed and isolated by and in his conference work, he received a cheering and unexpected degree of warmth and courtesy, if not real understanding, from a great range of people. He spoke to MPs of all parties at a meeting in the Commons, and later to Labour MPs who were the most sympathetic. He spent a weekend in Oxford where he met several influential academics, including A.D. Lindsay, Master of Balliol, and R. Coupland, Beit Professor of History, and had detailed discussions with Lord Lothian, Under-Secretary of State for India. Lothian later presided at a Chatham House meeting arranged by the Royal Institute of International Affairs, where Gandhi's moderate and largely factual presentation of Congress and India was much appreciated. Recognizing the significance of the educational establishment and their students he visited not only Oxford, but Cambridge, Manchester and Nottingham, and several leading public schools, including Eton. Similarly he realized that Christian leaders and groups would be important in the pressure they could exert on government, and he had easy access to such circles through Andrews and his Quaker friends, including Horace Alexander to whom earlier he had painstakingly explained his passion for public sanitation. He met the Archbishop of Canterbury and the famous 'Red Dean' of Canterbury, and the Bishops of Birmingham and Chichester; he spoke at Church House, Westminster, at a gathering of 32 bishops and other church leaders, presided over by the Archbishop of York. He also met Quakers in Birmingham and London, spoke at a missionary conference, and to a group dedicated to Franciscan ideals.

Gandhi also hoped, somewhat naïvely, to reach the middle class through working people. It was for this reason that he stayed in Bow rather than in a West End hotel or flat, and why he went out of his way to meet cotton mill operatives as well as mill owners when he went to Lancashire, the homeland of the cloth he had sought to boycott. He

Gandhi with Lancashire textile workers, 26 September 1931.

expressed concern for local poverty and unemployment to which his campaign had contributed, though he could not change his fundamental hostility to the Lancashire trade as a buttress of imperialism and a contributory factor in India's even worse poverty and unemployment. None the less, both employers and operatives were impressed by his sincerity and humanity. By the time he left for India, he had made a broad appeal for an understanding of his personal aims, and the nature of Congress and its claims, and he had gathered a small group of English friends who would, he hoped, continue this work of interpreting the Indian scene to the British public after his departure.

Although there was little to show for this broader aspect of his work in England beyond curiosity at the eccentric, spinning saint-politician, and some genuine sympathy for his cause, he had demonstrated that he was far more than a politician; this was to prove significant when in the circumstances of renewed conflict the government in Britain had to ward off criticisms about its treatment of him. Because he was so special in the eyes of a foreign public, American as well as British, his value to his colleagues in India increased. But the visit to Britain had produced no immediate political fruit except deadlock and recrimination, the opposite of national unity and the vindication of Congress legitimacy as the voice of an Indian nation, for which he had striven.

Renewed conflict

Gandhi hurried home to India in December, abandoning tentative plans to spend time appealing to a wider audience in Europe and possibly America, because he heard from his Congress colleagues of increasing tension between them and the government, even though his settlements with Irwin and Willingdon were technically still in operation. In three areas tension was particularly acute – Bengal, where terrorism was a real problem; the Frontier, where the 'Reds Shirts', nominally Congress-men and Gandhians, were locked in conflict with the authorities; and UP, where Congressmen, led by Jawaharlal Nehru, were supporting agriculturalists in their opposition to rent and revenue demands in a situation of falling agricultural prices, despite hesitations from senior Congressmen outside the province, including Vallabhbhai. In all three areas government took special powers by ordinance to deal with the situation, and Jawaharlal was gaoled as he started south to meet Gandhi in Bombay.

The government's swift and tough response to these local challenges was a symptom of the new policy which had been refined during the summer. A package of measures had been arranged for use if Congress reverted to civil disobedience: this included declaring the CWC and local Congress organizations illegal, the swift arrest of Gandhi and major provincial leaders, and a battery of ordinance powers. As Gandhi's ship neared Bombay Willingdon's Council decided that the Viceroy would not see him while the UP campaign continued, and that government would implement the prepared package if Congress resolved to restart civil disobedience, support the UP campaign, or boycott British goods. A provisional booking was made for the Mahatma in Yeravda, though the harrassed Bombay government would have preferred him to be shipped to inhospitable Aden or the penal Andaman Islands.[93]

When Gandhi reached Bombay he received a great public welcome, but almost immediately he went into conclave with the CWC. There were some in Congress like Ansari and Rajendra Prasad from Bihar who were reluctant to revert to conflict; they echoed the fears of Moderates and the Bombay commercial community. With the CWC's backing, Gandhi wired to request an interview with Willingdon. A meeting was offered, but on condition that Gandhi should denounce Congress activities in UP and the Frontier, and that there would be no discussion with Willingdon of government action in those areas and Bengal. Predictably Gandhi and the CWC denounced this reply, threatening civil disobedience if government did not make substantial concessions. Gandhi asked again to see Willingdon 'as a friend', under no conditions, but this, too, was refused. Very briefly it seemed as if a body of commercial and Moderate opinion would achieve a mediation attempt; Jayakar was involved, but significantly his old and experienced partner in mediation between Gandhi and government, T.B. Sapru, refused, thinking it would be fruitless. The plan collapsed when within hours of a conciliatory talk with Jayakar, Gandhi was arrested before dawn on 4 January and removed to Yeravda.

However much Gandhi had sincerely hoped for a more co-operative relationship with Delhi, the government now had no need of his services as a Congress spokesman and negotiator . It was determined not to boost his reputation and strength by any 'pacts' with him; and it was now confident of its powers to crush civil disobedience at the outset and to let the constitution-making process continue without Congress. Further, Willingdon was no Irwin. He felt that Gandhi was fundamentally two-faced: 'and while he may possibly have his saint-like side, on the other he is the most Machiavellian bargaining little political humbug I have ever come across.'[94] So the honoured conference delegate, welcomed in Whitehall and received by the Sovereign, was rebuffed and locked away. He was squeezed by his colleagues and the government into a position where conflict was the only way Congress could attempt to take the political initiative. A reluctant antagonist, he almost certainly felt a certain philosophical relief that Congress was returning to the way of non-violence and truth, as he saw it.

Once in Yeravda he relaxed both in body and in spirit. He admitted that gaol freed him from responsibility for insoluble problems such as the Frontier and the communal deadlock, and gave him rest essential if he were to avoid another collapse. He confided to his diary in January that he felt like lying down and sleeping much of the time. He now had no plans and was content that this should be so. 'As a matter of fact . . . my ship sails as the wind blows. I have no map of the course with me. How can I have one? Having such a map is contrary to the spirit of *bhakti* [devotion]. How can one who would dance as God wills choose deliberately a course?'[95]

In contrast to Gandhi's contentment, Congress as a whole found reversion to civil disobedience destructive and ultimately profoundly frustrating. It had laid no detailed plans for civil disobedience, and the CWC merely suggested variations on the old themes – boycott of foreign cloth and British goods, picketing of foreign cloth and liquor shops, breaking salt laws, and non-payment of taxes. Knowing the terms of the government's new policy, the central Congress recognized that each province, indeed each district, would be out on its own to a greater degree even than in 1930–1. This proved to be so, for immediately the CWC, AICC and many local Congress bodies were banned, their premises and funds were seized, and leaders were incarcerated. A hand-to-mouth all-India organization just managed to exist, none the less, sending erratic bursts of bulletins to PCCs, with news and suggestions. However, there was little surviving provincial organization to receive or act on these: Bombay and UP kept a skeletal organization going but most areas merely had emergency councils or 'dictators' according to who happened to be out of gaol. Further, money became an insuperable problem in most provinces even though Congress organizations had tried to hide their funds in anticipation of government seizure.

In the early months of 1932 there was surprising uniformity in the campaign throughout the country – processions, flag-raising, boycott, picketing, local conferences and raids to recapture buildings government had seized. Bombay Presidency, particularly the city, was again the storm centre, and only here and on the Frontier did government experience real problems of control. In contrast to 1930 the campaign never deepened and widened in appeal by linkage to local drives. It never really struck rural roots; and after the initial thrust it rapidly died away, from March 1932. Towards the end of the year the government considered it moribund. By the end of April 1933 nearly 75,000 had been convicted, but this was only a minute fraction of the population, even where the campaign was strongest – 0.64% in Bombay, for example. Very few Muslims were convicted except on the Frontier. Again, as in 1930, women and young people were prominent among the convicts, and literacy rates shot up in the gaols housing civil disobedience prisoners. Clearly the campaign's activists were mainly Hindus, urban and educated.[96]

Because of the government's draconian policy it was very hard for Congressmen to meet and make any plans; when they did contrive meetings it was plain that civil disobedience had landed them in a frustrating impasse. Conflict brought them nothing but gaol and hardship, and none of the political gains it had in 1930 – local support, an increasing reputation for leaders and Congress itself, and a government willing to do a deal in order to save the reforms under discussion. Now the government refused to have any dealings with Gandhi as their leader: 'talks' would, in the official view, only increase Gandhi's repute and leverage, and government was secure in the knowledge that Congress was not only laid low but isolated, and that it could control events in India and woo collaboration from outside Congress by the continuing processes of constitutional reform. Consistently Delhi squashed any attempts at mediation between government and Gandhi, from Moderates, businessmen and journalists; and even rebuffed the Secretary of State who was under pressure from an Archbishop of York, convinced that Gandhi was a man of peace.

It was not only Congressmen who felt frustrated by conflict. A broad range of politically conscious Hindus who were sympathetic to Congress also became increasingly disturbed at the deadlock – from Malaviya at the orthodox end of the spectrum, to Moderates such as Jayakar and Sapru, and many businessmen. Many of these people were undoubtedly ambivalent towards Congress and Gandhi, thinking they had landed political India in a mess from which there seemed no escape; yet their sympathies were fundamentally nationalist and consequently they detested any attack on Gandhi, and strongly disapproved of the methods used to crack down on Congress. Delhi officials were in fact

shaken by the vehemence of Hindu feeling, which was brought to their
notice by Moderates and their own local governments when they
enquired into the state of public opinion.[97]

Gandhi meanwhile settled peacefully down to life in gaol, this time
having as his companions Mahadev Desai and Vallabhbhai Patel.[98] The
three of them kept a regular and self-disciplined routine of praying,
reading, spinning, walking and, in Gandhi's case, of receiving and
writing letters. Their day started well before dawn, and Gandhi also
slept during the daytime, and they retired by 9.00 p.m. Gandhi lived on
a rather different diet from his companions – toast, fruit, vegetables,
nuts, honey and soda, and for some time milk, too. Mahadev made the
bread (which Gandhi insisted should be unrefined), and Vallabhbhai
turned from organizing *Patidars* to preparing the Mahatma's fruit and
vegetables. Friends outside gaol kept Gandhi supplied with certain
'luxury' foods, such as dates, oranges and other fruits, though he did not
hesitate to chide when some dates sent from Bombay arrived full of
grubs. On this regime he kept in good health: his digestive system
remained tranquil, his weight hardly varied, at about seven and a half
stone, and his only health problem was an elbow sore from spinning.
He was allowed a considerable range of newspapers, including his own
two journals, and he both took books to Yeravda and was sent many by
friends. He read on religion and political economy, among other topics,
continued to study Urdu and became increasingly fascinated by as-
tronomy. His companions were similarly well occupied: Vallabhbhai
took up Sanskrit, while Mahadev studied French and Urdu when he was
not cooking or doing secretarial work for the other two. At first Gandhi
received weekly visits from relatives, friends and colleagues who were
not involved in politics; but in June he gave up this concession after an
altercation with government over a visit from Mirabehn. She was not
permitted to visit because she had been gaoled for civil disobedience.

Gandhi also clashed with government over censorship procedures and
subsequent delays in his mail, but eventually this was resolved, and
much of his time was devoted to a huge correspondence with a broad
range of enquirers and friends, particularly people in the ashram. He
covered moral and religious questions and matters of health, but
eschewed political matters. His diary recorded the amazing number of
letters, and his hard-worked secretary commented in his own diary on
the advice he was continually showering on the ashram: 'Bapu's spiritual
ambition knows no bounds. He is introducing one reform after another
at Sabarmati.... How long will all the Ashramites be able to bear all
this strain?'[99] On top of his correspondence Gandhi also wrote for the
ashram a series of letters on the *Gita*, which he had begun in 1930 in
Yeravda, and a history of the ashram itself.[100] This was only briefly
historical: the greater part of it concerned ashram observances. Writing
this must have enabled him to make a broad-ranging review of his life's
principles and work. He covered not only obviously religious topics
such as prayer and truth, but also the application of religious principles

to life – in fasting, chastity, poverty, 'bread labour', swadeshi and caste. He touched on the most recent agricultural experiments at the ashram, on proper treatment of cows and dairying, and on his own and still controversial attitudes to education.

However, beneath this quiet and scholarly life led by the three prisoners a time bomb was ticking away: the problem of the future political position of India's untouchables on which Gandhi had promised to wager his life if need be. Gandhi remained interested in political life despite the constraints of gaol: he read the papers, discussed politics with his two companions, his gaolers and visiting officials. He also kept in touch with the highest levels of government, corresponding on particular issues. On 11 March when he gathered that a Communal Award was imminent, he wrote to remind the Secretary of State of his attitude. Certainly he wished for untouchables to be represented in the legislatures, preferably by adult suffrage. But he opposed separate electorates, basically on the religious grounds that it would only divide Hindus from Hindus and would do nothing about their 'crushing degradation'. From his discussions with Vallabhbhai and Mahadev Desai in Yeravda as he wrote the letter it was clear that although he underlined the religious argument, the political implications of separate electorates were very important to him. Compounding separate electorates for Muslims, a similar concession to untouchables would shatter the united polity for which he had worked so long, and would cast Congress in the role of sectarian religious party rather than representative of an Indian nation. But he did not want to publicize this dimension of the problem for he felt it would only exacerbate communal conflict. To Hoare he apologized if his intended action was an embarrassment to government and admitted that he would probably be condemned for introducing into politics methods which were 'hysterical, if not much worse. All I can urge in defence is that for me the contemplated step is not a method, it is part of my being. It is a call of conscience which I dare not disobey, even though it may cost whatever reputation for sanity I may now possess.'[101]

Hoare courteously recognized the strength of Gandhi's feelings; but government policy moved according to a different and more pressing logic – without an award there could be no vital decisions on federation, and government might lose Muslim co-operation in constitution-making just when Hindu opinion had turned so sullen and hostile in reaction to its tough handling of civil disobedience. On 4 August the London government made an award: untouchables were among those who would have separate constituencies.[102] Ambedkar felt even this was not enough to protect untouchables, but Muslims were generally contented. Many Hindus were uneasy but did nothing; but in Punjab and Bengal both Hindus and Sikhs violently condemned the proposals because they meant that in practice Muslims would have majorities in their provincial legislatures. Gandhi went quietly about his work the day he heard of the award as if nothing special had occurred. In the evening he began to draft a letter to the Prime Minister, announcing that he would fast from 20 September unless the decision relating to the untouchables was revoked and they were included in the general electorates with a common franchise.[103] No amount of persuasion and counter-argument by London or the Inspector-General of Prisons, who visited Gandhi twice, could make him budge. Indeed he was in a state of considerable spiritual exaltation, thinking this opportunity a rare privilege and his supreme *dharma*.[104]

Not even Gandhi's gaol companions wholly approved of his plan. Vallabhbhai could not understand its religious rationale, and thought it would damage Gandhi's reputation and invite imitative fasts. When the plan became public knowledge in mid-September there was an outburst of emotion: Yeravda was showered with messages of concern and pleas for him to desist, for no one doubted that Gandhi would do what he said. Even his closest friends and colleagues were nonplussed and angry: Gandhi had rightly predicted that Jawaharlal Nehru would be. Srinivasa Sastri probably spoke for many non-Congressmen when he privately deplored this flight from the way of reason and the inevitable moral coercion that it would impose.[105] Ambedkar predictably called it a political stunt. Officials, too, were sure the fast was a devious political manoeuvre, though they differed on what they thought it was meant to achieve. Willingdon and the Bombay government thought it was designed to revive the failing civil disobedience movement and reassert Gandhi's political authority. Gandhi argued publicly that his intention was religious – to throw his whole weight against untouchability and sting the consciences of caste Hindus into right action by using a means of penance and purification accepted in Hinduism, Islam and Christianity.[106] However, such public statements were an oversimplification both of his own reasoning and the likely effects of his action. For him nothing was 'only religious', religion and all life were inextricable, and this action was work for swaraj as he interpreted it just as much as civil disobedience; his talks with his gaol companions indicated that he was well aware of the political dimension of his action. Further, though he denied that he intended any coercion he realized that some people might experience the fast as such.[107]

Gandhi was a creature of pattern, whether it was in planning satyagraha, seeking compromise in high-level talks, or fasting. Now, as at other times of apparent impotence, he made the ulitmate personal gesture of which he was capable. It might be a response hallowed by religion; he might do his best to lay down restrictions on its use; but ultimately – and particularly from one of his standing – it exerted profound pressure, just as did a fasting mother in a Hindu family. Although Gandhi wanted to use techniques which were totally unambiguous, totally moral, he confronted the basic dilemma of the religious visionary – that ordinary life is never black and white, that practical decisions and actions are often misinterpreted and have unforeseen and unintended repercussions. The man of faith who involves himself in public life is therefore always enmeshed in ambiguities and compromises; none more so than a 'saint' who endeavours to be a national leader.

Although the government was prepared to let Gandhi fast in the ashram he preferred to stay in gaol, and was accordingly allowed to see and correspond with anyone he wished in order to discuss the untouchables' problem. Meanwhile, a wide range of Hindus had been planning to retrieve what threatened to become a disastrous situation, and Pandit Malaviya convened a conference in Bombay which Ambedkar also attended. A small deputation went in advance to Yeravda to sound out Gandhi's views and gathered that he would accept a compromise of reserved seats for untouchables provided they were not given separate electorates. This was duly reported to the conference. Understandbly Ambedkar felt he was in a situation of intolerable pressure, but eventually he agreed to a plan contrived by the indefatigable Sapru and Jayakar: a two-tiered system of election for the seats reserved for untouchables, in which only untouchables would vote in the primary elections.

Sapru and Jayakar, Birla, Devadas Gandhi and other Congressmen went by night train to Poona on the evening of the first day of the fast. They were soon joined by Ambedkar, and detailed discussions followed, as Gandhi grew frighteningly weaker. (Kasturbhai was even brought to be with her husband.) Eventually an agreed package was drawn up and signed by Ambedkar and representative Hindus, the so-called 'Poona Pact'. Ambedkar, though under pressure, had driven a hard bargain: in place of separate electorates he gained the compromise system of election, and almost double the number of reserved seats planned under the official award for untouchables in the provincial assemblies, plus a guaranteed percentage of seats in the federal assembly. Untouchables' education was also to receive a special sum in every provincial budget. Back in Bombay Malaviya's conference ratified the pact and passed a resolution Gandhi had drafted, that no Hindu should be regarded as untouchable because of his birth, and that all those who had once been untouchables would now have equal access with other Hindus to all public institutions, including wells, roads, and schools.

On 26 September Gandhi heard that the Cabinet had accepted the pact's provisions, and he ceremoniously ended his fast with a drink of orange juice after prayers, in the presence of 200 people, in a manner reminiscent of his great fast in Delhi on communal unity. Gandhi admitted that he suffered considerably during the fast, but the days of deprivation were also ones of real inner joy, even illumination, and he told his Quaker friend, Alexander, that 'God was never nearer to me than during the fast'.[108] He fairly quickly recovered, and by the end of October he was virtually back to normal health. Reaction to the pact and Gandhi's survival was almost hysterical. Temples and wells were opened to untouchables, caste Hindus publicly embraced those they had previously avoided as polluting, and inter-caste dinners were held. At a public meeting in Bombay an All-India Anti Untouchability League was formed with Birla as its president. However, this ebullient fraternity soon ebbed: in some places temples were re-purified after untouchables had entered them, and many caste Hindus began to count the political cost of the pact, particularly in Bengal and Punjab where they were a minority and realized that precious Hindu seats had been bartered away for a dubious all-India cause.

Gandhi hoped that this episode would herald a new era in Indian public life; he saw it, too, as a new beginning for himself. He not only expected to have continuing facilities in gaol for anti-untouchability work, he also hoped to resume relations with the government. A small group of Moderates and men on the periphery of Congress attempted to facilitate an agreement between the Mahatma and government; but Delhi shut down all visits and potential mediation, for it had no need of Gandhi's overtures and was determined not to allow him to re-establish himself in political life.

So Gandhi was totally boxed in by the government. His response was to turn from the prospect of arranging peace with the government to a campaign for the untouchables, the Harijans, or Children of God, as he now habitually called them, thereby not so much giving himself a new role as concentrating on one particular dimension of his work for swaraj. Even in the exhaustion following the fast he displayed his remarkable capacity for resilience and ingenuity: if one avenue to swaraj was closed he would walk up another, but his destination was the same. When the Delhi government was confronted with the fact that Gandhi intended to eat only gaol food unless he was allowed wide facilities for Harijan work (and would almost certainly become ill without his special diet) it agreed to let him have them, and Gandhi promised not to abuse this trust by discussing civil disobedience. Bombay thought this was a surrender, but Delhi had to protect its reputation in India and abroad, which was already besmirched by its treatment of Gandhi. More deviously, it hoped Gandhi's new emphasis would side-track both him and the public from civil disobedience, possibly reduce Gandhi's popularity among Hindus and provide him with a face-saving exit from political conflict.

Gandhi threw himself into his new Harijan work with the fanatical zeal characteristic of him when he was sure of his moral ground. It devoured his thoughts and energy and he even dreamed of it! His close ashram colleague, Chhaganlal Joshi, was transferred from another gaol to help with the volume of work the Mahatma generated. Gandhi himself had stopped spinning because of sore elbows and he now gave up reading to devote himself to correspondence and interviews. He regularly wrote twenty or more letters a day, and his visitors were so numerous that they had to be accommodated in a special yard.[109] In the week beginning 29 November, for example, he had on successive days 12, 8, 13, 22, 25, 42 and 37 callers! He produced a series of statements on aspects of untouchability, and he followed closely the work in Kerala to open Guruvayur temple to untouchables, because he felt temple-entry was the touchstone by which to judge whether caste Hindu attitudes had really changed. At one stage he had seriously considered fasting for this issue, too. To all this he added in February 1933 writing for a new paper, *Harijan*, which was effectively his mouthpiece.

The student of Gandhi's life is in danger of becoming immune to the extraordinary aspects of his career and his relationship with the government. What other nationalist leader in an anti-colonial struggle held a prayer meeting in the House of Commons? What other politician has conducted his work by means of hand-written notes on 'silence days'? And here he was, a self-professed rebel, and a prisoner, allowed to hold daily audiences in a prison yard, and to conduct a public campaign for social reform. His position in Yeravda says as much about the nature of the raj and its political acumen and flexibility as it does about Gandhi's concerns and reputation.

However, Gandhi seems to have become increasingly aware of the magnitude of the untouchability problem as he laboured after the Poona fast. At the same time he was disquieted at news from the ashram; for despite his stream of letters its problems and the moral standards of its members suggested that it was not, as he had thought, his best creation, his finely-tuned instrument for reform. So in late April he announced that he would embark on a three-week fast of purification. This time it was not aimed at any specific object, group or person, but was his individual attempt to generate inward power to fight an evil of incomparable proportions. He had taught that private and public life could not be disentangled, and that one person's purity and vision could touch the lives of others, so interdependent were people in the divine economy of life, and by this personal and private means he hoped to achieve some outflowing of purity and power from himself into the lives of his co-workers and the murky depths of Hindu society. His friends and colleagues were confused and hostile, wondering what on earth this had to do with the battle against the raj, and dreading the loss of the man they both revered and needed if they were to emerge from their current political frustration.[110] Government officials, too, could not fathom his reasoning, though the ever-suspicious Willingdon thought he might be attempting to regain the public gaze. But they could not risk his death in prison, and indeed saw advantages in releasing him on humanitarian grounds without a suspicion of 'negotiations'. On his release Gandhi advised Congress to suspend civil disobedience at least during the fast, and indicated that he would like to enter into discussions with the government, in fact to start afresh from where he had left off on his return from England in 1931.[111] The government immediately announced that it had no intention of negotiating or releasing prisoners until civil disobedience was totally abandoned.

Gandhi survived his fast in the house of a Poona friend, conserving his strength by giving up most of his correspondence and visitors, and devoting himself to meditation and hearing recitations from the *Gita* and other scriptures. As was now his customary pattern, he ended it with a devotional public ceremony. He had approached the fast as a great and divine gift, the answer of the 'inner voice' to several days of internal turmoil; it seems as if he felt he was breaking new ground in his experiments with truth. As he had written privately in January, 'My fasts never spring from despair or frustration. They have their source in my undying optimism and intense faith. Nor are they as cheap as you think.'[112]

Abandoning confrontation

To Gandhi's Congress colleagues his actions provided no answer to their immediate dilemma – how to extract themselves from a defunct campaign, and return to normal political life in as honourable a fashion as possible. The problem was becoming urgent because in March 1933 the government produced a White Paper containing its reform proposals of a federation between British and Princely India and an immediate grant of autonomy to the provinces of British India. From this it was clear just how much power would be on offer if they came in from the political wilderness and used the Congress name and organization for the purposes of constitutional politics. A broad range of Congressmen and non-Congress Hindus were deeply anxious that Gandhi should be persuaded to abandon civil disobedience. Prominent among them were the Nationalist Muslims so crucial to Gandhi's view of Congress as representative of all Indians. Yet there were those like Jawaharlal Nehru and Vallabhbhai and the men of the Frontier, whom he also valued and trusted, who felt that continued conflict, however hard, was better than ignominious acceptance of the raj's terms for their re-entry into ordinary political life. The Congress to which Gandhi returned in mid-1933 was thus divided and demoralized; yet no one had the authority or will to challenge Gandhi openly and break the stalemate. Jawaharlal, still in gaol, was beside himself with mixed emotions about Gandhi and his leadership. He wrote in his diary once he knew Gandhi had survived the three-week fast:[113]

As I watched the emotional upheaval during the fast I wondered more and more if this was the right method in politics. It is sheer revivalism and clear thinking has not a ghost of a chance against it. All India, or most of it, stares reverently at the Mahatma and expects him to perform miracle after miracle and put an end to untouchability and get Swaraj and so on – and does nothing itself! And Bapu goes on talking of purity and sacrifice. I am afraid I am drifting further and further away from him mentally, in spite of my strong emotional attachment to him. His continual references to God irritate me exceedingly. His political actions are often enough guided by an unerring instinct but he does not encourage others to think. And even he, has he thought out what the objective, the ideal should be. Very probably not. The next step seems to absorb him.

The leader of the largest party in India being unavoidably detained in gaol, it is anticipated that special arrangements will be made to discuss with him the new Indian Charter of Liberty.

ROUND TABLE CONFERENCE.

Cartoon from the London *Evening Standard*, 20 March 1933.

Nehru was right in thinking that Gandhi was no ordinary politician: his mind was fixed on the right means at all times, and for this reason he would never abandon satyagraha himself as both government and many of his colleagues seemed to be insisting. He spelt this out to one of the Nationalist Muslims in June.[114]

> I am ... unable to say anything on the present situation because I am still bed-ridden and have not been able to make an analytical study of it. I want you, however, to understand my fundamental difficulty which constitutes also my limitation. Non-violence for me is not a mere experiment. It is part of my life and the whole creed of Satyagraha, Non-co-operation, Civil Disobedience, and the like, are necessary deductions from the fundamental proposition that Non-violence is the law of life for human beings. For me it is both a means and an end and I am more than ever convinced that in the complex situation that faces India, there is no other way of gaining real freedom. In applying my mind to the present situation I must, therefore, test everything in terms of Non-violence.

However, in July he gathered a private conference of about 150 Congressmen in Poona in order to take soundings and suggest an appropriate strategy. It was just the sort of divided gathering, looking to him for leadership, in which his personal and political skills were most effective; the fact that most of the Congressmen were seeing him for the

first time for months and after the emotional tension of two fasts added
to his personal influence. The prevailing sense of the meeting was that
civil disobedience was dead: Congress must decide whether to abandon
it unilaterally or attempt to bargain with government for 'conditions' of
its formal termination. Gandhi was brooding on the idea of individual
civil disobedience as a way out of this dilemma, but the meeting threw
out this idea and resolved that Gandhi should see Willingdon to explore
the possibility of peace. But the Delhi government was adamant: even
though civil disobedience was moribund it had no intention of doing
anything that could be construed as 'negotiating' under the threat of
civil disobedience. Most Congressmen had dispersed while these
exchanges occurred and Gandhi was thus placed in a position where he
could personally advise action. His suggestion was – despite the Poona
meeting – individual civil disobedience for a few committed souls,
while most Congressmen should concentrate on constructive work. He
gave no guidance on the fraught question of co-operating in either the
existing or future constitutions. Furthermore, he felt that the Congress
organization, beijng illegal and therefore necessarily secret, should cease
to function.[115] So Gandhi once more attempted to turn Congress into a
sacrificial and constructive body, to preserve the purity of civil disobedience, and to further real work for swaraj. Cutting the link between the
Congress organization and civil disobedience might also pave the way
for a new relationship with government. But to his colleagues this
advice offered no escape from their confusion, no satisfactory strategy;
and worse, it presaged the loss of the organization they knew would be
vital in future politics. It was small wonder that Sapru wrote of 'utter
chaos and confusion in public life' and of 'despair & disappointment'
among Congressmen.[116]

Gandhi was in his element with the policy of individual civil disobedience. He announced that he was disbanding the Sabarmati ashram
and would march with chosen companions through Gujarat, preaching civil disobedience and the reforms vital for true swaraj. Blank incomprehension greeted this gesture, particularly as he offered the
ashram's fixed plant to the government. Almost certainly Gandhi, who
had been so concerned about the ashram's standards, wanted to start
afresh with colleagues whose reliability had been proved by individual
civil disobedience. Not surprisingly the government wished to prevent
any repetition of the 1930 march to Dandhi, and Gandhi rapidly found
himself back in Yeravda, leaving Congressmen leaderless, saddled with
a programme they neither wanted not understood.

Gandhi's term in gaol was brief despite his year's sentence. When he
realized that he would not have the extraordinary facilities for Harijan
work he had previously enjoyed he began to fast, and rapidly became
very ill. He was removed to hospital, and in fact prepared himself for
death. But when the authorities judged that his life was in danger he was
released unconditionally. Government had once again boxed Gandhi in,
though he was nominally a free agent. He could not play a public role

from gaol, and if he adopted civil disobedience he would be imprisoned and then released if he fasted – a humiliating cat and mouse position which would do nothing but harm to his reputation, his cause and his colleagues. He wanted to re-establish relations with government, but the government would not play.

As he agonized over the future he was bombarded with advice from a range of people he trusted. Sastri, for example, pleaded with him to free Congress from his grip and let it abandon civil disobedience and play a normal political role. With some truth Gandhi replied that compared with his 'surrender' to the Swarajists a decade earlier, there was now no alternative leadership or group to take over from him – just a jumble of confused and conflicting wishes to end the existing stalemate. But – prophetically – he concluded, 'The moment I feel that I can get out of it [Congress] to the benefit of the Congress, I will not fail.'[117] He was anxious to know Nehru's mind before he made any decisioins. Gandhi met his dearly loved 'son' in September, for the first time since his departure to London in 1931. Their main concern was Gandhi's immediate role, though they both realized that their opinions diverged widely on many political matters. From this meeting came Gandhi's decision to devote himself to Harijan work for the unexpired portion of his sentence. In his statement announcing this he once more publicized his wish to explore avenues of peace with the government.[118]

Although Gandhi had thus demarcated for himself a public role, his freelance activities did nothing to help his Congress colleagues. As he plunged into a mammoth Harijan tour from early November they began to confer and realign in most provinces, as the unpopular strategy of individual civil disobedience soon fizzled out. In some regions new 'Swaraj parties' were founded; but clearly outright opposition to Gandhi and the question of council entry were as divisive as the current strategy was frustrating. Among those who worked hardest for change were the Bombay politician, Nariman, who had felt so bitter about Gandhi's 'autocracy' at the time of the Gandhi – Irwin Pact; the leading Congress Muslim, Ansari; and the senior Calcutta Congressman, Dr B.C. Roy, who saw the erosion of support for Congress in his own region after the Poona Pact had compounded the problem posed by the Communal Award for Bengali Hindus.

At last in mid-March 1934 it seemed that Gandhi would not stand in their way; but until then they had not been prepared to force the issue. His opinion now was that the paralysis of the educated politicians must be ended and that he would welcome a party of Congressmen pursuing a policy of council entry rather than remaining sullen, discontented and inactive. If the majority so desired, they should even suspend or abandon civil disobedience.[119] Those who hoped for a new course gathered at Ansari's Delhi home – ironically where Gandhi had stayed when manoeuvring to end civil disobedience in 1931. The gathering ingeniously decided to side-step the question of civil disobedience and working the new constitution, and hit on an anodyne gesture – contesting the forthcoming elections to the existing central assembly, and to this end reviving the Swaraj Party. A small deputation, including Ansari and Roy, should put the idea in person to Gandhi.

To find Gandhi they had to go to Bihar, for his Harijan tour had been disrupted by the catastrophe which hit Bihar on 15 January. North Bihar was devastated by one of the world's largest recorded earthquakes: in an area of 6,000 square miles virtually all buildings were damaged or destroyed, 12 towns were effectively demolished, giant cracks opened in the earth, agriculture and communications were disrupted, and over 7,000 people were killed. Gandhi's response to the horror was a moral one which most of his compatriots could not stomach: he said it was punishment for sin, probably the sin of untouchability.[120] Bihar Congressmen, led by Rajendra Prasad, plunged into relief work, co-operating with government regardless of any policy of non-co-operation. When Prasad appealed for Gandhi's help in person he went immediately, bringing his repute and skills of organization and fund-raising. He urged Congressmen to co-operate with government, and used the tragedy as an occasion to continue his educative role in public life, underlining, for example, the need to end untouchability, village hygiene, and efficient accounting for public funds.

In this context of *de facto* co-operation with the government to meet human need, Gandhi met his friends from Delhi. But their tactful mission of persuasion proved unnecessary. Gandhi had already prepared a statement announcing his advice as the author of satyagraha, that Congressmen should give up civil disobedience in the cause of swaraj and leave it to him alone. This had been slowly evolving in his mind; many considerations must have converged in this decision – not just his immediate environment of unconditional co-operation with government, but his past experience of 'freeing' Congress from divisions, demoralization and inaction, and his conviction that satyagraha was the perfect weapon in the struggle for swaraj which must be protected and refurbished in the hands of true believers, not sullied by handling from those without commitment and self-discipline. It was this final argument that dominated his statement.[121] In a widely published letter to Ansari he blessed the revival of the Swaraj Party and offered it any help he could give, though his *personal* attitude to the worth of work in the legislatures had not changed. Increasingly he became convinced his decision and its timing were right. To the perplexed Vallabhbhai he wrote quizzically:[122]

I think it is our duty to give full freedom to Congressmen who favour entering the legislatures. It is but right that those who daily attend legislatures in their thoughts should do so physically as well. Then alone will they be able to judge the relative advantages and disadvantages of that policy. Is it not better that one who daily eats *jalebi* [sweetmeat] in his imagination should eat the real thing and know the wisdom or folly of doing so?

Once Gandhi had freed Congressmen from their impasse to follow their political inclinations, divisions among them became acute as they jostled to control the potential Congress electoral machine. It was the Mahatma, the sole remaining satyagrahi, who come to their resuce with his conciliatory and management skills in early May at meetings of the Swaraj Party and the AICC: his judicious compromises just held them together. But despite his success as broker and arranger his heart was not in Congress politics as it seemed to be developing – riddled with strife and struggles for position, in contrast to the single-minded, pure and constructive national body for public work he had striven to create. Congressmen had neither understood nor followed his advice at Poona in July 1933: now they were up to their old tricks. (As soon as Congress bodies were legal from mid-June Congressmen began to rend each other, and their infighting even led to violence in places.)

Gandhi's confidantes became aware that he was contemplating leaving Congress as he had 10 years before, so dispirited was he by the true values of Congressmen that were reasserting themselves, and his inability to infuse them with his own vision. In such a situation he felt it would be better to let Congress function without him and therefore without hypocrisy.[123] Many of his closest colleagues were horrified at the prospect, and in deference to them (and to test opinion in the proposed October Congress session in Bombay) he postponed any major step; though in mid-September he published a long statement about his intention because of fundamental differences between himself and Congress. Among these difference he noted *khadi*; his commitment to end untouchability; non-violence; and even his interpretation of swaraj. He also mentioned 'corruption' among Congressmen, meaning their unedifying struggles for power.[124]

Although he spoke of testing opinion in Bombay his letters showed that even before the session he was determined to go.

> My mind is certainly set on going out of the Congress. I feel sure that it will do good to the Congress and to me. I shall better influence the Congress by being outside. I shall cease to be the weight that I am just now, and yet I shall be passing my views on to the Congress whenever occasion demands it.[125]

As he contemplated the future he must have felt that remaining in a body so divided by region, faction and ideology, and lacking the finely tuned implement of satyagraha, would be imprisonment without Yeravda's walls. To be true to himself and his inner calling he must work unfettered. At Bombay he achieved what he wanted – a decorous departure from active Congress politics, yet the knowledge that those who trusted him controlled the nerve centre of the all-India organization and would be receptive to his advice. Further, Congress established an All-India Village Industries Association (AIVIA) to work under his guidance as an autonomous Congress body with its own organization and funds. The parallel with 1925 was close. Then he left Congress to

Gandhi at the Bombay Con-
gress, October 1934.

work through the AISA; now again he could leave Congress to a firm
leadership and with an established organization (which had been impossible when Sastri mooted it in 1933), and work for swaraj in his own
way through his own organization.

So ended a distinct and at times dramatic phase in Gandhi's life when
he was the towering figure in Congress and its relations with the British,
despite his months in gaol. The years had shown and increased his
unique standing in public life. Yet his public role was never static and his
all-India political dominance was ephemeral and fluctuating: it could and
did build and collapse, depending on whether his particular ideals and
skills performed an enabling and lubricant role in the interlocking
relationships amongst Indians and between Indians and British which
were the substance of continental politics. In late 1928 he had returned to
Congress because his skills and presence were desparately needed by his
countrymen, and in the ensuing months his dominance was confirmed
by the needs of Indians and the government for him as they jostled in
anticipation of a new political order and under pressure from an economic slump which profoundly dislocated many public relationships. But
from late 1931 his person and his strategies failed to provide what his
political contemporaries needed. Government refused to deal with him,
strong in its other alliances, and so he could decreasingly deliver the

political goods for his compatriots. The Mahatma and satyagraha proved divisive and inhibiting, as he himself came to recognize. Yet the ups and downs of his position (when judged by ordinary poltical standards) showed his immense resilience in public life, even when political opinion was flowing along a different course from his own; for then he was able to turn, as in gaol or when he left Congress in 1934, from ordinary politics to other styles of work, which were equally part of his vocation to nurture true swaraj.

Gandhi had approached this phase of his life when he became inextricable from Congress with the hope of achieving unity in an Indian nation and legitimacy for Congress as the voice of that nation. But in both respects his hopes were dashed. Muslim and Hindu became increasingly divided in politics, often bloodily so, and despite the National Muslims in Congress it could not speak for all communities, as the Round Table Conference made painfully clear. However Congress was increasingly seen by politically conscious Hindus as the voice of India and as their natural political ambience, because of its range of organization, its funds and its repute in the struggle with the raj. Few Hindus broke away from it, and those who did, whether Moderates or orthodox Hindus, did so reluctantly and retained personal links with it. The British, too, had recognized that these years, and particularly civil disobedience, were a test of their legitimacy as rulers. Gandhi's programme had rarely made government impossible but it had dangerously eroded British moral authority, a fact they recognized as they pushed ahead with constitutional reform to buttress their dominion. Now, late in 1934, it seemed that Congress would re-engage with India's rulers in creating a new political order in which both Indian and British had a legitimate role and prospects of power. The Mahatma had apparently chosen a prophetic role on the periphery of political life, but few believed that this astute *bania* and ascetic visionary had retired from politics. By extricating himself from the daily business of Congress politics he had achieved a new freedom to pursue his vision and confirmed his uniqueness in public life.

PART III

The crises of old age

'WHERE THERE IS NO VISION, THE PEOPLE PERISH'

In middle life Gandhi had embarked on a new and unexpected career. Far from becoming a social worker in Gujarat, as he had envisaged on his return to India, he had become a continental leader who confronted the raj with the weapon of non-violence and embarked on the great enterprise of defining and building an Indian nation. By late 1934 it seemed as if his vision of non-violence and true swaraj was hardly shared by his compatriots, while the policies he had suggested were very patchily and temporarily implemented. Now in his late sixties and seventies he faced old age and what it might mean for him and his public role. Old age is rightly seen in many philosophical and religious traditions as a time of necessary change for the individual, a time of challenge, even of crisis, as he or she adjusts to declining physical capacities, the rise of a new generation to its prime, and probably to a changing external environment. Some respond with anger and resentment, clinging on to old roles, reluctant to encourage successors: others welcome age with grace and humour, seeing restricted and changed roles as a release from former burdens and an invitation to explore new dimensions of life. If this is true of the private individual it is the more so of a public figure like Gandhi, who had had such a unique standing and an enormously wide and demanding range of activities.

Gandhi in effect faced not one crisis of old age, but a compound of several. He had to come to terms with himself as an individual, as his health and energy failed, and as some of his close colleagues and confidantes died. He had to meet and adjust his relationships with a new generation of political leaders and activists, many of whom were sceptical about the political worth of non-violence, and espoused ideologies generated in a world and age very different from the one in which Gandhi had been brought up. Moreover, because of his longevity he found himself working in a political context that was changing markedly – in terms of the issues at stake and the structures of political activity. The British pushed ahead with constitutional reform: the 1935

Government of India Act freed Delhi from much of the control London had previously exercised, and devolved government of the provinces almost totally into the hands of elected Indians. It was a strategy to salvage and sustain a minimal British raj, but it gave Indian politicians a whole new range of structures in which to compete for and exercise power. As it envisaged a federation with Princely India in the near future it also brought into play in the politics of British India the nature of Princely rule and the political aspirations of the Princes' subjects. Furthermore, now it was clear that the British would actually withdraw from India the issue of who constituted the Indian successor nation was critical. Gandhi therefore faced the question of whether a leader who had proved adept at contriving anti-imperial demonstrations and consolidating oppostion to a common antagonist could adapt to the new times, could learn new skills appropriate to the new structures and styles of politics, and could perform the changing functions now required of a continental leader.

Gandhi the visionary and prophet

Yet crises are also opportunities. The may generate deeper vision and enable the development of ideas and strategies, as well as being possible occasions for stagnation, failure and despair. This chapter largely stands back from chronology and contemplates Gandhi in the later 1930s as he met the changing external situation and began to cope within himself with the personal aspects of the experience of ageing. Congress's policy, despite initial misgivings, was to co-operate in the new structures of politics and administration, and in 1937 after elections with an enlarged franchise, it became the party of government in seven of the eleven provinces of British India, having won 716 out of the 1585 seats in the new provincial legislatures.[1] Gandhi meanwhile remained apart from the rough and tumble of politics and of administration, and pursued his dual vision of non-violence and swaraj through village work, grounding his life and work in an evidently profound sense of Truth as the ultimate and only reality. Without such a vision he believed that public life, including politics and government, would be corrupt, and independence would not be true swaraj in the sense of a reformation of India's society and polity, but an Indian version of the imperial raj with all its faults, in Gandhi's eyes, of violence and insensitivity to the wishes and needs of ordinary people. He often quoted the New Testament; had he known the Old Testament as well he would perhaps now have used words which typified his current concerns: 'Where there is no vision, the people perish.' (Proverbs, Ch. 29. v. 18)

As Gandhi was now so well known as a religious figure in India and abroad he was frequently asked how he saw himself. He denied that there was any such thing as 'Gandhism', or that he was trying to found a new doctrine or sect, and he asserted that his role was to apply truth and non-violence to life.[2] To those who complained that he was sometimes inconsistent, even inscrutable, he underlined his role as a truth-seeker, not as one who had a ready-made and unchanging philosophy. 'My aim is not to be consistent with my previous statements on a given question, but to be consistent with truth as it may present itself to me at a given moment. The result has been that I have grown from truth to truth . . .'[3] When people further suggested that his current aloofness from politics was a recognition of failure he again pointed to truth as his lodestar.[4]

> You say I have had the experience of being not successful and that I had retired for some time from political work. In the dictionary of a seeker of truth there is no such thing as being 'not successful'. He is or should be an irrepressible optimist because of his immovable faith in the ultimate victory of Truth which is God. And, I have not retired, temporarily or permanently from political work for I recognize no watertight compartments. What I have done is to retire from the Congress and Congress politics – and that I have done to serve the Congress and the politics of the country better than before.

The Hindu tradition might advocate 'retirement' for the ageing, to enable them to shed earthly burdens and prepare for death and the next stage of the soul's journey, but Gandhi was clear that his vocation was to continue working, and he aimed at a long life full of activity to the end.[5]

However he was becoming increasingly frail and his health was almost constantly in danger, not least from chronic overwork. He recognized that his closest friends and colleagues were deeply worried about this, yet, as he explained to his close supporter from Madras, Rajagopalachariar, he could not limit the energy and emotion he put into his work, or abandon problems some thought unimportant, because of his concern for truth. To do so would be to go against his very nature. 'For fifty years I have acted in the same way and I cannot change my spots now.'[6] The correspondence of his friends and secretaries shows how often Gandhi was on the verge of collapse or actually bedridden, as his blood pressure shot up at the slightest provocation. Late in 1935 when persistent pain in the back of his head was investigated he was found to have such high blood pressure that he had to take immediate bed rest: there was to be no correspondence and his harrassed secretary commented that Gandhi had neither learned to rest nor did he help those around him to relax. It took two months before he was in any sense well again, and then he had all his remaining teeth out. Mahadev Desai noted that though his laughter had changed as a result, it retained its original quality.[7]

In July 1937 he was again exhausted and agreed to rest. Late in October of the same year he collapsed again and after a partial recovery went for a month to Juhu beach outside Bombay, where he had convalesced after his operation in 1924. All through 1938 his blood pressure was still dangerously erratic. Mahadev Desai commented, 'Gandhiji is somehow standing the strain of the ever increasing work that he is called upon to bear. How long he can go on like that God alone knows.' Early in 1939 he was again forced to rest in bed to avoid another total collapse.[8] Gandhi did make some efforts to conserve his energy, in addition to the times when he reluctantly followed his doctors' advice and went to bed. He started keeping far longer periods of silence than his regular silence days – four weeks in March-April 1935, for example, and two months in mid-1938; he spoke of it as 'a wall of protection' which enabled him to cope better with his work.[9] He still travelled a considerable amount – to south India early in 1937 and to the North-West Frontier in late 1938. But he admitted at the close of that year that his touring days were probably over. As he concentrated his efforts for village uplift in one village in central India, Sevagram, he recognized that he had neither the strength nor the will to attempt the larger-scale work he had launched at Sabarmati.[10]

Gandhi's collapses were rarely due solely to overwork. The undoubted physical and mental strain to which he constantly exoposed himself was often overlaid with emotional tension or distress which precipitated a 'physical' collapse. Late in March 1938, for example, his dangerously high blood pressure was provoked by the visit of Kasturbhai and Mahadev Desai's wife to a temple in Puri which had not been opened to Harijans. He admitted that this 'upset me terribly', and there was a profound crisis in his immediate circle on the issue.[11] In mid-1938 and again later in the year his poor health had partly emotional origins – his angry and sad response to what he perceived as his personal failure in brahmacharya and to the violence he saw around him.[12]

Although the ageing Mahatma seemed to the public a tranquil spirit, he was often moody and experienced a turbulent anger with himself, his family and his close colleagues. He admitted that this was a besetting problem, and at times it disrupted his closest relationships and life in the new ashram he was forming at Sevagram.[13] He found that one of the benefits of his frequent silences was that it seemed to eat up his anger.[14] However, it seems that old age did not bring him to a sense of peace with himself, a charitable acceptance of his failings and foibles, and he was constantly doing battle with his deepest feelings and drives. His anger was one case in point. He was frustrated by his inability to do all his work without wrecking his health. He was also deeply humiliated and ashamed when he felt he was falling short of his standard of chastity, as when during his illness of late 1935–6 he experienced a vivid sense of sexual arousal while he was awake and in his opinion should have been in control of himself. In mid-April 1938 he had an involuntary discharge while awake, an experience he had not had for years, which he called 'dirty' and 'torturing', and it plunged him into a 'well of despair'.[15] To the modern and particularly the Western ear such self-castigation sounds prudish and cranky. But it has to be set in .the context of the religious tradition which had moulded Gandhi, and its insistence that the man who conserves his semen conserves his vital strength, which he can then put to good and spiritual use. To Gandhi the precondition of spiritual vision and power was inner purity.

Believing that he had a vocation to change Indian life and infuse it with his vision on non-violence, it is understandable that he was so distraught by these normal physical experiences which to him seemed to make him unfit for public service.

Some months after his experience in April 1938 he stated categorically that his own impurity was probably the chief stumbling block to the development of non-violence in India.[16] His despondency was deepened because he felt that impurity darkened man's eyes in the search for truth which was man's primary vocation. He called himself a scavenger or sweeper, both in the literal sense and it a spiritual way: 'I am endeavouring ... to clean my inside also, so that I may become a faithful interpreter of the truth as I may see it.'[17] Gandhi's anxieties about his spiritual and physical failings were further compounded by the knowledge that if he truly exercised the quality of detachment from the fruits of his actions which he believed was taught in the *Gita* he would not be so tossed about by human emotion or so liable to physical collapse. He felt this detachment was the hardest thing to achieve, yet essential if the individual were to experience peace and gain the vision of the true self as it related to ultimate reality. His failure to achieve detachment was yet further material for self-condemnation.[18]

Here evidently was a soul in travail, a visionary haunted by his own inadequacies. He was also a very lonely man, despite the crowds that thronged to see him, and the devotees and the curious who came to Sevagram from all parts of India and from far further afield. He confessed his loneliness of spirit to Jawaharlal in April 1938 when he felt the two of them were drifting apart. A year later a close woman friend told Nehru that Gandhi seemed to be constantly lonely.[19] He had very little support from his actual family, and some of its members were a constant worry to him. His eldest son, Harilal, was a continuing shame to him. In 1935 there was an apparent reconciliation between them, but the son broke away from the conditions of a 'pure' life which his faher expected, and thereafter Gandhi really washed his hands of him, and they were rarely directly in touch. However news of Harilal's debts, his drunkenness and sexual vices, and his scrounging for money reached Gandhi. So also did news of his conversion to Islam, in 1936, which Gandhi sadly and publicly considered to be no true conversion and change of life; had it been so he would have rejoiced. When he was later 'reconverted' to Hinduism Gandhi lamented that there had been no change, and all his son wanted was money for drink. He continued to blame himself for Harilal's life – because he was born when Gandhi was so young and had spent so many of his formative years away from his father. Yet he still prayed and hoped that God might touch his life, so convinced was he that man's journey was by nature towards a better life.[20]

Kasturbhai too, was a worry to her eccentric but caring husband. As she aged she became cantankerous and difficult to please; Gandhi told their daughter-in-law, Sushila, not to mind what she said.[21] She

evidently retained many of the family and wordly attachments that
Gandhi tried to lay aside, and he reluctantly accepted her interference in
the ashram life and the fact that her special tastes in food were pandered
to. His concern and tenderness towards her were very real, despite their
long times apart and their lack of a normal family home and life. He
assured her of his increasing love for her, though he made no outward
sign of this. When she joined a struggle in her native Rajkot it was
against his will, as he was aware of her age and physical weakness; and
when she was interned he wrote to her daily. He recognized that she had
faithfully stood by him though his was not the behaviour she would
have expected of a husband and father when she married him; he saw
that she had changed remarkably for a simple Indian wife, and paid
generous tribute to her strength of character.[22]

In the South African communities Gandh had created he had found
genuine frinedship, ease of companionship and support from those who
joined in his experiments with new styles for living. But just as the
Sabarmati ashram seems to have drained him of so much time and
energy and eventually failed him, so his new ashram at Sevagram was
hardly a source of true companionship and understanding. Amrit Kaur,
a Punjabi Christian of high birth and good education, who became a
colleague, amanuensis and companion in these later years, wrote vividly
to Jawaharlal of the 'lame ducks' who gathered round Gandhi in the
ashram. She realized that Nehru was profoundly irritated by the weak,
hapless and depressed to whom Gandhi was a magnet; but Gandhi
welcomed them, and she herself was learning to put up with them in
order to enjoy 'Bapu's' presence. Yet she noted, 'I feel too that if a
certain number of 'sane' people did surround Bapu things would be
easier & happier for him and he appreciates intellectual companionship.'[23] Gandhi himself joked to her that the ashram was 'an asylum for
the insane, the infirm, the abnormals and the like'; and he admitted that
the ashram community was full of bickering which might even make
him close it down.[24] Even his relationships with his trusted secretaries
were sometimes turbulent, partly because of the intensity of their
devotion to him, and his heavy reliance on them. The younger one,
Pyarelal, left at one stage in late 1937 after a bitter outburst. Mahadev
Desai considered leaving after Gandhi's storm over the visit of their two
wives to the Puri temple; he lamented,[25]

> To live with the saints in heaven
> Is a bliss and a glory,
> But to live with a saint on earth
> Is a different story.

Gandhi did have some genuinely close relationships with men and
women who were his intellectual equals, though inevitably the passing years took some of them. His doctor and Muslim friend and adviser, Ansari, died in 1936, leaving a significant political and personal
gap in his life. He grieved deeply, but he tried to realize that sorrow

was needless, as his friend's soul lived on and he would be living a life of service still, though in an unseen manner.[26] He was deeply attached to some of his political colleagues – Vallabhbhai Patel and Rajagopalachariar, for example – and took in good part their criticisms of and differences with him. But he knew that Patel could not understand or share the religious dimension of much of his 'reasoning', just as Jawaharlal Nehru could not. Perhaps his closest relationship was with this younger man whom he treated as a son and a colleague, and whose support he recognized was essential if he was to work with a new generation of the politically conscious and active. Nehru in turn saw the value of Gandhi to the formation of a genuinely popular nationalist movement, and political sense confirmed the deep bond of emotion between them. Yet his socialist aspirations and his knowledge of international affairs often divided him intellectually from the older man. It was when Gandhi felt that Jawaharlal was drifting away from him that he felt his loneliness most deeply. In July 1939 he even considered total retirement because he thought Nehru primarily, but others also, were fed up with him and his experiments with non-violence, particularly after an occasion when Nehru lost his temper with him. Vallabhbhai hurriedly warned Nehru of the depth of Gandhi's sense of isolation. 'I don't think that he loves anybody more than he loves you and when he finds that any action of his has made you unhappy he broods over it and feels miserable. Since that evening he has been thinking of retiring altogether ...'[27]

Gandhi seems to have gained much of his genuine emotional sustenance from relationships with mature women who co-operated in his constructive work, treated him as an honoured guest in their family homes, visited his ashram, and dedicated themselves to his walfare. It is a pattern of relationships not uncommon around 'saintly' celibates. The women found a new fulfilment in the tender concern he showed to them and in the public work he demanded of them, while he found companionship and service. The quality of these relationships can be seen in his correspondence with Amrit Kaur, for example. He called her 'idiot', and she addressed him as 'tyrant'; his letters were in turn tender, didactic and demanding, He chided her for overwork and illness: with friends he prescribed the medicine of relaxation that he was unable to give himself! He even suggested that her constant colds were caused by her private habits – wearing silk underwear, taking frequent baths, and 'the criminal use of soap' which destroyed natural protective oil on the face.[28] Amrit Kaur recognized the personal submission Gandhi seemed to require from his true devotees, and this she was not prepared to give. Gandhi's talent for eliciting love and admiration also drew to him many foreign friends: there was still C.F. Andrews (who died in 1940), and newer helpers such as Agatha Harrison and Horace Alexander. But though they could provide sympathy and understanding, they were rarely present to provide the companionship of equals he so sorely needed.

It was in the late 1930s that Gandhi really for the first time sensed that he was growing old. After his involvement in the same struggle in Rajkot as his wife he acknowledged that it seemed to have 'robbed me of my youth. I never knew that I was old. Now I am weighed down by the knowledge of decrepitude.'[29] Far from feeling 70 he now felt like an 80-year old. Given his increasing frailty, his battles with himself, his suppressed anger and his isolation, it is perhaps little wonder that as he aged he suffered from bouts of extreme dejection and loss of confidence. For some weeks in April–May 1938 he was in a deep trough of despondency and self-doubt which he mentioned constantly in public and private; again in mid-1939 he was so dispirited that he talked of totally abandoning a public role. Despite the anguish of these times of real depression he remained truly a prisoner of hope, bound by a conviction of the ultimate reality and power of truth. Significantly he now preferred to say that Truth is God, rather than that God is Truth. In 1936 he denied having any sense of defeat, humiliation or despair though he had retired from Congress politics. Even in the gloom of 1938 he still had a sense that his current depression was but a preparation for a new phase in his life. And as 1939 lengthened he spoke of his optimism, and his sense that he still had the energy to lead a far greater struggle than any they had so far undertaken.[30] Gandhi's optimism rested not only on his belief in the *ultimate* triumph of truth, but more nearly on his sense that each individual could change for the better, because in each there was a spark of truth or godliness – even in his apparently reprobate son. His buoyancy also flowed from his concentration on and concern for the present, rather than worrying about the long-term future. He told Jawaharlal, 'My difficulty is not about the remote future. It is always the present that I can concentrate upon and that at times worries me. If the present is well taken care of, the future will take care of itself.'[31]

Evidence from the late 1930s suggests that this was a time, despite Gandhi's swings of mood and emotion, when he experienced a deepening of his personal religious life. Although he tended to speak austerely of truth as God he evidently had a deeply intimate and personal sense of the Divine. He wrote of his journeying towards God, feeling the warmth of His presence, of yearning to lay his weary head in the lap of his Maker.[32] And for him the value of the silence he increasingly kept was not just the utilitarian function of enabling him to work more or deal with his anger: it was also a spiritual necessity for him as a truth seeker, for in silence he could best hold communion with God.[33]

In January 1937 he travelled south to Travancore, on what he described as a pilgrimage, now that its temples had been thrown open to Harijans. It was evidently a profound religious experience. In the past he had not used temples as part of his own devotions, particularly since he had worked for Harijans. Indeed he had severely criticized the current state of many temples. But now he realized from a deep personal vision that temples could be bridges between the individual and the unseen and indefinable God.[34] Recitation of the name of God, *Ramanama*, had long been part of his personal prayer, and this practice now became such a part of him that it was as natural and constant as breathing. Inevitably Gandhi, the Mahatma, was often questioned about his own beliefs, and what he considered to be 'Hinduism'; in the last months of 1936 his thoughts finally centred on the first stanza of the *Isha Upanished* as the essence and crystallization of Hinduism. Even if the rest of Hindu scripture vanished and this alone was left, then in his view Hinduism would live for ever.[35] His precious *Gita* was a commentary on this stanza.

> At the heart of this phenomenal world,
> > within all its changing forms,
> > dwells the unchanging Lord.
> So, go beyond the changing,
> > and, enjoying the inner,
> > cease to take for your self what to others
> > are riches.

   Much of Gandhi's discussion of religious matters expanded what he had said in the 1920s. He continued to speak of the nature of true religion as opposed to specific religions, and of how people should view religions other than their own. He argued that Hinduism should undergo a proper growth and reform, and, despite his lack of technical knowledge, he continued to expound the principles he felt were essential for the acceptance or rejection of the various Hindu scriptures. His radicalism was robust, even shocking: 'There is so much humbug in the so-called Shastras that revised editions should be brought out.'[36] Even earlier he had publicly argued

> ... that all that is printed in the name of scriptures need not be taken as the word of God or the inspired word. But everyone can't decide what is good and authentic and what is bad and interpolated. There should therefore be some authoritative body that would revise all that passes under the name of scriptures, expurgate all the texts that have no moral value or are contrary to the fundamentals of religion and morality, and present such an edition for the guidance of Hindus.[37]

Gandhi's discussion of social problems in Hindu society continued unabated, too, in the 1930s; his arguments for a new attitude to and role for women, his castigation of untouchability and his consideration of the nature of caste became even more forthright, as he based them on his judgement of all religious authority according to the standards of reason, morality and compassion. In relation to caste his leap into a truly radical stance had occurred late in the 1920s: now he was unhesitatingly outspoken. In 1935, for example, he stated categorically that caste as found in India, with its many divisions, its sense of inferior and superior, and its restrictions on social intercourse between castes, was

'the very antithesis of varnashrama': in a state of true *varnashrama* there
would be four equal groups with no barriers to their members eating
with each other or even marrying across caste boundaries.[38] Whereas
he had earlier hesitated to promote marriages across major caste
boundaries, now he exhorted those close to him to break down old
barriers as they arranged the marriages of their young folk. 'The barriers
ought to be broken. When the whole country is ours, why should we
keep ourselves confined to one community or province or region?'[39] On
untouchability he continued to argue that it was a terrible sin, and that
unless it was destryed it would destroy Hinduism, and he threw himself
into Harijan work with the energy and passion that Rajagopalachariar
exhorted him to avoid if he was to conserve his ebbing strength. Yes, he
acknowledged that he needed rest, 'but how can I rest? How can one
have rest with a raging fire within? How can any Hindu, knowing that
Hinduism is on the brink of an active volcano, afford to have a
moment's rest?'[40] His primary work for Harijans was now his work in
villages, for he argued that improvement of the quality of village life
would help them and alleviate the poverty and degradation they had
endured for centuries. He also concerned himself with opening temples
to Harijans, but he believed that this was not so much the spiritual need
of Harijans themselves but of the caste Hindus who considered themselves so pure. 'They can have no spiritual grace so long as they deny to
their fellows in faith the same right of worship that they claim for
themselves.'[41] But he could not but be aware that if caste Hindus did not
open temples to Harijans, the latter might well abandon their religious
heritage. For in 1935, Ambedkar, the untouchable leader who opposed
Gandhi's efforts to help Harijans, criticizing them as cosmetic charity
rather than radical reform, advised his fellow Harijans to choose any
other religion that gave them equal status and treatment. On hearing of
this Gandhi exhorted Harijans not to leave their ancestral tradition, and
argued as he had for years, that religious conversion was rarely genuine
and indeed was positively inimical to true religion.

> But religion is not like a house or a cloak which can be changed at
> will. It is more an integral part of one's self than of one's body.
> Religion is the tie that binds one to one's Creator and whilst the body
> perishes ... religion persists even after death.[42]

So Gandhi as he aged and did battle with his increasing limitations
drew more deeply on his religious inheritance for sustenance and
support. He restricted his energies and attention to those topics and
areas of work he considered central to his vocation and to the future of
India. Secluding himself somewhat from the high politics in which he
had been so prominent, he took on the role of the visionary and
prophet, the man on the margins of public life whose message concerned realities deeper than the bargains, alliances and strategies that
were the stuff of daily political life.

The vision of non-violence

To Gandhi the most important aspect of his vision of and for India was the practical working out of the principle of non-violence. This was, in his view, the means to true swaraj, and would be the hallmark or a swaraj society. His withdrawal from Congress politics was partly to enable him in 'voluntary isolation, to explore the yet hidden possibilities of non-violence.'[43] He seems to have felt that now in old age his own non-violence was on trial, and that he must try to express it so that it was like the sun at noon, whose warmth even the blind could feel.[44] For Gandhi still, despite all the evidence to the contrary around him, non-violence was the very law of human nature, the only way for men and women if they wished to be truly human: recognition of this law and its application in daily life was the fundamental distinction between humankind and the animals.[45] Furthermore, in the specifically Indian context he felt that swaraj that was truly swaraj for even the poorest could only be won through non-violence.[46] It was therefore understandable that he claimed non-violence was the root of all his activities. Although he undoubtedly saw it as a message for the whole world he felt his personal vocation was more limited. 'God has not given me the power to guide the world on the path of non-violence. But I have imagined that he has chosen me as His intrument for presenting non-violence to India for dealing with her many ills.'[47] Yet as his personal commitment to non-violence deepened he became increasingly disheartened by the evidence that his compatriots' 'non-violence' was but an expedient strategy and not a sincere belief: it was 'the non-violence of the calculating Bania'. He admitted that ever since the 1928 Bardoli satyagraha he had weakly shared the delusion that they had attained sufficient non-violence to strive for responsible government. Now, seeing the truth around him he would not lead another salt march to Dandi. Further, he would stiffen his qualifications for would-be satyagrahis in the future, even if that meant they were in worldly terms an insignificant number. Congress itself was not an effective vehicle for satyagraha, so unwieldy was it, so corrupt, ill-disciplined and divided. Any allegedly non-violent mass movement would almost certainly become violent, discredit Congress and wreck the struggle for independence.[48]

Gandhi's pursuit of the vision of non-violence led him into several specific areas of controversy. Within Congress itself there was now a group of younger men with radical sympathies who were overt in their rejection of Gandhi's ideals. Disillusioned by the apparent failure of civil disobedience, they joined together in 1934 to form the Congress Socialist Party (CSP). Their most prominent spokesmen were young, highly-educated, and tended to be northern Indians from urban, professional families. Their radicalism was a blend of various influences, including Marxism and socialism akin to that of the British Labour Party. They numbered among them R. Lohia, A. Mehta, M.R. Masani and Jayaprakash Narayan, who in old age himself became a great Gandhian figure in the politics of independent India. Gandhi was more than willing to talk to them and to read what they wrote, and he even teased them about the ill-health which seemed to afflict so many of them, and invited them to stay with him to be cured. However, he argued, in a fashion which must have been maddening for them, that socialism was no modern invention or insight: it was explicit in the first stanza of the *Isha Upanished* which he now quoted as the essence of Hinduism. Further, he claimed he had been a natural socialist long before these younger men had learned socialism from books; his stemmed from his non-violence which rose up against social injustice.[49] He argued that it was he who was now tackling the real problems of Indian society through his village work and his gospel of trusteeship, while they were just Westernized theorists. As he confided to a colleague,

> Among the Socialists there are many good people, and some have the spirit of self-sacrifice in them; there are some who possess a powerful intellect and some who are rogues. Almost all of them have Westernized minds. None of them knows the real conditions in Indian villages or perhaps even cares to know them.[50]

His fundamental difference with them was on the question of non-violence. They had no objection to coercion, and their programme indeed pre-supposed coercion, either through legislation or through the mechanism of class war. He believed that fundamental changes in society could only occur through conversion of people's hearts, and this belief rested ultimately on his conviction that the world was ordered by an active and living God. Other differences between them existed but were less critical: for example, Gandhi's stress on individual effort rather than collective work, and his willingness to envisage a longer time-scale for true reform through the processes of re-education among both the privileged and the deprived.[51] Gandhi was able to coexist with these young radicals as he himself aged and became surer of his priorities because of the strength of his supporters in the central Congress organization and because of Jawaharlal's peculiar relationship to the socialists. Although he shared many of their ideals, he saw that Gandhi was essential to a successful national movement against the British and would not break with or jettison him. The socialists felt let down by the young Nehru, one whom they saw as their natural ally and spokesman, but without whom as an alternative figurehead and leader they could not mount a serious challenge to the ageing Mahatma.

However, Gandhi's pursuit of an ever-deepening vision of non-violence brought him into conflict with even his closest colleagues, including Nehru, when he extended it in 1939 to Rajkot state. This episode was a small part of the much wider problem of relations between the Princely states and British India. During these years official negotiations to get the Princes to join the federation envisaged in the

1935 Government of India Act were painfully slow and unproductive. (They were finally abandoned after war broke out.) Meanwhile in many states popular agitations developed against Princely autocracy: these attracted the sympathy of many in Congress but were also considered by the central Congress leadership to the potentially destabilizing to Congress if small groups of Congress dissidents, such as the socialists, used the peoples' agitations in the Princely states as a popular springboard. In 1938 the CWC tried to ensure a measure of control over agitations in the states, and to draw a clear line of separation between them and Congress politics. Gandhi supported this strategy, encouraging the states' peoples to realize their potential power through satyagraha, yet urging the Princes to realize that times were changing and that they would have to grant their people responsible government and should see themselves as trustees for their people.[52] He became personally involved in states matters only when a issue arose that concerned his own Rajkot and his loyalty to Vallabhbhai Patel who was steering a struggle there.

Patel had eventually reached an agreement with the Rajkot ruler on a committee to plan a scheme of political reform for the state. But the ruler backed out of the agreement. Gandhi perceived this as a breach of faith with the people, and in late February 1939 he went to Rajkot on a mission of peace. Instead his intervention generated more bitterness and misunderstanding. Exasperated by the ruler's chief minister, who was adept at delays and changes of position, Gandhi wrote a stiff letter to the ruler, reminding him of his family ties with the state and his consequent paternal feelings towards the ruler; and he announced that he would fast until his suggestions were accepted. To the public he said the fast was the result of an undeniable inner compulsion, though he undertook it reluctantly. It was intended to touch the heart of the ruler. But he also hoped it would have a purificatory influence in the wider politics of Kathiawar, which he sensed on this brief visit were as corrupt and intrigue-ridden as they had been in his childhood.[53] He exhorted his anxious friends around the country not to be perturbed, and professed to be in a state of great peace and spiritual exaltation. However, to generate movement in the impasse beside the impact of the fast he let it be known that he hoped the Viceroy might intervene. Lord Linlitghow, concerned about the inevitably wider repercussions if Gandhi died, brushed aside time-consuming argument about the points at issue and referred the question to the Chief Justice of India, who eventually decided in favour of Patel's position. Gandhi accepted the Viceroy's move as a basis for breaking his fast, and did so with due ceremony on 7 March 1939.[54]

However, worse confusion followed this apparent triumph of non-violence, particularly over the accommodation of Muslims, landlords and Harijans on the committee of reform, and Gandhi found himself accused by them of breach of faith. He felt hurt and suffocated by this atmosphere of intrigue, and began to lose hope of a settlement. He agonized within himself why all this bitterness should have resulted from his intervention in the cause of good faith and peace. In a gesture of despair the 'released' the ruler from the necessity of observing the terms of the Chief Justice's award, thereby also neatly letting himself off the hook of having to placate the minority interests who had understood that he would protect them.

Hardly surprisingly, even his closest colleagues in Congress, including Nehru, were mystified and upset as the Mahatma appeared to play fast and loose with the interests of the state's people and to stir up conflict among the minorities. Gandhi himself argued that the bitterness that had attended his best efforts in Rajkot reflected what he now interpreted as his own failure of non-violence, and that his appeal to the Viceroy had been coercive.[55] To later, detached observers, the Rajkot conflict suggests that the politics of non-violence depend for their success very greatly on the nature of the opponent, and the clarity and dimensions of the issue at stake. Here Gandhi took a stand on an apparently simple and clear-cut moral issue, only to find it was far more complex than it had first appeared; and, moreover, that he had challenged an adversary that had no need of his services and no care for its wider moral repute, as had the supposedly powerful British raj with which he had been able to deal rather more easily. Gandhi made it clear in public and private that the whole Rajkot episode was deeply painful to him, not least because of the gulf it created between him and his friends: it was Rajkot which made him feel old and decrepid and prompted him briefly to consider total retirement. However, from the humiliation, failure and physical exhaustion he drew some signs of hope and renewal. He called Rajkot a 'laboratory' for the development of the science of non-violence, an experience critical for his deepening understanding of *ahimsa* and its implementation in India conditions. He now saw that if non-violence were to be a practical proposition in India, it could only be deployed by the truly disciplined and dedicated, perhaps only by one man.[56] As far as the states were concerned, Gandhi now deferred all questions to Nehru as president of the All-India States Peoples Conference and refused to become personally involved in their struggles.[57] Yet he remained convinced that change must come in the states, though he did not wish to eliminate the Princes, and he refused to countenance any deviation from the path of non-violence in the inevitable processes of readjustment.

Rajkot had shown how the rough realities of states' politics might not be malleable to Gandhi's non-violent political style, even where he felt he had the family ties with the ruler which might have made fasting an appropriate gesture in a Hindu context. In British India the deepening communal problem proved equally insoluble to him. He had found his failure to speak for Indian Muslims in London a searing and disheartening experience. Now that was compounded by the death of Dr Ansari who had been his 'infallible guide' in handling Muslim politics, and he cast around for another Muslim to take his place.[58]

Eventually Maulana A.K. Azad became the Muslim guide to Gandhi and the central Congress leadership, providing Congress with a Muslim voice and token presence at the highest levels of its decision-making to 'prove' Congress's cross-communal support and its legitimacy as a national mouthpiece.[59] Yet Azad was hardly of the all-India standing to perform this function, as an educated Bengali without a regional base or a solid organizational backing in his community. But if Azad could not speak for India's Muslims nor could anyone else make a legitimate claim to do this, so divided were Muslims by provincial loyalties and priorities.

The man who cast himself in the role of would-be Muslim spokesman was M.A. Jinnah, that severe and aloof figure who had opposed Gandhi's populist style and radical aims two decades before. In the late 1920s he had retired to London, his hopes for a strong centre in Indian government where Muslims shared power with Congress having been dashed on the rocks of Muslim provincialism and Congress obduracy. However, in 1934 he was back in Indian politics, working to revive the Muslim League and to gain the support of Muslim provincial majorities, where these existed, in order to speak legitimately for Indian Muslims in negotiations from a position of strength with Congress.[60] The 1937 elections, however, showed that although Congress could not claim to speak for India's Muslims, neither could the League It won only 109 of the 482 seats reservced for Muslims, gaining just under 5% of the Muslim vote. None the less Jinnah and the League increasingly stridently denounced Congress as a Hindu body, and publicized alleged Congress 'attacks' on Muslim minorities where Congress formed provincial governments under the new constitution. Even more ominously many Muslims began to feel that the constitutional structure so recently erected by the British could not protect their special identity, and some began under the banner of the League to perceive of themselves as a separate nation. In this atmosphere of fear and suspicion the League began to pick up increasing Muslim support.[61]

As communal relations deteriorated at many levels of public life there was much to be said for attempted negotiations between Gandhi and Jinnah, from Congress's point of view, though Gandhi was sensitive to Nehru's feelings in this matter. The younger man was locked in an acrid controversy with Jinnah, and he felt that the League was a reactionary force and profoundly anti-national. However Gandhi began to engage in a correspondence with Jinnah in October 1937 and eventually the two met in April and May of 1938 – with no result. The real stumbling block to any fruitful negotiations was Jinnah's insistence that Gandhi and Congress alike could only speak for Hindus, while the League alone could represent Indian Muslims. This Gandhi could not accept any more than he had accepted in London in 1931 that Congress was less than the nation's legitimate voice.[62] Gandhi had hoped to act as a bridge and peacemaker between Hindus and Muslims, as he told Jinnah; but the two men's mutual perceptions of their own and each other's role made this impossible, and Gandhi also found Jinnah's 'tough customer' political style distasteful and destructive.

Increasingly he felt that he and his generation had shot their bolt on the communal problem, and that it was time for younger men to take up the cause of unity.[63] As commual tension heightened and politics became polarized on communal lines, Gandhi was painfully aware of his own powerlessness, however profoundly he still hoped for communal unity: all he felt he could do was pray.[64] His personal non-violence seemed incapable of altering the situation; nor did his colleagues in Congress seem to take seriously his suggestion that the only way to win Muslim hearts was by serving Muslims, particularly in the villages, as opposed to the superficial ways of making mass political contacts or contriving high-level political compromises.[65] In the long-term, too, communal antagonism seemed to rule out any likelihood that non-violence could become a practical all-India option. The problem that had haunted Gandhi before he hit on the tactic of the salt satyagraha in 1930 was now immensely greater and apparently insoluble. He wrote in October 1939,

> Apart from the uncertainty of the observance of non-violence in Congress ranks is the tremendous fact that the Muslim League looks upon the Congress as the enemy of the Muslims. This makes it well-nigh impossible for the Congress to organize successful non-violent revolution through civil disobedience. It will mean Hindu–Muslim riots.[66]

It was a sad reflection for one who had retired five years earlier to ponder the new possibilities of non-violence.

Grass-roots reconstruction

When Gandhi made his well-managed exit from the public stage of Congress late in 1934 he gained Congress sanction for a new organization to promote village industries. In the following years his labours, inspired by a vision of true swaraj to be achieved by work in and for India's villages, was more public than his pursuit of the vision of non-violence, however central the latter was to him personally. The government was understandably suspicious of Gandhi's apparent seclusion, deep in the heart of the Indian countryside, suspecting that his new concentration on village work, and the AIVIA in particular, was a device to extend support for himself and for Congress, as a preliminary to renewed civil disobedience. This Gandhi firmly denied, declaring his aim to be the moral and material growth of villages, and that if he were ever to organized civil disobedience it would be independently and separate from his other constructive work.[67] But though he trod warily, consciously avoiding conflict with the government, now that he had at last gained room to work after the frustrations of the early 1930s, he was well aware of the long-term political implications of successful village work, and these included the organizational ability to perform satyagraha. He exhorted the trusted Vallabhbhai Patel to be 'quite firm about the constructive work. If the people do not overcome their lethargy and attend to the essential tasks, there will be no satyagraha and no swaraj. We must learn mutual co-operation.'[68]

Everything Gandhi did was in a sense political, just as it was in his own understanding religious, because his life was a whole, not divided up into separate compartments. What changed from time to time was his current emphasis. When he sensed that active politicians and those closest to him in constructive work saw themselves as two antagonistic and mutually exclusive groups he reminded the latter that there was no watertight division between 'the so-called political and the so-called constructive programmes ... Nevertheless I do maintain that for the sake of efficiency it is necessary for one to confine oneself to one item at a time or such items as conveniently run together.'[69] In the later 1930s village work was his main mode of pursuing his vision of true swaraj as a refashioning of India's society and polity. It was the flowering and integrating of many pre-existing aspects of his work: khadi, constructive work, food reform, educational change and Harijan uplift, to name but a few. He was himself aware that this marked a new phase in his life and work. He wrote early in 1935 of his heart being in village work, and in late 1936 of wishing to bury himself in the village he had chosen and to be forgotten.[70] To him work in India's villages, trying to solve the problems and change the lives of those who were the majority of India's population, was at this stage of his life his true sadhana, or spiritual path and discipline.[71] Gandhi's new public role and his willingness to tackle the diverse problems posed in the villages demonstrated his life-long adaptability as situations changed, and now his ability to use the constrictions of age rather than fighting them, to deepen his vision of a new India and to explore new ways of implementing it which would use to the full rather than dissipate his failing energy.

Many people, including his well-wishers and supporters, were perplexed by Gandhi's changed focus of attention. But as he constantly tried to explain, India lived in her villages: these were the homes of her teeming millions and it was here that radical change must take place if a new nation were to come into being, drawing on the inheritance of its great civilization rather than being corrupted by the modern economic and political modes that were taking root under the aegis of the raj. No longer did he feel that the key to a new national life lay in India's cities, as he had done on his return from South Africa.[72] Then he had believed that if urban Indians learned how to regulate their lives, to keep their streets clean and produce selfless citizens for civic government, they could then rightfully claim wider powers. Now after the experience of two decades of public work in India he believed that the cities and their people were strangling the villages, and living off their rustic compatriots, forcing them into poverty and idleness. What must be

done was to free the villagers from this crushing burden, and to give
them once more work and adequate remuneration.[73] Once this occurred
India's peasants would, he believed, stand forth as the heirs of India's
civilization, the true citizens of the swaraj society he envisaged. 'Take
away the encrustation [of crudeness], remove his chronic poverty and
his illiteracy and you have the finest specimen of what a cultured,
cultivated, free citizen should be.'[74] When people wondered whether his
new focus of work meant the end of his Harijan campaign Gandhi
immediately insisted that village work was a natural consequence and
complement of his earlier work for untouchables, for they were the
poorest and most despised of India's people; they in particular would
benefit from better food in the villages, a cleaner environment, and
more work.[75]

Gandhi's turning away from Congress politics to village work was
also a measure of his distrust of political power as commonly
understood. This was always implicit in his understanding of true
swaraj as self-regulation, from the individual and the local community
upwards, rather than as an Indian takeover of the institutions and style
of government forged by an alien, imperialist regime. He had publicly
argued the issue in 1931 with Congressmen who were insistent that he
should go to London to participate in constitution-making. Even then
his ideal had been a kind of enlightened anarchy, a situation in which
national life became self-regulating: political power, in as much as he
sought it for Congress, was not an end in itself but only a means of
enabling people to reform their lives through the work of national
representatives. Then he had quoted Thoreau, that the best government
was one which governed least. Now in the later 1930s he quoted him
again, and urged that it was a fatal fallacy to think that Indians must first
win political power before they could embark on reform. Vital reforms
were open to them now, without any need for government intervention: this was why he was concentrating on the mundane needs of
the poorest, discussing their food or their sanitation.[76] Gandhi's attention to self-reform and self-regulation was the more timely now,
and the more urgent, as Congress took office in so many of the
provinces and showed that as a party of government rather than of
opposition, enjoying the luxury of rhetoric, it often had neither the will
nor the financial resources to tackle the real social and economic
problems of India's masses.

Congress itself had sanctioned the two main institutional means at
Gandhi's disposal for village work. He still played a prominent role in
the AISA, though of course its work was confined to the production and
sale of *khadi*. By 1935 Gandhi was seriously concerned that this body
was merely a small-scale commercial operation, primarily producing for
an urban market. What he envisaged as a true contribution to village
welfare was a self-sustaining *khadi* operation, in order primarily to
clothe villagers and give them a realistic living wage, and only

secondarily to supply the cities with surplus *khadi*. As a result of his advice the association altered its policy in Ocotober 1935 so that each local *khadi* operation should become autonomous and should pay its workers a realistic wage based on food and clothing requirements. He meant this to be an act of faith in the vitality of village life and recognized that many of those who worked in the association were afraid that the inevitably higher price of *khadi* now commercially available would possibly lead to a drop in sales. However after the introductioin of the new policy in 1936 the reduction in sales was not as great as had been feared, and in 1937 sales began to increase, largely because of Congress's successful electioneering and its support when in provincial government. In 1937 the AISA's registered spinners numbered 171,760 compared with 103,383 in 1936; the value of production and sales by AISA branches rose from 1,713,400 rupees in 1936 to 2,353,045 rupees in 1937. The movement was strongest in UP, Tamilnadu, Maharashtra and Bihar. Even so, it was a small contribution to solving the overwhelming problem of India's rural poverty.[77]

The AIVIA was a far smaller operation, with less capital and a narrower geographical range; but it began to break new ground in fostering and experimenting with small-scale manufactures suitable for the village environment. Like the AISA after its 1935 shift of policy the AIVIA was to be decentralized and its workers were to be paid the sort of realistic wage that would make a significant contribution to village prosperity. It was formally founded in mid-December 1934, with its headquarters in Wardha, in central India, on land donated by Gandhi's generous and wealthy supporter, Jamnalal Bajaj. Its organizer was J.C. Kumarappa, a chartered accountant by training, who had worked in a Gandhian educational institution in Gujarat and had been prominent in Congress affairs, including the management of the funds collected for relief in Bihar after the earthquake early in 1934. He was assisted by a Board of Management, which included Shankerlal Banker, the secretary of the AISA. Gandhi had high hopes of what he called his 'new baby', if it could attract public support.

> ... it will give hope to the millions of villagers; it will turn the city-dwellers, who are today their exploiters, into real helpers and servants; it will establish a living link between the intelligentsia and the illiterate masses; it will be instrumental in abolishing all distinctions between man and man, and it will turn the villagers from being mere creaters of raw produce, which they have practically become, into self-sustained units and caterers for most of the requirements of city-dwellers.[78]

However, its funds were limited – in 1936 its credit balance was between forty and fifty thousand rupees; there was little India-wide interest in it, and most of its work occurred at the Wardha headquarters. There it embarked on paper-making, oil-pressing, rice-husking, tanning,

dairying and an apiary, as well as spinning and weaving. The local
government reported approvingly to Delhi on its efficiency and its lack
of overt political overtones.[79]

Although Gandhi was keenly interested in small-scale village production, and had been notorious for his hostility to large-scale
industrialization since he wrote *Hind Swaraj*, he took pains to correct
widespread misapprehensions – 'superstitions' as he called them – about
his real attitude. He was not in fact the fanatical opponent of all
machinery and industry he was often popularly supposed to be. In
mid-1935 he explained that he was hostile to machinery only if it
enriched the few at the expense of the many, or displaced useful labour,
and he recognized that 'heavy machinery for work of public utility
which cannot be undertaken by human labour has its inevitable place',
but in such cases it should be state-owned and used for the benefit of the
people. He was not totally hostile even to large-scale production, but it
could only be tolerated for articles that villagers could not easily
produce.[80] Even so, he was out of tune with most Congressmen, who
looked forward to a modern, industrialized economy on Western lines.
Nehru in particular was deeply influenced by what he had seen of
economic planning in Russia, and became Chairman of the National
Planning Committee that Congress had set up once it became a party of
government. Gandhi felt that Nehru was wasting his time and energy
on this, though he recognized that the younger man was only satisfied
with large-scale projects;[81] for himself it was the slower, less glamorous
work of economic change in the fields and lanes of India's villages by
personal example and persuasion.

His main personal contribution to village work was to bury himself in
rural India and tackle for himself the villagers' problems. After some
months near Wardha he moved in mid-1936 right out into the
countryside, though within range of Wardha, to the village of
Sevagram, chosen because it was a genuine village, small, with a
population of 600, and predominantly Harijan by caste. It was poor,
disease-ridden and isolated. Some of his colleagues, including
Vallabhbhai Patel and Bajaj, were deeply worried about the move: the
munificent Bajaj even built a proper road to the village through his own
land so that there were easier communications between Sevagram and
Wardha. At first the only habitation for Gandhi and the few who
accompanied him was a village-style house, made of local material with
mud walls, about 29 feet by 14 feet, with a seven foot verandah
surrounding it. A small kitchen and bathroom were contrived on the
verandah, and each person had a sleeping place allotted to him or her in
the one room. Despite the extreme simplicity – spartan even by
Gandhi's standards – he thoroughly enjoyed the experience and
described Sevagram as 'an inexhaustible source of joy'.[82] Others did not
share his enthusiasm. When Kasturbhai eventually joined him she found
the lack of privacy intolerable, and eventually Bajaj built her a special
house.

Soon the tiny community expanded and devotees joined Gandhi, though he did not plan it as an ashram or try to impose the kind of discipline he had envisaged at Sabarmati. There was no formal link between the members except Gandhi, and no manager as there had been at Sabarmati. Soon the lack of co-operation between the strange assortment of his companions was a strain and he began to look tired, though he would not let any one tell him so.[83] But he pressed on, emphasizing the new orientation of his village work in Sevagram. It was 'whole village work', and it was this he was now advocating to his supporters. Rather than campaigning on particular issues he now felt they must concentrate on a complete village community and attempt there to solve the country's basic problems.[84]

As Gandhi grappled with the nature of village life he did not only concern himself with economic issues and the small-scale industries that could alleviate poverty and prevent idleness. He carried on his crusade for cleanliness and proper sanitation. He described villages as dung heaps and judged that village sanitation was perhaps the AIVIA's most difficult task. In person and in the columns of *Harijan* he showed how waste of all kinds should be cleared, classified and disposed of. Rags and waste paper could be turned into paper; excreta should become manure. He described alternative designs for village latrines, and hammered home the message that a pure water supply was essential for good health.[85] He attacked the problem of a proper diet for village people – asking scientists and doctors about the relative merits of different kinds of food, and encouraging the use of natural, inexpensive and nutritional foods which village people could obtain locally. In terms that sound uncannily modern in the late twentieth century, when well-nourished, affluent people are increasingly aware of the dangers of over-abundasnce and a highly refined and processed diet, Gandhi exhorted villagers and their helpers to eat whole, unpolished rice; to choose wholewheat flour, hand-ground at home, which still retained the natural bran so valuable for the digestive system; to abandon refined sugar in favour of *gur*, traditional brown sugar from locally grown sugar cane. In line with his personal habit, he encouraged the growth of green vegatables for food and tried to spread knowledge about their value and how cooking could destroy the natural vitamins in vegetables. Laughingly he called himself a food missionary. With his natural humour and ability to use direct visual imagery he demonstrated his views to people who had come to Wardha in October 1935 to learn about village work by giving them a meal which was cheap, nourishing, and made of materials readily available in villages. It cost under 10 rupees for nearly 100 people, and included flour, vegetables, fruit and milk.

Good food and cleanliness were also part of his wider concern for village health. He was anxious to discover natural means of maintaining village people's health without resort to expensive drugs, or 'village quacks or incantations'. He was painfully aware that most of the people of Sevagram suffered from malaria or dysentry, and he was distressed that he had to go to hospital in Wardha as the result of an attack of malaria. This only strengthened his desire to improve village health for those whose poverty gave them no such escape.[86] One senses that a sight of this frail, laughing but grimly determined old man, tramping the muddy village lanes, reasoning with and demonstrating to his village neighbours, would give a truer impression of the deepest in Gandhi than the political campaigns or the negotiations with those in power which generated the bulk of the written historical records of his life.

Education deeply concerned Gandhi at this time and was integral to his vision of transforming villages and India as a whole. Just as 'whole village work' was the fruition of many of his previous endeavours, so in the late 1930s Gandhi contrived a scheme known as Basic Education, which was the working out on a national scale of convictions he had long held and publicized. Since his later years in South Africa he had criticized the Western-style, English medium education which had taken root in India from the early nineteenth century. He felt it hacked at the roots of Indian civilization, cut off the so-called educated from their rural and ill-educated compatriots, denigrated physical labour, demoralized and alienated people by its lack of spiritual content and its wearisome rote-learning, and turned out generations of Indians whose main ambition was to obtain a secure and sedentary job. It was no wonder that he turned to education as the source of new attitudes and skills in his grass-roots labour for a new India. At a more mundane level, education was becoming an urgent political question as Congress came to power in so many of the provinces, thereby taking on responsibility for education. But it lacked the financial resources to pour funds into a new system of education as it would have wished. Congress's acceptance of Gandhi's own argument for total prohibition and condemnation of raising money from the sale of alchohol only increased the dilemma of financing education.[87]

Gandhi's experience of Sevagram only served to convince him that radical change in India's education was vital. As a result of his new work he perceived even more clearly the division of India into two groups – the apparently educated who were the victims of the existing system, and the uneducated in the villages whose lives were grinding drudgery, condemning them to the level of animals, unilluminated by any spiritual or intellectual development: and he felt that the 'educated' were totally unfit to take up the sort of work for village revivification he had in hand.[88]

Late in October 1937 Gandhi chaired an education conference held at Wardha which was attended by the Education Ministers of the Congress provincial governments, among others. He intended to put before the conference a radical plan for a seven-year course of compulsory, free schooling for all Indian children, in which the essentials of education should be given through manual training rather than book learning. The solution to the problem of educational finance was that the pupils' labour should finance their schooling. Instruction should be given in the mother tongue. Higher education was left out of the scheme because Gandhi felt it could be left to private enterprise. The state's responsibility was to see that its future citizens and leaders were given a basic education which would enable their all-round development rather than perpetuating the current system and its ills. Following his proposition and its subsequent discussion at the conference, a committee was appointed under Zakir Husain to make detailed plans to implement the broad outlines of the scheme Gandhi had proposed and the conference had accepted.[89] It enshrined many of the ideals and innovations Gandhi had worked out in his succession of experiments in community living, though it omitted any provision for formal religious instruction, leaving this to parents – a sad reflection of the state of relationships between India's religious communities.

Now what had been a personal and idiosyncratic experiment became a serious item on the contemporary political agenda, considered by the British and by Indian politicians. Not surprisingly it generated much controversy. In many ways it challenged the ethos, values and life-style of those who held power in Congress and in government. Its practicality was doubtful, given not only the vested interests of so many in the existing system but also the financial constraints on government which militated against change, even though the new system was intended eventually to be self-financing. Yet it showed how Gandhi was even in old age addressing himself to fundamental problems in Indian life, and asking awkward questions (even if he could not ultimately and realistically answer them), which were to remain persistent long after his death. The implementation of his scheme of Basic Education was in the event thwarted by the outbreak of war in 1939 and the exit from provincial government of the Congress.

The issue of education was one which Gandhi thought out in terms of the Indian village, coming to his conclusions in the context of his village experience in Sevagram. But it showed how his work for swaraj could not be done without links with those who made political decisions and wielded political power, however much he mistrusted the exercise of power and the apparatus of the state. Despite his apparent seclusion and isolation he was evidently still very influential in Congress. He needed Congress, and many Congressmen still turned to him for advice and inspiration, such was his vision and continuing political skill, and his capacity for innovation, even in old age.

Gandhi and Congress

However, the Congress to which Gandhi had to relate in the late 1930s was in many ways profoundly different from the Congress in which he had first exerted authority in 1920; and which he had been called upon to lead in 1928–9; or even Congress in the mid-1920s when much of its political thrust was in the legislatures. Then it had been primarily a movement of opposition to the British raj, whether through the politics of agitation or of constitutional activity; Gandhi had for much of the time been the figure-head for this opposition and had helped Congress contrive new modes of reaction to the British which generated a considerable popular following. Now for the first time under the 1935 constitution Congressman had to come to terms with the possibility of becoming a party of government. Through 1935, 1936 and part of 1937 they agonized over the prospect of electioneering and taking office in provincial government; then in office they struggled with the problems of being the government in many areas. As a result of this major change in its political stance and manner of operation, Congress became the natural arena of political activity for most politically-minded Hindus. Given its repute and its continental spread of organization, few would-be political activists cared to operate as independents or in Hindu minority groups when Congress loomed as the potential giant with the contacts and funds that could smooth the electoral path to power. The consequence was a flow of new political recruits into Congress, and a resulting decrease in homogeneity among Congressmen, as they represented different areas and social backgrounds. The advent of men of rural origins in Congress and its positions of office was just one aspect of this, with its corollary, a new 'vernacular' style of politics unlike those more decorous and constitutional styles evolved by earlier and highly-educated Congressmen, and continued by their successors of Motilal Nehru's generation.

As Congress took up the reins of government it also experienced increasing tension between the centre of its organization and its peripheries. The priorities of local Congressmen could often clash with the needs of the centre to maintain a cohesive party with the ability to re-engage in conflict with the raj, should this again become necessary. For example, new legislators in provincial assemblies often found their need to satisfy constituents on economic questions such as land tenure and revenue conflicted with the all-India priorities of a Congress pledged to national unity across regional, religious and class divisions. Or bitter personal and factional struggles among provincial Congressmen could erupt into the counsels of the national body via cross-regional alliances, or the efforts of one group to use the centre to strengthen its local position against its rival.

The details of Congress politics in these years are tortuous.[90] What is crucial in the context of Gandhi's life is the fact that the 'job' of its leaders, the problems they had to solve, and consequently qualifications for successful leadership, were very different when compared with those of an earlier generation of influential Congressmen, Gandhi included. In the provinces there began to emerge a new breed of party men, who needed to be efficient electioneers, organizers and bargainers: local bosses who could satisfy their clients and bind local Congressmen into a disciplined political force in and outside the legislatures. But Congressmen who were to be all-India leaders needed the skills of the organizer and the disciplinarian; they needed to be able to deal with the discords and pressures generated in the localities and brought to bear on the party as a whole, by force of personality, choice of policy and strategy, by persuasion or ultimately the threat of expulsion. It was increasingly unlikely that one man could exercise all these skills and perform such a multiplicity of roles, and so the combination of men pooling their individual skills might well dominate Congress in the future. Vallabhbhai Patel thrived in the new environment, as a party organizer and disciplinarian *par excellence*, well suited to operating in a more abrasive and calculating politics. Rajagopalachariar from Madras proved adept at the new styles required of a Congress Chief Minister who now had to co-operate with a British Governor and the imperial administrative structure.

But what role was there for Gandhi, a Mahatma, a visionary who was basically mistrustful of political power and state structures; who had never held office in civic administration, as had a Patel or a Nehru, thus gaining an apprenticeship to government; who was, rather, notoriously skilled in embarrassing governments through opposition, agitation and taking a high moral stand; who wanted Congress to become a disciplined organization for social service? It was perhaps little wonder that whereas few Congressmen had wanted at least openly to criticize Gandhi, the national figure-head, during phases of agitational opposition to the raj, now that power in that raj's state structures was available there were many cross-currents of opposition to him. Some resented the supercilious 'holier-than-thou' attitude they sensed in those who grouped round Gandhi, as they battled for Congress to become an efficient political machine for men anxious to become effective provincial politicians in the new political structures. Others for local reasons of factional bonds or communal priorities opposed the all-India stance Gandhi personified. In Central Provinces, for example, a local political crisis generated such hostility to the central leadership that Gandhi was vilified as a fiend, demon and murderer.[91]

Although Gandhi's relationship with Congress was evidently much changed in the later 1930s, Congress was still of great importance to him, despite his apparent exit from its ranks and his growing realization that it was a frail and unreliable instrument for the implementation of his priorities in Indian public life. As in 1930–1 when he had worked for public and official acceptance of Congress as the one legitimate national representative, now he still thought it had a unique standing in Indian public affairs. In the context of British plans for a federation of British and Princely India he wrote in 1938, 'My ambition is to see the Congress recognized as the one and only party that can successfully resist the Government and deliver the political goods. It is the one party which, from its inception, has represented all minorities.'[92] Further, he still believed that it was a possible instrument for non-violent action against the British, though if and when this would occur was still unclear in his mind. When asked in mid-1935 when he was coming back into Congress he laughed and was reported as saying, 'If you have direct access to God, ask him when I am coming back to the Congress.... I do not know it myself.'[93] His trusted secretary, Mahadev Desai, told Jawaharlal shortly afterwards that Gandhi still felt that, despite its faults, Congress was the most effective instrument available for India's progress and could be used to prepare India for 'a final and successful effort for achieving freedom'. Even four years later when Congress was even less the disciplined organization for work among the masses that Gandhi hoped for, he judged that its record in administration was better than that of those governments which had preceded it in the provinces.[94]

Contemporaries recognized that although Gandhi's relationship with Congress was very different from that of agitational leader and major spokesman as in the immediately preceding years, his departure in 1934 was certainly not retirement. He maintained a lively interest in all Congress decisions, and kept a singular and important role in its decision-making processes. An official assessment of the political situation in May 1936, for example, noted Gandhi's important behind-the-scenes role at the recent Lucknow Congress session and subsequent CWC meetings, and concluded, 'Mr Gandhi is thus still the director of Congress and has lost none of his political astuteness or of his inveterate hostility to British rule.' When Congress met again in Faizpur in December 1936 the Bombay government reported that there was little doubt that Gandhi remained the most important figure in Congress.[95] Indian politicians made similar observations, sometimes with considerable rancour. One Maharashtrian lawyer complained in a private letter in mid-1938 that Congress had surrendered to the cult of personality, and predicted that when Gandhi died the Congress would be like the Mughal empire after Aurangzeb! His experienced colleague replied that their best option was to try to capture Congress and undermine its existing leadership rather than follow the 'mirage' of a rival party – a striking piece of evidence of the way Congress had become the one viable political arena for Hindus.[96] Such comments suggest that although Gandhi had not retired from Congress politics he had adapted his role in relation to Congress to suit the new situation of his own increasing years and declining physical capacity, and of the changing nature and position of Congress in political life.

Gandhi himself was articulate and clear about the way he perceived his position. In a press statement on his intentions late in October 1934 he affirmed that he was still interested in politics and the well-being of Congress, but now he would not concern himself with the day to day details of its working. 'And I shall certainly cease to shape the policy of the Congress organization as I have had the privilege of doing ...' Consistently thereafter he maintained that his role was to give advice rather than to control Congress, and that the true spokesmen for Congress were the president and the CWC members, to whom all questions should be referred.[97]

It was certainly true that Gandhi now withdrew from the rough and

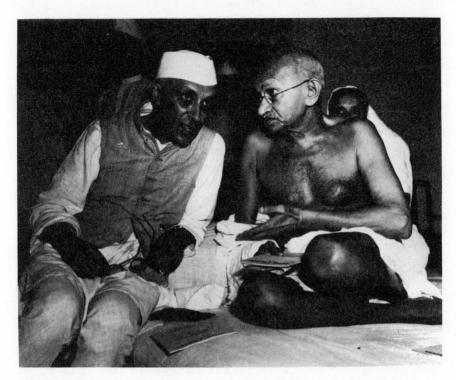

With Jarwaharlal Nehru, 1936.

Gandhi with Rajendra Prasad.

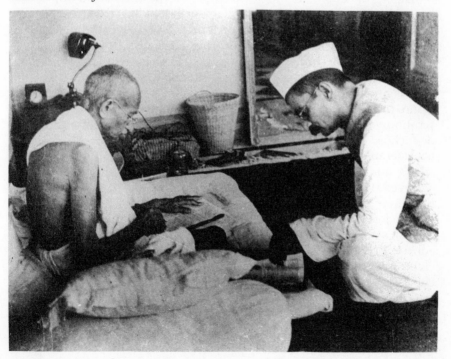

tumble of *local* Congress politics and reserved his energies for the all-India Congress arena. Even in his own Gujarat he delegated Congress matters completely to Vallabhbhai Patel; and he did not step in to intervene and mediate in local disputes between Patel and other senior Gujarati Congressmen. When Madras Congressmen complained to him about the way his friend and colleague, Rajagopalachariar, acted as Chief Minister, he refused to become embroiled in local controversy by exercising his very considerable influence with Rajaji. (But he made it plain in *Harijan* that he sympathized with Rajaji's problems and solutions.) In Punjab where Congressmen were warring against each other he recognized that he had no influence in their local conflict, and refused to become entangled. Further, he took no part in the selection of Ministers for Congress's provincial governments, would not interfere with their work, as people often asked him to do, and refused to listen to complaints against the Congress ministries, referring the aggrieved to the CWC. He had by the end of 1938 an unread file of papers which included complaints against Ministers, and told his readers that he had neither the time nor the inclination to deal with them.[98] Although Gandhi's refusal to become involved in the increasingly fractious and murky workings of local Congress politics resulted largely from lack of time and energy, it was also a recognition that he did not possess the qualifications in terms of skills, priorities and power bases necessary for successfully wielding influence in local Congress situations. His were abilities and resources of authority fitted to the all-India arena. By remaining operative only in all-India politics he also helped to preserve his national rather than local or factional standing; this was a most valuable asset when the outbreak of World War II dramatically changed the political environment and the role of Congress.

Gandhi's connection with Congress, the channel of his continuing influence over policies and the organization, was the CWC. Although he was not a member he often attended its meetings or was to hand if it wanted his advice; he often drafted its resolutions, though he did not scrutinize all of them. Under the 1934 Congress constitution the president chose the CWC, so it was hardly surprising that Gandhi also took considerable pains to steer the election of president. In late 1935 through letters and personal discussions with individuals and the CWC he achieved the selection of Jawaharlal as president for the coming year, in the hope and belief that this would dissolve many of the conflicts between the younger man and some of the older, more conservative of Gandhi's supporters, and would integrate many of Jawaharlal's radical adherents into a more unified Congress.[99] Now, as during the days of civil disobedience, Nehru was a crucial figure in Gandhi's method of coping with old age, and in his increasing delegation of roles he might once have performed himself. However, he could be ruthless if he felt the unity of Congress was threatened, or that its acceptance of non-violence was being compromised. Although he and his allies at the centre of Congress could not control the election of the president for

1939, the fiery and distinctly un–Gandhian S.C. Bose, they did, by passive resistance at the centre, make it virtually impossible for him to function as president, thereby forcing his resignation.[100]

This dramatic show-down, and the record of Gandhi's letters and meetings in these years, demonstrates that he relied for his continuing continental influence in Congress on an influential and recognizable core group of Congressmen who operated powerfully at the all–India level of politics, often as the result of pre-existing local power bases or institutional positions. They often predominated in the CWC, and also formed its Parliamentary Sub-committee, known as the 'High Command', which endeavoured to control and supervise the Congress parties in the legislatures. The 'High Command' were Patel from Gujarat; Rajendra Prasad, a Bihari, who had been staunchly behind Gandhi since his Champaran campaign in 1917; and A.K. Azad, the Muslim on whom Gandhi relied for advice and as a prominent (if unconvincing) example of the communal inclusiveness of Congress, after the death of Ansari and the defection of the Ali brothers in the 1920s. The core group also included J.B. Kripalani and Rajago-palachariar, among others. Nehru was always volatile and unique – tied to Gandhi because of personal affection and political calculation, co-operating uneasily with the others who formed what was sometimes called the 'Mahatmaji Group'.[101]

This men of this core group were not ideological 'Gandhians' in the same sense as those who gravitated to Sevagram or loyally laboured at constructive work in the villages. They tended to be hard–headed politicians rather than spiritual visionaries. They spanned a considerable political spectrum, but were united in their evaluation of Gandhi's role in India's natinal political development. In their eyes he was the focus of a broad national consensus behind the desire for independence, yet he stood for peaceful change rather than revolutionary destruction of society or the evolving structures of the state. They valued his public image in India and abroad, his widespread appeal, his influence with government, his restraining hand on Nehru, his tactical inventiveness, and, not least, his talent for raising funds. Many of them had first entered politics under his guiding hand, and his presence had been vital in the development of their political careers from local operators to very significant national leaders. Not surprisingly many of them were also bound to hm by deep personal affection, and in Rajaji's case by the marriage of their children.

In the later 1930s the Mahatma's agitational skills were not required. Nor did his advice to perform village work provide a compelling programme for a united Congress. But he had other abilities which his key group valued highly as they struggled to control Congress in the changing political situation: in particular as they strove to prevent local divisions and priorities from splitting and weakening it as a whole, thereby undermining it as a national voice and as an instrument for continued work for independence. A brief glimpse behind the scenes in

Congress or at the columns of *Harijan* confirms this, showing the unique role Gandhi still played in Congress.

His main skill, urgently needed at this juncture of Indian politics, was that of mediator and provider of a focus for Congress unity. This was abundantly clear in the long months between Congress's abandonment of civil disobedience in 1934 and its decision to take office in the provinces where it gained majorities in the 1937 elections. This issue of office acceptance bedevilled Congress unity. Some were eager to accept what the new constitution offered. Others, including Nehru, were reluctant to collaborate with the imperial regime after long years of opposition and deprivation, and to accept office without complete power, thus taking responsibility for actions that might alienate their constituents. Others who were not powerful in Congress realized that they would not share in the profits of office and were for more personal and mundane reasons reluctant to let Congress – which meant their local opponents in Congress – take the reins of government and pocket the perks of power. Time and again it was Gandhi who came up with a compromise solution which permitted Congress to maintain a semblance of unity – first by a series of postponements of the issue, and eventually by a compromise under which Congress would form provincial governments provided that the provincial governors would in practice limit the use of their emergency powers.[102]

At other times Gandhi was brought in or himself took steps to smooth over fraught personal conflicts among senior Congressmen. Late in April 1936, for example, there was a sharp clash of opinions in the CWC between Nehru as president and most of its members. (The issues included the sensitive ones of labour and agricultural conditions and agrarian relations.) The handwritten minutes of the proceedings at Wardha state somewhat laconically:

> There was a general desire to avoid a crisis and Gandhiji was invited to participate in the discussion and generally to give the benefit of his advice to the members. He heard the views of the members on the situation & his advice was that the Committee should pull together. This advice was accepted and the Committee proceeded with its business.[103]

The ensuing compromise proved temporary, and again it was Gandhi who patched up a more long-lasting agreement. After a crucial number of his key supporters, including Prasad, Patel, Rajaji, Kripalani and J. Bajaj, had resigned from the CWC in June, Gandhi talked at length to them and they withdrew their resignations; he also remonstrated privately with Nehru, and co-operation within the CWC was restored. Less successfully, Gandhi attempted to mediate between Patel and another Bombay Presidency politician over the leadership election within the Bombay Congress party in the legislature; and in 1938 at the Haripura session of Congress he tried to ease the tension between Patel and the Socialists, asking his close colleague to be less aggressive in manner.[104]

Gandhi's other qualification for influence in the turbulent Congress of the late 1930s was his 'saintliness', his repute as a Mahatma and as one devoted to the Indian nation and her poorest peoples. He became in person and through the columns of *Harijan* an educator and chastiser of Congressmen and critic of their priorities and political styles. It was he who was custodian of the Congress conscience, he who strove to burnish its national image, as it seemed often to come perilously close to disintegration, or to be little different from previous governments. Although his close political adherents might be embarrassed by his forthrightness, and might indeed disagree with some of his prescriptions for Congress ills, they saw the need to keep Congress as a working national machine with a credible national ideology in its relations with the British. Performing this didactic role Gandhi ranged widely in his criticisms and suggestions; these were the corollary of his gradual and reluctant acceptance that Congressmen would have to be allowed to enter government if they were to maintain their unity. At least their mode of government should, in his view, limit the damage office acceptance might do to them, their organization and their constituents, and inculcate patterns of public service and co-operation rather than encouraging autocratic behaviour and lust for power. At the outset of the Congress essay into government Gandhi insisted that Ministerships were not prizes for past deeds but avenues to public service. Saddened by the scramble for office, and the requests for his intervention in the selection of Ministers, he refused to interfere, and argued that Congressmen must be loyal and disciplined in relation to those who had been chosen. 'The grim fight in which the country is engaged cannot be won if Congressmen do not show in their conduct a sufficient measure of selflessness, discipline and faith in the means enunciated by the Congress for the attainment of the goal.'[105] A year later he was still having to remonstrate with Congressmen over the increasing tur- bulence of elections within the Congress organization as people fought to capture the high road to government office and its spoils.[106] Once it had become clear that Congress would take provincial power, he used *Harijan* to elaborate a programme of work for the new Ministers, though he took care to publicize the fact that these were his own ideas, not the official views of the CWC.[107]

Central to his plan was prohibition; the CWC's decision in August 1937 that all Congress Ministries should work for prohibition within three years he called the Committee's 'greatest act' since its formation. He reacted with horror to suggestions that gambling and brothels should be legalized, and argued that Congress could have nothing to do with income derived from any vice. Rather, Congressmen in power should strive to implement the constructive programme laid down since 1920 – including eradication of untouchability, social liberation of women, betterment of villagers' lives, an overhaul of education and

provision of free and compulsory primary schooling, and a radical
change in the country's legal machinery, including transformation of
gaols into reformatories.[108] He felt that Congress Ministers had voted
themselves excessive salaries; and though he realized he could not
overturn their decision he argued publicly that they should live simply
and work hard to deserve these payments.[109] In line with his arguments
over decades that true swaraj must include a radical change in
government, rather than an Indian version of the raj and a continuation
of imperial styles and structures of rule, he urged them to evolve new
modes of government. He told one high official to burn the accumulation of files on his desk. Red tape in his view was one hallmark
of the old order: it would only strangle the new. Congressmen must
eventually find a way to rule without using police and soldiers to keep
order; if this proved impossible they should leave office and again search
for non-violence in the apparent political wilderness. They should
establish new organs of local government, really designed for local
service; meanwhile local Congressmen elected to municipal government
should forthwith turn themselves into unpaid sweepers, road-makers,
health workers and teachers.[110]

Thinking beyond the actual practice of government he urged that in
its annual gatherings Congress should become a 'villagers' Congress'
without the amenities such as electricity or motor vehicles generally
thought necessary. Neither should anyone have better food or accommodation at the sessions just because he was educated or held
office.[111] He roundly condemned those who thought Congress rule was
a licence for lawlessness, and argued that Congress governments had the
right and duty to keep public order and restrain those who disturbed the
peace. He wrote in blunt terms against Congressmen who imported
violence into politics, in the form of violent picketing, seizure of
Congress offices, breaking up meetings, and reviling the rich and
inciting people to loot their property.[112] Perhaps strangely for one who
doubted the worth of state structures and had tried to turn Congress
into a social service organization, Gandhi was now in the changed
political circumstances and in a different type of leadership role still
exerting a moral force in Congress, still pursuing through it his vision of
true swaraj and non-violence.

*   *   *

The later 1930s saw the ageing Gandhi still an optimist – about human
nature, himself and India public life. But he was coming to terms with
the passing years painfully and not without struggle, his hope often
temporarily darkened by events as clouds blot out the sun but cannot
finally remove it. He achieved a new place in public life, and maintained
a very considerable measure of influence, because he was flexible enough
to adapt to a changing situation – by delegating former responsibilities
and areas of work, and by undertaking new but restricted work. His

profound spiritual vision of life as a pilgrimage generated in him a mental and emotional agility which responded to change as an opportunity to be welcomed rather than resisted with fear. His adaptability to new public roles was possible because he was not a career politician in the usual sense, but primarily a visionary, who believed that without vision a new Indian nation would perish before it was born. His own vision of truth and non-violence and of true swaraj he pursued at personal cost, paying the price of ill-health, exhaustion, self-doubt, loneliness and misunderstanding by others. He even interested himself in aspects of public life such as legislators' work which he had once avoided and even decried.

The outbreak of world war, however, radically changed Indian domestic politics, and demanded from Congress and from Gandhi further change. To him it would be the ultimate trial, inside India and beyond her borders, of the viability of non-violence as practical politics.

9

NON-VIOLENCE ON TRIAL

The outbreak of war in September 1939 profoundly altered India's political life and Gandhi's public role, dramatically changing the patterns that had seemed to be evolving in the later 1930s. Congress had embarked in 1937, despite its divisions and hesitations, on a course of co-operation with the British in governing India. It could be convincingly argued that this co-operation might have led to practical independence within a short time, as the British withdrew from the daily execution of governance, increasingly anxious for peaceful relations with a stable partner in the Empire–Commonwealth, rather than responsibility for a reluctant dependency which needed extensive and expensive manning. Now this potentially fruitful experiment collapsed.[1] Congress withdrew from provincial government in November 1939 (and former Congress provincess came under executive rule), and with much anguish and hesitation embarked on a policy of confrontation with the raj which developed from individual demonstrations of hostility to the war in 1940–1 to an all-out 'Quit India' campaign in 1942. This collapsed under a fierce imperial response, leaving the major Congress leaders in gaol until the end of the war, and their organization shattered and illegal. Ironically this supposedly supreme challenge to imperial rule occured just when the British had the motivation and might to suppress it. Now they sorely needed India as a source of money, materials and manpower, and increasingly as a base of operations in Asia once Singapore had fallen in 1942. Conciliation of a hostile Congress which made demands for a crucial role in central government might endanger India's ability to satisfy these imperial needs, and would be likely to provoke a major communal reaction from Indian Muslims. The British also had far more troops in India than in peacetime, and fewer worries about public opinion at home and among their American allies if it could be shown that an onslaught on Congress was essential for imperial security and allied success.

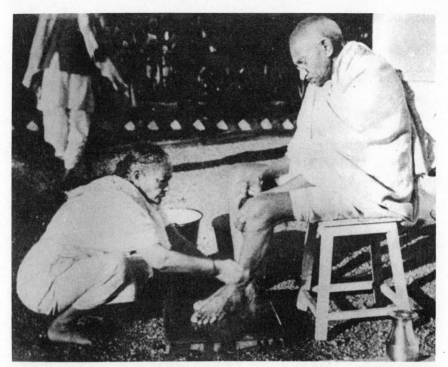

Kasturbhai helping Gandhi to wash, 1939.

Spinning, 1942.

The context of Gandhi's public role was thus drastically changed. From being Congress's conscience and the CWC's guiding spirit, he was offered and accepted once more a direct leadership role in Congress in what proved to be his own and Congress's last attempt at achieving a mass, non-violent opposition movement to the British raj. But could Gandhi in old age respond to this challenge? Could his ingenuity contrive a strategy to overcome the weaknesses and failures so visible in his earlier all-India campaigns? He knew full well that there was opposition to him and his priorities deep within Congress itself, as well as among orthodox Hindus, many old-style Moderates, and of course many Muslims. The Congress he had so often chided in the late 1930s was a weak instrument for his style of work. His own health, too, was frail. Only constant care by devoted friends and secretaries, and his own self-discipline in conserving his energy, kept his erratic blood pressure under control and preserved an amazing ability to sustain an arduous public role.[2]

He was also, not unnaturally at this time of life, increasingly having to bear the personal loss of many who had been close to him emotionally and had actively supported and co-operated in his public work. While he was in prison during and after the Quit India campaign he lost his wife and trusted secretary, Mahadev Desai, both of whom were with him in gaol in the Aga Khan's palace in Poona. Desai more than almost anyone else had come close to understanding Gandhi, and his loyalty, energy and efficiency had for years enabled Gandhi to maintain a massive correspondence and journalistic output. Even earlier, in February 1942, Jamnalal Bajaj collapsed and died unexpectedly of a brain haemorrhage. Gandhi had considered him as a son and had relied on him heavily of late for funds and organizational skill in a range of constructive work. Gandhi admitted to grief such as he had not experienced except when Maganlal died in 1928; Mahadev described him as being 'in greatest need of consolation'. Despite Gandhi's appeal for people to take up Bajaj's work inevitably his own burden increased.[3]

The apostle of non-violence

What primarily sustained the ageing Gandhi, gave him inner buoyancy and a measure of tranquillity, and allowed him even in old age to be inventive and ingenious was his abiding sense of vocation and guidance. To him as an apostle of non-violence, the war was a powerful moral challenge, as well as a source of personal grief. He wrote of being stirred to the depths at the thought of the devastation of London, and of his tears as he pictured Westminster Abbey and the Houses of Parliament and their possible destruction. He vented his anger and desolation on God.

I have become disconsolate. In the secret of my heart I am in perpetual quarrel with God that He should allow such things to go on. My non-violence seems almost impotent. But the answer comes at the end of the daily quarrel that neither God nor non-violence is impotent. Impotence is in men. I must try on [sic] without losing faith even though I may break in the attempt.[4]

But at this supreme international testing of his faith in non-violence his convictions became stronger and his faith brighter, even as the war, 'this unholy duel', intensified.[5] In relation to non-violence within India he had no well-laid plans. He believed profoundly that it was his personal vocation to present non-violence to India in its struggle against imperialism, and that his God would guide him as circumstances unfolded. Time and again he spoke of listening to 'the still small voice' as he fended off persistent questioning; he described how it was a sense of the ultimate power and directive force of the divine in human affairs which sustained him and gave him hope for the future. This clinging to and preaching of a vision of non-violence was the great duty that he had been called upon to perform in his closing years.[6] He even wondered whether it might also be his vocation to be a world peacemaker, and an international apostle of peace during the war.[7]

Just as Gandhi trusted in the abiding triumph of ulitmate reality, so he maintained, despite horrific evidence to the contrary in wartime, a belief in human nature as containing a spark of true divinity and as being capable of change and reformation when offered the good and the true without coercion. He spoke at a Sevagram prayer meeting of this belief.

My faith in human nature is progressively growing. I have concluded, on the basis of my experiments, that human nature can be easily moulded. We have come to assume, because of our inertia, that human nature is always the same and seldom amenable to progress. Churchill and Hitler are striving to change the nature of their respective countrymen by forcing and hammering violent methods on them. Man may be suppressed in this manner but he cannot be changed. Ahimsa, on the other hand, can change human nature and sooner than men like Churchill and Hitler can.[8]

However, it seems that by 1942 he had come to a cataclysmic sense that now within India, as Congress and empire seemed locked in conflict, such a profound challenge to his vision of non-violence and to the Indian nation was occurring that he must be prepared to take risks he would not have contemplated earlier in his life, in order to vindicate non-violence and test its efficacy against the raj at war. They would have to risk even violence and anarchy, rather than draw back from fear of human weakness; violence and anarchy, were, in the last resort, preferable to their current 'calamity of slavery'.[9]

As Gandhi wrestled with critical national and international issues in the light of his vision of ultimate values and realities, his home and the background to his life was the Sevagram community. It seems incongruous perhaps, and is certainly seldom emphasized in accounts of his life and work, that the man who dared to challenge the idea of world war, and to plan a new pattern of opposition to the imperial regime, continued to live in his spartan village setting, to concern himself with the food and illnesses of his village neighbours, and their precarious livelihoods. To Gandhi the man, as he really was, the evening walks with visitors who sought to know his mind, the constant battle against ignorance, dirt and poverty, and the round of prayer and work in Sevagram were of continuing significance, though they generated few historical sources. It was he who insisted that Sevagram was his true identity, where he was most fully himself. 'My true body is the Ashram. If the Ashram is nothing, then I am nothing.'[10] It was his holy place, where he could meet Truth; he likened it to the Himalayan Mount Kailas, the paradise of Siva, and to the river Ganges, sacred to Hindus as a source of salvation and a place of encounter between man and the divine.[11] It was there that he longed to come home in 1944 after his imprisonment and necessary convalescence near Bombay: the home he grieved at leaving when political events and duties called him away.

Gandhi's sense of the significance, even the sanctity, of the Sevagram attempt at community and constructive work, meant that there was no dichotomy in his life and thought between it and the great moral issues he was forced to consider afresh by the war and its impact on India. In 1940 he spoke of Sevagram as the place where non-violence could be tested and proved:

> My ahimsa is imperfect and that is why my surroundings are not saturated with ahimsa. Sevagram is to me a laboratory for ahimsa. If my experiment[s] here were successful and I could find a solution for the little problems that confront me here, I am sure the same formula would provide me a solution for the bigger issues that today face us in the country. That is why I am reluctant to leave Sevagram. It is my laboratory for satyagraha. It is there that I expect to discover the key to India's independence, not in Simla or New Delhi.[12]

In 1945 he used Sevagram for a most intimate testing his own chastity, by sleeping naked with some of the trusted women residents, though he soon abandoned this out of deference to the community's feelings. *Brahamacharya* was of course linked in his mind to his ability to be non-violent.[13] Less dramatically he felt that Sevagram could become the example of a village such as he envisaged as the bedrock of a truly free and self-governing India, and he exhorted his ashram inhabitants to eat, clothe and house themselves simply but well in ways that were possible for their village neighbours. They must extend their corporate example to co-operative farming and self-sufficiency, and must engage with the problem of education. Example was a surer way than argument to influence people. Thus should Sevagram eventually become a self-regulating, small-scale republic, and demonstrate in action an ideal and non-violent society.[14]

I am convinced that a non-violent society can be built only on the foundation of harmony and co-operation, without which society is bound to remain violent. If we argue that this cannot be done it will mean that a non-violent society can never come into being. In that case our entire culture would be meaningless.

Even when Gandhi was involved in affairs of state, likely to be whisked away for interviews in Simla or New Delhi, or urgently needed at CWC meetings, and even when he was personally guiding the first stages of the anti-British campaign, his concern in the running of Sevagram was constant and detailed. Since he had first moved out there to a single hut, the community had continually expanded. By 1945 its annual expenditure was around 100,000 rupees, largely provided by G.D. Birla's brother, Rameshwardas. Despite new buildings, more permanent in construction and made of brick, visitors flowed in and at times outnumbered the permanent residents. Gandhi insisted that the community was a so-called ashram, for they were a medley of persons with different aims, and only a few stayed permanently to pursue a common ideal.[15] Their life was guided by the same principles that had moulded life at Sabarmati. But Gandhi also wrote down simple instructions about courteous and self-effacing behaviour, and expected all who were there to observe high standards of industry and mutual co-operation in ordering daily life; he made detailed suggestions ranging from the proper way of washing up to the best manner of cleaning the teeth with a brush made from twigs. True to form, he included precise and intimate details on use of and cleanliness in the ashram latrines.[16]

The community now had a manager, Chimanlal Shah; but even so Gandhi found himself involved in the minutiae of the community's evolving life. He would advise on the best way to keep cooking utensils scrupulously clean, on how to guard against malaria or sunstroke; he was immediately critical if he noticed dirt and refuse lying around. He gave his opinion on the running of the kitchens. But his skills were most gravely taxed by constantly having to deal with difficult inmates, and to soothe the frictions that were so common among the residents. It was little wonder that he sensed that Sevagram produced in microcosm the basic issues of non-violence in the interaction of people, and attempted there to resolve strife and misunderstanding, even though it concerned petty issues and personal quirks. There was even serious talk about disbanding the ashram in 1944–5. It is surely a significant reminder of his age and the strain Sevagram imposed on him that even as early as 1941 he could not contemplate any new community venture.[17]

Non-violence – the international dimension

As Gandhi strove to realize non-violence in the intimate context of Sevagram, events compelled him also to consider the implementation of his vision of non-violence and to discern his own vocation on a far broader stage – in international relations, and then in the pressing circumstances of India's domestic politics. (Home and international affairs were, of course, closely intertwined: even more than in 1914–18, world war profoundly affected Indian politics, not least by the impact of its changing course on Gandhi's mind and on the emotional and rational responses of the Indians and Britons with whom he had to deal.) Gandhi was not well informed about international affairs; nor had he any experience of them. Nor indeed was he particularly interested in them, because he felt that his message must first be heard and acted out in India, and that therefore his role was to concentrate his energies on what he could do in India. He had been reluctant to comment on the Abyssinian crisis in 1935, for example, because he felt an opinion from him was valueless unless he could follow it up with action; all he would say was that he was praying and hoping for peace.[18] He tended to leave Congress pronouncements on foreign issues to Jawaharlal, for whom they were of great significance.

However, as tension increased in Europe, and the shadow of Hitler became ominously visible even in India, Gandhi was forced by events and public questioning to consider the international and world-wide relevance and practicability of non-violence. 'You see I have come out of my shell and begun to speak to Europe', he wrote to his old and intimate friend, C.F. Andrews, in October 1938.[19] He called the Munich agreement 'peace without honour' but confessed that he could not see how the French and British representatives would have acted otherwise, given that they spoke for democracies whose people naturally wanted peace, to dictators whose philosophy presupposed readiness for violence without moral compunction. In such a confrontation the presence in Europe of small nations such as the Czechs was bound to precipitate conflict, unless they were prepared to stand unaided, and not look to Britain and France for protection. His advice to the Czechs (through *Harijan*) was that they should offer Hitler unarmed resistance.[20] Some weeks later senior American and British representatives of an International Missionary Conference being held in India tried in person to argue with Gandhi that this sort of advice was unsound, because of the fundamental immorality of Hitler and Mussolini. Gandhi rejected the notion that any ruler was beyond moral regeneration and argued that until now such men had not had to face large-scale non-violent resistance – so nobody could predict the outcome in human terms; as for himself he believed the non-violent resister was fortified by God and was therefore indomitable. This sort of argument, that true non-violent resistance had never yet been tried, and that if it apparently 'failed' it would be the result of 'absence or inadequacy of non-violence' was unassailable because it put those who tried to urge reality upon Gandhi in a Catch 22 position.[21]

Nor did Gandhi waver from his position when questioned about the plight of Germany's threatened Jewish population. He sympathized deeply with them and thought (not entirely accurately) that there was a close parallel to be drawn with the position of India's untouchables. However, he argued that a solution to their problems did not lie in founding a homeland in Palestine: that land in his view belonged to the Arabs. He urged that they should instead work for better treatment of Jews in whatever land they were born and bred. Yet he recognized the enormity of their plight in Germany, and even admitted that, 'If there ever could be a justifiable war in the name of and for humanity, a war against Germany, to prevent the wanton persecution of a whole race, would be completely justified.' But, he added, 'I do not believe in any war'.

To Jews confronted by the hideous terror of naked violence, he offered the same remedy as he had to the beleaguered Czechs – non-violent resistance to preserve their self-respect, even if this resulted in a 'general massacre of the Jews'. Even so great and apparently terrible a measure of voluntary suffering could, he believed, be 'a day of thanksgiving and joy that Jehovah had wrought deliverance of the race even at the hands of the tyrant'. There was no way of arguing with one who passsionately believed that to the godfearing, death was no terror, but a 'joyful sleep' of refreshment. Interestingly he compared the Jews' potential for offering satyagraha with the South African Indians, whom he had led; he argued that they were better placed because they were a compact and homogeneous community, more gifted, and had organized world opinion supporting them. When questioned he reiterated his advice to German Jews, and again, as he had done in relation to the Czechs, underlined the novelty and potential of the situation. Hitler had never had to face such courageous, non-violent resistance as he was prescribing, and he would certainly bow before it. Without an apparent flicker of doubt he said his advice was 'infallible when taken in the right manner'. Yet he realized the weakness of his own *locus standi*: India, where he was working in person, had not totally accepted his advice. He therefore *expected* nothing from his advice, but felt morally bound to say what he felt, 'having got the prescription and being sure of its efficacy', if he saw situations in which it applied.[22]

Abiding faith in human nature and its ability to change and improve when exposed to the power of truth and love, of which he was to speak so movingly to his Sevagram friends, was a constant theme in his response to the nightmarish figure of a Hitler or a Mussolini.[23] Acting on this faith, he wrote to Hitler; as one 'who has deliberately shunned the method of war not without considerable success', he appealed to him to prevent a war which threatened to reduce humanity to the condition of savages.[24] The government did not permit this to be sent.

However, Gandhi realized that the reality of world war was a very difficult question for him to tackle; he did not know what India's national response should be and admitted to shirking the issue, though for himself he believed in 'unadulterated ahimsa'.[25] Eventually he left this decision to Congress, though its members knew that his personal view was that India could only offer the Allies moral support and refrain

from embarrassing the British raj, though his personal sympathy undoubtedly lay with the allied cause. When pressed by English supporters
as war broke out to give a message of leadership, he publicly proclaimed his faith in non-violence; but he wrote of treading the lonely
path of non-violence, as he recognized that many of his Congress
colleagues would be prepared, if Britain made suitable concessions to
India, to co-operate actively in the war.[26] At the outset Gandhi realized
that this war was a 'catastrophe without parallel', and as conflict
intensified and widened, enveloping more and more people and areas,
he likened it to the epic conflict of Hindu mythology depicted in the
Mahabharata, and increasingly came to believe that it was a threat to all
civilized life and would reduce the whole of mankind to savagery if
it continued.[27] In response he attempted to act as an international
peacemaker.

He wrote to the Viceroy in late May 1940, offering to go to Germany
to plead for peace, though he admitted this might be only a 'visionary's
idea'. Linlithgow politely but very firmly dismissed this as political
nonsense. But Gandhi did not stop there. Within weeks he penned an
appeal to Britons to lay down their arms and oppose Hitler with
non-violence – even at the price of invasion, the loss of home and life
itself. Again he offered his personal services in any way that the British
government might think was of practical use in achieving non-violence.
As 1940 closed, he wrote again to Hitler, a letter which the government
would not send, appealing to him to stop the war and refer the issues
at stake to an international tribunal.[28] Although his own hopes of
international mediation were a pipe-dream, he seems to have hoped that
America might prove a mediator in the war. He sadly noted American
entry into the war late in 1941, refusing to join in the welcoming 'chorus
of public opinion', because now there was no great power left which
could work to make peace between the antagonists.[29]

Very soon Gandhi was forced by the the advance of the Japanese and
India's vulnerability to consider whether India herself should respond to
the possibility of invasion in the same way he had recommended for the
Czechs and to the British themselves. He was still out of tune with the
thinking of many Congressmen who believed that they could not
commit India to total non-violence in the face of invasion. He continued
to argue that whether it was the Nazis or the Japanese, Indians should
respond only with non-violent resistance.[30] In Gandhi's mind behind
the Congress call in 1942 for the British to quit India was his ill-founded
belief that Japan had no designs on India as such, but was only hostile
to the British; therefore, if the British left, the reason for a Japanese
invasion would disapper. He even envisaged the possibility of a free
India then negotiating with Japan. This was beyond what most leading
Congressmen could accept, and they were realistic in thinking that even
if India gained freedom she would need the help of allied troops, though
they also recommended passive resistance against a Japanese advance on
to Indian soil.[31]

However, in mid-1942 the gap between Gandhi and most of his Congress colleagues closed, as the Mahatma, the apostle of total pacifism, came gradually round to a measure of political realism and agreed that India could not in the event of immediate independence do without the assistance of allied soldiers for her defence.[32] Pertinent questions by American journalists and long discussions with Nehru, with his greater knowledge of the possible implications of an allied collapse in Asia, and his passionate support for Russia and China against fascism, doubtless helped persuade the old man at this critical juncture.[33] Just before the Quit India campaign, he wrote an appeal 'to every Japanese' (which was actually published in Japan). He took care to make it plain that the demand for the British to quit India signalled no welcome for the Japanese but quite the reverse: they could expect to meet both allied troops and a resisting population if they invaded an India granted its liberty. Days later when the AICC passed the Quit India resolution, it envisaged a free India resisting aggression with all the armed and non-violent forces at its disposal, in cooperation with the Allied Powers and the United Nations.[34]

Gandhi accepted in mid-1942 the weakness of his grasp of international affairs. Throughout the war there had been no doubt of his high moral stand on non-violence and his personal integrity, as he offered it to those caught up in the great conflict, even though his public appeals always contained an element of publicity for the Indian cause. Few would have doubted that he would himself have faced death in similar situations. But there was then, and is now from a later perspective, a sense of unreality, an incomprehesion of the practicalities of political life when opposing international forces, both ideological and physical, were engaged, in comparison to the far smaller-scale and often face-to-face conflicts in which he had tested non-violence and attained a degree of success. It is not insignificant that he attempted to replicate such face-to-face politics in his attempts to be a world mediator. Furthermore, as he himself admitted, non-violence of the sort he envisaged, when put on trial in such a conflagration as had engulfed individuals and nations was only possible for those who had no fear of death, and moreover believed that deaths even on a massive scale, would forward their cause rather than leave the field open to their opponent. As he was fond of saying, in the vocabulary of the satyagrahi there was no enemy and no failure: only a common humanity which could not but be enriched and reformed by the practice of non-violence, however 'suicidal' that might seem to those who did not share his vision of truth and love.

Gandhi, Congress and the raj – the viability of non-violent politics

Few leading Congressmen shared Gandhi's complete commitment to *ahimsa*, and in the early years of the war, when they were still at liberty and could discuss India's manner of self-defence and possible participation in the war as a free nation, there were many agonized discussions among them on the issue of pacifism. Most of them were torn between a real sympathy with the allied cause against fascism and a desire to see the collapse of imperialism in India; in such a mental conflict degrees of co-operation with the raj seemed better than outright opposition, particularly if they were greeted with British assurances of a new order in India. However, the war as it affected Indian politics, and in particular the decisions of Indian politicians, did give the Mahatma a changed role in Congress, and at times a position of real leadership, in contrast to his low profile in Congress in the later 1930s. The war demanded of Congress a coherent all-India stand in relation to the raj; it thus consolidated the power of the central group of men close to Gandhi and enabled them to retain the initiative at the centre of Congress for which they had struggled in peacetime as the realities of provincial power had threatened to pull Congress apart. For these men who controlled the CWC Gandhi's active presence was crucial, as a unifier and a strategist. As so often in the past, he sought to soothe differences and effect compromises between conflicting points of view, and often the strategy of a potential, muted or outright campaign of non-violent opposition to the raj became a focus for an uneasy Congress unity.

From Gandhi's point of view the domestic political circumstances of the war gave him a final opportunity to 'experiment' with active non-violence as a way of dealing with the imperial presence – but only if the terms were acceptable to him. So the complex and often confusing swings in Congress policy[35] and its relations with the Mahatma from 1939 to 1942 become comprehensible if they are seen as the meshing and unmeshing of Gandhi's personal vision and intentions and the need of Congressmen for him, with his peculiar style of leadership, to perform for them certain vital functions – maintaining their internal cohesion and their relations with the Congress rank and file, and achieving a credible stance towards the raj at war.

The first phase of Gandhi's wartime relations with Congress was the prolonged and fitful progression of Congress into outright opposition to the imperial regime between September 1939 and September 1940. At the outbreak of war Gandhi had two meetings with the Viceroy, Lord Linlithgow, on 4 and 26 September. But he insisted that he represented no one and no politicial body, that he therefore had no power to 'negotiate' and that the most he could do was to act as an intermediary.[36] He knew he was out on a limb from his Congress colleagues on the issue of pacifism; it was therefore Jawaharlal Nehru rather than he who led Congress in trying to formulate a considered attitude to the war and to the raj, after Linlithgow had correctly but tactlessly proclaimed India to be at war without consultation with leaders of Indian political opinion either in or outside the Central Legislature. When his old Bengali colleague, Dr B.C. Roy (who had been so prominent in Congress's moves to disentangle the party from the policy of civil disobedience in 1934), urged him to reassert his dominance in Congress, Gandhi replied that it was Jawaharlal who alone had the drive to take his place, and that he felt totally unable to take up the burden Roy suggested. He felt that Jawaharlal was the crucial person through whom he could influence India now.[37]

Linlithgow was meanwhile interviewing a wide range of Indian politicians – including CWC members, Jinnah and Muslim League members, and the Chancellor of the Chamber of Princes; but his statement on 17 October after this opinion-seeking exercise was regarded as a poor reply by Congressmen to the AICC's demand that Britain should declare her war and peace aims, and that these should include India's independence. Linlithgow could offer no change of policy – only that enshrined in the 1935 act, though after the war they would negotiate any changes that seemed necessary with all parties concerned. This was a comfort to India's minorities rather than a recognition of Congress as the legitimate voice of the nation. It was little wonder that Gandhi publicly called it 'profoundly disappointing', and 'the old policy of divide and rule', and he felt that Congress could be no party to it, but would have 'to go into the wilderness again before it becomes strong and pure enough to reach its objectives.'[38]

Within days the CWC implemented Gandhi's wishes by directing all Congress provincial ministries to resign, and urged Congressmen to forget their internal conflicts and discipline themselves in case non-violent resistance should become necessary. Later Gandhi admitted that he had taken a leading part in this decision.[39] Although the resignation of the ministries seemed an act of political self-denial, even suicide, by the party that claimed to speak for the nation, in some ways it must have been a profound relief to the central leadership, anxious to preserve an untarnished, unified national image for Congress, because in the previous months they had realized how the exercise of power not only generated divisions within Congress but hostility to Congress, and Nehru admitted in December that for at least six months he had been wanting the Congress governments to resign.[40]

The CWC had in effect handed over 'control and management' of any subsequent civil disobedience campaign to Gandhi. He made it plain that he would require the strictest discipline in the Congress ranks, and that if this was not forthcoming he would retire at once.[41] Time and again in the subsequent weeks and months he made it clear in private and public that he felt that the atmosphere was not right for civil disobedience. His age and physical weakness meant that he was less able to move about and had far less contact with the public mind, and therefore less confidence in his skill and strength as a mass leader. He was also paintfully aware of Muslim hostility to Congress, and had grave doubts about Congressmen's own non-violence. Nor was it yet clear to him that they had no other option in relation to the British and he feared that too hasty decision for civil disobedience would plunge India into anarchy and would embarrass the raj, which he maintained he had no desire to do.[42]

Gandhi's newly resumed leadership role was plain at the Congress session at Ramgarh in March 1940. At his own request he addressed the Subjects Committee and the full session – for the first time since 1934 when at the Bombay session he had so publicly 'retired'. He wanted to see the material with which he would now have to deal; he warned Congressmen that like a general viewing his troops he was telling them the terms of his leadership, and that at present he could see no prospect of an immediate campaign. They could of course expect a dire response from a raj at war. Even more 'appalling' to him was the state of Congress itself – the bogus membership resulting from a lust for power, the entry into their ranks of the power-hungry, and their factionalism and internal violence. He could only lead disciplined devotees of non-violence, truth and the constructive campaign, and he would rather they rejected him if they could not follow the path he laid down.[43] Congress, despite these warnings, accepted the policy of civil disobedience – but only when the organization was considered ready – under Gandhi's control, its decision following the recommendation of the CWC at the beginning of March.

Government reports from various provinces confirm from the evidence of events at Ramgarh and reactions among Congressmen that Gandhi and his close all-India colleagues had unchallenged dominance in Congress, and that Gandhi himself, once retired and an isolated pilgrim on a lonely path by his own admission, was now again the only leader who had the policy and appeal to rally a broad range of Congressmen.[44] Gandhi at Ramgarh sounded like Gandhi at the Calcutta Congress of 1928 – stating his terms for leadership. But neither Calcutta nor Ramgarh were occasions of widespread conversions to *ahimsa* among Congressmen. In 1940, as in 1928, Congress was a disparate body with no clear policy in a time of political confusion, and turned to the Mahatma not so much for his ideals but for the utilitarian strategy he could offer. A *potential* rather then *actual* civil disobedience campaign was a convenient holding tactic for senior all-India Congressmen who needed to indicate opposition to the raj but neither wished for nor had the ability to organize and discipline a mass campaign of non-co-operation. Moreover, as an apparently more aggressive stance, it conciliated the radical and restive in Congress whose discontent with Congress inaction was widely apparent at the turn of the year, particularly the members of the CSP and those who were attracted to Bose's opposition to the central leadership in his new party, the Forward Bloc.[45]

The AICC office duly sent the results of the Ramgarh proceedings to PCCs, and drew attention to Gandhi's speeches there and to his writings in *Harijan*, particularly his instructions which appeared in the edition of 30 March. In this he called for whole-hearted discipline, not grudging acceptance of his terms because they wished to use, even exploit, him and what he could offer them. Every Congress committee should become a Satyagraha committee and register those who accepted non-violence and performed such constructive work as spinning and Harijan uplift; only those prepared to go to goal should be registered. An honest register of potential satyagrahis was the precendition for his ability to lead a struggle: 'a huge army' which he could not trust would leave him embarrassed and powerless.[46] The central Congress took discipline and organization with the utmost seriousness, and sent inspectors to each province to find out what was really happening. The reports on local readiness for a campaign such as Gandhi envisaged were far from encouraging.

It was also clear at a CWC meeting in mid-April that Gandhi was deeply worried about the Muslim dimension to the problem of effective civil disobedience – and whether a new campaign would provoke communal violence. Just as in early 1930, under similar but less intense pressures, when he had hit on the tactic of the salt satyagraha, now he began to evolve in his mind a carefully controlled and restricted movement which would be a successful demonstration of the weapon of non-violence. In conceiving a strategy he also had to consider his refusal to launch a movement that would embarrass the British government just at this critical juncture when Hitler had launched his *Blitzkrieg* in Europe.[47]

Persuaded by the new and terrifying vulnerability of Britain herself and the hope that the war crisis would elicit a new political deal from the raj, the central Congress leadership reached a different conclusion from Gandhi: non-embarrassment was not enough. The CWC played for positive co-operation with the raj, even to the point of joining in a national government, at the same time as it parted company with Gandhi on the question of possible armed defence of India. Gandhi was accordingly freed from responsibility for the Congress programme to pursue his path of non-violence.[48] Once more it was clear that, however uneasy and embarrassed men like Patel were at appearing to oppose Gandhi publicly, they were prepared to dispense with him if his policies seemed unproductive in a specific political situation. But Gandhi with his passion for unity and his personal friendship with most of them made the break with him easy, as Patel thankfully acknowledged to Jawaharlal.[49] In public, too, Gandhi was philosophical and conciliatory about the end of his guiding role in the CWC, but suggested that the apparent break with his colleagues might be only temporary. His article in *Harijan* was typical of him.[50]

I am both happy and unhappy.... Happy because I have been able to bear the strain of the break and have been given the strength to stand alone. Unhappy because my word seemed to lose the power to carry with me those whom it was my proud privilege to carry all these many years which seem like yesterday. But I know that, if God shows me the way to demonstrate the efficacy of non-violence of the strong, the break will prove to have been temporary. If there is no way, they will have justified their wisdom in bearing the wrench of letting me go my way alone. If the tragic discovery of my impotence is in store

for me, I hope still to retain the faith that has sustained me all these
years and to have humility enough to realize that I was not a fit
enough instrument to carry the torch of non-violence any further.

Gandhi's hope of a rapid reconvergence of his views with those of
leading Congressmen were quickly fulfilled – though as a result of the
failure of their strategy apart from him, rather than from his 'proving'
non-violence, as he had hoped. All the government could offer in
response was Linlithgow's statement on 8 August, the so-called 'August
Offer' of an expanded Executive Council and a new War Advisory
Council, on to both of which 'representative Indians' would be invited.
It also contained an assurance to the minorities that no future responsible
government would come into being which could not command the
willing loyalty of substantial sections of the population.[51]

The central Congress leaders, their hopes dashed, turned back to
Gandhi and the strategy of civil disobedience, and at an AICC meeting
in Bombay in mid-September following a CWC meeting they formally
requested him to resume guidance of Congress; they also left open the
question whether a free India would resort to armed self-defence.
Gandhi's response was one of extreme caution, as he made clear to
Thakurdas, a notable Bombay businessman he had known for years,
even before the resolution was passed. To the AICC he spoke of his
sense of increasing age and the fact that the passing years had altered his
relations with Congress: those he had first known and worked with in
Congress were gone, while another generation was replacing those who
had then been the young men. He was full of doubts whether he could
carry them with him, and the responsibility of leadership had never
seemed such a heavy burden. He had as yet no plan for civil disobedience though he knew it would not be a mass campaign. His first step
would be to seek an interview with the Viceroy.[52]

Already in late August he had put out feelers to Linlithgow, and on 29
August had told him that there were virtually no differences now
between him and most Congressmen, as there had been in mid-
summer. Now he asked to see the Viceroy both as a friend and as the
Congress guide. His aim was not to threaten the Viceroy but to make
quite sure whether or not he understood British policy correctly and
therefore whether there were grounds for civil disobedience.[53] Always a
creature of pattern, Gandhi was now acting out what had become
almost a ritual preliminary to any satyagraha – to seek a clarificatory and
possibly conciliatory interview with the opponent; memories of his
warm and productive relations with Smuts and latterly with Irwin were
doubtless vivid in his mind, for he often consciously and publicly
harked back to his earlier experiences and acted on them. Elaborate
courtesy surrounded the visit but the talks on 27 and 30 September
yielded nothing to change the situation, and Gandhi unveiled to the
Viceroy the heart of his new strategy which he had hinted at to the
AICC. He claimed for Indians the right to speak against the war and call

on their countrymen to refrain from assisting in the war, though he
emphasized that he did not wish to embarrass the war effort. He was
told that he could only have the same rights as conscientious objectors in
Britain: not to fight and to be free to proclaim their faith, but not to
persuade others against the war effort.[54]

So Congress moved into opposition to the war effort and Gandhi
confronted the Viceroy as its representative and leader, in contrast to
his stance twelve months before when he went to Simla as a mere
intermediary, summoned from rustic seclusion. In the intervening
months Congress leaders had twice turned to him again for leadership,
and now a civil disobedience campaign of his contriving appeared best
to answer their needs – to relate to the raj at war in a manner that
confirmed the idea of national solidarity and freedom, yet did not
seriously hamper the international fight against fascism, and to satisfy as
broad a range of Congressmen in the localities as possible, offering
opposition to the radicals, yet allowing those who still clung to power in
the organs of local government to continue in their positions.

The subsequent campaign of 'individual' civil disobedience lasted
until the end of 1941. It usually receives only a paragraph or two in
discussions of Gandhi and the Congress. Yet in a sense it was perhaps
the most 'Gandhian' of all his national campaigns, in that he chose the
issue, initiated and ended the movement, and carefully controlled its
course. It was a time when he exercised a unique degree of leadership in
Indian domestic politics, and it seems that he was profoundly conscious
that this was an opportunity for a singular 'experiment' in non-violence;
it was for this reason he valued it so highly, even when others were
becoming frustrated and disgruntled as a result of its. He saw himself in
the unique role of an active reformer, 'carrying on an experiment never
before tried in the political field.'[55] The issue he had chosen was a purely
symbolic one – the right to publicize the slogan, 'It is wrong to help the
British war effort with men or money. The only worthy effort is to
resist all war with non-violent resistance.' (This seems to have been his
own idea, just as salt was as an opening symbolic issue in 1930; he
described it as an answer to prayer for guidance.[56]) This was not a
campaign for independence: the British were not in a position to grant
that, particularly at this point of their dire peril in the war. Rather, it was
a campaign for free speech – because absence of such a basic freedom
was symbolic of India's present servile status. It was also of course a
demonstration of their commitment to non-violence.[57]

Just as salt had been his answer to the pressures and dangers
surrounding a decision about civil disobedience in 1930, now with
similar ingenuity he lifted the struggle on to the high moral ground,
above the entanglements and local factions and priorities which had
dogged Congress as a party in power, in a manner designed to appeal to
moderate Indian and world opinion, to avoid communal conflict, and to
refrain from really hampering the raj at war.

In a manner quite unlike non-co-operation in 1920–2 or civil disobedience a decade later, this campaign was tightly controlled and directed by Gandhi in person. Only by so doing could he really 'experiment' with non-violence and stage a limited opposition to the government which stopped short of outright conflict with no room for compromise, and all that that would mean for Congress as a present and future political force in India. He did not offer disobedience himself, because he knew that would inevitably produce an embarrassing position for the government; he also wished to be at liberty to organize the movement. Of course as other leading Congressmen were gaoled in the following months, this only increased his own significance as the arbiter of the campaign. He planned the overall shape of the movement: first, the demonstration of disobedience by prominent individuals, such as his committed disciple, Vinoba Bhave; then from mid-November the members of the CWC and AICC and Congress legislators; broadening out in January 1941 to include office-bearers of PCCs, DCCs and Tehsil Congress Committees; and eventually from April 1941 extending to all Congressmen and their sympathizers. At each stage he carefully controlled the actual people in these categories permitted to participate, and to facilitate this the AICC office in practice moved to Wardha. It was no wonder that in late 1940 he admitted to being 'fagged out', and having to cut back his work load.[58] There is evidence that he personally scrutinized all the lists of potential participants, and did not hesitate to refuse the names of those he considered unsuitable.[59] Those who had been released from gaol and wished to be exempted from courting gaol again had to apply for exemption to Gandhi; the records show that Gandhi made the decisions after soliciting the views of the relevant PCC. Various applicants, for example, were granted time out of the campaign to rest and recuperate after sentences, or were allowed to withdraw completely because of personal or domestic circumstances.[60]

Gandhi also produced advice on proper behaviour for satyagrahis – not to hold demonstrations, not to use secret methods, not to hide Congress funds, for example. All behaviour was to be courteous and peaceful, and satyagrahis should observe gaol rules and should, if fined, pay up. Students should not go on strike. Satyagrahis ignored by the authorities should even begin individual marches in the direction of Delhi. Gandhi also became involved in the vexed question of whether Congressmen should withdraw from district and municipal government – and on this issue he acquiesced in the wish of most to keep their hands on local power. In line with his own practice and previous arguments he still maintained that the bread and butter work of Congress was constructive action; this should go on, and he argued that it actually contributed to civil disobedience in its own way, expressing non-violence and preparing people for disciplined and obedient work. For him constructive work was the true construction of a swaraj society and polity, and he wrote a full *apologia* on this in mid-December 1941. It is as significant a statement of his priorities in old age as *Hind Swaraj* had been a sign of his new vision at the outset of his career. In contrast to grass-roots reconstruction civil disobedience had only a very limited use, and indeed with swaraj in view it was 'mere bravado' if not backed by mass participation in construction of the new order. With his eye for the haunting phrase he maintained, in conclusion, 'my handling of civil disobedience without the constructive programme will be like a paralysed hand attempting to lift a spoon'.[61]

In terms of numbers and public enthusiasm this very Gandhian campaign proved extremely low-key. The government reported little enthusiasm from the start, and increasing apathy as the months passed; by mid-1941 it had ceased to be a serious administrative problem.[62] It had not needed to have recourse to the comprehensive and tough policy it had been preparing in anticipation of a Congress campaign in the shape of an Emergency Powers Ordinance and a scheme for censorship of mail: the ordinary law and the Defence of India regulations sufficed.[63] About 1,200 people were 'eligible' in the first group stage of the campaign; by the end of 1940 about a half of these were in gaol, including many prominent Congress figures. Among them were 32 former ministers, of whom seven had been Provincial Premiers under the terms of the 1935 act. In the next stage about 15,000 were potential resisters and by mid-April about 13,300 had been convicted. Just over 8,600 were in gaol on 1 April. In the final stage the peak came in May 1941 when nearly 14,000 satyagrahis were in gaol. There were others of course who were fined rather than gaoled, or were ignored by provincial governments. By the end the government thought about 26,200 had been convicted, but by then only 6,000 were still in gaol. Statistics are not a reliable guide to the differential strength of the movement because provincial governments followed different policies about the numbers they gaoled. But CP, Madras and particularly UP seem to have been the heart of the support for Gandhi's plans.[64]

Official assessments that the movement was sharply declining in popularity by mid-1941, and that many people participated unenthusiastically but only with the long-term view of not damaging their careers by seeming disloyal to Congress and Gandhi, are confirmed by evidence of the many politicians who were openly restive at Gandhi's leadership. That old Moderate campaigner, T.B. Sapru, believed by mid-August that a 'good many Congress leaders are fed up with the barren programme of the Mahatma and though publicly they may decline to admit it . . . many of them have communicated their views to the Mahatma.'[65] Satyamurti from Madras was prominent both in public and private in urging Gandhi to let Congressmen leave civil disobedience to himself and a handful of others while most of them returned to work in the legislatures. The realistic Rajaji from Madras and the prominent Bombay Congressman, Bhulabhai Desai, also began to campaign for an end to Gandhi's policy in the hope of reaching a settlement with the government and getting Congressmen back into parliamentary work. When members of the Congress party in the Central Legislature met in New Delhi in early November 1941 many of them were deeply unhappy about Gandhi's policy, yet recognized that he was the only available leader with a popular appeal; they did not wish to lose him, but hoped he could be persuaded to be more flexible and accommodate all types of work. Asaf Ali even went as far as reminding Gandhi of the comparable situation of Congress disquiet in 1933, and said that differences were now being voiced more emphatically: in his view they had come to a turning-point which only Gandhi could help them manoeuvre.[66] But Sapru was deeply sceptical that men like Rajaji or Desai would be able to effect any change in Gandhi or Congress.[67]

Although Gandhi was well aware of Congress opinion, he was happily contemplating a long campaign, lasting even five years, and he joked about the desert air being good for Congress.[68] Even when evidence of discontent began to accumulate he seemed happy with the experiment he was making. In October 1941 Rajendra Prasad reported him as 'thoroughly satisfied. I have never seen him so very optimistic about the future. He is ordinarily not given to despondency but today he is more than ever satisfied and hopeful. So there can be no question of any fundamental change in our programme if he is to conduct the movement.'[69] Indeed, Gandhi feared that if parliamentary activity was resumed Congress would be so seriously demoralized, as he saw it, that this would jeopardize any future campaign.[70] He only had to recall the state of Congress in 1937–9 for evidence of the repercussions of power in a party he had hoped would be selfless and national in orientation. Birla had other fears. Even he was coming round to arguing that Gandhi should give up leadership of Congress, but as the Congress assembly members had recognized, there was no other leader who could do what Gandhi could to unite their heterogeneous body. He could not predict what Gandhi would decide, but on the evidence of later discussions between Gandhi, Rajaji and Bhulabhai Desai, it seemed that the Mahatma remained unconvinced of any need for change.[71] Gandhi's inner contentment with his 'experiment' very probably helps to account for his better health in 1941, despite the work he had to do.

In the end it was affairs external to Congress which broke the deadlock. Early in December the government announced that it would release all remaining satyagrahi prisoners – a relaxation of policy which resulted from the expansion of the Viceroy's Executive Council to include more Indians, as well as recognition of the stagnation of civil disobedience, and a hope that this gesture would encourage moderate opinion and Congressmen who were anxious about Gandhi-style politics.[72] Within days the Japanese had attacked Pearl Harbour and begun their drive through Burma. Once again the unresolved question of non-violence in India's own defence and the possibility of British concessions split the central Congress leadership. It was Gandhi himself, ever the mediator, the contriver of compromises within Congress for the sake of unity even at the apparent expense of his own leadership, who managed to let Congress off the hook of a moribund campaign and prevent a split on the issue of non-violence. It was 'his campaign' in its ending, as it had been in its initiation.

The CWC met in Bardoli in the last week of December. Significantly it was during the train journey from Wardha to Bardoli that Gandhi first drafted his manifesto on the constructive movement and its fundamental significance for swaraj, thereby indicating how his mind was working and where his priorities lay. At the meeting he realized how far he was from most of his colleagues on the fundamental question of non-violence. He maintained that Congress had taken a stand on non-violence in Bombay in 1940 as a matter of principle; most of the committee disagreed and said opposition to the war in its new form had been a matter of policy rather than principle. It seems to have been a profound crisis, generating controversy and even bitterness in Gandhi's immediate circle. Gandhi himself saved them by formally requesting them to relieve him of leadership of the Congress campaign so that he could continue his 'mission' alone or with people who believed in opposition to all war. This his colleagues accepted, thus opening the way to a change of strategy.

In public also Gandhi worked to retain Congress unity.[73] Two weeks later when the AICC met at Wardha he again pleaded for unity, exhorting them to accept what the Bardoli meeting had done. He felt its resolution reflected Congress's mind and could be a focus for unity, and he was deliberately not asking those closest to him like Rajendra Prasad and Patel to follow him in leaving the Congress.[74] So Gandhi recognized political reality, and by reserving civil disobedience for himself and encouraging Congress to get on with constructive and even parliamentary work, he managed once more to extricate himself to follow his vision of non-violence, and, as the Governor of UP put it, 'once again history has repeated itself and Gandhi with his usual cunning has welded Congress together with a formula which is capable of numerous interpretations.'[75]

Gandhi was pleased with his experiment with non-violence. It was indeed a personal *tour de force*, demanding his constant attention to Congress affairs and a stream of communications with the government, though at least he did not have to write for his journals at this stage, for he had temporarily withdrawn them as a protest against government censorship. Civil disobedience also demonstrated the efficiency of the Congress as a body that could maintain nationwide communications, though even at this juncture some local offices were negligent in sending information to the AICC. Gandhi's campaign never slipped form central control, but that was largely because it accommodated the political instincts and drives of many local activists, by permitting wide provincial flexibility in the matter of participation in local government, and because it never became a vehicle for popular discontent or distress, as had his previous campaigns. In broader terms it functioned as a holding strategy for a central leadership anxious to preserve Congress unity yet reluctant to meet the raj in all-out conflict. But it did not mollify Muslim opinion or persuade orthodox and moderate Hindu opinion of Congress's fitness or legitimacy as the voice of an Indian nation claiming freedom. Sapru, representing moderate nationalism, was becoming sick and tired in early 1941 of Congress manoeuverings and the fact that so many Congressmen would not openly say that they wanted a settlement with the government. 'The most sickening thing is that these Congressmen talk ... quite sensibly in private but when they go out or speak or write in public they adopt a different tone and language.'[76] However, by later 1941, civil disobedience had ceased to be a useful strategy in the eyes of many Congressmen, as it did not pressurize the government or gather public acclamation, and in fact began to divide them from each other, in a situation similar to the one in which they had found themselves in late 1933 – hence their willingness to let Gandhi pursue civil disobedience alone and to consider a new strategy.[77] What to put in place of civil disobedience, given the government's war-time priorities, remained their dilemma.

The Congress central leadership, adrift from Gandhi, could neither resolve its differences nor contrive a new strategy. Two of Gandhi's closest colleagues, Nehru and Rajagopalachariar, for example, held opposite views on the worth and possibility of collaboration with the raj at this moment of peril. Rajaji was frankly in favour of a settlement with the British and pleaded for compromise, and Nehru took him to task privately, arguing that such defeatist talk would weaken Congress and deflect its members from active constructive work and the strengthening of the Congress machine. 'For my part,' he wrote,

> ... I think it much too late for any real compromise to take place, for the very minimum conditions on our part are far beyond what the British Government might do. I think there can be nothing more dangerous than our being saddled with responsibility without complete power. Complete power is inconceivable in the present and partial power will make our position worse.[78]

Even by early March they had failed to reach any policy decisions; there were defections among the Congressmen who were members of the Central Legislature, there seemed little life in local Congress organizations, and the central leaders were keenly aware of being adrift in uncharted and dangerous waters. This pessimism coloured their meeting when eventually a CWC gathered in mid-March.[79] Although Nehru had complained that it was weak to wait to respond to some outside influence, this was precisely what Congress did. Only a government initiative ended the impasse.

In late March came a new British offer in the form of a declaration carried to India by Sir Stafford Cripps, who was known for his sympathy towards Congress, and Nehru in particular. It envisaged after the war a truly independent India as a Dominion united to Britain by a common allegiance to the Crown, the constitution of which would be decided by Indians, though any province would be at liberty to opt out of the new Indian state. In the meantime the political leaders of India would be invited to participate more fully in the government of their country and the war effort, in an expanded Executive Council.[80]

The origins of Cripps' mission to India lay in a request by Sapru that the British should do something significant to end the political stalemate, a suggestion which fortuitouly received added weight when a new War Cabinet was formed in February 1942 and Attlee became Deputy Prime Minister and Cripps became Lord Privy Seal and Leader of the House of Commons. The idea eventually got under way when Churchill unexpectedly backed it – not because he wished to see constitutional advance in India, but because he hoped to promote India's war effort and if the initiative failed at least to have shown to the British public and to the Americans that failure was due to Indian intransigence rather than a negative imperial policy.[81] Conceived and born in the cross-currents of domestic British and international politics, it was hardly surprising that it failed to attract the co-operation of Indian politicians. Its terms for the immediate changes envisaged were so general that when Cripps came down to the intricacies of negotiation and definition he soon found he could not satisfy Congress and retain the backing of Viceroy and Cabinet. The break between Cripps and Congress (whose negotiators were Azad as President and Nehru) eventually came on the issue of Indian control of defence and whether any new Executive Council would function like a Cabinet; for if not, in Congress's eyes, this was still imperial control in thin disguise. Not surprisingly, Congress also opposed any notion that parts of India might go their own way after the war.

Much bitterness and controversy surrounded the collapse of this initiative, and also the nature of Gandhi's role in the matter. Cripps himself and Sapru both felt that Gandhi was largely responsible.[82] Gandhi later denied outright that he had directly intervened in the final stages of discussion, and his denial was corroborated by Rajagopalachariar.[83] At the CWC meeting in mid-March he had advised that only the Congress President should see Cripps, and though he agreed to meet Cripps after a personal request, he insisted that only Azad and Nehru could negotiate on behalf of Congress.[84] When he met Cripps on 27 March he made it clear that he felt Congress would not accept the offer, primarily because of the support it appeared to give to the Princes, and the offer of non-accession to provinces that did not wish to join an Indian union. Probably on the same day he wrote a note to Jawaharlal saying he felt they could not accept what Cripps had come to offer.[85] On 29 March he described himself as 'out of all this thing' and said that the CWC had the matter in hand;[86] on 5 April he left Delhi for Wardha, while negotiations continued. When challenged later he told the press he had left the CWC to it and neither guided not interfered with their negotiations and decision, and he reiterated this to his friend, Horace Alexander, incidentally referring to the episode as 'that dismal mission'.[87] Certainly there seems no clear evidence of any dramatic last-minute intervention by Gandhi on the phone from Wardha as Cripps alleged. But Gandhi's views were well known to his colleagues before he left for the ashram; his very absence confirmed his lack of hope in the new move, because he of all people would have been the first to offer his mediatory services had he envisaged a positive outcome. But the man who had been Irwin's willing counter-player in 1931 had come to sense a new official hardness of attitude, particularly during the war. Quite apart from the personalities now involved compared with the sensitive and deeply religious Viceroy a decade before, now he felt that the offer was woefully divisive. He also loathed any idea of possible Congress co-operation in active warfare, and seems to have been deeply worried that in any violent resistance to the Japanese communal hostilities would erupt.[88] Ultimately his views coincided with Nehru's – that it was too late now for compromise and that anything less than full power and responsibility would be disastrous, though Nehru had negotiated in earnest with Cripps in the hope of a real breakthrough. It was doubtless with some personal relief that most of the CWC realized that they would not have to condemn their friend and guide to a solitary life at Sevagram while they trod the corridors of power in uneasy partnership with the British, nor be forced to risk a total rift in their ranks between those like Prasad and Patel who stood by Gandhi, and Nehru, Azad and of course Rajaji who were tempted to make the most of imperial need for collaboration in wartime.

Gandhi now turned his mind to the need to find an appropriate response to the failure of the mission. Within days of the breakdown he was seized and increasingly consumed by the idea which came to him on his silence day that the British should quit India at once and thus lessen the risk of a Japanese invasion. To Horace Alexander he admitted the enormity of what he was envisaging, and that such an orderly exodus

... would mean courage of a high order, confession of human limitations and right-doing by India. Britain cannot defend India, much less herself on Indian soil with any strength. The best thing she can do is to leave India to her fate. I feel somehow that India will not do badly then.[89]

At about the same time he drafted a resolution for an AICC meeting which he did not attend in person, putting forward this idea. It was not accepted by the gathering which on 1 May resolved that Congress could now only countenance independence, but refused to consider that the Japanese could 'liberate' India: any invasion would be resisted non-violently and Congressmen must work to make each area self-reliant and self-sufficient in anticipation of such a necessity.[90] Gandhi, however, continued to brood on a new campaign. Yet he was determined not to precipitate matters, and even at the end of May had no concrete plans, though he was mulling several over in his mind.[91]

It is almost impossible at this distance in time to understand how Gandhi's mind was working – particularly as both British and Indian observers close to him were amazed, disconcerted and critical. If he really thought the British would quit and leave India exposed to the Japanese, forgoing all her geographical and material imput into the war effort, he was naïve, to put it kindly. Some have suggested on little real evidence that he seriously thought this was the moment for a real revolution in India, to be born out of the anarchy of a breakdown of the present social and political order attendant on a British withdrawal.[92]

The records suggest, rather, that after the failure of Cripps' enterprise, Gandhi was aware that in Congress there was a terrible sense of helplessness. He had always argued that positive action was better than lethargy and despair; now once again, at a moment of dire crisis for his Congress colleagues and his nation, he offered his unique vision of the non-violence of the brave in spirit and flesh. For even anarchy if it occurred would be better than their present stagnation and impotence.[93] Now, if ever, non-violence was on trial, both as an answer to their domestic relations with their rulers and to the threat of invasion. So cataclysmic were the times, in his estimation, that he could not now exercise the caution he had for years, in restricting civil disobedience or stopping it if violence erupted. Now with grim foreboding rather than any sanguine anticipation of violence as the prelude to revolution, he began to say that a brief outburst of violence might be inevitable. He saw violence all around him, and resolved to put to the test his long-held belief that non-violence could 'sterilize' the atmosphere' if he did not act he sensed that he might be overwhelmed and engulfed by violence anyway. Seen in this light a new campaign, though fraught with risk, might be a pre-emptive strike in the cause of non-violence and freedom. 'Our ahimsa will remain lame as long as we do not get rid of the fear of anarchy. This is the time to prove that there is no power stronger than ahimsa in this world.'[94] Now that there seemed no other way to achieve freedom he would forge ahead rather than act the coward when India was enslaved. His response when challenged as to whether he was no longer the apostle of non-violence showed both his conviction and his inner turmoil:

But today we have to go a step further. We have to take the risk of violence to shake off the great calamity of slavery. But even for resort to violence one requires the unflinching faith of a non-violent man. There cannot be any trace of violence either in my plans or in my thoughts. A non-violent person has complete faith in God. My ahimsa was always imperfect and therefore it was ineffective to that extent. But I have faith in God. In this context I say: 'Rama is the strength of the weak.' There is no trace of violence in my consciousness or in the remotest corner of my being. My very being is full of consciousness. How can a man who has consciously pursued ahimsa for the last fifty years change all of a sudden? So it is not that I have become violent.[95]

Sapru's and Sastri's reading of Gandhi, after long experience of him, confirms that the Mahatma was convinced, with great intensity, that he was being guided to pursue non-violence, and that he realized his own time was running out and was prepared to make a last and risky throw to vindicate the guiding passions of a lifetime.[96]

By late June Gandhi had almost finalized a plan for a renewed struggle; at this point he was also coming round to agreeing that a free India would have to welcome allied troops in the fight against fascism, and the gap between him and the CWC was accordingly closing.[97] In mid-July the CWC resolved that a civil disobedience struggle led by Gandhi might be necessary if the British refused to withdraw. Once again Gandhi and most of his immediate colleagues had closed ranks and resumed co-operation in circumstances when Gandhi's strategy seemed the only viable option in a situation of political stalemate. Even Jawaharlal aligned with Gandhi after his earlier hesitations once Gandhi admitted his imperfect grasp of the international situation and had accepted the necessity for foreign troops to combat Japanese aggression. A few brave realists, aghast at what sudden British withdrawal might mean, and convinced that the very idea was a chimera, spoke out and entreated the Mahatma to desist. Chief among them was Rajagopalachariar, though this political rift did not harm their warm personal relations. But Gandhi pressed ahead, speaking of a swift and short mass campaign which would be open but non-violent rebellion, and he began to draft instructions for it. When he spoke of non-violent rebellion he later said that this meant the achievement of a peaceful transfer of power, not a violent seizure of it; indeed his suggestions stressed non-violence and in the opening *hartal* he envisaged that those in government services, including offices, factories and vital communications, should not participate since their object was not to encourage invasion. He expected students to leave government college, and envisaged non-payment of land revenue and illegal manufacture of salt. Grudgingly the Viceroy acknowledged both Gandhi's skill and his unique capacity to unite the Congress, and had rightly predicted that Rajaji's 'revolt' would be of little consequence:

> ... the old man has lost none of his political skill with age. I shall be astonished if he moves unless he really feels that he has got a sufficient degree of substantial support behind him (for if he tries again and fails, especially in the middle of the war, the blow to his own prestige and to that of Congress, both of them very dear to him, will be immense). On the other hand, I think him still, as I have always thought him, the one man capable of uniting all the various threads of thought in Congress, and I find it difficult to conceive of circumstances in which any lengthy resistance to him on the part of Congress leaders, however prominent, can be looked for.[99]

On 8 August 1942 the AICC endorsed the July CWC resolution and called for the British to quit India, envisaging in their place a provisional government formed from all major political groups whose primary task would be to defend India with all armed and unarmed strength available. It sanctioned 'for the vindication of India's inalienable right to freedom and independence, the starting of a mass struggle on non-violent lines on the widest possible scale' and asked Gandhi to lead and guide the nation. It was then that Gandhi made his famous call to do or die,[100] though the implications of this were imponderable, as he with all the other prominent Congress leaders were almost immediately arrested. There is however, conclusive evidence that even at this late stage, even after the 8 August resolution, Gandhi hoped for a respite in which he could have communicated with the Viceroy. Indeed, it would have been entirely out of keeping with his whole approach to conflict, and his harking back to old patterns of satyagraha, had he not done so. Sapru confirmed that Gandhi had hoped even at the beginning of August to avoid a crisis, and Gandhi himself had said publicly at the AICC meeting that he intended to contact Linlithgow and he was clearly offended that the government had not waited for him to do so before taking swift action.[101]

The British were well prepared to combat a new campaign. All members of the CWC were immediately detained, and the CWC, AICC and PCCs were proclaimed illegal, and in mid-August provincial governments were given Ordinance powers for emergency conditions to try offenders and levy collective fines where there was action against public order. The aim was to abort the movement at the outset by removing the leaders, but to do as little as possible to antagonize ordinary Indians.[102] In the subsequent weeks Congressmen learned to their cost that they had collided head-on with a powerful machine for repression, its strength greatly increased because of the presence of extra troops during the war. In government eyes 'Quit India' was outright sedition in wartime, and it responded with unprecedented toughness. Even the moderate businessman-politician, Thakurdas, lamented that government repression was threatening to create a second front in India.[103] In stark contrast to the raj's secret, careful planning, Gandhi and the central Congress leadership had no time to formulate a coherent strategy and to communicate with PCCs. Gandhi had hoped to consider his draft instructions with the AICC but was arrested before this could happen – so all that Congressmen had when the leadership was removed was the evidence of past satyagrahas and Gandhi's public comments in mid-summer. When government accused Gandhi and Congress of planning violent insurrection, Gandhi vehemently denied this.[104]

What seems to have occurred was that in some areas lesser Congressmen, often overt opponents of Gandhian non-violence, seized the initiative and engineered violence and destruction of government property and vital parts of the communications network. Consequently the Quit India movement was totally un-Gandhian in its form and intention. Yet some understanding of it is significant in tracing Gandhi's life because it not only coloured his subsequent thinking and relations with the raj, but also casts doubts on the viability of non-violence as a political mode except in very restricted, small-scale situations, where its exponents could be carefully disciplined and deployed.

'Quit India' as it erupted after the leaders' arrests was patchy, uncoor-
dinated and in some cases bloody, violent and destructive, the main
targets being government property, roads, railways and telegraphic
communications. By the end of September it was petering out, though
remnants of action and disturbance lingered on into 1943.[105] Bihar, UP
and Bombay were the storm centres of the eruption, and briefly
government in those areas was under very severe pressure. The UP
government observed that it had faced mass rebellion, and in certain
areas civil administration ceased to function. In Bihar not only were the
ordinary forces of law and order overwhelmed: normal sources of
government intelligence dried up, and the general population lapsed
into uncooperativeness. At one time the provincial government had to
use Tiger Moths of the Bihar Flying Club to keep open communications
with one of its districts, and had completely lost touch with the rest.
Disruption of communications in Bihar meant that Bengal and Assam
were temporarily isolated from the rest of India. By late 1943 the official
estimate was that 208 police stations and 749 other government buildings throughout India had been destroyed or badly damaged; there had
been hundreds of cases of sabotage to roads, and in all a loss to
government of 2,735,125 rupees. Police had had to fire hundreds of
times, and had killed or injured well over 2,500. Many police were also
injured. At the start of 1944 14,135 were still in gaol, having been
convicted under the law, while 5,189 were still detained under the
Defence of India rules. Over 66,000 had been convicted or detained in
all. Such leadership and co-ordination as there was came from lesser
Congressmen who rapidly went underground; from staff and students
such as those at Benares Hindu University in UP; and not least in Bihar
from disaffected left-wing Congressmen who appealed to a peasantry
disturbed for local reasons who followed them into mob violence. In
Bihar the collapse of normal administration also reflected the weakness
of the local police, the size of the districts, poor communications and the
tensions within the civilian administration. It is not surprising that,
given such a breakdown and the threat or actuality of mob violence,
government officials over-reacted and were harsh if not brutal in
response.

By mid-1943 the high echelons of the raj were well content that revolt
had been crushed and India secured as a vital element in the allied war
effort. The Secretary of State commented that 'it looks as if India had
never been so quiet politically as it is at this moment.' While Linlithgow
prepared to lay down his high office contentedly, believing India to be
'in pretty good trim.... The leaders of the revolt ... have neither
programme nor policy. The Working Committee are in jail and forgotten ... Gandhi is equally out of the way of doing mischief, and so long
as he maintains his present point of view I trust he will so remain.'[106]

Meanwhile Gandhi was housed in the Aga Khan's palace outside
Poona in company with Mahadev Desai, Mirabehn, the physician
Sushila Naiyar, sister of Pyarelal, and Kasturbhai who voluntarily

accompanied her husband. There had in fact been discussion of deport-
ing him, possibly to Aden. In physical terms his detention was scarcely
arduous. The palace was roomy and airy, and had extensive grounds.
Now as a museum it is a welcome haven of cool and quiet for the
visitor. Gandhi was allowed whatever food and medical attention he
wanted, and practically any books and papers. Although initially he was
allowed to correspond with his family on personal matters, again he
tried to insist on correspondence with ashram members on matters
broader than merely personal ones, including the ashram and the AISA;
when this was blocked he replied that he would write no letters.[107] His
life, as always in goal, was one of simple and healthy routine, though
now he rose later, around 6.30 a.m. and was in bed by 10.00 p.m. He
walked, ate and slept regularly each day, and was massaged daily by two
doctors. Each evening there was spinning and prayer. He was alert
about political affairs, reading the papers and discussing them with
Pyarelal, who later joined them, and Mirabehn; and each evening
several of them helped him index his many newspaper cuttings. In the
early months of the sentence he also wrote a guide to health which was a
revision of his earlier work in 1913.[108]

However, this detention, despite its pleasant physical conditions, was
not a time when Gandhi found nourishment of spirit or recouped his
health and strength. It was a time of distress and turmoil, as a result of
events outside and of the profound loss he suffered close at hand in the
deaths of Desai and Kasturbhai. Even the amount of news he received
about events after his arrest must have distressed him; but what hurt
him most was the government's insistence that he and Congress were
responsible for the nature of the campaign, and its violence. At the close
of the year he embarked on a correspondence with Linlithgow in an
attempt to convince him of him own commitment to non-violence and
the innocence of Congress and himself of responsibility for the violence
which had occurred. Right at the outset he said that fasting would be a
remedy in such a time of trial.[109] In late January Gandhi was still utterly
convinced of the rightness of his own case, and argued that violence was
in fact the government's fault because by repression it had goaded
people into violence. He announced his intention to fast for three weeks
from 9 February to 2 March. He did not intend to die, and said he would
drink citrus fruit juice with water to enable him to take enough water to
live.

Gandhi insisted that his fast was an appeal to a Higher Tribunal than
Linlithgow for justice, and that it was for the service of God in His
presence; he denied that it was intended as a form of political blackmail,
though he said he would not fast if he were set free, for then he would
have to review the situation completely. Those who visited him bore
witness to his unprecedented distress at the accusation laid against him.
The government and many acute observers of the Mahatma were at a
loss to understand the fast and its intentions. But others who knew him
well, like Srinivasa Sastri, were perturbed, even dismayed, and felt it

was moral coercion. Sapru, Rajaji and Bhulabhai Desai and Jayakar with others told Churchill that Gandhi was fasting to be able to review the situation as a free man.[110] The Delhi government was put in a profoundly embarrassing situation, urged by London to take a firm stand, yet aware of the pressure both in India and abroad for special treatment of the Mahatma, and knowing the risk of disturbances should he die in gaol. In the end the Viceroy, who personally would have been prepared to let Gandhi fast to death in gaol, was convinced of the primary necessity of keeping his expanded Executive Council in sympathy with him, and the final outcome of the lengthy official discussions was that Gandhi should be released only for the fast itself. When he refused this temporary release he was kept in detention.

The agonizings among officials over this decision on the treatment of Gandhi are a reflection of his enormous and unique public reputation, and the real fear of what might happen if he died in gaol. The Governor of Bombay noted grimly of his area, 'Here, Gandhi is a religion to very large numbers of people, and ordinary standards of logic and reason cannot be applied, where he is concerned, without grave risk.' The Governor of Bihar commented, 'it is a mad feature of the present situation in India that because of the "Mahatmic superstition" we have to employ police and troops all over the country in case the old zealot should die.'[111]

Before Gandhi undertook the fast there were very grave doubts about whether he would in fact survive, and the Bombay government made extremely detailed and cautious preparations for his care. In all, nine doctors attended him when Sushila Naiyar felt she could not take sole responsibility. Sarojini Naidu, poet and politician, became an unofficial matron-in-chief at the palace and according to the Governor of Bombay was the only one who retained some sense of humour during the proceedings; at the same time, one of the doctors, transferred from Yeravda gaol, became effective Master of Ceremonies and made sure that the many visitors stayed only long enough to receive Gandhi's *darshan*. Gandhi was keenly interested in this fast as a physiological experiment, quite apart from its moral meaning for him, and his powers of will and endurance proved remarkable, for they were taxed to the limit. He lost over one and a quarter stone in all, suffered severe nausea early on, and increasingly became very weak and drowsy. Half way through the fast he survived a real crisis when it was thought he would lapse into a coma. The Surgeon-General of the Presidency, who was in attendance, was surprised that Gandhi recovered, and, not having actually witnessed the event itself, strongly suspected that Gandhi might have unwittingly received glucose or extra fruit juice. He reported at the end that Gandhi was as weak as if he had been seriously ill, and would probably not be back to normal health for several months.[112] Gandhi professed by the end to be in an inner state of heavenly peace, and as usual he broke the fast with religious ceremonial – prayer, silence and the recitation of Hindu, Christian and Muslim devotions. Although

Gandhi said he had found peace, the question of responsibility for the outbreaks during the Quit India movement remained, and during the rest of his sentence he was involved in continuing controversy with the government.[113]

For Gandhi the Aga Khan's palace became also a place of personal sorrow. His faithful secretary, Mahadev Desai, died early in their detention, and Gandhi presided over the preparation of his body for cremation and over the cremation itself in the palace grounds. He described Desai as 'an associate beyond compare'. Then, early in 1944, Kasturbhai became increasingly dispirited and feeble, and she died on 22 February. The circumstances were particularly distressing because of her own unhappiness and the difficulties Gandhi encountered in getting the right treatment for her. He felt her death deeply, far more than he thought he would, on his own admission. Thereafter he paid tribute to her courage and faithfulness through all the strangeness of the life to which he had introduced her. It was a reflection of his grief, and typical of his courtesy spanning racial barriers, that when the Surgeon-General who had attended his fast lost his wife soon after Kasturbhai's death, Gandhi wrote to him in condolence, and added, 'I know from my own recent experience what the death of a lifelong partner must mean to the survivor.'[114] To the son of an old missionary friend he wrote of his abiding sense of Kasturbhai's presence.

Ba is ever with me though her body has been consigned to the flames. Though I see this truth through the reason and the heart, worldwide sympathy I have prized. It has made me realize the goodness of God as never before.[115]

Mirabehn wrote to Amrit Kaur at about the same time, saying that Gandhi's progress back to health was very slow and that he did not seem to be able to rest; she testified to the loss he felt when Kasturbhai died – an even greater loss that at the death of Mahadev. 'With Ba it was as if a part of Bapu departed. Such things we went through in that Palace. Things that are branded on one's memory with burning fire.'[116]

On 6 May 1944, after a severe attack of malaria, Gandhi had been unconditionally released because of his poor health, when the medical opinion of Dr B.C. Roy and the Surgeon-General indicated that he was never likely to be an active force in politics again. He was anaemic, had continuing blood pressure and kidney problems and these were thought likely to produce cerebral or coronary thrombosis. He also suffered from hookworm and amoebic dysentery. Churchill insisted that there could be no negotiations between Gandhi and the new Viceroy, Lord Wavell.[117] Gandhi went to Juhu beach to convalesce and decided to help himself by observing two weeks of silence; then he went to Poona and ultimately returned to Sevagram in early August. He made a steady but slow recovery – far slower that he had anticipated. But even this elicited a sharp retort from Churchill who had thought him to be terminally ill from the information given to him; Wavell however stuck to his opinion that their decision had been correct and told the Prime Minister in early July that Gandhi was still far from well and incapable of prolonged physical or mental effort.[118] Although he seemed stronger later in 1944, by late November he was again exhausted and decided to take a month's complete rest in order to avoid a total breakdown, very largely at the urging of Rajagopalachariar. It was now clear that age, overwork and the rigours of his life had severely weakened Gandhi, and as the months passed without his regaining his old capacity even he was forced to recognize that he could no longer cope with all the things he once had.[119]

Gandhi at large, however, was not really free to pursue his vision of non-violence in Indian public life, for he was boxed in by his own weakness and the refusal of the government to negotiate with him. Soon after his release he seems to have felt profoundly dispirited and even temporarily to have lost his vivid sense of God. But soon his faith and optimism returned and he began to take stock of the situation and his own position. He still maintained that all his past work and his present role was to see how truth and non-violence could be brought to operate in daily life, including politics and public affairs. He gently chided Congressmen who met him in June at their loss of faith in these two great affirmations. For his part he was not frustrated, and a private letter soon afterwards showed how he was wrestling with the practicalities of his faith.

> Of course, there must be organized resistance to organized evil. The difficulty arises when the organizers of satyagraha try to imitate the organizers of evil. I tried and failed hopelessly. The way of organizing forces of good must be opposite to the evil way. What it exactly is I do not yet know fully. I feel that it lies through perfection, as far as may be, of individuals. It then acts as the leaven raising the whole mass. But I am still groping.[120]

Immediately after his release he felt unable to comment authoritatively on how he viewed the events of 1942, though he recognized that bravery and violence had been intertwined. Later he was prepared to say that public violence in 1942 was a matter for sorrow, though he did not feel the movement had been in vain.[121] At first he was in no hurry to make any public statements and merely watched the situation. He felt that because he had been released for health reasons he was not at liberty to resume any role of authority in Congress. He did, however, make it clear to those Congressmen who had gone underground that he disapproved of all secrecy in the application of non-violence. He also felt that though there could be no co-operation with the government, neither could there now be any mass civil disobedience.[122]

As he regained strength Gandhi tried to break the political deadlock between Congress and government, and on 17 June wrote to Lord Wavell asking to see him and to consult with the CWC. People were expecting him to make 'some decisive contribution to the general good', but he could not until he knew how the CWC members were thinking. Wavell firmly declined both requests, but said he would gladly consider any definite and constructive policy Gandhi could make after further thought and convalescence.[123] Gandhi was not discouraged and made a further effort to contact the Viceroy and explain his present position, this time through the indirect method of using a London journalist who sought an interview. Gandhi saw him at length between 4 and 6 July and indicated that he felt the whole situation had changed since 1942. There was now no chance of civil disobedience and he felt the CWC should be allowed to review the whole situation with him. He would now be satisfied with a national government in full control of civil administration. Gandhi again contacted Wavell in person, but was rebuffed in the same terms as before: the Viceroy would only consider a definite and constructive plan.[124] In considerable disappointment at this official blockage of his role as mediator, the role in which he felt particularly experienced, with some justification, Gandhi then formally put to Wavell what he was prepared to advise the CWC.

I am prepared to advise the Working Committee to declare that in view of the changed conditions, mass civil disobedience envisaged by the resolution of August 1942 cannot be offered and that full cooperation in the war-effort should be given by the Congress, if a declaration of immediate Indian independence is made and a national government responsible to the Central Assembly be formed subject to the proviso that, during the pendency of the war, the military operations should continue as at present but without involving any financial burden on India.

He hoped this could be the basis for 'mutual friendly discussion'. He received a lengthy reply, the nub of which was that no purpose could be served by discussion on the basis Gandhi was suggesting.[125] Gandhi was convinced that it was the London part of the government (and Churchill in particular) which refused to consider a settlement with Congress. He would have been even more convinced had he known the battle Wavell had fought, unsuccessfully, for a reply warmer in tone than a blank refusal. Churchill had at one point accused Wavell of entering into negotiations with a Gandhi who should by now have been dead, politically if not physically. The beleaguered Viceroy, more atuned to the Indian situation, replied that there was no question of negotiation. To him it mattered greatly that the reply was not intransigent and discourteous: he felt that British insensitivity to the importance of good manners to the Indian mind was one of their great imperial mistakes.[126]

Hardly surprisingly this correspondence only increased Gandhi's scepticism about British intentions and their good faith in asserting that their goal was independence. But he maintained a sense of the guiding hand of the divine in his life and this saved him from falling into hopelessness. Later in the year he told a friend,

The secret of my peace and sense of humour lies in my unflinching faith in God, that is, Truth. I know that by myself I can do nothing. How can I be unhappy when God dwelling within me impels my every act? I know too that whatever He makes me do, is ultimately for my own good. I should be happy in this awareness.

And to an English sympathizer he admitted that though 'in the midst of a raging storm' he often hummed to himself 'Rock of Ages cleft for me ...'.[127] Gandhi apparently felt no sense of defeat, though he was clearly stifled and hurt by the attitude of the government in preventing him playing a prominent public role. He was also, in view of his health and age, taking thought for the future of those organizations he had set up to carry on his work, and was aiming to make them independent of him, at least financially. Such 'letting go' was in itself an act of faith that despite current circumstances and the likelihood that the future rulers of India would not share his ideals, his vision of peaceful, slow reconstruction of a new nation would not die with him.

Non-violence and communal relations

However, there was one area of Indian public life in which Gandhi's vision of a new India and his role as the apostle of non-violence were consistently challenged and with increasing force – communal relations. He had felt distressed and helpless on this issue even before the war years. But by the end of the war his understanding of the Indian nation was denied by Jinnah and the Muslim League, who insisted that India's Muslims were a separate nation needing a secure homeland, Pakistan (meaning in Urdu 'the land of the pure'), rather than a minority within a nation embracing several religious groups who needed reassurance and constitutional protection. Moveover, in dealing with Muslim hopes and fears, and the profound deterioration in communal relations at local level as well as among the politicians, Gandhi's prescription of non-violence seemed ineffective. Further, communal relations were the threatening background to his decisions about the viability of satyagraha as practical politics, because he was afraid it might precipitate communal violence. The presence and claims of the League were a standing challenge to Congress, too. They undermined Congress's longstanding claim to be the national voice, and complicated Congress's relations with the raj, as the British hesitated to alienate Muslims as well as Congress in wartime, not least because of their role in the army, and thereby confirmed the bargaining position of Jinnah and the League. The Congress leadership found that it could not deal realistically with the League without going back on its claims to represent all Indians, regardless of caste or creed, and found itself trapped in a position where it could not negotiate; Further, Congress Muslims proved to be token 'Muslims' and highly irritating to the League, rather than accurate guides to Indian Muslim thinking or proof of wide Muslim support for Congress.

Anyone returning to India in 1940 after a decade's absence would have found the position and claims of the League, and Jinnah's standing in all-India politics, as one of the most surprising changes on the political scene. In a sense Jinnah's rise to power was almost as curious and unpredictable as had been Gandhi's own assertion of political authority in 1920. When Congress swept to provincial power in Hindu majority areas in the 1937 elections the League had no similar success where Muslims were a majority, and it would have been impossible to talk of any coherent and unified 'Muslim politics' on the subcontinent. However, very rapidly this situation changed and Jinnah had begun to build the League as an all-India Muslim organization, as he realized that the 1935 constitution and its provisions offered poor protection against majority domination. His relations with the Muslim majority provinces, particularly Punjab and Bengal, were less than certain, however; for there, Muslim local strength sufficed and made Muslim politicians and their followers less susceptible to Jinnah's conviction that if Muslims were to be secure in the future they must be able to argue with Congress from a position of continental strength. However, Muslim thinking began rapidly to shift, and in this process the idea of a separate Muslim nation needing its own homeland gained popularity – a claim which was to exercise a profound popular appeal once it became the currency of the mosque and the market-place rather than the dreams of poets and students. In its Lahore meeting early in 1940 the League resolved that in the future no constitutional plan would be acceptable to Muslims unless it was based on the principle

> ... that geographically contiguous units are demarcated into regions which should be so constituted with such territorial readjustments as may be necessary that the areas in which the Muslims are numerically in a majority, as in the north-western and eastern zones of India, should be grouped to constitute 'independent states' in which the constituent units shall be autonomous and sovereign.

By no means all Muslims (and not even all the Muslim clerisy) supported this claim, and Muslim politicians and the ordinary Muslim had no clear idea what it might mean in precise geographical or constitutional terms. The Viceroy thought it a bargaining counter with which to challenge Congress's claims. Late in 1941 a British official reported after an extended tour that almost all Muslim League members interpreted Pakistan as being part of a confederation with Hindu India; few, he thought, were particularly enthusiastic about the idea, but they would not repudiate it for fear of alienating Jinnah or undermining Muslim solidarity which they thought was vital at this politial juncture.[128] In 1943 and even as late as 1946 Jinnah himself made it plain that the precise nature of Pakistan was open to discussion. However, the situation of India at war gave the League and its spokesmen a free field to co-operate with the British and entrench their positions, once the Congress had withdrawn its co-operation and launched civil disobedience. It was not only able to publicize its claims to a mass audience, but to form provincial governments in several Muslim majority provinces.

This further increased Muslim leverage over the British who, unaware of the eventual tragedy they were helping to stage, gave Muslims a virtual blocking veto on all constitutional change, as was made clear in the Viceroy's 'August Offer' of 1940 and the offer Cripps brought in 1942, when they sought to assuage minority fears in order to broaden their collaborative base in wartime.

Gandhi's basic position as he surveyed the way Indian politics were shaping was the same one he had maintained for years – as in London in 1931 for example – that Congress represented all Indians.[129] However, as he himself had failed to find a way of resolving the opposing claims of Congress and League and of ending communal conflict, he followed Jawaharlal Nehru late in 1939 and agreed to the younger man's proposal, accepted by the CWC in September 1939, that India should be allowed to frame her own constitution through a Constituent Assembly without outside (i.e. imperial) interference.[130] Through this means for achieving democratic swaraj, Gandhi argued, no group would be coerced, as all communities would be represented in their proportion of the population; it would be an exercise in political education and would lead to a truly indigenous constitution rather than an external import or imposition. This last argument took up a theme which he had long emphasized – that a Western-style government would not be true sawraj – and he likened India to the jackdaw in the fable who tried unsuccessfully to walk like a peacock wearing the latter's borrowed feathers. This suggestion failed to convince Jinnah who thought Congress would pack and manipulate any such assembly. His attitude was reflected in his exhortation to Muslims to celebrate a 'day of deliverance' in late December 1939 after Congress had withdrawn from provincial power. Although Gandhi had his own reasons for welcoming the Congress decision that its governments should step down, he was rightly perturbed that the kind of appeal Jinnah was making, couched in religious terms, would only publicize unproven allegations against Congress governments and spread communal bitterness.[131]

When the League began to espouse the idea that Muslims and Hindus were two separate nations, Gandhi was greatly hurt, for it denied an aspect of his personal vocation which he had for decades considered essential: working for communal harmony as a precondition of true swaraj for the Indian nation. He called the idea an untruth, and referred to a possible partition of India as vivisection. Furthermore he felt the idea was profoundly irreligious and actually harmful to Islam.

> Religion binds man to God and man to man. Does Islam bind Muslim only to Muslim and antagonize the Hindu? Was the message of the Prophet peace only for and between Muslims and war against Hindus or non-Muslims? Are eight crores of Muslims to be fed with this which I can only describe as poison? Those who are instilling this poison into the Muslim mind are rendering the greatest disservice to Islam. I know that it is not Islam.[132]

Earlier he had said that the argument that Hinduism and Islam were antagonistic doctrines and cultures was a denial of God, and his soul rebelled against it. Yet he acknowledged that as a man of non-violence, 'I cannot forcibly resist the proposed partition if the Muslims of India really insist upon it. But I can never be a willing party to the vivisection. I would employ every non-violent means to prevent it.' Late in 1940 he reiterated to the AICC that they might well have to use non-violent methods to prevent minorities from breaking India up, and, with tragic irony when viewed from a later perspective, he argued that they might have to test their non-violence in a situation of anarchy and disorder because of communal conflict.[133] He was by the second half of 1940 profoundly pessimistic and privately wrote in June, 'My own opinion is that the time for a settlement has not arrived. It will come but not without agony. I have not lost hope but am prepared for the worst.'[134]

Others, however, still hoped that if Gandhi and Jinnah met, some solution could be found. Late in 1940 the two businessmen, Birla and Thakurdas, corresponded about contriving such a meeting; but this idea collapsed after Thakurdas had talked to Jinnah for an hour and a half on 1 Jauuary 1941. Jinnah was quite prepared to talk to Gandhi or anyone from Congress, provided whoever it was agreed that he represented Hindus and that Jinnah represented Muslims, i.e., that each represented a community rather than a political party.[135] This of course would have been anathema to Gandhi. The indefatigable Sapru pursued a similar line early in 1941, but at the outset Gandhi indicated to his old colleague, so proficient in mediation, that he always seemed to antagonize Jinnah, and that he felt Jinnah did not yet want a settlement for reasons of his own.

> My impression is that he does not want a settlement till he has so consolidated the League position that he can dictate his terms to all the parties concerned including the rulers. I do not blame him for having taken up that position, if he has. But with this impression it is useless for me to approach him.[136]

One might observe that Gandhi was well placed to understand Jinnah's mind, not least because he himself had experience of trying to build up a party's status and strength as a preliminary to a successful deal, as at the time of his second civil disobedience movement.

As Sapru persevered it became clear that the real stumbling-block to a meeting was Jinnah's insistence to Sapru, as to Thakurdas, that Gandhi must come as a representative of Hindus: this Gandhi utterly refused.[137] Even so, Sapru did not give up the enterprise, and when Gandhi called on him in Allahabad late in February he again raised the question of such a meeting. But Gandhi remained very cautious and profoundly sceptical even of the idea of meeting Jinnah in a non-party conference, for he felt that failure would exacerbate the situation. But he encouraged Rajaji to do what he could.[138] Later in the year Sapru had grown far more doubtful whether any sort of meeting was possible because Jinnah would not meet Gandhi as an individual but only as a Hindu representative, which Gandhi could not accept. He confided to a prominent Indian journalist, 'Further to tell you the truth I am not so hopeful as some of you seem to be that Gandhiji will change. He is a firm believer in his own principles and, happen what may, he is not going to budge an inch.'[139]

As Gandhi became convinced that there was an unbridgeable gulf between Congress and the League there began to emerge more clearly in his pronouncements on the communal problem the idea that if the British quit then the League and Congress would have to come to a solution. He said publicly in April 1941 what he had said to the AICC in September 1940 – that then they might have to risk a brief outburst of violence. He also underlined the idea that he had stressed in connection with a Constituent Assembly, that after the British departed League and Congress could, 'devise a home-made solution to the Government of India. It may not be scientific; it may not be after any Western pattern; but it will be durable.'[140] In 1942 this insistence that the British departure was an essential precondition to communal unity became even stronger, adding to Gandhi's other arguments for a British withdrawal. In his opinion the British had created this essentially artificial division, and were now prolonging it. This accounted, so he said, for his apparent shift from his former argument that Hindu–Muslim unity must precede sawarj.

> Time is a merciless enemy, if it is also a merciful friend and healer. I claim to be amongst the oldest lovers of Hindu–Muslim unity and I remain one even today. I have been asking myself why every whole-hearted attempt made by all including myself to reach unity has failed, and failed so completely that I have entirely fallen from grace and am described by some Muslim papers as the greatest enemy of Islam in India. It is a phenomenon I can only account for by the fact that the third power, even without deliberately wishing it, will not allow real unity to take place. Therefore I have come to the reluctant conclusion that the two communities will come together almost immediately after the British power comes to a final end in India.[141]

In maintaining this position Gandhi was totally underestimating the strength of Muslim feelings and the appeal of the emotive slogan of Pakistan. More realistic was Rajagopalachariar who unsuccessfully tried to persuade Congress to accept Pakistan as a basis for a settlement with the League. To Gandhi the evidence of escalating distrust and violence between Hindus and Muslims was a matter for extreme sorrow; he dreaded that one or other would 'call in outside help', but all he could offer was non-violence, not political negotiation and concession on what he regarded as the fundamental issue of Indian national unity transcending religious barriers.[142] However, non-violence as a political mode proved counter-productive in the context of communal relations. When Congress under Gandhi's guidance embarked on civil disobedi-

ence in 1940 and 1942 Jinnah publicly branded it as an attempt to force
the British to yield to Congress demands and create a Hindu raj.
Gandhi's belief that the Muslim masses sympathized with the Congress
goal proved a naïve and tragic misreading of the communal situation.[143]

Two years later, years of much violence and hardening communal
attitudes, Gandhi emerged from detention, weak but more realistic –
about mass non-violence, about imperial determination in wartime, and
about the communal problem. Even while in detention Gandhi had made
an attempt to meet Jinnah, which the government promptly aborted. But
in mid-July 1944 as a free man he was able to contact Jinnah and suggest
a meeting. The solution of the communal problem seemed to him the
more urgent because the Viceroy had, on the insistence of Whitehall,
rebuffed his attempt to break the political deadlock by seeing the
Viceroy and the CWC. He realized of course that this contradicted his
words of mid-1942 on the divisive presence of the raj: 'Whilst I had said
and repeat that the presence of a third party effectively prevents a
solution, it was never meant to convey that I would make no attempt at
an honourable soltuion, even while the third party continued to dominate this land of ours.'[144] What Gandhi now hoped could be the basis for
'an honourable solution' was a formula worked out by the tireless realist
Rajaji: that the League would endorse the claim for independence and
co-operate with Congress in a transitional government, and a commission after the war should demarcate adjoining districts in north-west and
north-east India where Muslims were a majority, and there all adult
inhabitants should have the right to vote on the issue of separation from
India. If a majority favoured separation this would take place, but the
two successor states would enter mutual agreements on certain crucial
joint matters, such as defence, commerce and communications. Although this was considerably more flexible in tone and content that
Gandhi's castigations of Pakistan in 1942 he made his support for the
'Rajaji formula' public, but took care to point out that it was open to
amendment if Hindus or Sikhs found it unacceptable.[145] He was right in
issuing this caveat, because the formula and the prospect of Gandhi
attempting to do a deal with Jinnah, even on the basis of a limited
Pakistan, disturbed Sikhs, Hindus and Nationalist Muslims alike. Even
so moderate a man as Srinivasa Sastri was worried that the League
would use the formula as a bargaining counter which could never be
withdrawn, even it their talks failed to achieve a solution.[146]

Talks between Jinnah and Gandhi eventually took place in Bombay
at Jinnah's home, starting on 9 September and lasting nearly three
weeks. Despite the fact that Gandhi was still suffering from hookworm
and amoebic infection he found he could stand the strain; luckily their
two bases were very close to each other, and Gandhi's special food was
carried in every day for him. He wrote in the train to Bombay to Sapru,
'I am going in hope but without expectation. So if I return empty-
handed, I shall not be disappointed.'[147] Despite external courtesy the
talks yielded no positive step towards a solution of the communal

problem; indeed the mutual incompatibility of the two men, their styles and their claims became even clearer in their correspondence clarifying details raised in their discussions. One insoluble problem was that of Gandhi's status, just as it had been in 1940–1 when Thakurdas and Sapru had tried a contrive a meeting between Gandhi and Jinnah. Now Gandhi insisted that he represented nobody but himself, though he aspired to represent all Indians. Jinnah promptly replied:

> ... when you proceed to say that you aspire to represent all the inhabitants of India, I regret I cannot accept that statement of yours. It is quite clear that you represent nobody else but the Hindus, and as long as you do not realize your true position and the realities, it is very difficult for me to argue with you, and it becomes still more difficult to persuade you, and hope to convert you to the realities and the actual conditions prevailing in India today.[148]

Furthermore, they disagreed whether 'Pakistan' should be achieved before or after independence from British rule; Jinnah insisted that it should be before the British departed, otherwise they would be leaving Muslims at the mercy of the majority. They also clashed on what areas should constitute Pakistan and whether or not Muslims and others in Muslim majority areas should vote in any plebiscite. Towards the end of their correspondence Jinnah accused Gandhi of refusing to accept that Indian Muslims were a nation with a right to self-determination, which they alone could exercise. In this he was right – as Gandhi had proudly confirmed. He was only prepared to accept some division, he later noted of the talks, 'as between members of the same family and therefore reserving for partnership things of common interest. But [Jinnah] would have nothing short of the two-nation theory and therefore complete dissolution amounting to full sovereignty in the first instance.'[149] Evidently Gandhi, for all his espousal of the Rajaji formula was hostile to anything but a very limited Pakistan; it is significant that early on in the period of the talks he told Rajaji that he was basically trying to find out what Jinnah wanted. 'I am to prove from his own mouth that the whole of the Pakistan proposition is absurd. I think he does not want to break. On my part I am not going to be in a hurry. But he can't expect me to endorse an undefined Pakistan.' He felt that Jinnah would have to give up his claim if there was to be a settlement. 'He wants a settlement, but what he wants he does not know. I want to show him that your Formula is the only thing that he can reasonably ask for.'[150]

When the talks eventually collapsed both men publicly announced their regret and the hope that their failure would not create public bitterness. The Viceroy was irritated and disappointed. In the privacy of his journal he noted that he had hoped for something better of these two leaders: 'two great mountains have met and not even a ridiculous mouse has emerged.'[151] Hardly surprisingly, after this débâcle, Gandhi insisted that any future decision about possible Hindu–Muslim co-operation should be made by the CWC alone.

One of the most significant results of the failure of these discussions was hidden from the two protagonists and many observers – namely, the impetus it gave to Lord Wavell to push London hard towards a new political move in India.[152] Wavell has been a much-maligned and underestimated Viceroy. He fell foul of Congress, the League and his own Prime Minister, Churchill. He confided to his journal in mid-1944, 'I wonder if we shall ever have any chance of a solution till the three intransigent, obstinate, uncompromising principals are out of the way: Gandhi (just over 75), Jinnah (68), Winston (nearing 70).'[153] When he had been unceremoniously sacked, his successor was the more outgoing and glamorous Mountbatten who appeared to succeed where he had failed, though at an immense cost. As the wartime stop-gap appointment to the highest office in the raj, Wavell proved far more sensitive and realistic than his masters had anticipated or most subsequent authors have acknowledged. As early as August 1944, after being forced brusquely to close the door to Gandhi, Wavell was utterly convinced that the British would have to make a new political move, probably when war ended in Europe. He argued cogently that though the raj seemed comfortable and secure in the short term, in the long term the prospects for continuing imperial rule were very dubious. Once the war against Japan ended the political situation, now forcibly contained, would erupt: politicians would emerge from gaol, elections would be held, there would be high political expectations of early changes in the light of Britain's wartime offers, and the raj would have lost its wartime instruments of control. The civil service was badly stretched and its members were tired, and it would soon be seriously short of senior men. (He even referred to the British Services as moribund.) Further, British troops would be returning home and the Indian army might well be open to political influence. Moreover, there would be inevitable economic hardship and dislocation, a dangerous breeding ground for political opposition. As had even now become clear, any government's political options were limited by the expansion and Indianization of the Viceroy's Executive Council during the war.[154] He was convinced that they must provide educated Indians with opportunities to exercise their political and administrative energy – and this meant a solution to the political problem. He confronted Churchill with the blunt truth that despite Linlithgow's suppression of 'Quit India', 'there remains a deep sense of frustration and discontent amongst practically all educated Indians, which renders the present arrangements for government insecure and impermanent.' The present government, with all its weakness, could not continue indefinitely, and though Whitehall still had final responsibility it no longer had the power to take effective action. If it came to it, a comparatively small force might be able to hold India forcibly, but there was not the political will for that at home, nor would there be international support; in any case British soldiers would want to be home, not fighting colonial insurgents. So there would have to be Indian acquiescence if India was even to remain in the Commonwealth.

From this it was clear how strong and how diverse were the underlying forces making for the end of the raj: in crude, even cruel, terms, India was no longer as a dependency worth the expenditure of men, money and reputation to keep her so. From the point of view of Gandhi's political activity what is significant in Wavell's assessment is that his campaigns in themselves did not represent a threat to the raj. But the growth of Congress's legitimacy as a national voice and a political ambience for Hindus at least, in the development of which Gandhi's public image, preaching and campaigns were highly influential, constituted the central challenge to British legitimacy as India's rulers.

As Wavell tried to persuade Whitehall of the reality and urgency of the imperial dilemma in India his plans received little support. The Secretary of State was thinking not of political change in India, but of relaxing London's control. He also realized the passion in Churchill's conservative attitude to India, and his colleagues' reluctance to challenge him and wreck the wartime Cabinet.[155] Eventually late in March 1945 Wavell was allowed to fly home to put his plans to the government in person. There he languished until the very end of May, increasingly gloomy at the delays, rebuffs and misunderstandings he experienced. However on 31 May the Cabinet agreed on a new move which included the release of all members of the CWC who were still detained, and simultaneous announcements in London and India on 14 June by Amery and Wavell, that the offer made in March 1942 still held, but in the meantime the Viceroy would call a conference of leading Indian politicians with a view to selecting Indian political leaders to form a new Executive Council, which would be representative of India's main communities, and would include equal proportions of Caste Hindus and Muslims.[156]

By contrast with developments in London, events in India moved fast. The day after the announcement the CWC members were released, and ten days later the conference met in Simla. From the outset in 1944 Wavell had recognized that this was a risky throw and might fail. But what he fundamentally hoped for was not just a post-war safety-valve but a real bridge to making a new Indian constitution, if the different groups of politicians could by means of this new government become accustomed to working together. 'That is the whole basis of my re-commendations – that conferences and discussions will get us simply nowhere; and that practical participation in the Government, with all its dangers and difficulties, is the only hope of progress.'[157] He also hoped that if this interim government worked it might induce Muslims to abandon the idea of Pakistan[158] – an interesting observation in the light of accusations levelled by later writers that Wavell favoured the Muslims.

Gandhi, when invited by Wavell to attend the conference, agreed to be present in Simla for its duration, though he insisted that he could not represent Congress. That, he thought, was the proper role of the Congress President (Azad, a Muslim of course and a standing challenge

to Jinnah's probable claims) and the CWC's nominees; he could only be
an informal advisor.[159] His brief public statements in advance of the
conference were basically hopeful, though he made it plain in public and
to Wavell that he objected to the words 'Caste Hindus' and rejected the
idea that Congress represented them rather than all India's peoples.[160]
Wavell also in a personal meeting with him gained the impression that
he was favourable towards the proposals. When he raised the question
of whether Congress could propose names of Muslims or untouchables,
Wavell agreed, though underlined that the principle of parity as outlined
would be kept,[161] which Gandhi had reluctantly accepted despite his
initial observations.

Gandhi stayed with Amrit Kaur and her brother while he was in
Simla, cocooned in 'lavish affection' and considerable comfort. People
flocked to catch a glimpse of him and he chided them for their unruly
and destructive behaviour, both in Simla and on his journey there
during which wild demonstrations greeted the Frontier Mail in which
he was travelling at every station where it stopped.[162] The authorities
provided a special train for his journey home to Wardha.

Initially the conference seemed to go well and the atmosphere was
friendly, but within days it became obvious that Congress and League
representatives could not agree on the composition of a new Council. In
late June they agreed that all parties should send Wavell lists of suggestions from which he would try to form an acceptable Council, and to
enable this the conference adjourned until mid-July. The Congress duly
compiled a list of a complete Council, including Muslims and untouchables, a Christian (Amrit Kaur) and a Sikh still to be chosen; it envisaged
including three Muslim League members, among them Jinnah, as well
as two Congress Muslims. Gandhi was sad that Congress in its choice
had accepted parity – and would have preferred to see Congress as a
minority to remove the 'communal poison' and so bring freedom
nearer.[163] However, the conference finally collapsed because Jinnah,
despite firm pressure from Wavell in private towards the end of the
adjournment, refused to submit a list because he could not have the sole
right to nominate Muslims. With Cabinet approval Wavell then selected
a possible Council which included four Muslim League men and one
non-League Muslim from Punjab, who was unlikely to be offensive to
the League, but was not a Congress Muslim. When confronted with this
list Jinnah again insisted on the sole right to nominate Muslims and also
demanded a form of communal veto on topics sensitive to Muslims.
Wavell realized this would make a Council unworkable because it
would also have to be granted to other religious groups.

And so Wavell's prolonged initiative collapsed.[164] He publicly took
the blame on himself in his closing statement in order to prevent the
leaders indulging in bitter recrimination which would have worsened
the communal situation. Privately he felt that though the breakdown
had occurred because of Jinnah's intransigence, deeper still as the real
cause was Muslim mistrust of Congress. 'Their fear that the Congress,

by parading its national character and using Muslim dummies will permeate the entire administration of any united India is real, and cannot be dismissed as an obsession of Jinnah and his immediate entourage.'[165] Whether Wavell could have done anything else in this situation is highly debatable. He knew the governors were divided on the question of trying to push ahead with a new Council without League co-operation, and that the Bengal and Punjab governors, with their Muslim majorities, were firmly against it. He also knew that the government in London, which had been so reluctant to sanction his move, would have had no truck with the idea of a Council dominated by men who had so recently been in gaol for sedition. Moreover, his own aim had been to use co-operation in the nuts and bolts of government as a bridge to making a new constitution, and now the prospect of co-operation had gone the, plan lost its *raison d'être*.

For his part Gandhi, when told by Wavell of the débâcle an hour after the crucial interview with Jinnah, was calm and friendly, but he said he thought that ultimately the British would have to choose between Hindus and Muslims as they could not resolve their own differences. He doubtless sympathized with Wavell's dilemma in relations with Jinnah for it was on the key question of the League's status that he himself had clashed with its leader. In a generous letter to Wavell he said that Wavell bore no blame for the breakdown; but he wondered whether ultimately the cause of the breakdown was not an official reluctance to part with power.[166] However, to his closest co-workers in the ashram he counselled no frustration, no despair; their role was now an even greater effort in radical constructive work to strengthen their position and serve the masses.[167]

So the apostle of non-violence reverted to his fundamental aim – to create a new nation from the grass roots. Simla had shown him that the very existence of one Indian nation was still in question, despite nearly a lifetime's work and words. Some would in fact argue that Gandhi's manner of work, his religious style and very Hindu symbolism in his own person and in what he said were part of the problem: that the Mahatma, whatever he said to the contrary, was the representative of a Hindu-dominated Congress and the epitome of a future Hindu raj in the eyes of India's fearful minorities. Certainly his insistence on Congress's unique national status made it very difficult for Congress leaders to adopt a real negotiating position, particularly when they were faced in Jinnah with an adversary whose tactic was always to say no, to pitch his demands at their highest and leave his opponents to make the running.

* * *

The war years had taken their toll on Gandhi. Old age had caught up with him and he recognized his declining strength. He refused to become embroiled in matters he would once have taken up, and discouraged people from visiting him. It was also evident to people who

Gandhi age 75.

observed him that he was indeed slowing down in his capacity to cope with work. It was well known, however, that he hoped to live to 125 – an idea which first came to him as he spoke in the critical AICC meeting on 8 August 1942. It reflected his intense wish to live long enough to complete his allotted work which he saw as bidden in his precious *Isha Upanishad*; it also derived from his conclusions as an advocate of nature

cure that if a man truly believed in divine power and had conquered
desire the body would be transformed and enabled to live long.[168] His
own attitude to pressure of work and the sense of too little time was to
have patience, to do what seemed most useful and to leave the rest to
God, who might or might not grant more time to finish the labour.[169]

Yet the war years had shown Gandhi the grievous problems
associated with deploying non-violence in public life, and had indicated
that there were aspects of relationships between Indians where non-
violence seemed to be ineffective. He was also aware that his vision of
non-violence was not shared by many of those who surrounded him and
looked to him for leadership, and he realized that, not least because of
his commitment to non-violence, he would probably not be wanted in a
free India.[170] But even this did not perturb his tranquillity in the face of
declining strength and the passage of time. He maintained that there
never had been and never would be despair in his life: his hope rested on
increasing faith in an unseen God and therefore he did not try to see his
future role, but despite the seemingly insoluble problems before him
believed that through the workings of this divine power both people
and situations could be changed.

10

PRISONER OF HOPE

Gandhi had for years maintained that persistent hope was a hallmark of a satyagrahi, one who followed a vision of truth and tried to deploy the strength of truth and love in daily life. In his own experience, despite ups and downs of mood, battles with anger and frustration, and episodes of depression, hope grounded in religious conviction held him secure: he was in a real sense a 'prisoner of hope'.[1] An essential aspect of his basic optimism was the belief that people and therefore situations can radically change. In the final years of his life, from the end of the war, change there certainly was in India, but not of the kind he had hoped for. India indeed gained her independence from British rule in August 1947. The raj which had seemed so immovable, whose representatives had often seemed to Gandhi and his associates so insincere in their protestations about India's eventual status, now wound itself up with a rapidity that bewildered Indian politicians, Princes and civil servants alike, accustomed as they were to its cumbersome, bureaucratic style.

Wavell had for many months realized and tried to impress on the politicians in London just how weak the raj had become by the end of the war. Looking back on 1946 he noted that the Cabinet Mission that year had been 'our last chance to bring about a settlement in India, a temporary one which would have enabled us to leave India with peace and dignity.' Now he felt he was the head of a crumbling regime; the British still left in the ICS were tired and dispirited, the police were weak and unreliable, while he feared that the communalism which had begun to affect the police might soon corrode the loyalty and strength of the Indian army.

Meanwhile the administration has declined, and the machine in the Centre is hardly working at all now, my ministers are too busy with politics. And while the British are still legally and morally responsible for what happens in India, we have lost nearly all power to control events; we are simply running on the momentum of our previous prestige.[2]

In London at the end of the year he reiterated the importance of having a 'breakdown plan', such was British weakness and the apparent deadlock between Congress and the League in deciding on the form of the independent state or states which should inherit the raj. He had indeed prepared such a plan some months earlier. But it was only after he had been replaced by Mountbatten in the spring of 1947 that London was convinced that the raj must end within weeks rather than in 1948, as had been planned when Mountbatten was appointed.

However, Gandhi did not see Independence Day, 15 August 1947, as the coming of the swaraj he had envisaged and worked for. Not only did the manner and (to a significant extent) the personnel of government remain the same: freedom from imperialism was achieved at the price of India's unity. The 'vivisection' he had so dreaded occurred, and a curious two-winged Pakistan was split off from India to accommodate the fears and aspirations of Jinnah, the League and its followers. Moreover, in the process of deciding on the nature of the new nation states to emerge from the raj and in the course of the partition, violence and displacement of people occurred on a devastating scale. In August 1946 after an orgy of killing in Calcutta, the Governor of Bengal, formerly of the Guards and therefore not ignorant of death in battle, made a sickened report to Wavell, admitting that what he had seen was as bad as anything he had witnessed on the Somme.[3] It is impossible to give accurate figures for the numbers killed and injured as violence swept through Bengal and Bihar and then, at partition, engulfed Old Delhi and the Punjab, where the belligerent Sikh minority added a further dimension to the communal carnage. Possibly a million died in all, and nearly two million fled their homes and trecked to the 'right' religious side of the new international boundaries as Bengal and the Punjab were divided.

In this situation Gandhi's own arena of work also changed significantly, and he showed to the end an amazing adaptability and capacity in old age to respond to changing situations. He gradually disengaged from 'high politics', but did not retire, as so often in earlier years, to the ashram and his constructive work. Instead he went into the eye of the storm, into places where violence was most terrifying; he became the sole satyagrahi, a man who pitted himself totally against violence by personal demonstation as well as preaching and fasting, and ultimately by his own death.

So often Gandhi's life is portrayed in terms of the great political movements and changes in India and his role in them. But he was always ultimately concerned with the individual and his or her problems, and with achieving small-scale solutions that might have wider implications. And this continued to be true right up until his death. It would not be right to call this the 'private' side of Gandhi's life and work, because as he said, there could be no private compartment of life for the man of truth: he must be patent, open to all, both in his achievements and apparent failures. At one of his regular public prayer-meetings in the last months of his life, he explained the significance of his work with individuals: 'For me the smallest work is as important as the biggest. For me whatever is in the atoms and molecules is in the universe. I believe in the saying that what is in the microcosm of one's self is reflected in the macrocosm.'[4]

The Sevagram community, as an attempt to mould individuals into a non-violent and constructive core of new Indians, still commanded much of Gandhi's attention. Through 1945 and 1946 he was still consulted on a wide range of issues that arose in the ashram life, even when he was far away or involved in high level political discussions. But although he said his heart was in Sevagram he encouraged the senior residents to make decisions without him.[5] By late 1946 he had realized that he would probably never return to Sevagram. More urgent work claimed him among the terror-struck victims of communal violence. *Harijan* published a letter he had written to the ashram late in November explaining this.

> I am afraid you must give up all hope of my returning early or returning at all to the Ashram.... It is a Herculean task that faces me. I am being tested. Is the satyagraha of my conception a weapon of the weak or really that of the strong? I must either realize the latter or lay down my life in the attempt to attain it. That is my quest. In pursuit of it I have come to bury myself in this devastated village. His will be done.[6]

From then onwards the ashram people were exhorted to regulate their lives as they thought best, and as if he were no longer available for consultation. He evidently felt that, for all their good intentions and their acceptance of his ideals, they had all failed to exhibit the true quality and power of non-violence in this desperate moment in their country's history. In the light of his personal actions in 1946–7 it is significant that as early as August 1946 he had spoken at an ashram prayer meeting of the need ultimately to make a 'pure sacrifice' in the midst of violence – sacrifice of themselves backed by and infused with total purity, for without this even death would be thoughtless and desperate self-destruction.[7] This helps to explain his personal agonies of conscience and the stringent tests of purity to which he later subjected himself as he tried to pit himself against violence.

Another aspect of Gandhi's small-scale work with individuals in these last years was his new interest in establishing nature cure clinics which would be available for the poorest. He recognized with good humour that this was an amazing departure for one who was manifestly elderly; but it was an interest that had flowered in old age and he could not resist it.[8] Nature cure had been a concern of his even in South Africa. Now it had for him a dual significance, both spiritual and utilitarian. Following its precepts for healthy living meant being in touch with and living by the laws of nature. Being healthy meant being a true servant of God; and he had always felt that sickness in himself and in others was a cause for shame because it was a sign of disorderliness of spirit, for example overwork and lack of detachment, undisciplined or ignorant consumption of too rich a diet, or an otherwise unreformed life-style. Further, natural medicine was cheap and readily available; if it could be actively promoted he felt it could solve the problems of chronic sickness which afflicted India's poor who could never afford expensive Western-style medical treatment.

In 1945 he had accompanied Vallabhbhai Patel to a natural health clinic in Poona run by Dinshaw Mehta, to supervise Patel's treatment, as this hard-headed Gujarati had little faith in nature cure himself. Patel suffered from a spastic colon and looked very haggard and ill when he emerged from detention. (It is symptomatic of Gandhi's tenderness with his colleagues that he should expend such time on their personal well-being, and accounts not a little for their close bond to him.) Later in the same year Gandhi attempted to transform the clinic into one which could serve the poor.[9] However he rapidly realized that an urban clinic could not teach the villagers how to lead a healthy life, and he turned instead to a village-based experiment in nature cure in March 1946. He could not stay long in person, but left detailed instructions on a simple life-style and the type of natural treatments to be offered, including sun baths, mud packs and massage, and recitation of the *Ramanama*. A manager and medical instructor were left in charge, but Gandhi kept a keen eye on the development, even from far away: at the height of negotiations over India's future he took time to consider its building plans, including its sanitation and whether the doors were wide enough to take patients' beds.[10]

Gandhi also expended a great deal of his time on the problems of individual men and women. Perusal of the content of his correspondence, speeches and journalism is a valuable antidote to any portrayal of his life mainly in terms of Indian politics. He was, for example, always ready to give advice on health matters to friends, relatives and those who asked his counsel. In these closing months of his life there was his care for Vallabhbhai's ill-tempered intestines, and his nature-cure regime for his 'granddaughter' (actually his great-niece), Manu, who was his constant companion, which ended, to his humiliation, in her undergoing an appendicectomy, in May 1947 when his mud packs and diet had failed. Just days before his death he wrote a letter advising a women on avoiding pulses and spices, and having hip-baths, mud packs and rest to cure vaginal discharge; he added that if he could find time in the future, 'my first task will be to tackle all these diseases of women through nature cure'.[11]

Equally intimately Gandhi entered into the spiritual and emotional lives of many people, expending on each tenderness and care as if he or she were the only one who mattered to him. His natural family undoubtedly suffered from his public role, but his cutting of natural family ties by his vow of celibacy does seem to have freed him to be open and available to many hundreds of people from widely differing backgrounds, from aristocratic Indians like Amrit Kaur or the Nehrus themselves, to Mirabehn, an English Admiral's daughter, to the poorest in Sevagram village and those who came to his village clinic. He gave guidance on matters of vocation and spiritual devotion. He comforted the bereaved. He entered into marital problems – for example, late in November 1945 giving some very forthright advice to a close associate who had committed himself to celibacy before his marriage and had never told his wife, who was now longing not only for her husband's love but for children.[12] Yet even from such a role of personal guide he began to withdraw.[13] His capacity to cope with individual letters was further curtailed after he had revived *Harijan* in early 1946 in order to expound his deep belief in moral and spiritual strength, though events seemed to point to the power of physical force.

The Mahatma's more hidden work with individuals was rooted in a profound religious conviction of the sanctity and potential strength of each person. His more public speeches and writings on religious matters, particularly his talks at his regular prayer meetings, also reflected his deepest vision, and they still in these hectic days took up much of his time. Indeed one seasoned journalist who had watched Gandhi's career since his return from Africa commented to Srinivasa Sastri early in 1946 that Gandhi was no longer pre-eminently a political leader but more a spiritual one.[14] For Gandhi as he aged fundamental issues and profound truths became even sharper. He said that the essence of true religion was the realization by the individual that God was within, and if served and worshipped would infuse and transform the person whose body was His temple. The outward trappings of religion were inessentials compared with this inward search for reality.

> To seek God one need not go on pilgrimage or light lamps fed with ghee and burn incense before the image of the deity or anoint it or paint it with vermilion. For He resides in our hearts. If we could humbly obliterate in us the consciousness of our physical body, we would see Him face to face.[15]

As his own life ebbed away he had even less time for the quietism or the solitary, precious piety which passed as 'religion'. Real religious commitment showed itself in hard work for the realization of God on earth, and a religion which harped on the world after death was not worthy of the name, in his estimation. When critics accused him of using prayer meetings to propagate political ideas he rounded on them with the robust affirmation that the religious person could not divide his life into different compartments.[16] Of increasing significance to him in this process of self-realization, becoming infused with the divinity within, was constant, prayerful recitation of *Ramanama*, the name of Ram; though even in relation to this devotion he warned against vain babble and ostentatious display of the rosary.[17]

Gandhi's vision of God was broad and sustaining. Drawing on the Jain sense of the many-sidedness of truth, and the Hindu awareness of the many aspects of the divinity, he was not perturbed by the apparent problem of evil in the world:[18] since God was both Creator and Destroyer, 'what cause is there for grief and sorrow?'[19] In the tumultuous weeks before and after partition he wrote of dancing to God's tune, and of experiencing deeper communion with God and growing faith in His grace, the fiercer was the ordeal he faced. Just days before he died he told English people in Delhi who visited him with Amrit Kaur that to see God had been his hope for 60 years, and though he had not yet achieved that vision, 'I feel I am coming closer to it every day and that is enough for me.'[20] His own religious life was sustained by keeping silence every Monday (and he advocated a weekly day of silence for any one who would seek truth and abide in God), and by the practice of *Ramanama*. As the servant of Ram, as one who was held and guided by Him, what he hoped was that if his lot were to be killed he would be without anger in his heart towards the killer, and would die with the name of Ram on his lips.[21]

Although Gandhi sensed a divine purpose and pattern in his life, he could not help being aware that in the estimation of many others he was in these last years of his life an ebbing political influence, even an apparent political failure. The months following the Simla Conference were a time of disengagement from 'high politics' for him, though he never contemplated political retirement. Just before Independence Day he answered the question whether he would retire then: 'the life of the millions is my politics from which I dare not free myself without denying my life work and God. That my politics may take a different turn is quite possible.'[22] When questioned by someone about 'taking *sannyasa*', retiring to the forest for a contemplative life, a Hindu practice held desirable for the old, he showed the understanding of tradition that certainly underpinned his own continuing public role.

> I believe that the man who observes self-control in thought, word and deed in the midst of the world is verily a great ascetic. If things do not bind us, if we are not attached to things even when they are easily available that, according to me, is a greater test of our detachment than mere withdrawal to a lonely forest.[23]

Most obviously Gandhi's withdrawal from his earlier active role in all-India politics first occurred after the members of the CWC were released in mid-1945. He now steered all questions on Congress matters to them and privately acknowledged that his participation in the CWC's affairs was slight and growing slighter.[24] Further, there were clear differences of opinion between him, and even its most influential members who were closest to him. He came under fire for his dealings with Jinnah when they had been in detention, for example.[25] There was also a sharp difference between him and his much-loved protégé and acknowledged political heir, Nehru, because in contrast to the younger

man's vision of a free and modern India, Gandhi still adhered to the
vision he had expounded in *Hind Swaraj*. But intimate discussions
showed that there was no personal rift between them: as Gandhi put it,
their hearts were one even if ultimately their paths differed.[26]

When a Labour government came to power in Britain at the end of
July 1945 it was soon clear that there would be rapid political change in
India. The first step was to be fresh elections to the legislatures in the
coming winter, and later, selection of members to form a Constituent
Assembly. Gandhi played no part in the election work which immediately began to concern Congressmen, and hardly even discussed
the elections with Patel when they were together in the Poona clinic. He
did not attend CWC meetings to select candidates, and what little he
knew of the later selections with the Constituent Assembly in view
came from the papers.[27] He still personally attached very little importance to entering the legislatures. But compared with his earlier
attitude to parliamentary activity he was now more positive about it as
being right for some people, primarily because he felt the legislatures
could be used to promote constructive work.[28] On election matters he
deflected enquirers to the CWC, and as so often in the past was
distressed at rivalry among Congressmen during the electoral process,
and the fact that they saw seats as prizes and perks rather than positions
for service. The election results were a striking sign that Congress was
by far the most powerful political voice of politically active Hindus: it
won over 90% of the non-Muslim vote. (Ominously for the future of a
united India after British withdrawal, it was also clear that now the
League could legitimately claim to represent India's Muslims, in contrast to its status in the late 1930s. It swept up 439 of the 494 special
Muslim seats in the legislatures, and had large majorities in Bengal and
Punjab, the Muslim majority areas where previously it had been so
weak.)

As in 1937–9, now in 1946, Gandhi was anxious about the behaviour
of the successful Congressmen, for it did not seem to him that their
attitudes and standards of behaviour were fitting in those who would
soon be creating a free India and determining the quality of its public
life. Taking on the role of critic and chastiser, he underlined the theme
of service of the nation, and condemned rowdy behaviour, election
wrangles, place seeking, intrigue and factional strife. He condemned the
legislators and Ministers who merely retained the expensive life-style of
the *sahib log*, the British rulers, and even found time in *Harijan* to point
to their habit of using expensive, embossed official writing paper, and of
deflecting it for private use.[29] These were not the hallmarks of thrift and
honesty he expected in a true people's government.

Although Gandhi was now little concerned with the daily workings
of the Congress, the political initiative of the new Attlee government in
London early in 1946 drew him back for the last time into the heart of
deliberations and decisions about the nature of free India and the
mechanisms for achieving it. After prolonged discussions in London,
and between London and Delhi, in the second half of 1945 and early

1946,[30] when the Labour government took a fresh look at the whole Indian problem, it was decided that a Cabinet Mission should go to India. It consisted of the Secretary of State for India, Lord Pethick-Lawrence, Sir Stafford Cripps, who needed no introduction to Indian politicians, and A.V. Alexander, First Lord of the Admiralty, who had never been to India. They assumed at the start that Indian independence and right to self-determination was not now the main issue: it was the accepted premise of their work, which was now to consider the nature of the state or states which would inherit the raj, and the composition of a more popular and representative interim government which would see India through the phase of transition.[31]

The details of the Mission from 23 March to 29 June have been meticulously recorded elsewhere: here the exhausting labour of the three 'Magi' as Wavell called them, and their ultimate failure, are relevant only in brief because they were the context of Gandhi's last major political intervention and the background to his very changed role in the final months of the raj. The Mission's work can best be visualized in several phases: an initial period of exploring Indian opinion through interviews; the preparation of alternative plans; a conference in Simla when the politicians were invited to discuss the Mission's own elaborate and ingenious plan; the preparation of a statement on 16 May elaborating the Mission's plan after the failure of the leaders to agree; and finally gathering Indian reactions to the plan, and the attempt by Wavell and the Mission together to form an Interim Government.

The Mission's own plan[32] was a device to devolve power to one India, as they thought the variants of partition they could envisage were not viable options, but in so doing to make provision to alleviate the fears of minorities, primarily the Muslims. Its essence was a system of three tiers: a Union of British and Princely India, limited to foreign affairs, defence and communications; three Groups of Provinces and States, each dealing with topics the component units agreed to have in common; and at the base, the individual Provinces and States that would hold residuary powers. They proposed that the members of the provincial legislatures should elect a Constituent Assembly which would meet as a whole at the beginning and end of the constitution-making process. In the middle period the proposed second tier of Groups should meet to decide what should be Group matters and the constitution of the Provinces. (The Groups were to be the six Hindu majority provinces, the Muslim majority areas of North-West India and the Muslim majority areas of Eastern India.) It was, however, an attempt to accommodate two views of India – the Congress view that India was one nation though a religiously plural society, and the League view that Muslims by virtue of their religion were a distinct and separate nation with a right to self-determination and a homeland. By now these views were really incompatible because they had been refined in the previous months of acrimonious discussion between Congress and League leaders, and had generated far wider popular support. Eventually these opposing visions of national identity blew the attempts of the Mission and the Viceroy to bits, though the breakdown occurred on narrow issues which were none the less symoblic of this central division. The longer-term plan collapsed because Congress would not accept that the individual Provinces must participate in their Groups for the whole process, while the League insisted that they had to, because only if they did could some semblance of a homeland for Muslims be achieved. (If mainly Hindu Assam opted out of the North-East group, for example, as Gandhi was to encourage, the eastern Muslim core based on Bengal would not be viable.) The immediate attempt to form a representative Interim Government foundered on the issue that had wrecked Wavell's 1945 Simla Conference – whether the League was the sole representative of India's Muslims.

Gandhi's initial response to the prospect of the Cabinet Mission was friendly. He urged Indians to accept the Mission as a genuine attempt to give India her freedom, and to welcome the Ministers with the same courtesy as they would show to a debtor coming 'in contrition to repay his debt'; and he was convinced that the Mission signified that the British had at last decided on total withdrawal.[33] As at the Simla Conference in 1945, now during the Mission he maintained that he could not 'represent' Congress. But he was present in Delhi and Simla during most of the proceedings, and was constantly available to his colleagues and to the Cabinet Mission, his direct links with the members of the Mission being supplemented by the intermediary work of friends such as Horace Alexander and Agatha Harrison, who were now in India, and various Indians, including Amrit Kaur and a young executive from the Tata firm, Sudhir Ghosh.

Cripps had always believed that it was Gandhi's intervention which sabotaged his attempts in 1942; now he was determined to keep in touch with Gandhi, however unofficial the channels, and if possible to keep him friendly and constructive. Gandhi was one of the 'leaders' the Mission interviewed at the outset, and the Secretary of State deliberately sought his co-operation in the last days of decision-making on the Plan.[34] In the intervening weeks Gandhi constantly visited or corresponded with the Mission either directly or through his entourage, who scurried about to keep communications open. Wavell was 'frankly horrified at the degree of deference shown to Gandhi' by the Mission, and recorded on 3 April,

I thought the interview with Gandhi, naked except for a dhoti and looking remarkably healthy, was rather a deplorable affair. S. of S. began with his usual sloppy benevolence to this malevolent old politician, who for all his sanctimonious talk has, I am sure, very little softness in his composition.

He also heartily disapproved of the Secretary of State's attendance at some of Gandhi's prayers. In retrospect he felt the Mission should not have had such constant contact with the Congress leaders, and Gandhi in particular, and noted that they 'put exaggerated faith and belief in him'.[35]

Throughout the interchanges, discussions and numerous interviews, Gandhi still pursued the goal of a united, free India, and as Wavell realized, he could be very tough on what he perceived as crucial issues. Certainly he was firmly convinced that the 'Groupings' envisaged in the plan were not binding.[36] However, he was not prepared to force his intuitive feeling against co-operation in the Constituent Assembly on the CWC.[37] But it was on the communal composition of a new Interim Government that Gandhi's attitude was decisive, and, in the eyes of the Viceroy, destructive. Not surprisingly Jinnah insisted that in any transitional government he must nominate all the Muslim members, and that Congress and League should have equal membership; equally predictably, Congress rejected his challenge. When the Mission and Wavell then tried to contrive an acceptable list for a new government Gandhi stepped in and persuaded the CWC – against its initial intention – that a Nationalist Muslim must be included, even though Wavell had not accepted Jinnah's claim to parity between League and Congress.[38] Gandhi's commitment to Congress as nationally inclusive was of course of long standing; but now he also seems to have realized that an Interim Government imposed from above and founded on an unstable coalition, whose members had different fundamental aims, would be useless as a bridge to real freedom. His own proposal was that the government should have the courage in this deadlock to choose the names submitted either by Congress or the League[39] – echoing what he had said to Wavell just after the breakdown of the 1945 Simla Conference.

It was perhaps hardly surprising that Wavell, who had long thought Gandhi was a skilful political opportunist, distrusted him even more comprehensively after this failure to achieve an agreed Interim Government. His less than charitable assessment sent to King George VI is symptomatic of the frustration and misunderstanding of successive British administrators when faced with this enigmatic figure who was so unlike any politician to be encountered in British public life. It also reflects Wavell's extreme fatigue after weeks of diplomacy and hard labour, and his unease at the attitudes and style of at least two members of the Cabinet Mission.

> Gandhi ran entirely true to form: his influence is still great; his line of thought and action at any given moment and on any particular issue is as unpredictable as ever; he never makes a pronouncement that is not so qualified and so vaguely worded that it cannot be interpreted in whatever sense best suits him at a later stage; but however double-tongued he may be, he is quite single-minded on the one objective from which he has never swerved in the last 40 years, the elimination of the hated British influence from India. My distrust of this shrewd, malevolent, old politician was deep before the Conference started; it is deeper than ever now.[40]

Wavell had retreated into Lewis Carroll one evening towards the end of the Mission and found it reflected his thoughts about Indian politics! Capable of a lighter vein in his journal than in his letter to his King, he vented his frustration in a parody of Carroll's 'Jaberwock' in which the Mahatma figured thus:

> The Gandhiji, on wrecking bent,
> Came trippling down the bhangi ways,
> And woffled as he went.[41]

However, very soon the eruption of communal violence took Gandhi physically away from the centre of decision-making, and incidentally from 'the bhangi ways', a reference to the untouchables' quarter in Delhi where Gandhi had been staying during negotiations with the Mission. (He had decided in late March that wherever he went he must now live amongst untouchables.) Furthermore, as Wavell struggled to form an Interim Government, and eventually succeeded though initially it was without League participation, power in Congress swung towards Nehru, now Congress president and from the beginning of September the leading Congressman in that government, as Minister in charge of External Affairs, and to his colleagues, Patel, Prasad and Rajagopalachariar, who were also Ministers.[42]

Confronted with the practicalities of government and a deteriorating situation as violence sparked off more violence, the other leaders began to face reality, and Gandhi · sensed his ebbing authority. Some time in 1946 he told his friend and financier, G.D. Birla, 'My voice carries no weight in the Working Committee ... I do not like the shape that things are taking and, I cannot speak out.'[43] When the government convened a small conference in London in December to see if there was any way that the Congress and League could participate in the Constituent Assembly, it was Nehru who went to represent Congress. Then, early in March, when Gandhi was away in Bihar, the CWC reluctantly but realistically resolved that partition of the Punjab would be the only solution to the current violence. Gandhi was still deeply hostile to any partition based on communal grounds and the theory of two nations, Hindu and Muslim, and wrote to Nehru and Patel, asking why the Committee had so decided. Nehru replied as a realist: 'now a time for decision has come and mere passing of resolutions giving expression to our views meant little. I feel convinced and so did most of the members of the Working Committee that we must press for this immediate division so that reality might be brought into the picture.' Patel wrote back that the decision was only taken after the deepest deliberation, and told the man to whom he had so often deferred, 'you are, of course, entitled to say what you feel is right'.[44] Shortly afterwards Gandhi said at one of his prayer meetings, 'Whatever the Congress decides will be done; nothing will be according to what I say. My writ runs no more.... No one listens to me any more.... I am crying in the wilderness.'[45]

Gandhi's changed role and reputation as a political leader was nowhere clearer than during the last Viceroyalty. Mountbatten came to
India early in 1947, his mission being to wind up the raj by June 1948 at
the latest, and if possible to hand over power to a unitary state set up in
accordance with the Cabinet Mission Plan.[46] Not only were the objectives of his term of office different from those of his predecessors: his
whole open and easy style abadoned the old protocols of the raj. He and
his wife and hand-picked staff were readily available to Indians, and
deliberately cultivated easy social relations with those who had previously been kept at a distance or indeed detained for sedition. It was
evident that the Viceroy and Lady Mountbatten found Nehru a particularly attractive colleague and friend, and Mountbatten felt he could do
serious and constructive business with him and Patel. To Gandhi he
showed his great charm and courtesy, and, unlike Wavell, found the old
enigma fascinating, and was prepared to give much time for his ramb-
ling recollections of his life, as well as to discussions with him about the
immediate matters in hand. He apparently regarded him as 'an old
poppet'.[47] Certainly he felt Gandhi was still a figure of political importance and kept in constant touch with him; but the leadership of
Congress had by this stage clearly passed into other hands. For example,
in their first set of interviews early in April Gandhi floated to Mountbatten the idea that Jinnah should be invited to form an Interim Government with League members, to which Mountbatten should then hand
over power. The Viceroy's advisors were sure the scheme was totally
unworkable, and not surprisingly Nehru and the CWC almost almost
unanimously rejected it out of hand. Gandhi sadly reported this to
Mountbatten and virtually resigned from the decision-making process.

> I felt sorry that I could not convince them of the correctness of my
> plan from every point of view. Nor could they dislodge me from my
> position although I had not closed my mind against every argument.
> Thus, I have to ask you to omit me from your consideration.
> Congressmen, who are in the Interim Government, are stalwarts,
> seasoned servants of the nation and, therefore so far as the Congress
> point of view in concerned, they will be complete advisers.

But he said he would always be at the Viceroy's disposal should he need
his services.[48]

By May 1947 the new Viceroy had become convinced that there was
no future for the Cabinet Mission Plan and had begun in earnest
preparation of a new plan to devolve power to two dominions within
the Commonwealth. It was Nehru's voice to which Mountbatten
listened most attentively and whose acceptance he thought was critical
on the Congress side. Gandhi, meanwhile, was still hostile to any idea of
a partition of India, and told Mountbatten so in forthright terms. From a
private talk with a colleague it was clear that what he dreaded was that
partition now would be the prelude to further fragmentation, and
though his generation would not live to see the consequences, younger

Gandhi with the Mountbattens,
31 March 1947.

men would come to curse them for the kind of swaraj they would have
bequeathed.[49] In his distress and confusion he reiterated that the British
should leave the government of India to one party or the other, and even
began to back the virtually defunct Cabinet Mission Plan.[50] The Viceroy
took the precaution of trying to explain matters to him on 2 June, the
day he unveiled his own Viceregal plan for partition to the main leaders,
but communication was somewhat hampered by the fact that it was one
of Gandhi's silent Mondays and his comments were written on the back
of five old envelopes.[51] Although Patel though Gandhi would loyally
stand by any Congress decision, when Mountbattan was told that some
of the Congress leaders were fearful that Gandhi in his present emotional and unhappy state would denounce the Viceroy's carefully contrived
plan, even after the CWC had agreed to accept it, he saw the old man yet
again on 4 June in an attempt to soothe him.[52] Gandhi had however
realized how remote he now was from the thinking of even his closest
colleagues and he agonized in the early hours of 1 June about his
predicament for he did not want to be a party to his country's vivisection but feared there was now no alternative.[53] At the crucial CWC
meeting on 2 June he indicated that he would not stand in the way of
Congress's acceptance of the plan, despite his personal disapproval.
Patel was right in counting on Gandhi's loyalty to Congress: for in
subsequent days he made it clear that he would not launch an agitation
against Congress, and indeed supported the CWC's stand at the ensuing
AICC meeting in mid-June which followed the CWC lead.[54]

Gandhi and Mountbatten, 2 June 1947.

Having gained the agreement of the leaders, after tense days of cliff-hanging negotiations, Mountbatten pushed ahead with breath-taking speed towards the 15 August deadline for solving the host of problems attendant on independence and partition. These ranged from the division of the army and civil service, and the even greater but hitherto virtually unconsidered problem of the integration of India's Princes and their peoples into either India or Pakistan, down to division even of office furniture in government departments. Mountbatten ruthlessly and consciously worked the politicians harder than they had probably ever been before in their lives, and all as the temperatures soared.

As independence came so near, Gandhi's heart was neither in the planning nor in the euphoria of public celebration. Rather, he was deeply fearful that what was now so near at hand was not the true independence he had so long envisaged and for which he had tried to prepare his countrymen. To him swaraj had never been mere political freedom from imperial rule: it lay rather in the self-reliance of the people who would work together to create a harmonious society in which all were safe, whatever their faith, and in which all had a sufficiency. Now he preached the need for radical constructive work, and sorrowfully criticized the attitudes and behaviour which seemed to be the opposite of those needed in a true swaraj society and polity – anger, intolerance, rowdyism, carelessness and lack of discipline.[55] He still ultimately held to the views he had expounded in *Hind Swaraj*, as he told two English visitors.

> The foreign power will be withdrawn before long, but for me real freedom will come only when we free ourselves of the dominance of Western education, Western culture and [the] Western way of living which have been ingrained in us, because this culture has made our living expensive and artificial.... Emancipation from this culture would mean real freedom for us.[56]

By early May Gandhi was saying that he no longer wished to live to be 125 because he saw falsehood all around him; and as independence approached he was increasingly appalled by what he called the stench of violence, and said that the swaraj he had dreamed of was still far away.[57] After 15 August his message remained the same. Communal violence meant that this was no true swaraj, nor *ramrajya*, the rule of God; military expenditure was rising and he saw around him 'madness and the vain imitation of the tinsel of the West'. Yet he had not lost hope, for he still hoped that out of this blood-bath and apparent imitation of Western modes and priorities of government, India would arise, new and robust, with a message of moral strength for the world.[58]

If India was to survive the present violence and confront its real problems, Gandhi realized that Congress must change. For years he had periodically tried to reform it into a body of dedicated constructive workers, but always the competitive political instincts of its members had turned it back again into a political party. Now in the last months of his life he reverted to his old hope of creating a body of servants of their country. Discussion about a new constitution for Congress had been going on at least since 1946,[59] and from the outset Gandhi made his views plain. In the final days, even hours, of his life he worked out his suggestions more fully for the drafting committee, but its members had no time to discuss these with him as they had hoped, for his death intervened. Now often called his last will and testament, this document, dated 29 January 1948, summarized his vision of decades: of a Congress which was not a power-seeking political party but a body of servants of the people, whose main labours would be in the villages, educating villagers in agriculture and handicrafts, so that they could become self-supporting, preaching public health, organizing basic education, and encouraging them to exercise the franchise. *Khadi* would be the hallmark of these servants, and to their parent organization would be affiliated all the constructive bodies he had set in motion, including the AISA and the AIVIA. Congress as it was had, in his opinion, outlived its usefulness: now it must be a body which would help India's masses to attain real social, moral and economic independence.[60]

Gandhi's vision was not that of a practical government in the difficult circumstances of 1947, nor was his hope for Congress likely to commend itself to Congressmen who saw it as the vehicle for political careers and influence, as well as the means of manifesting a genuine patriotism. His skills and dreams had suited Congressmen while their primary objective was to agitate for independence and to spread the ideal of a new nation. Now they were involved in the endgame of an imperial raj, and facing the real problems of government, and the leadership naturally fell into the hands of those who had the skills suited to the times. Gandhi was acutely aware that there was little need of him now. He spoke of being 'a lone voice', of ceasing to be useful for achieving anything but unity.[61] He wondered aloud what place he had in this new India and had stopped thinking about aspiring to a long life, because he now felt so helpless, apparently unable to serve his country.[62] But there was one area of public life where he still had a unique role – to throw himself into the places where violence had been most horrific and to try to stop the downward spiral of fear and revenge. In his last months he had the opportunity to test out his belief in non-violence in extreme circumstances; and though in political terms he was virtually powerless, even obsolete, in retrospect men and women far beyond India's borders and his own times have sensed that morally this was his finest and most significant hour.

The combination of causes and the actual mechanics of the communal violence that cut a horrific swathe across nothern India in 1946–7 will probably never be fully known. There was certainly no historical inevitability about it. For generations Hindus and Muslims had lived and intermingled in many parts of the subcontinent in a basic, if a times uneasy, peace. There had been potential for misunderstanding and strife in some of their mutually conflicting religious attitudes and activities; but on the other hand there had also been significant social, economic and political co-operation between members of the two communities. What had increasingly occurred in the twentieth century was the politicization of religion, or conversely, the 'communalization' of politics, as the British began to devolve power through mechanisms which reflected their understanding of Indian society as a plural one of different peoples who needed special outlets in political life. Furthermore, local conflicts of long standing, often economic rather than basically religious, tended to become infused with a communal passion. In this process the overtly religious appeals of politicians in search of a following were as significant as British perceptions of India, and by the 1940s they had let loose a tiger they could not control.

The immediate trigger for the great conflagration was the announcement by Jinnah and the League that Muslims should observe 16 August 1946 as Direct Action Day, and the public assertion that now Muslims would bid farewell to constitutional methods. This unleashed communal violence and a train of retaliation which even a joint appeal for peace by Gandhi and Jinnah in April 1947 could not control.[63] Almost certainly as order temporarily collapsed in some places gangs of thugs exploited the opportunity, and old scores were settled. When the Punjab erupted roving bands of Sikhs added a further dimension to the murderous violence, and Muslims fleeing to Pakistan were butchered by the train-load. Ultimately no community and probably no politician could escape some responsibility for what occurred.

Gandhi's reaction to this violence was deep distress – both at the butchery and the cowardice of those who fled or resorted to violent retaliation. He told his daughter-in-law that he was far weaker in bearing the pain of this than he had thought, and was now filled with agony by what was happening. In a prayer-meeting he vented his anguish:

> But today we seem to have given up reason altogther. Reason can hold sway only when we have courage. There is nothing brave about what is going on today. It is a sheer negation of humanity. We have well-nigh turned into beasts.[64]

Trying to fathom the deep origins of this bestiality he argued that communalism was an outcome of urbanization – for in villages Hindus and Muslims were used to living in mutual interdependence.[65] Although he denied that he and Congress were in any way directly responsible for creating communal violence, he had begun to feel that the violence of 1942 in Bihar at least had been the seed-bed of the Hindu violence against Muslims in that province, which followed the Muslim massacres of Hindus in Calcutta and Bengal.[66]

Increasingly he lamented that their earlier 'non-violence' was 'bankrupt', that it was now proved to have been the non-violence of the weak who had no alternative, not the creative and purifying non-violence of the strong and courageous. Almost at the end of his life he published a private letter in which he confessed not the failure of *ahimsa* itself but

> ... [that] what I had mistaken for ahimsa was not ahimsa, but passive resistance of the weak, which can never be called ahimsa even in the remotest sense. The internecine feud that is going on today in India is the direct outcome of the energy that was set free during the thirty years' action of the weak. Hence, the proper way to view the present outburst of violence ... is to recognize that the technique of unconquerable non-violence of the strong has not been discovered as yet.[67]

To a prayer-meeting in New Delhi he lamented that there was no satyagraha and no *ahimsa* left now – all seemed to have become votaries of violence.[68] But he also blamed the presence of British troops in India, seeing them as an invitation to Hindus and Muslims to look to them as a third party for protection, rather than relying on their own strength.[69]

From his confused understanding of the origins of communal strife and his horror at its dimensions he drew the lesson that now non-violence was on trial as never before. He told the people at Sevagram this in November 1946 when he warned them that he might never come back to the ashram, and he often returned to this theme. In December 1946 he wrote, 'Ahimsa is indeed put to the test now.' And in February 1947 he told A.K. Azad, 'If the ahimsa about which I have written so much and which I have striven to realize all these years does not answer in a crisis, it ceases to have any value in my eyes.'[70]

What had perplexed him as he emerged from detention in 1944 was whether or not the forces of non-violence could be marshalled and directed on any scale: now he was only thinking whether in his own person non-violence could be shown to be efficacious. The greater part of his life had been built on this assumption, and for his own sake he needed to know whether he had acted on illusion or spiritual reality.[71] This was indeed an intensely personal crisis for him, as the apostle of *ahimsa*. He believed profoundly that this was his allotted role in life; *ahimsa* itself could never fail, but if it appeared now not to work he thought it must be his fault, his failure to find the right mode of implementation.[72] His life had been a record of experiments with spiritual forces, as he had indicated in the subtitle to his autobiography; he had seen public life as his laboratory, as he had proclaimed when he appeared to fail in Rajkot in 1939. Now was the ultimate test. He was bowed down with an enormous sense of responsibility for what had happened, and for the vindication now of real *ahimsa*. To Congressmen he said in October 1947, 'It is I who am to be blamed. There has been some flaw somewhere in my ahimsa. And this was bound to have its effect on the people.' To a Swiss Friend he wrote some weeks later,

> . . . we are daily paying the heavy price for the unconscious mistake we made or, better still, I made in mistaking passive resistance for non-violent resistance. Had I not made the mistake, we would have been spared the humiliating spectacle of a weak brother killing his weak brother thoughtlessly and inhumanly.[73]

It was no wonder that now he tested to the utmost, in the only ways he knew how, his courage and purity of heart, the prerequisites for the exercise of *ahimsa*.

His first step was in late October 1946 to go to Noakhali district in Bengal where Hindus had been the victims of murder, forcible conversion, abduction, and destruction of property. Not surprisingly many had fled in terror to nearby districts of Bengal and Bihar where Hindus were a majority. Despite his age and physical frailty he plunged into a punishing regime of travel and speeches, trying to confront the terror and bitterness, absorbing it and calming and comforting those he met. He preached the protection of God as the remedy for fear, exhorted Hindus to return home, and called for a Hindu and a Muslim in each village to accompany the returning refugees and stand surety for their safety. Then in mid-November he decided to test himself still further by burying himself virtually alone in one village, Srirampur, among Muslims, to see whether in one place his presence could radiate non-violence and bring peace.

Ahimsa which to me is the chief glory of Hinduism has been sought to be explained away by our people as being meant for sannyasis only. I do not share that view. I have held that it is *the* way of life and India has to show it to the world. Where do I stand? Do I represent this ahimsa in my person? If I do, then deceit and hatred that poison the atmosphere should dissolve. It is only by going into isolation from my companions, those on whose help I have relied all along, and standing on my own feet that I shall find my bearing and also test my faith in God.[74]

Using the slogan he had given Congress in 1942, now applying it to himself, he said he must do or die. Likening himself to a gardener raising seedlings, he occupied himself with one small area in the hope of planting and raising *ahimsa*. But he was evidently, as one of two companions reported, searching in the darkness, perplexed and deeply upset, feeling uncertainty, anxiety and anger with an intensity which was unaccustomed and distressing.[75] He worked 18 hours a day, learning Bengali, cooking, mending his clothes, coping with correspondence and meetings, conducting prayers, and walking through the surrounding villages to spread his message. Then in January he embarked on a walking tour, a plan which had gradually been forming in his mind. In seven weeks he visited 47 villages and covered 116 miles – a considerable feat for one who in 1944 was thought to be incapable of ever playing a public role again. Almost the only concession he made to his age and fatigue was to stop getting up at 3.00 a.m. He did however have police protection – at a discreet distance as they walked. He went barefoot now, as if on pilgrimage for peace, as he passed through the evidence of devastation and inhumanity. Yet Muslim hostility to him was rife and he felt increasingly unwelcome in Bengal. In March he left for Bihar, where the Hindus had been the aggressors and Muslims the victims; and, basing himself in Patna, the provincial capital, he began the same work of reconciliation and restoration of courage.

There was no doubt of Gandhi's courage as he went where anger and fear ran high. But in his anguish and self-examination he began to question the inner purity of his spirit. For years he had believed that purity of heart, lack of attachment and desire, was the precondition both of a vision of God and the path to Him, and of the strength to follow that vision, to walk that path, holding fast to truth and *ahimsa*. Now he wrestled with the problem, in the belief that 'If I succeed in emptying myself utterly, God will possess me.'[76] His solution was to test his own *brahmacharya* in extreme conditions, for only if he retained his purity and detachment could he hope to be the embodiment of *ahimsa*.

So began in Bengal an experiment of sleeping naked with young women he knew well, principally Manu, his constant companion and handmaid at the end of his life. This caused immense concern among his friends and well-wishers; some left his company, and he hastened to explain to those who valued and revered him such as Birla and Vinoba

Bhave why he was doing this.[77] Eventually he gave it up in the face of this disquiet. It is an episode which is discreetly omitted in some of the most serious accounts of Gandhi's life – and, indeed, the Bengali interpreter, N.K. Bose, who later wrote about his days with Gandhi in Bengal could not find an Indian publisher after Gandhi's death. On the other hand, it is a widely known fact of Gandhi's life which readily gives rise to superficial jokes about his 'sexual hang-ups', or ill-qualified pseudo-psychiatric interpretations. Probably no one doubted that Gandhi's relationship with Manu was totally platonic and moral. But in his anxiety about his own spiritual state and his concern not to end his life as a failure but to demonstrate the guiding truths of a life's work, he chose a means which gave rise to malicious gossip and was possibly hurtful to the people he chose to use as partners in his experiment, particularly the young and impressionable. Not to recognize this episode, and see its place in Gandhi's crisis of old age and apparent defeat, is to portray a plaster saint rather than an old and sometimes confused and misguided human being who could make unfortunate choices and decisions in his zeal and sense of urgency. To ignore it is also to ignore the continuing importance in Gandhi's self-perception of his Hindu background.

Gandhi was not content to pit himself against violence just by means of his personal presence and self-abnegation. When further violence erupted at the time of partition he also used again the weapon of the fast, the attempt to muster spiritual power to transform an apparently deadlocked situation and to change people's attitudes. The first occasion was in Calcutta, where once again the city was in turmoil. With his usual talent for choosing the significant symbolic gesture, he proposed that he should live with the Muslim Chief Minister, whom Hindus held responsible for the continuing disturbances in the city. They chose for their demonstration of unity an abandoned Muslim house in a dirty and riot-afflicted part of Calcutta, unprotected by police or soldiers. It was, as he admitted to Vallabhbhai Patel, 'a big risk'.[78] But amazingly within hours Muslims and Hindus began to embrace each other, attend each other's mosques and temples, and freely walk in streets they would so recently have considered dangerous. Rajagopalachariar, now Governor of Bengal, visited him to congratulate him on the 'miracle'. Indeed Gandhi went deaf from the friendly shouting and was tired out at having to give his *darshan*. Part of him revelled in the experience, so much did it remind him of South Africa and of the Khilafat campaign, when he had felt secure in the friendship and co-operation of Muslims. Yet he was also sceptical whether the apparent change of heart was real or a momentary enthusiasm.[79]

Sadly his apprehensions proved well-founded, and at the end of the month rioting broke out again, triggered by news of atrocities in Punjab as Muslims and Sikhs became locked in conflict. A Hindu crowd surged round the house where Gandhi was staying, angered by tales of Muslim violence in Calcutta, and Gandhi proved unable to pacify them when he was roused from sleep by the noise. Brooding sadly on the scene, wondering where his duty lay, he decided rapidly that he would fast until sanity should return to the city, despite the counter arguments and admonitions of the worried Rajagopalachariar.[80] Gandhi hoped that a rapid decision to fast would prevent further attacks on Calcutta's Muslims, and would touch those Hindus whose sympathy and passive support was aiding those who actually took to the streets in violence: it was an appeal for everyone to search and purify their hearts.[81] Soon the violence died down; deputations reached the house; Hindus were surrendering their illegal arms; and leaders of the Hindus, Muslims and Sikhs pledged themselves to prevent violence erupting again in their city.

On 4 September Gandhi broke the fast, hoping that he could now go on to the Punjab on his mission of peace. Rajagopalachariar was to say that his victory over violence in Calcutta was one of Gandhi's greatest achievements, and on 6 September Mountbatten's press attaché commented dryly:

Hardened Press correspondents report that they have seen nothing comparable with this demonstration of mass influence. Mountbatten's estimate is that he has achieved by moral persuasion what four Divisions would have been hard pressed to have accomplished by force.[82]

(Mountbatten had earlier wired to 'My Dear Gandhiji', paying tribute as a serving officer to this 'One Man Boundary Force' – referring obliquely to the Punjab Boundary Force which was signally failing to keep order on the opposite side of the country, though his congratulations had proved somewhat premature.)[83]

Thus released from Calcutta in early September 1947, Gandhi travelled to Delhi, hoping to proceed to the Punjab. But in the capital of free India he found communal strife of such dimensions that Mountbatten, no stranger to armed conflict, wrote to his daughter, Patricia, 'I've never been through such a time in my life. The War, the Viceroyalty were jokes, for we have been dealing with life and death in our own city.'[84] So Gandhi stayed – this time not in the Harijan quarters which were now overflowing with refugees, but in Birla House, the large and comfortable home of his wealthy friends. This was to be his home until his death a few short months later. He held daily prayer-meetings at which he discoursed upon the matters that were concerning him, he received deputations and visitors, dealt with his usual large correspondence, he toured the city, and visited the many refugee camps which housed Muslims who had fled for protection in numbers from their Delhi homes, and Sikhs and Hindus who had migrated from what was now Pakistan. He spoke publicly of many matters, but primarily of communal unity. What distressed him most was the evidence of huge migrations of fearful people across the the new national border; he urged that there would never be real peace until people of every community returned to their original homes, their safety guaranteed by the government of the dominion in which they lived.[85]

To observers he seemed to have become deeply sad, even pessimistic, and to have lost the zest for living which had been so characteristic of him, even in old age. Certainly he felt increasingly isolated, adrift from his Congress colleagues, and now in Delhi struggling for unity, without Muslim help such as he had had in Calcutta, and he admitted that those Muslims in Congress on whom he had relied for so long now proved useless as intermediaries and interpreters. In November he compared Delhi with Calcutta.

> Here I don't find a single Muslim who can approach the Hindus, if only to die, or whose word weighs with the Muslims. Maulana Saheb [A.K. Azad] and the nationalist Muslims have also lost this strength. Hence my work here is much more difficult than it was in Calcutta. I am doubtful whether I shall fulfil my vow of doing something here. But my other vow, that of dying, will certainly be fulfilled. For that I have not the least worry. May God take from me whatever work He intends me to do.[86]

Despite and indeed because of his sense of helplessness Delhi was to be the scene of what he called his greatest fast.[87] The fast was his answer to helplessness, the last weapon of a true satyagrahi, where the violent man would use a sword. His decision was made suddenly, though after considerable thought – he gave no hint of it even to Nehru and Patel who were with him shortly before he announced his intention at a prayer-meeting on 12 January 1948. He said he would fast until communal peace was restored, real peace rather than the calm of a dead city imposed by police and troops.[88] Patel and the government took the fast partly as a condemnation of their decision to withhold a considerable cash sum still outstanding to Pakistan as a result of the allocation of undivided India's assets, because of the hostilities that had broken out in Kashmir; it seems that Mountbatten had invoked Gandhi's support on this issue. The Mountbattens actually visited the fasting Mahatma as a symbol to the world that they supported him. But even when the government agreed to pay out the cash, Gandhi would not break his fast: that he would only do after a large number of important politicians and leaders of communal bodies agreed to a joint plan for restoration of normal life in the city.[89] Although this six-day fast was a considerable physical strain, during it Gandhi experienced a great feeling of strength and peace.[90]

Underlying the apparent success of Gandhi's fasts in Calcutta and Delhi, and the moral influence he still exerted, there were clear signs that in the turmoil accompanying partition many Hindus bitterly distrusted this 'Mahatma' and resented his role which they interpreted as weakness towards Muslim demands. This was no new phenomenon, as some orthodox Hindus had always disliked the accommodating policy the central Congress leadership of a supposedly inclusive body had tried to achieve. Dr B.S. Moonje, for example, continually complained to his diary of Gandhi's lack of political instinct, and his over-conciliatory attitude to Muslims;[91] he represented many who supported the more orthodox Hindu Mahasabha which aimed to strengthen Hindus and create a truly Hindu rather than a plural India. Partition sharpened this underlying mistrust of Gandhi, for all his Hindu style. During his last months in Delhi even his prayer-meetings were disturbed by angry Hindus. On 16 September, for example, people objected to recitation from the Koran and shouted, 'Death to Gandhi', and the prayers had to be abandoned. Gandhi admitted, too, that he was receiving abusive letters from Hindus, who accused him of appeasing Muslims and helping to destroy Hindus. He realized that much of the veneration accorded to him yielded little practical work, and was saddened that many people were deceiving him, rather than being honest about their opinion of him. Privately he wrote in December,

> I know that today I irritate everyone. How can I believe that I alone am right and all others are wrong? What irks me is that people deceive me. They should tell me frankly that I have become old, that I am no longer of any use and that I should not be in their way. If they thus openly repudiate me I shall not be pained in the least.[92]

As the weeks in Delhi passed, close observers of Gandhi sensed that he was feeling isolated and lonely, even pessimistic. His smile was seldom seen, and his voice had lost its magnetic quality, though that might have been the result of a cough which plagued him in the Delhi winter and for which he refused to take antibiotics. He admitted to being so totally exhausted by the end of each day that he was lost to the world. His work seemed endless, and visitors came in a constant stream, often greatly upsetting him with their tales of their harrowing experiences in the strife. He experienced swings of mood, and often he felt he was fumbling in the dark. Yet fundamentally he seemed still to sense that despite all the evidence around him God was filling him with strength. He often spoke in the second half of 1947 of going through a fiery ordeal, yet of being sustained by God and having even deeper faith and closer communion with the divine. Under the heading, 'Apt Lines', he published a stanza a friend had sent him which reflected his inner calm.[93]

> It is by my fetters that I can fly;
> It is by my sorrows that I can soar;
> It is by my reverses that I can run;
> It is by my tears that I can travel;
> It is by my Cross that I can climb into the heart of humanity;
> Let me magnify my Cross, O God!

Although the events around him distressed him acutely, he likened them to dirt coming to the surface when the Ganges was in flood, soon to be replaced by calmer and clearer waters when the flood subsided, he hoped.[94] Hope indeed was still the hallmark of his thinking: he insisted that he had never lost hope and never would, because it was an essential ingredient of his undimmed faith in non-violence.[95]

Gandhi knew in his last days that his life was in danger. A bomb went off on 20 January at his prayer-meeting, and police guards around him were strengthened, though he refused Patel's urgent plea that the police should be allowed to search the prayer congregations. He had constantly maintained that God would protect him while his services were still required, and in place of fear he experienced a great peace. From a letter of late December it seems as if he almost longed to die – provided death came in the service of God. 'In the end it will be as Rama commands me. Thus I dance as He pulls the strings. I am in His hands and so I am experiencing ineffable peace.'[96] Late in January, talking with Birla about the extra police protection, he said he only accepted it to assuage the anxiety of Patel and Nehru, not because he himself believed it was of any use.

> Today perhaps I am the only one left who has faith in ahimsa. I pray to God that he may grant me the strength to demonstrate this ahimsa even if it be in my own person. So it is all the same to me whether there are or there are not all these police and military personnel posted here for my protection. Because it is Rama who protects me ... I become more and more convinced that everything else is futile.[97]

In the midst of danger he went quietly on with his work, a solitary figure of faith in the midst of turmoil; and in what were to be his final hours he concentrated on matters typical of his priorities and patterns of a lifetime – planning a new constitution for Congress, and attempting to mediate in a dispute between Nehru and Patel. Indeed, his last talk with Patel on 30 January was so important and prolonged that he was slightly late in going to the evening prayer-meeting. Flanked by two young relatives he walked through the crowd as usual, giving the Hindu greeting with folded hands as he went. A figure jostled through the crowd and roughly pushed Manu away – a young Hindu, deeply offended by Gandhi's work for peace and unity. When he was directly in front of Gandhi he fired three shots at point-blank range. The frail old body slumped to the ground; but his last words were, as he had wished, to call on the name of Ram, the God whose presence had sustained him and made him a prisoner of hope.

Mountbatten as Governor-General went at once to Birla House where all was confusion outside. Within there was the dazed atmosphere of shock and grief. Mountbatten at once brought Nehru and Patel to-gether, saying that in his last talk with Gandhi the Mahatma had said how deeply he wished for their reconciliation. The body lay supported by praying, weeping women, and Mountbatten's press attaché was deeply moved by the scene.

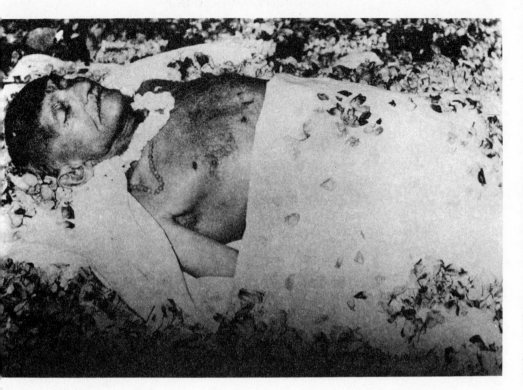

Gandhi's body, January 1948.

Gandhi's face was at peace, and looked rather pale in the bright light. Also they had taken away the steel-rimmed glasses which had become almost an integral part of his features. The smell of the incense, the sound of the women's voices, the frail little body, the sleeping face and the silent witnesses – this was perhaps the most emotionally charged moment I have ever experienced. As I stood there I felt fear for the future, bewilderment at the act, but also a sense of victory rather than defeat; that the strength of this little man's ideas and ideals, from the very force of the devotion he was commanding here and now, would prove too strong for the assassin's bullets and the ideas that they represented.[98]

Gandhi had left instructions with Pyarelal that his body should not be revered or preserved. So the next day he was cremated according to Hindu custom. Thousands flocked to pay their last devotions to this indomitable spirit and remarkable patriot; officials, the unknown, the high-born and the outcast, thronging together. It was Nehru who, in a broadcast on 30 January, put into words the overpowering emotions of the time, and spoke a fitting tribute to the man and master, with infectious smile and laughing eyes, who strove to see the real behind the unreal, and to realize truth and love in the midst of human living.

... the light has gone out of our lives and there is darkness everywhere ... The light has gone out, I said, and yet I was wrong. For the
light that shone in this country was no ordinary light ... that light
represented something more than the immediate present, it represented the living, the eternal truths, reminding us of the right path,
drawing us from error, taking this ancient country to freedom ... A
great disaster is a symbol to us to remember all the big things of life
and forget the small things of which we have thought too much. In
his death he has reminded us of the big things of life, the living truth,
and if we remember that, then it will be well with India.

EPILOGUE

When India achieved independence in August 1947 the president of Congress hailed Gandhi as the father of the Indian nation. But that was too easy an epigram on his life, and is too simple an epitaph after his death. Certainly Gandhi was and is the individual who most clearly personifies free India for Indians and foreigners alike. The frail man with his long walking-staff, his round spectacles and his spinning-wheel is the symbol of India's movement for freedom from imperialism; and the hagiography of the early historians of Indian nationalism has been confirmed vividly in the eyes of a later generation by Richard Attenborough's film of Gandhi's life which was widely shown in the 1980s. Yet India's nationalist movement existed before Gandhi and would have attained its goal without him. For far deeper economic and political forces than the leadership of one man were at work loosening the links between Britain and India – forces that had their origins in India, in Britain, and in the wider world economy and balance of power. Yet his skills and his particular genius marked the nationalist movement and gave it a character unlike that of any other anti-imperial nationalism of the century.

Gandhi was an ingenious and sensitive artist in symbols. In his own person as a self-denying holy man, by his speeches full of pictorial images and references to the great Hindu myths, by his emphasis on the *charkha* and on the wearing of *khadi* as a uniform to obliterate distinctions of region and caste, he portrayed and publicized in a world with few mass communications and low literacy, an ideal of an Indian nation which was accessible even to the poor and unpoliticized. For many, at least for a time, the ideal of the nation and a sense of national identity were lifted out of the rough and often sordid world of politics, although the inevitable struggles and intrigues accompanying any shifts of power in a complex polity jostled uneasily with the vision of nationhood and often threatened to engulf it. A new nation had to be fashioned out of the numerous loyalties and contests for dominance which were the stuff of Indian politics. Gandhi knew this full well as he agonized over political strategies, as he attempted to minimize conflict among Indians and generate a moral community which encompassed and purified old loyalties. His long march to Dandi to make salt in 1930, his fasts in Poona in 1932 and in Delhi in 1948 were not personal idiosyncracies but a careful understanding and weighing of some of the realities of Indian society and politics that militated against nationhood. Those who clustered round him and formed the central Congress leadership realized that in the Mahatma they had a living symbol and a man of considerable political creativity, whose background and beliefs particularly suited him for this role of popularizing a new Indian identity, whereas the early Congress leaders, inhibited by their back- grounds and ideals, had failed to create more than a minority political movement in the name of the nation.

Many ideological and political struggles are watered with the blood of martyrs. Under Gandhi's presiding genius India's campaign for political identity and freedom was sealed with common experiences of conscious and conscientious law-breaking, of feeling the blows of police *lathis*, and of going to gaol. Where once such experiences would have been considered demeaning and insulting, Gandhi helped to turn them into badges of high moral and emotional commitment. British imperial administrators had long emphasized the importance of *izzat*, of the prestige of place and power in their imperial regime; now Gandhi turned *izzat* on its head, making ignominy and pain the hallmarks of a new and greater esteem according to the logic of nationalism. Where once so many Indians had felt alienated from their roots, living in a no man's land between their own and Western civilization, Gandhi helped to rekindle a proper pride and a new courage deeply embedded in Indian culture. Yet this powerful manipulation of symbol in the national cause had its grave drawbacks: chief among them was the growing disquiet of many Muslims at the Hindu tenor of Congress politics as it broadened its appeal; as Gandhi, a Hindu Mahatma, became its leader, preaching in revivalist tones the coming of a new kingdom of God on earth when swaraj was attained. Increasingly for Muslims such a vision meant the coming of Ram rather than Allah, and in concrete terms the dominance of Ram's devotees, the Hindu majority.

Gandhi's other great contribution to India's national movement was his technique of non-violent protest. It was such a contrast to the politics of petitioning or the terrorist tactics that had preceded it that it was little wonder that the rulers were perplexed by it, Indians were sceptical of it, and later observers have seen it as the Gandhian hallmark. Yet, as this book has endeavoured to show, when the myth and exaggerations are stripped away, it becomes clear that non-violent forms of opposition to the British raj rarely achieved major or immediate political concessions; and satyagraha on a national scale certainly did not evict the British from the sub-continent. Satyagraha worked, in the ordinary political sense of procuring a remedy for a complaint or making a substantial moral demonstration (rather than in the peculiar Gandhian sense of inevitably purifying its true adherents and their opponents), when it was deployed on a limited and clearly demarcated issue, by a small number of highly committed and disciplined adherents, against an opponent who was particularly vulnerable, either to pressure from a higher authority which had different priorities (as in Champaran in 1917) or to public opinion at home and abroad.

However, the British raj was in the long term a vulnerable superstructure raised over a complex and ancient society over which it had little control. As its civil servants and military officers alike realized, it remained stable and functioning as long as it retained the formal or informal collaboration of certain key groups of Indians, and the acquiescence of the vast majority. Dislodging the imperial power was in large part a battle for the mind, both of Indians and the British rulers and electorate, and their foreign allies. In this, satyagraha and Gandhi's preaching of its meaning proved highly significant because it encouraged Indians to shed their ingrained fear and acceptance of the raj, and to realize their own strength. It also alienated from the imperial regime many moderate men and those who were educated yet did not play an active political role, not least because of the treatment its exponents suffered at the hands of the raj, and it cast the British in the role of moral villain in the eyes of her essential allies across the Atlantic. Increasingly the British realized that smashing such a movement on a large scale would be too costly in moral and material terms for what it could achieve. In the economic and political world order from the 1930s, and increasingly after the second world war, a contented ally and trading partner within the Commonwealth was a much better proposition than a restless dependency, held down by unconvinced soldiers and civil servants, which was anyway far less significant in terms of jobs, investment, trade and strategic protection of British world interests than it had been in the later nineteenth century when the raj was at its most secure and most profitable to its British rulers.

Non-co-operation also played a politically significant educative and incorporative role in the development of Indian nationalism. It could be adapted to suit the immediate and local needs of a wide range of people, in stark contrast to the politics of the early Congress which were accessible only to the highly educated and the English-speaking. Gandhi's campaigns offered modes of opposition to the old and young, to men and women, to the educated as well as the poor and illiterate. Children could sing patriotic songs in procession, students could leave their desks and take part in demonstrations, women could picket liquor and foreign cloth shops and visualize themselves as latter-day Sitas, peasants could cut grass and graze their cattle in prohibited places, owner-cultivators could withhold their land revenue, townsmen could enjoy a good bonfire of foreign cloth, while professional people could ostentatiously boycott the legislatures and the courts. Yet this very inclusiveness, incorporating different and often pre-existing struggles into one national movement and reinterpreting them as facets of nationalism, had its dangers. Mass movements very easily slipped from central control and an apparently national campaign could rapidly disintegrate into its disparate and often conflicting parts, and into violence which was the negation of everything for which Gandhi claimed to stand.

In the end after many attempts to organize, lead and control a broadly based campaign, Gandhi recognized that he had failed to find the right formula; he ended his life trying to exert non-violence as a lone individual who could at least control his own actions and try to purify his own intentions. Furthermore, Gandhi never converted more than a handful into true believers in *ahimsa*. For the vast majority of politicial activists, even among his closest and most influential political colleagues, non-violence was a desirable and often very useful political strategy in a specific situation rather than a total moral commitment as it was for him. Consequently satyagraha could easily degenerate into violence among some on the radical wing of Congress, as in 1942, or shade off into constitutional co-operation among other Congressmen who always intended eventually to use the established political structures and saw in non-co-operation a way of extending those structures and generating a political following which would ultimately elect them to positions of power.

The experience of participating in non-co-operation undoubtedly also helped to bond several generations of Indians, to recruit, train and incorporate many who might have become angry and uncontrollable young men, and to unite Indians across regional and language boundaries in one national movement. Furthermore, Gandhi's passion for order and organization, his vision of a disciplined body of national servants and his eye for minute detail also played a part in binding together a national Congress. It was not for nothing that Gandhi was a *bania* by caste; he sometimes laughingly used and played on this image of the careful businessman, keeping his books, watching his finances and minding his stock. The zeal that prompted him to send G.D. Birla meticulous accounts of the way he spent all his benefactor's munificent donations took another form in his repeated attempts to reform the Congress organization into a body able to receive and act on national commands, which spanned every province and reached down to every village. His ideal of a fully functional popular body never materialized, nor did his vision of a dedicated body of public servants. But in considerable part because of his emphasis on effective organization, shared by Nehru and Patel, the Congress particularly from the 1930s onwards became a far more streamlined and broadly based party than the ramshackle affair he had attended on his return from South Africa. In the long term the range and experience of the Congress as an organization for protest stood it in good stead when it became the party of government: it was one of the institutions that helped to keep the Indian union intact in the first difficult years after independence and partition. In contrast, the fact that the Muslim League had so comparatively little time to organize its supporters, to become a natural arena for Muslim politics, and to put down real roots in the social soil of the areas which became Pakistan, accounts in part for the instability of democracy in Pakistan and the ultimate disintegration of Jinnah's Pakistan with the creation of Bangladesh.

Yet it would be wrong to see Gandhi, for all his skills of organization, publicity and strategy, as the great driving force of Indian nationalism. He was used by India's politicians, followed for his skills and potential, and at times tactfully ignored by them when his priorities and practices seemed unproductive or divisive. He recognized this with a cheerful realism, and was content to be put on the shelf in ordinary political terms, provided that he was permitted to get on with what he perceived as his life's work – the construction of a new Indian polity and society infused with non-violence and godliness – by other means. Ironically it was precisely because he was not a career politician that he had such a long career in politics, survived what to others would have been political retirement or even suicide, and was able to come back again and again to play a formidable political role when events made him a valuable resource to a significant number of his compatriots. He did indeed have a charismatic effect on individuals and on vast crowds; but it was utility rather than charisma or mass conversion to his ideals which gave him at times such influence in national politics. Once this is understood it becomes clear why his influence in independent India was so limited. He himself sensed this would be so in the closing months of his life: that there would be no place for his ideals of self-denial and service when power was within the politicians' grasp, that there would be no scope for his modes of action once Congress was the government rather than opposing the established regime.

Most Indian towns indeed have their statues of Gandhi, there are many roads named after him, and many institutions trade under his name. Yet on the issues that deeply concerned him there is little evidence that Gandhi is the father of contemporary India. During his life he confronted many of the real problems of India in a basic and forthright way which contrasted strongly with the intellectual nationalism of so many of his generation of politicians and even earlier Congressmen. In the pages of this book we have seen him dealing not only with 'high politics' but with the varied concerns of ordinary people – health, food, agriculture, education, caste, marriage customs, women's role (even their jewellery), public cleanliness, the meaning of religion and the best way to pray, to name but a few. Indeed one problem has been to know where to draw the line. For example, much could have been written about his attitude to cows, as part of his relationship with Hindu tradition as well as his concern for good farming practices and humane animal husbandry. Or there could have been more consideration of his attitude to contraception and his response to foreign women who advocated its virtues for India. His handling of the problem of a national language was also significant both in his nationalism and in the way it elicited increasing hostility from some, most obviously Indian Muslims.

Yet in contemporary India so much that he strove to change in order to achieve real swaraj has remained or indeed has developed in directions alien to Gandhi's thinking. Although he accepted that a Western style of democratic state was probably necessary in India, at least in the short term, his ideal was the diffusion of power down to local level so that village communities could organize their own affairs as far as possible. In modern India the state has increased massively in power since the days of imperial rule. The British raj was a light-handed, amateur affair compared to the Indian state of the later twentieth century, with its greatly increased numbers of employees and functionaries, its bigger revenues, higher expenditure on the army and the police, its economic planning and control of the economy through directives and a pervasive system of licences. It is also far more intrusive into personal life with its policies for development, education, welfare, and family planning. Even the new structures of village-based local government bear no resemblance to Gandhi's ideals, but are the instruments of government control and often the arenas for local factional struggles and the exercise of power rather than service of the community.

Gandhi's economic ideals have similarly been shelved. Whereas he had envisaged a very small role for modern-style industry and a dominant place in the economy for small-scale, rural industry complementing agriculture, India has become one of the world's most highly industrialized nations, its range of products and its development of a consumer-orientated economy a far cry from the austere economy of sufficiency advocated by Gandhi. Handicrafts are an aspect of tourism and interior decor rather than a local supplying of basic needs of clothing, and domestic and agricultural equipment; those village-based industries that have developed have tended to eliminate jobs and line the pockets of those who have the capital to invest in plant and machinery, whereas he had advocated them as a means of alleviating rural unemployment and giving the poorest an additional source of income to ensure their dignity of life. India is still a land of villages and villagers – only about 20% of Indians live in towns. Yet percentages belie numbers. Because the population has risen so steeply in the last half of the century, as a result of greatly improved health and nutrition, and a falling death-rate, millions more Indians now actually experience what Gandhi felt were the degrading and de-Indianizing influences of urban life than ever did in his day.

In social relations, too, there are few signs of change as a direct reflection of Gandhi's work. Certainly his growing hostility to caste as he found it in India and his abhorrence of untouchability were significant in moulding the Congress mind; and when an independent government, freed from the inhibitions of an alien, imperial regime, took power it rapidly and robustly legislated against the public observance of untouchability and proclaimed the equality of all citizens, regardless of caste. But as Gandhi knew full well, laws need public support, and he was realistic in his assertion that the critical change needed was one of attitudes. Many of India's apparently radical legislative reforms of social customs have been honoured in the breach rather than in observance. Untouchability, for example, persists with its degradation; it rests on unchanged attitudes and the harsh facts of economic life which prevent most untouchables from gaining access to essential credit, to new employment and to new wealth. As change does slowly occur in caste perceptions and relationships it is the result of new values inculcated through mass education, which in form and content reflects Western values and practices in a way which would have horrified Gandhi who had formulated such distinctive and Indian plans for Basic Education.

Much the same could be said of the role of women. The phenomenon of a woman Prime Minister in the 1970s is no indication of the role of most Indian women. Their place in public and private is still constrained by traditional attitudes and values, by the custom of arranged marriages, and by women's economic dependence on men. Indeed modern feminists accuse Gandhi of confirming women's dependent position by his use of traditional Hindu models of femininity, by his appeals to women to play a public and private role distinct from men and not in competition with them, and by his rejection of modern forms of birth control. Further, his reliance on women devotees also confirmed the subservience of women in the context of nationalist politics. Such criticism from the perspective of the late twentieth century is misplaced. Gandhi was a man of his own time, indeed a Victorian by birth, and many of his ideas about women were genuinely reformist if not radical in that context. Arguing on similar lines many would now question whether Gandhi was radical in his vision of Indian society and his work for change, though he claimed to be more radical than the young socialists who chafed at his leadership. His advocacy of gradual reform, of including different economic groups in one national movement and his opposition to class conflict confirmed Congress in a basic social conservatism which still persists, indeed has grown, despite Nehru's socialism and the state's commitment to a socialist pattern of society, not least because of Congress's reliance on the votes of a substantial peasantry who have prospered as prices of agricultural crops have risen, and who would not countenance radical change in the countryside. It would be possible to go on demonstrating the facets of modern Indian life that would have distressed Gandhi. Not the least would be the tragic evidence of continuing violence in public life, often stemming from persisting communal loyalties and hostilities, Muslim set against Hindu, Sikh in conflict with Hindu, as a plural society searches for appropriate political forms to contain its tensions and channel its ambitions.

This bleak assessment of contemporary India in the light of Gandhi's vision of true swaraj as distinct from mere Indian assumption of political power in an unreformed polity suggests how strong and pervasive were many of the social and political forces that constrained Gandhi in his life. In recognizing them one is more able to perceive the true stature of the man and to see the depth of his struggle to create a new order free from what he saw as the evil effects of imperialism and tradition alike. It is in his struggles with himself and his society that some of his most powerful and lasting contributions to this century lie. He was not a trained philosopher or interested in producing a coherent body of thought. Rather, he was inspired by a powerful religious vision which prompted him to grow through experience, to be courageous enough to be pragmatic, and to refine his views in the light of reality. Consequently his lines of thought are sometimes hard follow, and the British thought him a slippery customer. But in his strivings, his set-backs and even his self-contradictions he faced crucial human questions which find resonances in almost any time and place. It is because of his confrontations with fundamental religious, philosophical and moral questions in the context of an active public lilfe that he still exercises such a fascination, can still inspire hostility as well as hope.

In Gandhi's eyes men and women were human in virtue of their capacity for religious vision. It was this which distinguished them from the rest of creation; if this was stifled by the individual or by political and economic structures then people were degraded and dehumanized. This was as strong and striking an attack on secular materialism as could be made. Yet he was equally pungent in his criticism of much that passed for religion in many of the world's major traditions, though inevitably his main criticisms were of his own. Observance of religious forms, belonging to organized religious bodies were of themselves, nothing to him; true religion lay in the deepest places of the heart, when and where a man strove to realize his origins and true being. It was a search for fundamental truth, for an undergirding reality which, if genuine, would overflow into love for others and a life of service. It was from this understanding of the true nature of humanity and personhood that Gandhi developed his increasingly radical conception of the equality of people across boundaries of creed, sex, race and social or economic background. Given this underlying sense of equality, Gandhi's sense of fraternity also flowered, ultimately into a passionate identification with the poor and despised. His glorification of poverty and his difficult phrases about finding God in the poor jarred on the ears of men like Nehru who thought poverty a shameful curse and rebelled at the idea of giving it any aroma of sanctity rather than working to obliterate it; just as Gandhi's sentiments still alienate those who feel that such an attitude only serves to reinforce the status quo and to generate charity rather than equality.

As an avowed and genuine religious seeker and visionary who felt compelled by his vision to participate in a wide range of public activity rather than retire to a contemplative seclusion, Gandhi not only rejected religious quietism and a purely private piety. He also confronted the problem of means and ends, from which none can escape, particularly those who handle public power and influence the minds and destinies of many. Gandhi's response to this age-old dilemma was first a strong affirmation that there could be no distinction between public and private life; that public life did not permit a different and more utilitarian moral stance. In his own mind there was then only one unfailing solution to the problem – to adopt a means which was in a sense itself the end, which would generate the qualities that would effectively transform any situation. Non-violent striving after truth, satyagraha, was just such a means. It recognized that no person or group had a total grasp of truth, and ensured that in conflict none was coerced beyond the dictates of conscience. (In practice, of course, 'non-violence' could be very different from Gandhi's ideal, and even his fasts exerted a moral pressure for which non-violence was a dubious description.) What he discovered to his cost – but not at the expense of continuing hope and action – was that all men of vision find that life is full of unavoidable contradictions, constraints and compromises. There is rarely a choice between absolute good and evil, clear truth and falsehood, but generally between lesser and greater evil, a further or nearer approximation to a vision of truth.

As Gandhi explored the implications of human equality and farternity he also pondered on the nature of community and the meaning of family, kinship and wider forms of society, including ashrams, villages and nations. His hope was for organic communities bound by common ties of vision and service rather than physical attraction, blood or, at a higher lever, state compulsion or religious exclusiveness and dogmatism. This led him to cut his own physical ties of marriage, to expose his family and close relatives to hardship and experimentation. Kasturbhai, their sons, and at the end Manu were all in different ways the objects, even the victims, of his experiments in true community; it was because of his treatment of them that he felt able to 'mother' a broad spectrum of people, that he was liberated to be the friend and advisor of so many.

Contemporary and later observers criticized Gandhi's asceticism, his attitude to sexuality, his negation of the body as harsh and joyless, and have traced its roots to deep tensions within his own personality. There is considerable truth in this. His was not a personality at peace with itself. Often he was tormented with self-questioning, anger and frustration; yet it is only out of tension, stress and conflict that lasting resolutions of fundamental problems are born. Further, against the harshness and self-distrust, against the demands he made on others and himself, must be set the evidence of humour and tenderness which did so much to attract men and women to him, the personal concern for the individual which made so many feel at his death a personal bereavement and the extinguishing of a guiding light. Gandhi's experiments with simple, communal living and with health for villagers which did not rely on expensive drugs, even led him to consideration of mankind's relations with the environment, human obligations towards animals, and use of air, water and soil. Unlike most politicians of his day, his breadth of concern again led him to ask fundamental questions about life. They make him sound distinctly modern as his ideals of simplicity and smallness of scale echo the fears of people in the later part of the century who have glimpsed some of the darker aspects and unsuspected repercussions of industrialization, the driving force of the Western civilization he so condemned.

Gandhi was no plaster saint. Nor did he find lasting and real solutions to many of the problems he encountered. Possibly he did not even see the implications of some of them. He was a man of his time and place, with a particular philosophical and religious background, facing a specific political and social situation. He was also deeply human, capable of heights and depths of sensation and vision, of great enlightenment and dire doubt, and the roots of his attitudes and actions were deep and tangled, as are most people's. He made good and bad choices. He hurt some, yet consoled and sustained many. He was caught in compromises inevitable in public life. But fundamentally he was a man of vision and action, who asked many of the profoundest questions that face human-kind as it struggles to live in community. It was this confrontaton out of a real humanity which marks his true stature and which makes his struggles and glimpses of truth of enduring significance. As a man of his time who asked the deepest questions, even though he could not answer them, he became a man for all times and all places.

NOTES

CHAPTER 1

1 Gandhi subtitled his autobiography, 'The Story of My Experiments with Truth'. He wrote it in 1927 in the form of a series of newspaper articles as a teaching medium for those who wished to understand his life and work. It was subsequently republished in book form in India and abroad many times.

2 For example, in 1939 when he was charged with inconsistency he wrote in his newspaper, *Harijan*, of 30. September: 'At the time of writing I never think of what I have said before. My aim is not to be consistent with my previous statements on a given question, but to be consistent with truth as it may present itself to me at a given moment. The result has been that I have grown from truth to truth ...' (*The Collected Works of Mahatma Gandhi*, vol. 70, p. 203). These volumes, published in Delhi by the Government of India between 1958 and 1984, are the main published source for this study. Henceforward they are referred to as *CWMG*.

3 An excellent account of the life of an ordinary Briton who went into the Indian Civil Service in the early twentieth century is W. Saumarez Smith, *A Young Man's Country* (Michael Russell, Salisbury, 1977). More detailed introductions to India at the turn of the century can be found in Judith M. Brown, *Modern India. The Origins of an Asian Democracy* (OUP, Oxford, 1985); and B.S. Cohn, *India: The Social Anthropology of a Civilization* (Prentice Hall, Englewood Cliffs, New Jersey, 1971). Two valuable Indian accounts of growing up at this time are P. Tandon, *Punjabi Century* (Chatto & Windus, London, 1963); and N.C. Chaudhuri, *The Autobiography of an Unknown Indian* (Macmillan, London, 1951).

4 The best account of the early Congress is J.R. McLane, *Indian Nationalism And The Early Congress* (Princeton University Press, Princeton, 1977).

5 See an excellent description of a traditional trading and financial centre which became 'the Manchester of India'; K.L. Gillion, *Ahmedabad. A Study in Indian Urban History* (UCLA Press, Berkeley and Los Angeles, 1968).

6 Understanding the cluster of traditions which make up the Hindu inheritance is still difficult for outsiders who assume that a religion must have a credal core like the world's great monotheisms, and are perplexed by the range of deities within the Hindu pantheon and their depiction in art and image. Particularly helpful in overcoming these barriers to understanding are B.S. Cohn, *op.cit.*; K.M. Sen, *Hinduism* (Penguin Books, Harmondsworth, 1961); L.A. Babb, *The Divine Hierarchy: Popular Hinduism in Central India* (Columbia University Press, New York and London, 1975);

D.L. Eck, *Darsan. Seeing the Divine Image in India* (Anima Books, Chambersberg PA, 1981)

7 See C.H. Heimsath, *Indian Nationalism and Hindu Social Reform* (Princeton University Press, Princeton, 1964).

8 For Gandhi's childhood see his *Autobiography*, Part I (the edition referred to here is Jonathan Cape, London, 1966.

9 *Ibid.*, p. 27.

10 *Ibid.*, p. 29.

11 The missionary influence Gandhi encountered was Irish Presbyterian. For the turbulence which resulted in Rajkot see S. Hay, 'Between Two Worlds: Gandhi's First Impressions of British Culture', *Modern Asian Studies*, III, 4 (1969), pp. 308–10. The best account of Gandhi's religious background and development is M. Chatterjee, *Gandhi's Religious Thought* (Macmillan, London, 1983).

12 A most illuminating account of the Indian experience of childhood within the Hindu extended family is S.Kakar, *The Inner World. A Psycho-analytic Study of Childhood and Society in India* (OUP, Delhi, 1978).

13 Gandhi, *An Autobiography*, p. 10.

14 For, example, E. Victor Wolfenstein, *The Revolutionary Personality. Lenin, Trosky, Gandhi* (Princeton University Press, Princeton, 1967).

15 See Kakar, *The Inner World*, particularly chs. III and IV.

16 Gandhi, *An Autobiography*, p. 26.

17 *Ibid.*, p. 32.

18 S. Sinha's memory of Gandhi in February 1890, quoted in B. R. Nanda, *Mahatma Gandhi. A Biography* (Beacon Press, Boston, 1958), p. 28.

19 Gandhi, *An Autobiography*, p. 41.

20 *Ibid.*, p. 57.

CHAPTER 2

1 M.K. Gandhi, *Satyagraha in South Africa* (Navajivan, Ahmedabad, 1961 impression), p. 338. (This account was first published in 1928. It and the relevant sections in Gandhi's *Autobiography* are his own account of his South African experience.)

2 Gandhi, *An Autobiography*, p. 109.

3 *Ibid*, pp. 93–8.

4 For the background to the Indian community in South Africa and a detailed account of its constitutional position and struggle for rights, see

R.A. Huttenback, *Gandhi in South Africa. British Imperialism and the Indian Question, 1860–1914* (Cornell University Press, Ithaca & London, 1971); R.A. Huttenback, 'Indians in South Africa, 1860–1914; the British Imperial Philosophy on Trial', *English Historical Review* (EHR) vol. LXXXI April 1966, pp. 273–91.

As these titles suggest Huttenback writes from the viewpoint of investigating imperial policy and philosophy; his works are not an account of Gandhi's experiences in South Africa, although they are invaluable in placing Gandhi's personal work in its local and imperial setting. In contrast M. Swan starts her study in the nature of the Indian community in South Africa, its divisions and its organized politics; *Gandhi. The South African Experience* (Ravan Press, Johannesburg, 1985).

5 *Natal Mercury*, 24 January 1895, quoted in Huttenback, *Gandhi in South Africa*, p. 40.

6 Johannesburg *Star*, 1 March 1899, quoted in *ibid.*, p. 117.

7 Gandhi, *An Autobiography*, p. 109.

8 Hardinge to Sir George Clarke, 16/19 April 1912, University Library (UL), Cambridge, Hardinge Mss., 1912, Letters & Telegrams, India, vol. III, 83.

9 Hardinge to Crewe, 23 July 1913, UL, Cambridge, Hardinge Mss., 1913, Letters, Secretary of State, vol. III, 119.

10 Gandhi to Dadabhai Naoroji, 5 July 1894, *CWMG*, vol. 1, p. 106.

11 M. Chatterjee calls Gandhi's turning away from selfishness and self-righteousness to service, his sense of expansion, one of his 'most seminal contributions to the understanding of spiritual growth'. Chatterjee, *Gandhi's Religious Thought*, (Macmillan, London, 1983) p. 48.

12 For example, 'An Appeal to every Briton in South Africa', 16 December 1895, *CWMG*, vol. 1, p. 283; 'The Grievances of the British Indians in South Africa. An Appeal to the Indian Public', 14 August 1896, *CWMG*, vol. 2, p. 17; Petition to the Governor of the Transvaal, 8 June 1903, *CWMG*, vol. 3, pp. 330–1.

13 Gandhi to the editor, *Natal Mercury*, 13 April 1897, published on 16 April 1897, *CWMG*, vol. 2. p. 305. See also

press interview published in *Natal Advertiser*, 14 January 1897, *ibid.*, p. 163.

14 For Gandhi's ashram or community, see Chapter 4.

15 In Hindu thought men and women pass through phases of life, each of which has its *dharma* or duty attached to it. The child gives place to the student, who then becomes a householder, until in old age he or she increasingly withdraws from worldly obligations and concerns, even to the extent of becoming a religious recluse. This ideal is sometimes still enacted in the late twentieth century.

16 Gandhi, *An Autobiography*, p. 112.

17 *Ibid.*, p. 155.

18 *Ibid.*, p. 185.

19 *Ibid.*, p. 232.

20 *Ibid.*, p. 172.

21 *Ibid.*, p. 233.

22 *Ibid.*, pp. 167–8; Gandhi to Maganlal Gandhi, 18 May 1911, Gandhi to Harilal Gandhi, 14 March 1913, *CWMG*, vol. 11, pp. 77–8, 484–5.

23 Gandhi, *An Autobiography*, p. 222.

24 Gandhi to H. Polak, 2 September 1909, Gandhi Papers, Sabarmati Collection, no. 5042. See also his letters of instruction to Chhaganlal Gandhi, 19 April and 6 May 1905, Gandhi Papers, Sabarmati Collection, nos. 4233 and 4236. [Papers from this collection are now noted as SN no.]

25 Accounts of these two settlements are in Gandhi, *An Autobiography*, pp. 250ff., 276ff., and Gandhi, *Satyagraha in South Africa*, pp. 232ff. The ideals behind Phoenix and Tolstoy Farm are explored in the following chapter.

26 Article on the 1858 Royal Proclamation, *Indian Opinion*, 9 July 1903, *CWMG*, vol. 3, pp. 357–8.

27 Gandhi to Parsi Rustomji, 1 March 1902, *ibid.*, p. 227. See also the record of the founding of the NIC, 22 August 1894, *CWMG*, vol. 1, pp. 130–5; 1st Report of NIC, August 1895, *ibid.*, pp. 231–9; 2nd Report of NIC, late 1899, *CWMG*, vol. 3, pp. 96–110; chapter on NIC, Gandhi, *An Autobiography*, pp. 123ff. Further evidence on the range of NIC activities is in Gandhi's correspondence, Sabarmati Collection.

28 Gandhi, *Satyagraha in South Africa*, p. 47.

29 *Indian Opinion*, 26 August 1905, *CWMG*, vol. 5, p. 50.

30 Gandhi to A. Ali, 6 September 1909, SN no. 5055; Gandhi to Maganlal Gandhi, 29 January 1909, SN no 4918.

31 Gandhi to P. S. to Secretary of State for India, 18 September 1909. SN no. 5083; Gandhi to H. Polak, 16 September 1909, SN no. 5104a.

32 *Hind Swaraj*, *CWMG*, vol. 10. p. 29.

33 *Indian Opinion*, 4 June 1903, *CWMG*, vol. 3, p. 313.

34 Gandhi, *An Autobiography*, p. 119. The petitions referred to are in *CWMG*, vol. 1.

35 Lord Ampthill to L.W. Ritch (Secretary of the Committee), 28 July 1909, SN no. 4964; Lord Ampthill to Gandhi, 29 July 1909, SN no 4967; Gandhi to H. Polak, 30 July 1909, SN no. 4970. Evidence of the establishment of the Committee is in the same collection.

36 Gandhi to Viceroy, 30 November 1896, re-the compulsory movement of Indians into locations in the Transvaal, *CWMG*, vol. 2, p. 137.

37 *CWMG*, vol. 2, pp. 350–6; vol. 3, pp. 183–6.

38 These are all available in *CWMG*, vol. 1.

39 *CWMG*, vol. 2, pp. 1–51.

40 *CWMG*, vol. 3, pp. 213–15.

41 Gandhi to Lord Ampthill, 4 August 1909, *CWMG*, vol. 9, p. 329. Polak's full letters to Gandhi from India during August–October 1909 are in the Sabarmati Collection.

42 *Indian Opinion*, 4 June 1903, *CWMG*, vol. 3, p. 313. The journal's maximum number of subscribers was c.3,500.

43 Gandhi to G.A.Natesan, 9 December 1910, *CMWG*, vol. 10, pp. 379–81; *Indian Opinion*, 17 December 1910, *ibid.*, p. 385.

44 Gandhi, *Satyagraha in South Africa*, p. 129.

45 Gandhi's accounts in 1896 of his expenditure of the £75 entrusted to him, *CWMG*, vol. 2, pp. 139–53; Gandhi, *Satyagraha in South Africa*, pp. 122–3.

46 Gandhi, *Satyagraha in South Africa*, p. 102.

47 *Ibid.*, p. 114; Gandhi to Editor, 1 July 1907, *Rand Daily Mail*, 2 July 1907, *CWMG*, vol. 7, p. 67.

48 *Indian Opinion*, 8 September 1906, *CWMG*, vol. 5, p. 414.

49 Parsi Rustomji to Gandhi, 5 March 1921, SN no. 7497.

50 Gandhi, *An Autobiography*, p. 128.
51 *Indian Opinion*, 20 May 1905, *CWMG*, vol. 4, p. 430.
52 Gandhi to C. Gandhi, 21 April 1907, *CWMG*, vol. 6, p. 435.
53 Gandhi on his gaol experiences, *Indian Opinion*, 30 January 1909 *CWMG*, vol. 9, p. 181; speech by Gandhi, 15 July 1914, *Indian Opinion*, 5 August 1914, *CWMG*, vol. 12, p. 495.
54 Gandhi, *Satyagraha in South Africa*, pp. 276–85.
55 Gandhi, *An Autobiography*, p. 235.
56 One of the best accounts of the life of C.F. Andrews, one-time missionary and Anglican priest, who became an admirer and close colleague of Gandhi is H. Tinker, *The Ordeal of Love. C.F. Andrews and India* (OUP, Delhi, 1979. Andrews and Gandhi first met in South Africa, when Andrews went there as Gokhale's representative at the climax of the Indian campaign.
57 Gandhi's articles on his gaol life are in *CWMG*, vols. 8 and 9.
58 *Indian Opinion*, 9 January 1909, *CWMG*, vol. 9, p. 131. See also *ibid.*, pp. 120, 147; *CWMG*, vol. 8, p. 119.
59 *Indian Opinion*, 5 June 1909, *CWMG*, vol. 9, p. 240. See also *ibid.*, p. 182; *CWMG*, vol. 8, p. 119.
60 On Gandhi's gaol reading see *ibid.*, p. 159, *CWMG*, vol. 9, pp. 181–2, 241–2.
61 See, for example, *CWMG*, vol. 1, pp. 162–3; vol. 5, pp. 45, 116–18; vol. 7, pp. 6–7; vol. 8, pp. 246, 273.
62 *CWMG*, vol. 1, p. 285, Gandhi, *An Autobiography*, pp. 142–3.
63 *Indian Opinion*, 31 March 1906, *CWMG*, vol. 5, p. 250. See also *CWMG*, vol. 2, pp. 47, 365; vol. 3, p. 334.
64 *Indian Opinion*, 21 January 1905, *CWMG*, vol. 4, p. 113.
65 Gandhi to the Colonial Secretary, 19 October 1899, *CWMG*, vol. 3, pp. 113–14. For Gandhi's reasoning see *An Autobiography*, pp. 129, 261; *Satyagraha in South Africa*, pp. 71–3.
66 *Indian Opinion*, 27 August 1903, *CWMG*, vol. 3, p. 426.
67 *Indian Opinion*, 3 December 1910, *CWMG*, vol. 10, p. 376; Gandhi to High Commissioner, 3 December 1907, *CWMG*, vol. 7, p. 409; *Indian Opinion*, 20 August 1904, *CWMG*, vol. 4, pp. 240–1.
68 *Indian Opinion*, 2 October 1909, *CWMG*, vol. 9, pp. 388–9; Gandhi to

Polak, 14 October 1909, *ibid.*, pp. 478–81.
69 *Indian Opinion*, 2 April 1910, *CWMG*, vol. 10, p. 189. The text of *Hind Swaraj* is in *ibid.*, pp. 6–68.
70 *Ibid.*, p. 15.
71 *Indian Opinion*, 24 June 1911, *CWMG*, vol. 11, pp. 111–114.
72 Gandhi, *An Autobiography*, p. 148.
73 *Ibid.*, pp. 187–91.
74 Gandhi to G.A. Natesan, probably late October 1909, *Indian Opinion*, 27 November 1909, *CWMG*, vol. 9, pp. 506–7; Gandhi to Polak, 6 October 1909, *ibid.*, pp. 463–4.
75 Gandhi to Dr P. Mehta, 22 October 1911, *CWMG*, vol. 11, p. 169.
76 Gandhi to Gokhale, 30 October 1911, Gandhi to Dr P. Mehta, 11 and 17 November 1911, *ibid.*, pp. 176–8, 183, 185.
77 *Indian Opinion*, 1 August 1908, *CWMG*, vol. 8, pp. 418–9.
78 Gandhi to Dr P. Mehta, 8 May 1911, *CWMG*, vol. 11, pp. 64–5.
79 *Young India*, 13 July 1921, *CWMG*, vol. 20, p. 371.
80 Crewe to Hardinge, 6 December 1912, UL, Cambridge, Hardinge Mss., 1912, Letters, Secretary of State, vol. II, 118.
81 Gandhi to Maganlal Gandhi, 27 January 1910, *CWMG*, vol. 10, p. 139.
82 Gandhi to Gokhale, 27 February 1914, *CWMG*, vol. 12, pp. 360–1; Gandhi to Gokhale, 30 October 1911, *CWMG*, vol. 11, p. 178.
83 Fragment of letter from Gandhi to unknown recipient, 22 April 1914, *CWMG*, vol. 12, pp. 410–411; C.F. Andrews to Gandhi, 5 April 1914, SN no. 5956; Polak to Gandhi, 19 October 1909, SN no. 5138.
84 Natesan's speech at Allahabad Congress, 1910, SN no. 5201; Polak to Gandhi, 7 October 1909, SN no. 5116.
85 Crewe to Hardinge, 26 March 1914, UL, Cambridge, Hardinge Mss., 1914, Letters, Secretary of State, vol. IV, 120. The Hardinge papers for 1913–14 are an invaluable source for government attitudes to Gandhi at this time.
86 Gandhi to Dr P. Mehta, early July 1911, 24 September 1911, 10 October, 1911, *CWMG*, vol. 11, pp. 117, 161, 166; Gandhi to Gokhale, 30 October 1911, *ibid.*, p. 178.
87 Gandhi to Maganlal Gandhi, late

September 1913, *CWMG*, vol. 12, pp. 209–10; speech in Durban, 9 July 1914, *Indian Opinion*, 15 July 1914, *ibid.*, p. 455; Gandhi to P. Desai, 15 November 1914, *ibid.*, p. 554.

CHAPTER 3

1 Smuts to Sir Benjamin Robertson, 21 August 1914, quoted in W.K. Hancock, *Smuts. The Sanguine Years 1870–1919* (CUP, Cambridge, 1962), p. 345.
2 Gandhi, *An Autobiography*, pp. 109, 132.
3 *Indian Opinion*, 15 June 1907, *CWMG*, vol. 7, p. 44.
4 Gandhi, *An Autobiography*, p. 114.
5 *Ibid.*, pp. 73–5.
6 Questions and answers, 1894, *CWMG*, vol. 32, pp. 593–602.
7 Gandhi's reminiscences of Raychandbai, November 1926 and June 1930, *CWMG*, vol. 32, pp. 1–13, vol. 43, pp. 98–9.
8 Gandhi, *An Autobiography*, pp. 221.
9 *Ibid.*, p. 114.
10 Speech on centenary of Tolstoy's birth, 10 September 1928, *CWMG*, vol. 37, p. 262; article, 18 November 1909, *Indian Opinion*, 25 December 1909, *CWMG*, vol. 10, p. 1.
11 *Indian Opinion*, 2 September 1905, *CWMG*, vol. 5, pp. 56–7.
12 Speech on centenary of Tolstoy's birth, 10 September 1928, *CWMG*, vol. 37, pp. 265, 268.
13 Gandhi–Tolstoy correspondence, 1909–1910, *CWMG*, vol. 9, pp. 444–6, 593; vol. 10, pp. 210, 505, 306–7, 512–14. For Gandhi's publication of Tolstoy's 'Letter to a Hindu', see his English and Gujarati prefaces, dated 18 and 19 November 1909, in *Indian Opinion*, 25 December 1909, *CWMG*, vol. 10, pp. 1–5.
14 Gandhi, *An Autobiography*, pp. 249–50.
15 Gandhi's articles, entitled *Sarvodaya*, 'the welfare of all', published in *Indian Opinion*, 1908, are in *CWMG*. vol. 8.
16 This is one of the themes in M. Chatterjee, *Gandhi's Religious Thought*; for example, pp. 3–4.
17 Discourses given at ashram morning prayers, 24 February to 27 November 1926, *CWMG*, vol. 32, pp. 94–376; Gandhi on 'Gandhism' to R. Nehru, 7 June 1946, *CWMG*, vol. 84, p. 303.
18 Interview to a Negro journalist, *c.*30

May 1945, *CWMG*, vol. 80, p. 209.
19 This was how Gandhi described the central tenets of Hinduism in a speech to the Theosophical Society on 25 March 1905, reported in *Indian Opinion*, 15 April 1905, *CWMG*, vol. 4, p. 408. It seems that this reflected his own view, and he barely mentioned the variety of philosophical traditions within Hinduism or the deities of the Hindu pantheon. On salvation, the soul and God, see also Gandhi to J. Gandhi, 30 May 1913, *CWMG*, vol. 12, pp. 92–3.
20 Gandhi, *An Autobiography*, pp. 282–3.
21 *Indian Opinion*, 26 August 1905, *CWMG*, vol. 5, pp. 49–50; ch. x of *Hind Swaraj*, *CWMG*, vol. 10, p. 29.
22 Gandhi to J. Gandhi, 30 May 1913, *CWMG*, vol. 12, p. 94.
23 Speech to Theosophical Society on 25 March 1905, reported in *Indian Opinion*, 15 April 1905, *CWMG*, vol. 4, p. 408. An examination of *dharma* in Gandhi's thinking is in M. Chatterjee, *op. cit.*, pp. 17ff.
24 Gandhi to P. Kantak, 3 August 1932, *CWMG*, vol. 50, p. 326.
25 Gandhi to M. Gandhi, 11 November 1910, *CWMG*, vol. 10, p. 350.
26 Discussion in August 1936, *Harijan*, 29 August 1936, *CWMG*, vol. 63, p. 240.
27 Gandhi, *An Autobiography*, p. 145.
28 *CWMG*, vol. 10, p. 51.
29 *CWMG*, vol. 10, p. 43.
30 Gandhi, *Satyagraha in South Africa*, p. 339.
31 *CWMG*, vol. 10, pp. 50–3.
32 Gandhi, *An Autobiography*, pp. 291–2.
33 *Ibid.*, pp. 171–7, 264–6.
34 *Ibid.*, pp. 172, 264.
35 *CWM 9, p. 396.*
39 *Gandhi to Editor, 26 November 1894, Natal Mercury, 3 December 1894, Gandhi to Editor, 21 January 1895, Natal Advertiser, 1 February 1895, CWMG*, vol. 1, pp. 139–40, 165–6.
40 *Indian Opinion*, 20 August 1903, *CWMG*, vol. 3, pp. 414–15.
41 *Indian Opinion*, 18 July 1908, *CWMG*, vol. 8, p. 374.
42 Gandhi to H. Polak, 14 October 1909, *CWMG*, vol. 9, pp. 479–81.
43 9, p. 396.
39 Gandhi to Editor, 26 November 1894, *Natal Mercury*, 3 December 1894, Gandhi to Editor, 21 January 1895, *Natal Advertiser*, 1 February 1895,

CWMG, vol. 1, pp. 139–40, 165–6.

40 *Indian Opinion*, 20 August 1903, *CWMG*, vol. 3, pp. 414–15.

41 *Indian Opinion*, 18 July 1908, *CWMG*, vol. 8, p. 374.

42 Gandhi to H. Polak, 14 October 1909, *CWMG*, vol. 9, pp. 479–81.

43 *CWMG*, vol. 10, p. 36.

44 *Ibid.*, p. 37.

45 Gandhi to H. Polak, 14 October 1909, *CWMG*, vol. 9, p. 480.

46 Ibid., p. 481.

47 Gandhi to C. Gandhi, 11 March 1914, *CWMG*, vol. 12, pp. 380–3.

48 *Indian Opinion*, 2 January 1909, *CWMG*, vol. 9, p. 118.

49 *CWMG*, vol. 10, pp. 58–9, 63.

50 *Indian Opinion*, 4 April 1908, *CWMG*, vol. 8, p. 171; congratulatory address, March 1898, *Natal Advertiser*, 19 March 1898, *CWMG*, vol. 3, p. 6.

51 Arrangements for education at Phoenix, *Indian Opinion*, 9 January 1909, *CWMG*, vol. 9, pp. 135–9.

52 *Indian Opinion*, 30 January 1909, *CWMG*, vol. 9, pp. 177–8.

53 Speech at Gujarati meeting in London, 5 October 1909, *Indian Opinion*, 20 November 1909, *CWMG*, vol. 9, pp. 457–60.

54 *CWMG*, vol. 10, pp. 53–57.

55 Gandhi, *An Autobiography*, pp. 278–84.

56 Gandhi to C. Gandhi, 6 May 1905, *CWMG*, vol. 4, p. 424.

57 *CWMG*, vol. 10, pp. 35–6, 63.

58 Gandhi, *Satyagrapha in South Africa*, p. 240.

59 Ibid., pp. 247–8, 254–6.

60 These are in *CWMG*, vols. 11 and 12.

61 *Indian Opinion*, 16 August 1913, *CWMG*, vol. 12, p. 165.

CHAPTER 4

1 Gandhi to A.H. West, 20 November 1914, *CWMG*, vol. 12, p. 557.

2 Gandhi to A.H. West, 23 December 1914, *ibid.*, p. 556.

3 Gandhi to Mr Lazarus, a Durban grocer, January 1915, SN no. 612.

4 Gandhi, *An Autobiography*, pp. 297–300; Gandhi to Maganlal Gandhi. 25 October 1914, 10 December 1914, *CWMG*, vol. 12, pp. 545–6, 561; Gandhi to A.H.West, 20 November 1914, *ibid.*, pp. 556–7.

5 Details of Gandhi's work in this connection, including the controversies over control of the volunteers are in

CWMG, vol. 12 and Gandhi, *An Autobiography*, pp. 269ff.

6 Gandhi, *An Autobiography*, pp. 291–3; Gandhi to Maganlal Gandhi, 18 September 1914, Gandhi to P. Desai, 5 November 1914, *CWMG*, vol. 12, 531–2, 554–5.

7 Gandhi, *An Autobiography*, p. 318.

8 Ibid., p. 325.

9 Entry for 27 February 1915, diary of V.S.S. Sastri (SIS, Madras). Crucial evidence of this episode is Gandhi, *An Autobiography*, pp. 321–2; Bombay Presidency Police, Secret Abstract of Intelligence, vol. xxviii of 1915, paras 169(a) and 186; Gandhi to V.S.S. Sastri, 13 January 1916, *CWMG* vol. 13, p. 200; V.S.S. Sastri to Dr H.S. Deva, 21 January 1916, V.S.S. Sastri Papers, Corr. File 1916, Letters to and from Sastri, no. 164 (National Archives of India [NAI], Delhi).

10 V.S.S. Sastri to his brother, V.S.R. Sastri, 10 January 1915, T.N. Jagadisan (ed.), *Letters of the Right Honourable V.S. Srinivasa Sastri* (2nd edn., Asia Publishing House, Bombay, 1963), p. 41.

11 K. Natarajan, editor of the *Indian Social Reformer*, to Gandhi, 26 May 1915, SN no. 6195.

12 NAI Home Political Files, July 1916, no. 23, Deposit.

13 Article in the *Indian Review*, October 1917, *CWMG*, vol. 13, pp. 533–4.

14 For the early days of the ashram see Gandhi, *An Autobiography*, pp. 329–33. Evidence of Gandhi's contacts with Ahmedabad businessmen and Maganlal Gandhi's mission to discover whether financial support would be given is in the Gandhi Papers for February–April 1915, SN nos. 6154, 6157–9, 6163, 6175.

15 *CWMG*, vol. 13, pp. 91–8.

16 For Gandhi's belief at this stage that the caste system itself should be retained as it was a reasonable and useful form of social order, see an article in *Bharat Sevak*, October 1916, *CWMG*, vol. 13, pp. 301–3.

17 On this crisis see Gandhi, *An Autobiography*, pp. 331–3; Gandhi to V.S.S. Sastri, 23 September 1915, *CWMG*, vol. 13, pp. 127–8; P.C. Gandhi to C.K. Gandhi, 30 September 1915, SN no. 6234; Gandhi to Maganlal Gandhi, 3 November 1915, *CWMG*, vol. 13, p. 137; Bombay Presidency Police, Secret Abstract of

Intelligence, vol. xxviii of 1915, para. 1259.

18 'War and the Search for a New Order', chapter iv of Judith M. Brown, *Modern India*, pp. 187ff.; Judith M. Brown, 'War and the Colonial Relationship: Britain, India and the War of 1914–18', in M.R.D.Foot (ed.), *War and Society* (Paul Elek, London, 1973), pp. 85–106.

19 Gandhi, looking back on 1917–18, to C.F. Andrews, 6 August 1918, *CWMG*, vol. 15, p. 4.

20 On the whole question of indentured labour see H. Tinker, *A New System of Slavery. The Export of Indian Labour Overseas 1830–1920* (OUP for the Institute of Race Relations, London, 1974). For Gandhi's activities see, e.g., Gandhi, *An Autobiography*, pp. 333ff.; resolution in 1916 Congress, *CWMG*, vol. 13 pp. 320–1; speeches by Gandhi in February 1917, *ibid.*, pp. 338–9, 342, 343, 347–51.

21 Speech in Surat, 26 February 1917, *ibid.*, pp. 348–9.

22 Foreword to new edition of *Hind Swaraj*, May 1919, *CWMG*, vol. 15, p. 330.

23 Speech at missionary conference, Madras, 14 February 1916, *CWMG*, vol. 13, pp. 219–25.

24 Speech at Muir College Economic Society, Allahabad, 22 December 1916, *ibid.*, pp. 310–7.

25 Gandhi to K. Mehta, 18 January 1917, *ibid.*, p. 331; plan for national Gujarati school, January 1917, *ibid.*, pp. 332–4.

26 Circular letter appealing for funds for ashram, July 1917, *ibid.*, p. 652; other examples of Gandhi's critical speeches on contemporary education are 21 December 1916, *ibid.*, pp. 318–9, 20 October 1917, *CWMG*, vol. 14, pp. 8–36.

27 Speech on 29 December 1916, *CWMG*, vol. 13, pp. 321–2; speech on 20 October 1917, *CWMG*, vol. 14, pp. 8–36.

28 Gandhi, *An Autobiography*, pp. 316–17. Other evidence of Gandhi's involvement on this issue are speech on 12 December 1915, *CWMG*, vol. 13, p. 151; resolution proposed at Bombay Provincial Conference, 21/22/23 October 1916, Bombay Presidency Police, Secret Abstract of Intelligence, vol. xxix of 1916, para. 1460.

29 Gandhi to Maganlal Gandhi, 10 April

1917, *CWMG*, vol. 13, pp. 360–1. Sources for the account of Gandhi's Champaran work which follows are: Gandhi, *An Autobiography*, pp. 337ff.; *CWMG*, vol. 13; Rajendra Prasad, *Satyagraha In Champaran* (2nd revised edn., Navajivan, Ahmedabad, 1949); B.B. Misra (ed.), *Select Documents on Mahatma Gandhi's Movement in Champaran 1917–18* (Govt. of Bihar, 1963); Judith M. Brown, *Gandhi's Rise To Power. Indian Politics 1915–1922* (CUP, Cambridge, 1972), pp. 52–83; S. Henningham, 'The Social Setting of the Champaran Satyagraha: The Challenge to an Alien Elite', *The Indian Economic and Social History Review*, vol. xiii, No. I (Jan.–March 1976), pp. 59–73.

30 W.H. Lewis to W.B. Heycock, 29 April 1917, NAI, Appendix D to Proceeding no. 323 of Home Political Files, A, July 1917, nos. 314–40.

31 Gandhi to V.S.S. Sastri, 30 September 1917, *CWMG*, vol. 13, p. 559.

32 On Kaira district and Gandhi's satyagraha campaign, see Gandhi, *An Autobiography*, pp. 362–7; D. Hardiman, *Peasant Nationalists of Gujarat. Kheda District 1917–1934* (OUP, Delhi, 1981); Brown, *Gandhi's Rise To Power*, pp. 83–111.

33 Gandhi to ed., 15 April 1918, *Bombay Chronicle*, 17 April 1918.

34 Lord Willingdon to Sir Harcourt Butler, Lt-Governor of UP, 5 May 1918, India Office Library (IOL), Harcourt Butler Papers, Mss. EUR.F.116 (53).

35 Gandhi to Ambalal Sarabhai, 1 March 1918, *CWMG*, vol. 14, pp. 229–30. Background to and accounts of the Ahmedabad dispute are in Gillion, *Ahmedabad*; E. Erikson, *Gandhi's Truth. On the Origins of Militant Nonviolence* (Faber and Faber, London, 1970); Brown, *Gandhi's Rise to Power*, pp. 111–20; Gandhi, *An Autobiography*, pp. 355–7, 358–62; Mahadev Desai, *A Righteous Struggle* Navajivan, Ahmedabad, 1951).

36 Speech at a prayer meeting, 17 March 1918, *CWMG*, vol. 14, p. 262.

37 Leaflet no. 6, March 1918, *ibid.*, pp. 232–4; Gandhi to Ambalal Sarahai, 21 December 1917, *ibid.*, p. 115.

38 *Navajivan*, 8 and 29 February 1920, *CWMG*, vol. 17, pp. 19, 47–51. For Gandhi's attitude to social and economic relations, see P.J. Rolnick, 'Charity, Trusteeship and Social Change in

India. A Study of a Political Ideology', *Word Politics*, no. 3 (April 1962), pp. 439–60.

39 *Young India*, 3 December 1925, *CWMG*, vol. 29, p. 290.

40 Gandhi, *An Autobiography*, p. 420.

41 Gandhi to A.H. West, 13 February 1918, *CWMG*, vol. 14, pp. 192–4.

42 Gandhi to S. Banerjea, 10 August 1918, to B.G. Tilak, 25 August 1918, *CWMG*, vol. 15, pp. 15, 31; Gandhi at provincial conference in Belgaum, 29 April–1 May 1916, Bombay Presidency Police, Secret Abstract of Intelligence, vol. xxix of 1916, para. 757.

43 26 November 1917, E.S. Montagu, *An Indian Diary* (Heinemann, London, 1930), p. 58.

44 Gandhi to M. Ali, 18 November 1918, NAI, Home Political Files, December 1918, no. 3 Deposit; Gandhi, *An Autobiography*, pp. 367–9.

45 Gandhi to B.G. Tilak, 25 August 1918, *CWMG*, vol. 15, p. 31.

46 Speech at Gujarat Political Conference, 3 November 1917, *CWMG*, vol. 14, pp. 52ff.; also foreword to booklet by G.A. Natesan, 27 September 1917, *CWMG*, vol. 13, p. 556.

47 Gandhi to N.M. Samarth, 20 August 1918, to B.G. Tilak, 25 August 1918, *CWMG*, vol. 15, pp. 29, 31–2.

48 Gandhi to Dr Pranjivan Mehta, 2 July 1918, *CWMG*, vol. 14, p. 468.

49 Gandhi to Esther Faering, 30 June 1918, *ibid.*, pp. 462–3. See also Gandhi to Hanumantrao, 17 July 1918, *ibid.*, pp. 484–5; Gandhi to Maganlal Gandhi, 25 July 1918, *ibid.*, pp. 504–5; leaflet by Gandhi appealing for recruits in Kaira, 22 June 1918, *ibid.*, pp. 439–43; Gandhi to V.S.S. Sastri, 18 July 1918, *ibid.*, pp. 488–9.

50 Gandhi to C.F. Andrews, 6 July 1918, *ibid.*, pp. 474–8.

51 Gandhi to V.S.S. Sastri, 5 November 1918, *CWMG*, vol. 15, p. 61. Gandhi's comments on his illness are scattered through letters in the early part of *CWMG*, vol. 15; see also Gandhi, *An Autobiography*, pp. 374–9.

52 Gandhi, *An Autobiography*, pp. 378–9; Gandhi to Maganlal Gandhi, 10 January 1919, Gandhi to Narahari Parikh, 21 and 27 January 1919, *CWMG*, vol. 15, pp. 70–1, 73–5, 78–9.

53 Mr. Justice Rowlatt chaired the committee, appointed in 1917, which reported in 1918: *Report of Committee Appointed to Investigate Revolutionary Conspiracies in India*, Cd. 9190, London, 1918.

54 Gandhi to P. Desai, 9 February 1919, *CWMG*, vol. 15, p. 88.

55 See P.G. Robb, *The Government of India and Reform. Policies toward Politics and the Constitution 1916–1921* (OUP, 1976), pp. 148ff. E.S. Montagu's attitude to the Rowlatt Report was voiced in his letter to the Viceroy, 10 October 1918, Chelmsford Papers, IOL, Mss. EUR. E. 264(4).

56 Gandhi to V.S.S. Sastri, 9 February 1919, *CWMG*, vol. 15, pp. 87–8.

57 Gandhi to E.S. Montagu, 14 June 1919, *ibid.*, p. 368.

58 Gandhi to Sir Dinshaw Wacha, 25 February 1919, *ibid.*, p. 107.

59 For the Rowlatt Satyagraha see Gandhi, *An Autobiography*, pp. 379ff.; Brown, *Gandhi's Rise to Power*, pp. 160–189; R. Kumer (ed.), *Essays on Gandhian Politics. The Rowlatt Satyagraha of 1919* (Clarendon Press, Oxford, 1971).

60 Pledge, 24 February 1919, *CWMG*, vol. 15, pp. 101–2.

61 Gandhi to C.F. Andrews, 25 February 1919, *ibid.*, pp. 104–5; Gandhi to Viceroy, telegram, 24 February 1919, *ibid.*, pp. 102–3.

62 V.S.S. Sastri to S.G. Vaze, 1 April 1919, NAI, Sastri Papers, Correspondence File 1919, letters to and from Sastri.

63 These problems are investigated in the context of several regions in R. Kumar (ed.), *Essays on Gandhian Politics*.

64 Gandhi to J.L. Maffey, 14 April 1919, NAI, Home Political Files, May 1919, nos. 455–72 A.

65 Gandhi to Sir Stanley Reed, 15 April 1919, *CWMG*, vol. 15, pp. 227–31.

66 Gandhi to secretaries, Satyagraha Committee, 12 June 1919, *ibid.*, pp. 364–5.

67 Gandhi to G. Arundale, 4 July 1919, *Bombay Chronicle*, 12 August 1919.

68 Gandhi to S. Schlesin, 2 June 1919, SN no. 6635. Gandhi on the significance of the 1919 Congress in *An Autobiography*, p. 405.

69 Sir D.E. Wacha to G.A. Natesan, 12 April 1919, Nehru Memorial Museum and Library (NMML), G.A. Natesan Papers; V.S.S. Sastri to S.G.

Vaze, 17 April 1919, NAI, Sastri Papers, Correspondence File 1919, letters to and from Sastri.

70 Lord Chelmsford to E.S. Montagu, 9 April 1919, IOL, Montagu Papers, Mss. EUR.D.523 (8).

71 J.L. Maffey to Gandhi, 13 March, 20 April, 7 May 1919, SN nos. 6456, 6551, 6593. Gandhi's approach to Maffey requesting such a 'hot line' during the satyagraha, reminiscent of South Africa, 11/12 March 1919, SN no. 6449.

72 Sir George Lloyd to E.S. Montagu, 2 and 23 May 1919, IOL, Montagu Papers, Mss. EUR. D. 523 (24).

73 NAI, Home Political Files, August 1919, nos. 261–272 and K–W, A.

CHAPTER 5

1 Account of Gandhi's trial, 18 March, 1922, Young India, 23 March 1922, CWMG, vol. 23, pp. 110–20.

2 Young India, 28 July 1920, CWMG, vol. 18, p. 89; speech at Shantiniketan, 17 September 1920, ibid., p. 265; speech at Lucknow, 15 October 1920, ibid., p. 350; letter to parents of Aligarh students, Young India, 3 November 1920, ibid., p. 421.

3 Gandhi to C.F. Andrews, 23 November 1920, CWMG, vol. 19, p. 14.

4 For a fuller account of the Khilafat movement, see Brown, Gandhi's Rise to Power, pp. 190–229; G.M. Minault, The Khilafat Movement: Religious Symbolism and Political Modernization in India, (Columbia University Press, New York 1982).

5 Young India, 5 May 1920; Navajivan, 29 February 1920, CWMG, vol. 17, p. 59; Young India, 28 April 1920.

6 Gandhi to Maganlal Gandhi, 4 May 1920, CWMG, vol. 17, pp. 386–7; Gandhi to S. Chowdhrani, 30 April 1920, ibid., p. 359.

7 On the Punjab issue, see Brown, Gandhi's Rise To Power, pp. 230–49. The 'Hunter Report' is a parliamentary paper, Report of the Committee Appointed by The Government of India to Investigate Disturbances in the Punjab, etc., Cd. 681, London, 1920.

8 M. Nehru to G. Misra, 12 March 1920, NMML, AICC Papers, 1920, File no. 8. The Congress report on events in the Punjab, published 25

March 1920, CWMG, vol. 17, pp. 114–292.

9 Young India, 9 June 1920, ibid., pp. 480–3.

10 Lord Reading to E.S. Montagu, 19 May 1921, IOL, Reading Papers, Mss. EUR.E.238 (3). On British discussion of policy towards Gandhi in mid-1920, see NAI, Home Political Files, September 1920, nos. 100–3 a. This includes an important policy letter from Government of India to all local governments, 4 September 1920.

11 Gandhi to V.S.S. Sastri, 18 March 1920, CWMG, vol. 17, pp. 96–8. For Motilal Nehru's backing for this proposal, see this letter to Sastri, and Motilal to Jawaharlal Nehru, 13 March 1920, NMML, Nehru Papers.

12 Young India, 28 April, 1920, CWMG, vol. 17, pp. 347–9.

13 Fortnightly report from Bombay for first half of October 1920, NAI, Home Political Files, December 1920, no. 59, Deposit; Bombay Presidency Police, Secret Abstract of Intelligence of 1920 (June–December), paras. 1360 and 1382 (25); resignation letter, 27 October 1920, M.R. Jayakar, The Story of My Life, vol. 1, 1873–1922 (Asia Publishing House, Bombay, 1958). p. 405.

14 Gandhi, An Autobiography, p. 407.

15 Young India, 12 May 1920, CWMG, vol. 17, p. 406. In Young India, 19 January 1921, he reiterated this: 'I enter politics only in so far as it develops the religious faculty in me'. CWMG, vol. 19, p. 238.

16 Gandhi to N.C. Sinha, 14 May 1920, SN no. 7249A.

17 Gandhi to K. Natarajan and to Sir Dinshaw Wacha, both on 25 February 1919, CWMG, vol. 15, pp. 106, 107.

18 Young India, 22 September 1920, CWMG, vol. 18, pp. 270–3; Gandhi's speech on non-cooperation in Congress, 8 September 1920, Young India, 15 September 1920, ibid., pp. 245–9. Gandhi still felt in 1921 that swaraj could be achieved in a year provided that Indians fulfilled certain conditions such as non-violence and communal unity; Young India, 23 February 1921, CWMG, vol. 19, pp. 383–5.

19 Young India, 26 January 1921, ibid., pp. 277–8; Young India, 4 May 1921, CWMG, vol. 20, p. 58; Young India,

27 October 1921, *CWMG*, vol. 21, p. 354.

20　J. Nehru, *An Autobiography*, (John Lane The Bodley Head, London, 1936), p. 76.

21　*Young India*, 4 August 1920.

22　J. Nehru, *An Autobiography*, p. 73.

23　The intricate details of these manoeuvres and of events in the two Congress sessions are available in Brown, *Gandhi's Rise to Power*, pp. 250–306.

24　Chunilal Gandhi to Sir P. Thakurdas, 20 and 21 October 1920, NMML, P. Thakurdas Papers, File no 24, p. 2, 1920–2.

25　Sir Dinshaw Wacha to G.A. Natesan, 6 October 1920, NMML, G.A. Natesan Papers.

26　*Times of India*, 27 December 1920.

27　Note by S.P. O'Donnell, Secretary to Govt of India, Home Dept, 14 January 1921, NAI, Home Political Files, July 1921, no. 3 and K.-W., Deposit.

28　*Bombay Chronicle*, 27 December 1920.

29　Sir Frank Sly to Viceroy, 1 January 1921, IOL, Chelmsford Papers, Mss. EUR. E. 264 (26).

30　Krishnadas, *Seven Months with Mahatma Gandhi* (Navajivan, Ahmedabad, 1951), pp. 26–7, 34.

31　*Ibid.*, p. 117.

32　Gandhi to Mahadev Desai, 31 October 1921, *CWMG*, vol. 21, p. 375.

33　*Young India*, 24 November 1921, *ibid.*, p. 465.

34　*Navajivan*, 9 October 1921, *ibid.*, p. 268.

35　Lord Willingdon to E.S. Montagu, 11 February 1922, I.O.L., Willingdon Papers, Mss. EUR.F.93 (4).

36　Accounts of non-co-operation are in Brown, *Gandhi's Rise to Power*, pp. 307–351; C. Baker, 'Non-cooperation in South India', C.J. Baker and D.A. Washbrook *South India: Political Institutions and Political Change 1880–1940* (Macmillan India, Delhi, 1975), pp. 98–149. A contemporary account prepared for the government by a senior official in the intelligence department, republished by Deep Publications, Delhi, 1974, is P.C. Bamford, *Histories of the Non-co-operation and Khilafat Movements* (Government of India, Delhi, 1925).

37　Reading to E.S. Montagu, 4 August 1921, I.O.L., Reading Papers, Mss. EUR.E.238 (3).

38　Bombay Presidency Police. Secret Abstract of Intelligence of 1922, no. 7,

vol. xxxv, para. 32; Bamford, *op.cit.*, pp. 46–7.

39　See C. Baker's study cited in fn. 36 above.

40　Gandhi's instructions to UP peasants when he visited the province in 1921 are in *Young India*, 9 March 1921, *CWMG*, vol. 19, pp. 419–20.

41　Leaflet issued on 18 November 1921, and published in *Young India*, 24 November 1921, *CWMG*, vol. 21, p. 465.

42　Appeal to Bombay citizens, 19 November 1921, published in *Young India*, 24 November 1921, *CWMG*, vol. 21, pp. 466–7.

43　Statement on breaking fast, 21 November 1921, published in *Young India*, 24 November 1921, *CWMG*, vol. 21, pp. 475–7.

44　Gandhi to J. Nehru, 19 February 1922, NMML, J. Nehru Papers, File no. G. 11, 1922 (ii).

45　On the events leading up to and including the Working Committee meeting in mid-February, see CID report, 13 February 1922, NAI, Home Political Files, 1922, no. 580-II.

46　*Navajivan*, 21 August 1921, *CWMG*, vol. 21, p. 3.

47　Quoted in weekly report of Director, Intelligence Bureau, 10 March 1921, NAI, Home Political Files, Deposit, June 1921, no. 53.

48　Lord Willingdon to Lord Reading, 3 April 1921, I.O.L., Willingdon Papers, Mss. EUR. F. 93 (5).

49　For example, fortnightly report from U.P. for first half of May 1921, NAI, Home Political Files, Deposit, June 1921, no. 63; Bombay Presidency Police. Secret Abstract of Intelligence of 1921, no. 7. volume xxxiv, para. 441 (11); fortnightly report from U.P. for second half of August 1921, NAI, Home Political Files, Deposit, 1921, no. 18.

A fascinating discussion of Gandhi's image among the peasantry of one village, based on stories circulating about him, is S. Amin, 'Gandhi as Mahatma: Gorakhpur District, Eastern UP, 1921-2' in R. Guha (ed.), *Subaltern Studies III. Writings on South Asian History and Society* (OUP, Delhi, 1984), pp. 1–61.

50　Note by T.B. Sapru, 9 October 1921, NAI, Home Political Files, 1921, no. 303.

51　The details of this crumbling of Gandhi's power bases in 1921–2 are worked out in Brown, *Gandhi's Rise to Power*, pp. 328–42.

52 Government policy is analysed in D.A. Low, 'The Government of India and the first non-cooperation movement, 1920–1922', R. Kumar (ed.), *Essays on Gandhian Politics*, pp. 298–323. The manoeuvres between government, the Moderates and Gandhi are documented in the Reading Papers and *CWMG*, vol. 22.

53 Letter of invitation to conference, 3 January 1922, sent to a range of people, signed by M.M. Malaviya, M.A. Jinnah, P. Thakurdas, M.R. Jayakar, A. Sarabhai, K. Natarajan, and G.M. Bhurgri, published in *Indian Social Reformer*, 8 January 1922.

54 *Indian Social Reformer*, 5 February 1922.

55 Bombay Presidency Police, Secret Abstract of Intelligence of 1921, para. 382 (10).

56 See D.A. Low's detailed study of government policy cited above, fn. 52.

57 G. Krishna, 'The Development of the Indian National Congress as a Mass Organization, 1918–1923', *Journal of Asian Studies*, vol. xxv, no. 3 (May 1966), pp. 413–30; Brown, *Gandhi's Rise to Power*, pp. 320–2; C. Baker, 'Non-cooperation in South India', Baker and Washbrook, *South India*, pp. 134–5.

CHAPTER 6

1 One historian referred to the mid-1920s as a time of 'partial eclipse' in Gandhi's life: P. Moon, *Gandhi and Modern India* (English Universities Press, London, 1968), title of chapter x.

2 Lord Birkenhead to Lord Reading, 22 October 1925, IOL, Reading Papers, Mss. EUR. E. 238 (8).

3 Lord Irwin to Lord Birkenhead, 16 June 1926 and 3 November 1927, IOL, Halifax Papers, Mss. EUR. C. 152 (2) and (3).

4 Gandhi to Konda Venkatappayya, 4 March 1922, to T. Prakasam, 7 March 1922, *CWMG*, vol. 23, pp. 1–4, 20–1; article in *Young India*, 23 October 1924, *CWMG*, vol. 25, pp. 258–60.
Congress had launched its own civil disobedience enquiry in 1922

and concluded that India was not yet ready for mass civil disobedience; Viceroy to Secretary of State, telegram, 7 November 1922, IOL, Reading Papers, Mss. EUR. E. 238 (11).

5 Government discussed whether to release Gandhi unconditionally or to try to extract from him an undertaking not plunge into active anti-government campaigning: eventually Delhi acceded to Bombay's wishes for immediate, unconditional release in the light of extreme public pressure for this. See IOL, Reading Papers, Mss. EUR. E. 238 (13) and (18).

6 Gandhi to Abdul Bari, *c.* mid-March 1922, to M. Trikumji, 13 March 1922, to H. A. Khan, 14 April 1922, *CWMG*, vol. 23, pp. 92, 94, 133.

7 Gandhi to H.A. Khan, 14 April 1922, *ibid.*, pp. 133–4. Gandhi's brief diaries in gaol are in *ibid.*, pp. 144–53, 178–88: these record little more than his reading, visitors, changes in food and health.

8 *Young India*, 17 April 1924, *CWMG*, vol. 23, p. 449. His articles on his gaol experiences are available in *CWMG*, , vols. 23–5.

9 Evidence of his reading is in his diaries (see fn. 7); three articles in *Young India*, 4, 11 and 25 September 1924, *CWMG*, vol. 25, pp. 82–7, 125–9, 153–6.

10 *Young India*, 4 September 1924, *CWMG*, vol. 25, p. 86.

11 *Young India*, 4 September 1924, *ibid.*, pp. 86–7.

12 Gandhi to D.R. Majli, 23 March 1924, *CWMG*, vol. 23, pp. 302–3.

13 Gandhi to H.A. Khan, 14 April 1922, *ibid.*, p. 134.

14 Speech in Gujarat, 2 January 1925, *Navajivan*, 11 January 1925, *CWMG*, vol. 25, p. 536.

15 On the political situation Gandhi faced in 1924, see Judith M. Brown, *Gandhi and Civil Disobedience. The Mahatma in Indian Politics 1928–1934* (CUP, Cambridge, 1977), pp. 6–11; D.E.U. Baker, 'The Break-Down of Nationalist Unity and the Formation of the Swaraj Parties, India, 1922 to 1924', *University Studies in History*, vol. v, no. 4 (1970), pp. 85–113.

16 *Young India*, 3 April 1924, *CWMG*, vol. 23, p. 340.

17 *Young India*, 17 April 1924, *ibid*, pp. 453, 459.

18 Statement, 22 May 1924, *The Hindu*, 23 May 1924, *CWMG*, vol. 24, pp. 109–11.

19 Gandhi's speech at AICC meeting, 28 June 1924, *Navajivan*, 17 July 1924, *ibid.*, pp. 306–11. In advance Gandhi had published his proposed resolutions in an article, 'The Acid Test', *Young India*, 19 June 1924, *ibid.*, pp. 267–70.

20 The AICC meeting is documented in *CWMG*, vol. 24; Viceroy to Secretary of State, telegram, 21 July 1924, IOL, Reading Papers, Mss. EUR. E. 238 (12); 'Defeated and Humbled', *Young India*, 3 July 1924, *CWMG*, vol. 24, pp. 334–40; Gandhi's 'emotional breakdown' was largely on the issue of non-violence, Mahadev Desai to J. Nehru, 27 December 1935, NMML, J. Nehru Papers.

21 Gandhi to J. Nehru, 15 September 1924, *CWMG*, vol. 25, p. 148.

22 Speech in Poona, 4 September 1924, *Navajivan*, 14 September 1924, *ibid.*, p. 89.

23 The Calcutta Agreement between Das, Nehru and Gandhi in November 1925 and the Belgaum Congress are documented in *CWMG*, vol. 25.

24 *Young India*, 16 April 1925, *CWMG*, vol. 26, p. 515.

25 AICC resolutions at Patna meeting, 22 September 1925, *Young India*, 1 October 1925, *CWMG*, vol. 28, pp. 475–7. Gandhi's original suggestion was in letter to M. Nehru, 19 July 1925, *CWMG*, vol. 27, p. 398.

26 M. to J. Nehru, 30 March, 14 April and 11 August 1927, NMML, J. Nehru Papers, Part I, vol. LXIX.

27 Interviews given in February and March 1924, *CWMG*, vol. 23, pp. 196, 239. He distinguished between the parliamentary swaraj he was working for immediately and the state he had depicted in *Hind Swaraj*, *CWMG*, vol. 24, p. 548.

28 Presidential address at Congress, 26 December 1924, *Young India*, 26 December 1924, *CWMG*, vol. 25, pp. 481–2; see also *Young India*, 29 January 1925, *CWMG*, vol. 26, p. 50.

29 Speech at Gauhati Congress, 28 December 1926, *CWMG*, vol. 32, p. 468; reaction to Madras Congress resolutions, *Young India*, 5 and 12 January 1928, *CWMG*, vol. 35, pp. 437–9, 454–7. On Gandhi's strained relations with Jawaharlal Nehru as a result, see letters to J. Nehru, 4, 11 & 17 January 1928, NMML, J. Nehru Papers, Part I, vol. XXII, J. Nehru, *A Bunch of Old Letters* (Asia Publishing House, Bombay, 2nd edn, 1960), pp. 58–60. On the Madras Congress see Brown, *Gandhi and Civil Disobedience*, pp. 21–2.

30 *Young India*, 17 March 1927, 23 February 1928, *CWMG*, vol. 32, p. 164, vol. 36, p. 43.

31 Gandi to J. Nehru, 20 July 1927, *CWMG*, vol. 34, p. 207; M. to J. Nehru, 30 March & 14 April 1927, N.M.M. & L., J. Nehru Papers, vol. LXIX.

32 Gandhi to M. Ali, 7 February 1924, *CWMG*, vol. 23, pp. 20–1.

33 *Young India*, 1 May 1924, Gandhi to Dr Satyapal, 25 March 1924, *ibid.*, pp. 512, 311.

34 *Navajivan*, 12 March 1922, *ibid.*, p. 76.

35 *Young India*, 29 May and 5 June 1924, *CWMG*, vol. 24, pp. 136–54, 188–90.

36 *Young India*, 18 September 1924, *CWMG*, vol. 25, pp. 166–9. See also Gandhi to G.D. Birla, 25 August 1924, *ibid.*, p. 39.

37 Statement, 18 September 1924, *Young India*, 25 September 1924, *ibid.*, pp. 171–2.

38 Gandhi to C.F. Andrews, 17 September 1924, *ibid.*, p. 157.

39 Discussions with Mahadev Desai and Shaukat Ali, 18 and 19 September 1924, *Young India*, 23 October 1924, *ibid.*, pp. 174–6, 181–4; *Young India*, 25 September 1924, *ibid.*, pp. 199–202.

40 Gandhi to M. Nehru, 27 September 1924, *ibid.*, pp. 215–16; press statement on Unity Conference, 24 September 1924, draft resoultion for conference, *ibid.*, pp. 209–10, 214–15.

41 Speech on 9 December 1924, *Navajivan*, 14 December 1924, *ibid.*, p. 414.

42 These two controversies are documented in *CWMG*, vol. 26. Gandhi insisted in making his disagreement with Shaukat Ali public as an object lesson in mutual toleration.

43 Speech on 7 March 1925, *The Hindu*, 9 March 1925, *CWMG*, vol. 26, p. 244. See also press interview, 5 March 1925, *The Hindu*, 6 March 1925, *ibid.*, pp. 232–4.

44 *Young India*, 3 April 1924, *CWMG*, vol. 23, p. 340; Gandhi to A.W. Baker, 18 March 1924, *ibid.*, p. 267.

45 *Young India*, 3 April 1924, 1 October 1925, *CWMG*, vol. 23, p. 349, vol. 28, p. 269.

46 *Young India*, 7 January 1926, 9 September 1924, *CWMG*, vol. 29, p. 382, vol. 25, p. 117.

47 Gandhi to Dr N. Leys, 28 May 1926, *CWMG*, vol. 30, p. 492.

48 Gandhi to D. Hanumantrao, 16 March 1924, *CWMG*, vol. 23, p. 261.

49 Gandhi to K. Bajoria, 7 September 1926, *CWMG*, vol. 31, p. 365.

50 Gandhi to Mrs Maddock, 14 March 1924, *CWMG*, vol. 23, p. 243. On his 'nationalism', *Amrita Bazar Patrika*, 15 August 1925, *CWMG*, vol. 28, p. 23. On possible foreign visits, *Young India*, 17 September 1925, *ibid.*, pp. 186–91, *Navajivan*, 20 December 1925, *CWMG*, vol. 29, pp. 335–6.

51 On his humiliation at their weakness, Gandhi to M. Nehru, 30 October 1924, *CWMG*, vol. 25, p. 270; *Navajivan*, 2 November 1925, *ibid.*, pp. 280–1. On his role of concentrating on internal growth and strengthening, *New India*, 29 April 1925, *CWMG*, vol. 26, p. 560; *Young India*, 25 February 1926, *CWMG*, vol. 30, p. 49.

52 Gandhi to S.S. Caveesar, 12 March 1926, *CWMG*, vol. 30, p. 107.

53 *Young India*, 14 July and 1 December 1927, *CWMG*, vol. 34, p. 173, vol. 35, p. 353.

54 *Young India*, 20 August 1925, 6 May 1926, *CWMG*, vol. 28, p. 87, vol. 30, p. 415.

55 *Navajivan*, 26 September 1926, *CWMG*, vol. 31, p. 454; Gandhi to Bal Kalelkar, 12 August 1927, *CWMG*, vol. 34, p. 334.

56 *Young India*, 25 February 1926, *CWMG*, vol. 30, p. 16.

57 *Young India*, 19 March 1925, *CWMG*, vol. 26, p. 333.

58 *Navajivan*, 17 May 1925, *Young India*, 6 May 1926, *CWMG*, vol. 27, p. 108, vol. 30, p. 415.

59 Gandhi to S. Karamchand, 21 March 1924, to A. Mirbel, 12 February 1926, *CWMG*, vol. 23, p. 298, vol. 30, p. 9.

60 Gandhi to A.W. Baker, 18 March 1924, *Young India*, 25 September 1924, 13 August 1925, *CWMG*, vol. 23, p. 267, vol. 25, p. 188, vol. 27, p. 448.

61 28 July 1925, *CWMG*, vol. 27, p. 439; Gandhi to K. Natarajan, 6 August 1924, to A.W. Baker, 18 March 1924, *CWMG*, vol. 24, p. 515, vol. 23, p. 267.

62 21 December 1925, *CWMG*, vol. 29, p. 341.

63 Gandhi to P.S. Lall, 11 September 1926, *CWMG*, vol. 31, p. 395: on art's meaning, discussion with G. Ramachandran, 21–22 October 1925, *CWMG*, vol. 25, p. 249.

64 Gandhi to S.C. Das Gupta, late March 1927, *CWMG*, vol. 33, pp. 195–6.

65 *Young India*, 7 January 1926, *CWMG*, vol. 29, pp. 380–1.

66 Gandhi to M.A. Ansari, 28 April 1927, to H. Kallenbach, 13 May 1927, *CWMG*, vol. 33, pp. 274–5, 314–15. *CWMG*, vols. 33 and 34 are full of evidence of his convalescence.

67 See above, pp. 146–7; answers to questions, February 1924, *CWMG*, vol. 23, p. 196.

68 *Young India*, 31 July & 25 September 1924, *CWMG*, vol. 24, p. 476, vol. 25, p. 179.

69 Gandhi to I. Bamlet, 22 May 1927, *CWMG*, vol. 33, p. 353.

70 'We often prate about spirituality as if it had nothing to do with the ordinary affairs of life and had been reserved for anchorites lost in the Himalayan forest or concealed in some inaccessible Himalayan cave. Spirituality that has no bearing on and produces no effect on every day life is "an airy nothing".' *Young India*, 5 August 1926, *CWMG*, vol. 31, pp. 260–1.

71 Gandhi's attitude to *shuddhi*: *Young India*, 6 January 1927, *CWMG*, vol. 32, p. 515; Gandhi to G.D. Birla, 24 January 1927, *CWMG*, vol. 33, p. 8. Gandhi felt that Christian missionaries were guilty of supporting the raj as well as proselytizing; but he recognized their charitable work, and their impetus to Hindus to put their own religious house in order. *Young India*, 31 July 1924, 17 December 1925, *CWMG*, vol. 24, p. 476, vol. 29, p. 326. Gandhi recognized with gratefulness that compared with his searing memories of missionaries in Gujarat in his boyhood,

there was now among them a spirit of greater tolerance and appreciation of other faiths; *Young India*, 4 March 1926, *CWMG*, vol. 30, pp. 70–1.

72 *Navajivan*, 5 October 1924, *CWMG*, vol. 25, p. 221; speech on 7 May 1925, *CWMG*, vol. 27, pp. 61–2; *Young India*, 2 September 1926, *CWMG*, vol. 31, p. 351; *Young India*, 20 October 1927, *CWMG*, vol. 35, pp. 166–7.

73 *Young India*, 14 October 1926, *CWMG*, vol. 31, p. 494; Gandhi to B.S. Moonje, 14 May 1927, *CWMG*, vol. 33, pp. 322–3.

74 *Young India*, 24 April 1924, 8 April 1926, 13 October 1927, *CWMG*, vol. 23, p. 485, vol. 29, pp. 443–5, vol. 35, pp. 123–4.

75 *Navajivan*, 15 February 1925, *CWMG*, vol. 26, p. 131; *Young India*, 2 September and 14 October 1926, *CWMG*, vol. 31, pp. 351, 494.

76 *CWMG*, *Young India*, 4 December 1924, vol. 25, p. 390.

77 Gandhi to M. Trikumji, 6 March 1922, *CWMG*, vol. 23, p. 20; *Young India*, 21 January 1926, *CWMG*, vol. 29, p. 411.

78 For example, *Navajivan*, 18 May, 29 June 1924, 3 May 1925, *CWMG*, vol. 24, pp. 70–1, 319–21, vol. 27, p. 21; *Young India*, 1 October 1925, *CWMG*, vol. 28, p. 264; *Navajivan*, 11 October 1925, *ibid.*, pp. 316–321; *Navajivan*, 20 June, 18 July 1926, *CWMG*, vol. 31, pp. 23–4, 158; Gandhi to Jayanti, 11 August 1927, *CWMG*, vol. 34, pp. 330–1.

79 Discourses on the *Gita*, February–November 1926, published in 1955, *CWMG*, vol. 32, pp. 94–376. On Gandhi's interpretation of the *Gita*, see M. Chatterjee, *Gandhi's Religious Thought*, pp. 35–40; A. Bharati, Gandhi 'Gandhi's Interpretation of the Gita. An Anthropological Analysis', S Ray (ed.), *Gandhi, India and the world. An International Symposium* (Temple University Press, Philadelphia, 1970), pp. 57–70.

   Gandhi saw in the *Gita* 'a perennial guide to conduct', 'a solace' (speeches, 1 and 28 July 1925, *CWMG*, vol. 27, pp. 315, 435), 'more and more the only infallible guide, the only dictionary of reference' (Gandhi to G. Nanda, 28 May 1927, *CWMG*, vol. 33, p. 384). See also *Navajivan*, 11 October 1925,

CWMG, vol. 28, pp. 318–21; Gandhi to S. Maharaj, 2 July 1927, *CWMG*, vol. 34, p. 90.

80 Gandhi to S.D. Nadkarni, 4 June 1927, *CWMG*, vol. 33, p. 432; *Young India*, 8 September 1927, *CWMG*, vol. 34, p. 438; speeches, 25 September 1927, 24 January 1928, *CWMG*, vol. 35, pp. 37, 486.

81 *Navajivan*, 18 July 1926, *CWMG*, vol. 31, p. 157; Gandhi to P.D. Gupta, 19 November 1926, *CWMG*, vol. 32, p. 67.

82 *Young India*, 28 August 1924, *CWMG*, vol. 25, p. 46; *Navajivan*, 3 May 1925, *CWMG*, vol. 27, p. 21.

83 *Young India*, 1 September 1927, *CWMG*, vol. 34, p. 431.

84 On prayer: Gandhi to S. Karamchand, 21 March 1924, *CWMG*, vol. 23, p. 298; *Navajivan*, 20 September 1925, *CWMG*, vol. 28, pp. 207–9; Gandhi to D.G. Mukerji, 29 July 1926, to V.M. Tarkunde, 30 October 1926, *CWMG*, vol. 31, pp. 225, 542.

85 *Young India*, 22 January 1925, *CWMG*, vol. 26, p. 28; letter, 13 July 1927, *CWMG*, vol. 34, pp. 162–3.

86 Some of Gandhi's attempts to describe how he saw the Deity: speech, 18 May 1924, *CWMG*, vol. 24, p. 86; *Young India*, 25 September 1924, 5 March 1925, 21 January 1926, *CWMG*, vol. 25, p. 178, vol. 26, p. 224, vol. 29, pp. 411–12.

87 Answers to questions, 5 August 1927, *CWMG*, vol. 34, p. 290; Gandhi to N.C.Dey, 21 December 1927, *CWMG*, vol. 35, pp. 403–4.

88 Speech, 21 December 1925, *CWMG*, vol. 29, p. 340.

89 Gandhi to B. Matthews, 8 June 1927, *CWMG*, vol. 23, p. 452.

90 *Navajivan*, 1 November 1925, *CWMG*, vol. 28, p. 407; *Young India*, 3 December 1925, *CWMG*, vol. 29, p. 291; speech, 1 February 1928, *CWMG*, vol. 36, p. 1.

91 *Young India*, 3 December 1925, 14 June 1928, *CWMG*, vol. 29, p. 290, vol. 36, p. 409; ashram trust deed, 2 February 1926, *CWMG*, vol. 29, p. 435.

92 Gandhi to K.G. Rekhade, 25 March 1924, *CWMG*, vol. 23, p. 307.

93 Speech, 11 February 1925, *CWMG*, vol. 26, p. 129.

94 *Young India*, 3 December 1925, *CWMG*, vol. 29, pp. 289–91.
In mid-1928 Gandhi made a further 3-day fast because of a 'moral lapse' in the ashram.

95 *Young India*, 17 December 1925, *CWMG*, vol. 29, pp. 315–19.

96 Gandhi to Manilal Gandhi, 3 April 1926, *CWMG*, vol. 30, pp. 229–30.

97 Gandhi to M. and S. Gandhi, January 1928, *CWMG*, vol. 35, p. 460.

98 Gandhi to J. Nehru, 24 April 1928, *Young India*, 26 April 1928, *CWMG*, vol. 36, pp. 258, 263.

99 *Young India*, 27 August 1925, *CWMG*, vol. 28, p. 112. Examples of Gandhi's refusal to become involved in communal questions, *Young India*, 24 September 1925, *ibid.*, p. 222; *Young India*, 26 November 1925, 21 January 1926, *CWMG*, vol. 29, pp. 278–9, 423.

100 Gandhi to G.D. Birla, 27 April 1926, *CWMG*, vol. 30, p. 372; see also Gandhi to M. Shafee, 22 June 1926, to S.C. Mukherjee, 15 October 1926, *CWMG*, vol. 31, pp. 32, 504, *Young India*, 22 September 1927, *CWMG*, vol. 35, p. 16.

101 *Young India*, 1 December 1927, *CWMG*, vol. 35, pp. 352–4. For his abiding hope for unity see also speech, 16 January 1927, *CWMG*, vol. 32, p. 572.

102 *Young India*, 17 March 1927, *CWMG*, vol. 33, p. 166.

103 *Young India*, 8 May, 12 June 1924, *CWMG*, vol. 24, pp. 14, 238; *Navajivan*, 11 January 1925, *CWMG*, vol. 25, pp. 536–7; *Young India*, 1 October 1925, *CWMG*, vol. 28, p. 265; *Young India*, 17 March 1927, *CWMG*, vol. 35, pp. 165–6.

104 *Young India*, 24 July 1924, *CWMG*, vol. 24, p. 431; *Young India*, 29 January 1925, *CWMG*, vol. 26, p. 50; *Young India*, 27 August 1925, *Navajivan*, 30 August 1925, *CWMG*, vol. 28, pp. 123, 135–6; *Young India*, 9 September 1926, *CWMG*, vol. 31, p. 369.

105 *Navajivan*, 11 January 1925, *CWMG*, vol. 25, p. 536.

106 *Young India*, 4 February 1926, *CWMG*, vol. 29, p. 365.

107 For example, *Young India*, 30 July 1925, *CWMG*, vol. 27, p. 450.

108 *Young India*, 1 October 1925, *CWMG*, vol. 28, pp. 264–8; draft constitution, *ibid.*, pp. 227–30.

109 *Young India*, 8 October 1925, *ibid.*, p. 302.

110 Gandhi to D.D. Gupta, 10 February 1926, to D. Hanumantharao, 21 February 1926, *CWMG*, vol. 29. p. 453, vol. 30, p. 38; Gandhi to G.D. Birla, 16 April 1926, *ibid.*, p. 299.
Total collections in south India and Ceylon are documented in *CWMG*, vol. 35, pp. 526–30. In Tamil Nadu and Kerala, for example, 157,851 rupees were collected.

111 *Young India*, 26 August 1926, 11 August 1927, *CWMG*, vol. 31, p. 327, vol. 34, pp. 320–1; statistics for the first year, *Young India*, 23 December 1926, *CWMG*, vol. 32, p. 450, for the second year, *Young India*, 5 April 1928, *CWMG*, vol. 36, pp. 186–7.

112 Gandhi's ideas on industrial relations are evident in Gandhi to S. Saklatvala, 10 May 1927, to G. Nanda, 15 June 1927, *CWMG*, vol. 33, pp. 301–3, 479–81; speech in Ahmedabad, 1 May 1928, *CWMG*, vol. 36, pp. 288–9. On his attitude to landowners, *Young India*, 4 February 1926, *CWMG*, vol. 29, p. 363. A general discussion of Gandhi's theory of trusteeship is P.J. Rolnick, *loc. cit.* (see chapter 4, n. 38).

113 *Navajivan*, 11 May 1924, *CWMG*, vol. 24, p. 33; *Young India*, 25 March 1926, *CWMG*, vol. 30, p. 170.

114 *Navajivan*, 20 April 1924, *Young India*, 1 May 1924, *CWMG*, vol. 23, pp. 465, 519; *Young India*, 21 August 1924, *CWMG*, vol. 24, pp. 25–6.

115 *Young India*, 24 April 1924, *CWMG*, vol. 23, p. 485; *Navajivan*, 18 May 1924, *CWMG*, vol. 24, p. 40.

116 *Young India*, 10 September 1925, *CWMG*, vol. 28, p. 168.

117 *Young India*, 25 March 1926, *CWMG*, vol. 30, p. 170.

118 Gandhi to G.D. Birla (reporting discussion with Pandit M.M. Malaviya), 20 July 1927, *CWMG*, vol. 34, p. 208; conversation with deputations of untouchables, 15 October 1927, *CWMG*, vol. 35, p. 142.

119 Article, October 1916, *CWMG*, vol. 13, pp. 301–3.

120 *Young India*, 25 February 1926, *CWMG*, vol. 30, p. 47. For his earlier pronouncements, speech, 27 December 1924, *CWMG*, vol. 25, pp. 511–13; *Young India*, 5 February 1925, 12 March 1925, speech, 22 March 1925, *CWMG*, vol. 26, pp.

64–7, 289, 374–5; *Young India*, 21 January 1926, *CWMG*, vol. 29, pp. 410–11.

121 Speeches, 16 September 1927, 4 October 1927, c. 10 October 1927, *Young India*, 17 November 1927, *CWMG*, vol. 35, pp. 1–3, 81, 105–7, 259–63. See also D. Dalton, 'The Gandhian View of Caste, and Caste after Gandhi', P. Mason (ed.). *India and Ceylon: Unity and Diversity* (OUP, 1967), pp. 159–81.

122 *Navajivan*, 11 May 1924, *CWMG*, vol. 24, pp. 33–4.

123 On marriage between people of different sub-castes, *Navajivan*, 11 May 1924, *ibid*, p. 34; *Navajivan*, 13 July 1924, *ibid.*, p. 382; *Navajivan*, 3 May 1925, *CWMG*, vol. 27, p. 20. On a wider restriction of choice of marriage partner, *Young India*, 12 March 1925, *CWMG*, vol. 26, p. 285.

124 *Young India*, 19 March 1925, 30 April 1925, *CWMG*, vol. 26, pp. 328, 569–70.

125 Speech, 30 January 1927, *CWMG*, vol. 33, p. 30.

126 Gandhi to M Gandhi, 8 February 1927, *ibid.*, pp. 55–6.

127 *Navajivan*, 17 August 1924, *CWMG*, vol. 25, p. 7. Gandhi disapproved profoundly of divorce and of artificial means of birth control. He began to deal publicly with the latter topic in March 1925. See *Young India*, 12 March 1925, *CWMG*, vol. 26, pp. 279–80. Articles on the topic in 1926 are in *CWMG*, vol. 31. Gandhi felt that there was an undoubted need to limit births, but that the only moral means was sexual abstinence.

128 Speech, 16 January 1925, *CWMG*, vol. 26, p. 2; *Young India*, 26 August 1925, *CWMG*, vol. 31, p. 330; *Young India*, 28 June 1928, *CWMG*, vol. 36, p. 470.

129 *Young India*, 28 June 1928, *idem.*; *Young India*, 5 August 1926, *CWMG*, vol. 31, p. 263.

130 *Navajivan*, 22 June 1924, *CWMG*, vol. 24, p. 278; *Navajivan*, 24 May 1925, *CWMG*, vol. 27, pp. 151–2; speech, 27 September 1927, *CWMG*, vol. 35, p. 44.

131 Gandhi to ashram women, 13 December 1926, *CWMG*, vol. 32, p. 430.

132 Gandhi to K. Chakravarti, 1 April 1926, *CWMG*, vol. 30, pp. 216–7.

133 *Navajivan*, 25 December 1927, *CWMG*, vol. 35, pp. 419–20.

134 *Young India*, 15 October 1925, *CWMG*, vol. 28, pp. 327–8.

135 *Navajivan*, 28 June 1925, *CWMG*, vol. 27, p. 308.

136 Gandhi to Dr B.C. Roy, 1 May 1928, *CWMG*, vol, 36, p. 287.

CHAPTER 7

1 Press interview, 1 November 1928, *Young India*, 26 April 1928, *CWMG*, vol. 38, p. 5, vol. 36, p. 266.

2 The most accessible specialist accounts of the political environment at this stage of Gandhi's life are (general) Brown, *Modern India*; (political negotiations between Indian groups and the British) R.J. Moore, *The Crisis of Indian Unity 1917–1940* (Clarendon Press, Oxford, 1974); (Gandhi's political role) Judith M. Brown, *Gandhi and Civil Disobedience. The Mathatma in Indian Politics 1928–34* (CUP, 1977).

Because my *Gandhi and Civil Disobedience* deals with this phase with such detailed evidence the minimum of footnotes are given here, being mainly sources for direct quotations; readers will find further evidence in the earlier specialist study.

3 The Simon Commission reported in 1930, but by then its recommendations were obsolete because of rapidly developing British policy in 1929–30. Its report remains a valuable historical source, particularly its survey of society and politics (vol. I: Cmd. 3568, 1930) and its auxiliary committee's report on education (Cmd. 3407, 1929).

4 Gandhi to M. Nehru, 29 February 1928, *CWMG*, vol. 36, p. 67; Gandhi to C.F. Andrews, 21 September 1928, *CWMG*, vol. 37, p. 291.

5 Gandhi to A. Moore, 10 June 1928, *CWMG*, vol. 36, p. 391.

6 Gandhi to B. W. Tucker, 24 February 1928, *ibid.*, p. 49; see also *Young India*, 9 February 1928, *ibid.*, pp. 14–15.

7 Gandhi to J. B. Pennington, 8 June 1928, *ibid.*, pp. 376–77.

8 *All Parties Conference, 1928*; *Report of the Committee appointed by the Conference to determine the principles of the Constitution for India* (Allahabad, 1928). This is described and quoted

extensively in R. Coupland, *The Indian Problem 1833–1935. Report on the Constitutional Problem in India. Part I* (OUP, 1942), pp. 87–96.

9　Jawaharlal was made deeply unhappy by the Nehru Report, but restrained himself as much as possible from making public criticisms of it in mid-1928, not least because his father had so set his heart on the Report. He felt it was too supportive of vested economic interests; but his main criticism was its goal of dominion status rather than total independence. See J. Nehru, *An Autobiography*, pp. 171–3; J. Nehru to N.S. Hardikar, 8 October 1928, NMML, N.S. Hardikar Papers, File no. II.

10　S. Ali to Gandhi, 23 October 1928, *CWMG*, vol. 38, pp. 436–7. For Gandhi's interest in the Conference see Brown, *Gandhi and Civil Disobedience*, p. 27, fn. 54.

11　Gandhi to M. Nehru, 29 February 1928, *CWMG*, vol. 36, p. 68.

12　*Young India*, 23 August, 6 September, 6 December 1928, *CWMG*, vol. 37, pp. 196–7, 233–4, vol. 38, p. 137. Gandhi did realize that it was an entirely Western-style constitution, the logical outcome of their present structures of government, and the work to be expected of a man experienced in the existing central legislature. But this did not detract from his support for it: 'if it does not suit the genius of the people . . . they will destroy it and raise another into being.' Gandhi to M. Zafarulmulk, 8 September 1928, *CWMG*, vol. 37, p. 243.

13　Gandhi to M. Nehru, 3 March 1928, *CWMG*, vol. 36, p. 76–7.

14　For the Bardoli satyagraha see the first-hand account by Gandhi's secretary, Mahadev Desai, *The Story of Bardoli* (Navajivan, Ahmedabad, 1929). Later analyses are Brown, *Gandhi and Civil Disobedience*, pp. 29–33; B.G. Gokhale, 'Sardar Vallabhbhai Petel: the Party Organizer as Political Leader', R.L. Park & I. Tinker (ed.), *Leadership and Political Institutions in India* (Princeton University Press, 1959), pp. 87–99; A. Bhatt, 'Caste and Political Mobilisation in a Gujarat District', R. Kothari (ed.), *Castle in Indian Politics* (Orient Longman, New Delhi, 1970), pp. 299–339.

15　*Navajivan*, 22 July 1928, *CWMG*, vol. 37, p. 85.

16　*Young India*, 8 March 1928, *CWMG*, vol. 36, p. 90. See also *Navajivan*, 9 September 1928, *CWMG*, vol. 37, p. 249.

17　*Young India*, 17 May 1928, *Navajivan*, 10 June 1928, *CWMG*, vol. 36, pp. 321–2, 384; *Young India*, 9 August 1928, *CWMG*, vol. 37, pp. 146–7.

18　*Navajivan*, 3 June, 19 August 1928, *CWMG*, vol. 36, p. 360, vol. 37, pp. 190–1.

19　Gandhi to C.F. Andrews, 24 August 1928, *CWMG*, vol. 37, p. 200. For similar sentiments see *Young India*, 12 July, 6 September 1928, Gandhi to R.B. Gregg, 14 August 1928, *ibid.*, pp. 46, 234, 176.

20　*Young India*, 6 December 1928, *CWMG*, vol. 38, pp. 162–3; see also *Young India*, 27 December 1928, *ibid.*, p. 245.

21　For details of the 1928 Calcutta Congress see Brown, *Gandhi and Civil Disobedience*, pp. 36–9; main speeches by Gandhi and resolutions are in *CWMG*, vol. 38.

22　Gandhi to M. Nehru, 17 January 1929, NMML, Motilal Nehru Papers, File G-1; *Young India*, 20 March 1930, *CWMG*, vol. 43, p. 43.

23　Speech in Subjects Committee, 28 December 1928, *CWMG*, vol. 38, p. 289.

24　Answers to questions during visit to Burma, 10 March 1929, *CWMG*, vol. 40, p. 122; speech in Calcutta, 4 March 1929, *ibid.*, p. 80.

25　For example, Sir Grimwood Mears, Chief Justice, Allahabad High Court, to Lord Irwin, 26 March and 29 April 1929, I.O.L., Halifax Papers, Mss. EUR. C. 152 (23); diary of Dr B.S. Moonje, 25 October 1929, NMML, microfilm of Moonje Diaries.

26　*Young India*, 5 September 1929, *CWMG*, vol. 41, p. 276.

27　*Young India*, 7 March 1929, *CWMG*, vol. 40, p. 92.

28　Gandhi's proposed scheme, *Young India*, 24 January 1929, *CWMG*, vol. 38, pp. 388–9.

29　Gandhi to Mirabehn, 5 May 1929, *CWMG*, vol. 40, p. 344.

30　*Young India*, 5 September 1929, *CWMG*, vol. 41, p. 351.

31　Gandhi to J. Nehru, 1 February

1929, NMML, J. Nehru Papers, Part I, vol. XXII.

32 Sri Prakasa to J. Nehru, 5 May 1929, NMML, AICC Papers, 1929, File No. P 24. For further evidence on Congress organization, finances and recruitment see Brown, *Gandhi and Civil Disobedience*, pp. 49–53.

33 Speech at AICC, 27 July 1929, *CWMG*, vol. 41, pp. 228–9; compare Gandhi's original attitude, *Young India*, 13 June 1929, *ibid.*, pp. 42–3.

34 On this episode see Brown, *Gandhi and Civil Disobedience*, pp. 56–7; *Young India*, 1 August, 12 September 1929, *CWMG*, vol. 41, pp. 239–41, 378–9; J. to M. Nehru, 30 August 1929, NMML, M. Nehru Papers.

35 Gandhi to H. Alexander, 22 June 1928, *CWMG*, vol. 36, p. 449.

36 *CWMG*, vol. 40, pp. 283–4, vol. 41, pp. 445–8.

37 *Young India*, 28 March 1929, *CWMG*, vol. 40, pp. 63–4.

38 'My Shame and Sorrow', originally published in *Navajivan*, 7 April 1929, *ibid.*, pp. 209–12.

39 Gandhi to Chhaganlal Joshi, 6 October 1929, *CWMG*, vol. 41, p. 519.

40 Gandhi to G.D. Birla, 3 June 1929, *ibid.*, p. 13. *CWMG*, vol. 41 contains Gandhi's articles on the raw food experiment.

41 Gandhi to C. Joshi, 16 September 1929, *ibid.*, pp. 412–13.

42 Secretary, Home Dept., Govt. of India, to all local govts, 21 February 1929, IOL, L/PJ/6/1976.

Local governments were urged to use the ordinary law efficiently to retain the initiative against Congress and its activities, but not to act against major leaders without careful consideration and consultation with Delhi.

An analysis of the government's policy is D.A. Low, '"Civil Martial Law": the Government of India and the Civil Disobedience Movements, 1930–34', D.A. Low (ed.), *Congress And The Raj. Facets of the Indian Struggle 1917–47* (Heinemann, London, 1977), pp. 165–198.

43 Irwin to Peel, 24 January 1929, IOL, Halifax Papers, Mss. EUR. C. 152 (5).

44 For the Irwin Declaration and the cross-currents of politics which accompanied and very nearly des-

troyed it, see Brown, *Gandhi and Civil Disobedience*, pp. 62–3; Moore, *The Crisis of Indian Unity 1917–1940*, pp. 51–94.

45 H. Haig to J. Hotson, 25 May 1930, NAI, Home Political Files, 1930, no. 257/V & K.-W.

46 The intricacies of negotiations and shifts in opinions and relationships among Congressmen and Liberals in these weeks are worked out with substantial references to sources in Brown, *Gandhi and Civil Disobedience*, pp. 63–74.

47 Sherwood Eddy to Irwin, 3 December 1929, IOL, Halifax Papers, Mss. EUR. C. 152 (23).

Gandhi's worries about the strength of the Labour Party as an ally were evident also in *Navajivan*, 8 December 1929, *CWMG*, vol. 42, p. 251.

48 V.S.S. Sastri to Sir P.S. Sivaswami Aiyar, 2 December 1929, Jagadisan (ed.), *Letters of the Right Honourable V.S. Srinivasa Sastri* (2nd edn, Asia Publishing House, Bombay, 1963), pp. 183–4.

49 For details of the Lahore Congress see Brown, *Gandhi and Civil Disobedience*, pp. 74–80: Gandhi's many speeches at Lahore are in *CWMG*, vol. 42.

50 *Young India*, 20 March 1930, *CWMG*, vol. 43, p. 43.

51 Quoted in Punjab Fortnightly Report for second half of December 1929, NAI, Home Political Files, 1929, No. 17.

52 *Young India*, 9 January 1930, *CWMG*, vol. 42, pp. 376–7.

53 Gandhi to J. Nehru, 10 January 1930, NMML, AICC Papers, 1930, File no. Misc. 26.

54 Gandhi to C.F. Andrews, 2 February 1930, *CWMG*, vol. 42, p. 444.

55 *Young India*, 30 January 1930, *ibid.*, pp. 434–5.

56 Gandhi to Irwin, 2 March 1930, IOL, Halifax Papers, Mss. EUR. C. 152 (4).

57 J. Nehru's *Foreword*, 30 June 1951, D.G. Tendulkar, *Mahatma*, vol. 1, 1869–1920 (2nd ed., Govt. of India Delhi, 1960), p. xii.

58 Collector of Ahmedabad to Home Dept., Govt. of Bombay, 2 April 1930, NAI, Home Political Files, 1930, No. 247/II; Viceroy to Secretary of State, 7 April 1930, IOL, Hali-

fax Papers, Mss. EUR.C. 152 (6).

59 Speech on 26 March 1930, *CWMG*, vol. 43, p. 126; see also press interview, *c*.11 March 1930, *ibid*, p. 39. Gandhi's speeches during the march are in *CWMG*, vol. 43.

60 Viceroy to Secretary of State, 26 March 1930, IOL, Halifax Papers, Mss. EUR. C. 152 (6).

61 Viceroy to Secretary of State, 24 April 1930, *idem*.; Bombay Govt. to Govt. of India, Home Dept., telegram, 26 April 1930, IOL, Sykes Papers, Mss. EUR. F. 150 (2).

62 Viceroy to Secretary of State, 13 March, 7 April 1930, IOL, Halifax Papers, Mss. EUR. C. 152 (6).

63 F.G. Griffith to G.F.S. Collins (Secretary, Govt. of Bombay), 5 May 1930, *Source Material for a History of the Freedom Movement in India. Vol. III. Mahatma Gandhi. Part III: 1929–1931* (Govt. of Maharashtra, Bombay, 1969), p. 124 (henceforth *HFM III, III*)

For the details of government policy towards Gandhi during the salt march see Brown, *Gandhi and Civil Disobedience*, pp. 106–12.

64 See Brown, *ibid*., pp. 112–152.

65 Note by H. Haig, 13 June 1930, NAI, Home Political Files, 1930, no. 257/V & K.-W.

66 Sapru to Irwin, 19 September 1930, IOL, Halifax Papers, Mss. EUR. C. 152 (25).

67 Gandhi to Mirabehn, and to N. Gandhi, 12 May 1930, *CWMG*, vol. 43, pp. 402, 403.

68 Gandhi to E.E. Doyle, 10 May 1930, to N. Gandhi, 12 May 1930, to Saraladevi, 25 May 1930, *ibid*., pp. 401, 403–4, 421. Evidence on Gandhi's life in gaol is in *CWMG*, vols. 43 and 44; and in *HFM III, III*.

69 Gandhi to N. Gandhi, 22/23 June 1930, *CWMG*, vol. 43, p. 441.

70 Comments by Kalelkar after his release in late November, *Bombay Chronicle*, 1 January 1931, *CWMG*, vol. 44, p. 347, fn.1; Gandhi to N. Gandhi, 25/30 September 1930, *ibid*, p. 186.

71 Note by R.V. Martin, 19 December 1930, *HFM III, III*, p. 178. (The regular official medical reports on Gandhi are in this volume.)

72 Gandhi to N. Gandhi, 20/26 January 1931, *CWMG*, vol. 45, p. 124; NMML, microfilm of B.S. Moonje

diaries, 2 August 1930, noting Jayakar's observation.

73 Interview to the *Daily Herald*, 20 May 1930, *CWMG*, vol. 43, pp. 415–17; Gandhi to W. Wellock, Birmingham MP, 11 July 1930, *CWMG*, vol. 44, p. 15.

74 Viceroy to Secretary of State, telegram, 2 June 1930, IOL, Halifax Papers, Mss. EUR. C. 152 (11); Secretary of State to Viceroy, 20 June 1930, *ibid*. (6). A full account of British policy and the abortive mediation between Congress and government in mid-1930 is in Brown, *Gandhi and Civil Disobedience*, pp. 155–168.

75 See Moore, *The Crisis of Indian Unity 1917–1940*, pp. 103–64.

76 Press interview, 26 January 1931, *CWMG*, vol. 45, p. 125.

77 Gandhi to Irwin, 14 February 1931, IOL, Cunningham Papers, Mss. EUR. D. 670. (This is the original: copies are in IOL, Halifax Papers, Mss. EUR. C. 152 (6) and (26).)

78 Irwin to Wedgwood Benn, 16 February 1931, IOL, Halifax Papers, Mss. EUR. C. 152 (6).

79 V.S.S. Sastri to T.R.V. Sastri, 17 February 1931, Jagadisan (ed.), *Letters of Srinivasa Sastri*, p. 209. Details of the talks are in Brown, *Gandhi and Civil Disobedience*, pp. 178–86. Irwin's later warm tribute to Gandhi is remarkable: Halifax, *Fulness of Days* (Collins, London, 1957), pp. 146–51. Gandhi's appreciation of Irwin was generous and public: press statement, 5 March 1931, *CWMG*, vol. 45, p. 250.

80 Press statement, 5 March 1931, interview to journalists, 6 March 1931, *Navajivan*, 15 March 1931, *ibid*., pp. 250–6, 263–7, 296.

81 On the Karachi Congress, see Brown, *Gandhi and Civil Disobedience*, pp. 200–4; important resolutions and Gandhi's speeches *CWMG*, Vol. 45; Congress official report on Karachi session, IOL, microfilm pos. 2274.

82 K.F. Nariman to S.A. Brelvi, 1 March 1931, NMML, S.A. Brelvi Papers.

83 Gandhi to C.F. Andrews, 29 April 1931, *CWMG*, vol. 46, p. 50.

84 Gandhi argued that the CWC decision was to save money, keep good workers in India where real work for

swaraj was done, and ensure that Congress spoke with one voice: *Young India*, 9 April 1931, *CWMG*, vol. 45, pp. 403–4. See also *Young India*, 18 June 1931, *CWMG*, vol. 47, pp. 1–3.

85 The appallingly intricate details of Gandhi's role in April-August 1931 are unravelled in Brown, *Gandhi and Civil Disobedience*, pp. 206–41.

86 Willingdon to Hoare, 28 August 1931, IOL, Templewood Papers, Mss. EUR. E. 240 (5).

87 M. Desai to J. Nehru, 31 August 1931, NMML, J Nehru Papers, Part I, vol. xvii. For details of Gandhi's time in England, see Brown, *Gandhi and Civil Disobedience*, pp. 242–62; Gandhi's speeches at the Round Table Conference, other speeches in England and a brief diary of meetings, 14 October–31 December 1931, are in *CWMG*, vol. 48. Further analysis of the Round Tabel Conference is in Moore, *The Crisis of Indian Unity 1917–1940* pp. 218–239.

88 Interview to press, 5 September 1931, Gandhi Papers, Sabarmati, SN no. 17643.

89 J. Nehru to Gandhi 11 September 1931, setting out minium Congress demands, NMML, J. Nehru Papers, Part I, vol. xxiii. Also V. Patel to Gandhi, 10 September 1931, Gandhi Papers, Sabarmati, SN no. 17681.

90 Speech at Minorities Committee meeting, 13 November 1931, *CWMG*, vol. 48, pp. 293–8.

91 Hoare to Willingdon, 19 November 1931, IOL, Templewood Papers, Mss. EUR. E. 240 (1).

92 Interview to press, 3 December 1931, *CWMG*, vol. 48, p. 381.

93 On the details of government plans to deal with Gandhi's return and the possible renewal of civil disobedience, see Brown, *Gandhi and Civil Disobedience*, pp. 271–4.

94 Willingdon to Hoare, 10 January 1932, IOL, Templewood Papers, Mss. EUR. E. 240 (5). Interestingly Hoare thought Willingdon did not understand Gandhi's personality: he guessed Irwin would have seen Gandhi without imposing conditions: Templewood, *Nine Troubled Years* (Collins, London, 1954), pp. 66–7.

95 Gandhi to N. Gandhi, 25 January 1932, *CWMG*, vol. 49, p. 32. On his

weariness and need of rest, Gandhi to H. Alexander, 25 March 1932, *ibid.*, p. 236; diary entries, 10 and 29 January 1931, *ibid.*, pp. 506, 509. See also 17 March 1932, *The Diary of Mahadev Desai, Volume I* (Navajivan, Ahmedabad, 1953), p. 17.

96 A survey of the 1932–3 civil disobedience campaign is in Brown, *Gandhi and Civil Disobedience*, pp. 282–311.

97 *Ibid.*, pp. 307–10.

98 Evidence of his life in gaol is in *The Diary of Mahadev Desai, vol. I*; and Gandhi's own brief diaries, *CWMG*, vol. 49, pp. 505–27; vol. 50, pp. 453–65; vol. 51, pp. 440–53.

99 28 June 1932, *The Diary of Mahadev Desai, vol. I*, p. 199.

100 Letters on the *Gita*, *CWMG*, vol. 49, pp. 111–49; history of the ashram, *CWMG*, vol. 50, pp. 188–236.

101 Gandhi to Sir S. Hoare, 11 March 1932, IOL, Templewood Papers, Mss. EUR. E. 240 (16); 10 March 1932, *The Diary of Mahadev Desai, vol. I*, pp. 4–5.

102 *East India (Constitutional Reforms) Communal Decision*, Pp. 1931–2, xviii, Cmd. 4147.

103 Gandhi to R. MacDonald, 18 August 1932, IOL, Templewood Papers, Mss. EUR. E. 240 (16).

104 Gandhi to M. M. Bhatt, Devadas Gandhi, Kasturbhai Gandhi, N. Gandhi, all on 13 September 1932, to Mirabehn, 15 September 1932, *CWMG*, vol. 51, pp. 50–3, 56–7.

105 'But my general recoil from his method is so great that if the use of single words were not open to serious objection, I should call it moral coercion and the result achieved *whitemail* (formed on the analogy of blackmail).' V.S.S. Sastri to P. Kodanda Rao, 10 October 1932, Jagadisan (ed.), *Letters of Srinivasa Sastri*, p. 238. See also 22 September 1932, entry in J. Nehru's prison diary, *Selected Works of Jawaharlal Nehru, Volume Five* (Orient Longman, Delhi, 1973), pp. 407–8 (henceforth *SWJN*).

106 Press statements, 16, 20 and 23 September 1932, *CWMG*, vol. 51, pp. 62–5, 116–20, 132–3; Gandhi to B. Bijoria, 10 October 1932, *ibid.*, p. 226.

107 Gandhi to S.M. Mate, 2 October 1932, *ibid.*, p. 167.

108 Gandhi to N. Gandhi, 2 October 1932, to H. Alexander, 4 October 1932, to E. Menon, 4 October 1932, *ibid.*, pp. 174–5, 186, 187. This whole episode is discussed and documented in detail in Brown, *Gandhi and Civil Disobedience*, pp. 318–323.

109 Gandhi's gaol diary, 16 November 1932 to 31 December 1932 gives an idea of his work; *CWMG*, vol. 51, pp. 315–27.

110 For a discussion of this fast, see Brown, *Gandhi and Civil Disobedience*, pp. 336–8; Gandhi's announcement of fast, 30 April 1933, *Harijan*, 6 May 1933, *CWMG*, vol. 55, pp. 74–5; letter to J. Nehru, 2 May 1933, NMML, J. Nehru Papers, Part I, vol. XXIII. In the Gandhi Papers the file for May 1933 is full of his friend's and colleagues' complaints at his plan.

111 Gandhi's 8 May 1933 statement on civil disobedience, NAI, Home Political Files, 1933, no. 4/11.

112 Gandhi to P.K. Kapadia, 8 January 1933, *CWMG*, vol. 52, p. 399, Further evidence is Gandhi's attitude to his fasts is a statement on 4 December 1932, *ibid.*, pp. 112–14.

113 4 June 1933 entry, *SWJN*, 5, p. 478.

114 Gandhi to M. Asaf Ali, 26 June 1933, Gandhi Papers, SN no. 19108.

115 Statement, 26 July 1933, NAI, Home Political Files, 1933, no. 4/11. For details of the Poona conference and subsequent developments see Brown, *Gandhi and Civil Disobedience*, pp. 343–6.

116 T.B. Sapru to S. Sinha and to M. R. Jayakar, both 13 August 1933, IOL, Sapru Papers, 2nd Series.

117 V.S.S. Sastri to Gandhi, 27 August, 4 September 1933, Gandhi to V.S.S. Sastri, 30 August, 9 September 1933, Jagadisan (ed.), *Letters of Srinivasa Sastri*, pp. 258–265.

118 Statement, 14 September 1933, NAI, Home Political Files, 1933, no. 3/17. On the basic ideological rift between them displayed in the tactful device of an exchange of letters, see Brown, *Gandhi and Civil Disobedience*, pp. 355–6. These letters are in NAI, Home Political Files, 1933, no. 4/11.

119 Gandhi to M.A. Ansari, 18 March 1934, NAI, Home Political Files, 1934, no. 3/6. On the search by many Congressmen for a new prog-

ramme, see Brown, *Gandhi and Civil Disobedience*, pp. 360–373.

120 *Harijan*, 2 February 1934, *CWMG*, vol. 57, pp. 86–7.

121 Press statement, released on 7 April 1934, *CWMG*, vol. 57, pp. 348–50.

122 Gandhi to Vallabhbhai Patel, 18 April 1934, *ibid.*, pp. 403–5; see also Gandhi to M.A. Ansari, 5 April 1933, and to J. Nehru, 14 April 1933, *ibid.*, pp. 352–3, 388.

123 For example, Gandhi to Agatha Harrison, 7 August 1934, Gandhi Papers, Letter File, Aug.-Dec. 1934; Gandhi to Vallabhbhai Patel, 19 August 1934, *CWMG*, vol. 58, pp. 329–30; Gandhi to C. Rajagopalachariar, 3 September 1934, also sent by M. Desai to R. Prasad, NAI, R. Prasad Papers, File no. VII/35, Coll. 1.

124 Press statement, 17 September 1934, *CWMG*, vol. 59, pp. 3–12.

125 Gandhi to Mirabehn, 12 October 1934, Gandhi Papers, File, Aug.-Dec. 1934.

CHAPTER 8

1 On the new constitutional experiment, see Brown, *Modern India*, pp. 284–305.

2 Speech, 3 March 1936, *CWMG*, vol. 62, pp. 223–5.

3 *Harijan*, 30 September 1939, *CWMG*, vol. 70, p. 203.

4 Gandhi to M. Sevenich, 13 August 1937, *CWMG*, vol. 66, p. 43.

5 Gandhi to Mirabehn, 20 January 1939, *CWMG*, vol. 68, pp. 310–11.

6 Conversation with C. Rajagopalachariar, 7 January 1938, *Harijan*, 15 January 1938, *CWMG*, vol. 66, pp. 329–30.

7 This breakdown is documented in letters from M. Desai to J. Nehru, 13, 19 December 1935, 10, 15, 22 January 1936, NMML, J. Nehru Papers; see also references in *CWMG*, vol. 62.

8 Gandhi to J.C. Kumarappa, 2 February 1939, to Lord Linlithgow, 12 February 1939, *CWMG*, vol. 68, pp. 362, 409. The late 1937 collapse is documented in *CWMG*, vol. 66. See also M. Desai to V.S.S. Sastri, 28 April 1938, NMML, V.S.S. Sastri Papers.

9 Speech at Bannu, 25 October 1938, *CWMG*, vol. 68, p. 55. On the 1935

silence see speech, 19 April 1935, *CWMG*, vol. 60, p. 434.

10 Gandhi to C. Tyagi, 15 September 1936, *CWMG*, vol. 63, p. 288; *Harijan*, 5 November 1938, *CWMG*, vol. 68, p. 53.

11 Gandhi to Amrit Kaur, 2 April 1938, *CWMG*, vol. 67, p. 2; see M. Desai's account of the affair, *Harijan*, 9 April 1938, *ibid.*, pp. 445–447.

12 See correspondence between Gandhi and Amrit Kaur in mid-1938, NMML, A. Kaur Papers, File no. G1; Amrit Kaur to J. Nehru, 9 September 1938, NMML, J. Nehru Papers.

13 *Harijan*, 6 February 1937, *CWMG*, vol. 64, p. 347; Gandhi to Amrit Kaur, 8 September 1937, *CWMG*, vol. 66, p. 115.

14 Gandhi to Devadas Gandhi, 27 August 1938, *CWMG*, vol. 67, p. 288.

15 On the earlier experience see *Harijan*, 29 February 1936, and Gandhi to P. Kantak, 21 May 1936, *CWMG*, vol. 62, pp. 211–12, 428–30. On his 1938 experience see Gandhi to Mirabehn, 3 May 1938, to Amrit Kaur, 7 May 1938, *CWMG*, vol. 67, pp. 61, 69.

16 Gandhi to Amrit Kaur, 24 October 1938, *CWMG*, vol. 68, p. 49. He spelt out the connection between chastity and power in *Harijan*, 23 July 1938, *CWMG*, vol. 67, pp. 195–8; *Harijanbandhu*, 22 October 1939, *CWMG*, vol. 70, pp. 287–9.

17 Speech, 16 January 1937, *CWMG*, vol. 64, p. 253.

18 Speech, 16 February 1936, *Harijan*, 29 February 1936, *CWMG*, vol. 62, pp. 192, 211–12; *Harijan*, 6 February 1937, *CWMG*, vol. 64, pp. 347–8.

19 Gandhi to J. Nehru, 25 April 1938, NMML, J. Nehru Papers; Amrit Kaur to J. Nehru, 29 May 1939, NMML, J. Nehru Papers.

20 *Harijan*, 18 August 1940, *CWMG*, vol. 72, pp. 354–5; press statement on Harilal's 'conversion' to Islam, 2 June 1936, *CWMG*, vol. 63, pp. 5–7.

21 Gandhi to S. Gandhi, 20 August 1938, *CWMG*, vol. 67, p. 271.

22 Gandhi to Devadas Gandhi, 15 May 1940, *CWMG*, vol. 72, p. 70.

23 Amrit Kaur to J. Nehru, 16 March and 24 May 1938, NMML, J. Nehru Papers.

24 Discussion with a friend, *c.* 10 October 1939, Gandhi to Amrit Kaur, 29 October 1939, *CWMG*, vol. 70, pp. 247, 309. Gandhi's letters are full of references to disagreements in Sevagram: see *CWMG*, vol. 65.

25 *Harijan*, 9 April 1938, *CWMG*, vol. 67, p. 447; see also Gandhi to Pyarelal, 22 November 1937, *CWMG*, vol. 66, p. 307.

26 Gandhi to Amrit Kaur, 18 May 1936. NMML, Amrit Kaur Papers, File no. G1.

27 Vallabhbhai Patel to J. Nehru, 3 July 1939, Amrit Kaur to J. Nehru, 6 July 1939, NMML, J. Nehru Papers.

28 Gandhi to Amrit Kaur, 8 April 1936, NMML, Amrit Kaur Papers, File no. G1. On the 'surrender' Gandhi seemed to require, see Amrit Kaur to J. Nehru, 18 February 1940, NMML, J. Nehru Papers.

29 Press statement, 24 April 1939, *CWMG*, vol. 69, p. 168. See also press interview, 27 April 1939, *ibid.*, p. 178.

30 See *Harijan*, 13 June 1936, *CWMG*, vol. 63, p. 58; Gandhi to Amrit Kaur, 7 May 1938, NMML, Amrit Kaur Papers, File no. G1; discussion with J.R. Mott, December 1938, *Harijan*, 28 January 1939, *CWMG*, vol. 68, pp. 169, 321. On Gandhi's definition of Truth as God, see interview with a Christian student, May 1935, *CWMG*, vol. 61, p. 81.

31 Gandhi to J. Nehru, 30 July 1936, NMML, J. Nehru Papers.

32 *Harijan*, 18 April 1936, *CWMG*, vol. 62, p. 334.

33 Discussion with J.R. Mott, December 1938, *CWMG*, vol. 68, pp. 172–3.

34 Speech at Trivandrum, 13 January 1937, interview to temple trustee, 18 January 1937, *CWMG*, vol. 64, pp. 238–9, 280.

35 Speech at Quilon, 16 January 1937, *ibid.*, pp. 258–60. For an examination of Gandhi's relationship to the Hindu tradition at this stage of his career, see Judith M. Brown, 'Mahatmas as Reformers: Some Problems of Religious Authority in the Indian Nationalist Movement', *South Asia Research*, vol. 6, no. 1 (May 1986), pp. 15–26.

36 Gandhi to D.B. Kalelkar, early September 1938, *CWMG*, vol. 67, p. 321.

37 *Harijan*, 28 November 1936, *CWMG*, vol. 64, p. 85.

38 'Caste has to Go', *Harijan*, 16 November 1935, 'Caste and Varna', *Harijanbandhu*, 19 January 1936, *CWMG*, vol. 62, pp. 121–2, 142–3.

39 Gandhi to Ganagabehn Vaidya, 3 August 1937, *CWMG*, vol. 66, p. 9.

40 Speech, 2 January 1935, *CWMG*, vol. 60, pp. 46–7.

41 Gandhi to E. Menon, 5 January 1935, *ibid.*, p. 57.

42 Press statement, 15 October 1935, *CWMG*, vol. 62, p. 37. On the work of Gandhi and Ambedkar and their differences on the untouchable problem, see E. Zelliot, 'Gandhi and Ambedkar – A Study in Leadership', in J. Michael Mahar (ed.), *The Untouchables in Contemporary India* (University of Arizona Press, Tucson, Arizona, 1972), pp. 69–95.

43 Gandhi to C. Heath, 3 January 1935, *CWMG*, vol. 60, p. 50.

44 Gandhi to A. Harrison, 7 March 1935, *ibid.*, p. 277.

45 *Harijan*, 5 and 26 September 1936, *CWMG*, vol. 63, pp. 262, 320–1.

46 Gandhi to P. Kantak, 10 September 1935, *CWMG*, vol. 61, p. 404.

47 *Harijan*, 23 July 1938, *CWMG*, vol. 67, pp. 194–8; also *Harijan*, 12 October 1935, *CWMG*, vol. 62, p. 30.

48 Speech, 31 May 1939, *Harijan*, 24 June and 8 July 1939, *CWMG*, vol. 69, pp. 312–14, 359–61, 389–92.

49 *Harijan*, 20 February 1937, 20 April 1940, *CWMG*, vol. 64, p. 385, vol. 71, p. 424.

50 Gandhi to P. Kantak, 10 September 1935, *CWMG*, vol. 61, p. 403.

51 Gandhi to M. Rolland, March 1935, *CWMG*, vol. 60, p. 326; speech, 4 March 1936, *CWMG*, vol. 62, p. 231; *Harijan*, 14 April 1940, *CWMG*, vol. 71, p. 425.

52 On Gandhi's attitude to the States, see, for example, *Harijan*, 9 July and 3 December 1938, *CWMG*, vol. 67, pp. 157–8, vol. 68, pp. 151–3.

53 Gandhi to ruler of Rajkot, 2 March 1939, press statements, 2 and 3 March 1939, *CWMG*, vol. 69, pp. 1–5, 9–10, 10–13.

54 Press statement, 7 March 1939, *ibid.*, pp. 33–7; on the broader view of Lord Linlithgow see J. Glendevon, *The Viceroy at Bay. Lord Linlithgow in India 1936–1943* (Collins, London, 1971), p. 115.

55 Press statement, 17 May 1939, *CWMG*, vol. 69, pp. 269–71. Gandhi's internal agonizings prior to this are documented in *ibid.*, pp. 162–6, 168–71, 255–8.

56 Press statement, 24 April 1939, answers to questions, 5 May 1939, speech, 7 May 1939, *ibid.*, pp. 168–71, 216, 241–2.

57 Gandhi to J. Nehru, 29 July 1939, *Harijan*, 5 August 1939, *CWMG*, vol. 70, pp. 42, 45.

58 Gandhi to Z. Husain, 25 May 1936, *CWMG*, vol. 62, pp. 441–2.

59 Gandhi to S.B. Ahmed, late September 1937, Gandhi to M.A. Jinnah, 24 February 1938, *CWMG*, vol. 66, pp. 182, 387.

60 There are no really adequate accounts of M.A. Jinnah's life and work. The following are helpful: H. Bolitho, *Jinnah. Creator of Pakistan* (John Murray, London, 1954); S.A. Wolpert, *Jinnah of Pakistan* (OUP New York, 1984); A. Jalal, *The Sole Spokesman. Jinnah, the Muslim League and the Demand for Pakistan* (CUP, 1985).

61 The rise of the Muslim League and the rapid deterioration of communal relations in the late 1930s is a complex and ideologically loaded subject. For a consideration of it, see Brown, *Modern India*, pp. 297–305. More recently Ian Talbot's work on the growth of the League in the Muslim majority provinces, which would make a Pakistan viable, has stressed the local reasons Muslim politicians had for this move, and the shallowness of the League's political roots: *Provincial Politics and the Pakistan Movement. The Growth of the Muslim League in North-West and North-East India 1937–47* (OUP, Karachi, 1988).

62 The exchange of letters between Gandhi and Jinnah from 19 October 1937 to 8 March 1938 is available in *CWMG*, vol. 66, pp. 257, 470, 349–50, 479–80, 387, 480–1, 395–6. Gandhi's remarks on Jinnah's toughness in negotiating style are in letter to Amrit Kaur, 22 May 1938, NMML, A Kaur Papers, File no. G 1.

63 Speech in Peshawar, 4 May 1938, *CWMG*, vol. 67, p. 62.

64 Gandhi to P. Kantak, 5 April 1935, *CWMG*, vol. 60, pp. 388–9; *Hari-*

jan, 2 October 1935, *CWMG*, vol. 62, p. 28; Gandhi to M.A. Jinnah, 22 May 1937, *CWMG*, vol. 65, p. 231.

65 Gandhi on the way of substantial village work among Muslims, to J. Nehru, 30 July 1937, NMML, J. Nehru Papers; discussion with colleagues, 26 March 1938, *CWMG*, vol. 66, p. 430.

66 *Harijan*, 4 November 1939, *CWMG*, vol. 70, p. 315.

67 Press interview, 21 January 1935, *CWMG*, vol. 60, p. 104.

68 Gandhi to Vallabhbhai Patel, 26 December 1934, *ibid.*, pp. 32–3. P. Spear, then a young lecturer at St Stephen's College, Delhi, and later a distinguished historian of India, was well aware that though Gandhi's work was avowedly non-political, everything he did was connected with Congress, and Congress would ultimately gain. P. Spear to H. Alexander, 17 April 1935, NMML, Letters of H. Alexander.

69 Speech, 3 March 1936, *CWMG*, vol. 62, p. 227.

70 Gandhi to Amrit Kaur, 11 April 1935, NMML, Amrit Kaur Papers, File no. G1; Gandhi to J. N. Parekh, 22 September 1936, *CWMG*, vol. 63, p. 306.

71 *Harijan*, 5 and 19 September 1936, *ibid.*, pp. 257, 295.

72 Speech at Gujarat Political Conference, 3 November 1917, *CWMG*, vol. 14, p. 56. Cf. Gandhi's statement in *Harijan*, 19 September 1936, that India lived in her villages, *not* in her cities; *CWMG*, vol. 63, p. 295.

73 *Harijan*, 4 January 1935, *CWMG*, vol. 60, pp. 54–5. Gandhi's castigation of urban as exploitative is in speech, 12 April 1936, *CWMG*, vol. 62, p. 324.

74 *Harijan*, 28 January 1939, *CWMG*, vol. 68, p. 266.

75 Gandhi to P. N. Reddy, 10 February 1935, *CWMG*, vol. 60, p. 202.

76 'A Fatal Fallacy', *Harijan*, 11 January 1936, *CWMG*, vol. 62, pp. 92–3. For Gandhi's views in 1931, see *Young India*, 2 July and 6 August 1931, *CWMG*, vol. 47, pp. 90–2, 252; and discussion in Brown, *Gandhi and Civil Disobedience*, p. 224.

77 Gandhi on the needful change in AISA policy, *Harijan*, 6 July 1935, *CWMG*, vol. 61, pp. 232–3; October resolution of AISA, *CWMG*, vol. 62, pp. 471–2; evidence on the AISA is in NMML, AICC Papers, File nos. G-67 (1934–6), G-27 (1937–8).

78 *Harijan*, 21 December 1934, *CWMG*, vol. 60, p. 17; the AIVIA's objectives and constitution were set out in the same issue of *Harijan*, *CWMG*, vol. 59, pp. 449–453. Evidence on the AIVIA is in NMML, AICC Papers, File No. G-22 (1935).

79 Fortnightly Reports from CP for first half of October and December 1935, NAI, Home Political Files, 1935, nos. 18/10 and 18/12.

80 *Harijan*, 22 June 1935, *CWMG*, vol. 61, pp. 187–8; *Harijan*, 28 January 1939, *CWMG*, vol. 68, pp. 258–9, 266.

81 Gandhi to Amrit Kaur, 29 June 1939, *CWMG*, vol. 69, p. 384; Gandhi to J. Nehru, 11 August 1939, *CWMG*, vol. 70, p. 86.

82 Gandhi to Amrit Kaur, 4 May 1936, *CWMG*, vol. 62, p. 369; Gandhi to A.V. Thakkar, 12 August 1936, *CWMG*, vol. 63, p. 218. For glimpses into the life and work at Sevagram, see Balvantsinha, *Under the Shelter of Bapu*, (Navajivan, Ahmedabad, 1962).

83 Amrit Kaur to J. Nehru, 7 March 1937, NMML, J. Nehru Papers.

84 Press interview, 22 May 1935, *CWMG*, vol. 61, p. 86; *Harijan*, 5 September 1936, *CWMG*, vol. 63, pp. 257–8.

85 *Harijan*, 8 February 1935, *CWMG*, vol. 60, pp. 190–2. Gandhi's considerations of village food, health, etc. are to be found in the volumes of *CWMG*, relating to the later 1930s.

86 *Harijan*, 19 September 1936, *CWMG*, vol. 63, pp. 295–7.

87 *Harijan*, 31 July 1937, *CWMG*, vol. 65, pp. 447–53; *Harijan*, 21 August 1937, *CWMG*, vol. 66, p. 59.

88 *Harijan*, 8 May and 3 July 1937, *CWMG*, vol. 65, pp. 72–4, 361–2.

89 Gandhi's proposals in anticipation of the conference, *Harijan*, 2 October 1937, *CWMG*, vol. 66, pp. 194–5; Gandhi's speeches at conference, *Harijan*, 30 October 1937, *ibid.*, pp. 263–7, 273. The committee's report appeared in *Harijan*, 11 December 1937.

90 A detailed study is available in B.R. Tomlinson, *The Indian National Congress and the Raj, 1929–1942. The*

Penultimate Phase (MacMillan, London, 1976).

91 M. Desai to J. Nehru, 14 September 1938, NMML, J. Nehru Papers.

92 20 January 1938, *CWMG*, vol. 66, p. 344.

93 *Bombay Chronicle*, 23 May 1935, *CWMG*, vol. 61, p. 88; Bombay Fortnightly Report for second half of May 1935, NAI, Home Political Files, 1935, no. 18/5.

94 M. Desai to J. Nehru, 6 September 1935, NMML, J. Nehru Papers; *Harijan*, 12 August 1939, *CWMG*, vol. 70, p. 67.

95 Viceroy (Home Dept) to Secretary of State, telegram, 18 May 1936, NAI, Home Political Files, 1936, no. 31; Bombay Fortnightly Report for second half of December 1936, *ibid.*, File no. 18/12.

96 D. Mangalmurti to M.S. Aney, 31 July 1938, Aney's reply, 2 August 1938, NMML, M.S. Aney Papers, Subject File no. 10.

97 Prss statement, 30 October 1934, *CWMG*, vol. 59, p. 263; Gandhi to S. Gupta, 6 August 1935, *CWMG*, vol. 61, p. 314; message to American newspaper readers, 12 April 1937, *CWMG*, vol. 65, pp. 74–5; 'Am I all-powerful?', *Harijan*, 12 August 1939, *CWMG*, vol. 70, pp. 65–7.

98 *Harijan*, 12 November 1938, *CWMG*, vol. 68, p. 92; see also *Harijan*, 12 August 1939, *CWMG*, vol. 70, p. 66. On Gandhi's role in local Gujarat Congress matters see report by Bombay DIGP, 9 May 1935, NAI, Home Political Files, 1935, no. 3/8. For Gandhi's non-intervention in Madras politics, see *Harijan*, 10 September 1938, *CWMG*, vol. 67, pp. 323–6. For Gandhi's non-intervention in Punjab disputes, see Gandhi to Dunichand, 20 July 1939, and *Harijan*, 19 August 1939, *CWMG*, vol. 70, pp. 13, 91.

99 On the interaction between Gandhi and Nehru on this issue, see secret government report, 4 December 1935, NAI, Home Political Files, no. 4/13; M. Desai to J. Nehru, 6 September 1935, *CWMG*, vol. 61, p. 473.

100 A detailed investigation of Bose' re-election and the subsequent conflicts is in Tomlinson, *The Indian National Congress and the Raj*, pp. 126–30.

101 G.D. Birla to Sir P. Thakurdas, 20 April 1936, NMML, P. Thakurdas Papers, File no. 177.

102 See, for example, as evidence of Gandhi's strategies for and success in maintaining unity on this issue, B. Desai's diary entry, 28 June 1936, after CWC meeting, NMML, Bhulabhai Desai Papers, Diary 1935–1936; file re Faizpur Congress, December 1936, NAI, Home Political Files, 1936, no. 4/40 and K.-W.; account of 27–28 February 1937 CWC meeting in Bajaj's Wardha home, in which Gandhi took an active part, CP and Berar Fortnightly Report for second half of February 1937, NAI, Home Political Files, 1937, No. 18/2.

103 Handwriteen minutes of 27–29 April 1936 CWC meeting, NMML, AICC Papers, File no. G-31 (1936). Later correspondence between members of the CWC and Gandhi is in NMML, J. Nehru Papers, and in *CWMG*, vol. 63. On the restored amity within the CWC, see M. Desai to J. Nehru, 26 August 1936, NMML, AICC Papers, File no. G-85 (i) (1936).

104 Gandhi to V.Patel, 20 February 1938, *CWMG*, vol. 66, p. 382.

105 *Harijan*, 7 August 1937, *ibid.*, p. 16.

106 *Harijan*, 3 September 1938, *CWMG*, vol. 67, pp. 303–4; speech at CWC, 23 September 1938, *ibid.*, p. 370.

107 M. Desai to R. Prasad, 23 July 1937, NAI, Rajendra Prasad Papers, File No. VI/37, Col. no. 1; *Harijan*, 21 August 1937, *CWMG*, vol. 66, p. 61.

108 *Harijan*, 28 August and 4 September 1937, *ibid.*, pp. 81–3, 102–3, 104–5.

109 *Harijan*, 21 August 1937, *ibid.*, pp. 61–2.

110 *Harijan*, 17 and 24 December 1938, 18 February 1939, *CWMG*, vol. 68, pp. 193–5, 222–4, 338–40.

111 *Harijan*, 19 March 1938, *CWMG*, vol. 66, pp. 402–3.

112 *Harijan*, 23 October 1937, 13 August 1938, *CWMG*, vol. 66, pp. 268–9, vol. 67, pp. 245–6.

CHAPTER 9

1 This experiment was, however, already becoming imperilled by Muslim hostility to Congress, and by Princely opposition to the plan for a federation with British India.

(Negotiations with the Princes were abandoned during the war.) There were also of course those in British ruling circles who would have bitterly opposed any rapid Indian advance towards independence; principal among them being Churchill, whose emotional resistance to the idea was ill-founded in political judgement.

On the fundamental economic change in India's long term 'worth' to Britain, see B.R. Tomlinson, *The Political Economy Of The Raj 1914–1947. The Economics of Decolonization in India* (MacMillan, London, 1979). The interlocking problem of actually manning the empire in India is discussed by D.C. Potter in 'Manpower Shortage and the End of Colonialism. The Case of the Indian Civil Service', *Modern Asian Studies*, vol. 7, part 1 (January 1973), pp. 47–73; and in *India's Political Administrators 1919–1983* (Clarendon, Oxford, 1986).

2 See letters from Amrit Kaur to Syed Mahmud, 30 November, 17 and 23 December 1940, NMML, Syed Mahmud Papers.

3 On Bajaj's death, see M. Desai to C. Rajagoplachariar, 14 February 1942, *CWMG*, vol. 75, pp. 454–5. Gandhi's writings on the significance of the death, *Harijan*, 15 February 1942, letter to *c*.190 friends of Bajaj, 14 February 1942, *Harijan Sevak*, 22 February 1942, letter to V.J. Pancholi, 26 February 1942, *ibid.*, pp. 306, 315–16, 323, 365.

4 Press statement, 5 September 1939, *CWMG*, vol. 70, p. 162.

5 Interview to *The New York Times*, April 1940, *CWMG*, vol. 72, pp. 11–12; Gandhi to Agatha Harrison, 22 October 1941, *CWMG*, vol. 75, pp. 37–8; press interview to an Australian, April 1942, *CWMG*, vol. 76, p. 3.

6 *Harijan*, 30 September, 2 and 5 December 1939, *CWMG*, vol. 70, pp. 205–6, 386, vol. 71, p. 11; speech, 22 February 1940, *CWMG*, vol. 71, p. 264.

7 *Harijan*, 20 October 1940, *Sarvodaya*, May 1941, *CWMG*, vol. 73, pp. 107, 407.

8 Speech at prayer meeting, 22 October 1941, *CWMG*, vol. 75, p. 45.

9 Speech to young people, 28 May 1942, *Harijanbhandu*, 14 June 1942,

CWMG, vol. 76, pp. 159–60, 219–20.

10 Gandhi to Balvantsinha, 28 March 1945, *CWMG*, vol. 79, p. 323.

11 Gandhi to K.G. Mashruwala, 2 July 1945, *CWMG*, vol. 80, p. 397.

12 Discussion with Pyarelal and M. Desai, June 1940, *CWMG*, vol. 72, p. 211.

13 See *CWMG*, vol. 79 for references to this.

14 Speech at prayer meeting, 22 October 1941, *CWMG*, vol. 75, pp. 40–5.

15 *Harijan*, 28 June 1942, *CWMG*, vol. 76, p. 232.

16 8 December 1941, *CWMG*, vol. 75, pp. 139–41.

17 Gandhi to K. G. Mashruwala, 13 May 1941, *CWMG*, vol. 74, p. 55. Evidence of Gandhi's involvement in the community's life and the debilitating disagreements which plagued it are in *CWMG* volumes for the 1940s.

18 *Hindustan Times*, 2 August 1935, *CWMG*, vol. 61, pp. 301–2.

19 Gandhi to C.F. Andrews, 5 October 1938, *CWMG*, vol. 67, p. 402.

20 'If I were a Czech', *Harijan*, 15 October 1938, and subsequent article in same issue, *ibid.*, pp. 404–6, 413–5.

21 Discussion reported in *Harijan*, 24 December 1938, *CWMG*, vol. 68, p. 205.

22 'The Jews', *Harijan*, 26 November 1938, 'Some questions answered', *Harijan*, 17 December 1938, *ibid.*, pp. 137–41, 191–9.

23 Discussion with missionary leaders reported in *Harijan*, 24 December 1938, *ibid.*, p. 205; 'Is non-violence ineffective?' *Harijan*, 7 January 1939, *ibid.*, pp. 276–8. (In this Gandhi dealt with the sufferings of Pastor Niemoeller and other Lutherans who opposed Hitler. He believed their suffering was not in vain: they had preserved their self-respect and proved their faith, but so far they had not generated sufficient moral energy to melt Hitler's heart.)

24 Gandhi to Hitler, 23 July 1939, *CWMG*, vol. 70, pp. 20–1.

25 Gandhi to Satyanand (S.E.Stokes), 8 June 1939, *CWMG*, vol. 69, p. 332; also Gandhi to A. Harrison, 4 May 1939, *ibid.*, p. 201.

26 Press statement, *Harijan*, 2 September 1939, *CWMG*, vol. 70, pp. 126–

7; 'On Trial', *Harijan*, 14 October 1939, *ibid.*, pp. 243–5.

27 Press statement, 5 September 1939, *ibid.*, p. 162; *Harijan*, 6 July 1940, *CWMG*, vol. 72, p. 229; *Sarvodaya*, January 1942, *Harijan*, 15 February 1942, *CWMG*, vol. 75, pp. 272, 305.

28 Gandhi to Linlithgow, 26 May 1940, *CWMG*, vol. 72, pp. 100–1; 'To every Briton', 2 July 1940, *Harijan*, 6 July 1940, *ibid.*, pp. 229–31; Gandhi to Hitler, 24 December 1940, *CWMG*, vol. 73, pp. 253–5.

29 Press statement, 20 December 1941, *CWMG*, vol. 75, p. 180.

30 For example, *Harijan*, 15 February 1942, *ibid.*, p. 305; *Harijan*, 12 April 1942, Gandhi to Mirabehn (spelling out in detail what he envisaged), 31 May 1942, *CWMG*, vol. 76, pp. 5–7, 173–5.

31 'Foreign soldiers in India', *Harijan*, 26 April 1942, *ibid.*, pp. 49–50; draft resolution by Gandhi for AICC, late April 1942, *ibid.*, pp. 63–5; resolution as finally passed by AICC, 1 May 1942, *ibid.*, pp. 424–5.

32 Interview to American press man, 10 June 1942, *Harijan*, 21 June 1942; answers to questions, *Harijan*, 21 June 1942; *Harijan*, 28 June 1942; Gandhi to F.D. Roosevelt, 1 July 1942; *ibid.*, pp. 207–8, 215–16, 240–1, 265.

Gandhi's change of view appears to have occurred in the first week of June 1942. See L. Fischer, *A Week With Gandhi* (Duell, Sloane & Pierce, New York, 1942): also an article about Fischer's visit and his questions to Gandhi, written on 6 June 1942, *Harijan*, 14 June 1942, *CWMG*, vol. 76, pp. 186–8.)

33 Gandhi to Linlithgow, 14 August 1942, *The Transfer of Power 1942–7, Volume II*, p. 705. (This 12 volume collection of documents, published by HMSO, London, 1970–83, is a massive source for the final years of the raj, from the angle of the departing rulers. It will be referred to henceforth as *TP*, followed by the volume number. It editors were N. Mansergh, E.W.R. Lumby and P. Moon.)

34 'To every Japanese', 18 July 1942, *Harijan*, 26 July 1942, *CWMG*, vol. 76, pp. 309–12; AICC resolution, 8 August 1942, *TP* 2, pp. 621–4.

35 For more detailed accounts of Congress politics during the war, and British policies, see B.R. Tomlinson, *The Indian National Congress and the Raj, 1929–1942*, pp. 142–158; Moon, *Gandhi and Modern India*, pp. 203–26; R.J. Moore, *Churchill, Cripps and India, 1939–1945* (Clarendon Press, Oxford, 1979); S. Gopal, *Jawaharlal Nehru. A Biography*, vol. 1, pp. 249–302; P. Moon (ed.), *Wavell. The Viceroy's Journal* (OUP, London, 1973); *TP*, 1–5.

36 Press statement, 5 September 1939, *CWMG*, vol. 70, pp. 161–2; Gandhi to J. Nehru, 24 September 1939, *ibid.*, p. 197.

37 Gandhi to Dr B.C. Roy, 12 October 1939, *ibid.*, pp. 248–9.

38 Press statement, 18 October 1939, *ibid.*, pp. 267–8.

39 Gandhi to Sampurnanand, 1 December 1939, *CWMG*, vol. 71, p. 1; the CWC's resolution on 22 October 1939 is in *CWMG*, vol. 70, pp. 419–20.

40 J. Nehru to S. Mahmud, 12 December 1939, NMML, Syed Mahmud Papers. Further evidence of the negative effects on Congress of having governmental power is in V. Patel to R. Prasad, 17 July 1939, and Prasad's reply, 22 July 1939, NAI, R. Prasad Papers, File no. 1-C/39, Col. 2; V. Patel to R. Prasad, 14 October 1939, NAI, R. Prasad Papers, File no. 3-RP/PSF (I) – 1939.

41 Statement (24 October 1939) in *Harijan*, 28 October 1939, *CWMG*, vol. 70, pp. 291–3.

42 Gandhi to J. Nehru, 26 October, 4 November 1939, *ibid.*, pp. 297, 328; *Harijan*, 4 November, 21 December 1939, *ibid.*, pp. 315–16, 388–90; *Harijan*, 20 January, 10 February 1940, *CWMG*, vol. 71, pp. 114–17, 190–1.

43 Speech at Subjects Committee, 18 March 1940, at full Congress, 20 March 1940, *ibid.*, pp. 348–54, 357–60.

44 Bombay, Punjab and Bihar Fortnightly reports for second half of March 1940, NAI, Home Political Files, 1940, no. 18/3.

45 Bihar Fortnightly report for first half of December 1939, UP. Fortnightly report for second of December 1939, NAI, Home Political Files, 1939, no. 18/12. UP had reported, 'Many people think that Mr Gandhi will have

to take some action if he is to prevent a split. What that action will be, however, no one can guess.' See also Bombay and UP Fortnightly reports for first half of January 1940, NAI, Home Political Files 1940, no. 18/1.

46 *Harijan*, 30 March 1940, *CWMG*, vol. 71, pp. 368–70; AICC circulars to PCCs, 23 and 29 March 1940, NMML, J. Nehru Papers, Subjects File No. 42.

47 Reports of Provincial Inspectors, 1940, NMML, AICC Papers, File no. Misc. 65 (Parts I, II, and III) (1940); report of CWC meeting, 15–19 April 1940, *CWMG*, vol. 72, pp. 4–7; *Harijan*, 27 April, 18 and 25 May, 1 June, 4 August 1940, *ibid.*, pp. 19–21, 64–66, 80–2, 103–5, 339–41.

48 The crucial CWC meetings at which this break between Gandhi and the CWC occurred were 17–21 June and 3–7 July (Delhi). At the latter the resolution offering co-operation in a national government after an unequivocal British commitment to Indian independence (at an unspecified date) was largely the work of Rajagoplachariar, *CWMG*, vol. 72, p. 467. The Delhi resolution was confirmed at an AICC meeting in Poona, 25–28 July 1940.

49 V. Patel to J. Nehru, 8 August 1940, NMML, J. Nehru Papers.

50 Written on 24 June 1940, appeared in *Harijan*, 29 June 1940, *CWMG*, vol. 72, p. 195. J. Nehru also issued a conciliatory statement denying any break between Gandhi and Congress despite their different approaches at present, *ibid.*, p. 197, fn. 1.

51 Text of 8 August 1940 statement, *ibid.*, pp. 472–4.

52 Account of Bombay meetings of CWC and AICC, mid-September 1940, Bombay Fortnightly report for first half of September 1940, NAI, Home Political Files, 1940, no. 18/9; P. Thakurdas to G. Birla, 16 September 1940, NMML, P. Thakurdas Papers, File no. 239., Pt 1; Gandhi's speeches at AICC, *CWMG*, vol. 73, pp. 4–13, 14–21, 22–6.

53 Press statement, 20 September 1940, *ibid.*, p. 37; Gandhi to Linlithgow, 29 August, 6, 18 and 28 September 1940, *CWMG*, vol. 72, pp. 425–7, 445–6, vol. 73, pp. 33, 62–3.

54 Gandhi's accounts of meeting, *Harijan*, 6 and 13 October 1940, *ibid.*, pp. 74–5, 77–80; Linlithgow's account is in letter to Gandhi, 30 September 1940, *ibid.*, pp. 450–1.

55 Gandhi to Sir R. Maxwell, 2 December 1940, *ibid.*, p. 208. See also Gandhi to *Times of India*, 31 July 1941, *CWMG*, vol. 74, p. 199.

56 Speech at AICC meeting, 16 September 1940, *CWMG*, vol. 73, p. 23.

57 Speech at AICC meeting, 15 and 16 September 1940, press statement, 5 October 1940, *Harijan*, 20 October 1940, *ibid.*, pp. 10, 22–3, 80, 106.

58 Gandhi to Sir R. Maxwell, 2 December 1940, *ibid.*, p. 208.
Source for a study of 'individual' civil disobedience and Gandhi's role include *CWMG*, vols. 73–5; History of the Civil Disobedience Movement – 1940–41, prepared by the Govt. of India, NAI, Home Political Files, 1942, No. 3/6; NMML, AICC Papers, e.g., File no. P1 (1940).

59 Instructions to satyagrahis, 8 November 1940, *CWMG*, vol. 73, p. 157; AICC Circular, No. 32, 21 January 1941, NMML, AICC Papers, File no. P1 (1940); note by W. Jenkin, 14 May 1941, NAI. Home Political Files, 1940, no. 3/3.

60 File relating to exemptions, NMML, AICC Papers, File no. 65 (Pt. 2) (1941).

61 'Constructive Programme: its meaning and place', *CWMG*, vol. 75, pp. 146–166. See also press statement re National Week, 6–13 April 1941, NMML, AICC Papers, File no. Misc. 2 (1941); press statement, 28 October 1941, *CWMG*, vol. 75, pp. 61–2.

62 Home Dept to Secretary of State, wire, 17 July 1941, NAI, Home Political Files, 1941, No. 3/31.

63 A summary of government policy, which indicates the restraint London placed upon Delhi, is in History of the Civil Disobedience Movement – 1940–41, NAI, Home Political Files, 1942, No. 3/6. Further evidence is available in Home Political Files, 1940, Nos. 3/11, 3/13, 3/16, 3/31, 6/8, 6/13, 14 A, 160.

64 Figures are taken from History of the Civil Disobedience Movement – 1940–41, NAI, Home Political Files, 1942, no. 3/6; also Home Political

Files, 1941, nos. 3/2, 3/13, 18/16; AICC General Secretary's report, 1940–2, NMML, AICC Papers, File no. Misc. 55 (1940).

65 T.B. Sapru to B. Shiva Rao, 16 August 1941, NMML, B. Shiva Rao Papers.

It is significant that through 1941 Sapru was unwilling to take up the role of mediator again between Congress and government, despite urgings from some Congressmen and his old partner, M.R. Jayakar. However, he was prominent in Moderate moves in 1941, centring on a Bombay conference in March, to persuade the government to make some political concessions. Evidence is in NMML, B. Shiva Rao Papers and P. Thakuradas Papers, File no. 239, Pt 1.

66 Evidence of Congressmen's unrest: Satyamurti to Gandhi, 27 August 1941, NAI, Home Political Files, 1941, no. 32/14; wide range of evidence in Home Political Files, 1941, no. 4/8; Asaf Ali to B. Desai, 16 October 1941, to Gandhi, 17 November 1941, NMML, Bhulabhai Desai Papers, Corr. File I – Re Congress Assembly Party 1941–4; notes on 3–5 November 1941 meeting, *idem*.

67 T.B. Sapru to B. Shiva Rao, 31 October and 10 December 1941, NMML, B Shiva Rao papers.

68 On 23 July 1941, *CWMG*, vol. 74, p. 183; see also Gandhi to G. Bardoloi, 30 June 1941, press statement, 6 July 1941, *ibid.*, pp. 131, 150.

69 Rajendra Prasad to Syed Mahmud, 11 October 1941, NMML, Syed Mahmud Papers. Also speech at Sevagram, 12 October 1941, *CWMG*, vol. 75, p. 7.

70 K. Rangaswami to K. Srinivasan, 13 October 1941, NAI, Home Political Files, 1941, no. 4/8.

71 G. Birla to P. Thakurdas, 8 November 1941, NMML, P. Thakurdas Papers, File no. 239, part 2; Intelligence report from CP and Berar, 2 December 1941, on late November discussions at Wardha, NAI, Home Political Files, 1941, no. 4/8.

72 File dealing with release of satyagrahi prisoners, NAI, Home Political Files, 1941, no. 3/36.

73 AICC General Secretary's report, 1940–1, NMML, AICC Papers, File no. Misc 55 (1940); intelligence report on Bardoli meeting, NAI, Home Political Files, 1942, no. 33/30; Gandhi to A.K. Azad, 30 December 1941, *CWMG*, vol. 75, pp. 189–90; CWC resolutions, 30 December 1941, *ibid.*, pp. 450–52; press statement, 30 December 1941, *ibid.*, pp. 189–92.

74 Speech at AICC, 15 January 1942, *ibid.*, pp. 219–29; Shiva Rao (who had been at Wardha) to T.B. Sapru, 26 January 1942, NMML, B. Shiva Rao Papers.

75 Sir M. Hallett to Linlithgow, 19 January 1942, *TP* 1, p. 39.

76 T.B. Sapru to B. Shiva Rao, 15 May 1941, also his letters to Shiva Rao, 4 January and 14 April 1941, NMML, B. Shiva Rao Papers.

77 Bombay's Governor stressed in interpreting the Bardoli decisions, '... I am inclined to think that the real meaning behind the move is that they want to move out of the negative position into which Gandhi has led them, and want to make the best bargain they can, and are therefore taking their first bargaining position.' Sir R. Lumley to Linlithgow, 1 January 1942, *TP* 1, p. 2.

78 J. Nehru to C. Rajagopalachariar, 26 January 1942, NMML, J. Nehru Papers.

79 Asaf Ali to B. Desai, 4 March 1942, NMML, Bhulabhai Desai Papers, Corr. File I Re Congress Assembly Party 1941–4; J. Nehru to A.K. Azad, 4 March 1942, NMML, J. Nehru Papers; CWC proceedings, Wardha, 17–18 March 1942, NMML, AICC Papers, File no. G-32 (1942).

80 Cripps' document for discussion with Indian leaders, 30 March 1942, Cripps' broadcast, 30 March 1942, *TP* 1, pp. 565–6, 566–71. Full documentation and discussion of this abortive mission is in *TP* 1, and Moore, *Chruchill, Cripps, and India, 1939–1945*.

81 L. Amery (Secretary of State for India) to Linlithgow, 13 February 1942, Churchill to Linlithgow, 10 March 1942, telegram, *TP* 1, pp. 160–61, 395.

82 Cripps' report on his mission, 6 July 1942, *TP* 2, no. 227, especially p. 342; T.B. Sapru to B. Shiva Rao, 14 April 1942, NMML, B. Shiva Rao Papers.

83 Press statement, 4 May 1945, *CWMG*, vol. 80, p. 66. Rajagopalachariar had publicly denied Gandhi's responsibility for the failure of the mission in September 1942; cited in Moore, *Churchill, Cripps, and India, 1939–1945*, p. 128.

84 Gandhi to Cripps, 25 March 1942, *CWMG*, vol. 75, p. 428.

85 Note by Cripps on interview with Gandhi, 27 March 1942, *TP* 1. pp. 498–500; Gandhi to J. Nehru, *c*.27 March 1942, *CWMG*, vol. 75, p. 440.

86 Gandhi to B.S. Moonje, 29 March 1942, *ibid.*, p. 444.

87 Press interviews, 15 April and 19 June 1942, *CWMG*, vol. 76, pp. 40–1, 235; Gandhi to H. Alexander, 22 April 1942, *ibid.*, pp. 60–1.

88 J. Kripalani to R. Prasad, 23 April 1942, on a discussion with Gandhi, NAI, R. Prasad Papers, File no. 2-A/42, col. no. 1.

89 Gandhi to H. Alexander, 22 April 1942, *CWMG*, vol. 76, p. 61; see also Fischer, *A Week with Gandhi*, pp. 102–3 (recording his experiences on 9 June 1942).

90 Gandhi's draft resolution, before 24 April 1942, resolution as passed, which was J. Nehru's, 1 May 1942, *CWMG*, vol. 76, pp. 63–5, 424–5. See also Governor of UP, Sir M. Hallett, to Linlithgow, reporting on AICC meeting and giving text of various drafts and final resolution, *TP* 2, pp. 63–70.

91 Gandhi to Mirabehn, 22 May 1942, press interview, 28 May 1942, *CWMG*, vol. 76, pp. 136, 163.

92 See comments by A. Copley, *Gandhi. Against the Tide* (Historical Association Studies, Basil Blackwell, Oxford, 1987), pp. 90–91; F.G. Hutchins is the exponent of the 'revolutionary' explanation in *India's Revolution, Gandhi and the Quit India Movement* (Harvard University Press, Cambridge, Massachusetts, 1973).

93 Evidence of an atmosphere of stagnation and helplessness in Congress and Gandhi's anxiety on this count: Asaf Ali to B. Desai, 30 May 1942, NMML, Bhulabhai Desai Papers, Corr. File 1 – Re Congress Assembly Party 1941–4; Amrit Kaur to J. Nehru, 31 May 1942, NMML,

J. Nehru Papers; Sri Prakasa to J. Nehru, 14 July 1942, NMML, J. Nehru Papers; *Harijan*, 28 June 1942, *CWMG*, vol. 76, p. 237.

94 *Harijanbandhu*, 14 June 1942, *CWMG*, vol. 76, p. 220. For further evidence that Gandhi realized he had to change his long-held position of caution and run the risk of violence *in the cause of non-violence and freedom*, see also Gandhi to Mirabehn, 22 May 1942, conversation with young volunteers, 28 May 1942, Gandhi to Chiang Kai-Shek, 14 June 1942, *Harijan*, 28 June and 5 July 1942, *ibid.*, pp. 136, 159–60, 225, 237, 253.

95 Conversation with young volunteers, 28 May 1942, *ibid.*, p. 160.

96 T.B. Sapru to B. Shiva Rao, 29 July 1942, NMML, B. Shiva Rao Papers; V.S.S. Sastri to K. Natarajan, 14 February 1943, NMML, V.S.S. Sastri Papers.

97 Gandhi to G.D. Birla, 24 June 1942, *CWMG*, vol. 76, p. 246; see also fn. 32 of this chapter.

98 Press statement, 14 July 1942, *CWMG*, vol. 76, pp. 294–7; draft instructions, early August 1942, *ibid.*, pp. 365–7. See also discussion in May 1944, *CWMG*, vol. 77, p. 267; discussion with Congressmen in December 1945, *CWMG*, vol. 82, p. 278.

99 Linlithgow to L. Amery, 15 June 1942, *TP* 2, p. 213.

100 Gandhi's last message, 9 August 1942, *CWMG*, vol. 76, p. 403; (he had offered this *mantra* at the AICC meeting, *ibid.*, p. 392); AICC resolution, 8 August, *ibid.*, pp. 458–61.

101 Gandhi to T.B. Sapru, 4 August 1942, *ibid.*, pp. 369–70; T.B. Sapru to M.S. Aney, 8 September 1942, NMML, Aney Papers, Subject File no. 19; Gandhi to Linlithgow, 14 August 1942, and to Home Secretary, Govt. of India, 23 September 1942, *CWMG*, vol. 76, pp. 406, 414; speech at AICC, 8 August 1942, *ibid.*, p. 394.

102 Govt of India, Home Dept, to Secretary of State, 3 August 1942, *TP* 2, pp. 534–7; NAI, Home Political Files, 1942, nos. 3/15, 25/1.

103 Sir P. Thakurdas to Sir V.T. Krishnamachari, 7 September 1942, NMML, Sir P. Thakurdas Papers, File No. 239 Pt 2.

104 Gandhi to Secretary, Home Dept., Govt. of India, 23 September 1942, *CWMG*, vol. 76, pp. 414–15; answers to questions, March 1943, *CWMG*, vol. 77, p. 71; press statement, 4 May 1945, *CWMG*, vol. 80, p. 65.

105 Sources for this brief discussion of 'Quit India' are *TP* 2: NAI, Home Political Files, 1942, nos. 3/30, Part I, 3/42, 3/16, 18/14, 8/11; 1943, nos. 3/15, 3/52, 3/66, 3/70: M. Harcourt, 'Kisan Populism and Revolution in Rural India: The 1942 Disturbances in Bihar and East United Provinces', D.A. Low (ed.), *Congress and the Raj*, pp. 315–48; F.G. Hutchins, *India's Revolution*.

106 L. Amery to Linlithgow, 28 June 1943, Linlithgow to Amery, 4 October 1943, *T.P.* 4, pp. 36, 349.

107 Gandhi to Secretary, Home Dept, Govt of Bombay, 26 September 1942, *CWMG*, vol. 76, pp. 415–16; file containing discussions on terms of Gandhi's detention, NAI, Home Political Files, 1942, no. 3/21, vol. 1. There is considerable documentation of Gandhi's detention period in *CWMG*, vol. 77.

108 'Key to Health', *ibid.*, pp. 1–48, Original version in article form is in *CWMG*, vols. 11 and 12.

109 Gandhi to Linlithgow, 31 December 1942, *CWMG*, vol. 77, pp. 49–53. Further evidence on the fast and events leading up to it is in *ibid.*, and *TP* 3, and NAI, Home Political Files, 1943, no. 33/4.

110 V.S.S. Sastri to K. Natarajan, 14 February 1943, NMML, V.S.S. Sastri Papers; T.B. Sapru and others to Churchill, telegram, 21 February 1943, *TP* 3, p. 711.

111 Sir R. Lumley to Linlithgow, 4 March 1943, *ibid.*, p. 755; T. Rutherford to Linlithgow, 5 March 1943, *ibid.*, p. 765.

112 Detailed accounts of the fast from a medical point of view are in *ibid.*, pp. 756–61, 767, 769–71.

113 Long letter from Gandhi to Govt of India, Home Dept, 15 July 1943 (in reply to an official pamphlet released in February 1943 *Congress Reponsibility for the Disturbances, 1942–43*), *CWMG*, vol. 77, pp. 105–99.

114 Gandhi to Major-General R.H. Candy, 7 March 1944, *ibid.*, p. 244.

115 Gandhi to C.M. Doke, 26 July 1944, *ibid.*, p. 421; also Gandhi to Wavell, 9 March 1944, *ibid.*, pp. 244–5; foreword to biography of Kasturbhai Gandhi, 18 February 1945, *CWMG*, vol. 79, p. 133; talk on 8 June 1947, *CWMG*, vol. 88, pp. 105–6.

116 Mirabehn to Amrit Kaur, 10 July 1944, NMML, Amrit Kaur Papers, file no. M8.

117 Memorandum by Secretary of State for India, 5 May 1944, *T.P.* 4, pp. 952–3.

118 Churchill to Wavell, telegram, 5 July 1944, Wavell's reply, telegram, 8 July 1944, *ibid.*, pp. 1070, 1073–4.

119 Gandhi to S. Salemna, 23 May 1945, to K. Gandhi, 7 July 1945, *CWMG*, vol. 80. pp. 167, 405.

120 Gandhi to A. Chakravarty, 20 July 1944, *CWMG*, vol. 77, p. 407; also speech, 29 June 1944, *ibid.*, p. 339.

121 Press interview, 19 July 1944, *ibid.*, pp. 404–5; discussion, December 1945, *CWMG*, vol. 82, p. 277; Gandhi to J.P. Bhansali, 19 April 1946, *CWMG*, vol. 84, p. 27.

122 Discussion with Bombay Congressmen, late July 1944, *CWMG*, vol. 77, p. 433; press statement, 5 August 1944, *CWMG*, vol. 78, pp. 9–11.

123 Gandhi to Wavell, 17 June 1944, and Wavell's reply, 22 June 1944, *TP* 4, pp. 1032, 1039–40.

124 Accounts of 4–6 July interview between Gandhi and S. Gelder, *CWMG*, vol. 77, pp. 347–8, 349–52, 474–7. Gandhi's intention of reaching Wavell via Gelder is clear in press statement, 12 July 1944, *ibid.*, pp. 368–70. Gandhi to Wavell, 15 July 1944, and Wavell's reply, 22 July 1944, *TP* 4, pp. 1096, 1115.

125 Gandhi to Wavell, 27 July 1944, Wavell's reply, 15 August 1944, *ibid.*, pp. 1136, 1197–9.

126 Moon (ed.), *Wavell. The Viceroy's Journal*, pp. 82–7; Churchill to Wavell, 4 August 1944, Wavell's reply, 4 August 1944, boith telegrams, *TP* 4, pp. 1158, 1159–60. (This volume of *TP* also includes documentation of the long discussion in London and between London and Delhi on the text of the Viceroy's reply to Gandhi.)

127 Gandhi to A. Hingorani, 24 October 1944, to C. Heath, 13 November

1944, *CWMG*, vol. 78, pp. 230, 290.

128 Note by H.V. Hodson on his tour in November–December 1941 of Madras, Orissa, Bengal and Bihar, *TP* 1, pp. 66–7. (The text of the Pakistan resolution is in *CWMG*, vol. 71, pp. 444–5).

129 *Harijan*, 21 October, 4 and 18 November 1939, *CWMG*, vol. 70, pp. 258–61, 318–19, 341–2.

130 *Harijan*, 25 November 1939, 30 March 1940, *ibid.*, pp. 262–5, *CWMG*, vol. 71, pp. 371–2.

131 Press statement, 9 December 1939, *CWMG*, vol. 71, pp. 18–19.

132 *Harijan*, 4 May 1940, *CWMG*, vol. 72, p. 28. See also *Harijan*, 6 April 1940, *CWMG*, vol. 71, pp. 388–90.

133 *Harijan*, 13 April 1940, *ibid.*, pp. 412–13; speech at AICC, 16 September 1940, *CWMG*, vol. 73, pp. 25–6.

134 Gandhi to Shiva Rao, 7 June 1940, *CWMG*, vol. 72, p. 148.

135 G.D. Birla to P. Thakurdas, 18 and 22 December 1940, 4 January 1941, Thakurdas to Birla, 19 and 20 December 1940, and note by Thakurdas on meeting with Jinnah, 2 January 1941, NMML, P. Thakurdas Papers, File no. 177.

136 Gandhi to T.B. Sapru, 25 January 1941, *CWMG*, vol. 73, p. 297.

137 Gandhi to T.B. Sapru, 1 and 16 February 1941, *ibid.*, pp. 310, 337; Sapru to Gandhi, 28 January and 12 February 1941, *ibid.*, pp. 461–3, 463–5; Sapru to Shiva Rao, 6 and 20 February 1941, NMML, B. Shiva Rao Papers, File of correspondence between Shiva Rao and Sapru.

138 T.B. Sapru to Shiva Rao, 3 March 1941, *idem.*; Gandhi to Sapru, 7 March 1941, *CWMG*, vol. 73, pp. 362–3. See also Gandhi to G.D. Birla, 1 March 1941, *ibid.*, pp. 352–3.

139 T.B. Sapru to Shiva Rao, 8 August 1941, NMML, B. Shiva Rao Papers.

140 Press statement, 25 April 1941, *CWMG*, vol. 74, pp. 14–15.

141 *Harijan*, 21 June 1942, *CWMG*, vol. 76, p. 213. For similar pronouncements see press interview, 16 May 1942, *Harijan*, 24 May and 7 June 1942, *ibid.*, pp. 112, 120–1, 167.

142 *Bombay Chronicle*, 25 April 1942, *ibid.*, pp. 24–5 (see also n. 88 of this chapter). Gandhi worked out in some detail in 1941 how Congressmen should react non-violently to communal violence: e.g. *CWMG*, vol. 74, pp. 26–9, 74–6.

143 See L. Fischer, *A Week with Gandhi*, pp. 92–3.

144 Press interview, 30 July 1944, *CWMG*, vol. 77, p. 440; Gandhi to Jinnah, 17 July 1944, *ibid.*, p. 393. For Gandhi's attempt in 1943 to correspond with Jinnah see Gandhi to Jinnah, 4 May 1943 (*ibid.*, pp. 75–6), which the government blocked: government discussion is documented in *TP* 3; final decision of Cabinet was wired from L. Amery to Linlithgow, 19 May, 1943, *TP* 3, p. 996.

145 Answers to press questions, 20 July 1944, *CWMG*, vol. 77, p. 411; interview with S.P. Mookerjee, President of Hindu Mahasabhabha, 5 August 1944, *CWMG*, vol. 78, pp. 12–13; press interview, 18 August 1944, *ibid.*, p. 40.

146 V.S.S. Sastri to Gandhi, 4 August 1944, NMML, V.S.S. Sastri Papers. M.R. Jayakar made a similar point after the abortive talks, in letter to Gandhi, 29 September 1944, *CWMG*, vol. 78, p. 145, fn. 1. For orthodox Hindu hostility see entries for 25 June and 16 July 1944 in B.S. Moonje's Diary no. 5 – 1944, NMML, B.S. Mooje Papers.

147 Gandhi to T.B. Sapru, 8 September 1944, *CWMG*, vol. 78, p. 87. The course of the talks and the letters between Gandhi and Jinnah are in *ibid.*

148 Jinnah to Gandhi, 17 September 1944, *ibid.*, p. 408, in reply to letter from Gandhi, 15 September 1944, *ibid.*, p. 103.

149 Answer to Sapru's questions, 26 February 1945, *CWMG*, vol. 79, p. 169: see also Gandhi to Jinnah, 15 September 1944, Jinnah to Gandhi, 25 September 1944, *CWMG*, vol. 78, pp. 101–2, 413.

150 Discussion between Gandhi and Rajagopalachariar, 12 September 1944, *ibid.*, p. 97.

151 Moon (ed.), *Wavell. The Viceroy's Journal*, p. 91.

152 Wavell to L. Amery, 2 telegrams, 5 October 1944, *TP* 5, pp. 85, 87.

153 Moon (ed.), *Wavell. The Viceroy's Journal*, p. 79.

154 Wavell's clearest analyses of the probable post-war situation are in discussions during a Governors' con-

ference, 31 August 1944; in memorandum, September 1944, sent to Amery on 20 September 1944; Wavell to Churchill, 24 October 1944; *TP* 5, pp. 1–2, 37–41, 126–33.

155 L. Amery to Wavell, 10 October 1944, *ibid.*, pp. 96–7. See also Wavell's account of Churchill's 40-minute 'jeremiad' about India on 29 March 1945, Moon (ed.), *Wavell. The Viceroy's Journal*, p. 120.

156 Cabinet decision, 31 May 1945; policy statement by Secretary of State for India, 14 June 1945; Wavell's broadcast from New Delhi, 14 June 1945; *TP* 5, pp. 1083–6, 1118–21, 1122–4.

157 Wavell to L. Amery, 20 December 1944, *ibid.*, p. 315. Also note by Sir E. Jenkins, 30 September 1944; Wavell to Amery, 15 November 1944, *ibid.*, pp. 58, 207.

158 Wavell to Sir B. Glancy, Governor of Punjab, 8 June 1945, *ibid.*, p. 1104.

159 Gandhi to Wavell, telegrams 14 and 15 June 1945; press statement, 15 June 1945; Gandhi to Wavell, 16 June 1945, *CWMG*, vol. 80, pp. 327, 329, 331, 335–6.

160 Press statement, 15 June 1945, Gandhi to Wavell, telegram, 18 June 1945; press interview, 18 June 1945; *ibid.*, pp. 331–3, 345–6, 350.

161 Moon (ed.), *Wavell. The Viceroy's Journal*, pp. 144–6; also account of their meeting in telegram from Wavell to L. Amery, 25 June 1945, *TP* 5, pp. 1152–3.

162 Speech at prayer meeting, 12 July 1945, *CWMG*, vol. 80, pp. 421–2; press statement, 18 July 1945, *CWMG*, vol. 81, p. 4; 'Bread and butter letter' to Amrit Kaur, 19 July 1945, *ibid.*, p. 5.

163 Congress list, *TP* 5, p. 1208; Gandhi on this list to G.B. Pant, 29 June 1945, to Wavell, 8 July 1945, *CWMG*, vol. 80, pp. 381–2, 406–7.

164 For Wavell's account of the conference see Moon (ed.), *Wavell. The Viceroy's Journal*, pp. 144–56; note sent by Wavell to L. Amery on 15 July 1945, *TP* 5, pp. 1258–63. Documents relating to the conference are conveniently indexed as Ch. 4 in *ibid.*

165 Wavell's note sent to L. Amery, 15 July 1945, *ibid.*, p. 1263.

166 Account of Wavell's interview with Gandhi, 11 July 1945, Moon (ed.), *Wavell. The Viceroy's Journal*, p. 154; Gandhi to Wavell, 15 July 1945, *CWMG*, vol. 80, p. 426.

167 Address to ashram workers, 19 July 1945, *CWMG*, vol. 81, p. 8.

168 Article, *c.* 12 June 1945, *CWMG*, vol. 80, pp. 299–300.

169 26 May 1945, *ibid.*, p. 433.

170 *Harijan*, 9 August 1942, *CWMG*, vol. 76, p. 351. His fundamental hope is evident in letter to P. Kantak, 1 March 1945, *CWMG*, vol. 79, p. 188; note to B. Desai, 11 June 1945, *CWMG*, vol. 80, p. 296.

CHAPTER 10

1 This phrase is taken from Zechariah, 9:12: 'Turn you to the strong hold, ye prisoners of hope.'

2 Moon (ed.), *Wavell. The Viceroy's Journal* p. 402. On the need for a 'breakdown plan', *ibid.*, pp. 386–9; *TP* 8, pp. 454–65 (note by Wavell outining his plan, 7 September 1946). Detailed doucmentation on the final decisions about British rule in India is in *TP* 6–12, covering 1 August 1945 onwards. Good introductions to these fraught months are R.J. Moore, *Escape From Empire. The Attlee Government and the Indian Problem* (Clarendon Press, Oxford, 1983); P. Ziegler, *Mountbatten* (Fontana/Collins, 1986 paperback edn., first pub. Glasgow, 1985), Part III dealing with 1946–8. Eye-witness accounts are P. Moon, *Divide and Quit* (University of California Press, Berkeley and Los Angeles, 1962); A. Campbell-Johnson, *Mission with Mountbatten* (Robert Hale, London, 1951).

3 Sir F. Burrows to Wavell, 22 August 1946, *TP* 8, p. 298.

4 4 April 1947, *CWMG*, vol. 87, p. 207.

5 Gandhi to Manilal Gandhi, 28 August 1946, *CWMG*, vol. 85, p. 217. An example of Gandhi's reluctance to impose decisions when he was not resident is his letter to Krisnachandra, 7 June 1946, *CWMG*, vol. 84, pp. 304–5.

6 *Harijan*, 8 December 1946, *CWMG*, vol. 86, p. 143. Gandhi's urging ashram people to do without his advice is in letter to one of them, 26 May 1947, *CWMG*, vol. 88, p. 10: see also *ibid.*, p. 299.

7   24 August 1946, *CWMG*, vol. 85, pp. 202–3.

8   Gandhi to G.D. Birla, 18 November 1945, *CWMG*, vol. 82, p. 93.

9   Press statement, 21 November 1945, *ibid.*, pp. 101–2.

10 Gandhi's instructions for the new village clinic at Uruli-Kanchan, March 1946, *CWMG*, vol. 83, pp. 336–7; further observations on the experiment, *Harijan*, 26 May and 2 June 1946, *CWMG*, vol. 84, pp. 179–80, 203; letter to manager, Manibhai Desai, 2 June 1946, on the building plans, *ibid.*, pp. 262–3.

11 Fragment of letter, 4 January 1948, *CWMG*, vol. 90, p. 353.

12 Gandhi to M.G. Shah, 3 November 1945, *CWMG*, vol. 82, pp. 19–20.

13 Gandhi to K.T. Bhashyam, 6 January 1946, *ibid.*, p. 361; Gandhi to M.J. Mehta, 23 April 1946, *CWMG*, vol. 84, p. 55.

14 K. Natarajan to V.S.S. Sastri, 8 February 1946, NMML, V.S.S. Sastri Papers. P. Moon comments on the last 15 months of Gandhi's life, 'The politician gave place to the saint', Moon, *Gandhi and Modern India* (English Universities Press, London 1968), p. 250. (Gandhi would of course have disagreed, seeing no such distinctions in his life.)

15 Letter, 10 June 1947, *CWMG*, vol. 88, p. 122: see also 26 October 1945, *CWMG*, vol. 81, p. 462.

16 Speech at prayer meeting, 10 March 1947, *CWMG*, vol. 87, p. 65; also discussion on 2 January 1946, and 'Thought for the Day', 15 December 1945, *CWMG*, vol. 82, pp. 334, 447.

17 *Harijan*, 17 February 1946, 29 June 1947, *CWMG*, vols. 83, p. 107–8, 88, pp. 184–6.

18 *Harijan*, 24 February 1946; talk with an English friend, late March 1946; *CWMG*, vol. 83, pp. 141, 305.

19 *Harijanbandhu*, 22 September 1946, *CWMG*, vol. 85, p. 312.

20 31 December 1947, *CWMG*, vol. 90, p. 337: also note to Pyarelal, December 1946, *CWMG*, vol. 86, p. 225; *Harijan*, 8 June 1947, *CWMG*, vol. 88, p. 58; letter, 10 June 1947, *ibid.*, p. 120; fragment of letter, 21 December 1947, *CWMG*, vol. 90, p. 273.

21 Fragment of letter, 24 January 1948, *ibid.*, p. 489.

22 7 August 1947, published in *Harijan*, 17 August 1947, *CWMG*, vol. 89, p. 13.

23 Fragment of letter, 5 November 1947, *ibid.*, pp. 475–6.

24 Press statement, 4 August 1945, *CWMG*, vol. 81, p. 74; letter to G. Ramachandra Rao, 27 October 1945, *ibid.*, p. 426.

25 Gandhi to V. Patel, 12 August 1945, *ibid.*, pp. 109–10.

26 Gandhi to J. Nehru, 5 October and 13 November 1945, *ibid.*, pp. 319–21, *CWMG*, vol. 82, pp. 71–2. Nehru's reply to 5 October letter, setting out his views, 9 October 1945, J. Nehru, *A Bunch of Old Letters* (Asia Publishing House, Bombay, 1960), pp. 507–11.

27 Gandhi to C. Setalvad, 3 October 1945, *CWMG*, vol. 81, p. 310; *Harijan*, 14 July 1946, *CWMG*, vol. 84, p. 414.

28 Speech to Congressmen, 20 December 1945, Gandhi to R. Nehru, 15 January 1946, *CWMG*, vol. 82, pp. 247, 424; 'The Lure of Legislatures' *Harijan*, 17 February 1946, *CWMG*, vol. 83, pp. 95–6.

29 *Harijan*, 16 June, 29 September 1946, *CWMG*, vols. 84, p. 308, 85, p. 344.

30 The Labour re-assessment of the Indian problem is documented in *TP* 6.

31 Sources for study of the Cabinet Mission are *TP* 7; Moon (ed.), *Wavell. The Viceroy's Journal*, pp. 226–317; *CWMG*, vols 84 and 85. See also the meticulous and detailed study in Moore, *Escape From Empire*, chs 1–3. A more succinct account is in Moon, *Gandhi and Modern India*, pp. 241–7.

32 Statement of Cabinet Mission and Viceroy, 16 May 1946, *TP* 7, pp. 582–91.

33 Speeches at prayer meetings, 11 March and 13 April 1946, *CWMG*, vol. 83, pp. 243, 403.

34 Note of interview, 3 April 1946, *TP* 7, pp. 116–18; Pethick-Lawrence to Gandhi, 25 May 1946, *ibid.*, pp. 687–8.

35 Moon (ed.), *Wavell. The Viceroy's Journal*, pp. 236, 314.

36 Speech at prayer meeting, 17 May 1946, *CWMG*, vol. 84, p. 162; Gandhi's analysis of Cabinet Mission Plan, *Harijan*, 26 May 1946, *ibid.*, pp. 169–72. Record of meeting between Gandhi, Patel, the Cabinet Mission and Wavell, 24 June 1946, *TP* 7, pp. 1026–9; record of meeting of Cabinet

Mission and Wavell, 25 June 1946, *ibid.*, pp. 1042–3.

37 Speech at CWC, 25 June 1946, *CWMG*, vol. 84, p. 368; speech at AICC, 7 July 1946, *ibid.*, p. 419. Text of CWC resolution (ratified by AICC in July) 25 June 1946, *TP* 7, pp. 1036–8.

38 Evidence of Gandhi's intervation on the Nationalist Muslim issue: Secretary of State's information about CWC's attitude, given in meeting of Mission with Wavell, 19 June 1946, *TP* 7, pp. 972–3; interview between Cripps, Azad and Gandhi, 19 June 1946, *ibid.*, pp. 985–6; Sir W. Croft to Sir D. Monteath, 22 June 1946, *ibid.*, pp. 1007–9; Wavell to Sir F. Mudie, 29 June 1946, *ibid.*, p. 1082.

39 Gandhi to Wavell, 13 June 1946, *CWMG*, vol. 84, pp. 328–9; Gandhi to Cripps, 13 June 1946, *ibid.*, p. 330.

40 Wavell to the King, 8 July 1946, *TP* 7, pp. 1092–3.

41 Moon (ed.), *Wavell. The Viceroy's Journal*, p. 316.

42 The formation of an Interim Government is doucmented in *TP* 8.

43 Undated note to G.D. Birla which *CWMG*, places at end of 1946, *CWMG*, vol. 86, p. 295.

44 Text of CWC resolution on partition of Punjab, taken at meeting in Delhi, 6–8 March 1947, *CWMG*, vol. 87, p. 538. Gandhi to J. Nehru, 20 March 1947, to V. Patel, 22 March 1947, *ibid.*, pp. 124–5, 138; Nehru to Gandhi, 25 March 1947, Patel to Gandhi, 24 March 1947, *ibid.*, pp. 125, fn. 1, 138, fn. 2.

45 Speech at paryer meeting in Delhi, 1 April 1947, *ibid.*, p. 187.

46 The 1948 deadline was made public in policy statement of 20 February 1947, *TP* 9, pp. 773–5; see also Attlee to Mountbatten, 18 March 1947, containing his 'instructions', *ibid.*, pp. 972–4. Mountbatten's term of office is covered in *TP* 10–12.

47 Ziegler, *Mountbatten*, p. 369.

48 Gandhi to Mountbatten, 11 April 1947, *TP* 10, pp. 197–8. (Even on 4 April 1947 Shiva Rao, the journalist, wrote to Sapru that Gandhi was telling Mountbatten to consult Nehru, Patel and the other Congressmen in the Interim Government on political matters: NMML, B. Shiva Rao Papers.)
Records of interviews between Gandhi and Mountbatten when Gandhi raised the idea of a Jinnah government, 1, 2, 3 and 4 April, are in *TP* 10, pp. 69–70, 83–4, 102–3, 120–1. Also record of interview on 12 April 1947, *ibid.*, pp. 211–13.

49 Talk with K.S. Roy, 3 May 1947, *CWMG*, vol. 87, pp. 402–3; Gandhi to Mountbatten, 8 May 1947, *ibid.*, pp. 434–7.

50 Speeches at prayer meetings, 26 and 29 May 1947, *CWMG*, vol. 88, pp. 13, 39.

51 Records of interview on 2 June 1947, *TP* 11, pp. 48, 74, 160.

52 Record of interview, 4 June 1947, *ibid.*, pp. 131–2.

53 Early-morning talk with Manu Gandhi, 1 June 1947, *CWMG*, vol. 88, pp. 50–2.

54 Speech at CWC, 2 June 1947, *ibid.*, p. 61; letter, *c.* 2 June 1947, *ibid.*, p. 63; speech at AICC, 14 June 1947, *ibid.*, pp. 153–7.

55 For example, talk, 9 April 1947; talk with Congressmen, 17 April 1947; speech at prayer meeting, 17 April 1947; advice to constructive workers, 13 May 1947; *CWMG*, vol. 87, pp. 242–3, 295, 298–9, 463–4.

56 19 April 1947, *CWMG*, vol. 87, p. 310.

57 Talk with close colleagues, 4 May 1947, *ibid.*, p. 408; speech at prayer meeting, 9 July 1947, *CWMG*, vol. 88, pp. 306–7.

58 Speech at prayer meeting, 19 October 1947, *CWMG*, vol. 89, p. 365; Gandhi to Y. Privat, 29 November 1947, *CWMG*, vol. 90, p. 130.

59 NMML, AICC Papers, File nos Misc. 34 (1946–7); G-11 (Pt 1) (1947–8). See also Gandhi's ideas in *Harijan*, 3 August 1947, *CWMG*, vol. 88, p. 426.

60 Gandhi's draft constitution for Congress, 29 January 1948, *CWMG*, vol. 90, pp. 526–8.

61 Discussion with J.B. Kripalani, 25 September 1947, *CWMG*, vol. 89, p. 237; speech at prayer meeting, 24 October 1947, *ibid.*, p. 399.

62 Speech at prayer meeting, 2 October 1947, *ibid.*, p. 275; *Harijan*, 12 October 1947, *ibid.*, p. 286; Gandhi to S. Schlesin, 1 November 1947, *ibid.*, p. 449.

63 Appeal by Gandhi and Jinnah, released to the press on 15 April 1947, *CWMG*, vol. 87, p. 261.

64 Speech at prayer meeting, 29 May 1947; Gandhi to S. Gandhi, 2 July 1947; *CWMG*, vol. 88, pp. 38, 257.

65 Letter to a student, 9 April 1947, *CWMG*, vol. 87, p. 240.

66 Discussion with Aruna Asaf Ali and Ashok Mehta, 6 May 1947, *ibid.*, p. 424; also discussion with close colleagues, 4 May 1947, *ibid.*, p. 406.

67 Gandhi to K. Struve, 1 January 1948, *CWMG*, vol. 90, p. 337. Similar assessments of past 'non-violence' are speech at prayer meeting, 15 June 1947, interview, 8 July 1947, *CWMG*, vol. 88, pp. 160, 300; talk with S. Nelson, August 1947, *CWMG*, vol. 89, p. 62.

68 Speech at prayer meeting, 8 January 1948, *CWMG*, vol. 90, p. 386.

69 Discussion with English journalist, October 1946, *CWMG*, vol. 86, p. 49; message to a British magazine, 12 March 1947, *CWMG*, vol. 87, pp. 72–3.

70 Gandhi to K. Dewan, 2 December 1946, to A.K. Azad, 12 February 1947, *CWMG*, vol. 86, pp. 181, 458.

71 Re-Gandhi in Bengal, 5 December 1946, N.K. Bose, *My Days with Gandhi* (Nishana, Calcutta, 1953), p. 97; interview, 9 December 1946, *CWMG*, vol. 86, pp. 211–12.

72 Press interview, early December 1946, talk with journalists, 18 January 1947, *CWMG*, vol. 86, pp. 183, 368; speech at prayer meeting, 15 June 1947, interview, 8 July 1947, *CWMG*, vol. 88, pp. 160, 300.

73 Gandhi to Y. Privat, 29 November 1947, *CWMG*, vol. 90, p. 130; see also talk with Sindhi Congressman, 21 October 1947, *CWMG*, vol. 89, p. 379.

74 Talk in November, published in *Harijan*, 8 December 1946; also press interviews, 20 November and 2 December 1946; *CWMG*, vol. 86, pp. 134, 138–9, 182–3.

75 N.K. Bose, *My Days with Gandhi* gives a vivid sense of Gandhi's state of mind.

76 Gandhi to Mirabehn, 4 January 1947, NMML, Mirabehn Papers.

77 Gandhi to Vinoba Bhave, 10 February 1947, to G.D. Birla, 15 February 1947, *CWMG*, vol. 86, pp. 452–3, 464–5. N.K. Bose's recollections are in *My Days with Gandhi*.

78 Gandhi to V. Patel, 13 August 1947, *CWMG*, vol. 89, p. 35.

A detailed study of Gandhi's work in Calcutta during partition is D.G. Dalton, 'Gandhi During Partition: a Case Study in the Nature of Satyagraha', pp. 222–4 of C.H. Philips and M.D. Wainwright (eds), *The Partition Of India. Policies and Perspectives 1935–1947* (George Allen and Unwin, London, 1970).

79 'Miracle or Accident', 16 August 1947, *Harijan*, 24 August 1947; Gandhi to Amrit Kaur, 16 August 1947; Gandhi to V. Patel, 17 August 1947; *CWMG*, vol. 89, pp. 48–9, 50, 55.

80 Press statement, 1 September 1947; Gandhi to V. Patel, 1/2 September 1947; *ibid.*, pp. 129–32, 133–4.

81 Discussions with Rajagopalachariar (1 September 1947) and S.C. Bose (2 September 1947), *ibid.*, pp. 132–3, 137.

82 Campbell-Johnson, *Mission with Mountbatten*, p. 181.

83 Mountbatten to Gandhi, 26 August 1947, cited by D. Dalton in Philips and Wainwright (eds), *The Partition of India*, p. 234, fn. 5.

84 28 September 1947, cited in Ziegler, *Mountbatten*, p. 436.

85 Gandhi's prayer meeting speeches in Delhi for September 1947 to January 1948 are collected in M.K. Gandhi, *Delhi Diary* (Navajivan, Ahmedabad, 1948).

86 Fragment of letter, 13 November 1947, *CWMG*, vol. 90, pp. 23–4.

87 Gandhi to Mirabehn, 16 January 1948, to Amtussalaam, 25 January 1948, *ibid.*, pp. 430, 491.

88 Speech at prayer meeting, 12 January 1948, *ibid.*, pp. 408–11.

89 Ziegler, *Mountbatten*, p. 462; speech at prayer meeting, 16 January 1948, speech before breaking fast, 18 January 1948, *CWMG*, vol. 90, pp. 435–7, 444–8.

90 Speeches at prayer meetings, 16 and 17 January 1948, *ibid.*, pp. 435, 440.

91 26 April and 26 June 1946 entries, for example, NMML, B.S. Moonje Papers, Diary no. 6, 1945–6.

92 Fragment of letter, 18 December 1947, *CWMG*, vol. 90, p. 253.

93 'Apt Lines', *Harijan*, 12 October 1947, *CWMG*, vol. 89, p. 277.

For Gandhi's sense of God, see letters, 10 June and 2 July 1947, *CWMG*, vol. 88, pp. 120–1, 258; talk, 8 November 1947, *CWMG*, vol. 89, pp. 499–500.

94 Interview, 28 May 1947, *CWMG*, vol. 88, p. 26; Bose, *My Days with Gandhi*, pp. 270–1.

95 Talk with Muslims, 22 October 1947, *CWMG*, vol. 89, p. 385; *Harijan*, 23 November 1947, *CWMG*, vol. 90, pp. 2–3.

96 Fragment of letter, 21 December 1947, *ibid.*, p. 273.

97 Talk with G.D. Birla, 21 January 1948, *ibid.*, pp. 469–70.

98 Campbell-Johnson, *Mission with Mountbatten*, p. 275.

SUGGESTIONS FOR FURTHER READING

Detailed references to primary sources and academic studies relating to Gandhi's life and the environment in which he worked are provided in the notes to each chapter. What follows are suggestions for reading on various aspects of Gandhi's life and twentieth-century India which would be available and of interest to the general reader.

For a general background: primarily on politics, a comprehensive survey with its own suggestions for reading arranged by subjects is J.M. Brown, *Modern India. The Origins of an Asian Democracy* (OUP, 1985); on Indian Muslims there is P. Hardy, *The Muslims Of British India* (CUP, 1972). A brief but useful background on Hinduism is K.M. Sen, *Hinduism* (Harmondsworth, 1961).

On Gandhi's life and thought: two very different but useful studies are A. Copley's succinct Historical Association Study, *Gandhi. Against the Tide* (Basil Blackwell, 1987); and the more journalistic and personal enquiry into Gandhi and his followers by V. Mehta, *Mahatma Gandhi and His Apostles* (Viking Press, New York, 1976). Taking up controversial aspects of Gandhi's thought and work is B.R. Nanda, *Gandhi and His Critics* (OUP, Delhi, 1985).

The best study of Gandhi's religious thinking is M. Chatterjee, *Gandhi's Religious Thought* (Macmillan, 1983); from a broader perspective there is the useful and compact study, though it is less readable, by G. Richards, *The Philosophy of Gandhi. A Study of his Basic Ideas* (Curzon Press, 1982). Far more detailed and academic in approach, but excellent for those interested in philosophy, is the weighty study by R.N. Iyer, *The Moral and Political Thought of Mahatma Gandhi* (OUP, New York, 1973). A major psychological interpretation of Gandhi is the idiosyncratic and thought-provoking work of E. Erikson, *Gandhi's Truth. On the Origins of Militant Nonviolence* (Faber and, Faber 1970). An old but still interesting enquiry into satyagraha as a social and political technique is J.V. Bondurant, *Conquest of Violence. The Gandhian Philosophy of Conflict* (Revised edn., University of

Californa Press, 1969). Two detailed studies of Gandhi as a political activist in the Indian context are J.M. Brown, *Gandhi's Rise To Power. Indian Politics 1915–1922* (CUP, 1972) and *Gandhi and Civil Disobedience. The Mahatma in Indian Politics 1928–34* (CUP, 1977). An original and interesting study of Gandhi's handling of tradition is Part Two, 'The Traditional Roots Of Charisma: Gandhi', in L.I. and S.H. Rudolph, *The Modernity Of Tradition. Political Development in India* (University of Chicago Press, 1967).

Primary sources: readily available are Gandhi's own *Autobiography* and J. Nehru, *An Autobiography* (see notes for publication details). The Clarendon Press, Oxford, has published (1986–7) an immensely valuable three-volume selection of Gandhi's works edited by R.N. Iyer, *The Moral And Political Writings Of Mahatma Gandhi*. A delightful insight into the closing years of the raj from the British angle, and the reaction of one Viceroy to Gandhi is P. Moon (ed.), *Wavell. The Viceroy's Journal* (OUP, London, 1973).

Of related interest: the major biography of J. Nehru in three volumes by S. Gopal, published by Jonathan Cape, (London, 1975–84); introductions to India since independence, R.L. Hardgrave, *India. Government and Politics in a Developing Nation* (3rd. edn, Harcourt, Brace Jovanovich, 1980), and W.H. Morris-Jones, *The Government and Politics of India* (London, 3rd. edn, 1988) which has a significant discussion of 'the saintly idiom' in Indian politics.

INDEX

PHOTOGRAPHIC
ACKNOWLEDGEMENTS

Frontispiece: National Gandhi Museum, Rajghat, New Delhi.

p. xiv: Reproduced from Brian Lapping, *The End of Empire*, Channel 4 Books, 1985; original source, *A Historical Atlas of South Asia*, University of Chicago Press.

pp. 38 (below), 39 (below), 150, 178 (both pictures), 307 (top): © Associated Press Photo.

p. 239 Illustrated London News Picture Library.

p. 258 Copyright The British Library.

p. 271 Centre for the Study of Cartoon and Caricature, © Solo Syndication, London.

All other photographs provided by Weidenfeld and Nicolson.